UNDERSTANDING HUMAN MOTIVATION

revised edition

Compiled and Edited by
   Manfred F. DeMartino

   DREAMS AND PERSONALITY DYNAMICS
   SEXUAL BEHAVIOR AND PERSONALITY CHARACTERISTICS

   Chalmers L. Stacey
   Manfred F. DeMartino

   COUNSELING AND PSYCHOTHERAPY WITH THE MENTALLY RETARDED

UNDERSTANDING HUMAN MOTIVATION

REVISED EDITION

Compiled and Edited by
Chalmers L. Stacey
and
Manfred F. DeMartino

THE WORLD PUBLISHING COMPANY
CLEVELAND AND NEW YORK

Published by The World Publishing Company
2231 West 110th Street, Cleveland, Ohio 44102

Revised Edition
Copyright © 1965 by The World Publishing Company

Published simultaneously in Canada by
Nelson, Foster & Scott Ltd.

Printed In The United States Of America

To Our Wives

Katherine and Grace

PREFACE TO REVISED EDITION

The present revision was undertaken for a number of reasons among which were: 1) to include some additional concepts such as that of homeostasis (Paper No. 4 by R. Stagner) and that of competency (Paper No. 5 by R. W. White), which have become recognized and accepted as important in the study of human motivation; 2) to present some of A. H. Maslow's current thinking on self-actualization and psychological health (Paper No. 8); 3) to include a paper which deals with the measurement of the Achievement motive (Paper No. 11 by D. C. McClelland); 4) to include a section on Motivation and Emotion which was originally contemplated for inclusion in our first edition; 5) to include extensive references for each section.

It is hoped that these additions will better serve the needs of those individuals interested in understanding human motivation.

Syracuse University
January, 1963

Chalmers L. Stacey
Manfred F. DeMartino

PREFACE TO FIRST EDITION

⎰ In recent years, social scientists have been focusing more and more interest and attention upon the dynamics of *human behavior*⎰ This, we feel, is a very healthy sign: unless and until we really understand the fundamental or basic strivings of human beings in all their interrelationships our theories of personality and our attempts at psychotherapy will, at best, leave much to be desired./Credit for the pioneer work in the field of *human motivation* must be attributed for the most part to Sigmund Freud and other psychoanalysts. Although no one can deny the inestimable value of their contributions in understanding the dynamics of human behavior, there has still remained a great need for experimental research/

Actually, psychologists had been aware of this need for some time, as can be attested by the many studies during the last three decades on motivation with rats and other animals. But because of the relatively simple nature of these animal subjects as compared with complex human beings, and because the results of animal research can not be directly and wholly applied to an understanding of *human behavior,* such studies yielded a paucity of information on the dynamics of *human motivation.* It would seem, therefore, that if we are to acquire a more thorough and extensive understanding of human motivation, we need to deal primarily with human beings. Fortunately, an increasing emphasis has been devoted, in the last two decades, to theoretical discussions and experimental studies pertaining to *human motivation.* This book of readings has been conceived and organized in line with this trend of thought.

Our primary aim in bringing together these articles was to provide a readable, interesting and basic introductory text on human motivation for undergraduate courses. One of the editors (C.L.S.) has taught such a course in *human motivation* for the past ten years, and most of the articles were selected on the basis of first hand classroom experience with them. While not all aspects of *human motivation* have been included in this book, we do feel that the basic or core areas have been covered.

We would like to extend our thanks to the individual authors and publishers who kindly granted permission to reproduce the various selections contained in this volume of readings. Acknowledgement is given to the various authors and publishers (except those authors whom we were unable to locate or who are deceased) in the footnote of each paper.

We would also like to express our appreciation and thanks to Dr. A. H. Maslow for his stimulating discussions and many valuable suggestions in the preparation of this volume. To Dr. Calvin S. Hall and Dr. Gordon W. Allport we would like to express our gratitude for their encouragement and support. Finally, we would like to thank Mrs. Cecile Gitlin for her untiring efforts in the typing of the manuscript.

Syracuse University
April, 1958

C.L.S.
M.F.D.

CONTENTS

CURRENT STATUS

Present day thinking in human motivation theory has changed greatly from the time when motivational theory was centered around the concept of instinct. The theories of William James, William McDougall, and Edward L. Thorndike no longer govern the thinking in the field of motivation. Some of the early critics of the instinct theory instrumental in bringing about this change were Knight Dunlap, Luther Bernard, and Z. Y. Kuo.

Actually, the area of human motivation is so highly complex and inclusive that theoretically the entire field of human behavior could be included under this heading. There are a number of reasons why the study of human motivation is so complex and so difficult. First, motivation is concerned with the "why" rather than with the "how" of human behavior. In other words, its problem is one of explanation and causation, not simply one of description. Second, it is always a *total* organism in a social environment that responds or reacts, not just one segment of it. Third, motives can only be inferred from behavior; they are not *directly* observable. For example, although a number of people may exhibit very similar behavior, the underlying motives governing the behavior of each person may be quite different. Moreover, persons with essentially similar motives may express them in markedly different ways. Fourth, the "why" of a specific act may be due primarily to physio-

1

logical factors, or to social factors, or more often to the interaction of the two. Frequently it is difficult to differentiate the relative significance of these determinants.\

In Paper No. 1 Graffam presents a succinct historical introduction to motivation. He discusses the changes in thinking regarding motivation, beginning with some of the very early philosophers and concluding with a discussion of the ideas of contemporary theorists. Symonds (Paper No. 2) presents in organized form what he believes to be the fundamental human urges or drives. He divides these fundamental drives into three types; the process of adjustment as a drive, the first order appetites and aversions, and derived or learned drives. He discusses in detail and illustrates the meaning of each of these three types of drives. Seward (Paper No. 3) stresses the point that an item of behavior must be evaluated not in isolation, but interpreted rather in terms of the total situation.

\In Paper No. 4 Stagner proposes that the biological concept of homeostasis "can be expanded into a major generalization in the field of personality theory. This principle can be shown to have value in illuminating personality considered both as a universal and as a unique phenomenon." That is, homeostatic principles apply not only at the "microscopic level (tissue conditions) but also at macroscopic levels (objects in the physical environment, and persons in the social environment)." The major portion of Stagner's article is devoted to a consideration of the value of homeostatic principles to the study of personality.

One of the most important and pertinent papers on the overall problems of motivation from a theoretical standpoint, published in recent years, is that by Robert W. White (Paper No. 5). The ideas expressed in this paper have already exerted a marked influence on the thinking of serious students (ranging from those in the field of animal psychology to those in the field of psychoanalytic ego psychology) concerned with the complex problems of motivation. White emphasizes the fact that there is widespread dissatisfaction with motivational theories based principally upon primary drives. This dissatisfaction has been evidenced in the fields of animal psychology as well as psychoanalytic ego psychology. Various workers in both of these areas have attempted to overcome the existing theoretical inadequacies, but it is White's contention that such attempts, thus far, have been unsuccessful. White, believing that the time has arrived for a broader and more adequate conceptualization in motivational theory, in Paper No. 5 introduces, develops, and explains in detail, his concept of *com-

petence. As used by White, *competence* refers "to an organism's capacity to interact effectively with its environment."

Among the various theories of human motivation which have been presented by social scientists one of the most promising, well organized and intriguing is that formulated by A. H. Maslow (Paper No. 6). He believes that human needs arrange themselves in hierarchies of prepotency (i.e. predominance) and that the appearance of one need usually rests on the prior satisfaction of another more prepotent need. It is Maslow's feeling that the hierarchy of needs is arranged as follows: 1) The Physiological Needs, 2) The Safety Needs, 3) The Love Needs, 4) The Esteem Needs, 5) The Need for Self-Actualization. He also contends that there are important differences between those needs called "higher" and those called "lower" (Paper No. 7). In describing his theory of human motivation, however, Maslow states clearly that it should be "considered to be a suggested program or framework for future research," and the validity of which needs to be determined by future research and clinical evidence. Paper No. 8 represents an expansion and further development of the ideas discussed by Maslow in his two other papers (Nos. 6 and 7). In it he presents a comprehensive view of human nature which he labels a "holistic-dynamic psychology." He discusses his current thinking in terms of thirty-seven propositions.

Kilby (Paper No. 9) presents a partial verification of Maslow's theory. Gordon Allport is another outstanding social scientist who has been greatly concerned with the problem of human motives and the ways in which they are revealed. One of the major points emphasized in his Paper No. 10 is that with well-integrated personalities as much importance should be attached to their *conscious* verbal reports of emotions, wishes, desires and interests, as is usually given to those motives uncovered by projective (indirect) methods, motives of which the individual presumably is unaware.

In the paper by McClelland (No. 11) there is reported a number of preliminary experiments designed to meet the need for a satisfactory method of measuring human motivation. The main objective of McClelland and his associates was to measure "the strength of the Achievement motive in phantasy." Essentially, McClelland's paper is concerned with a presentation of methodology, and the relation of the Achievement motive to other aspects of human behavior such as performance, learning, level of aspiration, perception, and memory.

While on the surface there may appear to be much diversity of opinion and disagreement regarding current human motivation theory, a careful analysis of the various approaches tends to show a good deal of agreement. For example, psychologists no longer accept the instinct theory but instead recognize the importance of: a) the physiological as well as the social or learned needs, b) the unconscious motives, and c) the defense mechanisms (projection, repression, rationalization) in explaining motivation. They also agree that the problem of human motivation is highly complex and that practically all human behavior is motivated. It is quite probable that future research will reinforce this trend even more.

1. Brief Historical Introduction to Motivation

Donald T. Graffam

MAN'S interest in finding out why he behaves as he does, what forces operate within and without his skin to make him do what he does, in short, what *motivates* him, has undoubtedly existed long before he learned how to record his thoughts by means of language. While we cannot spend much space in this brief introduction on motivational concepts of the great thinkers of the ancient, medieval, and early modern periods of history, we pause to note the emphasis on *hedonism* in Aristotle's *Rhetoric* 23 centuries ago, in More's *Utopia,* Descartes' *The Passions of the Soul,* Hobbes' *Leviathian,* and the writings of Beccaria, Adam Smith, and Jeremy Bentham over a century later. While these writers differed as to their application of hedonism, they seemed to regard the mainspring of human activity as a self-interested desire to seek comfort and pleasure and to avoid discomfort and pain. They regarded this search as arising out of man's conscious purposes and overcomplimented man as being essentially a *rational* being who knew what he wanted and who was capable of being responsible for his actions. This splendid idea is still held by many people, and possibly the increasing knowledge about man and his potentiali-

Abridged and published by permission of the author.

ties gained from the study of psychology and other sciences of man may assist in its actualization.

Then we could mention the stream of thought stemming from the religionists from times of antiquity to the present which has emphasized man's *emotional* drive to seek that which is good and ethical and holy and eschew that which is evil and unethical and unholy as another powerful concept about motivation. But we shall pick up our story with the thoughts of William James, who has been called the "father of American psychology." In his *Principles of Psychology,* he recognized an *unconscious* source of motivation, called *instincts,* which may be modified by *habits,* which are learned. Included in his long list of unlearned behaviors were crying, locomotion, curiosity, imitation, sociability, pugnacity, sympathy, fear of dark places, acquisitiveness, love, jealousy and many others which psychologists now recognize to be at least partly learned.

The instinct theory of motivation, that is, the basis of much of man's behavior stems from unlearned, innate tendencies, was furthered by the work of William McDougall and Edward L. Thorndike, who extended or revised James' list, but these two men differed in the role which they assigned to emotion in instincts. To McDougall, emotions were the core of instincts, while Thorndike looked upon them as unlearned patterns of behavior. Freud also believed that man's behavior was motivated by instincts, chiefly two: those of sex and of self-preservation. Later he added the notion of Thanatos, a death instinct. Two of his associates, Jung and Adler, also emphasized the role of instincts in human motivation, but broke with Freud in 1911 partly because of their different viewpoints on which instincts were of primary importance. Whereas Freud believed that the energizing force of man (libido) is sexual in nature, Jung added the need for nutrition and gregariousness as prime movers, while Adler stressed the drive for power as a compensation for the weakness and helplessness suffered by all men in their infancy. Thus the problem of motivation from the respective standpoints of the "schools" founded by these men may be put thus: the psychoanalytic school stressed the need of "being good" (i.e., controling sexual energies in harmony with the mores); the school of individual psychology (Adler) stressed the importance of "making good" (i.e., gaining power and prestige, avoiding weakness and "failure"); the analytical psychology of Jung stressed the development of the individual in harmony with his structural type (introvert or extravert) and finding eventually peace and harmony within his own soul.

In 1924, the instinct theory ran into serious trouble when Luther Bernard, a sociologist, reviewed the various ideas of many instinct theorists and found that the list of so-called instincts included nearly 6000 activities, from generalized urges such as "social behavior" to specific ones like an "instinct to avoid eating apples in one's own orchard." No wonder that the term "instinct" became unpopular with psychologists thereafter. Even before this time, several psychologists were attacking the doctrine of instinct. In 1918, Robert Woodworth of Columbia University pointed out that habits can become drives, that doing a thing repetitively carries its own motivation. In 1919, Knight Dunlap and John B. Watson, both of Johns Hopkins, made separate attacks on the instinct theory. Concurrently, the rise of experimental method in psychology and the influence of anthropology served further to weaken the hold of the instinct doctrine in the field of social psychology which it had enjoyed from the time of McDougall's *An Introduction to Social Psychology*. The upshot of all this was that human motivation is not a matter of unlearned built-in mechanisms but is shaped largely through learned reactions and subtle influences of the culture into which one is born. For example, Margaret Mead observed that fathers, not mothers, in the Manus tribe of New Guinea brought up the children and that her presents of dolls attracted the attention of boys rather than girls. Ruth Benedict found, contrary to Adler's postulate of the power drive in man, that the Zuni Indians invoked penalties on members of the tribe who were too aggressive or who frequently won in contests. And one looks in vain for a "warlike" instinct among Eskimo tribes, who cannot grasp why groups of people should try to exterminate one another. "Instinctive behavior" now refers to the innate patterns found among the sub-human species.

But another term was made ready to slip into the place of "instinct," namely *drive*. This term was first used as a psychological explanation of motivation by Woodworth in his *Dynamic Psychology*, 1918. He got the idea from mechanics and used "drive" to refer to the supply of energy that puts the machine (or organism) in motion; thus he spoke of *drive* as a general term for supply of energy, not of specific *drives* as used by F. A. Moss in 1924. Moss spoke of *a* drive as a specific directional force leading to a specific goal; e.g., sex drive, hunger drive, etc. In 1928, C. J. Warden, famous for his experiments with his Columbia obstruction box, used "drive" to mean a *behavioral tendency* directed toward or away from some specific goal object, such as food, water, etc. He did not use it to mean the physiological state of tension or imbalance implied in Cannon's concept of homeostasis. Warden found experimentally that in rats the relative strength of five drives is as follows: maternal, thirst, hunger; then sex; and weakest, exploratory.

Dashiell, Tolman and Richter were others who employed the term drive, presumably adopting it from Woodworth. In 1931, E. B. Holt used the term in a double sense: (1) the chemical energy stored in the sense organs, nerves and muscle tissues, and (2) the agencies which release stored energy—stimuli acting on sense organs without and within. Thus Holt brings the meaning of drive to a peak of confusion by overdefining it and confusing it with *incentive*. Young summarizes five meanings of incentive and six meanings of drive and Brown decries the confusion in present usage of the term with habit and denies that drive provides direction to action in addition to energy. Perhaps the term drive will go the way of the term instinct, unless a careful delimitation of its meaning is agreed upon.

Regardless of whether "drive" is scraped, another term has been brought into play as more befitting to the complexity of human behavior: *motive*. This term definitely includes the concept of direction and includes social urges as well as physiological energizers, drives, needs, urges, etc. In 1923, W. I. Thomas, sociologist, presented his four wishes, which he believed every normal individual desired to fulfill; namely, the desire for new experiences, security, response, and recognition. (An earlier version of these four fundamental motives appeared in a work by Thomas and Znaniecki, 1918.) As Dewey and Humber point out, while this formulation of basic motives has been criticized by certain social psychologists as being inadequate and incomplete, they have been found useful to others in the absence of an integrated system of social motivation formulated by the social psychologists themselves. A similar and later statement of basic motives is given by A. H. Maslow, whose components of motivation include safety needs, love needs, esteem (of self and of others) needs, need for self-actualization, and the desire to know and understand. He proposes a hierarchy of motives in the following order of prepotency: physiological, safety, love, esteem, self-actualization.

Many other attempts have been made in classifying motives by sociologists, psychoanalysts, cultural anthropologists, personologists, and social psychologists, using various frames of reference and revising and extending the simple classification of Thomas. Thus the list of motives grows longer and more confusing, including such disparate components underlying behavior as emotion, habitual activity, sex attraction, ambition, bodily comfort, interests, conformity, mastery or domination, submission, unconscious motives expressed through the various defense mechanisms (or dynamisms, such as rationalization, projection, identification and the like), gregariousness or desire to be with one's kind, acquisitiveness, pugnacity, concern for the welfare of others, etc. In passing over the list, one notes their secondary rather than primary nature; i.e., for the most part they are learned in a social setting rather than innately endowed. Obviously, there is need for integrating and organizing human motives, lest they too, like instincts, ultimately come to be abandoned.

The reasons for this confusion are well summarized by Sargent. First, the classification of motives is concerned with the difficult task of trying to explain rather than merely to describe behavior. It is always easier to describe events than to ascertain their cause. Second, motives are never directly observable, but have to be inferred from overt acts, which opens the way to errors of the "personal equation." Third, confusion arises from semantic difficulties besetting students of motivation. Meanings of the terms employed are not clear, as noted above in references to criticism of Young and Brown. Even the definition of motive involves disagreement. Fourth, motives may be primarily physiological or primarily social in origin. Fifth, motives vary within and between individuals. In arguing for a fresh start on the problem of motivation, Sargent reminds the reader of the concept of behavior as a function of an organism (O) in a social situation (S): $B=f(OS)$. Motives arise and operate within the field of interaction between the organism and the situation. O has physiological and psychological tensions in addition to the equipment for perceiving S, and the latter takes on significance according to O's perception of it. On the other hand, S stimulates O. Thus there are two aspects of motives: (1) the relationship between tensions and positive or negative aspects of S and (2) the development of motives which have a situational rather than a physiological basis. It is this second aspect which leads us to the discussion of another important concept in motivation: *incentives*.

The idea that rewards and punishments influence behavior is a natural legacy of hedonism; indeed, it probably existed ages before hedonism got its name. It has always been a firmly intrenched notion in the minds of common men and of scholars as well. The role of incentives, for example, has been a favorite theme among philosophers, economists, industrial psychologists, and animal experimentalists. Even Thorndike's cats and Tolman's rats were found to require rewards in order to learn to escape puzzle boxes and run mazes, and to require penalties to avoid making "errors." Grades and switches have been chief motivational tools throughout the history of education as have been verbal praise and reproof of pupils by teachers.

Hurlock, in a well known study, showed varying gains for children in learning arithmetic under conditions of being ignored (slight loss), reproof (some gain), and praise (best gain). Thorndike's experiment with blindfolded subjects attempting to draw a line four inches long showed how knowledge of results improved efficiency. No improvement in the seven subjects was made in 400 tries (average error about one inch). Allowing them to look after each try for 25 tries reduced the average error to three-sixteenths of an inch. This illustrates, in one way, his law of effect. Recent emphasis is given to incentives by Harlow's principle of exteroception derived from experiments with visual rewards and learning in monkeys.

The importance of incentives in motivation has been appreciated by industrial psychologists ever since Hugo Munsterberg initiated that branch in 1913 with his *Psychology and Industrial Efficiency*. In 1927 an extensive study of the effect of various kinds of working conditions, wage plans, rest pauses, and other incentives on production was begun in the Hawthorne Plant of Western Electric Company. To the surprise of the investigators, the output of several units studied over a period of several years kept increasing even when unfavorable conditions supplanted more favorable ones. It finally dawned on them that hitherto overlooked factors of motivation, such as ego-involvements and social attitudes of workers toward each other and the company, were responsible for the improvement in production. Great emphasis on these aspects of human motivation has been given in recent years by social psychologists and leaders in a new movement known as human relations in industry. At long last, it is coming to be recognized that good human relations based on recognition of personal worth and integrity of individuals, effective communication, congeniality, and participation of employees in company goals—which promote feelings of belongingness and security among the employees—are even more important factors of motivation than financial incentives and working conditions per se.

A quick review of our story thus far yields the interesting observation that each aspect of motivation brought into view involves a higher level of consciousness or awareness, from instinct, which requires no awareness or conscious attention on the part of the organism for its operation, and drive, which involves at least a dim awareness, to incentive, which requires perceptual contact with outer reality, learning, reinforcement, and in humans, at least, conscious attention. Midway in this continuum might be placed the concept of the *functional autonomy of habits* in the line of James, Woodworth, and Gordon Allport; that is, that habits apparently provide their own motivation even when the original motives which caused them to be formed no longer exist. Because of differing views of the nature of motivation, i.e., whether it simply involved energy transfer within tissues of an organism resulting in mere motion, or motion directed toward some goal or incentive, it was inevitable that writers in this field should produce some confusion in the mind of a student who was seeking to acquire a clear distinction between drive, habits, and rewards. A recent criticism of this state of affairs is made by Brown, who denies the power of drives to *direct* behavior and assigns them three functions: (1) to energize latent associative tendencies; (2) to reinforce responses whose elicitation is followed by a reduction in drive; (3) to punish the organism when abrupt increases in drive follow a response. Language also further confuses the issue, as when persons speak of a drive for affection, a drive for money, etc. What is more to the point, he says, is that they have learned to be anxious in the absence of such goals; thus, man does not work *for money* so much as he is motivated *to reduce the anxiety of not having money* (in a pecuniary culture). The same reasoning applies to prestige, affection, or other motives considered of importance in a given society. In answering the question, "Does a monkey open the window of an opaque box in order to see out, or in order to avoid anxiety of not seeing out?" Brown would point to the latter while Harlow would point to the former.

In an experiment with three white male albino rates (mature) in the Dickinson College laboratory recently, effectiveness in learning an elevated multiple-T maze constructed of 2″ x 2″ fir, containing eight choice points of the pattern rrllrrll and sixteen blind alleys, was tested under four conditions of "motivation": (1) manipulative-exploratory without reinforcement; (2)

hunger-as-drive and food-as-reward as a design for primary drive-primary reinforcement experiment; (3) fear as a learned drive (elicited through using a wired grid as starting platform) and escape from fear as acquired drive reduction; (4) placing the animal's own cage on the finish platform. None of the animals "learned" the maze under conditions 1, 2, or 3. All of them promptly learned to run the maze without errors under condition four. Thus, of four possible theories of motivation, (exteroception, homeostasis, pain and fear reduction, and anxiety reduction), Brown's theory seemed to be the most plausible explanation of the behavior of the rats in this experiment. It is planned to conduct the experiment a number of times using split-litter technique before definite conclusions are drawn.

Another aspect of motivation somewhere on the cycle between zero awareness and full awareness of its operation is that which stems from cultural influences. Thanks are due to the cultural anthropologists, or ethnologists, for stressing the importance of the social matrix and the fruitlessness of studying motives apart from the cultural milieu. The work of Margaret Mead and Ruth Benedict, pioneers in the field, have been mentioned earlier in the article and will not be elaborated on further.

We complete the cycle by returning to the level of the unconscious, although not in the same sense as implied in connection with the instinct theory. Here we mean *unconscious motivation* as implied by Freud, the psychoanalysts, and depth psychologists. Although the existence of an unconscious aspect of mind was posited by Leibnitz about 1700 and by Herbart in the first textbook in psychology (1816), it was Freud who must be credited with first postulating a psychodynamic theory of unconscious motivation. It was developed in the 1880's in connection with a case of hysteria. One of the symptoms had to do with the young lady's disgust for drinking a glass of water without knowing why. In a hypnotic state, she was able to recall that she had once seen a pet dog drink from a glass. Fearing to show disgust in the presence of the owner, whom she admired, she *repressed* her feelings and was unable to remember the incident thereafter until the aid of a therapist made its recovery possible. Freud realized that "forgotten" painful memories, actually repressed rather than forgotten, could still play a vital part in human motivation. Thus began the seed of a system of psychology which could cope with a vast reservoir of human motivation which could never be tapped by the classical psychology of his day which limited its study to man's *conscious* states.

Investigations of the powerful dynamisms springing from the unconscious which drive men in ways they do not understand and aberrate them in ways they do not appreciate have been carried on with increasing zeal by Freud's associates, even by his opponents, until today psychologists and medical doctors accept some of his basic notions while disagreeing with other Freudian tenets. All, however, give the master his due credit for his indefatigable scholarship and personal sacrifice which resulted in opening up a new vista of man's behavior. While he covered many aspects of behavior, his ideas on neurotic motivation are germane to the present discussion. Put most simply, he believed that the neurotic's problems arose because of a too-severe super-ego (conscience) probably resulting from too-strict parental discipline; and that treatment consisted in allowing the patient to express his fears and anxieties in a permissive atmosphere provided by the therapist. In this way repression is gradually unlearned and the tensions from oversocialized anxiety thus disappear.

Quite an opposite view of this theory is taken by one of the leading psychologists of the day, O. H. Mowrer, who avers that the neurotic's problem is not one of having a superego as tyrant, but who lacks the character and honesty to measure up even to an ordinary conscience. Thus his motivation comes from internal tensions expended to cover up feelings of guilt (self-punishment) and avoid criticisms (social punishment) which usually attend irresponsible behavior. Thus the problem of therapy is not one of providing catharsis, but of helping the patient grow in moral capacity to meet responsibilities in such a way that guilt and criticism will not be necessary.

We close this brief treatment of the history of motivation with a reference to a new attack on the subject made by A. H. Maslow, *Motivation and Personality*, (Harper & Bros., 1954). He points out that most of what we know about human motivation comes from inferences drawn by psychotherapists about their patients. What we need, he says, is a positive orientation to the subject based on study of healthy persons as well as neurotics. Unlike Mowrer, Maslow believes that the neurotic personality is one which feels unsafe and afraid and who retains his childhood ways of meeting the world—he is insecure, rather than dishonest—although he states that there are exceptions. In constructing a theory of motivation for healthy individuals, Maslow proceeds to construct a heirarchy of needs in the following order of prepotency: physiological, safety, belongingness and love, esteem, self-actualization, cognitive, and aesthetic. The basic principle, heretofore overlooked, is that our needs emerge only when the more prepotent ones have been gratified. There is much more to his theory; but it is of importance to note it in closing as the best attempt to date in formulating a positive, wholesome, and *human* psychology of motivation.

2. Human Drives

Percival M. Symonds

THIS paper is concerned with a restatement of the problem of the drives or urges at work within the human organisms which make the individual go, in the first place, and make him go in one direction rather than another, in the second. This problem is perennially important in education. All learning must take place in response to the demands of the organism. These drives are not to be brooked, and when normal satisfactions are not easily obtainable an individual is driven to abnormal or pathological behavior. A knowledge of what drives are fundamental is essential, then, for an understanding of what adjustments an individual must make, and why certain kinds of adjustments frequently are made.

As a term applied to human beings *instinct* has been practically defunct in psychological discussions of motivation for the past decade. The theory of motivation based on the concept of instinct was first formally stated by William James in a series of magazine articles in 1887 and later in his two volume work on Psychology. James, however, received inspiration and suggestions from two earlier writers on instinct, one, W. Preyer, who in 1881 wrote a book on development psychology based largely on a complete diary of his own son kept from birth to the end of his third year, and the other, G. H. Schneider's more theoretical works on animal and human impulses.

Although the concept of instinct has been vaguely traced to the Greeks and to mediaeval scholars, the real impetus to the modern formulation came from the work of the great biologists of the nineteenth century, particularly Darwin, (Preyer was a follower of Darwin), Herbert Spencer, Lloyd Morgan, and others, and the modern concept of instinct may be said to have developed from the biological study of animals on the one hand, and the physiological study of the nervous system and basic organic reactions on the other.

Thorndike, a student of James, elaborated James' theory of instinct, and applied it definitely to educational theory. Thorndike in his *Human Nature*

Abridged from *The Journal of Educational Psychology*, 1934, 25, 681-694. Reprinted by permission of the author and *Warwick and York, Inc.*

Club gave an early statement of the point of view which he has since persistently held.

> We inherit certain connections between nerve-cells which make us act in certain circumstances in definite ways, without our learning how, or thinking about the matter at all, or hearing what we are going to do. Our inherited constitution makes us breathe and suckle and smile and reach for things and walk and be afraid in the dark, just as it makes us sleep and digest food and grow. We call such unlearned activities, *instincts,* or *native reactions.* Such activities may appear before birth or at birth or be delayed till after birth. They may be transitory, that is, may stay for a while and then disappear if not exercised and rendered habitual. Some of them we have in common with a great many of the lower animals. Some of them are peculiar to the human race. On the basis of these instinctive acts develop all our later acquisitions.

William McDougall has been another champion of instinct as the "essential springs or motive powers of all thought and action." McDougall defines instinct as an "*innate specific* tendency of the mind." With dogmatic abruptness he rejects the possibility of what he defines as instinctive actions being learned.

> Or what could be more strained and opposed to hundreds of familiar facts than Herbert Spencer's doctrine that the emotion of fear provoked by any object consists in faint revivals, in some strange cluster, of ideas of all the pains suffered in the past upon contact with, or in the presence of, that object?

Guided by the weight of these authorities instinct was accepted quite universally (passively, at least) as the basis of human motivation by 1919. But the lists of specific instincts became longer and longer and finally the elaborate theoretical structure broke beneath its own weight. The initial demolishing shot came from Knight Dunlap in a critical paper read before the American Psychological Association in Cambridge, Mass., December 29, 1919. In this paper although Dunlap does not deny that "there is a great deal of instinctive activity, both conscious and unconscious, and probably both volitional and non-volitional," he claimed that the recent classifications of instincts had lost touch with physiological realities and that it were better not to refer to specific instincts.

Certain sociologists, approaching the problem of human motivation from a fresh point of view, found the concept of instinct not sufficient for a proper interpretation of social behavior. Bernard says

> The category of instinct, which serves very well the purposes of describing the activities of lower organisms, proves to be entirely inadequate for an account of human social behavior. Only habit and constantly and easily modified acquired reactions can serve his complicated and voluminous adjustment needs.

and as a result of his survey of the problem Bernard states

> The instincts are very early overlaid by acquired habits in the process of adapting the individual to his environment . . . the child who has reached a rational age is reacting in nine-tenths or ninety-nine one-hundredths of his character directly to environment, and only in the slight residual fraction of his nature directly to instinct.

In the meantime and apparently independently the attack on instinct was gathering force from within psychology itself. In an excellently written paper Kuo proposed that the concept of instinct had no place whatever in the interpretation of human behavior, basing his argument on purely behavioristic grounds. After demonstrating how many of the so-called instincts could have developed by the process of learning from more elementary acts or reflexes he states,

> If we watch the stages of development of human behavior closely enough, we shall not have any difficulty to trace the sources of social influences. To call an acquired trend of action an instinct is simply to confess an ignorance of the history of its development.

Kuo gives as his positive theory of man's native equipment as follows:

> The human infant is endowed with a great number of units of reaction. By units of reaction I mean the elementary acts out of which various coordinated activities of later life are organized. The reaction units are what we find in the child's spontaneous activities and random acts. The new-born baby is characterized by being easily aroused to action; it is exceedingly active . . . . These reaction units are the elements out of which all the coordinated acts of the organism are integrated.

Kuo, while presenting no new evidence, illustrated the possibility of acts, formerly thought instinctive, to be the product of learning.

Finally John B. Watson, on the basis of his experiments in conditioning infant emotions comes out with extreme statements doing away with instincts altogether.

> There are then for us no instincts—we no longer need the term in psychology. Everything we have been in the habit of calling an "instinct" today is a result largely of training—belong to man's *learned behavior* . . . . The infant is a graduate student in the subject of *learned responses* (he is multitudinously conditioned) by the time behavior such as James describes—imitation, rivalry, cleanliness, and the other forms he lists—can be observed.

(Watson at the same time goes to such absurd extremes as to claim that "there is no such thing as an inheritance of *capacity, talent, temperament, mental constitution* and *characteristics*.")

Having reached this point in throwing over instincts, psychologists have been busy for a decade peering into infant behavior to discover and describe how it is possible for the manifold activities of a baby's day to be learned.

The question of what motivates human behavior can not be so easily disposed, however. James, Thorndike, and McDougall may have oversimplified the problem of human behavior by suggesting that it is built on an original structure of performed instructive behavior. But whatever the accuracy of their theories one is convinced by reading their descriptions of instinct that they are dealing with something so universal and with such a driving quality that it cannot be wholly subsumed under the guise of habits built on purely random activities.

Tolman was one of the first to propose a substitute theory of "driving adjustment." Tolman's theory in brief is that excitement of the smooth muscles of the visceral and organic systems of the body causes a change in adjustment or disequilibrium which has a tendency of its own to seek equilibrium again. This change in adjustment in turn stimulates the somatic system of the body to activity which will initiate behavior, at first random, later learned, leading to a reduction of the autonomic disequilibrium. Any act of the somatic system is successful which provides new stimuli for neutralizing or opposing the autonomic adjustment, thus bringing it back to equilibrium.

To give a familiar concrete illustration, hunger is known to consist of a series of rhythmical contractions of the smooth muscle wall of the stomach. This disequilibrium initiates restless searching movements until food is found and delivered to the stomach whence the muscle contraction waves cease and equilibrium is restored.

Tolman apparently received help on his theory from four sources. W. Craig had already formulated a theory of appetites and aversions as the constituents of instinct as a result of his observation of the sexual anomalies of male doves reared in isolation in which the variability of instincts was demonstrated.

Woodworth had earlier elaborated a very similar theory in his lectures on *Dynamic Psychology,* although in those lectures the nature of a "consummatory reaction" was not very explicitly stated.

A third source for Tolman's theory was the work of his own teacher, Ralph Barton Perry, Professor of Philosophy at Harvard, who in a series of articles indicated the possibility of an "autonomic" explanation of adjustment.

Finally Kempf presented a theory of the autonomic nervous system which provided a framework for the physiological phases of the theory.

Tolman shortly after preparing his theory of "driving adjustment" elaborated the theory by preparing a list of the "fundamental drives." Tolman describes drives into two main categories, the *appetities* and *aversions*. Appeties are initiated by internal physiological disturbances, rhythmical in nature. "When the rhythm reaches the proper part in its cycle, the organism becomes restless and embarks upon exploratory movements, until finally it came by chance," upon the appropriate stimulus which is capable of reducing the disturbance. Appetites lead to *seeking* activity.

Aversions, on the other hand, are drives to get away from external situations which cause physiological disturbances (injury, pain, physiological blocking, etc.). "In the case of the aversion the physiological inciting state tends to be a more enduring and constant affair." Aversions lead to *avoiding* behavior.

Tolman then proposed that drives originating directly from physiological disturbance be called first-order drives while acts which in the past have proven that they serve the direct physiological drives by helping to bring the organism in contact with the necessary reduction stimulus (or in the case of aversions, away from the irritating stimulus) be called second-order drives. Curiosity, for instance, would be a second-order drive, for it helps to bring distant objects within closer range, and hence may serve both hunger and sex, the first-order drives. In many respects these second-order drives are more like the aversions than like the appetites.

In his recent book, *Purposive Behavior in Animals and Men,* Tolman gives a list of fundamental drives derived from his mature consideration of the problem.

Appetites	*Aversions*	*Second-Order Drives*
Food-hunger.	Fright (injury-	Curiosity.
Sex-hunger.	avoidance).	Gregariousness.
Excretion-hungers.	Pugnacity (inter-	Self-assertion.
Specific-contact-	ference-avoidance).	Self-abasement.
hungers.		Imitativeness.
Rest-hunger.		
Sensory-motor-hungers		
(i.e., the esthetic and		
play hunger).		

H. L. Hollingworth in his recent book on Educational Psychology has woven this point of view in a thorough-going discussion of human motives as applied to education. He says,

> Action was found to be the result of disturbance, stress, or upset of equilibrium. We may suppose that the so-called instinctive acts are also responses to some mental or bodily disturbance, to some irritant, which produces restlessness and activity until it is relieved.

In the same chapter Hollingworth gives a list of twenty-three "distresses" which he calls a "sample list of man's original activities or fundamental adjustments." In presenting such an extended list Hollingworth tends to lead back to the same overloaded system which caused the breakdown of the instinct theory.

It is the purpose of this paper to explore the question of the fundamental human urges or drives with the purpose of arriving at a formulation which is useful to educators who wish to understand the springs of human behavior. Certain wishes or urges or activities of a child may be so easily turned aside that it is evident that they are not very deep-rooted. One may substitute (with a little tact) a peach for a pear or a toy automobile for a picture book without creating any pronounced disturbance. On the other hand, depriving a hungry child of food has unmistakable results.

It is also evident that it is not possible or practicable in every case to go back to hunger, sex, thirst, desire for sleep, etc. as the urge of the moment. In most social activity it would require a considerable stretch of the imagination to make such an interpretation of the urge which is at work.

As early as 1923 W. I. Thomas, a sociologist, influenced by the work of John B. Watson, attempted such a formulation. He says

> We understand . . . that . . . expressions of emotion mean a preparation for action which will be useful in preserving life (anger), avoiding death (fear), and in reproducing the species (love), but even if our knowledge of the nervous system of man were complete we could not read out of it all the concrete varieties of human experience. The variety of expressions of behavior is as great as the variety of situations arising in the external world, while the nervous system represents only a general mechanism for action. We can, however, approach the problem of behavior through the study of the forces which impel to action, namely, the wishes, and we shall see that these correspond in general with the nervous mechanism.
>
> The human wishes have a great variety of concrete forms but are capable of the following general classification:
> 1. The desire for new experience.
> 2. The desire for security.
> 3. The desire for response.
> 4. The desire for recognition.

Reading on, one finds that these are simply new terms for the tendencies expressing the following dominant urges (1) fighting (hunting), (2) fear, (3) sex, (4) ego, (food getting?). In short Thomas' list presents in less conventional terms Tolman's two aversions and the two most important appetities. It requires some stretching of the imagination, however, to see how these basic physiological drives carry over into the derived forms as described by Thomas' four wishes.

At the end of this chapter Thomas adds the significant statement,

> We may assume also that an individual cannot be called normal in which all the four types of wishes are not satisfied in some measure and in some form.

Thomas' list with two additions has been presented by Watson and Spence in their *Educational Problems for Psychological Study*. They say,

> There are a few fundamental drives which lead to a restless series of behaviors designed to bring about a change from the unsatisfactory state of affairs in a given direction of adjustment. There

are a thousand ways of satisfying hunger, and perhaps even more specific behaviorisms any one of which might be employed in satisfying an urge toward mastery and success. For understanding people, nothing seems more important than insight into the ways in which they are moved by these fundamental psychological pressures. Six major trends may be mentioned.

1. Human beings tend to behave in ways making movement from physical deprivations (pain, hunger, sex demands, needs for sleep), toward physical well-being, euphemia.

2. Human beings tend to behave in ways involving movement from failure, thwarting, disappointment, toward success, mastery and achievement.

3. Human beings tend to behave in ways involving movement from being ignored or looked down upon, toward being looked up to, recognized, approved, admired.

4. Human beings tend to behave in ways involving movement from being unwanted toward being loved and given intimacy, tenderness, and a sense of belonging.

5. Human beings tend to behave in ways involving movement from being worried, anxious, fearful, toward release, security, and peace of mind.

6. Human beings tend to behave in ways involving movement from being bored, finding life dull and monotonous, toward adventure, new experience and zestful activity.

One should note that four of Watson and Spence's drives are identical with Thomas'. In addition, Watson and Spence have included the physical demands (which Thomas implies were subsumed in his more derived list) and *success* which Thomas does not mention, although it is so closely related to recognition that some have debated whether one exists apart from the other.

It should be noted that Spence and Watson have made each drive partake of the nature of both aversion and appetite, that is, tendency *away from* and *toward*.

As a result of this survey I wish to propose a new formulation of the fundamental human urges or drives. There seems to be at least three distinct types which can be distinguished.

1. The first type consists of descriptions or characterizations of the process of adjustment itself, looking at this process from various angles. For instance, adjustment is a drive toward the reduction of organic, visceral, or postural tensions and away from tissue destruction. The gestaltists have recognized this in their principle of *closure*. A dominant chord struck on the piano sets up tensions which require a tonic chord to restore the equilibrium. Any movement initiated in an attempt to reduce tensions set up has its own drive to completion. Regardless of the nature of the tension or of the process

set in motion to relieve it there is a drive toward *success*. I have found in studies of the adjustment of school children that the drive toward success, whatever the nature of the activity, is the most potent of all drives. In every individual there is a drive, strong or weak as it may be, to the successful completion of what one undertakes.

A second characterization of adjustment is a tendency to seek a situation and to repeat an act which in the past has relieved a tension or distress and has led to equilibrium. This is a tendency toward *familiarity*—the conservative tendency in men. Opposed to this is a third characteristic of adjustment— a tendency to random and restless behavior seeking for a situation and stimulus which will relieve the distress in case no familiar stimulus which has served successfully in the past is at hand. This leads to a tendency toward *exploration*. With the young and those with urgent drives the tendency is toward exploration, while the old and successful are conservative and tend to strive to retain the usual and the familiar.

It is quite possible that there are, besides these three, other characteristics of adjustment in general apart from the particular type of tension or disturbances from which equilibrium is sought.

2. The second type consists of the first order appetites and aversions which are groups of visceral or organic disturbances or tensions to be relieved by appropriate stimuli. Here I am quite willing to follow Tolman's list.

3. The third type consists of derived drives—similar in character to Tolman's second-order drives—drives which have been learned or acquired in the process of discovering ways and means of satisfying the primary organic drives. It is here that the greatest differences are found in the lists proposed by psychologists. It should be obvious that there is nothing necessarily universal in the nature of these derived drives except as the conditions of nurture throw all infants into approximately the same situations for the satisfactions of their primary drives. It is for this reason that I would criticize most lists of instincts and even the list of "primary distresses" proposed by Hollingworth. For instance, Hollingworth mentions as a primary distress "nakedness, shame, feelings of low worth" leading to such behavior as "decoration and exhibition of person and belongings or attainments." One has only to watch the entire unconcern of infants playing happily in a "state of nature" or the equal unconcern of primitive tribes to realize that this is a learned distress and is not "primary." It is true that maladjustments are found which seem to include a component of distress at nakedness, but such maladjustments can be understood only by going back to the really primary drives on which this sense of shame or feelings of inferiority have been built.

In like manner we would object to listing "ugliness, discord, and lack of harmony in surroundings" as a "primary distress" leading to such behavior as "decorative arrangement and disposition of materials provocative of relief (production of beauty)" when it is so evident that this tendency is learned in response to some other drive which is more fundamental. The urge toward beauty is by no means so universal, as evidenced by the millions of people who live in utterly mean and wretched surroundings, that it could be called primary. It develops too late in life to be a universal urge.

These second-order derived drives, to be at all *fundamental,* must have learnings attached to the primary drives in the first few weeks or months of life, and under conditions which are practically universal for every human being. Such reactions are those learned in connection with the acts of feeding, urinating and defecating and in avoiding pain, all of which, in the helpless state of infancy, require the assistance of others, particularly the mother. Any list, therefore, which may be made of the "fundamental" second-order drives must be the personal choice of some individual. As the list is added to, the drives become less and less universal and fundamental. There is no sharp dividing line between the second-order drives which may be counted on to operate in everyone and the very personal and specific wants of each individual.

We will list here nine second-order drives which seem to be of fundamental importance in interpreting problems of human adjustment. One is the desire to be with or in the presence of other persons, the old instinct of gregariousness. If this drive has good reason for being first on the list, it is because the baby is by force attended by others from birth onwards as a necessary part of his existence. Practically every satisfaction which he gains has associated with it the presence of another person. Little wonder, then, that the presence of other persons is demanded and enjoyed.

A second derived drive is the desire for attention from other people, closely related to the first, but possessing elements of its own. The baby not only wants other persons around but wants them to respond to him by looking at him, by speaking to him, by fondling him, and the like. This demand for attention from others continues as the baby matures into childhood and is a potent drive all through life.

Growing out of the last as a third drive is the desire for praise and approval. Not only does the baby want to be noticed but he has learned to crave certain kinds of notice such as smiles, friendly nods, pats and the whole complex behavior of sympathetic understanding, for these evidences of approval have occurred and have been associated with occasions when he has satisfied his desires of feeding, etc. These experiences which we call evidences of approval of themselves probably cause nervous relaxation and a pleasant body tone because of their associations. Consequently, everyone has learned to do the things which bring on these tokens of esteem and admiration which are valued for their relaxing powers. The desire for approval, applause, praise, and the like, becomes one of the strongest driving forces which human beings respond to.

Fenton speaks of

A certain satisfaction (in the infant), dim and unformed enough, to be sure, but none the less distinguishable, in producing results himself, not only for the sake of the particular result, but in part also for the sake of a rudimentary sense of power awakened in him by his own activity in causing the result . . . . Toward the end of the first year delight in doing things for himself becomes a motive for him, he must manage alone every activity that he could possibly achieve, and correspondingly as his abilities increased, his desire for independence and self-sufficiency waxed stronger, more compelling.

This is something the same as Thorndike had in mind when he said,

To do something and have something happen as the consequence is, other things being equal, instinctively satisfying, whatever be done and whatever be the consequent happening . . . . For example, a baby likes not only to see a pile of blocks tumble or a wheel go around, but also to find the blocks tumbling *when he hits them,* or the wheel revolving *when he pushes a spring.*

It is not necessary to assume that the satisfaction here is instinctive but that the relationship noticed is built up in situations which have their own satisfactions. It is quite possible that this simple drive is also the root of *mastering behavior.* Early in life we enjoy finding that we can control the actions of other people by what we say or do, especially when this gets us some other satisfaction which at the moment is desired. It is also possible that this simple drive is the origin of the drive toward the establishment of the self. Sooner or later, of course, this interest in and concern for the self acquires its own drive. So many of the adjustments of life, such as striving to win a game, are driven on by this tendency to exalt the self or maintain its integrity. If one can be persuaded that " it does not make any difference to himself personally" he will immediately let down in his striving to win or to excel others. These three separate drives—drive to be a cause, drive to mastery, and drive to maintain the self—may be different levels of a continuous development.

Opposed to this drive is the need for protection. The infant finds relief, comfort and protection at its mother's breast; later in his bed or his room; later the home affords a haven from the outside. There is a natural tendency to run to the mother or father for protection. That the infant finds its first satisfactions in a place that is warm, soft, and associated with a person (the mother) is the start for a need, expressed throughout life, for protection, shelter, security. No form of shelter is as effective as that of belonging to a group which indicates that this drive is closely related to the gregarious tendency. Out of the first intimate relations with the mother develop a need for affection, intimacy and tenderness.

Perhaps for completeness sake, curiosity should be mentioned as a third primary second-order drive to take care of the variety of early learned reactions to *objects* in the outside world. There are, for instance, the reaching and grasping movements which aid in food getting, exploration with the eyes and manipulation with the hands, and later the manipulation of words and ideas. The extent to which any of these components of curiosity become urges in their own right depends on how well they serve to satisfy the fundamental organic urges.

It should be noted how many of these drives are merely aspects of the mother-child relationship—the fact that the mother is present, that she gives her attention to the baby, that she responds to it approvingly, that he learns to control her, that she provides security and affection—and that these simple relationships become so firmly tied to the infant's satisfaction that they become primary needs for the rest of life. These second-order drives are in a sense fundamental because by the very conditions imposed by infant nurture no infant can escape them.

Postural tensions set up in the course of the pursuit of situations which can relieve fundamental urges themselves become drives, seeking relief, and easement. Muscular "sets" aroused by some stimulus which in the past has been associated with satisfying activity send repeated kinaesthetic nervous impulses which have driving force. Of these, "goal ideas" loom as being especially important. Presumably goal ideas are kept alive by unrelieved organic tensions which cause ends to persist in mind which experience has proven in the past to be satisfying or which the imagination promises to be satisfying. Naturally such postural states are too individual and too numerous to be listed or catalogued.

In conclusion, then, three types or levels of driving forces or urges in the human being are recognized:

I.   Fundamental characteristics of adjustment.
    (a)   Drive toward success.
    (b)   Drive toward the familiar.
    (c)   Drive toward new experiences.
II.   Appetites and aversions. (Tolman's list.)
    Food-hunger.   Fright (injury-avoidance).
    Sex-hunger.   Pugnacity (interference-avoidance).
    Excretion-hunger.
    Specific contact-hunger.
    Rest-hunger.
    Sensory-motor-hunger.
III. Derived drives.
    (a)   Desire to be with other persons.
    (b)   Desire for attention from other persons.
    (c)   Desire for praise and approval.
    (d)   Desire to be a cause.
    (e)   Desire for mastery.

(f)   Desire to maintain the self.
(g)   Desire for security, protection.
(h)   Desire for affection, tenderness, intimacy, sense of belonging.
(i)   Curiosity (reaching, grasping, manipulation, exploration).

These tendencies are present in every individual, but each individual satisfies them uniquely according to his experiences. To understand a person's adjustment one would do well in each case to inquire what situations or stimuli the individual has learned to require to satisfy these fundamental drives.

3. The 'Validation' of Drives

Georgene H. Seward

THE ambiguous categories of the McDougall generation have gradually given way to operationally defined concepts. This has led to the identification of drive with behavior. In line with this trend Anderson distinguishes between 'drive,' by which he refers to the neural mechanism underlying behavior, and 'need,' the instigating physiological state. Thus although the hunger drive is aroused by the changes taking place within the organism, this fact does not justify equating the hunger drive with these physiological conditions. He further suggests that learning may effect a shift in dependence for arousal from the original *internal* to a new set of *external* stimuli. Starting from this basic assumption, Anderson has deduced an impressive array of theorems which he is subjecting to experimental attack. The value of this step for progress in elucidating the important relationships between motivation and learning is undeniable. A grave danger lurks, however, in assuming equivalence between operationally identical behaviors regardless of origin. As Lewin reminds us, we are no more justified in postulating absolutes in the field of motivation than in that of perception. If we do we shall encounter the same difficulties that would result from assuming constancy of meaning for identifiable objects. Long ago Köhler pointed out

Abridged from the *Psychological Review,* 1942, 49, 88-95. Reprinted by permission of the author and the American Psychological Association, Inc.

the distinction between a branch perceived as part of a tree and the same branch perceived as an instrument for obtaining food. Similarly a chair when one wants to sit down is a different 'object' from the same chair when one wants to obtain something beyond reach. It was to avoid such ambiguities that Tolman introduced his concept of 'Sign-Gestalt.' In the field of motivation it is all the more necessary to recognize that a given behavorial item has different significance in the life economy of the organism according to the whole in which it is embedded. Therefore we should not regard as equivalent two examples of food-seeking behavior, one of which occurs in connection with food deficiency, the other as a result of conditioning. In other words, eating to satisfy physiological hunger has a different meaning for the organism from eating to satisfy an acquired 'social hunger.'.

Unless careful evaluation of behavior is made in terms of the total situation in which it occurs, we shall find ourselves in the paradoxical position of confusing, by over simplifying, the very issues we are striving to clarify. In the writer's opinion we may avoid this pitfall by a kind of 'validation' procedure. Instances of behavior associated with vegetative drives should always be checked against some criterion of internal need. This would in no way sacrifice objectivity because our indices could be as objective and as readily quantified as the behaviors correlated with them. If, for example, food-seeking behavior were found to occur regardless of deprivation interval, or female receptivity in the 'wrong' genital phase, we should have to designate these externalized forms in terms different from those used to describe their more 'valid' prototypes.

The importance of such distinctions is shown by the wide-spread prevalence of externalization. Not only does this trend characterize individual development, but the literature suggests a phylogenetic parallel. In the absence of systematic comparative studies bearing on this point, we can do little more than assume increasing susceptibility to external influences in correlation with increasing capacity for learning. At the lowest levels we should expect to find the behavior appropriate to a given need more rigidly bound to that need, but as we ascend the evolutionary scale this relationship should become more flexible. We should then anticipate greater mobility of the behavior, i.e., an easier shifting from the original need to the service of other needs. A survey of the experimental literature on motivation among vertebrates lends some support to our assumption, but proof awaits a systematic attack on this important problem.

In the case of feeding, the influence of social as well as physiological factors have been demonstrated as far down the scale as the fishes. Welty, using a variety of fishes, showed that more food was consumed by groups of four than by isolated individuals. At the level of the birds, the most conclusive evidence is that of Katz and his students, who reported in the case of the hen, transposability of behavior from an originally internal need to an external stimulus situation. In some of their experiments the amount of food presented—a purely environmental factor—was the chief determiner of the amount consumed. Another external factor, the presence of other hens, also produced striking effects. The resumption of eating by satiated animals followed the introduction of hungry members of the species, and the amount of food consumed varied directly with the number of other animals present. It was by means of such findings that Katz confirmed his two-component (external-internal) theory of hunger. Among mammals apart from Anderson's current work on externalization, Harlow was able to demonstrate social facilitation of feeding in the rat.[1] He found that more food was consumed when hungry rats were fed in pairs than when alone. Competition was apparently the factor responsible for the difference. The social effect failed to appear when satiated animals were used. The same author collaborating with Yudin attacked a similar problem in a group of rhesus monkeys. The results follow our theoretical expectation by showing a greater susceptibility to social influences in the higher form. This was true even in situations where competition was ruled out. In the chimpanzee, a pertinent observation reported by Nissen and Crawford in their work on food-sharing, was the absence of correlation between begging for food and degree of hunger. The importance of social factors in the feeding behavior of humans is a matter of common observation. The multiplicity of motives served by eating and drinking does not demand an excursion to the Kwakiutls but may be discovered directly by introspection.

Another line of evidence suggesting a loose tie between nutrition and feeding is adduced by Levy. He reports that under conditions where sufficient food was obtained but with a curtailment of eating responses, the latter were continued long after physiological hunger was satisfied, and appeared in pathological forms. His material included pecking in chicks, licking in dogs, and thumb-sucking in babies.[2]

We have chosen our examples from different phylogenetic levels in the hope of revealing a trend toward increasing susceptibility to social factors. Such a trend may be more clearly shown in forms of behavior that are not vital for individual survival. In life-preservative functions, *e.g.,* nutrition, one may expect a closer association with physiological conditions, and consequently less in the way of environmental modification. Other forms of behavior which subserve a vegetative but not a vital function, however, may be more easily shaken from their somatic moorings and subjected to outside influences. Sexual behavior affords the best illustrations of this trend and most clearly reveals the difficulties in which we may become involved unless

[1]Drinking in the rat has also been found subject to social facilitation.

[2]That the relation between food need and eating is variable may also be shown in converse by the many instances where hunger does not induce eating even in the presence of food. The most frequent cause of this anomaly is conflict with other drives.

we keep constantly before us the setting in which the behavior occurs. In an effort to find more general confirmation of Katz' two-component theory, Skard set up a series of experiments on sexual need in hens which roughly paralleled the earlier ones on hunger. The results indicated extra-somatic factors in sexual motivation. For example, increasing the amount of sexual stimulation led to greater sexual indulgence, just as increasing the amount of food presented had led to a continuation of eating beyond the point of physiological replacement. Moreover, thwarting of other needs, *e.g.*, lack of food, led to an intensification of sexual zeal, the sexual indulgence thus becoming what one might be tempted to call, 'sublimated eating!'

In the lower mammals represented by various rodents, sexual behavior seems to be closely associated with hormonal conditions, especially in the female. In the cat, on the other hand, Winslow reported situations in which male and female copulatory positions were assumed as expressions of dominance-subordination status, and apparently were devoid of sexual significance.

It is at the primate level, however, where transposability of sexual behavior reaches its peak and confusion of interpretation is rife. It has been noted by many investigators that sexual behavior is frequently used to mediate non-sexual motivation. Hamilton recognized its role in connection with escape from an enemy. Kempf saw in it a means of procuring food and protection. In an attempt to bring order out of chaos, Maslow, like Katz, set up a two-factor theory. Working with a variety of primates, he distinguished between sexual behavior which is a direct product of physiological tensions, and sexual behavior which expresses the impulse to dominate, and is used as a 'power weapon.' He pointed out that it is often interchangeable with bullying and fighting to subdue an annoying partner. This theory would explain why primate sexual behavior apparently occurs independently of periodicity although hormonal cycles can be demonstrated. It also explains the frequent appearance of various perversions that do not seem to have an endocrine basis. Recently, Yerkes and Yerkes and Elder have been able to reveal in the chimpanzee a period of 'heat' which is correlated with a condition of genital skin swelling. Copulation is likely to be limited to this time in the case of experienced and congenial consorts mated under controlled conditions. It does not, however, necessarily imply receptivity in the female, and may occur regardless of oestrous phase as a defensive or accommodating reaction to a dominant male.

Our knowledge of the primate should guide our interpretation of human sexual behavior. But again we find that the tendency to isolate a given behavioral item from its total motivational context has beclouded the issue. Malinowski could dichotomize man and animals thus: "The sexual impulse is not confined to any season, not conditioned by any bodily process . . . . It is there to affect at any moment the life of man and woman . . . " "When the animal instinctive endowment and physiological change throw male and female into a situation out of which they have to extricate themselves by the simple play of natural impulses, with man the control comes, as we know, from culture and tradition." Miller attempted to clear things up by pointing out the relation between the reproductive behavior of man and that of the lower mammals. Tinklepaugh also stressed the continuity in mammalian sexual behavior. He reminded us that psychological factors are so marked in the human that they obscure a biological cycle which is really homologous with the oestrous cycle of lower forms. He also made the interesting suggestion that demonstration of affection has developed by conditioning so that it readily leads to sexual stimulation and coitus. This is another way of saying that the human sexual drive has become externalized.

These illustrations which we have presented from food-seeking and sexual behavior may suffice to indicate the danger of identifying drive with isolated behavior. We have noted in the course of development of the species as well as in that of the individual, a tendency for drives to become externalized. This process involves an increasing readiness for transposability, *i.e.,* for the behavior originally associated with one drive to become elicited in the service of another. An integrative drive like dominance for example, may utilize as channels of expression, the behaviors properly belonging to the 'simpler' drives of hunger and mating. To avoid confusion and to achieve clearer insights we have suggested validating each behavior item and interpreting it in terms of its total setting.

4. Homeostasis as a Unifying Concept in Personality Theory

Ross Stagner

THE task of personality theory is to achieve generalizations having maximum applicability with maximum predictive value. Such generalizations may relate to personality as a feature of all human organisms, or to personality as the unique totality of a single individual. The most fruitful generalizations would seem to be those which are useful in both of these areas.

Abridged from the *Psychological Review*, 1951, *58*, 5-17. Reprinted by permission of the author and the American Psychological Association, Inc.

It is proposed here that the principle of homeostasis—the law that organisms seek to maintain constancy of inner tissue conditions—can be expanded into a major generalization in the field of personality theory. This principle can be shown to have value in illuminating personality considered both as a universal and as a unique phenomenon.

While the concept of homeostasis in itself needs no restatement here, the particular sequence of ideas to be developed calls for a beginning at the basic physiological level. Treating this very briefly, we shall then discuss in more detail some broader implications of the concept.

Homeostasis was first identified as a major biological concept in connection with the maintenance of essential tissue equilibria, such as the oxygen, temperature, glucose and other inner constants. These inner constancies correspond to the basic biological needs upon which behavioristic theorists develop their conception of personality dynamics.

According to this view, any disturbance of essential constancy leads to tension, restless activity, contacting the needed substance, and restoration of equilibrium. As metabolism consumes glucose, for example, the hunger tension arises. Seeking-behavior results in the location and ingestion of food; the return to equilibrium is accompanied by quiescence.

It is, however, obvious that the organism does not simply continue to restore those biological equilibria which are essential to the existence of our protoplasm. While critics of homeostatic theory have suggested that this view offers only a static explanation of behavior, a recurrent restoration of a pre-existing state, such interpretations are unfair to the theory. When a given tissue constancy is first disturbed, the organism mobilizes energy for action which ceases when the equilibrium is restored. *Recurrence* of this same disturbance is another matter. (1) The organism perceives minimal physiological changes as *cues* and *anticipates* the disturbance. Forestalling action therefore becomes possible. (We eat before we experience intense hunger pangs.) We suggest that energy mobilization for forestalling tactics must be explained in terms of a *cortical tension* which reflects the visceral-proprioceptive pattern of the original biological disequilibration. (2) The organism perceives environmental objects as potential sources of equilibrium-restoration and behaves differently toward them (hoarding food, building houses or nests, etc.). Thus, repeated disequilibration results in continuous modification of the organism and its perception of the external world. *Dynamic homeostasis* involves the maintenance of tissue constancies by establishing a constant physical environment—by reducing the variability and disturbing effects of external stimulation. Thus the organism does not simply restore the prior equilibrium. A new, more complex and more comprehensive equilibrium is established.

But it is not only the changes in physical situations which disturb tissue constancies. Persons become increasingly important to us from birth onward. To the infant the presence of mother is a *sign* of tissue constancy and physical-milieu constancy. The absence of mother becomes a sign of disequilibrium and threat. Thus, the mother's appearance, voice, etc., can become valued as a means to biological equilibrium. In the same way other changes in the social environment may come to function as signals for biological disturbance, and set off anxiety tensions, energy mobilization, and vigorous action toward the restoration of social-milieu constancy. The organism may then take anticipatory measures to prevent change in the *social* environment on subsequent occasions.

This sequence of events leads to the view of personality sketched in Figure 1, where it is suggested that the individual, dynamically striving to preserve his inner tissue constancies, moves successively to build a constant physical environment (second level), and a constant social environment (third level). These may be thought of as envelopes protecting the biological constancies. It is assumed that, in the typical sequence, demand for physical constancy emerges first and demand for social constancy second, the latter being based in considerable part upon the need for physical uniformity. This leads to the prediction that threats to the organism's physical environment will generally produce more vigorous energy-mobilizations than threats to the social constancies; and that actual biological disequilibrium will dominate over either of the others. For the most part this prediction is verified: under the pressure of physical hazard, social amenities disappear; and under extreme hunger or pain, the physical environment is likely to be disregarded. We shall consider later the case in which this prediction is not verified.

HOMEOSTASIS AND PERCEPTUAL CONSTANCY

Before elaborating further on the motivational aspects of homeostatic theory, it is desirable that we introduce a new thread into the pattern. An important part of stage two (the establishment of a constant physical milieu) is perceptual in character. The so-called "perceptual constancies" (size constancy, color constancy, etc.) must be introduced here if we are to get a clear picture of the extensive role played by the homeostatic principle in personality organization.

Every undergraduate student of psychology learns that objects tend to be visually perceived as having a constant size, shape and color under varying illuminations and at varying distances. It is noted that these external conditions make it physically impossible to have a constant retinal image; perceptual constancies are therefore central in basis. The teacher does not always point out to the undergraduate that such constancies have survival value; but it is fairly obvious that man could not have survived under primitive conditions if he failed to identify the small image of a sabor-tooth tiger before it reached the size associated with immediate physical danger.

When observed from this point of view, the perceptual constancies appear to be another facet of homeostasis. The organism needs a constant external environment if it is to maintain constant tissue states. In attempting to reduce the variability of external stimuli (threats to equilibrium or sources of needed substances), the organism must deal with objects. But objects, as stimuli affecting the distance receptors, are protean in size, shape and color. Under such conditions adjustment is most difficult. The organism therefore *learns* to perceive identical objects as possessing these constant attributes.

The excellent treatment by Hebb of the problem of perception has made it unnecessary to defend this suggestion. As Hebb has noted, the Gestalt emphasis on native factors in object perception should be restricted to the perception of *unity*; that is, the awareness of form and closure. The evidence he cites bears rather convincingly on the notion that *identity* must be a product of learning; indeed, it would seem that more than normal faith in mysterious organismic powers would be required to explain size-constancy on a nativistic basis.[1]

Hebb has placed rather less emphasis than seems justified upon the fact that perception is itself a purposive, need-directed process dominated by organismic homeostasis. It is interesting in this connection to consider the work of Adelbert Ames, Jr., and the variety of research activities stimulated thereby. It appears from these findings that even so simple a perception as that of two lines of light in a dark room is modified by the set or purpose of the observer, and that the perceived characteristics (size, shape and distance) of objects inhere in their relations to the purpose of the perceiver. Since— as the first section of this paper indicated—purposive activities can be subsumed under the homeostatic category, this line of reasoning confirms the view that the perceptual constancies are also to be considered as homeostatic manifestations.

Helson has argued persuasively, and the data of other researchers agree, that the frame of reference of the individual tends toward a constant organization about a point determined by the geometric mean of his experiences with the class of stimuli presented. This suggests that the organism builds not merely a constancy for characteristics of individual objects, but also constancy for classes of objects. Thus Hastorf notes that subjects make a projected rectangle of light larger when operating under the task-set of representing an envelope than when representing a calling card.

This is possibly the explanation for the finding of Bruner and Goodman

---

[1]There is even reason, according to Raney and Carmichael, to believe that both sensitivity and response are determined initially by inner, metabolic factors; and that outside stimuli acquire "meaning" in their function of interrupting or facilitating such endogenous behavior.

that poor children make a circle representing a 25-cent piece larger than it is made by well-to-do children. It may be that the "physically real" value (purchasing power) was greater for the poorer children; thus constancy would favor the larger size.

Physical perception of objects, and of classes of objects, as possessing constant characteristics, will aid survival. It becomes possible to contact needed substances and avoid noxious stimuli, to deal adaptively with physical reality; whereas reactions based directly upon the protean, ever-changing peripheral receptor process would induce only behavioral confusion.[2] We must maintain external as well as internal constancy.

CONSTANCIES IN SOCIAL PERCEPTION

Perceptual constancies may very well contribute in a major way to the establishment of the uniform social milieu which has been suggested as the third level of homeostatic adjustment. Successful adaptation of the child to demands of his parents is unquestionably facilitated if he behaves on a "constancy hypothesis" with respect to them. Where reality constantly frustrates this tendency (very inconsistent real behavior by a parent), maladjustment seems invariably to result.

In later social development the same pattern appears. Our perception of individual personalities follows the constancy principle. If I observe Mr. Smith behaving in a weak, futile, ineffectual manner today, I shall be predisposed to perceive those same characteristics in his actions tomorrow (the so-called "halo" effect). This phenomenon is likewise adaptive and homeostatic in character. The person, in his efforts to achieve tissue constancy, must operate on some hypothesis as regards external reality. Since the constancy hypothesis proves useful in dealing with inanimate objects, it tends to be transferred to dealing with people. Further, infantile experiences usually reinforce the constancy hypothesis. Mother has a dependable relationship with food, comfort and security. Strangers are often associated with disturbance of equilibrium, thwarting of needs, pain, discomfort and insecurity. Thus the perception of specific individuals, and of classes of people, may become organized as constants and this may aid in adjustment. Unfortunately, or fortunately, as one chooses to view the phenomenon, humans do not in reality manifest such constancy as does an inanimate object. The perception of personality-constancy is thus projective and inaccurate in many instances, but is adhered to nevertheless.

---

[2]We are intrigued, in this connection, with the work reported by Eysenck and others on dark-vision of anxiety neurotics. It appears that such patients show a far greater loss of visual efficiency under dark adaptation than normals or hysterics. Could this be due, in anxiety cases, to the presence of a deep insecurity about these perceptual constancies? Does it mean that children who, for any reason, fail to stabilize firmly these percepts—under widely varying physical conditions—are prone to develop anxiety neurosis?

Once a delineated percept for a given individual or group is established, it tends to persist. We overlook in our friends behavior that we bitterly criticize elsewhere. Undesirable characteristics simply are not perceived. Conversely, disliked individuals are seen as having "bad" traits even when no objective basis for this perception can be identified.[3]

Leeper demonstrated the establishment of a constant percept for an ambiguous figure. By showing a picture which allowed only one alternative (from the ambiguous drawing) to be seen, he was able to fix the perception so that it was virtually impossible for subjects to get the other object. Edwards verified the existence of a selective tendency based on established perceptions, tending to maintain constancy. He presented a speech containing an identical number of pro-New Deal and anti-New Deal statements to his subjects. Republicans remembered mostly anti-New Deal items (and distorted some favorable remarks into hostile comments); Democrats remembered pro-New Deal facts and ignored the others. Thus a percept of an idea or social object, once established, obeys the constancy principle.

The effect of reality (experience followed by action directed toward the object) no doubt is in the direction of modifying constancies established on an unrealistic basis. This process, in the field of physical reality, probably proceeds promptly and reliably. In social perceptions it is slower and less dependable. As the various studies of stero-types of social groups indicate, such pictures develop without much basis in reality. Even when world events clearly have a bearing on the qualitative nature of this stereotype, it is modified but slowly. Thus we may generalize that a fundamental tendency of personality seemed to be one of perceiving constancy in individuals (or groups of individuals), and to behave toward them in terms of these perceived constancies.

There is reason to believe that the preservation of a constant external environment is an aid to the development of a well-integrated ego. While we need not accept the analytic metaphor that "objects are internalized," we are on safe ground in stating that habits will function smoothly, and perceptual expectancies will be adequately related to objective reality, if this physical constancy is maintained.

The constancy of the social milieu is also important. The child establishes certain expectancies with regard to his parents—their personalities and behavior. He attains security as their actions fit into these expectancies. Furthermore, he imitates them, and develops certain expectancies for his own behavior patterned on theirs (the Freudian ego-ideal). Now, as Jacobson and Plant have noted, the effect of disappointment as regards their characteristics can be quite destructive of ego-integration, especially about the Oedipus age.

[3]A methodical analysis of perceptual constancies in the social field will be found in the recent monograph by Gustav Ichheiser. While we are in disagreement with minor parts in this treatment, it is generally supplementary to the basic thesis presented here.

It is worthy of note that both of these authors equate disappointment to disillusion. In our scheme this is equivalent to the disturbance of a perceptual constancy in the social field.

NEED AND PREFERENCE

Let us now turn to a criticism of homeostatic theory which is of considerable importance. This approach may be represented by P. T. Young, who has pointed out cogently that rats and humans may be motivated to more vigorous action by preference than by homeostatic need. The answer to this criticism can best be given in terms of perceptual phenomena.

We have already emphasized that the organism responds selectively to external stimuli when motivated by homeostatic tensions. Thus, certain perceived qualities of objects come to function as *cues* directing behavior toward these objects. It seems likely (1) that some such cues are innately given, in the sense that selective threshold differences are built into our nervous system. For example, mother's milk must be acceptable to the infant if the latter is to survive. We may therefore hypothesize that mammalian strains not provided with differential sensitivity to warm, sweet liquids were eliminated early in biological history. It is true, of course, that there are other substances whch offer these cues (*cf.* Young's rats who choose saccharine solutions) but which are not homeostatic in character.

A realistic approach to behavior theory requires a consideration of the fact that modern conditions face the organism with new objects of indeterminate homeostatic significance. Man (presumably by Darwinian selection processes) is so biologically constituted that he has sensory mechanisms capable of reporting on most of the noxious stimuli having any considerable probability of occurrence in primitive life. Furthermore, these sensory selectivities are triggered to visceral tensions in such a way that violent activity is released by the perception of this cue (physical pain, for example).

Man has not, however, evolved sensory mechanisms for the detection of X-rays, gamma rays, and other noxious stimuli present in modern life. This does not constitute a criticism of homeostatic theory, but only a recognition of the fact that some new sources of tissue disequilibrium have been invented. Organic disturbances must set off behavioral activity by way of afferent fibers. When the sensory mechanism is inadequate to detect a harmful stimulus, no homeostatic protective action is possible.

Similarly, modern living presents us with many stimulus objects *perceived as identical* with those having homeostatic value. If these are preferred, though useless, it may mean an "error" on the part of the integrating mechanism; it does not invalidate the theory.

A further point merits consideration, namely the fact (2) that learning to identify objects as equilibrium-restoring is never mathematically perfect. The organism operates on a probability basis. In the language of hypothesis-learning, we may say something like this: "In the past, most warm, sweet liquids have served as tension-reducers. The probabilities are high that this warm, sweet liquid is also need-satisfying in character." The phenomena of stimulus equivalence and positive transfer suggest that, within certain limits of discrimination threshold, objects presenting similar cues wll be perceived as identical. Thus rats and men may *prefer* substances which are not homeostatic in function, but are incorrectly identified as such.

Preference for foods may be changed either by satiating with the preferred food or by creating a need for the non-preferred substance. However, in the latter case it is necessary to break up the physically perceivable situation so that the preferred food does not affect the distance receptors simultaneously with the non-preferred. Otherwise the constancy based on former needs and tensions appears capable of blocking the establishment of a new habit adequate to the new need.

This seems to have considerable bearing on the success of reform or therapy. If the delinquent (or neurotic) is simply replaced in the environment which led him to develop maladjustive patterns of perceiving and acting, these are likely to be reinstated and to continue to dominate the motor system.

Young's own experiments show conclusively that preferences can be built upon a homeostatic need. It thus appears far more defensible to hold that homeostasis is the primary motivational principle involved, and that preference (palatability, affectivity) is simply a derivative based upon (1) inherent sensitivity thresholds of homeostatic significance, or (2) non-discriminable differences from signs of homeostatic goal-objects.

At this point it will be well also to deal briefly with two less fundamental criticisms of homeostatic motivation theory. One of these calls attention to the fairly obvious fact that, in the short run at least, people often indulge in behavior which is disequilibrating; the other, that behavior directed to the maintenance of a constant state sometimes takes such a form as to prevent the achievement of that state. Neither of these objections seems to carry much weight.

The relationship between short-run disequilibrium and long-run equilibrium has been dealt with rather adequately by Freeman, following the excellent analysis by Freud. That men do in fact go on fasts, climb mountains, hunt dangerous animals and in other ways disturb constant states is a truism. That such behavior violates the principle of homeostasis is not a truism.

The organism is constantly faced with the necessity for maintaining a variety of constant states and hence with the task of determining priorities. It seems safe to assume that within the biological needs, the relative survival significance of a given demand is keyed to dominance of the motor system: that is, that the hierarchy of physiological drives is a function of the threat to survival implied by a given deprivation. As we move from this level to the maintenance of a constant physical and a constant social environment, we encounter more difficulty in ascertaining the principles upon which dominance is based. It should be clear, nonetheless, that the organism in some way evolves standards of value, in terms of which choice is made as to the particular constancy which gets priority. Probably the history of the individual is decisive in this respect.

The facts indicate that the epithet "coward" may be more disturbing to equilibrium than the physical danger of facing a wild animal. Or, the humiliation of losing valued social status may be more upsetting than the physiological disequilibrium induced by mountain climbing. In terms of the view presented here, such choices will be functions of the perception of these alternatives, and this in turn will depend upon the number and kind of reinforcements related to such percepts. In one boy's family, physical prowess is constantly praised and rewarded; in another, it is ignored or depreciated. There is a significant relationship here to Freud's reality-principle; a short-run or minor disequilibrium may be accepted in order to achieve a long-run or major equilibrium. A fruitful approach to this problem is that of Mowrer, which utilizes the observation that some people orient their behavior to the rewards or punishments physically present or near in *time*, neglecting those to follow in the future. In the context of the present paper, the phenomenon is one of *perceiving as larger* that which is closer in time.

The second objection refers to those acts which ostensibly aim at restoring equilibrium but in fact prevent it. Thus we have the instance of the insecure, affection-starved woman who, in demanding love from people, so frightens them that she becomes even more insecure. When phrased thus, the problem promptly vanishes. No proponent of homeostatic theory has ever claimed that the organism did not make errors. Probably a young lion, trying to catch game, often is overeager and loses his dinner; this may be considered unfortunate—for him—but does not deny the applicability of homeostasis to his behavior.

This difference, of course, needs to be noted; the lion learns to correct his seeking behavior, or else he dies. The neurotic does not, without guidance learn to identify and eliminate his errors; on the contrary, he is most likely to establish an artificial constancy, perhaps on a fantasy level, in which his acts are not errors. That such inherently unstable equilibria lead to a piling up of residual tension and so eventually to breakdown has been aptly stated by Freeman, as in a different context by all the psychoanalysts. Sex conflicts lead to neuroses, whereas conflicts about food do not, because an unstable equilibrium with regard to food-need results in the destruction of the organism. Perception of non-food objects as edible, and of food as inedible, means suicide. Such a perceptual constancy, as regards sex, may be extremely uncomfortable—and yet, as the patient sees it, more acceptable than the apparent alternative. It seems likely that neurotic equilibria become stabilized only with regard to conflicts which do not violate the most comprehensive constancy of all—the maintenance of the total organism as a going concern.

EGO-CONSTANCY AND EGO-MOTIVATION

Let us now return to the problem raised in an earlier passage, the problem of the dominance of social constancies over biological constancies. This is the problem raised by exceptions to the suggestion made earlier, that biological demands finally control perception and behavior. How can homeostatic theory deal with the artist who starves in a garret to express his ideas, the martyr who prefers physical pain to an abandonment of his beliefs?

The solution to this problem seems to depend upon the evolution of a new perceptual object, the self or ego, and the establishment of a perceptual constancy with regard to it. The theory of the development of the ego as an object of perception has been presented adequately elsewhere. The tendency toward perceptual constancy will operate to hold constant the self-image. Since the ego will be repeatedly perceived as part of a total situation involving the restoration of biological equilibrium, physical constancy and social uniformity, it can become a highly-valued cue-object for the maintenance of all needed equilibria. The possibilities of mutual reinforcement (by different inner tensions) and of overvaluing the ego as object are therefore obvious.

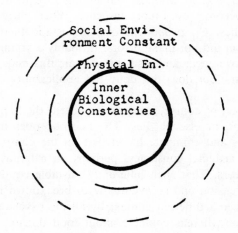

Fig. 1. The inner tissue constancies are most resistant to disturbance, and mobilize maximum energy to restore equilibrium. The physical environment is maintained constant by perceptual and functional activities, as is the social environment. Individuals differ in the extent to which physical or social constancies will be defended.

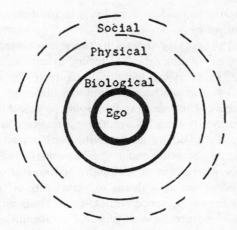

FIG. 2. In some personalities, ego-constancies come to dominate the motor system even to the exclusion of biological constant states.

The maintenance of ego-constancy may involve physical, social or individual uniformities. The child may seek to maintain himself in relation to physical patterns of security or symbols of prestige, such as toys, clothing, etc.; or he may focus on dominance or submission, exhibitionism or withdrawal, as social patterns; or he may try to act out verbal labels attached to him by adults, such as studious, "bad boy," artistic, or stupid.

The self-image (including the relation of self to environment) so evolved represents a "constant state" which the organism seeks to preserve. As such it may dominate the motor system and may even prevent homeostatic action based on earlier physical or social constancies. The person defending his ego-system of percepts and values may accept social ostracism or even physical disequilibrium. The mature ego, therefore, has its own constancy function; it tends to render the personality more independent of random changes in the physical or social milieu.

In this connection it should (unfortunately, perhaps) be emphasized that only a modest percentage of people really come to value ego-constancy as highly as often-cited examples would suggest. Thus, we need only look at Germany, where most people, even in the professional classes, abandoned valued portions of the self-image in order to preserve biological, physical and social constancies under the Nazi regime.

We suggest, however, that in some individuals a modification of the schema shown in Fig. 1 is necessary. For these persons the self or ego becomes a perceptual object, the constancy of which is highly valued. It may dominate over the social milieu, as when a person suffers ostracism for his ideals; or even over the physical environment, as in the man who indulges in hazardous activities for ego-gratification. Finally, in extreme forms, it may be represented as in Fig. 2, where the individual actually is more disturbed by loss of ego integrity than by hunger or pain.

The motivational potency of threats to the ego will depend, then, on the pattern of constancies an individual is trying to maintain, and upon their relative dominance. In everyday life this is likely to be ascertained by observing the types of disequilibrating stimuli which are most effective in mobilizing his energies. Thus we may find John (a viscerotonic, in Sheldon's schema) concerned mostly with his vegetative functions; he lives to eat, and is most profoundly disturbed by any stimulus which interferes with his visceral peace. Harry, on the other hand (perhaps an Adlerian case), may be concerned primarily with status equilibrium; his motivation is ego-centered, and any stimulus perceived as a threat to status sets off a violent reaction. Tom (studied by a Freudian, hence an anal-erotic) has an equilibrium based on order, scheduling and precision of physical arrangement; any interference with these patterns may be profoundly disturbing to him. Obviously, any number of such illustrations could be offered.

For the purposes of clinical personality study, it is more fruitful to investigate the particular *pattern of perceptual constancies* most characteristic of the person, rather than to hunt for behavioral constancies. Thus the orthodox analytic procedure is likely to determine father-figures, mother-figures, situations symbolizing traumatic (disequilibrating) stimuli, and so on. The non-directivists are concerned to obtain knowledge of the client's self-image, as well as his perception of reassuring and threatening social objects.

Action, of course, is directed by perception, not by the "physically real" stimulus. Under most conditions this is adaptive; it is, indeed, our justification for the survival value of the perceptual constancies. When the physically presented stimulus is so contrived as to give a perception of a radically different object (as in certain of the Ames demonstrations), behavior is governed by the percept, not by the intellectually known reality.

Clinical psychologists are, of course, familiar with this phenomenon. The patient perceives a harmless situation as involving a drastic threat to his ego. He may rationally know the threat to be non-existent; it may be demonstrated logically or even empirically to be non-threatening. Nevertheless, as long as the perception holds, the behavior is governed by perception, not by knowledge.

The importance of this point for social psychology was developed by Kurt Lewin in a penetrating essay. Rational, intellectual education against prejudice, in favor of new ways of dealing with human-relations problems, is doomed to failure unless it is accompanied by education for a new way of perceiving the situation. If minority groups continue to be perceived as having undesirable characteristics, behavior toward them will be discriminatory. We may even say that, within this restricted frame of reference, prejudice is rational; if the physically real minority group member had these traits, it would be proper to discriminate. The same, of course, can be said of the neurotic; a man would be a fool if he were not defensive when surrounded by the terrifying dangers which people the neurotic's environment. It is only by undermining the "unreal" perception that we can make progress.

In social relationships, behavioral constancy also reinforces perceptual constancy. If a man enters a group and perceives the other men as aggressive toward him, he will probably behave in such a way as to evoke aggression. A woman who attends a tea expecting to be snubbed may stay away from others and thus elicit non-accepting responses; she then concludes that her original perception of the situation was correct. There is, consequently, a major difference between the homeostatic process in the perception of physical and of social situations. Erroneous perceptions of physical constancies are automatically selfcorrecting; in the quest for need-gratification, behavior based on inadequate perceptions will fail of reinforcement. Because of the mechanism just sketched, behavior based on erroneous perceptions of social situations may be reinforced; thus an artificial constancy of the perceived environment is perpetuated.

According to the work of Frenkel-Brunswik and her collaborators, intolerance of ambiguity is in itself a major personality variable. The secure individual is not seriously disturbed by unclear physical percepts or equivocal emotional relationships. Certain insecure personalities, on the other hand, seem to be quite upset by any deviation from clearly defined structures, either perceptual or emotional. This quest for security through rigidity may be a function of having change and uncertainty forced upon the child before he is mature enough, or the ego-system well enough organized, to accept them. Many neurotics are capable of normal functioning in a constant environment, but they are thrown into panic by even minor changes. Clearly, in these cases, ego-constancy has *not* been successfully developed to replace physical and social constancies.

PROJECTIVE TESTS

Projective tests reveal the inner personality to the extent that they expose perceptual constancies. If, in a series of Rorschach blots, the person repeatedly perceives objects in disturbed motion, or if he seems able to see only minute, carefully delineated forms, the clinician is provided with supposedly valuable information. When a series of TAT productions gives repeated characterizations of father-figures as stern, punishing and repressive, we feel that something of importance has been ascertained. The relative value of specific tests is largely a function of the extent to which they tap important percepts, particularly if the characteristics of these percepts are, for one or another reason, not available to conscious report.

Projective tests are more useful than reality situations for diagnostic purposes. The percept in the latter case is likely to be a compromise between a value corresponding to true "constancy" and that dictated by the physical stimulus.[4] Even the neurotic does not perceive all social situations as equally threatening. While his "constancy" hypothesis may be that all adult males are threatening, the smile, voice, etc., of a specific male acquaintance may give him some reassurance. The ambiguous projective situation thus gives a more valid insight into this inner determinant of behavior than many reality situations.

THERAPY

The purpose of therapy, of course, is to help the patient achieve a realistic equilibrium in place of the unstable neurotic pattern he has evolved. Behavior aimed at the achievement of realistic need-gratifications and inner homeostasis is blocked by a pattern of inappropriate perceptual constancies. Therapy, then, must operate by modifying these perceptions of the self and the environment. Just as suggestion from a person of prestige may modify the perception of a social object, so suggestion from the respected therapist may induce modification of a perceived personal relationship. In the analytic situation, reactivation of infantile emotions without punishment and without rejection often leads to restructuring of percepts involved. This is not accomplished without extensive disturbances of equilibrium, and profound tensions within the patient.

As with projective tests, it is apparently possible in therapy (specifically, in the transference relationship) to evoke relatively "pure" emotions freed of reality factors. That is, if the therapist succeeds in keeping himself unclearly structured, the patient may project onto the therapist his image of one or more emotion-arousing figures; and the patient's experienced emotion in this case is uncomplicated by the reality features of the immediate situation. Since this makes an excellent opening for the therapist to demonstrate the projective character of the patient's perceptions, it offers an optimal chance for corrective work.

The modern trend in therapy calls for guided efforts at reality-testing by the patient. It is important that this be done if therapeutic gains are to transfer to everyday life, but it is futile to urge reality experimentation prior to insight and perceptual modification. Indeed, the neurotic at the onset of therapy will claim that he has tested reality and found it wanting. What he does not realize is that he never actually contacted reality; he perceived only his own projected universe of constant threats and frustrations. Thus a change

[4]This happens also in the laboratory. . . .

in perception of the self and the environment is a necessary preliminary to practice of new patterns.[5]

Implicit in the foregoing is the notion that therapy, in the early stages, leads to a disturbance of equilibrium. Neurosis is homeostatic in character; the neurotic has established his stable environment, with some dependable need-gratifications; even a painful symptom serves its purpose in the psychic economy. Phobias, compulsions, paralyses and other psycho-pathologies aid in the preservation of a precarious balance between gratification and threat.

If therapy is to be successful, this stable environment must be restructured. The patient immediately reacts to this as a threat, with consequences familiar to all clinicians. As Bergler has noted, "what neurotics fear most" is a disturbance of this formula, or "basic fallacy," which we have shown to be a form of perceptual constancy. It should not be surprising, furthermore, if modes of perceiving practiced for twenty or thirty years cannot be modified overnight.

Motivation is necessary if this restructuring is to be achieved. A person comes for therapy only when he is aware of a discrepancy between the equilibrium he has attained and that formerly possessed, or that believed to be attainable. There is nothing about the concept of homeostasis that is defeatist in character. While it is true that some pathological equilibria seem so stable as to defy therapeutic intervention (schizophrenias), it is generally possible to set up for the patient a fantasied new situation with a more favorable balance than he has achieved. Such phenomena as the positive transference can be utilized to provide some gratification, counterbalancing the painful effects of disequilibration as therapy proceeds. As therapy approaches its conclusion, many patients also show symptoms of disturbance as this new equilibrium must in turn be abandoned. Only the presence of these motivational factors makes possible the therapeutic modification of perceptions; the neuromuscular system is subservient to the vegetative system.

SUMMARY

Homeostasis is accepted as a general biological law. Since personality is developed on a biological foundation, it must follow homeostatic principles

---

[5]It is perhaps worth noting that the same symptomatic pattern of constancies can be produced by quite divergent series of events. Let us consider (a) a young woman who felt rejected by her parents, although she was in fact physically secure; who developed a fantasy of being orphaned, of being punished for some mysterious but enormous guilt; and who in consequence perceived herself as inadequate and worthless. Contrast (b) a young woman who was in fact orphaned, treated brutally by a family with whom she was placed, and indoctrinated with feelings of sin and guilt in a religious orphanage. The perceptual constancies which characterize the two personalities may be superficially quite similar; but in case (b) they have been reinforced so much more regularly and intensely that the therapeutic task is vastly harder. Even years of life under relatively secure economic and domestic conditions may fail to modify these constancies.

to some extent. Actually, these principles recur in many aspects of the psychology of personality.

Considering personality as a universal, we find the maintenance of constant states not only at the microscopic level (tissue conditions) but also at macroscopic levels (objects in the physical environment, and persons in the social environment). Physical and social constancies are shown to function in the service of tissue constancies. Disturbances at these macroscopic levels set off vigorous energy mobilizations comparable with those induced by disequilibrium on the tissue level. Constancies may be perceptual (uniform percept with varying "real" stimuli) or functional (manipulation of the "real" environment to reduce variation).

With reference to personality as a unique individual phenomenon, it is suggested that the homeostatic approach is useful in several ways. (1) The personality is characterized by the particular equilibria, disturbance of which gives rise to maximum energy mobilization, and by the particular perceptual constancies, especially social and ego constancies, which have been developed. (2) Neurotic, unrealistic equilibria can develop with reference to needs not directly involved in organismic survival, *e.g.*, sex. Such unrealistic equilibria involve perceptual constancies not appropriate to the "real" situation, but often reinforced because resultant behavior seems to lead to confirmation of the constancy hypothesis. (3) Projective tests may give a more adequate picture of these constancies than would result from observation in "real" situations. (4) Therapy involves disturbing the neurotic equilibrium, restructuring the unrealistic percepts, and evolving a new equilibrium providing more need-gratification.

5. Motivation Reconsidered: The Concept of Competence

Robert W. White

WHEN parallel trends can be observed in realms as far apart as animal behavior and psychoanalytic ego psychology, there is reason to suppose that we are witnessing a significant evolution of ideas. In these two realms, as in

From the *Psychological Review*, 1959, *66*, 297-333. Reprinted by permission of the author, the American Psychological Association, Inc. and the Dorsey Press, Inc.

psychology as a whole, there is evidence of deepening discontent with theories of motivation based upon drives. Despite great differences in the language and concepts used to express this discontent, the theme is everywhere the same: Something important is left out when we make drives the operating forces in animal and human behavior.

The chief theories against which the discontent is directed are those of Hull and of Freud. In their respective realms, drive-reduction theory and psychoanalytic instinct theory, which are basically very much alike, have acquired a considerable air of orthodoxy. Both views have an appealing simplicity, and both have been argued long enough so that their main outlines are generally known. In decided contrast is the position of those who are not satisfied with drives and instincts. They are numerous, and they have developed many pointed criticisms, but what they have to say has not thus far lent itself to a clear and inclusive conceptualization. Apparently there is an enduring difficulty in making these contributions fall into shape.

In this paper I shall attempt a conceptualization which gathers up some of the important things left out by drive theory. To give the concept a name I have chosen the word *competence*, which is intended in a broad biological sense rather than in its narrow everyday meaning. As used here, competence will refer to an organism's capacity to interact effectively with its environment. In organisms capable of but little learning, this capacity might be considered an innate attribute, but in the mammals and especially man, with their highly plastic nervous systems, fitness to interact with the environment is slowly attained through prolonged feats of learning. In view of the directedness and persistence of the behavior that leads to these feats of learning, I consider it necessary to treat competence as having a motivational aspect, and my central argument will be that the motivation needed to attain competence cannot be wholly derived from sources of energy currently conceptualized as drives or instincts. We need a different kind of motivational idea to account fully for the fact that man and the higher mammals develop a competence in dealing with the environment which they certainly do not have at birth and certainly do not arrive at simply through maturation. Such an idea, I believe, is essential for any biologically sound view of human nature.

As a first step, I shall briefly examine the relevant trends of thought in several areas of psychology. From this it will become clear that the ideas advanced in this paper have already been stated, in one way or another, by workers in animal behavior, child development, cognitive psychology, psychoanalytic ego psychology, and the psychology of personality. If there is novelty in this essay, it lies in putting together pieces which are not in themselves new. They already lie before us on the table, and perhaps by looking once more we can see how to fit them into a larger conceptual picture.

One of the most obvious features of animal behavior is the tendency to explore the environment. Cats are reputedly killed by curiosity, dogs characteristically make a thorough search of their surroundings, and monkeys and chimpanzees have always impressed observers as being ceaseless investigators. Even Pavlov, whose theory of behavior was one of Spartan simplicity, could not do without an investigatory or orientating reflex. Early workers with the obstruction method, such as Dashiell (1925) and Nissen (1930), reported that rats would cross an electrified grid simply for the privilege of exploring new territory. Some theorists reasoned that activity of this kind was always in the service of hunger, thirst, sex, or some other organic need, but this view was at least shaken by the latent learning experiments, which showed that animals learned about their surroundings even when their major needs had been purposely sated. Shortly before 1950 there was a wave of renewed interest not only in exploratory behavior but also in the possibility that activity and manipulation might have to be assigned the status of independent motives.

Exploratory Behavior

In 1953 Butler reported an experiment in which monkeys learned a discrimination problem when the only reward was the opening of a window which permitted them to look out upon the normal comings and goings of the entrance room to the laboratory. The discriminations thus formed proved to be resistant to extinction. In a later study, Butler and Harlow (1957) showed that monkeys could build up a series of four different discriminations solely for the sake of inspecting the entrance room. Butler concluded that "monkeys—and presumably all primates—have a strong motive toward visual exploration of their environment and that learning may be established on the basis of this motive just as it may be established on the basis of any motive that regularly and reliably elicits responses." Montgomery, in 1954, reported a study with rats in which the animals, their major organic needs satiated, learned to avoid the short arm of a Y maze and to take the path which led them into additional maze territory suitable for exploration. Similar findings have been described by Myers and Miller (1954), whose rats learned to press a bar for the sake of poking their heads into a new compartment and sniffing around. Zimbardo and Miller (1958) enlarged upon this study by varying the amount of novelty in the two compartments. In their report "the hypothesis advanced is that opportunity to explore a 'novel' environment or to effect a stimulus change in the environment is the reinforcing agent."

These experiments make a strong case for an independent exploratory motive. The nature of this motive can be more fully discerned in situations in which the animals are allowed a varied repertory of behavior. In 1950 Berlyne published a searching paper on curiosity, a theme which he further developed in subsequent years (1955, 1957, 1958). The rats in his experiments were confronted with an unfamiliar space and later with various novel objects placed in it. Approaching, sniffing, and examining were readily elicited by each novelty, were fairly rapidly extinguished, but were restored nearly to original strength when a fresh novelty was added. Exploration on the part of chimpanzees have been studied by Welker (1956), who put various pairs of objects before the animals and observed the course of their interest. The objects were often first approached in a gingerly manner, with signs of uneasiness, then examined and handled quite fully, then discarded. Introducing a new pair of objects promptly reproduced the whole sequence, just as it did with the rats in Berlyne's experiments. Welker used pairs of objects to find out whether or not the chimpanzees would have common preferences. Bigness and brightness evoked more interest, and greater time was spent upon objects which could be moved, changed, or made to emit sounds and light.

Recent reviews by Butler (1958) and Cofer (1959) show that a great deal of similar work is going on in animal laboratories, generally with similar results.

Exploration as a Drive

The designers of these experiments have favored the idea that exploration should be listed as an independent primary drive. In all cases the experimental plan calls for the elimination of other primary drives by satiation. It is recognized, however, that a confirmed advocate of orthodoxy might bring up two objections to the proposed enlargement of the list of primary drives. He might claim that exploratory behavior could be explained as a consequence of secondary reinforcement, or he might contend that it is reinforced by reduction of anxiety.

The first argument meets an immediate difficulty in Butler's finding that discriminations learned on the basis of visual exploration are resistant to extinction. When reinforcement of primary drive never takes place in the experimental situation, it is to be expected that secondary reinforcement will not prevent extinction (Miller, 1951). But even in those cases where extinction is rapid, as it was with Berlyne's rats and Welker's chimpanzees, serious problems are raised by the quick recovery of exploratory behavior when a novel stimulus is introduced (Berlyne, 1950). In order to sustain the idea that secondary reinforcement accounts for this fact, we should have to suppose that primary rewards have often been connected with the exploration of novelties. It would have to be assumed, for instance, that the securing of food by young animals occurred with considerable frequency in connection with the investigation of novel objects. This image may seem to fit mature animals who search the environment for their food, but it certainly cannot apply to young mammals before they are weaned. Here the learning process can do virtually nothing to reinforce an interest in novelties. Gratification comes from following the same old cues to the same old consummatory responses, and the animal whose attention strays to some novel variation of the breast will only find himself frustrated. One can say that the whole mammalian pattern of infancy works in the opposite direction. The mother is more active than the young in providing gratifications, and the babies must be pursued and retrieved if they stray from the scene of her ministry. However one looks at it, the hypothesis of secondary reinforcement seems to me to demand improbable assumptions about the relationship in the lives of young animals between exploration and primary need gratification.

The hypothesis that exploratory behavior is related to fear and receives its reinforcement from the reduction of anxiety is at first glance considerably more plausible. It seems justified by the observation that Welker's chimpanzees showed uneasiness on first contact with novel objects, and it fits the behavior of rats in a new maze, as reported by Whiting and Mowrer (1943), where initial terror gave place to an exploration so feverish that the food reward was not eaten. Montgomery and Monkman (1955) have undertaken to challenge this hypothesis by a direct experimental attack. They showed that fear induced in rats before entering a novel situation did not increase exploratory behavior, and that fear induced within the novel situation decreased exploration to an extent correlated with the intensity of the fear. They find it more reasonable to suppose that fear and exploration are conflicting forms of behavior, and this view can also be defended on purely logical grounds. Fear shows itself in either freezing or avoidance, whereas exploration is clearly an instance of approach. There is hardly a more perfect example of conflict between incompatible responses than that of an animal hesitating between investigation and flight. It is clear that exploration can sometimes serve to reduce anxiety, but the proposition that it comes into existence only for this purpose cannot be so easily accepted.

What assumptions have to be made to support the thesis that exploration is motivated by anxiety reduction? It has to be assumed that certain characteristic stimuli arouse anxiety and that exploration of these stimuli is then found to reduce the anxiety. If the characteristics in question are those of novelty and unfamiliarity, we must heed Berlyne's reminder that for the infant all experience is novel and unfamiliar. Berlyne (1950) proposes that the exploratory reaction "may be one that *all* stimuli originally evoke, but which disappears (becomes habituated) as the organism becomes familiar with them." But if all stimuli at first arouse anxious tension, we would have to deduce that all response would consist of avoidance in the interest of reducing that tension. Approaching a stimulus and taking steps to increase its impact could not occur. An exploratory tendency must be there in the first place before it can achieve the function of reducing anxiety. As Wood-worth (1958) expresses it, "if there were no exploratory drive to balance and overbalance the fear drive, an animal would be helpless in a novel situation." I find it hard to believe that creatures so liberally endowed with fear could ever achieve a working mastery of the environment if they were impelled toward it only by the pressure of organic needs.

Both hypotheses thus far examined—secondary reinforcement and anxiety reduction—require us to make improbable assumptions. There remains the possibility that exploration should simply be added to the list of primary drives and otherwise treated in orthodox fashion. Myers and Miller (1954) suggest that this is the appropriate course, provided the new drive shows the same functional properties as those already known. "If an exploratory tendency can produce learning like other drives such as hunger, and also show a similar pattern of satiation and recovery, these functional parallels to already known drives would help to justify its classification in the same category." Logically the problem can be dealt with in this way, but we must consider very carefully what happens to the category of drive if we admit this new applicant to membership.

Using hunger as the chief model, the orthodox conception of drive involves the following characteristics: (a) there is a tissue need or deficit external to the nervous system which acts upon that system as a strong persisting stimulus; (b) this promotes activity which is terminated by a consummatory response with consequent reduction of need; (c) the reduction of need brings about the learning which gradually shapes behavior into an economical pursuit of suitable goal objects. In this scheme the tension of an aroused drive is interpreted as unpleasant, at least in the sense that the animal acts in such a way as to lower the drive and becomes quiescent when it is lowered. There are probably no living champions of so simple an orthodoxy, yet the scheme remains pervasive, and it is therefore worth while to observe that the proposed exploratory drive hardly fits it at all.

In the first place, the exploratory drive appears to bear no relation whatever to a tissue need or deficit external to the nervous system. It is, of course, clearly related to certain characteristics of stimulation from the external environment, a source of motivation which Harlow (1953) would like to see restored to a serious place in contemporary psychology; but it certainly cannot be correlated with a visceral need comparable to hunger, thirst, or sex. Considering the pattern of satiation and recovery shown by Welker's chimpanzees, Woodworth (1958) remarks that "what becomes satiated is not the exploratory tendency in general, but the exploring of a particular place or object." It is possible, as Hebb (1955) has pointed out, that the so-called "reticular activation system" in the brain stem creates a kind of general drive state, and this mechanism might indeed be flexibly responsive to changes in sensory stimulation. This interesting suggestion, however, is still a far cry from viscerogenic drives; it commits us instead to the novel idea of a neurogenic motive, one in which the state of the nervous system and the patterns of external stimulation conspire to produce motivated behavior. There is even a good deal of trouble in supposing that the adequate stimuli for exploration are either strong or persistent. Novelty certainly cannot be equated with strength or persistence, and animals seem readily able to disregard the stimuli to exploration when they are weary.

In the second place, exploratory behavior cannot be regarded as leading to any kind of consummatory response. It is usual for the animal's investigation to subside gradually. If the animal at some point turns away and leaves the once novel object we may say that its curiosity is "satisfied," but we do not mean by this that the equivalent of a consummatory response has just taken place. The sequence suggests rather the curiosity wears out and slowly falls to a level where it no longer guides behavior, at least until a fresh novelty comes into view.

Finally, in the case of exploratory behavior there is real difficulty in identifying reinforcement with need reduction. Montgomery (1954), describing the learning of the Y maze, points out that the short arm, essentially a dead end, would tend to reduce the exploratory drive, whereas the long arm, itself a complex maze, would increase it—but the long arm is chosen. If the long arm functions as a reinforcing agent, "the mechanism underlying this reinforcement is an *increase*, rather than a decrease, in the strength of the exploratory drive." In this experiment, as in their natural habitat, animals do not wait to have novelty thrust upon them, nor do they avoid situations in which novelty may be found. Such behavior can be most readily conceptualized by admitting that under certain circumstances reinforcement can be correlated with an increase in arousal or excitement rather than a decrease. A drive which has no consummatory climax seems almost to require this formulation. It is distinctly implausible to connect reinforcement with the waning of an agreeable interest in the environment or with a general progress from zestful alertness to boredom.

If we admit exploration to the category of drive we are thus committing ourselves to believe that drives need have no extraneural sources in tissue deficits or visceral tensions, that they are not necessarily activated by strong or persistent stimuli, that they do not require consummatory responses, and that drive increase can sometimes be a mechanism of reinforcement.

Activity and Manipulation

Exploration is not the only motive proposed by critics of drive orthodoxy, and novelty is not the only characteristic of the environment which appears to incite motivated behavior. Some workers have suggested a need for activity, which can be strengthened by depriving animals of their normal opportunities for movement. Kagan and Berkun (1954) used running in an

activity wheel as the reward for learning and found it "an adequate reinforcement for the instrumental response of bar pressing." Hill (1956)
showed that rats will run in an activity wheel to an extent that is correlated
with their previous degree of confinement. It is certain that the activity
wheel offers no novelty to the animals in these experiments. Nevertheless,
they seem to want to run, and they continue to run for such long times that
no part of the behavior can readily be singled out as a consummatory response. Perhaps an unpleasant internal state created by inactivity is gradually
worked off, but this is certainly accomplished by a tremendous increase of
kinaesthetic stimulation and muscular output which would seem to imply
increased excitation in the system as a *whole*.

Harlow and his associates (Harlow, 1953; Harlow, Harlow, & Meyer,
1950) maintain that there is also a manipulative drive. It is aroused by certain patterns of external stimulation and reduced by actively changing the
external pattern. The experiments were done with rhesus monkeys, and
they involve the solving of a mechanical problem which, however, leads to
no further consequences or rewards. The task might be, for instance, to
raise a hasp which is kept in place by both a hook and a pin; all that can
be accomplished is to raise the hasp, which opens nothing and leads to no
fresh discoveries. When the hasp problem is simply installed in the living
cages, the monkeys return to it and solve it as many as 7 or 8 times over
several days. It seems unlikely that novelty can be postulated as the essential
characteristic of the stimulus which evokes this repeated behavior. The
simplest interpretation is rather that value lies for the animal in the opportunity, as Zimbardo and Miller (1958) express it, "to effect a stimulus
change in the environment." This formulation suggests something like the
propensities toward mastery or power that have often been mentioned in
discussions of human motivation.

The addition of activity and manipulation to the list of primary drives
can only make more serious the difficulties for the orthodox model that
resulted from admitting exploration. But recent research with animals has
put the orthodox model on the defensive even on its home grounds. It has
become increasingly clear that hunger, thirst, and sex cannot be made to fit
the simple pattern that seemed so helpful 40 years ago.

Changing Conceptions of Drive

In a brief historical statement, Morgan (1957) has pointed out that
the conception of drive as a noxious stimulus began to lose its popularity
among research workers shortly after 1940. "On the whole," he says, "the
stimulus concept of drive owed more to wishful thinking than to experimental fact." When technical advances in biochemistry and brain physiology
made it possible to bring in an array of new facts, there was a rapid shift
toward the view that "drives arise largely through the internal environment

acting on the central nervous system." One of the most influential discoveries was that animals have as many as a dozen specific hungers for particular kinds of food, instead of the single hunger demanded by Cannon's model of the hunger drive. If an animal's diet becomes deficient in some important element such as salt, sugar, or the vitamin-B complex, foods containing the missing element will be eagerly sought while other foods are passed by, a selectivity that obviously cannot be laid to contractions of the stomach. Similarly, a negative food preference can be produced by loading either the stomach or the blood stream with some single element of the normal diet. The early work of Beach (1942) on sexual behavior brought out similar complications in what had for a time been taken as a relatively simple drive. Hormone levels appeared to be considerably more important than peripheral stimulation in the arousal and maintenance of the sex drive. Further work led Beach (1951) to conclude that sexual behavior is "governed by a complex combination of processes." He points out that the patterns of control differ tremendously from one species to another and that within a single species the mechanisms may be quite different for males and females. Like hunger, the sex drive turns out to be no simple thing.

New methods of destroying and of stimulating brain centers in animals have had an equally disastrous effect on the orthodox drive model. The nervous system, and especially the hypothalamus, appears to be deeply implicated in the motivational process. Experimental findings on hypothalamic lesions in animals encourage Stellar (1954) to believe that there are different centers "responsible for the control of different kinds of basic motivation," and that in each case "there is one main excitatory center and one inhibitory center which operates to depress the activity of the excitatory center." As research findings accumulate, this picture may seem to be too cleanly drawn. Concerning sexual behavior, for example, Rosvold (1959) concludes a recent review by rejecting the idea of a single center in the cerebrum; rather, the sex drive "probably has a wide neural representation with a complex interaction between old and new brain structures and between neural and humoral agents." Nevertheless, Miller's (1958) careful work seems to leave little doubt that motivated behavior in every way similar to normal hunger and normal pain-fear can be elicited by electrical stimulation of quite restricted areas of the hypothalamus. It is clear that we cannot regress to a model of drives that represents the energy as coming from outside the nervous system. Whatever the effects of peripheral stimulation may be, drives also involve neural centers and neural patterns as well as internal biochemical conditions.

What sort of model becomes necessary to entertain these newly discovered facts? In 1938 Lashley expressed the view that motivation should not be equated with disturbance of organic equilibrium but rather with "a partial excitation of a very specific sensori-motor mechanism irradiating to affect other systems of reaction." Beach (1942) postulated that there must be in the nervous system "a condition analogous to Sherrington's central excitatory state." Morgan, in 1943, undertook to capture the facts in a systematic theory which seems to have been well sustained by subsequent research (Morgan, 1957). He distinguished two types of process which he called *humoral motive factors* and *central motive states.* The humoral factors consist of chemical or hormonal constituents of the blood and lymph, and they are conceived to influence behavior chiefly by a direct sensitizing action on neural centers. The central motive states have several properties: They are partly self-maintaining through neural circuits, they tend to increase the organism's general activity, they evoke specific forms of behavior not strongly controlled by the environment, and they prime or prepare consummatory responses which will occur when adequate stimulation is found. This is a far cry from the orthodox model, but we must nowadays admit that the orthodox model is a far cry from the facts.

In view of this radical evolution of the concept of drive, it is not surprising to find the drive reduction hypothesis in serious difficulties. The earlier identification of reinforcement with drive reduction has been directly attacked in a series of experiments designed to show that learning takes place when drive reduction is ruled out.

In 1950 Sheffield and Roby showed that instrumental learning would take place in hungry rats when the reward consisted not of a nutritive substance but of sweet-tasting saccharine in the drinking water. This finding appeared to be "at variance with the molar principle of reinforcement used by Hull, which identifies primary reinforcement with 'need reduction.'" The authors naturally do not question the vital importance of need reduction, but they point out that need-reducing events may accomplish reinforcement through a mechanism more direct and speedy than the reduction of the need itself. They think that "stimulation and performance of a consummatory response appears to be more important to instrumental learning—in a primary, not acquired, way—than the drive satisfaction which the response normally achieves." Their findings are in line with an earlier experiment with chickens by Wolfe and Kaplon (1941), who used different sizes of food pellets so that the number of pecks and the amount of food received could be thrown out of their usual close connection. The chickens, we might say, would rather peck than eat; learning was more strongly reinforced when four pecks were necessary than when one peck was enough to take the same amount of food.

The substitution of the consummatory response for need reduction as the immediate reinforcing mechanism is a step in advance, but it soon turns out that another step is required. Can it be shown that an aroused need which does not reach consummation has a reinforcing effect? To test this possibility Sheffield, Wulff, and Backer (1951) provided male rats with the reward of copulating with a female, but not enough times to produce ejaculation.

This reward was favorable to instrumental learning even though there was no need reduction and no performance of the final consummatory act. The results were supported by Kagan (1955), whose animals showed substantial learning under the same conditions, though learning was still faster when ejaculation was permitted. Sheffield, Roby, and Campbell (1954) have proposed a *drive-induction* theory according to which the property of reinforcement is assigned to the excitement of an aroused drive. We have already seen that some such assumption is essential if exploration is to be assigned the status of a drive. Here it can be added that the whole theory of pregenital sexuality involves motivation without consummatory acts and without any but the most gradual need reduction. And as a final blow to the orthodox hypothesis comes the finding by Olds and Milner (1954) that positive reinforcement can be brought about by direct electrical stimulation of certain areas of the brain. Once again we learn that neural centers are deeply implicated in the plot of motivation. The simple mechanics of need reduction cannot possibly serve as the basis for a theory of learning.

Twenty years of research have thus pretty much destroyed the orthodox drive model. It is no longer appropriate to consider that drives originate solely in tissue deficits external to the nervous system, that consummatory acts are a universal feature and goal of motivated behavior, or that the alleviation of tissue deficits is the necessary condition for instrumental learning. Instead we have a complex picture in which humoral factors and neural centers occupy a prominent position; in which, moreover, the concept of neurogenic motives without consummatory ends appears to be entirely legitimate. Do these changes remove the obstacles to placing exploration, activity, and manipulation in the category of drives?

Perhaps this is no more than a question of words, but I should prefer at this point to call it a problem in conceptual strategy. I shall propose that these three new "drives" have much in common and that it is useful to bring them under the single heading of competence. Even with the loosening and broadening of the concept of drive, they are still in important respects different from hunger, thirst, and sex. In hunger and thirst, tissue deficits, humoral factors, and consummatory responses retain an important position. The mature sex drive depends heavily on hormonal levels and is sharply oriented toward consummation. Tendencies like exploration do not share these characteristics, whatever else they have in common with the better known drives. It is in order to emphasize their intrinsic peculiarities, to get them considered in their own right, without a cloud of surplus meanings, that I prefer in this essay to speak of the urge that makes for competence simply as motivation rather than as drive.

THE TREND IN PSYCHOANALYTIC EGO PSYCHOLOGY

Rather an abrupt change of climate may be experienced as we turn from the animal laboratory to the psychoanalytic treatment room, but the trends of thought in the two realms turn out to be remarkably alike. Here the orthodox view of motivation is to be found in Freud's theory of the instincts—they might be known to us as drives if an early translator had been more literal with the German *Trieb*.

Freud's Theories of Instinct and Ego

In his final work, Freud (1949) described instincts as "somatic demands upon mental life" and as "the ultimate cause of all activity." He wrote further:

It is possible to distinguish an indeterminate number of instincts and in common practice this is in fact done. For us, however, the important question arises whether we may not be able to derive all of these instincts from a few fundamental ones. . . . After long doubts and vacillations we have decided to assume the existence of only two basic instincts, *Eros* and the *destructive instinct* (Freud, 1949, p. 20).

The history of Freud's long doubts and vacillations has been lucidly related by Bibring (1941). Up to 1914 Freud used a two-fold classification of sexual instincts and ego instincts. The ego instincts made their appearance in his case histories in a somewhat moral character, being held responsible for the disastrous repression of sexual needs, but in systematic usage they were conceived as serving the goal of self-preservation, and hunger was generally taken as an appropriate model. In 1914, when he evolved the concept of narcissism and saw that it threatened to blur the line between sexual and ego tendencies, Freud (1925b) still expressed himself as unwilling to abandon an idea which followed the popular distinction of love and hunger and which reflected man's dual existence "as reproducer and as one who serves his own ends." Various facts, particularly those of sadism and masochism, served to overcome his reluctance, so that he finally united self-preservation and preservation of the species under the heading of Eros or life instincts, establishing destructiveness or the death instinct as the great antagonist in a profound biological sense (Freud, 1948). This highly speculative step proved to be too much for some of his otherwise loyal followers, and the earlier orthodoxy did not become entirely extinct.

It is easier to follow Freud's reasoning when we bear in mind the simultaneous development of his ideas about the mental apparatus. Bibring (1941) points out that even in his early thinking a sharp contrast was always drawn between instinct and mental apparatus. Instinct supplied the energy in the form of powerful, persisting internal stimuli; the apparatus guided it into channels which produced organized behavior and eventually put a stop to the persisting stimulation. In 1915 Freud wrote:

The nervous system is an apparatus having the function of abolishing stimuli which reach it or of reducing excitation to the lowest possible level; an apparatus which would even, if this were feasible, maintain itself in an altogether unstimulated condition. . . . The task of the nervous system is—broadly speaking—*to master stimuli* (Freud, 1925c, p. 63).

During the next decade there was a considerable growth in his ideas about the mental apparatus, culminating in the well known division into id, ego, and superego. The activities of the ego now received much fuller recognition. Freud (1927) assigned to it "the task of self-preservation," which it accomplished through its several capacities of perception, memory, flight, defense, and adaptive action. One can see Freud's thought moving from a mechanical analogy—an engine and its fuel—toward a much more adaptational conception of the mental apparatus. Ego instincts did not wholly disappear, but the decline in their systematic importance was compensated by the insight that self-preservative tendencies were to some extent built into the whole living system. It is significant that as he took this course he came to question the earlier tension-reduction theory. In the last year of his life he declared it to be probable "that what is felt as pleasure or unpleasure is not the *absolute* degree of the tensions but something in the rhythm of their changes" (Freud, 1949).

Freud's tendency to revise his thinking makes it difficult to pin down an orthodox doctrine, but most workers will probably agree that his main emphasis was upon somatically based drives, a mental apparatus which received its power from the drives, and, of course, the multitude of ways in which the apparatus controlled, disguised, and transformed these energies. His treatment of the ego was far from complete, and it was not long before voices were raised against the conception that so vital and versatile a part of the personality could be developed solely by libidinal and aggressive energies.

An Instinct to Master

In 1942 Hendrick proposed that this difficulty be met by assuming the existence of an additional major instinct. "The development of ability to master a segment of the environment," he wrote, and the need to exercise such functions, can be conceptualized as an "instinct to master," further characterized as "an inborn drive to do and to learn how to do." The aim of this instinct is "pleasure in exercising a function successfully, regardless of its sensual value." The simpler manifestations are learning to suck, to manipulate, to walk, to speak, to comprehend and to reason; these functions and others eventually become integrated as the ego. "The central nervous system is more than a utility," Hendrick declared. The infant shows an immediate desire to use and perfect each function as it ripens, and the adult secures gratification from an executive function efficiently performed regardless of its service to other instincts.

Hendrick's procedure in this and two supporting papers (1943a,

1943b) is quite similar to that of the animal psychologists who propose listing exploration as an additional primary drive. The instinct to master has an aim—to exercise and develop the ego functions—and it follows hedonic principles by yielding "primary pleasure" when efficient action "enables the individual to control and alter his environment." It is to this extent analogous to the instincts assumed by Freud. But just as an exploratory drive seemed radically to alter the whole conception of drive, so the instinct to master implied a drastic change in the psychoanalytic idea of instinct. Critics were quick to point out that Freud had always conceived of instincts as having somatic sources external to the ego apparatus, a condition not met by the proposed instinct to master. There was nothing comparable to erogenous zones, to orgasm, or to the sequence of painful tension followed by pleasurable release. Mastery, the critics agreed, could not be an instinct, whatever else it might be.

It is of interest that Fenichel (1945), who definitely rejected Hendrick's proposal, gives us another close parallel to the animal work by attributing mastering behavior to anxiety-reduction. He argued that mastery is "a general aim of every organism but not of a specific instinct." He agreed that there is "a pleasure of enjoying one's abilities," but he related this pleasure to cessation of the anxiety connected with not being able to do things. "Functional pleasure," he wrote, "is pleasure in the fact that the exercise of a function is now possible without anxiety," and he contended that when anxiety is no longer present, when there is full confidence that a given situation can be met, then action is no longer accompanied by functional pleasure. We must certainly agree with Fenichel that anxiety *can* play the part he assigns it, but the proposal that all pleasure in ego functions comes from this source raises the same difficulties we have already considered in connection with exploratory behavior. That we exercise our capacities and explore our surroundings only to reduce our fear of the environment is not, as I have already argued, an assumption that enjoys high probability on biological grounds.

Hartmann on the Ego

A less radical change in the orthodox model is proposed by Hartmann, who, in a series of papers since 1939, often in conjunction with Kris and Loewenstein, has been refining and expanding Freud's views on the ego and the instincts. While the ego is conceived as a "substructure" of the personality, this term is somewhat metaphorical because in practice the ego has to be defined by its functions. The list of functions, which includes grasping, crawling, walking, perceiving, remembering, language, thinking, and intention, covers much the same ground that was indicated by Hendrick, but Hartmann does not attribute their growth to an instinct. On the other hand, Hartmann (1950) early came to the conclusion that development could not be explained, as Freud had seemed to conceive it, simply as a consequence of conflict between instinctual needs and frustrating realities. The instincts alone would never guarantee survival; they require mediation by the innate ego apparatus if they are to meet "the average expectable environmental conditions." He therefore proposed that we conceive of an autonomous factor in ego development, an independent maturation of functions taking place in a "conflict-free ego sphere." Functions such as locomotion ripen through maturation and through learning even when they are not caught up in struggles to obtain erotic and aggressive gratification or to avoid anxiety. As Anna Freud (1952) has pointed out, walking becomes independent of instinctual upheavals a few weeks after its beginning; thereafter, it serves the child impartially in situations of conflict and those that are free from conflict.

Hartmann's idea of autonomous ego development has of course been assumed all along by workers in child psychology, but it is an important step to relate it to Freud's disclosures concerning unconscious motivation. In what now looks like an excess of enthusiasm for his own concepts, Freud (1925a) undertook to explain the outgrowing of the pleasure principle and the substituting of the reality principle as a simple and direct consequence of the frustration of instinctual needs. However, the reality principle contained the idea of postponing an immediate gratification in favor of a future one, and Hartmann (1956) properly notes that the capacities for postponement and anticipation cannot be conjured into existence simply by the collision of frustrating reality and ungratified need. Important as frustrations may be, these capacities must already be available, "some preparedness for dealing with reality" must already exist, before the frustration can produce its momentous educative effect. It can be seen from this example that Hartmann's analysis opens the way for profitable commerce between developmental psychologies inside and outside of psychoanalysis.

Hartmann's emphasis on adaptation permits him to perceive much more that is autonomous about the ego than was ever seriously included in Freud's systematic thought. He allows, for instance, that aims and interests which develop in the beginning as defenses against instincts may later become part of conflict-free spheres of activity—become interests in their own right—and thus achieve "secondary autonomy," a concept very close to Allport's (1937) functional autonomy of motives (Hartmann, 1950). He deals with the possibility that adaptive skills developing in the conflict-free sphere may have a decisive influence on the handling of conflicts. These skills have a history of their own, shaped jointly by the child's abilities and by the responses evoked from parents. As Monroe (1955) has expressed it, they have "a very important role in the development of the conscious and semiconscious psychological self." They may thus have a direct influence upon the outcome when a child becomes involved in conflict. Rapaport (1958) sees Hartmann's ideas on the autonomy of the ego as vital to the proper understanding not only of healthy development but also of psychopathology itself.

In explaining the autonomous growth of the ego, Hartmann makes generous use of the concept of maturation, but he naturally does not exclude learning. Hartmann (1950) entertains the possibility, mentioned casually from time to time by Freud (1916, 1949), that ego functions are supplied with their own sources of energy independent of instincts, and that there is pleasure connected with their mere exercise. However, he makes little systematic use of this idea, relying instead upon a concept more central in Freud's thinking, that of the neutralization of drive energies. Freud (1927) found that he could "make no headway" in accounting for the varied activities of the ego without assuming "a displaceable energy, which is in itself neutral, but is able to join forces either with an erotic or with a destructive impulse, differing qualitatively as they do, and augment its total cathexis." He speculated that the neutral energy came from Eros and could be conceived as desexualized libido. Hartmann, Kris, and Loewenstein (1949) carried the idea forward a logical step by proposing that the energies of aggressive instincts could similarly be neutralized and placed at the disposal of the ego. Neutralized energy contributes to the development of the ego and makes possible a continuing interest in the objects of the environment regardless of their immediate relation to erotic or aggressive needs. Hartmann (1955) finds this concept particularly helpful in unscrambling the confusions that have arisen over the concept of sublimation.

The doctrine of neutralized instinctual energies is a curious one, and we should bear in mind the complex clinical findings that perhaps suggested it. Freud was an unquestioned genius in detecting the subtle operation of erotic urges and aggressive fantasies, along with elaborate mechanisms of defense, behind the seemingly objective or "neutral" activities of everyday life. Remarkable transformations of interest could sometimes be observed in the course of development. For example, a patient's childhood erotic rivalry and aggressive competition with his father might later disappear beneath a strong objective interest in running the family business; then suddenly, on the brink of success, this interest might come to a total halt, paralyzed by anxiety because the underlying instinctual goals came too close to symbolic fulfillment. The reappearance of instinctual preoccupations in such a case lends a certain color to the idea that they have somehow been driving the behavior all the time, even though the daily pursuit of business goals seems utterly remote from instinctual gratifications.

It is worth noticing that Freud's procedure in making the assumption of neutralized instinctual energy is similar to the one followed by orthodox behaviorists in connection with primary drives. These theorists started from the assumption that all behavior was powered by a limited number of organic drives, and then, in order to protect this assumption, they developed further hypotheses, such as secondary reinforcement, to account for motivated behavior that bore no obvious relation to primary goals. At the point where he could "make no headway" without postulating neutralization, Freud could conceivably have made a good deal of headway if he had been willing to assume that neutral energy, neither sexual nor aggressive, was available as a natural endowment in the first place. But he preferred to protect his assumption of two primary drives and to interpret other energies as transformations of these drives. Even so, the concept seems superfluous if we take Freud at his word about the nature of the life instincts. Freud (1949) made it clear that Eros included more than instincts having a sexual aim; its larger goal was "to establish even greater unities and to preserve them thus—in short, to bind together." Under this formula, it would seem possible to include energies inherently directed toward building up the integrated functions of the ego. But Freud did not exploit the full range of his theory of Eros and proposed only that neutral energies should be conceived as desexualized.

The concept of neutralization has in some respects had a good effect on psychoanalytic ego psychology. In Hartmann's writings, as we have seen, and in Rapaport's (1951, 1954) work on thinking, it has encouraged a strong interest in autonomous ego functions and a fresh analysis of their place in personality. Nevertheless, it seems to me an awkward conceptualization, one which in the end is likely to lead, as Colby (1955) has expressed it, to a "metapsychological snarl." The theory requires that instinctual energies can completely change their aims, which makes one wonder what purpose was served in the first place by defining them as having aims. It preserves an image of mobility of energies that seems much out of line with recent research on animal motivation, where energy is being conceived in a constantly closer relation to specific structures. To my mind it thus compares unfavorably with its quite straight-forward alternative, which is that the alleged neutralized energies are there in the first place as part of the natural make-up of an adaptive organism. I shall later develop this possibility by means of the concept of competence in its motivational aspect, and I believe that this concept gains support from certain other lines of work in the psychoanalytic tradition.

Motility and a Sense of Industry

The trend away from instinct orthodoxy is illustrated by the work of Kardiner (1947) on what he calls "the development of the effective ego." Kardiner's reflections arose from his work on the traumatic neuroses of war. In these disorders the main threat is to self-preservation, and some of the most important symptoms, such as defensive rituals and paralyses, are lodged in the action systems that normally bring about successful adaptive behavior. It thus becomes pertinent to study the growth of action systems, to discover how they become integrated so as to maintain "controlled contact" with the environment and "controlled exploitation of objects in the outer world," and to work out the conditions which either favor or disrupt this acquired integration. Thinking along these lines, Kardiner is led to conclusions just about the opposite of Freud's: It is the successful and gratifying experiences, not the frustrations, that lead to increasingly integrated action and to the discrimination of self from outer world. Frustration produces chiefly disruptions and inhibitions which are unfavorable to the early growth of the ego. Children are gratified when they discover the connection between a movement executed and the accompanying and subsequent sensations. They are still more gratified when they carry out actions successfully; this "gives rise to the triumphant feeling of making an organ obedient to the will of the ego." Such experiences build up "a definite self- or body-consciousness which becomes the center and the point of reference of all purposeful and coordinated activity." Growth of the ego, in short, depends heavily upon action systems and the consequences of action. The course and vicissitudes of this development have to be studied in their own right, and they cannot be understood as side effects of the stages of libidinal development.

A similar theme is pursued to even more radical conclusions by Mittelmann (1954) in his paper on motility. Mittelmann regards motility, which manifests itself most typically in skilled motor actions such as posture, locomotion, and manipulation, as an "urge in its own right" in the same sense that one speaks of oral, excretory, or genital urges. From about 10 months of age it has a distinctly "driven" character, and there is restlessness and anger if it is blocked. During the second and third years the motor urge "dominates all other urges," so that it is proper to "consider this period the motor level of ego and libido development." The child makes tremendous efforts to learn to walk, and to walk well, and he exhibits joyous laughter as he attains these ends. Restrictions of motility may occur because the parents are anxious or because the child's assertiveness troubles them, and a lasting injury to the parent-child relationship may result. Clumsiness in motor or manipulative accomplishments may lead to self-hatred and dependence, for "the evolution of self-assertiveness and self-esteem is intimately connected with motor development." Motility is of central importance in many of the most characteristic functions of the ego. Partly by its means the infant differentiates himself from other objects, and the child's knowledge of objects depends on an extensive activity of manipulation and examination. "Thus motility becomes one of the most important aspects of reality testing." Because it is an element in all cognitive behavior, it can also be considered "the dominant integrative function." Mittelmann bases motor development, in short, on an independent urge, and he sees this urge as the really crucial motive behind the development of the ego.

Like Kardiner, Mittelmann does not attempt to formulate in detail the nature of the motility urge. It is likened not to an instinct but to a "partial instinct," and this seems to place it somewhere between Hendrick's instinct to master and Hartmann's dimly sketched independent energies of the ego. This indefiniteness may irk the systematic theorist, but Mittelmann's account of the part played by motility in ego development easily stands as a significant contribution. Even more influential in this respect is the work of Erikson (1953), who has given a highly detailed timetable of ego development. Erikson stays with the libido theory as far as it will go, but he passes beyond its reach in his account of the latency period and some of the later crises of growth. It is clear that something more than the orthodox instincts is involved in the "enormous value" with which the child in the second year "begins to endow his autonomous will." Something more would seem to be implied in the expanding imagination and initiative of the "phallic" child. Certainly more is involved during the school years, when children address themselves to motor, manual, and intellectual achievements and need "a sense of being able to make things and make them well and even perfectly: this is what I call the *sense of industry*." Erikson's (1952) theory of play is also influenced by the idea that learning to deal with the animate and inanimate worlds is an important preoccupation of childhood: "the playing child advances forward to new stages of real mastery." Action systems, motility, and a sense of industry all direct our attention to behavior which can scarcely be contained in the old bottle of instinct theory.

Glancing back over these trends in psychoanalytic ego psychology, we cannot fail to be impressed by striking similarities to the trend in animal work. Using Reik's familiar metaphor, we might say that those who listen with their two ears and those who listen with the third ear have apparently been hearing much the same sounds. In both realms there is discontent with drive orthodoxy. In both there is persistent pointing to kinds of behavior neglected or explained away by drive orthodoxy: exploration, activity, manipulation, and mastery. Similar theories have been proposed to account for the energies in such behavior: (*a*) they are derived or transformed in some way from the primary drives or instincts (secondary reinforcement, neutralization of drive energies); (*b*) they are powered by the need to reduce anxiety; (*c*) they can be accounted for only by postulating a new primary drive (exploratory drive, instinct to master). When these explanations are considered to have failed, the one remaining course is to work out a different idea of motivation. In his study of action systems, Kardiner prefers to leave the question of energy sources unanswered, but Erikson's sense of industry and Mittelmann's motility urge point to a motivational base which is only remotely analogous to primary drives or fundamental instincts. I believe that the difficulties in this undertaking can be greatly reduced by the concept of competence, to which we shall shortly turn.

RELATED DEVELOPMENTS IN GENERAL PSYCHOLOGY

If a systematic survey were in order, it would be easy to show a parallel drift of opinion in other parts of the psychological realm. Among theorists of personality, for example, something like drive orthodoxy is to be found in the work of Dollard and Miller (1950), who have translated the main concepts of Freud's psychoanalysis, including processes such as repression and displacement, into the language of reinforcement theory. With them we might put Mowrer (1950), whose searching analysis of fear as an acquired drive has led him to postulate anxiety-reduction as the master motive behind the development of the ego. Discontent with drive orthodoxy has long been expressed by Allport (1937, 1946), who not only argues for a functional autonomy of motives from their infantile roots in primary drives but also seriously questions the law of effect, the very cornerstone of reinforcement theory. Little comfort for the orthodox can be found in Murray's (1938) detailed taxonomy of needs, especially when it comes to needs such as achievement and construction, which can be tied to primary drives only by conceptual acrobatics. Murray and Kluckhohn (1953), moreover, have made a case for pleasure in activity for its own sake, reviving the *Funktionslust* proposed many years ago by Karl Bühler (1924) and recently developed in some detail by French (1952). They also argue for intrinsic mental needs: "the infant's mind is not acting most of the time as the instrument of some urgent animal drive, but is preoccupied with *gratifying itself.*" Murphy (1947) takes the view that all tissues can become seats of tension and thus participants in drive; in addition to visceral drives, he postulates two independent forms, activity drives and sensory drives. Then there are workers such as Goldstein (1939) who approach the whole problem with a holistic philosophy which precludes the dictatorship of any isolated or partial drives. Goldstein (1940) assumes one master tendency, that toward self-actualization, of which the so-called visceral drives are but partial and not really isolated expressions, and which can find expression also in an urge toward perfection—toward completing what is incomplete, whether it be an outside task or the mastery of some function as walking. It has been shown by the Ansbachers (1956) that Adler, never a friend of instinct orthodoxy, in his later years reached an idea very similar to the urge toward perfection. Maslow (1954, 1955), too, belongs with the heterodox. He insists that we should take account of growth motivation as well as the deficiency motivation implied in the visceral drives, and he offers the valuable idea of a hierarchy of motives, according to which the satisfaction of "lower" needs makes it possible for "higher" needs to emerge and become regnant in behavior.

Mention of these names must suffice here to show that the trends observed in animal psychology and psychoanalytic ego psychology are pervasive in contemporary psychological thought. Doubtless the same controversies and problems could be pointed out in child development, in cognitive psychology, and in other fields. But in order to advance to my main theme, I shall select only certain developments which bear directly on the concept of competence.

Needs for Excitement and Novelty

Human experience provides plentiful evidence of the importance of reducing excessive levels of tension. Men under wartime stress, men under pressure of pain and extreme deprivation, men with excessive work loads or too much exposure to confusing social interactions, all act as if their nervous systems craved that utterly unstimulated condition which Freud once sketched as the epitome of neural bliss. But if these same men be granted their Nirvana they soon become miserable and begin to look around for a little excitement. Human experience testifies that boredom is a bad state of affairs about which something must be done. Hebb (1949) has been particularly insistent in reminding us that many of our activities, such as reading detective stories, skin-diving, or driving cars at high speeds, give clear evidence of a need to raise the level of stimulation and excitement. Men and animals alike seem at times bent on increasing the impact of the environment and even on creating mild degrees of frustration and fear. Hebb and Thompson (1954) reflect upon this as follows:

> Such phenomena are, of course, well known in man: in the liking for dangerous sports or roller coasters, where fear is deliberately courted, and in the addiction to bridge or golf or solitaire, vices whose very existence depends upon the level of difficulty of the problems presented and an optimal level of frustration. Once more, when we find such attitudes toward fear and frustration in animals, we have a better basis for supposing that we are dealing with something fundamental if a man prefers skis to the less dangerous snowshoes, or when we observe an unashamed love of work (problem solving and frustration included) in the scientist, or in the business man who cannot retire. Such behavior in man is usually accounted for as a search for prestige, but the animal data make this untenable. It seems much more likely that solving problems and running mild risks are inherently rewarding, or, in more general terms, that the animal will always act so as to produce an optimal level of excitation (Hebb & Thompson, 1954, p. 551).

The concept of optimal stimulation has been developed by Leuba (1955), who sees it as helpful in resolving some of the problems of learning theory. Believing that most theorizing about motivation has been based upon "powerful biological or neurotic drives," Leuba bids us look at the much more common learning situations of nursery, playground, and school, where "actions which increase stimulation and produce excitement are strongly reinforced, sometimes to the dismay of parents and teachers." He proposes that there is an optimal level of stimulation, subject to variation at different times, and that learning is associated with movement toward this optimal level, downward when stimulation is too high and upward when it is too low. A similar idea is expressed by McReynolds (1956) concerning the more restricted concept of "rate of perceptualization." Monotonous conditions provide too low a rate, with boredom; excessive stimulation produces too high a rate, with disruptive excitement; the optimal rate yields the experience of pleasure. These ideas are now amply supported by recent experimental work on sensory deprivation (Lilly, 1956; Hebb, 1958).

In recent papers Young (1949, 1955) has argued for an hedonic theory of motivation, one in which affective processes "constitute a form of primary motivation." According to Young's theory, "an organism behaves so as to maximize positive affective arousal (delight, enjoyment) and to minimize negative arousal (distress)." McClelland (1953) has offered a version of hedonic theory which is of particular value in understanding the significance of novelty. Affective arousal occurs when a stimulus pattern produces a discrepancy from the existing adaptation level. Small discrepancies produce pleasant affect and a tendency to approach; large ones produce unpleasantness and a tendency toward avoidance. The child at play, like the young chimpanzee and the exploring rat, needs frequent novelty in the stimulus field in order to keep up his interest—in order to maintain pleasant discrepancies from whatever adaptation level he has reached. Hebb's (1949) theory of the neurological correlates of learning also deals with novelty, though in a somewhat different way. He equates sustained interest with a state of neural affairs in which "phase sequences" are relatively complex and are growing, in the sense of establishing new internal relations. Such a state follows most readily from a stimulus field characterized by difference-in-sameness; that is, containing much that is familiar along with certain features that are novel. If the field is entirely familiar, phase sequences run off quickly, are short-circuited, and thus fail to produce sustained interest. Hebb's theory, which has the engaging quality of being able to explain why we enjoy reading a detective story once but not right over again, expresses in a neurological hypothesis the familiar fact that well-learned, habituated processes do not in themselves greatly interest us. Interest seems to require elements of unfamiliarity: of something still to be found out and of learning still to be done.

It seems to me that these contributions, though differing as to details, speak with unanimity on their central theme and would force us, if nothing else did, to reconsider seriously the whole problem of motivation. Boredom, the unpleasantness of monotony, the attraction of novelty, the tendency to vary behavior rather than repeating it rigidly, and the seeking of stimulation and mild excitement stand as inescapable facts of human experience and clearly have their parallels in animal behavior. We may seek rest and minimal stimulation at the end of the day, but that is not what we are looking for the next morning. Even when its primary needs are satisfied and its homeostatic chores are done, an organism is alive, active, and up to something.

Dealing with the Environment

If we consider things only from the viewpoint of affect, excitement, and novelty, we are apt to overlook another important aspect of behavior, its effect upon the environment. Moving in this direction, Diamond (1939) invites us to consider the motivational properties of the sensorineural system, the apparatus whereby higher animals "maintain their relations to the environment." He conceives of this system as demanding stimulation and as acting in such a manner as to "force the environment to stimulate it." Even if one thinks only of the infant's exploring eyes and hands, it is clear that the main direction of behavior is by no means always that of reducing the impact of stimulation. When the eyes follow a moving object, or when the hand grasps an object which it has touched, the result is to preserve the stimulus and to increase its effect. In more elaborate explorations the consequence of a series of actions may be to vary the manner in which a stimulus acts upon the sense organs. It is apparent that the exploring, manipulating child produces by his actions precisely what Hebb's theory demands as a basis for continuing interest: he produces differences-in-sameness in the stimulus field.

In a critical analysis of Freud's views on the reality principle, Charlotte Bühler (1954) makes a strong case for positive interests in the environment, citing as evidence the responsiveness and adaptiveness of the newborn baby as well as the exploratory tendencies of later months. The problem is worked out in more detail by Schachtel (1954) in a paper on focal attention. Acts of focal attention are characteristically directed at particular objects and they consist of several sustained approaches "aimed at active mental grasp" while excluding the rest of the field. These qualities can be observed even in the infant's early attempts to follow a moving object with his eyes, and they show more clearly in his later endeavors to learn how objects are related both to himself and to one another. Such behavior bespeaks "a relatively autonomous capacity for object interest." Schachtel makes the proposal that this interest is pursued precisely at those times when major needs are in abeyance. High pressure of need or anxiety is the enemy of exploratory play and is a condition, as every scientist should know, under which we are unlikely to achieve an objective grasp of the environment. Low need pressure is requisite if we are to perceive objects as they are, in their constant character, apart from hopes and fears we may at other times attach to them. Schachtel doubts that "the wish for need-satisfaction alone would ever lead to object perception and to object-oriented thought." Hence an autonomous capacity to be interested in the environment has great value for the survival of a species.

Being interested in the environment implies having some kind of satisfactory interaction with it. Several workers call attention to the possibility that satisfaction might lie in having an effect upon the environment, in dealing with it, and changing it in various ways. Groos (1901), in his classical analysis of play, attached great importance to the child's "joy in being a cause," as shown in making a clatter, "hustling things about," and playing in puddles where large and dramatic effects can be produced. "We demand a knowledge of effects," he wrote, "and to be ourselves the producers of effects." Piaget (1952) remarks upon the child's special interest in objects that are affected by his own movements. This aspect of behavior occupies a central place in the work of Skinner (1953), who describes it as "operant" and who thus "emphasizes the fact that the behavior *operates* upon the environment to generate consequences." These consequences are fed back through the sense organs and may serve to reinforce behavior even when no organic needs are involved. A rat will show an increased tendency to press a bar when this act produces a click or a buzz. A baby will continue to investigate when his efforts produce rattling or tinkling sounds or sparkling reflections from a shiny object. The young chimpanzees in Welker's experiment spent the longest time over objects which could be lighted or made to emit sounds. Skinner finds it "difficult, if not impossible, to trace these reinforcing effects to a history of conditioning." "We may plausibly argue," he continues, "that a capacity to be reinforced by any feed-back from the environment would be biologically advantageous, since it would prepare the organism to manipulate the environment successfully before a given state of deprivation developed."

Woodworth's Behavior-Primacy Theory

The most far-reaching attempt to give these aspects of behavior a systematic place in the theory of motivation is contained in Woodworth's recent book, *Dynamics of Behavior* (1958). Woodworth takes his start from the idea that a great deal of human behavior appears to be directed toward producing effects upon the environment without immediate service to any aroused organic need. "Its incentives and rewards are in the field of behavior and not in the field of homeostasis." This is illustrated by exploratory behavior, which is directed outward toward the environment.

Its long-range value as the means of making the child acquainted with the world he has to deal with later, and so equipping him through play for the serious business of life, can scarcely lie within the little child's horizon. His goals are more limited and direct: to see this or that object more closely, to find what is behind an obstacle, to hear the noise an object makes when it strikes the floor, to be told the name of a thing or person (Woodworth, 1958, p. 78).

More complex play, such as building with blocks, illustrates the same outgoing tendency and reveals more plainly the element of finding out what one can and cannot do with objects. Even social play falls into the pattern. Playmates do not chiefly supply affection or satisfy organic needs; rather, they "afford the opportunity to do something interesting in the environment."

Woodworth draws a contrast between *need-primacy* theories of motivation and the *behavior-primacy* theory. The latter holds that "all behavior is directed primarily toward dealing with the environment." It is to be noted that "dealing with the environment" means a good deal more than receiving stimuli and making responses. Stimuli must be taken as indicators of objects in space, and responses must be adapted to produce effects upon these objects. Even the so-called "mental" capacities, such as memory and ideational thinking, become in time high-level methods of dealing with the environment. Woodworth leaves no doubt as to what he considers basic in motivation. "We are making the claim that this direction of receptive and motor activity toward the environment is the fundamental tendency of animal and human behavior and that it is the all-pervasive primary motivation of behavior." Organic drives have to break into this constantly flowing stream of activity and turn it in a special direction. But the goals of drives cannot be achieved without effective action upon one's surroundings. The ever-present, ever-primary feature of motivation is the tendency to deal with the environment.

It may appear to some workers that Woodworth has overshot the mark by making primary what has commonly been regarded as secondary, and by reducing the familiar drives to what sounds a little like a subordinate station. Woodworth's theory, however, like Goldstein's concept of self-actualization, probably should be construed not as an attempt to down-grade the drives but rather as an insistence that they be kept in the context of a whole living organism which during its waking hours is more or less constantly active. Woodworth's emphasis on dealing with the environment makes his theory a point of culmination for many of those drifting away from drive orthodoxy which we have found to be persistent in so many different areas of psychology. It will soon appear that the concept of competence, to which I now turn, represents in many respects a similar way of thinking. It emphasizes dealing with the environment, and it belongs in the trend away from drive *orthodoxy*, but it is not intended to supplant, or even to subsume, such dynamic forces as hunger, sex, aggression, and fear, which everyone knows to be of huge importance in animal and human nature.

COMPETENCE AND THE PLAY OF CONTENTED CHILDREN

A backward glance at our survey shows considerable agreement about the kinds of behavior that are left out or handled poorly by theories of motivation based wholly on organic drives. Repeatedly we find reference to the familiar series of learned skills which starts with sucking, grasping, and visual exploration and continues with crawling and walking, acts of focal attention and perception, memory, language and thinking, anticipation, the exploring of novel places and objects, effecting stimulus changes in the environment, manipulating and exploiting the surroundings, and achieving higher levels of motor and mental coordination. These aspects of behavior have long been the province of child psychology, which has attempted to measure the slow course of their development and has shown how heavily their growth depends upon learning. Collectively they are sometimes referred to as adaptive mechanisms or as ego processes, but on the whole we are not accustomed to cast a single name over the diverse feats whereby we learn to deal with the environment.

I now propose that we gather the various kinds of behavior just mentioned, all of which have to do with effective interaction with the environment, under the general heading of competence. According to Webster, competence means fitness or ability, and the suggested synonyms include capability, capacity, efficiency, proficiency, and skill. It is therefore a suitable word to describe such things as grasping and exploring, crawling and walking, attention and perception, language and thinking, manipulating and changing the surroundings, all of which promote an effective—a competent—interaction with the environment. It is true, of course, that maturation plays a part in all these developments, but this part is heavily overshadowed by learning in all the more complex accomplishments like speech or skilled manipulation. I shall argue that it is necessary to make competence a motivational concept; there is a *competence motivation* as well as competence in its more familiar sense of achieved capacity. The behavior that leads to the building up of effective grasping, handling, and letting go of objects, to take one example, is not random behavior produced by a general overflow of energy. It is directed, selective, and persistent, and it is continued not because it serves primary drives, which indeed it cannot serve until it is almost perfected, but because it satisfies an intrinsic need to deal with the environment.

No doubt it will at first seem arbitrary to propose a single motivational conception in connection with so many and such diverse kinds of behavior. What do we gain by attributing motivational unity to such a large array of activities? We could, of course, say that each developmental sequence, such as learning to grasp or to walk, has its own built-in bit of motivation—its "aliment," as Piaget (1952) has expressed it. We could go further and say that each item of behavior has its intrinsic motive—but this makes the concept of motivation redundant. On the other hand, we might follow the lead of the animal psychologists and postulate a limited number of broader motives under such names as curiosity, manipulation, and mastery. I believe that the idea of a competence motivation is more adequate than any of these alternatives and that it points to very vital common properties which have been lost from view amidst the strongly analytical tendencies that go with detailed research.

In order to make this claim more plausible, I shall now introduce some specimens of playful exploration in early childhood. I hope that these images will serve to fix and dramatize the concept of competence in the same way that other images—the hungry animal solving problems, the child putting his finger in the candle flame, the infant at the breast, the child on the toilet, and the youthful Oedipus caught in a hopeless love triangle—have become memorable focal points for other concepts. For this purpose I turn to Piaget's (1952) studies of the growth of intelligence from its earliest manifestations in his own three children. The examples come from the first year of life, before language and verbal concepts begin to be important. They therefore represent a practical kind of intelligence which may be quite similar to what is developed by the higher animals.

As early as the fourth month, the play of the gifted Piaget children began to be "centered on a result produced in the external environment," and their behavior could be described as re-discovering the movement which by chance exercised an advantageous action upon things" (1952, p. 151.) Laurent, lying in his bassinet learns to shake a suspended rattle by pulling a string that hangs from it. He discovers this result fortuitously before vision and prehension are fully coordinated. Let us now observe him a little later when he has reached the age of three months and ten days.

> I place the string, which is attached to the rattle, in his right hand, merely unrolling it a little so that he may grasp it better. For a moment nothing happens. But at the first shake due to chance movement of his hand, the reaction is immediate: Laurent starts when looking at the rattle and then violently strikes his right hand alone, as if he felt the resistance and the effect. The operation lasts fully a quarter of an hour, during which Laurent emits peals of laughter (Piaget, 1952, p. 162).

Three days later the following behavior is observed.

> Laurent, by chance, strikes the chain while sucking his fingers. He grasps it and slowly displaces it while looking at the rattles. He then begins to swing it very gently, which produces a slight movement of the hanging rattles and an as yet faint sound inside them. Laurent then definitely increases by degrees his own movements. He shakes the chain more and more vigorously and laughs uproariously at the result obtained. (Piaget, 1952, p. 185).

Very soon it can be observed that procedures are used "to make interesting spectacles last." For instance, Laurent is shown a rubber monkey which he has not seen before. After a moment of surprise, and perhaps even fright, he calms down and makes movements of pulling the string, a procedure which has no effect in this case, but which previously has caused interesting things to happen. It is to be noticed that "interesting spectacles" consist of such things as new toys, a tin box upon which a drumming noise can be made, an unfolded newspaper, or sounds made by the observer such as snapping the fingers. Commonplace as they are to the adult mind, these spectacles enter the infant's experience as novel and apparently challenging events.

Moving ahead to the second half of the first year, we can observe behavior in which the child explores the properties of objects and tries out his repertory of actions upon them. This soon leads to active experimentation in which the child attempts to provoke new results. Again we look in upon Laurent, who has now reached the age of nine months. On different occasions he is shown a variety of new objects—for instance a notebook, a beaded purse, and a wooden parrot. His carefully observing father detects four stages of response: (*a*) visual exploration, passing the object from hand to hand, folding the purse, *etc.*; (*b*) tactile exploration, passing the hand all over the object, scratching, *etc.*; (*c*) slow moving of the object in space; (*d*) use of the repertory of action: shaking the object, striking it, swinging it, rubbing it against the side of the bassinet, sucking it, *etc.*, "each in turn with a sort of prudence as though studying the effect produced" (1952, p. 255).

Here the child can be described as applying familiar tactics to new situations, but in a short while he will advance to clear patterns of active experimentation. At 10 months and 10 days Laurent, who is unfamiliar with bread as a nutritive substance, is given a piece for examination. He manipulates it, drops it many times, breaks off fragments and lets them fall. He has often does this kind of thing before, but previously his attention has seemed to be centered on the act of letting go. Now "he watches with great interest the body in motion; in particular, he looks at it for a long time when it has fallen, and picks it up when he can." On the following day he resumes his research.

He grasps in succession a celluloid swan, a box, and several other small objects, in each case stretching out his arm and letting them fall. Sometimes he stretches out his arm vertically, sometimes he holds it obliquely in front of or behind his eyes. When the object falls in a new position (for example on his pillow) he lets it fall two or three times more on the same place, as though to study the spatial relation; then he modifies the situation. At a certain moment the swan falls near his mouth; now he does not suck it (even though this object habitually serves this purpose), but drops it three times more while merely making the gesture of opening his mouth (Piaget, 1952, p. 269).

These specimens will furnish us with sufficient images of the infant's use of his spare time. Laurent, of course, was provided by his studious father with a decidedly enriched environment, but no observant parent will question the fact that babies often act this way during those periods of their waking life when hunger, erotic needs, distresses, and anxiety seem to be exerting no particular pressure. If we consider this behavior under the historic headings of psychology we shall see that few processes are missing. The child gives evidence of sensing, perceiving, attending, learning, recognizing, probably recalling, and perhaps thinking in a rudimentary way. Strong emotion is lacking, but the infant's smiles, gurgles, and occasional peals of laughter strongly suggest the presence of pleasant affect. Actions appear in an organized form, particularly in the specimens of active exploration and experimentation. Apparently the child is using with a certain coherence nearly the whole repertory of psychological processes except those that accompany stress. It would be arbitrary indeed to say that one was more important than another.

These specimens have a meaningful unity when seen as transactions between the child and his environment, the child having some influence upon the environment and the environment some influence upon the child. Laurent appears to be concerned about what he can do with the chain and rattles, what he can accomplish by his own effort to reproduce and to vary the entertaining sounds. If his father observed correctly, we must add that Laurent seems to have varied his actions systematically, as if testing the effect of different degrees of effort upon the bit of environment represented by the chain and rattles. Kittens make a similar study of parameters when delicately using their paws to push pencils and other objects ever nearer to the edge of one's desk. In all such examples it is clear that the child or animal is by no means at the mercy of transient stimulus fields. He selects for continuous treatment those aspects of his environment which he finds it possible to affect in some way. His behavior is selective, directed, persistent—in short, motivated.

Motivated toward what goal? In these terms, too, the behavior exhibits a little of everything. Laurent can be seen as appeasing a stimulus hunger, providing his sensorium with an agreeable level of stimulation by eliciting from the environment a series of interesting sounds, feels, and sights. On the other hand we might emphasize a need for activity and see him as trying to reach a pleasurable level of neuromuscular exercise. We can also see another possible goal in the behavior: the child is achieving knowledge, attaining a more differentiated cognitive map of his environment and thus satisfying an exploratory tendency or motive of curiosity. But it is equally possible to discern a theme of mastery, power, or control, perhaps even a bit of primitive self-assertion, in the child's concentration upon those aspects of the environment which respond in some way to his own activity. It looks as if we had found too many goals, and perhaps our first impulse is to search for some key to tell us which one is really important. But this, I think, is a mistake that would be fatal to understanding.

We cannot assign priority to any of these goals without pausing arbitrarily in the cycle of transaction between child and environment and saying, "This is the real point." I propose instead that the real point is the transactions as a whole. If the behavior gives satisfaction, this satisfaction is not associated with a particular moment in the cycle. It does not lie solely in sensory stimulation, in a bettering of the cognitive map, in coordinated action, in motor exercise, in a feeling of effort and of effects produced, or in the appreciation of change brought about in the sensory field. These are all simply aspects of a process which at this stage has to be conceived as a whole. The child appears to be occupied with the agreeable task of developing an effective familiarity with his environment. This involves discovering the effects he can have on the environment and the effects the environment will have on him. To the extent that these results are preserved by learning, they build up an increased competence in dealing with the environment. The child's play can thus be viewed as serious business, though to him it is merely something that is interesting and fun to do.

Bearing in mind these examples, as well as the dealings with environment pointed out by other workers, we must now attempt to describe more fully the possible nature of the motivational aspect of competence. It needs its own name, and in view of the foregoing analysis I propose that this name be *effectance*.

EFFECTANCE

The new freedom produced by two decades of research on animal drives is of great help in this undertaking. We are no longer obliged to look for a source of energy external to the nervous system, for a consummatory climax, or for a fixed connection between reinforcement and tension-reduction. Effectance motivation cannot, of course, be conceived as having a source in tissues external to the nervous system. It is in no sense a deficit motive. We must assume it to be neurogenic, its "energies" being simply those of the living cells that make up the nervous system. External stimuli play an important part, but in terms of "energy" this part is secondary, as one can see most clearly when environmental stimulation is actively sought. Putting it picturesquely, we might say that the effectance urge represents what the neuromuscular system wants to do when it is otherwise unoccupied or is gently stimulated by the environment. Obviously there are no consummatory acts; satisfaction would appear to lie in the arousal and maintaining of activity rather than in its slow decline toward bored passivity. The motive need not be conceived as intense and powerful in the sense that hunger, pain, or fear can be powerful when aroused to high pitch. There are plenty of instances in which children refuse to leave their absorbed play in order to eat or to visit the toilet. Strongly aroused drives, pain, and anxiety, however, can be conceived as overriding the effectance urge and capturing the energies of the neuromuscular system. But effectance motivation is persistent in the sense that it regularly occupies the spare waking time between episodes of homeostatic crisis.

In speculating upon this subject we must bear in mind the continuous nature of behavior. This is easier said than done; habitually we break things down in order to understand them, and such units as the reflex arc, the stimulus-response sequence, and the single transaction with the environment seem like inevitable steps toward clarity. Yet when we apply such an analysis to playful exploration we lose the most essential aspect of the behavior. It is constantly circling from stimulus to perception to action to effect to stimulus to perception, and so on around; or, more properly, these processes are all in continuous action and continuous change. Dealing with the environment means carrying on a continuing transaction which gradually changes one's relation to the environment. Because there is no consummatory climax, satisfaction has to be seen as lying in a considerable series of transactions, in a trend of behavior rather than a goal that is achieved. It is difficult to make the word "satisfaction" have this connotation, and we shall do well to replace it by "feeling of efficacy" when attempting to indicate the subjective and affective side of effectance.

It is useful to recall the findings about novelty: the singular effectiveness of novelty in engaging interest and for a time supporting persistent behavior. We also need to consider the selective continuance of transactions in which the animal or child has a more or less pronounced effect upon the environment—in which something happens as a consequence of his activity. Interest is not aroused and sustained when the stimulus field is so familiar that it gives rise at most to reflex acts or automatized habits. It is not sustained when actions produce no effects or changes in the stimulus field. Our conception must therefore be that effectance motivation is aroused by stimulus conditions which offer, as Hebb (1949) puts it, difference-in-sameness. This leads to variability and novelty of response, and interest is best sustained when the resulting action affects the stimulus so as to produce further difference-in-sameness. Interest wanes when action begins to have less effect; effectance motivation subsides when a situation has been explored to the point that it no longer presents new possibilities.

We have to conceive further that the arousal of playful and exploratory interest means the appearance of organization involving both the cognitive and active aspects of behavior. Change in the stimulus field is not an end in itself, so to speak; it happens when one is passively moved about, and it may happen as a consequence of random movements without becoming focalized and instigating exploration. Similarly, action which has effects is not an end in itself, for if one unintentionally kicks away a branch while walking, or knocks something off a table, these effects by no means necessarily become involved in playful investigation. Schachtel's (1954) emphasis on focal attention becomes helpful at this point. The playful and exploratory behavior shown by Laurent is not random or casual. It involves focal *attention* to some object—the fixing of some aspect of the stimulus field so that it stays relatively constant—and it also involves the focalizing of *action* upon this object. As Diamond (1939) has expressed it, response under these conditions is "relevant to the stimulus," and it is change in the *focalized* stimulus that so strongly affects the level of interest. Dealing with the environment means directing focal attention to some part of it and organizing actions to have some effect on this part.

In our present state of relative ignorance about the workings of the nervous system it is impossible to form a satisfactory idea of the neural basis of effectance motivation, but it should at least be clear that the concept does not refer to any and every kind of neural action. It refers to a particular kind of activity, as inferred from particular kinds of behavior. We can say that it does not include reflexes and other kinds of automatic response. It does not include well-learned, automatized patterns, even those that are complex and highly organized. It does not include behavior in the service of effectively aroused drives. It does not even include activity that is highly random and discontinuous, though such behavior may be its most direct forerunner. The urge toward competence is inferred specifically from behavior that shows a lasting focalization and that has the characteristics of exploration and experimentation, a kind of variation within the focus. When this particular sort of activity is aroused in the nervous system, effectance motivation is being aroused, for it is characteristic of this particular sort of activity that is selective, directed, and persistent, and that instrumental acts will be learned for the sole reward of engaging in it.

Some objection may be felt to my introducing the word *competence* in connection with behavior that is so often playful. Certainly the playing child is doing things for fun, not because of a desire to improve his competence in dealing with the stern hard world. In order to forestall misunderstanding, it should be pointed out that the usage here is parallel to what we do when we connect sex with its biological goal of reproduction. The sex drive aims for pleasure and gratification, and reproduction is a consequence that is presumably unforeseen by animals and by man at primitive levels of understanding. Effectance motivation similarly aims for the feeling of efficacy, not for the vitally important learnings that come as its consequence. If we consider the part played by competence motivation in adult human life we can observe the same parallel. Sex may now be completely and purposefully divorced from reproduction but nevertheless pursued for the pleasure it can yield. Similarly, effectance motivation may lead to continuing exploratory interests or active adventures when in fact there is no longer any gain in actual competence or any need for it in terms of survival. In both cases the motive is capable of yielding surplus satisfaction well beyond what is necessary to get the biological work done.

In infants and young children it seems to me sensible to conceive of effectance motivation as undifferentiated. Later in life it becomes profitable to distinguish various motives such as cognizance, construction, mastery, and achievement. It is my view that all such motives have a root in effectance motivation. They are differentiated from it through life experiences which emphasize one or another aspect of the cycle of transaction with environment. Of course, the motives of later childhood and of adult life are no longer simple and can almost never be referred to a single root. They can acquire loadings of anxiety, defense, and compensation, they can become fused with unconscious fantasies of a sexual, aggressive, or omnipotent character, and they can gain force because of their service in producing realistic results in the way of income and career. It is not my intention to cast effectance in the star part in adult motivation. The acquisition of motives is a complicated affair in which simple and sovereign theories grow daily more obsolete. Yet it may be that the satisfaction of effectance contributes significantly to those feelings of interest which often sustain us so well in day-to-day actions, particularly when the things we are doing have continuing elements of novelty.

THE BIOLOGICAL SIGNIFICANCE OF COMPETENCE

The conviction was expressed at the beginning of this paper that some such concept as competence, interpreted motivationally, was essential for any biologically sound view of human nature. This necessity emerges when we consider the nature of living systems, particularly when we take a longitudinal view. What an organism does at a given moment does not always give the right clue as to what it does over a period of time. Discussing this problem, Angyal (1941) has proposed that we should look for the general pattern followed by the total organismic process over the course of time. Obviously this makes it necessary to take account of growth. Angyal defines life as "a process of self-expansion"; the living system "expands at the expense of its surroundings," assimilating parts of the environment and transforming them into functioning parts of itself. Organisms differ from other things in nature in that they are "self-governing entities" which are to some extent "autonomous." Internal processes govern them as well as external "heteronomous" forces. In the course of life there is a relative increase in the preponderance of internal over external forces. The living system expands, assimilates more of the environment, transforms its surroundings so as to bring them under greater control. "We may say," Angyal writes, "that the general dynamic trend of the organism is toward an increase of autonomy. . . . The human being has a characteristic tendency toward self-determination, that is, a tendency to resist external influences and to subordinate the heteronomous forces of the physical and social environment to its own sphere of influence." The trend toward increased autonomy is characteristic so long as growth of any kind is going on, though in the end the living system is bound to succumb to the pressure of heteronomous forces.

Of all living creatures, it is man who takes the longest strides toward autonomy. This is not because of any unusual tendency toward bodily expansion at the expense of the environment. It is rather that man, with his mobile hands and abundantly developed brain, attains an extremely high level of competence in his transactions with his surroundings. The building of houses, roads and bridges, the making of tools and instruments, the domestication of plants and animals, all qualify as planful changes made in the environment so that it comes more or less under control and serves our purposes rather than intruding upon them. We meet the fluctuations of outdoor temperature, for example, not only with our bodily homeostatic mechanisms, which alone would be painfully unequal to the task, but also with clothing, buildings, controlled fires, and such complicated devices as self-regulating central heating and air conditioning. Man as a species has developed a tremendous power of bringing the environment into his service, and each individual member of the species must attain what is really quite an impressive level of competence if he is to take part in the life around him.

We are so accustomed to these human accomplishments that it is hard to realize how long an apprenticeship they require. At the outset the human infant is a slow learner in comparison with other animal forms. Hebb (1949) speaks of "the astonishing inefficiency of man's first learning, as far as immediate results are concerned," an inefficiency which he attributes to the large size of the association areas in the brain and the long time needed to bring them under sensory control. The human lack of precocity in learning shows itself even in comparison with one of the next of kin: as Hebb points out, "the human baby takes six months, the chimpanzee four months, before making a clear distinction between friend and enemy." Later in life the slow start will pay dividends. Once the fundamental perceptual elements, simple associations, and conceptual sequences have been established, later learning can proceed with ever increasing swiftness and complexity. In Hebb's words, "learning at maturity concerns patterns and events whose parts at least are familiar and which already have a number of other associations."

This general principle of cumulative learning, starting from slowly acquired rudiments and proceeding thence with increasing efficiency, can be illustrated by such processes as manipulation and locomotion, which may culminate in the acrobat devising new stunts or the dancer working out a new ballet. It is especially vivid in the case of language, where the early mastery of words and pronunciation seems such a far cry from spontaneous adult speech. A strong argument has been made by Hebb (1949) that the learning of visual forms proceeds over a similar course from slowly learned elements to rapidly combined patterns. Circles and squares, for example, cannot be discriminated at a glance without a slow apprenticeship involving eye movements, successive fixations, and recognition of angles. Hebb proposes that the recognition of visual patterns without eye movement "is possible only as the result of an intensive and prolonged visual training that goes on from the moment of birth, during every moment that the eyes are open, with an increase in skill evident over a period of 12 to 16 years at least."

On the motor side there is likewise a lot to be cumulatively learned. The playing, investigating child slowly finds out the relationships between what he does and what he experiences. He finds out, for instance, how hard he must push what in order to produce what effect. Here the S-R formula is particularly misleading. It would come nearer the truth to say that the child is busy learning R-S connections—the effects that are likely to follow upon his own behavior. But even in this reversed form the notion of bonds or connections would still misrepresent the situation, for it is only a rare specimen of behavior that can properly be conceived as determined by fixed neural channels and a fixed motor response. As Hebb has pointed out, discussing the phenomenon of "motor equivalence" named by Lashley (1942), a rat which has been trained to press a lever will press it with the left forepaw, the right forepaw, by climbing upon it, or by biting it; a monkey will open the lid of a food box with either hand, with a foot, or even with a stick; and we might add that a good baseball player can catch a fly ball while running in almost any direction and while in almost any posture, including leaping in the air and plunging forward to the ground. All of these feats are possible because of a history of learnings in which the main lesson has been the effects of actions upon the stimulus fields that represent the environment. What has been learned is not a fixed connection but a flexible relationship between stimulus fields and the effects that can be produced in them by various kinds of action.

One additional example, drawn this time from Piaget (1952), is particularly worth mentioning because of its importance in theories of development. Piaget points out that a great deal of mental development depends upon the idea that the world is made up of objects having substance and permanence. Without such an "object concept" it would be impossible to build up the ideas of space and causality and to arrive at the fundamental distinction between self and external world. Observation shows that the object concept, "far from being innate or ready-made in experience, is constructed little by little." Up to 7 and 8 months the Piaget children searched for vanished objects only in the sense of trying to continue the actions, such as sucking or grasping, in which the objects had played a part. When an object was really out of sight or touch, even if only because it was covered by a cloth, the infants undertook no further exploration. Only gradually, after some study of the displacement of objects by moving, swinging and dropping them, does the child begin to make an active search for a vanished object, and only still more gradually does he learn, at 12 months or more, to make allowance for the object's sequential displacements and thus to seek it where it has gone rather than where it was last in sight. Thus it is only through cumulative learning that the child arrives at the idea of permanent substantial objects.

The infant's play is indeed serious business. If he did not while away his time pulling strings, shaking rattles, examining wooden parrots, dropping pieces of bread and celluloid swans, when would he learn to discriminate visual patterns, to catch and throw, and to build up his concept of the object? When would he acquire the many other foundation stones necessary for cumulative learning? The more closely we analyze the behavior of the human infant, the more clearly do we realize that infancy is not simply a time when the nervous system matures and the muscles grow stronger. It is a time of active and continuous learning, during which the basis is laid for all those processes, cognitive and motor, whereby the child becomes able to establish effective transactions with his environment and move toward a greater degree of autonomy. Helpless as he may seem until he begins to toddle, he has by that time already made substantial gains in the achievement of competence.

Under primitive conditions survival must depend quite heavily upon achieved competence. We should expect to find things so arranged as to favor and maximize this achievement. Particularly in the case of man, where so little is provided innately and so much has to be learned through experience, we should expect to find highly advantageous arrangements for securing a steady cumulative learning about the properties of the environment and the extent of possible transactions. Under these circumstances we might expect to find a very powerful drive operating to insure progress toward competence, just as the vital goals of nutrition and reproduction are secured by powerful drives, and it might therefore seem paradoxical that the interests of competence should be so much entrusted to times of play and leisurely exploration. There is good reason to suppose, however, that a strong drive would be precisely the wrong arrangement to secure a flexible, knowledgeable power of transaction with the environment. Strong drives cause us to learn certain lessons well, but they do not create maximum familiarity with our surroundings.

This point was demonstrated half a century ago in some experiments by Yerkes and Dodson (1908). They showed that maximum motivation did not lead to the most rapid solving of problems, especially if the problems were complex. For each problem there was an optimum level of motivation neither the highest nor the lowest, and the optimum was lower for more complex tasks. The same problem has been discussed more recently by Tolman (1948) in his paper on cognitive maps. A cognitive map can be narrow or broad, depending upon the range of cues picked up in the course of learning. Tolman suggests that one of the conditions which tend to narrow the range of cues is a high level of motivation. In everyday terms, a man hurrying to an important business conference is likely to perceive only the cues that help him to get there faster, whereas a man taking a stroll after lunch is likely to pick up a substantial amount of casual information about his environment. The latent learning experiments with animals, and experiments such as those of Johnson (1953) in which drive level has been systematically varied in a situation permitting incidental learning, give strong support to this general idea. In a recent contribution, Bruner, Matter, and Papanek (1955) make a strong case for the concept of breadth of learning and provide additional evidence that it is favored by moderate and hampered by strong motivation. The latter "has the effect of speeding up learning at the cost of narrowing it." Attention is concentrated upon the task at hand and little that is extraneous to this task is learned for future use.

These facts enable us to see the biological appropriateness of an arrangement which uses periods of less intense motivation for the development of competence. This is not to say that the narrower but efficient learnings that go with the reduction of strong drives make no contribution to general effectiveness. They are certainly an important element in capacity to deal with the environment, but a much greater effectiveness results from having this capacity fed also from learnings that take place in quieter times. It is then that the infant can attend to matters of lesser urgency, exploring the properties of things he does not fear and does not need to eat, learning to gauge the force of his string-pulling when the only penalty for failure is silence on the part of the attached rattles, and generally accumulating for himself a broad knowledge and a broad skill in dealing with his surroundings.

The concept of competence can be most easily discussed by choosing, as we have done, examples of interaction with the inanimate environment. It applies equally well, however, to transactions with animals and with other human beings, where the child has the same problem of finding out what effects he can have upon the environment and what effects it can have upon him. The earliest interactions with members of the family may involve needs so strong that they obscure the part played by effectance motivation, but perhaps the example of the well fed baby diligently exploring the several features of his mother's face will serve as a reminder that here, too, there are less urgent moments when learning for its own sake can be given free rein.

In this closing section I have brought together several ideas which bear on the evolutionary significance of competence and of its motivation. I have sought in this way to deepen the biological roots of the concept and thus help it to attain the stature in the theory of behavior which has not been reached by similar concepts in the past. To me it seems that the most important proving ground for this concept is the effect it may have on our understanding of the development of personality. Does it assist our grasp of early object relations, the reality principle, and the first steps in the development of the ego? Can it be of service in distinguishing the kinds of defense available at different ages and in providing clues to the replacement of primitive defenses by successful adaptive maneuvers? Can it help fill the yawning gap known as the latency period, a time when the mastery of school subjects and other accomplishments claim so large a share of time and energy? Does it bear upon the self and the vicissitudes of self-esteem, and can it enlighten the origins of psychological disorder? Can it make adult motives and interests more intelligible and enable us to rescue the concept of sublimation from the difficulties which even its best friends have recognized? I believe it can be shown that existing explanations of development are not satisfactory and that the addition of the concept of competence cuts certain knots in personality theory. But this is not the subject of the present communication, where the concept is offered much more on the strength of its logical and biological probability.

SUMMARY

The main theme of this paper is introduced by showing that there is widespread discontent with theories of motivation built upon primary drives. Signs of this discontent are found in realms as far apart as animal psychology and psychoanalytic ego psychology. In the former, the commonly recognized primary drives have proved to be inadequate in explaining exploratory behavior, manipulation, and general activity. In the latter, the theory of basic instincts has shown serious shortcomings when it is stretched to account for the development of the effective ego. Workers with animals have attempted to meet their problem by invoking secondary reinforcement and anxiety reduction, or by adding exploration and manipulation to the roster of primary drives. In parallel fashion, psychoanalytic workers have re ied upon the concept of neutralization of instinctual energies, have seen anxiety reduction as the central motive in ego development, or have hypothesized new instincts such as mastery. It is argued here that these several explanations are not satisfactory and that a better conceptualization is possible, indeed that it has already been all but made.

In trying to form this conceptualization, it is first pointed out that many of the earlier tenets of primary drive theory have been discredited by recent experimental work. There is no longer any compelling reason to identify either pleasure or reinforcement with drive reduction, or to think of motivation as requiring a source of energy external to the nervous system. This opens the way for considering in their own right those aspects of animal and human behavior in which stimulation and contact with the environment seem to be sought and welcomed, in which raised tension and even mild excitement seem to be cherished, and in which novelty and variety seem to be enjoyed for their own sake. Several reports are cited which bear upon interest in the environment and the rewarding effects of environmental feed-back. The latest contribution is that of Woodworth (1958), who makes dealing with the environment the most fundamental element in motivation.

The survey indicates a certain unanimity as to the kinds of behavior that cannot be successfully conceptualized in terms of primary drives. This behavior includes visual exploration, grasping, crawling and walking, attention and perception, language and thinking, exploring novel objects and places, manipulating the surroundings, and producing effective changes in the environment. The thesis is then proposed that all of these behaviors have a common biological significance: they all form part of the process whereby the animal or child learns to interact effectively with his environment. The word *competence* is chosen as suitable to indicate this common property. Further, it is maintained that competence cannot be fully acquired simply through behavior instigated by drives. It receives substantial contributions from activities which, though playful and exploratory in character, at the same time show direction, selectivity, and persistence in interacting with the environment. Such activities in the ultimate service of competence must therefore be conceived to be motivated in their own right. It is proposed to designate this motivation by the term effectance, and to characterize the experience produced as a *feeling of efficacy*.

In spite of its sober biological purpose, effectance motivation shows itself most unambiguously in the playful and investigatory behavior of young animals and children. Specimens of such behavior, drawn from Piaget (1952), are analyzed in order to demonstrate their constantly transactional nature. Typically they involve continuous chains of events which include stimulation, cognition, action, effect on the environment, new stimulation, *etc.* They are carried on with considerable persistence and with selective emphasis on parts of the environment which provide changing and interesting feed-back in connection with effort expended. Their significance is destroyed if we try to break into the circle arbitrarily and declare that one part of it, such as cognition alone or active effort alone, is the real point, the goal, or the special seat of satisfaction. Effectance motivation must be conceived to involve satisfaction—a feeling of efficacy—in transactions in which behavior has an exploratory, varying, experimental character and produces changes in the stimulus field. Having this character, the behavior leads the organism to find out how the environment can be changed and what consequences flow from these changes.

In higher animals and especially in man, where so little is innately provided and so much has to be learned about dealing with the environment, effectance motivation independent of primary drives can be seen as an arrangement having high adaptive value. Considering the slow rate of learning in infancy and the vast amount that has to be learned before there can be an effective level of interaction with surroundings, young animals and children would simply not learn enough unless they worked pretty steadily at the task between episodes of homeostatic crisis. The association of interest with this "work," making it play and fun, is thus somewhat comparable to the association of sexual pleasure with the biological goal of reproduction. Effectance motivation need not be conceived as strong in the sense that sex, hunger, and fear are strong when violently aroused. It is moderate but persistent, and in this, too, we can discern a feature that is favorable for adaptation. Strong motivation reinforces learning in a narrow sphere, whereas moderate motivation is more conducive to an exploratory and experimental attitude which leads to competent interactions in general, without reference to an immediate pressing need. Man's huge cortical association areas might have been a suicidal piece of specialization if they had come without a steady, persistent inclination toward interacting with the environment.

REFERENCES

Allport, G. W. *Personality: A psychological interpretation.* New York: Holt, 1937.
Allport, G. W. Effect: A secondary principle of learning. *Psychol. Rev.,* 1946, *53*, 335-347.
Angyal, A. *Foundations for a science of personality.* New York: Commonwealth Fund, 1941.
Ansbacher, H. L., & Ansbacher, R. R. (Eds.) *The individual psychology of Alfred Adler.* New York: Basic Books, 1956.
Beach, F. A. Analysis of factors involved in the arousal, maintenance and manifestation of sexual excitement in male animals. *Psychosom. Med.,* 1942, *4*, 173-198.
Beach, F. A. Instinctive behavior: Reproductive activities. In S. S. Stevens (Ed.), *Handbook of experimental psychology.* New York: Wiley, 1951. Pp. 387-434.
Berlyne, D. E. Novelty and curiosity as determinants of exploratory behavior. *Brit. J. Psychol.,* 1950, *41*, 68-80.
Berlyne, D. E. The arousal and satiation of perceptual curiosity in the rat. *J. comp. physiol. Psychol.,* 1955, *48*, 238-246.
Berlyne, D. E. Attention to change, conditioned inhibition (S^IR) and stimulus satiation. *Brit. J. Psychol.,* 1957, *48*, 138-140.
Berlyne, D. E. The present status of research on exploratory and related behavior. *J. indiv. Psychol.,* 1958, *14*, 121-126.
Bibring, E. The development and problems of the theories of the instincts. *Int. J. Psychoanal.,* 1941, *22*, 102-131.
Bruner, J. S., Matter, J., & Papanek, M. L. Breadth of learning as a function of drive level and mechanization. *Psychol. Rev.,* 1955, *62*, 1-10.
Bühler, C. The reality principle. *Amer. J. Psychotherap.,* 1954, *8*, 626-647.
Bühler, K. *Die geistige Entwicklung des Kindes.* (4th ed.) Jena: Gustav Fischer, 1924.
Butler, R. A. Discrimination learning by rhesus monkeys to visual-exploration motivation. *J. comp. physiol. Psychol.,* 1953, *46*, 95-98.
Butler, R. A. Exploratory and related behavior: A new trend in animal research. *J. indiv. Psychol.,* 1958, *14*, 111-120.
Butler, R. A. & Harlow, H. F. Discrimination learning and learning sets to visual exploration incentives. *J. gen. Psychol.,* 1957, *57*, 257-264.
Cofer, C. N. Motivation. *Ann. Rev. Psychol.,* 1959, *10*, 173-202.
Colby, K. M. *Energy and structure in psychoanalysis.* New York: Ronald, 1955.
Dashiell, J. F. A quantitative demonstration of animal drive. *J. comp. Psychol.,* 1925, *5*, 205-208.
Diamond, S. A neglected aspect of motivation. *Sociometry,* 1939, *2*, 77-85.

Dollard, J., & Miller, N. E. *Personality and psychotherapy.* New York: McGraw-Hill, 1950.

Erikson, E. H. *Childhood and society.* New York: Norton, 1952.

Erikson, E. H. Growth and crises of the healthy personality. In C. Kluckhohn, H. A. Murray, & D. Schneider (Eds.), *Personality in nature, society, and culture.* (2nd Ed.) New York: Knopf, 1953. Pp. 185-225.

Fenichel, O. *The psychoanalytic theory of neurosis.* New York: Norton, 1945.

French, T. M. *The integration of behavior.* Vol. I. *Basic postulates.* Chicago: Univer. Chicago Press, 1952.

Freud, A. The mutual influences in the development of ego and id: Introduction to the discussion. *Psychoanal. Stud. Child,* 1952, *7,* 42-50.

Freud, S. *Wit and its relation to the unconscious.* New York: Moffat, Yard, 1916.

Freud, S. Formulations regarding the two principles in mental functioning. *Collected papers.* Vol. 4. London: Hogarth Press and Institute of Psycho-analysis, 1925. Pp. 13-21. (a)

Freud, S. On narcissism: An introduction. *Collected papers.* Vol. 4. London: Hogarth Press and Institute of Psycho-analysis, 1925. Pp. 30-59. (b)

Freud, S. Instincts and their vicissitudes. *Collected papers.* Vol. 4. London: Hogarth Press and Institute of Psycho-analysis, 1925. Pp. 60-83. (c)

Freud, S. *The ego and the id.* (Trans. by J. Riviere) London: Hogarth Press, 1927.

Freud, S. *Beyond the pleasure principle.* London: Hogarth Press, 1948.

Freud, S. *An outline of psycho-analysis.* (Trans. by J. Strachey) New York: Norton, 1949.

Goldstein, K. *The organism.* New York: American Book, 1939.

Goldstein, K. *Human nature in the light of psychopathology.* Cambridge, Mass.: Harvard Univer. Press, 1940.

Gross, K. *The play of man.* (Trans. by E. L. Baldwin) New York: D. Appleton, 1901.

Harlow, H. F. Mice, monkeys, men, and motives. *Psychol. Rev.,* 1953, *60,* 23-32.

Harlow, H. F., Harlow, M. K., & Meyer, D. R. Learning motivated by a manipulation drive. *J. exp. Psychol.,* 1950, *40,* 228-234.

Hartmann, H. Comments on the psychoanalytic theory of the ego. *Psychoanal. Stud. Child,* 1950, *5,* 74-95.

Hartmann, H. Notes on the theory of sublimation. *Psychoanal. Stud. Child,* 1955, *10,* 9-29.

Hartmann, H. Notes on the reality principle. *Psychoanal. Stud. Child,* 1956, *11,* 31-53.

Hartmann, H. *Ego psychology and the problem of adaptation.* (Trans. by D. Rapaport) New York: International Univer. Press, 1958.

Hartmann, H., Kris, E., & Loewenstein, R. Notes on the theory of aggression. *Psychoanal. Stud. Child,* 1948, *3/4,* 9-36.

Hebb, D. O. *The organization of behavior.* New York: Wiley, 1949.

Hebb, D. O. Drives and the c.n.s. (conceptual nervous system). *Psychol. Rev.,* 1955, *62,* 243-254.

Hebb, D. O. The motivating effects of exteroceptive stimulation. *Amer. Psychologist,* 1958, *13,* 109-113.

Hebb, D. O., & Thompson, W. R. The social significance of animal studies. In G. Lindzey (Ed.), *Handbook of social psychology.* Vol. I. Cambridge, Mass.: Addison-Wesley, 1954, Pp. 532-561.

Hendrick, I. Instinct and the ego during infancy. *Psychoanal. Quart.,* 1942, *11,* 33-58.

Hendrick, I. Work and the pleasure principle. *Psychoanal. Quart.,* 1943, *12,* 311-329. (a)

Hendrick, I. The discussion of the 'instinct to master.' *Psychoanal. Quart.,* 1943, *12,* 561-565. (b)

Hill, W. F. Activity as an autonomous drive. *J. comp. physiol. Psychol.,* 1956, *49,* 15-19.

Johnson, E. E. The role of motivational strength in latent learning. *J. Comp. physiol. Psychol.,* 1953, *45,* 526-530.

Kagan, J. Differential reward value of incomplete and complete sexual behavior. *J. comp. physiol. Psychol.,* 1955, *48,* 59-64.

Kagan, J., & Berkun, M. The reward value of running activity. *J. comp. physiol. Psychol.*, 1954, *47*, 108.

Kardiner, A., & Spiegel, H. War stress and neurotic illness. New York: Hoeber, 1947.

Lashley, K. S. Experimental analysis of instinctive behavior. *Psychol. Rev.*, 1938, *45*, 445-471.

Lashley, K. S. The problems of cerebral organization in vision. In H. Kluver, *Visual mechanisms*. Lancaster, Pa.: Jaques Cattell, 1942. Pp. 301-322.

Leuba, C. Toward some integration of learning theories: The concept of optimal stimulation. *Psychol. Rep.*, 1955, *1*, 27-33.

Lilly, J. C. Mental effects of reduction of ordinary levels of physical stimuli on intact, healthy persons. *Psychiat. res. Rep.*, 1956, No. 5.

Maslow, A. H. *Motivation and personality*. New York: Harper, 1954.

Maslow, A. H. Deficiency motivation and growth motivation. In M. R. Jones (Ed.), *Nebraska symposium on motivation 1955*. Lincoln, Neb.: Univer. Nebraska Press, 1955. Pp. 1-30.

McClelland, D. C., Atkinson, J. W., Clark, R. A. & Lowell, E. I. *The Achievement motive*. New York: Appleton-Century. 1953.

McDougall, W. *Introduction to social psychology*. (16th ed.) Boston: John Luce, 1923.

McReynolds, P. A restricted conceptualization of human anxiety and motivation. *Psychol. Rep.*, 1956, *2*, 293-312. Monogr. Suppl. 6.

Miller, N. E. Learnable drives and rewards. In S. S. Stevens (Ed.), *Handbook of experimental psychology*. New York: Wiley, 1951. Pp. 435-472.

Miller, N. E. Central stimulation and other new approaches to motivation and reward. *Amer. Psychologist*, 1958, *13*, 100-108.

Mittelmann, B. Motility in infants, children, and adults. *Psychoanal. Stud. Child*, 1954, 9, 142-177.

Montgomery, K. C. The role of the exploratory drive in learning. *J. comp. physiol. Psychol.*, 1954, *47*, 60-64.

Montgomery, K. C., & Monkmann, J. A. The relation between fear and exploratory behavior. *J. comp. physiol. Psychol.*, 1955, *48*, 132-136.

Morgan, C. T. *Physiological psychology*. New York: McGraw-Hill, 1943.

Morgan, C. T. Physiological mechanisms of motivation. In M. R. Jones (Ed.), *Nebraska symposium on motivation 1957*. Lincoln, Neb.: Univer. Nebraska Press, 1957. Pp. 1-35.

Mowrer, O. H. *Learning theory and personality dynamics*. New York: Ronald, 1950.

Munroe, R. *Schools of psychoanalytical thought*. New York: Dryden, 1955.

Murphy, G. *Personality: A biosocial approach to origins and structure*. New York: Harper, 1947.

Murray, H. A. *Explorations in personality*. New York & London: Oxford Univer. Press, 1938.

Murray, H. A. & Kluckhohn, C. Outline of a conception of personality. In C. Kluckhohn, H. A. Murray, & D. M. Schneider (Eds.), *Personality in nature, society, and culture*. (2nd ed.) New York: Knopf, 1953.

Myers, A. K., & Miller, N. E. Failure to find a learned drive based on hunger; evidence for learning motivated by "exploration." *J. comp. physiol. Psychol.*, 1954, *47*, 428-436.

Nissen, H. W. A study of exploratory behavior in the white rat by means of the obstruction method. *J. genet. Psychol.*, 1930, *37*, 361-376.

Olds, J., & Milner, P. Positive reinforcement produced by electrical stimulation of septal area and other regions of rat brain. *J. comp. physiol. Psychol.*, 1954, 47, 419-427.

Piaget, J. *The origins of intelligence in children*. (Trans. by M. Cook) New York: International Univer. Press, 1952.

Rapaport, D. *Organization and pathology of thought*. New York: Columbia Univer. Press, 1951.

Rapaport, D. On the psychoanalytic theory of thinking. In R. P. Knight & C. R. Friedman (Eds.), *Psychoanalytic psychiatry and psychology*. New York: International Univer. Press, 1954. Pp. 259-273.

Rapaport, D. The theory of ego autonomy: A generalization. *Bull Menninger Clin.,* 1958, *22,* 13-35.

Rosvold, H. E. Physiological psychology. *Ann. Rev. Psychol.,* 1959, 10, 415-454.

Schachtel, E. G. The development of focal attention and the emergence of reality. *Psychiatry,* 1954, *17,* 309-324.

Sheffield, F. D. & Roby, T. B. Reward value of a non-nutritive sweet taste. *J. comp. physiol. Psychol.,* 1950, *43,* 471-481.

Sheffield, F. D., Roby, T. B., & Campbell, B. A. Drive reduction vs. consummatory behavior as determinants of reinforcement. *J. comp. physiol. Psychol.,* 1954, 47, 349-354.

Sheffield, F. D., Wulff, J. J., & Backer, R. Reward value of copulation without sex drive reduction. *J. comp. physiol. Psychol.,* 1951, *44,* 3-8.

Skinner, B. F. *Science and human behavior.* New York: Macmillan, 1953.

Stellar, E. The physiology of motivation. *Psychol. Rev.,* 1954, *61,* 5-22.

Tolman, E. C. Cognitive maps in rats and men. *Psychol. Rev.,* 1948, *55,* 189-208.

Welker, W. L. Some determinants of play and exploration in chimpanzees. *J. comp. psychol.,* 1956, *49,* 84-89.

Whiting, J. W. M. & Mowrer, O. H. Habit progression and regression—a laboratory study of some factors relevant to human socialization. *J. comp. Psychol.,* 1943, *36,* 229-253.

Wolfe, J. B., & Kaplon, M. D. Effect of amount of reward and consummative activity on learning in chickens. *J. comp. Psychol.,* 1941, *31,* 353-361.

Woodworth, R. S. *Dynamics of behavior.* New York: Holt, 1958.

Yerkes, R. M. & Dodson, J. D. The relation of strength of stimulus to rapidity of habit-formation. *J. comp. Neurol. Psychol.,* 1908, *18,* 459-482.

Young, P. T. Food-seeking drive, affective process, and learning. *Psychol. Rev.,* 1949, *56,* 98-121.

Young, P. T. The role of hedonic processes in motivation. In M. R. Jones (Ed.), *Nebraska symposium on motivation 1955.* Lincoln, Neb.: Univer. Nebraska Press, 1955. Pp. 193-238.

Zimbardo, P. G., & Miller, N. E. Facilitation of exploration by hunger in rats. *J. comp. physiol. Psychol.,* 1958, *51,* 43-46.

6. A Dynamic Theory of Human Motivation

A. H. Maslow

IN a previous paper various propositions were presented which would have to be included in any theory of human motivation that could lay claim to being definitive. These conclusions may be briefly summarized as follows:

Abridged from the *Psychological Review,* 1943, 50, 370-396. Reprinted by permission of the author and the American Psychological Association, Inc.

1. The integrated wholeness of the organism must be one of the foundation stones of motivation theory.

2. The hunger drive (or any other physiological drive) was rejected as a centering point or model for a definitive theory of motivation. Any drive that is somatically based and localizable was shown to be atypical rather than typical in human motivation.

3. Such a theory should stress and center itself upon ultimate or basic goals rather than partial or superficial ones, upon ends rather than means to these ends. Such a stress would imply a more central place for unconscious rather than conscious motivations.

4. There are usually available various cultural paths to the same goal. Therefore conscious, specific, local-cultural desires are not as fundamental in motivation theory as the more basic, unconscious goals.

5. Any motivated behavior, either preparatory or consummatory, must be understood to be a channel through which many basic needs may be simultaneously expressed or satisfied. Typically an act has *more* than one motivation.

6. Practically all organismic states are to be understood as motivated and as motivating.

7. Human needs arrange themselves in hierarchies of prepotency. That is the appearance of one need usually rests on the prior satisfaction of another, more prepotent need. Thus man is a perpetually wanting animal . . . .

8. *Lists* of drives will get us no place for various theoretical and practical reasons. Furthermore any classification of motivations must deal with the problem of levels of specificity or generalization of the motives to be classified.

9. Classifications of motivations must be based upon goals rather than upon instigating drives or motivated behavior.

10. Motivation theory should be human-centered rather than animal-centered.

11. The situation or the field in which the organism reacts must be taken into account but the field alone can rarely serve as an exclusive explanation for behavior. Furthermore the field itself must be interpreted in the organism's terms. Field theory cannot be a substitute for motivation theory.

12. Not only the integration of the organism must be taken into account, but also the possibility of isolated, specific, partial or segmented reactions.

It has since become necessary to add to these another affirmation.

13. Motivation theory is not synonymous with behavior theory. The motivations are only one class of determinants of behavior. While behavior is almost always motivated, it is also almost always biologically, culturally and situationally determined as well.

The present paper is an attempt to formulate a positive theory of motivation which will satisfy these theoretical demands, meanwhile, conforming to the known facts, clinical and observational as well as experimental. This theory is, I think, in the functionalist tradition of James and Dewey, corrected by the holism of Wertheimer, Goldstein and Gestalt Psychology, and by the dynamicism of Freud and Adler. This fusion or synthesis may arbitrarily be called a "general-dynamic" theory.

It is far easier to perceive and to criticize the lacks in motivation theory than to remedy them. Mostly this is because of the very serious lack of sound data in this area. I conceive this lack of sound facts to be due primarily to the absence of a valid theory of motivation. The present theory then must be considered to be a suggested program or framework for future research and must stand or fall, not so much on facts available or evidence presented, as upon researches yet to be done, researches suggested, perhaps, by the questions raised in this paper.

I

A. THE PHYSIOLOGICAL NEEDS

The needs that are usually taken as the starting point for motivation theory are the so-called physiological drives. Two recent lines of research make it necessary to revise our customary notions about these needs, first, the development of the concept of homeostasis, and second, the finding that appetites (preferential choices among foods) are a fairly efficient indication of actual needs or lacks in the body.

Homeostasis refers to the body's automatic efforts to maintain a constant, normal state of the blood stream. Cannon has described this process for a) the water content of the blood, b) salt content, c) sugar content, d) protein content, e) fat content, f) calcium content, g) ogyxen content, h) constant hydrogen-ion level (acid-base balance) and i) constant temperature of the blood. Obviously this list can be extended to include other minerals, the hormones, vitamins, etc.

Young in a recent article has summarized the work on appetite in its relation to body needs. If the body lacks some chemical, the individual will tend to develop a specific appetite or partial hunger for that food element

Thus it seem impossible as well as useless to make any list of fundamental physiological needs for they can come to almost any number one might wish, depending on the degree of specificity of description. We can not identify all physiological needs as homeostatic. If sexual desire, sleepiness, sheer activity and maternal behavior in animals, are homeostatic, this has not yet been demonstrated. Furthermore, this would not include the various sensory pleasures (tastes, smells, tickling, stroking) which are probably physiological and which may become the goals of motivated behavior.

In a previous paper it has been pointed out that these physiological drives or needs are to be considered unusual rather than typical because they are isolable, and because they are localizable somatically. That is, they are relatively independent of each other, of other motivations and of the organism as a whole, and secondly, in many cases, it is possible to demonstrate a localized, underlying somatic base for the drive. This is true less generally than has been thought (exceptions are fatigue, sleepiness, maternal responses) but it is still true in the classic instances of hunger, sex, and thirst.

It should be pointed out again that any of the physiological needs and the consummatory behavior involved with them serve as channels for all sorts of other needs as well. That is the person who thinks he is hungry may actually be seeking more for comfort, or dependence, than for vitamins or proteins. Conversely, it is possible to satisfy the hunger need in part by other activities such as drinking water or smoking cigarettes. In other words, relatively isolable as these physiological needs are, they are not completely so.

Undoubtedly these physiological needs are the most important of all needs. What this means specifically, is that in the human being who is missing everything in life in an extreme fashion, it is most likely that the major motivation would be the physiological needs rather than any others. A person who is lacking food, safety, love, and esteem would most probably hunger for food more strongly than for anything else.

If all the needs are unsatisfied, and the organism is then dominated by the physiological needs, all other needs become simply non-existent or are pushed into the background. It is then fair, for instance, to characterize the whole organism by saying simply that it is hungry, for consciousness is almost completely preempted by hunger, all capacities are put into the service of hunger-satisfaction, and the organization of these capacities is almost entirely determined by the one purpose of satisfying hunger. The receptors and effectors, the intelligence, memory, habits, all may now be defined as hunger-gratifying tools.[1] Capacities that are not useful for this purpose lie dormant, or are pushed into the background. The urge to write poetry, the desire to acquire an automobile, the interest in American history, the desire for a new pair of shoes are, in the extreme case, all forgotten or pushed into the background. For the man who is extremely and dangerously hungry, no other interests exist but food. He dreams food, he remembers food, he thinks about food, he emotes only about food, he perceives only food and he wants only food. The more subtle determinants that ordinarily fuse with the physiological drives in organizing even feeding, drinking or sexual behavior, may now be so com-

[1] Whenever a drive is studied as an isolated phenomenon, this will make us blind to the many other things that happen to the individual. In other words, with a limited theory we will look only for limited things and not perceive the many other happenings that our limited theory makes us blind to. In all motivational phenomena, many things happen simultaneously and in succession in the organism, e.g., in the fields of perception, thinking, feeling, wanting, and in every other field. Since we see usually what we look for, we must enlarge our position to look for all the happenings in motivation.

pletely overwhelmed, as to allow us to speak at this time (but *only* at this time) of pure hunger drive and behavior, with the one unqualified aim of relief.

Another peculiar characteristic of the human organism when it is dominated by a certain need is that the whole philosophy of the future tends also to change. For our chronically and extremely hungry man, Utopia can be defined very simply as a place where there is plenty of food. He tends to think that, if only he is guaranteed food for the rest of his life, he will be perfectly happy and will want nothing more, ever again. Life itself tends to be defined in terms of eating. Anything else will be defined as unimportant. Freedom, love, community feeling, respect, philosophy, may all be waved aside as fripperies which are useless since they fail to fill the stomach. Such a man may fairly be said to live by bread alone.

It cannot possibly be denied that such things are true but their *generality* can be denied. Emergency conditions are, almost by definition, rare in the normally functioning society. That this truism can be forgotten is due mainly to two reasons. First, rats have few motivations other than physiological ones, and since so much of the research upon motivation has been made with these animals, it is easy to carry the rat-picture over to the human being. Secondly, it is too often not realized that culture itself is an adaptive tool, one of whose main functions is to make the physiological emergencies come less and less often. In most of the known societies, chronic extreme hunger of the emergency type is rare, rather than common. In any case, this is true in the U. S. The average American citizen is experiencing appetite rather than hunger when he says "I am hungry." He is apt to experience sheer life-and-death hunger only by accident and then only a few times through his entire life.

Obviously a good way to obscure the "higher" motivations, and to get a lopsided view of human capacities and human nature, is to make the organism extremely and chronically hungry or thirsty. Anyone who attempts to make an emergency picture into a typical one, and who will measure all of man's goals and desires by his behavior during extreme physiological deprivation is certainly being blind to many things. It is certainly quite true that man lives by bread alone—when there is no bread. But what happens to man's desires when there *is* plenty of bread and when his belly is chronically filled?

At once other (and "higher") needs emerge and these, rather than physiological hungers, dominate the organism. And when these in turn are satisfied, again new (and still "higher") needs emerge and so on. This is what we mean by saying that the basic human needs are organized into a hierarchy of relative prepotency.

One main implication of this phrasing is that gratification becomes as important a concept as deprivation in motivation theory. Instead of assuming that deprivation is the only instigation, we are forced to recognize that gratification is in a manner of speaking an instigation as well, for it releases the organism from the domination of a relatively more physiological need, permitting thereby the emergence of other more social goals. The physiological needs, along with their partial goals when chronically gratified, cease to exist as active determinants or organizers of behavior. They now exist only in a potential fashion in the sense that they may emerge again to dominate the organism if they are thwarted. But a want that is satisfied is no longer a want. The organism is dominated and its behavior organized only by unsatisfied needs. If hunger is satisfied, it becomes unimportant in the current dynamics of the individual.

This statement is somewhat qualified by a hypothesis to be discussed more fully below, namely, that it is precisely those individuals who have been satisfied all their lives in a certain need who are best equipped to tolerate deprivation of that need in the future, and that furthermore, those who have been deprived in the past will react differently to current satisfactions than the one who has never been deprived.

B.   THE SAFETY NEEDS

If the physiological needs are relatively well gratified, there then emerges a new set of needs, which we may categorize roughly as the safety needs. All that has been said of the physiological needs is equally true, although in lesser degree, of these desires. The organism may equally well be wholly dominated by them, they may serve as the almost exclusive organizers of behavior, recruiting all the capacities of the organism in their service, and we may then fairly describe the whole organism as a safety-seeking mechanism. Again we may say of the receptors, the effectors, of the intellect and the other capacities that they are primarily safety-seeking tools. Again, as in the hungry man, we find that the dominating goal is a strong determinant not only of his current world-outlook and philosophy but also of his philosophy of the future. Practically everything looks less important than safety, (even sometimes the physiological needs which being satisfied, are now underestimated). A man, in this state, if it is extreme enough and chronic enough, may be characterized as living almost for safety alone.

Although in this paper we are interested primarily in the needs of the adult, we can approach an understanding of his safety needs perhaps more efficiently by observation of infants and children, in whom these needs are much more simple and obvious. One reason for the clearer appearance of the threat or danger reactions in infants, is that they do not inhibit this reaction at all, whereas adults in our society have been taught to inhibit it at all costs. Thus even when adults do feel their safety to be threatened we may not be able to see this on the surface. Infants will react in a total fashion and as if they are endangered if they are disturbed or dropped suddenly, startled by loud noises, flashing light, or other unusual sensory stimulation, by rough handling, by general loss of support in the mother's arms, or by inadequate support.[2]

In infants we can also see a much more direct reaction to bodily illnesses of various kinds. Sometimes these illnesses seem to be immediately and *per se* threatening and seem to make the child feel unsafe. For instance, vomiting, colic or other sharp pains seem to make the child look at the whole world in a different way. At such a moment of pain, it may be postulated that, for the child, the appearance of the whole world suddenly changes from sunshine to darkness, so to speak, and becomes a place in which anything at all might happen, in which previously stable things have suddenly become unstable. Thus a child who because of some bad food is taken ill perhaps, for a day or two may develop fear, nightmares, and a need for protection and reassurance never seen in him before his illness.

Another indication of the child's need for safety is his preference for order-liness, and for a kind of undisrupted routine or rhythm. He seems to want a predictable, orderly world. For instance, injustice, unfairness, or inconsistency in the parents seems to make a child feel anxious and unsafe. This may be not so much because of the injustice *per se* or any particular pains involved, but rather because of the fact that this threatens to make the world look un-reliable, or unsafe, or unpredictable. Young children seem to thrive better under a system which has at least a skeletal outline of rigidity, in which there is a schedule of a kind, some sort of routine, something that can be counted upon, not only for the present but also far into the future. Perhaps one could express this more succinctly by saying that the child needs an organized world rather than an unorganized or unstructured one.

The central role of the parents and the normal family setup are indisputable. Quarreling, physical assault, separation, divorce or death within the family may be particularly terrifying. Also parental outbursts of rage or threats of punishment directed to the child, calling him names, speaking to him harshly, shaking him, handling him roughly or actual physical punishment sometimes elicit such total panic and terror in the child that we must assume more is involved than the physical pain alone. While it is true that in some children this terror may represent also a fear of loss of parental love, it can also occur in completely rejected children, who seem to cling to the hating parents more for sheer safety and protection than because of hope of love.

Confronting the average child with new, unfamiliar, strange, unmanageable stimuli or situations will too frequently elicit the danger or terror reaction. Examples are: getting lost or even being separated from the parents for a short time, being confronted with new faces, new situations or new tasks, the

---

[2]As the child grows up, sheer knowledge and familiarity as well as better motor development make these "dangers" less and less dangerous and more and more manageable. Throughout life it may be said, that one of the main conative functions of education is the neutralizing of apparent dangers through knowledge, e.g., I am not afraid of thunder because I know something about it.

sight of strange, unfamiliar or uncontrollable objects, illness or death. Particularly at such times, the child's frantic clinging to his parents is eloquent testimony to their role as protectors, (quite apart from their roles as food-givers and love-givers.)

From these and similar observations, we may generalize and say that the average child in our society generally prefers a safe, orderly, predictable, organized world, which he can count on, and in which unexpected, unmanageable or other dangerous things do not happen, and in which in any case, he has all powerful parents who protect and shield him from harm.

That these reactions may so easily be observed in children is in a way a proof of the fact that children in our society, feel too unsafe, (or, in a word, are badly brought up). Children who are reared in an unthreatening, loving family do *not* ordinarily react as we have described above. In such children the danger reactions are apt to come mostly to objects or situations that adults too would consider dangerous.[3]

The healthy, normal, fortunate adult in our culture is largely satisfied in his safety needs. The smoothly running society ordinarily makes its members feel safe enough from wild animals, extremes of temperature, criminals, assault and murder, tyranny, etc. Therefore, in a very real sense, he does not any longer have any safety needs as active motivators (just as he has no active need for water or oxygen). This is not meant as any mere play on words, or for the sake of paradox. Just as a sated man no longer feels hungry, a safe man no longer feels endangered. If we wish to see these needs directly and clearly we must turn to neurotic or near-neurotic individuals, and the economic and social underdogs. In between these extremes, we can perceive the expressions of safety needs only in such phenomena as, for instance, the common preference for a job with tenure and protection, the desire for a savings account, and for insurance of various kinds (medical, dental, unemployment, disability, old age.)

Other broader aspects of the attempt to seek safety and stability in the world are seen in the very common preference for the familiar rather than the unknown. The tendency to have some religion or world-philosophy that organizes the universe and the men in it into some sort of satisfactorily coherent, meaningful whole is also an example of safety-seeking. Here too we may list science and philosophy in general as partially motivated by the safety needs (we shall see later that there are also other motivations to scientific, philosophical or religious endeavor).

---

[3]A "test battery" for safety might be confronting the child with a small exploding firecracker, or with a bewhiskered face, having the mother leave the room, putting him upon a high ladder, a hypodermic injection, having a mouse crawl up to him, etc. Of course I cannot seriously recommend the deliberate use of such "tests" for they might very well harm the child being tested. But these and similar situations come up by the score in the child's ordinary day-to-day living and may be observed. There is no reason why these stimuli should not be used with, for example, young chimpanzees.

Otherwise the need for safety is seen as an active and dominant mobilizer of the organism's resources only in emergencies, e.g., war, disease, natural catastrophies, crime waves, societal disorganization, neurosis, brain injury, chronically bad situations.

Some neurotic adults in our society are, in many ways, like the unsafe child in their desire for safety, although in them it takes on a somewhat special appearance. Their reaction is often to unknown, psychological dangers in a world that is perceived to be hostile, overwhelming and threatening. Such a person behaves as if a great catastrophe were almost always impending, i.e., he is usually responding as if to an emergency. His safety needs often take specific expression in a search for a protector, or a stronger person on whom he may depend.

Such a man may be described in a slightly different way with some usefulness as a grown-up person who retains his childish attitudes toward the world. That is, a neurotic adult may be said to behave "as if" he were actually afraid of a spanking, or of his mother's disapproval, or of being abandoned by his parents, or having his food taken away from him. It is as if his childish attitudes of fear and threat reaction to a dangerous world have gone underground, remaining untouched by the growing up and learning processes, and were now ready to be called out by any stimulus that would make a child feel endangered and threatened.

Not all neurotic individuals feel unsafe. Neurosis may have at its core a thwarting of the affection and esteem needs in a person who is generally safe.

The neurosis in which the search for safety takes its clearest form is in the compulsive-obsessive neurosis. Compulsive-obsessives try frantically to order and stabilize the world so that no unmanageable, unexpected or unfamiliar dangers will ever appear. They hedge themselves about with all sorts of ceremonials, rules and formulas so that every possible contingency may be provided for and so that no new contingencies may appear. They are much like the brain injured cases, described by Goldstein, who manage to maintain their equilibrium by avoiding everything unfamiliar and strange and by ordering their restricted world in such a neat, disciplined, orderly fashion that everything in the world can be counted upon. They try to arrange the world so that anything unexpected (dangers) cannot possibly occur. If, through no fault of their own, something unexpected does occur, they go into a panic reaction as if this unexpected occurrence constituted a terrific danger. What we can see only as a none-too-strong preference in the healthy person, e.g., preference for the familiar, becomes a life-and-death necessity in abnormal cases.

C. THE LOVE NEEDS

If both the physiological and the safety needs are fairly well gratified, then there will emerge the love and affection and belongingness needs, and the whole cycle already described will repeat itself with this new center. Now the person will feel keenly, as never before, the absence of friends, or a sweetheart or a wife, or children. He will hunger for affectionate relations with people in general, for a place in his group, and he will strive with great intensity to achieve these goals. He will want these more than anything else in the world and may even forget that once, when he was hungry, he sneered at love.

In our society the thwarting of these needs is the most commonly found core in cases of maladjustment and more severe psychopathology. In our society, love and affection, as well as their possible expression in sexuality, are generally looked upon with ambivalence and are customarily hedged about with many restrictions and inhibitions. Practically all theorists of psychopathology have stressed thwarting of the love needs as basic in the picture of maladjustment. Many clinical studies have therefore been made of this need and we know more about it perhaps than any of the other needs except the physiological ones.

One thing that must be immediately stressed is that love is not synonymous with sex. Sex may be studied as a purely physiological need. Ordinarily sexual behavior is multi-determined, that is, determined not only by sexual needs but also by others, chief among which are the love and affection needs. Also not to be overlooked is the fact that the love needs involve both giving *and* receiving love.

Very frequently there is confusion between love needs and other needs. For instance, the concept of psychological security has been used customarily to express the love needs but most writers have at one time or another confused with it the safety needs and the self-esteem needs, as well. We must be very careful to differentiate them. However, even after we exclude the safety needs and the self-esteem needs we still may sub-divide the love needs.

First, we have the need for affectional or love relationship with other individuals. This expresses itself in our society mostly between sweethearts and married people, between parents and children and between very close friends. Secondly, we have what has been called a desire for belongingness. That is, there seems to be the necessity for members of our society to have not only close love relations with one or two or three people but to have more diffuse love or affection relations with a wide number of other people, which may be seen as a desire to be a practicing, functioning accepted member of a group of some kind. The thwarting of the first aspect we may call rejection, of the second isolation. More widely used terms are "secure and insecure" and we may for the moment use them even if they are rather vague, simply because they are customarily used. In the table that follows there is a list of the various characteristics of insecure and secure people which has been worked out in previous research.

1. Feeling of rejection, of not being loved, of being treated coldly and without affection, of being hated, of being despised.

2. Feelings of isolation, ostracism, aloneness or being out of it, feelings of "uniqueness," of being essentially unlike or inferior to other human beings.

3. Perception of the world and life as dangerous, threatening, dark, hostile, or challenging; as a jungle in which every man's hand is against every other's, in which one eats or is eaten.

4. Perception of other human beings as essentially bad, evil, or selfish; as dangerous, threatening, hostile or challenging.

5. Constant feelings of threat and danger; anxiety.

6. Feelings of suspicion and mistrust; of envy or jealousy toward others; much hostility, prejudice, hatred.

7. Tendency to expect the worst; general pessimism.

8. Tendency to be unhappy or discontented.

9. Feelings of tension and strain and conflict; together with various consequences of tension, e.g., "nervousness," fatigue, irritability, nervous stomach and other psychosomatic disturbances, nightmares; emotional instability; vacillation, uncertainty and inconsistency.

10. Tendency to compulsive introspectiveness, morbid self-examination, acute consciousness of self.

11. Guilt and shame feelings, sin feelings, feelings of self-condemnation, suicidal tendencies, discouragement.

12. Disturbances of various aspects of the self-esteem complex, e.g., craving for power and for status, compulsive ambition, overaggression, hunger for money, prestige, glory, possessiveness, jealousy of jurisdiction and prerogative, over competitiveness; and/or the opposite masochistic tendencies, overdependence, compulsive submissiveness, ingratiation. Inferiority feelings, feelings of weakness and helplessness.

1. Feeling of being liked or loved, of acceptance, or being looked upon with warmth.

2. Feelings of belonging, or being at home in the world, of having a place in the group.

3. Perception of the world and life as pleasant, warm, friendly or benevolent, in which all men tend to be brothers.

4. Perception of other human beings as essentially good, pleasant, warm, friendly or benevolent.

5. Feeling of safety, rare feelings of threat and danger; unanxious.

6. Feeling of friendliness and trust in others; little hostility; tolerance of others; easy affection for others.

7. Tendency to expect good to happen; general optimism.

8. Tendency to be happy or contented.

9. Feelings of calm, ease and relaxation. Unconflicted. Emotional stability.

10. Tendency to outgoingness; interest in the outside world, in other people.

11. Self-acceptance, tolerance of self, acceptance of the impulses.

12. Desire for strength or adequacy with respect to problems rather than for power over other people. Firm, positive, well-based self-esteem. Feeling of strength. Courage.

13. Continual striving for, and hunger for safety and security, various neurotic trends, inhibitions, defensiveness, escape trends, ameliorative trends, false goals, fixations on partial goals. Psychotic tendencies, delusions, hallucinations, etc.

13. Relative lack of neurotic or psychotic tendencies.

14. Selfish, egocentric, individualistic trends.

14. "Social interest" (in Adlerian sense); cooperativeness, kindliness, interest in others, sympathy.

D. THE ESTEEM NEEDS

All people in our society (with a few pathological exceptions) have a need or desire for a stable, firmly based, (usually) high evaluation of themselves, for self-respect, or self-esteem, and for the esteem of others. By firmly based self-esteem, we mean that which is soundly based upon real capacity, achievement and respect from others. These needs may be classified into two subsidiary sets. These are first, the desire for strength, for achievement, for adequacy, for confidence in the face of the world, and for independence and freedom.[4] Secondly, we have what we may call the desire for reputation or prestige, (defining it as respect or esteem from other people), recognition, attention, importance or appreciation.[5] These needs have been relatively stressed by Alfred Adler and his followers, and have been relatively neglected by Freud and the psychoanalysts. More and more today however, there is appearing widespread appreciation of their central importance.

Satisfaction of the self-esteem need leads to feelings of self-confidence, worth, strength, capability and adequacy of being useful and necessary in the world. But thwarting of these needs produces feelings of inferiority, of weakness and of helplessness. These feelings in turn give rise to either basic discouragement or else compensatory or neurotic trends. An appreciation of the necessity of basic self-confidence and an understanding of how helpless people are without it, can be easily gained from a study of severe traumatic neurosis.

E. THE NEED FOR SELF-ACTUALIZATION

Even if all these needs are satisfied, we may still often (always?) expect

---

[4]Whether or not this particular desire is universal we do not know. The crucial question, especially important today, is "Will men who are enslaved and dominated, inevitably feel dissatisfied and rebellious?" We may assume on the basis of commonly known clinical data that a man who has known true freedom (not paid for by giving up safety and security but rather built on the basis of adequate safety and security) will not willingly or easily allow his freedom to be taken away from him. But we do not know that this is true for the person born into slavery. The events of the next decade should give us our answer.

[5]Perhaps the desire for prestige and respect from others is subsidiary to the desire for self-esteem or confidence in one's self. Observation of children seems to indicate that this is so, but clinical data give no clear support for such a conclusion.

that a new discontent and restlessness will soon develop. That is, it will appear unless the individual is doing what he is fitted for, what his talents allow him to do. A musician must make music, an artist must paint, a poet must write, if he is to be ultimately happy. What a man *can* be, he *must* be. This need we may call self-actualization.

This term, first coined by Kurt Goldstein, is being used in this paper in a much more specific and limited fashion. It refers to the desire for self-fulfillment, for full flowering of the capacities and potentialities of the person, to the tendency for him to become actualized in what he is pontentially. This might be phrased as the desire to become more and more what one is, to become everything that one is capable of becoming.

The specific form that these needs will take will of course vary tremendously from person to person. In one individual it may take the form of the desire to be an ideal mother, in another it may be expressed athletically and in still another one it may be to paint pictures or create inventions. It is not necessarily a creative urge although in people who have any capacities for creation it will take this form.

The clear emergence of these needs rests upon prior satisfaction of the physiological, safety, love and esteem needs. We shall call people who are satisfied in these needs, basically satisfied people, and it is from these that we may expect the fullest (and healthiest) creativeness.[6] Since, in our society, basically satisfied people are the exception, we do not know much about self-actualization, either experimentally or clinically. It remains a challenging problem for research.

F.   THE PRECONDITIONS FOR THE BASIC NEED SATISFACTIONS

There are certain conditions which are very immediate prerequisites for the basic need satisfactions. Danger to these is reacted to almost as if it were a direct danger to the basic needs themselves. Such conditions as freedom to speak, freedom to do what one wishes so long as no harm is done to others, freedom to express one's self, freedom to investigate and seek for information, freedom to defend one's self, justice, fairness, honesty, orderliness in the group are examples of such preconditions for basic need satisfactions. Thwarting in these will be reacted to with a threat of emergency response. These conditions are not ends in themselves but they are *almost* so since they are so closely related to the basic needs, which are apparently the only ends in them-

[6]Clearly creative behavior, like painting, is like any other behavior in having mutliple determinants. It may be seen in "innately creative" people whether they are satisfied or not, happy or unhappy, hungry or sated. Also it is clear the creative activity may be compensatory, ameliorative or purely economic. It is my impression (as yet unconfirmed) that it is possible to distinguish the artistic and intellectual products of basically satisfied people from those of basically unsatisfied people by inspection alone. In any case, here too, we must distinguish, in a dynamic fashion, the overt behavior itself from its various motivations or purposes.

selves. These conditions are defended because without them the basic satisfactions are quite impossible, or at least, very severely endangered.

If we remember that the cognitive capacities (perceptual, intellectual, learning) are a set of adjustive tools, which have, among other functions, the satisfaction of our basic needs, then it is clear that any danger to them, any
deprivation or blocking to their free use, must also be indirectly threatening
to the basic needs themselves. Such a statement is partial solution of the
general problems of curiosity, the search for knowledge, truth and wisdom,
and the ever-persistent urge to solve the cosmic mysteries.

We must therefore introduce another hypothesis and speak of degrees of
closeness to the basic needs, for we have already pointed out that *any* conscious desires (partial goals) are more or less important as they are more or
less close to the basic needs. The same statement may be made for various
behavior acts. An act is psychologically important if it contributes directly to
satisfaction of basic needs. The less directly it so contributes, or the weaker
this contribution is, the less important this act must be conceived to be from
the point of view of dynamic psychology. A similar statement may be made
for the various defense mechanisms or coping mechanisms. Some are very
directly related to the protection or attainment of the basic needs, others are
only weakly and distantly related. Indeed if we wished, we could speak of
more basic and less basic defense mechanisms, and then affirm that danger to
the more basic defenses is more threatening than danger to less basic defenses
(always remembering that this is so only because of their relationship to the
basic needs.)

G.   THE DESIRES TO KNOW AND TO UNDERSTAND

So far, we have mentioned the cognitive needs only in passing. Acquiring
knowledge and systematizing the universe have been considered as, in part,
techniques for the achievement of basic safety in the world, or, for the intelligent man, expressions of self-actualization. Also freedom of inquiry and
expression have been discussed as preconditions of satisfactions of the basic
needs. True though these formulations may be, they certainly do not constitute satisfactorily definitive answers to the question as to the motivation role
of curiosity, learning, philosophizing, experimenting, etc. They are at best
no more than partial answers.

This question is especially difficult because we know so little about the
facts. Curiosity, exploration, desire for the facts and for the truth, desire to
know may certainly be observed easily enough. The fact that they often are
pursued even at great cost to the individual's safety is an earnest of the partial
character of our previous discussion. In addition, the writer must admit that,
though he has sufficient clinical evidence to postulate the desire to know as a
very strong drive in intelligent people, no data are available for unintelligent

people. It may then be largely a function of relatively high intelligence. Rather tentatively, then, and largely in the hope of stimulating discussion and research, we shall postulate a basic desire to know, to be aware of reality, to get the facts, to satisfy curiosity, or as Wertheimer phrases it, to see rather than to be blind.

But even this postulation is not enough. Even after we know, we are impelled to know more and more minutely and microscopically on the one hand, and on the other, more and more extensively in the direction of a world philosophy, religion, etc. The facts that we acquire, if they are isolated or atomistic, inevitably get theorized about, and either analyzed or organized or both. This has been phrased by some as the search for "meaning." We shall then postulate a desire to understand, to systematize, to organize, to analyze, to look for relations and meanings.

Once these desires are accepted for discussion, we see at once that they too form themselves into a small hierarchy in which the desire to know is prepotent over the desire to understand. All the characteristics of a hierarchy of prepotency that we have described above, seem to hold for this one as well.

We must guard ourselves against the too easy tendency to separate these desires from the basic needs we have discussed above, i.e., to make a sharp dichotomy between "cognitive" and "conative" needs. The desire to know and to understand are themselves conative, i.e., have a striving character, and are as much personality needs as the "basic needs" we have already discussed.

II

FURTHER CHARACTERISTICS OF THE BASIC NEEDS

1. *The degree of fixity of the hierarchy of basic needs.* We have spoken so far as if this hierarchy were a fixed order but actually it is not nearly as rigid as we may have implied. It is true that most of the people with whom we have worked have seemed to have these basic needs in about the order that has been indicated. However, there have been a considerable number of exceptions.

a) There are some people in whom, for instance, self-esteem seems to be more important than love. This most common reversal in the hierarchy is most commonly due to the development of the notion that the person who is most likely to be loved is a strong or powerful person, one who inspires respect or fear, and who is self-confident or aggressive. Therefore such people who lack love and seek it, may try hard to put on a front of aggressive, confident behavior. But essentially they seek high self-esteem and its behavior expressions more as a means-to-an-end than for its own sake, for the sake of love rather than self-esteem itself.

b) There are other, apparently innately creative people in whom the drive to creativeness seems to be more important than any other counter-determin-ant. Their creativeness might appear not as self-actualization released by basic satisfaction, but in spite of lack of basic satisfaction.

c) In certain people the level of aspiration may be permanently deadened or lowered. That is, the less prepotent goals may simply be lost, and may dis-appear forever, so that the person who has experienced life at a very low level, i.e., chronic unemployment, may continue to be satisfied for the rest of his life if only he can get enough food.

d) The so-called "psychopathic personality" is another example of per-manent loss of the love needs. These are people who, according to the best data available, have been starved for love in the earliest months of their lives and have simply lost forever the desire and the ability to give and to receive affection (as animals lose sucking or pecking reflexes that are not exercised soon enough after birth).

e) Another cause of reversal of the hierarchy is that when a need has been satisfied for a long time, this need may be underevaluated. People who have never experienced chronic hunger, are apt to underestimate its effects and to look upon food as a rather unimportant thing. If they are dominated by a higher need, this higher need will seem to be the most important of all. It then becomes possible, and indeed does actually happen, that they may, for the sake of this higher need put themselves into the position of being de-prived in a more basic need. We may expect that after a long-time deprivation of the more basic need there will be a tendency to reevaluate both needs so that the more prepotent need will actually become consciously propotent for the individual who may have given it up very lightly. Thus, a man who has given up his job rather than lose his self-respect, and who then starves for six months or so, may be willing to take his job back even at the price of losing his self-respect.

f) Another partial explanation of *apparent* reversals is seen in the fact that we have been talking about the hierarchy of propotency in terms of consciously felt want or desires rather than of behavior. Looking at behavior itself may give us the wrong impression. What we have claimed is that the person will *want* the more basic of two needs when deprived in both. There is no necessary implication here that he will act upon his desires. Let us say again that there are many determinants of behavior other than the needs and desires.

g) But perhaps more important than all these exceptions are the ones that involve ideals, high social standards, high values and the like. These are the people who become martyrs, who will give up everything for the sake of a particular ideal, or value. These people may be understood, at least in part, by reference to one basic concept (or hypothesis) which may be called "in-creased frustration-tolerance through early gratification." People who have been satisfied in their basic needs throughout their lives, particularly in their earlier years, seem to develop exceptional power to withstand present or future thwarting of these needs simply because they have strong, healthy character structure as a result of basic satisfaction. They are the "strong" people who can easily weather disagreement or opposition, who can swim against the stream of public opinion and who can stand up for the truth at great personal cost. It is just the ones who have loved and been well-loved, and who have had many deep friendships who can hold out against hatred, rejection or persecution.

I say all this in spite of the fact that there is a ceratin amount of sheer habituation which is also involved in any full discussion of frustration tolerance. For instance, it is likely that those who have been accustomed to relative starvation for a long time, are partially enabled thereby to withstand food deprivation right now. What sort of balance must be made between these two tendencies, of habituation on the one hand, and of past satisfaction breeding present frustration tolerance on the other hand, remains to be worked out by future research. Meanwhile we may assume that they are both operative, side by side, since they do not contradict each other. In respect to this phenomenon of increased frustration tolerance, it seems probable that the most important gratifications come in the first two years of life. That is, people who have been made secure and strong in the earliest years, tend to remain secure and strong thereafter in the face of whatever threatens.

2. *Degrees of relative satisfaction.* So far, our theoretical discussion may have given the impression that these five sets of needs are somehow in a step-wise, all-or-none relationship to each other. We have spoken in such terms as the following: "If one need is satisfied, then another emerges." This might give the false impression that a need must be satisfied 100% before the next need emerges. In actual fact, most members of our society who are normal, are partially satisfied in all their basic needs and partially unsatisfied in all their basic needs at the same time. A more realistic description of the hierarchy would be in terms of decreasing percentages of satisfaction as we go up the hierarchy of prepotency. For instance, if I may assign arbitrary figures for the sake of illustration, it is as if the average citizen is satisfied perhaps 85% in his physiological needs, 70% in his safety needs, 50% in his love needs, 40% in his self-esteem needs, and 10% in his self-actualization needs.

As for the concept of emergence of a new need after satisfaction of the prepotent need, this emergence is not a sudden, saltatory phenomenon but rather a gradual emergence by slow degrees from nothingness. For instance, if prepotent need A is satisfied only 10% then need B may not be visible at all. However, as this need A becomes satisfied 25%, need B may emerge 5%, as need A becomes satisfied 75%, need B may emerge 90%, and so on.

3. *Unconscious character of needs.* These needs are neither necessarily conscious nor unconscious. On the whole, however, in the average person,

they are more often unconscious rather than conscious. It is not necessary at this point to overhaul the tremendous mass of evidence which indicates the crucial importance of unconscious motivation. It would by now be expected, on a priori grounds alone, that unconscious motivations would on the whole be rather more important than the conscious motivations. What we have called the basic needs are very often largely unconscious although they may, with suitable techniques, and with sophisticated people become conscious.

4. *Cultural specificity and generality of needs.* This classification of basic needs makes some attempt to take account of the relative unity behind the superficial differences in specific desires from one culture to another. Certainly in any particular culture an individual's conscious motivational content will usually be extremely different from the conscious motivational content of an individual in another society. However, it is the common experience of anthropologists that people, even in different societies, are a lot more alike than we would think from our first contact with them, and that as we know them better we seem to find more and more of his commonness. We then recognize the most startling differences to be superficial rather than basic, e.g., differences in style of hairdress, clothes, tastes in food, etc. Our classification of basic needs is in part an attempt to account for this unity behind the apparent diversity from culture to culture. No claim is made that it is ultimate or universal for all cultures. The claim is made only that it is relatively *more* ultimate, more universal, more basic, than the superficial conscious desires from culture to culture, and makes a somewhat closer approach to common-human characteristics. Basic needs are *more* common-human than superficial desires or behaviors.

5. *Multiple motivations of behavior.* These needs must be understood *not* to be *exclusive* or single determiners of certain kinds of behavior. An example may be found in any behavior that seems to be physiologically motivated, such as eating, or sexual play or the like. The clinical psychologists have long since found that any behavior may be a channel through which flow various determinants. Or to say it in another way, most behavior is multi-motivated. Within the sphere of motivational determinants any behavior tends to be determined by several or *all* the basic needs simultaneously rather than by only one of them. The latter would be more an exception than the former. Eating may be partially for the sake of filling the stomach, and partially for the sake of comfort and amelioration of other needs. One may make love not only for pure sexual release, but also to convince one's self of one's masculinity, or to make a conquest, to feel powerful, or to win more basic affection. As an illustration, I may point out that it would be possible (theoretically if not practically) to analyze a single act of an individual and see in it the expression of his physiological needs, his safety needs, his love needs, his esteem needs and self-actualization. This contrasts sharply with

the more naive type of trait psychology in which one trait or one motive accounts for a certain kind of act, i.e., an aggressive act is traced solely to a trait of aggressiveness.

6. *Multiple determinants of behavior.* Not all behavior is determined by the basic needs. We might even say that not all behavior is motivated. There are many determinants of behavior other than motives.[6] For instance, one other important class of determinants is the so-called "field" determinants. Theoretically, at least, behavior may be determined completely by the field, or even by specific isolated external stimuli, as in association of ideas, or certain conditioned reflexes. If in response to the stimulus word "table," I immediately perceive a memory image of a table, this response certainly has nothing to do with my basic needs.

Secondly, we may call attention again to the concept of "degree of closeness to the basic needs" or "degree of motivation." Some behavior is highly motivated, other behavior is only weakly motivated. Some is not motivated at all (but all behavior is determined).

Another important point which will be discussed fully in another publication, is that there is a basic difference between expressive behavior and coping behavior (functional striving, purposive goal seeking.) An expressive behavior does not try to do anything; it is simply a reflection of the personality. A stupid man behaves stupidly, not because he wants to, or tries to, or is motivated to, but simply because he *is* what he is. The same is true when I speak in a bass voice rather than tenor or soprano. The random movements of a healthy child, the smile on the face of a happy man even when he is alone, the springiness of the man's walk, and the erectness of his carriage are other examples of expressive, unmotivated behavior. Also the *style* in which a man carries out almost all his behavior, motivated as well as unmotivated, is also often expressive.

We may then ask, is *all* behavior expressive or reflective of the character structure? The answer is "No." Rote, habitual, automatized, or conventional behavior may or may not be expressive. The same is true for most "stimulus-bound" behaviors.

It is finally necessary to stress that expressiveness of behavior, and goal-directedness of behavior are not mutually exclusive categories. Average behavior is usually both.

7. *Goals as centering principle in motivation theory.* It will be observed that the basic principle in our classification has been neither the instigation nor the motivated behavior but rather the functions, effects, purposes, or goals of the behavior. It has been proven sufficiently by various people that this is the most suitable point for centering in any motivation theory. The in-

---

[6]I am aware that many psychologists and psychoanalysts use the term "motivated" and "determined" synonymously, e.g., Freud. But I consider this an obfuscating usage. Sharp distinctions are necessary for clarity of thought, and precision in experimentation.

terested reader is referred to the very excellent discussion of this point in Murray's, "Explorations in Personality."

8. *Animal—and human—centering.* This theory starts with the human being rather than any lower and presumably "simpler" animal. Too many of the findings that have been made in animals have been proven to be true only for animals but not for the human being. There is no reason whatsoever why we should start with animals in order to study human motivation. The logic, or rather illogic behind this general fallacy of "pseudo-simplicity" has been exposed often enough by philosophers and logicians as well as by scientists in each of the various fields. It is no more necessary to study animals before one can study man than it is to study mathematics before one can study geology or psychology or biology.

We may also reject without further ado the old, naive, behaviorism which assumed that it was somehow necessary, or at least more "scientific" to judge human beings by animal standards. One consequence of this belief was that the whole notion of purpose and goal was excluded from motivational psychology simply because one could not ask a white rat about his purposes. Tolman has long since proven in animal studies themselves that this exclusion was not necessary.

9. *Motivation and the theory of psychopathogenesis.* The conscious motivational content of everyday life has been above conceived to be relatively important or unimportant accordingly as it is more or less closely related to the basic goals. A desire for an ice-cream cone might actually be an indirect expression of a desire for love. If it is, then this desire for the ice-cream cone becomes extremely important motivation. If however the ice cream is simply something to cool the mouth with, or a casual appetitive reaction, then the desire is relatively unimportant. Everyday conscious desires are to be regarded as symptoms, as *surface indicators of more basic needs.* If we were to take these superficial desires at their face value we would find ourselves in a state of complete confusion which could never be resolved, since we would be dealing seriously with symptoms rather than with what lay behind the symptoms.

Thwarting of unimportant desires produces no psychopathological results; thwarting of a basically important need does produce such results. Any theory of psychopathogenesis must then be based on a sound theory of motivation. A conflict or frustration is not necessarily pathogenic. It becomes so only when it threatens or thwarts the basic needs, or partial needs that are closely related to the basic needs.

10. *The role of gratified needs.* It has been pointed out above several times that our needs usually emerge only when more prepotent needs have been gratified. Thus gratification has an important role in motivation theory. Apart from this, however, needs cease to play an active determining or organizing role as soon as they are gratified.

What this means is that, e.g., a basically satisfied person no longer has the needs for esteem, love, safety, etc. The only sense in which he might be said to have them is in the almost metaphysical sense that a sated man has hunger, or a filled bottle has emptiness. If we are interested in what *actually* motivates us, and not in what has, will, or might motivate us, then a satisfied need is not a motivator. It must be considered for all practical purposes simply not to exist, to have disappeared. This point must be hammered because it has been either overlooked or contradicted in every theory of motivation I know. See, for instance, how it necessitates basic revision of Freudian theory. The perfectly healthy, normal, fortunate man has no sex needs or hunger needs, or needs for safety, or for love, or for prestige, or self-esteem, except in stray moments of quickly passing threat. If we were to say otherwise, we should also have to aver that every man had all the pathological reflexes, e.g., Babinski, etc., because if his nervous system were damaged, these would appear.

It is such considerations as these that make it possible to postulate boldly that a man, who is thwarted in any of his basic needs may fairly be defined as a sick man. This is a fair parallel to our designation as "sick" of the man who lacks vitamins or minerals. Who is to say that a lack of love is less important than a lack of vitamins? Since we know the pathogenic effects of love starvation who is to say that we are invoking value-questions in an unscientific or illegitimate way, any more than the physician does who diagnoses and treats pellagra or scurvy? If I were permitted this usage, I should then say simply that a healthy man is primarily motivated by his needs to develop and actualize his fullest potentialities and capacities. If a man has any other basic needs in any active sense, then he is simply an unhealthy man. He is surely sick as if he suddenly developed a strong salt-hunger or calcium-hunger.

If this seems unusual or paradoxical the reader may be assured that this is only one among many such paradoxes that will appear as we revise our ways of looking at man's deeper motivations. When we ask what man wants of life, we deal with his very essence.

III

SUMMARY

1.   There are at least five sets of goals, which we may call basic needs. These are briefly physiological, safety, love, esteem, and self-actualization. In addition, we are motivated by the desire to achieve or maintain the various conditions upon which these basic satisfactions rest and by certain more intellectual desires.

2.   These basic goals are related to each other, being arranged in a hier-

archy of prepotency. This means that the most prepotent goal will monopolize consciousness and will tend of itself to organize the recruitment of the various capacities of the organism. The less prepotent needs are minimized, even forgotten or denied. But when a need is fairly well satisfied, the next prepotent ("higher") need emerges, in turn to dominate the conscious life and to serve as the center of organization of behavior, since gratified needs are not active motivators.

Thus man is a perpetually wanting animal. Ordinarily the satisfaction of these wants is not altogether mutually exclusive, but only tend to be. The average member of our society is most often partially satisfied and partially unsatisfied in all of his wants. The hierarchy principle is usually empirically observed in terms of increasing percentages of non-satisfaction as we go up the hierarchy. Reversals of the average order of the hierarchy are sometimes observed. Also it has been observed that an individual may permanently lose the higher wants in the hierarchy under special conditions. There are not only ordinarily, multiple motivations for usual behavior, but in addition many determinants other than motives.

3. Any thwarting or possibility of thwarting of these basic human goals, or danger to the defenses which protect them, or to the conditions upon which they rest are considered to be psychological threats. With a few exceptions, all psychopathology may be partially traced to such threats. A basically thwarted man may actually be defined as a "sick" man.

4. It is such basic threats which bring about the general emergency reactions.

5. Certain other basic problems have not been dealt with because of limitations of space. Among these are a) the problem of values in any definitive motivation theory, b) the relation between appetites, desires, needs and what is "good" for the organism, c) the etiology of the basic needs and their possible derivation in early childhood, d) redefinition of motivational concepts, i.e., drive, desire, wish, need, goal, e) implication of our theory for hedonistic theory, f) the nature of the uncompleted act, of success and failure, and of aspiration-level, g) the role of association, habit and conditioning, h) relation to the theory of inter-personal relations, i) implications for psychotherapy, j) implication for theory of society, k) the theory of selfishness, l) the relation between needs and cultural patterns. These as well as certain other less important questions, must be grappled with as motivation theory attempts to become definitive.

7. *Higher* and *Lower* Needs

A. H. Maslow

THIS paper attempts to prove that there are "real" psychological and operational differences between those needs called "higher" and those called "lower." This should be sufficient to establish that the organism itself dictates hierarchies of values, values which the scientific observer reports rather than creates. It is necessary thus to prove the obvious because so many still consider that values can never be more than the arbitrary imposition upon data of the writer's own tastes, prejudices, "intuitions," or other unproved or unprovable assumptions.

This casting out of values from psychology not only weakens it, and prevents it from reaching its full growth, but also abandons mankind either to supernaturalism or to ethical relativism. But if it could be demonstrated that the organism itself chooses between a prior and a subsequent, a stronger and a weaker, a "higher" and a "lower," then surely it would be impossible to maintain that one good has the same value as any other good, or that it is impossible to choose between them on any permanent basis. One such "principle of choice" has already been set forth in previous papers. The basic needs arrange themselves in a fairly definite hierarchy on the basis of the principle of relative potency. Thus the safety need is stronger than the love need, because it dominates the organism in various demonstrable ways when both needs are frustrated. In this sense, the physiological needs (which are themselves ordered in a sub-hierarchy) are stronger than the safety needs, which are stronger than the love needs, which in turn are stronger than the esteem needs, which are stronger than those idiosyncratic needs we have called the need for self-actualization.

But this is also an order which ranges from "lower" to "higher" in various other senses which are listed in this paper.

1. *The higher need is a later phyletic or evolutionary development.*

Abridged from *The Journal of Psychology*, 1948, 25, 433-436. Reprinted by permission of the author and The Journal Press.

We share the need for food with all living things, the need for love with (perhaps) the higher apes, the need for self-actualization (at least through creativeness) with nobody. The higher the need the more specifically human it is.

2. *Higher needs are later ontogenetic development.* Any individual at birth shows physical needs, and probably also, in a very inchoate form, needs safety, e.g., it can probably be frightened or startled, and probably thrives better when its world shows enough regularity and orderliness so that it can be counted upon. It is only after months of life that an infant shows the first signs of interpersonal ties and selective affection. Still later we may see fairly definitely the urges to autonomy, independence, achievement, and for respect and praise over and above safety and parental love. As for self-actualization, even a Mozart had to wait until he was three or four.

3. *The higher the need the less imperative it is for sheer survival, the longer gratification can be postponed, and the easier it is for the need to disappear permanently.* Higher needs have less ability to dominate, organize, and press into their service the autonomic reactions and other capacities of the organism, e.g., it is easier to be single minded, monomaniac, and desperate about safety than about respect. Deprivation of higher needs does not produce as desperate a defense and emergency reaction as is produced by lower deprivations. Respect is a dispensable luxury when compared with food or safety.

4. *Living at a higher need level means greater biological efficiency, greater longevity, less disease, better sleep, appetite, etc.* The psychosomatic researchers prove again and again that anxiety, fear, lack of love, domination, etc., tend to encourage undesirable physical, as well as psychological results.

5. *Higher needs are less urgent subjectively.* They are less perceptible, less unmistakable, more easily confounded with other needs by suggestion, imitation, by mistaken belief or habit. To be able to recognize one's own needs, i.e., to know what one really wants, is a considerable psychological achievement. This is doubly true for the higher needs.

6. *Higher need gratifications produce more desirable subjective results, i.e., more profound happiness, serenity, and richness of the inner life.* Satisfactions of the safety needs produce at best a feeling of relief and relaxation. In any case they cannot produce, e.g., the ecstasy and happy delirium of satisfied love.

7. *Pursuit and gratification of higher needs represents a general health-ward trend, a trend away from psychopathology.* The evidence for this statement is presented in another paper.

8. *The higher need has more preconditions.* This is true if only because prepotent needs must be gratified before it can be. Thus it takes more quanta of satisfactions for the love need to appear in consciousness than for the safety need. In a more general sense, it may be said that life is more complex

at the level of the higher needs. The search for respect and status involves more people, a larger scene, a longer run, more means, and partial goals, more subordinate and preliminary steps than does the search for love. The same may be said in turn of this latter need when compared with the search for safety.

9. *Higher needs require better outside conditions to make them possible.* Better[1] environmental conditions (familial, economic, political, educational, etc.) are all more necessary to allow people to love each other than merely to keep them from killing each other.

10. *A greater value is usually placed upon the higher need than upon the lower by those who have been chronically gratified in both.* Such people will sacrifice more for the "higher" satisfaction, and furthermore will more readily be able to withstand "lower" deprivation. For example, they will find it easier to live ascetic lives, to withstand danger for the sake of principle, to give up money and prestige for the sake of self-actualization.

11. *The higher the need, the wider is the circle of love-identification, i.e., the greater is the number of people love-identified with, and the greater is the average degree of love-identification.*[2] We may define love-identification as in principle, a merging into a single hierarchy of prepotency of the needs of two or more people. This is, of course, a matter of degree. Two people who love each other well will react to each other's needs and their own indiscriminately. Indeed the other's need *is* his own need.

12. *The pursuit and the gratification of the higher needs have desirable civic and social consequences.* To some extent, the higher the need the less selfish it must be. Hunger is highly egocentric; the only way to satisfy it is to satisfy oneself. But the search for love and respect necessarily involves other people. Moreover, it involves satisfaction for these other people. Moreover, people who have enough basic satisfaction to look for love and respect (rather than just food and safety) tend to develop such qualities as loyalty, friendliness, and civic consciousness, and to become better parents, husbands, teachers, public servants, etc.

13. *Satisfaction of higher needs is closer to self-actualization than is lower need satisfaction.* If the theory of self-actualization be accepted, then this is an important difference. Among other things, it means that we may expect to find in people living at the higher need level, a larger number and greater degree of the qualities found in self-actualizing people.

14. *The pursuit and gratification of the higher needs lead to greater,*

---

[1]It should be easy enough to define "better" impersonally, e.g., of two educational systems which purport to teach arithmetic, that system is better which actually does so.

[2]The writer considers the principle of love-identification of prime importance to the theory of inter-personal relations and of sociological phenomena in general. Of course, it also supplies the answer to those, e.g., the Gestalt psychologists who consider any need to be a selfish need, and who synonymize the study of motivation and the study of selfishness.

stronger, and truer individualism. This may seem to contradict the previous statement that living at higher need levels means more love-identification, i.e., more socialization. However it may sound logically, it is nevertheless an empirical reality. People living at the level of self-actualization are, in fact, found simultaneously to love mankind most and to be the most developed idiosyncratically. This completely supports Fromm's contention that self-love (or better, self-respect) is synergic with rather than antagonistic to love for others. His discussion of individuality, spontaneity, and robotization is also relevant.

8. Some Basic Propositions of a Growth and Self-Actualization Psychology

A. H. Maslow

WHEN the philosophy of man (his nature, his goals, his potentialities, his fulfillment) changes, then everything changes, not only the philosophy of politics, of economics, of ethics and values, of interpersonal relations and of history itself, but also the philosophy of education, the theory of how to help men become what they can and deeply need to become.

We are now in the middle of such a change in the conception of man's capacities, potentialities and goals. A new vision is emerging of the possibilities of man and of his destiny, and its implications are many not only for our conceptions of education, but also for science, politics, literature, economics, religion, and even our conceptions of the non-human world.

I think it is now possible to begin to delineate this view of human nature as a total, single, comprehensive system of psychology even though much of it has arisen as a "Third Force" reaction *against* the limitations (as philosophies of human nature) of the two most comprehensive psychologies now available, behaviorism (or associationism) and classical, Freudian psycho-

Abridged from the 1962 Yearbook of the Association for Supervision and Curriculum Development. *Perceiving, Behaving, Becoming: A New Force For Education,* A. W. Combs (Ed.). Reprinted by permission of Dr. A. H. Maslow.

analysis. Finding a single label for it is still a difficult task, perhaps a premature one. In the past I have called it the "holistic-dynamic" psychology to express my conviction about its major roots. Some have called it "organismic" following Goldstein. Sutich and others are calling it the Self-Psychology or Humanistic Psychology. We shall see. My own guess is, that in a few decades, if it remains suitably eclectic and comprehensive, it will be called simply "Psychology."

I think I can be of most service by speaking primarily for myself and out of my own work rather than as an "official" delegate of this large group of thinkers, even though I am sure that the areas of agreement among them are very large. . . . Because of the limited space I have, I will present only some of the major propositions of this point of view, especially those of importance to the educator. I should warn you that at many points I am way out ahead of the data. Some of these propositions are more based on private conviction than on publicly demonstrated facts. However, they are all in principle confirmable or disconfirmable.

1. We have, each one of us, an essential inner nature which is instinctoid, intrinsic, given, "natural," i. e., with an appreciable hereditary determinant, and which tends strongly to persist.

It makes sense to speak here of the hereditary, constitutional and very early acquired roots of the *individual* self, even though this biological determination of self is only partial, and far too complex to describe simply. In any case, this is "raw material" rather than finished product, to be reacted to by the person, by his significant others, by his environment, etc.

I include in this essential inner nature instinctoid needs, capacities, talents, anatomical equipment, physiological balances, prenatal and natal injuries, and traumata to the neonate. This inner core shows itself as natural inclinations, propensities or inner bent. Whether defense and coping mechanisms, "style of life," and other characterological traits, all shaped in the first few years of life, should be included is still a matter for discussion. I would say "yes" and proceed on the assumption that this raw material very quickly starts growing into a self as it meets the world outside and begins to have transactions with it.

These are potentialities, not final actualizations. Therefore they have a life history and must be seen developmentally. They are actualized, shaped or stifled mostly (but not altogether) by extra-psychic determinants (culture, family, environment, learning, etc.). Very early in life these goaless urges and tendencies become attached to objects ("sentiments") by canalization but also by arbitrarily learned associations.

This inner core, even though it is biologically based and "instinctoid," is weak in certain senses rather than strong. It is easily overcome, suppressed or repressed. It may even be killed off permanently. Humans no longer have instincts in the animal sense, powerful, unmistakable inner voices which tell them unequivocally what to do, when, where, how and with whom. All that we have left are instinct-remnants. And furthermore, these are weak, subtle and delicate, very easily drowned out by learning, by cultural expectations, by fear, by disapproval, etc. They are *hard* to know, rather than easy. Authentic selfhood can be defined in part as being able to hear these impulse-voices within oneself, i.e., to know what one really wants or doesn't want, what one is fit for and what one is *not* fit for, etc. It appears that there are wide individual differences in the strength of these impulse-voices.

2. Each person's inner nature has some characteristics which all other selves have (species-wide) and some which are unique to the person (idiosyncratic). The need for love characterizes every human being that is born (although it can disappear later under certain circumstances). Musical genius, however, is given to very few and these differ markedly from each other in style, e.g., Mozart and Debussy.

3. It is possible to study this inner nature scientifically and objectively (that is, with the right kind of "science") and to discover what it is like (*discover*,—not invent or construct). It is also possible to do this subjectively, by inner search and by psychotherapy, and the two enterprises supplement and support each other.

Many aspects of this inner, deeper nature are either (a) actively repressed, as Freud has described because they are feared or disapproved of or are ego-alien, or (b) "forgotten," (neglected, unused, overlooked, unverbalized or suppressed) as e.g., Schactel has described. Much of the inner, deeper nature is therefore unconscious. This can be true not only for impulses (drives, instincts, needs) as Freud has stressed, but also for capacities, emotions, judgments, attitudes, definitions, perceptions, etc. Active repression takes effort and uses up energy. There are many specific techniques of maintaining active unconsciousness, such as denial, projection, reaction-formation, etc. However, repression does not kill what is repressed. The repressed remains as one active determinant of thought and behavior.

Both active and passive repressions seems to begin early in life, mostly as a response to parental and cultural disapprovals.

However, there is also some clinical evidence that repression may arise also from intra-psychic, extra-cultural sources in the young child, or at puberty, out of fear of being overwhelmed by its own impulses, of becoming disintegrated, of "falling apart," exploding, etc. It is theoretically possible that the child may spontaneously form attitudes of fear and disapproval toward its own impulses and may then defend himself against them in various ways. Society need not be the only repressing force, if this is true. There may also be intra-psychic repressing and controlling forces. These we may call "intrinsic, counter-cathexes."

It is best to distinguish unconscious drives and needs from unconscious ways of cognizing because the latter are often easier to bring to consciousness and therefore to modify. Primary process cognition (Freud) or archaic thinking (Jung) are more recoverable by, e.g., creative art education, in dance education, and other non-verbal educational techniques.

4. Even though "weak," this inner nature rarely disappears or dies, in the usual person, in the U. S. (such disappearances or dying is possible early in the life history, however). It persists underground, unconsciously, even though denied and repressed. Like the voice of the intellect, it speaks softly but it *will* be heard, even if in a distorted form. That is, it has a dynamic force of its own, pressing always for open, uninhibited expression. Effort must be used in its suppression or repression from which fatigue can result. This force is one main aspect of the "will to health," the urge to grow, the pressure to self-actualization, the quest for one's identity. It is this that makes psychotherapy, education and self-improvement possible in principle.

5. However, this inner core, or self, grows into adulthood only partly by (objective or subjective) discovery, uncovering and acceptance of what is "there" beforehand. Partly it is also a creation of the person himself. Life is a continual series of choices for the individual in which a main determinant of choice is the person as he already is (including his goals for himself, his courage or fear, his feeling of responsibility, his ego-strength or "will power," etc.). We can no longer think of the person as "fully determined" where this phrase implies "determined only by forces external to the person." The person, insofar as he *is* a real person, is his own main determinant. Every person is, in part, "his own project" and makes himself.

6. If this essential core (inner nature) of the person is frustrated, denied or suppressed, sickness results, sometimes in obvious forms, sometimes in subtle and devious forms, sometimes immediately, sometimes later. These psychological illnesses include many more than those listed by the American Psychiatric Association. For instance, the character disorders and disturbances are now seen as far more important for the fate of the world than the classical neuroses or even the psychoses. From this new point of view, new kinds of illness are most dangerous, e.g., "the diminished or stunted person," i.e., the loss of any of the defining characteristics of human-ness, or personhood, the failure to grow to one's potential; valuelessness.

That is, general-illness of the personality is seen as any falling short of growth or of self-actualization or of fullhumanness. And the main source of illness, (although not the only one) is seen as frustration (of the basic needs, of the B-values, of idiosyncratic potentials, of expression of the self, and of the tendency of the person to grow in his own style) especially in the early years of life. That is, frustration of the basic needs is not the only source of illness or of human dimunition.

7. This inner nature, as much as we know of it so far, is definitely not "evil," but is either what we adults in our culture call "good," or else it is neutral. The most accurate way to express this is to say that it is "prior to

good and evil." There is little question about this if we speak of the inner nature of the infant and child. The statement is much more complex if we speak of the "infant" as he still exists in the adult. And it gets still more complex if the individual is seen from the point of view of B-psychology rather than D-psychology.

This conclusion is supported by all the truth-revealing and uncovering techniques, that have anything to do with human nature; psychotherapy, objective science, subjective science, education and art. For instance, in the long run, uncovering therapy lessens hostility, fear, greed, etc., and increases love, courage, creativeness, kindness, altruism, etc., leading us to the conclusion that the latter are "deeper," more natural, and more basic than the former, i.e., that what we call "bad" behavior is lessened or removed by uncovering, while what we call "good" behavior is strengthened and fostered by uncovering.

We must differentiate the Freudian type of superego from intrinsic conscience and intrinsic guilt. The former is in principle a taking into the self of the disapprovals and approvals of persons other than the person himself, fathers, mothers, teachers, etc. Guilt then is recognition of disapproval by others.

Intrinsic guilt is the consequence of betrayal of one's own inner nature or self, a turning off the path to self-actualization, and is essentially justified self-disapproval. It is therefore not as culturally relative as is Freudian guilt. It is "true" or "deserved" or "right and just" or "correct" because it is a discrepancy from something profoundly real within the person rather than from accidental, arbitrary or purely relative localisms. Seen in this way it is good, even *necessary*, for a person's development to have intrinsic guilt when he deserves to. It is not just a symptom to be avoided but is rather an inner guide for growth toward actualization of the real self, and of its potentialities.

8. "Evil" behavior has mostly referred to unwarranted hostility, cruelty, destructiveness, "mean" aggressiveness. This we do not know enough about. To the degree that this quality of hostility is instinctoid, mankind has one kind of future. To the degree that it is reactive (a response to bad treatment), mankind has a very different kind of future. My opinion is that the weight of the evidence so far indicates that *destructive* hostility is reactive, because uncovering therapy reduces it, and changes its quality into "healthy" self-affirmation, forcefulness, righteous indignation, etc. In any case, the *ability* to be aggressive and angry is found in all self-actualizing people who are able to let it flow forth freely when the external situation "calls for" it.

The situation in children is far more complex. At the very least, we know that the healthy child is also able to be justifiably angry, self-protecting and self-affirming, i.e., reactive aggression. Presumably, then, a child should learn not only how to control his anger, but also how and when to express it.

Behavior that our culture calls evil can also come from ignorance and from childish misinterpretations and beliefs (whether in the child or in repressed or forgotten child-in-the-adult). For instance, sibling rivalry is traceable to the child's wish for the exclusive love of his parents. Only as he matures is he in principle capable of learning that his mother's love for a sibling is compatible with her continued love for him. Thus out of a childish version of love, not in itself reprehensible, can come unloving behavior.

The commonly seen hatred or resentment of or jealousy of goodness, truth, beauty, health or intelligence, ("countervalues") is largely (though not altogether) determined by threat of loss of self-esteem, as the liar is threatened by the honest man, the homely girl by the beautiful girl, or the coward by the hero. Every superior person confronts us with our own shortcomings.

Still deeper than this, however, is the ultimate existential question of the fairness and justice of fate. The person with a bad heart may be jealous of the healthy man who is no more deserving than he.

Evil behaviors seem to most psychologists to be reactive as in these examples, rather than instinctive. This implies that though "bad" behavior is very deeply rooted in human nature and can never be abolished altogether, it may yet be expected to lessen as the personality matures and as the society improves.

Many people still think of "the unconscious," of regression, and of primary process cognition as necessarily unhealthy, or dangerous or bad. Psychotherapeutic experience is slowly teaching us otherwise. Our depths can also be good, or beautiful or desirable. This is also becoming clear from the general findings from investigations of the sources of love, creativeness, play, humor, art, etc. Their roots are deep in the inner, deeper self, i.e., in the unconscious. To recover them and to be able to enjoy and use them we must be able to "regress."

9. No psychological health is possible unless this essential core of the person is fundamentally accepted, loved and respected by others and by himself, (the converse is not necessarily true, i.e., that if the core is respected, etc., then psychological health must result, since other prerequisite conditions must also be satisfied).

The psychological health of the chronologically immature is called healthy growth. The psychological health of the adult is called variously, self-fulfillment, emotional maturity, individuation, productiveness, self-actualization, authenticity, full-humanness, etc.

Healthy growth is conceptually subordinate, for it is usually defined now as "growth toward self-actualization," etc. Some psychologists speak simply in terms of one overarching goal or end, or tendency of human development, considering all immature growth phenomena to be only steps along the path to self-actualization (Goldstein, Rogers).

Self-actualization is defined in various ways but a solid core of agreement is perceptible. All definitions accept or imply, (a) acceptance and expression of the inner core or self, i.e., actualization of these latent capacities, and potentialities, "full functioning," availability of the human and personal essence. (b) They all imply minimal presence of ill health, neurosis, psychosis, of loss or diminution of the basic human and personal capacities.

10. For all these reasons, it is at this time best to bring out and encourage, or at the very least, to recognize this inner nature, rather than to suppress or repress it. Pure spontaneity consists of free, uninhibited, uncontrolled, trusting unpremediated expression of the self, i.e., of the psychic forces, with minimal interference by consciousness. Control, will, caution, self-criticism, measure, deliberateness are the brakes upon this expression made intrinsically necessary by the laws of the social and natural worlds outside the psychic world, and secondarily, made necessary by fear of the psyche itself. Speaking in a very broad way, controls upon the psyche which come from *fear of the psyche*, are largely neurotic or *psychotic*, or not intrinsically or theoretically necessary. (The healthy psyche is not terrible or horrible and therefore doesn't have to be feared, as it has been for thousands of years. Of course, the *unhealthy* psyche is another story.) This kind of control is usually lessened by psychological health, by deep psychotherapy, or by any *deeper* self-knowledge and self-acceptance. There are also, however, controls upon the psyche which do not come out of fear, but out of the necessities for keeping it integrated, organized and unified ("intrinsic counter-cathexes"). And there are also "controls," probably in another sense, which are necessary as capacities are actualized, and as higher forms of expression are sought for, e.g., acquisition of skills through hard work by the artist, the intellectual, the athlete. But these controls are eventually transcended and become aspects of spontaneity, as they become self.

The balance between spontaneity and control varies, then, as the health of the psyche and the health of the world vary. Pure spontaneity is not long possible because we live in a world which runs by its own, non-psychic laws. It *is* possible in dreams, fantasies, love, imagination, the first stages of creativity, artistic work, intellectual play, free association, etc. Pure control is not permanently possible, for then the psyche dies. Education must be directed then *both* toward cultivation of controls and cultivation of spontaneity and expression. In our culture and at this point in history, it is necessary to redress the balance in favor of spontaneity, the ability to be expressive, passive, unwilled, trusting in processes other than will and control, unpremeditated, creative, etc. But it must be recognized that there have been and will be other cultures and other areas in which the balance was or will be in the other direction.

11. In the normal development of the normal child, it is now known that *most* of the time, if he is given a really free choice, he will choose what is good for his growth. This he does because it tastes good, feels good, gives

pleasure or *delight*. This implies that *he* "knows" better than anyone else what is good for him. A permissive regime means not that adults gratify his needs directly but make it possible for *him* to gratify his needs, and make his own choices, i.e., let him *be*. It is necessary in order for children to grow well, that adults have enough trust in them and in the natural processes of growth, i.e., not interfere too much, not *make* them grow, or force them into pre-determined designs, but rather *let* them grow and *help* them grow in a Taoistic rather than an authoritarian way.

12. Coordinate with this "acceptance" of the self, of fate, one's call, is the conclusion that the main path to health and self-fulfillment for the masses is via basic need gratification rather than via frustration. This contrasts with the suppressive regime, the mistrust, the control, the policing that is necessarily implied by basic evil in the human depths. Intrauterine life is completely gratifying and non-frustrating and it is now generally accepted that the first year or so of life had better also be primarily gratifying and non-frustrating. Asceticism, self-denial, deliberate rejection of the demands of the organism, at least in the West, tend to produce a diminished, stunted or crippled organism, and even in the East, bring self-actualization to very few, exceptionally strong individuals.

13. But we know also that the *complete absence* of frustration is dangerous. To be strong, a person must acquire frustration-tolerance, the ability to perceive physical reality as essentially indifferent to human wishes, the ability to love others and to enjoy their need-gratification as well as one's own (not to use other people only as means). The child with a good basis of safety, love and respect-need-gratification, is able to profit from nicely graded frustrations and become stronger thereby. If they are more than he can bear, if they overwhelm him, we call them traumatic, and consider them dangerous rather than profitable.

It is *via* the frustrating unyieldingness of physical reality and of animals and of other people that we learn about *their* nature, and thereby learn to differentiate wishes from facts (which things wishing makes come true, and which things proceed in complete disregard of our wishes), and are thereby enabled to live in the world and adapt to it as necessary.

We learn also about our own strengths and limits by overcoming difficulties, by straining ourselves to the utmost, by meeting challenge, even by failing. There can be great enjoyment in a great struggle and this can displace fear.

Overprotection implies that the child's needs are gratified *for* him by his parents, without effort of his own. This tends to infantilize him, to prevent development of his own strength, will and self-assertion. In one of its forms it may teach him to use other people rather than to respect them. In another form it implies a lack of trust and respect for the child's own powers and choices, i.e., it is essentially condescending and insulting, and can help to make a child feel worthless.

14. To make growth and self-actualization possible, it is necessary to understand that capacities, organs and organ systems press to function and express themselves and to be used and exercised, and that such use is satisfying, and disuse irritating. The muscular person likes to use his muscles, indeed, *has* to use them in order to "feel good" and to achieve the subjective feeling of harmonious, successful, uninhibited functioning (spontaneity) which is so important an aspect of good growth and psychological health. So also for intelligence, for the uterus, the eyes, the capacity to love. Capacities clamor to be used, and cease their clamor only when they *are* well used. That is, capacities are also needs. Not only is it fun to use our capacities, but it is also necessary for growth. The unused skill or capacity or organ can become a disease center or else atrophy, thus diminishing the person.

15. The psychologist proceeds on the assumption that for his purposes there are two kinds of worlds, two kinds of reality, the natural world and the psychic world, the world of unyielding facts and the world of wishes, hopes, fears, emotions, the world which runs by non-psychic rules and the world which runs by psychic laws. This differentiation is not very clear except at its extremes, where there is no doubt that delusions, dreams and free associations are lawful and yet utterly different from the lawfulness of logic and from the lawfulness of the world which would remain if the human species died out. This assumption does not deny that these worlds are related and may even fuse.

I may say that this assumption is acted upon by *many* or *most* psychologists, even though they are perfectly willing to admit that it is an insoluble philosophical problem. Any therapist *must* assume it or give up his functioning. This is typical of the way in which psychologists bypass philosophical difficulties and act "as if" certain assumptions were true even though unprovable, e.g., the universal assumption of "responsibility," "will power," etc. One aspect of health is the ability to live in both of these worlds.

16. Immaturity can be contrasted with maturity from the motivational point of view, as the process of gratifying the deficiency-needs in their proper order. Maturity, or self-actualization, from this point of view, means to transcend the deficiency-needs. This state can be described then as a meta-motivated, or unmotivated (if deficiencies are seen as the only motivations.) It can also be described as self-actualizing, Being, expressing, rather than coping. This state of Being, rather than of striving, is suspected to be synonymous with selfhood, with being "authentic," with being a person, with being fully human. The process of growth is the process of *becoming* a person. *Being* a person is different.

17. Immaturity can also be differentiated from maturity in terms of the

cognitive capacities (and also in terms of the emotional capacities). Immature and mature cognitions have been best described by Werner and Piaget. We can now add another differentiation, that between D-cognition and B-cognition (D = Deficiency; B = Being). D-cognition can be defined as the cognitions which are organized from the point of view of basic needs or deficiency-needs and their gratification and frustration. That is, D-cognition could be called selfish cognition, in which the world is organized into gratifiers and frustrators of our own needs, with other characteristics being ignored or slurred. The cognition of the object, in its own right and its own Being, without reference to its need-gratifying or need-frustrating qualities, that is, without primary reference to its value for the observer or its effects upon him, can be called B-cognition (or self-transcending, or unselfish, or objective cognition). The parallel with maturity is by no means perfect, (children can also cognize in a selfless way) but in general, it is mostly true that with increasing selfhood or firmness of personal identity (or acceptance of one's own inner nature) B-cognition becomes easier and more frequent. (This is true even though D-cognition remains for *all* human beings, including the mature ones, the main tool for living-in-the-world).

To the extent that perception is desire-less, and fear-less, to that extent is it more veridical, in the sense of perceiving the true, or essential or intrinsic whole nature of the object (without splitting it up by abstraction). Thus the goal of objective and true description of any reality is fostered by psychological health. Neurosis, psychosis, stunting of growth, all are, from this point of view, cognitive diseases as well, contaminating perception, learning, remembering, attending and thinking.

18. A by-product of this aspect of cognition is a better understanding of the higher and lower levels of love. D-love can be differentiated from B-love on approximately the same basis as D-cognition and B-cognition, or D-motivation and B-motivation. No ideally good relation to another human being, especially a child, is possible without B-love. Especially is it necessary for teaching, along with the Taoistic, trusting attitude that it implies. This is also true for our relations with the natural world, i.e., we can treat it in its own right, or we can treat it as if it were there only for our purposes.

19. Though, in principle, growth towards self-actualization is easy, in practice it rarely happens (by my criteria, certainly in less than 1 per cent of the adult population.) For this, there are many, many reasons at various levels of discourse, including all the determinants of psychopathology that we now know. We have already mentioned one main cultural reason, i.e., the conviction that man's intrinsic nature is evil or dangerous, and one biological determinant for the difficulty of achieving a mature self, namely that humans no longer have strong instincts.

There is a subtle but extremely important difference between regarding psychopathology as blocking or evasion or fear of growth toward self-actualization, and thinking of it in a medical fashion, as akin to invasion from without by tumors, poisons or bacteria, which have no relationship to the personality being invaded. Human dimunition (the loss of human potentialities and capacities) is a more useful concept than "illness" for our theoretical purposes.

20. Growth has not only rewards and pleasures but also many intrinsic pains and always will have. Each step forward is a step into the unfamiliar and is possibly dangerous. It also means giving up something familiar and good and satisfying. It frequently means a parting and a separation, with consequent nostalgia, loneliness and mourning. It also often means giving up a simpler and easier and less effortful life, in exchange for a more demanding, more difficult life. Growth forward *is in spite* of these losses and therefore requires courage, will, choice and strength in the individual, as well as protection, permission and encouragement from the environment, especially for the child.

21. It is therefore useful to think of growth or lack of it as the resultant of a dialectic between growth-fostering forces and growth-discouraging forces (regression, fear, pains of growth, ignorance, etc.). Growth has both advantages and disadvantages. Non-growing has not only disadvantages, but also advantages. The future pulls, but so also does the past. There is not only courage but also fear. The total ideal way to growing healthily, is, in principle, to enhance all the advantages of forward growth and all the disadvantages of not-growing, and to diminish all the disadvantages of growth forward and all the advantages of not-growing.

Homeostatic tendencies, "need-reduction" tendencies, and Freudian defense mechanisms are not growth-tendencies but defensive, pain-reducing postures of the organism. But they are quite necessary and not always pathological. They are generally prepotent over growth tendencies.

22. All this implies a naturalistic system of values, a by-product of the empirical description of the deepest tendencies of the human species and of specific individuals. The study of the human being by science or by self-search can discover where he is heading, what is his purpose in life, what is good for him and what is bad for him, what will make him feel virtuous and what will make him feel guilty, why choosing the good is often difficult for him, what the attractions of evil are. (Observe that the word "ought" need not be used. Also such knowledge of man is relative to man only and does not purport to be "absolute").

A neurosis is not part of the inner core but rather a defense against or an evasion of it, as well as a distorted expression of it (under the aegis of fear). It is ordinarily a compromise between the effort to seek basic need gratification in a covert or disguised or self-defeating way, and the fear of these needs, gratifications and motivated behaviors. To express neurotic needs, emotions, attitudes, definitions, actions, etc., means *not* to express the inner core or real self fully. If the sadist or exploiter or pervert says "Why shouldn't I express myself (e.g. by killing)?" or "Why shouldn't *I* actualize myself?" the answer to them is that such expression is a denial of and not an expression of instinctoid tendencies, (or inner core).

Each neuroticized need, or emotion or action is a *loss of capacity* to the person, something that he cannot do or *dare* not do except in a sneaky and unsatisfying way. In addition he has usually lost his subjective well-being, his will, and his feeling of self-control, his capacity for pleasure, his self-esteem, etc. He is diminished as a human being.

23. The state of being without a system of values is psychopathogenic, we are learning. The human being needs a framework of values, a philosophy of life, a religion or religion-surrogate to live by and understand by, in about the same sense that he needs sunlight, calcium or love. This I have called the "cognitive need to understand." The value-illnesses which result from valuelessness are called variously anhedonia, anomie, apathy, amorality, hopelessness, cynicism, etc., and can become somatic illness as well. Historically, we are in a value interregnum in which all externally given value systems have proven to be failures (political, economic, religious, etc.) e.g., nothing is worth dying for. What man needs but doesn't have, he seeks for unceasingly, and he becomes dangerously ready to jump at *any* hope, good or bad. The cure for this disease is obvious. We need a validated, usable system of human values that we can believe in and devote ourselves to (be willing to die for), because they are true rather than because we are exhorted to "believe and have faith." Such an empirically based Weltanschauung seems now to be a real possibility, at least in theoretical outline.

Much disturbance in children and adolescents can be understood as a consequence of the uncertainty of adults about their values. As a consequence, many youngsters in the U.S. live not by adult values but by adolescent values, which of course are immature, ignorant and heavily determined by confused adolescent needs. An excellent projection of these adolescent values is the cowboy, "Western" movie.

24. At the level of self-actualizing, many dichotomies become resolved, opposites are seen to be unities and the whole dichotomous way of thinking is recognized to be immature. For self-actualizing people, there is a strong tendency for selfishness and unselfishness to fuse into a higher, superordinate unity. Work tends to be the same as play, vocation and avocation become the same thing. When duty is pleasant and pleasure is fulfillment of duty, then they lose their separateness and oppositeness. The highest maturity is discovered to include a childlike quality, and we discover healthy children to have some of the qualities of mature self-actualization. The inner-outer split, between self and all else, gets fuzzy and much less sharp, and they are seen to be permeable to each other at the highest levels of personality development.

25. One especially important finding in self-actualizing people is that

they tend to integrate the Freudian dichotomies and trichotomies, i.e., the conscious, preconscious and the unconscious (as well as id, ego, superego). The Freudian "instincts" and the defenses are less sharply set off against each other. The impulses are more expressed and less controlled; the controls are less rigid, inflexible, anxiety-determined. The superego is less harsh and punishing and less set off against the ego. The primary and secondary cognitive processes are more equally available and more equally valued (instead of the primary processes being stigmatized as pathological). Indeed in the "peak-experience" the walls between them tend to fall together.

This is in sharp contrast with the classical Freudian position in which these various forces were sharply dichotomized as (A) mutually exclusive, (B) with antagonistic interests, i.e., as antagonistic forces rather than as complementary or collaborating ones, and (C) one "better" than the other.

Again we imply here (sometimes) a healthy unconscious, and desirable regression. Furthermore, we imply also an integration of rationality and irrationality with the consequence that irrationality may, in its place, also be considered healthy, desirable or even necessary.

26. Healthy people are more integrated in another way. In them the conative, the cognitive, the affective and the motor are less separated from each other, and are more synergic, i.e., working collaboratively without conflict to the same ends. The conclusions of rational, careful thinking are apt to come to the same conclusions as those of the blind appetites. What such a person wants and enjoys is apt to be just what is good for him. His spontaneous reactions are as capable, efficient and right as if they had been thought out in advance. His sensory and motor reactions are more closely correlated. His sensory modalities are more connected with each other (physiognomical perception). Furthermore, we have learned the difficulties and dangers of those ago-old rationalistic systems in which the capacities were thought to be arranged dichotomously—hierarchically with rationality at the top, rather than in an integration.

27. This development toward the concept of a healthy unconscious, and of a healthy irrationality, sharpens our awareness of the limitations of purely abstract thinking, of verbal thinking and of analytic thinking. If our hope is to describe the world fully, a place is necessary for preverbal, ineffable, metaphorical, primary process, concrete-experience, intuitive and esthetic types of cognition, for there are certain aspects of reality which can be cognized in no other way. Even in science this is true, now that we know (1) that creativity has its roots in the non-rational, (2) that language is and must always be inadequate to describe total reality, (3) that any abstract concept leaves out much of reality, and, (4) that what we call "knowledge," (which is usually highly abstract and verbal and sharply defined) often serves to blind us to those portions of reality not covered by the

abstraction. That is, it makes us more able to see some things, but *less* able to see other things. Abstract knowledge has its dangers as well as its uses.

Science and education, being too exclusively abstract, verbal and bookish don't have enough place for raw, concrete, esthetic experience, especially of the subjective happenings inside oneself. For instance, organismic psychologists would certainly agree on the desirability of more creative education in perceiving and creating art, in dancing, in (Greek style) athletics and in phenomenological observation.

The ultimate of abstract, analytical thinking, is the greatest simplification possible, i.e., the formula, the diagram, the map, the blueprint, certain types of abstract paintings. Our mastery of the world is enhanced thereby, but its richness may be lost as a forfeit, *unless* we learn to value B-cognition, perception-with-love-and-care, free floating attention, all of which enrich the experience instead of impoverishing it. There is no reason why "science" should not be expanded to include both kinds of knowing.

28. This ability of healthier people to dip into the unconscious and preconscious, to use and value their primary processes instead of fearing them, to accept their impulses instead of always controlling them, to be able to regress voluntarily without fear, turns out to be one of the main conditions of creativity. We can then understand why psychological health is so closely tied up with certain universal forms of creativeness (aside from special talent), as to lead some writers to make them almost synonymous.

This same tie between health and integration of rational and irrational forces (conscious and unconscious, primary and secondary processes) also permits us to understand why psychologically healthy people are more able to enjoy, to love, to laugh, to have fun, to be humorous, to be silly, to be whimsical and fantastic, to be pleasantly "crazy" and in general to permit and value and enjoy emotional experiences in general and peak experiences in particular and to have them more often. And it leads us to the strong suspicion that learning *ad hoc* to be able to do all these things may help the child move toward health.

29. Esthetic perceiving and creating and esthetic peak-experiences are seen to be a central aspect of human life and of psychology and education rather than a peripheral one. This is true for several reasons. (1) All the peak-experiences are (among other characteristics) integrative of the splits within the person, between persons, within the world, and between the person and the world. Since one aspect of health is integration, the peak-experiences are moves toward health and are themselves, momentary healths. (2) These experiences are life-validating, i.e., they make life worthwhile. These are certainly an important part of the answer to the question "Why don't we all commit suicide?" (3) They are worthwhile in themselves, etc.

30. Self-actualization does not mean a transcendance of all human problems. Conflict, anxiety, frustrations, sadness, hurt, and guilt can all be

found in healthy human beings. In general, the movement, with increasing maturity, is from neurotic pseud-problems to the real, unavoidable, existential problems, inherent in the nature of man (even at his best) living in a particular kind of world. Even though he is not neurotic he may be troubled by real, desirable and necessary guilt rather than neurotic guilt, (which isn't desirable or necessary), by an intrinsic conscience (rather than the Freudian superego). Even though he has transcended the problems of Becoming, there remain the problems of Being. To be untroubled when one *should* be troubled can be a sign of sickness. Sometimes, smug people have to be scared *"into* their wits."

31. Self-actualization is not altogether general. It takes place *via* femaleness *or* maleness, which are prepotent to general-humanness. That is, one must first be a healthy, femaleness-fulfilled woman before general-human self-actualization becomes possible.

There is also a little evidence that different constitutional types actualize themselves in somewhat different ways (because they have different inner selves to actualize).

32. Another crucial aspect of healthy growth to selfhood is dropping away the techniques used by the child, in his weakness and smallness for adapting himself to the strong, large, all-powerful, omniscient, god-like adults. He must replace these with the techniques of being strong and independent and of being a parent himself. This involves especially giving up the child's desperate wish for the exclusive, total love of his parents while learning to love others. He must learn to gratify his own needs and wishes, rather than the needs of his parents, and he must learn to gratify them himself, rather than depending upon the parents to do this for him. He must give up being good out of fear and in order to keep their love, and must be good because *he* wishes to be. He must discover his own conscience and give up his internalized parents as a sole ethical guide. All these techniques by which weakness adapts itself to strength are necessary for the child but immature and stunting in the adult. He must replace fear with courage.

33. From this point of view, a society or a culture can be either growth-fostering or growth-inhibiting. The sources of growth and of humanness are essentially within the human person and are not created or invented by society, which can only help or hinder the development of humanness. just as a gardener can help or hinder the growth of a rosebush, but cannot determine that it shall be an oak tree. This is true even though we know that a culture is a *sine qua non* for the actualization of humanness itself, e.g., language, abstract thought, ability to love; but these exist as potentialities in human germ plasm prior to culture.

This makes theoretically possible a comparative sociology, transcending and including cultural relativity. The "better" culture gratifies all basic human needs and permits self-actualization. The "poorer" cultures do not.

The same is true for education. To the extent that it fosters growth toward self-actualization, it is "good" education.

As soon as we speak of "good" or "bad" cultures, and take them as means rather than as ends, the concept of "adjustment" comes into question. We must ask "What kind of culture or subculture is the 'well adjusted' person well adjusted *to*." Adjustment is, very definitely, *not* necessarily synonymous with psychological health.

34. The achievement of self-actualization (in the sense of autonomy) paradoxically makes *more* possible the transcendance of self, and of self-consciousness and of selfishness. It makes it *easier* for the person to be homonomous, i.e., to merge himself as a part in a larger whole than himself. The condition of the fullest homonomy is full autonomy, and to some extent, *vice versa*, one can attain to autonomy only *via* successful homonomous experiences (child dependence, B-love, care for others, etc.). It is necessary to speak of levels of homonomy, (more and more mature), and to differentiate a "low homonomy" (of fear, weakness, and regression) from a "high homonomy" (of courage and full, self-confident autonomy), a "low Nirvana" from a "high Nirvana," union downward from union upward.

35. An important existential problem is posed by the fact that self-actualized persons (and *all* people in their peak-experiences) occasionally live out-of-time and out-of-the-world, (atemporal and aspatial) even though mostly they *must* live in the outer world. Living in the inner psychic world (which is ruled by psychic laws and not by the laws of outer-reality), i.e., the world of experience, of emotion, of wishes and fears and hopes, of love, of poetry, art, and fantasy, is different from living in and adapting to the non-psychic reality which runs by laws he never made and which are not essential to his nature even though he has to live by them. The person who is not afraid of this inner, psychic world, can enjoy it to such an extent that it may be called Heaven by contrast with the more effortful, fatiguing, externally responsible, world of "reality," of striving and coping, of right and wrong, of truth and falsehood. This is true even though the healthier person can also adapt more easily and enjoyably to the "real" world, and has better "reality testing," i.e., doesn't confuse it with his inner psychic world.

It seems quite clear now that confusing these inner and outer realities, or having either closed off from experience, is highly pathological. The healthy person is able to integrate them both into his life and therefore has to give up neither, being able to go back and forth voluntarily. The difference is the same as the one between the person who can *visit* the slums and the one who is forced to live there always. (*Either* world is a slum if one can't leave it). Then paradoxically that which was sick and pathological and the "lowest" becomes part of the healthiest and "highest" aspect of human nature. Slipping into "craziness" is frightening only for those who are not fully confident of their sanity. Education must help the person to live in both worlds.

36. The foregoing propositions generate a different understanding of the role of action in psychology. Goal-directed, motivated, coping, striving, purposeful action is an aspect or by-product of the necessary transactions between a psyche and a non-psychic world.

(a) The D-need gratifications come from the world outside the person not from within. Therefore adaptation to this world is made necessary, e.g., reality-testing, knowing the nature of this world, learning to differentiate this world from the inner world, learning the nature of people and of society, learning to delay gratification, learning to conceal what would be dangerous, learning which portions of the world are gratifying and which dangerous, or useless for need-gratification, learning the approved and permitted cultural paths to gratification and techniques of gratification.

(b) The world is in itself interesting, beautiful and fascinating. Exploring it, manipulating it, playing with it, contemplating it, enjoying it are all motivated kinds of action (cognitive, motor, and esthetic needs).

But there is also action which has little or nothing to do with the world, at any rate at first. Sheer expression of the nature or state or powers (Funktionslust) of the organism is an expression of Being rather than of striving. And the contemplation and enjoyment of the inner life not only is a kind of "action" in itself but is also antithetical to action in the world, i.e., it produces stillness and cessation of muscular activity. The ability to wait is a special case of being able to suspend action.

37. From Freud we learned that the past exists *now* in the person. Now we must learn, from growth theory and self-actualization theory that the future also *now* exists in the person in the form of ideals, hopes, goals, unrealized potentials, mission, fate, destiny, etc. One for whom no future exists is reduced to the concrete, to hopelessness, to emptiness. For him, time must be endlessly "filled." Striving, the usual organizer of most activity, when lost, leaves the person unorganized and unintegrated.

Of course, being in a state of Being needs no future, because it is already *there*. Then Becoming ceases for the moment and its promissory notes are cashed in the form of the ultimate rewards, i.e., the peak-experiences, in which time disappears.

9. Psychoneurosis in Times of Trouble: Evidence for a Hierarchy of Motives

Richard W. Kilby

IN the *New Yorker* of August 9, 1947, there appeared an a r t i c l e written by Berton Roueché of the *New Yorker's* staff reporting an interview with Dr. Hans Lowenbach, of the Department of Neuro-psychiatry, School of Medicine, Duke University, upon the latter's return from Germany. The article is mainly on Dr. Lowenbach's findings on medical progress (or lack of it) in Germany during the Nazi regime. But he makes several observations of interest to psychologists about mental health in Germany today.

The statement which caught my attention is the following, quoted by Roueché from Lowenbach:

> It (Germany) is like all Central Europe—hunger and sour trouble. The misery is so complete that even psychoneurosis has become rare. There is other mental illness, of course, but not much of that. The psychoneurotic, you know, often deals with

Abridged from the *Journal of Abnormal and Social Psychology*, 1948, 43, 544-545. Reprinted by permission of the author and the American Psychological Association, Inc.

distasteful problems of reality by developing ailments that compel others to pity and care for him, but his ailments frequently vanish when the people around him stop paying attention to them. That is the way it is in Germany now. Everyone has so much trouble that he has neither the time nor the energy to pity or care for others.

Lowenbach's point about part of the neurotic pattern being the presence of someone to pay attention to the "sufferer" is thought provoking in itself, but it was his observation on the low incidence of neurosis which caught my attention because of its apparent partial verification of A. H. Maslow's hierarchy of motives theory.

Briefly stated (and oversimplified) Maslow postulates that most human needs or motives can be arranged in the following five groups: (1) physiological needs, (2) safety needs, (3) love needs, (4) esteem needs, and (5) need for self-actualization. These needs from a hierarchy with the physiological needs being most basic, the others following in importance in the order listed, with the self-actualization need being least basic and least psychologically important. Maslow postulates that because of this hierarchial nature of motives the person who is in physical want—of food when starving, of water, of warmth when cold, etc.—will have his behavior dominated by these physiological needs, and as long as the physiological needs are dominant the other less basic needs (safety, love, esteem, self-actualization) will be nonexistent or, more correctly stated, latent.

This theory, therefore, would predict that the extremely hungry person gives little or no attention to whether or not he is liked or loved, has status with his associates, or has a normally high self-regard. Since a majority of maladjustment and neurosis is thought to come from frustration of love and esteem needs (usually lumped together and called "need for security"), the theory would predict that the hungry person, because he doesn't experience love or esteem needs as long as he is hungry, would not become neurotic in situations where these two groups of needs were otherwise being frustrated. (I am not overlooking the strong possibility that some form of neurosis will be directly caused by deprivation of the basic physiological needs.)

If the relation of Lowenbach's observation to Maslow's theory is not already evident, it may be pointed out that Maslow's theory predicts the situation Lowenbach observed, because there exists in Germany today, for many people, a situation in which life is taken up with gaining satisfaction of physiological needs, including the subjective behaviors of perceiving, thinking, and emoting about physical satisfiers, and the distraction caused by hunger, cold, and other discomforts.

A letter was written to Dr. Lowenbach asking, in part, whether he felt his observations were broad enough to permit a generalization on the extent of neurosis in Germany. He replied that the question was difficult to answer and continued as follows:

> . . . it is not easy to make observations in Germany under present day circumstances and I base my statement on the opinions as expressed to me by all the psychiatrists that I visited in the different universities. On the other side, the Germans are extremely restless and one could argue whether this is an expression of psychoneurotic anxiety. I was inclined to explain it on the grounds of inability to find work and social security in one place and of the wish to explore the pasture on the other side of the fence. I picked up dozens of German hitchhikers in my travels throughout Germany and found a good ability to cope with reality.

Other evidence on the primacy of physical needs comes from (1) the human guinea-pig hunger experiments and (2) the newspaper interviews of men who were adrift at sea without food for long periods during the war. Both show that food dominated attention; other previously important individual concerns lost their importance and often were forgotten for the duration of the hunger state.

Still another source of evidence on shifting of motivation is the decrease in neurosis among civilians in England during the Blitz. R. D. Gillespie, in his *Psychological Effects of War on Citizen and Soldier* confirms the findings of other British psychiatrists regarding this decrease in neurosis. But such a complex of motivational factors seems to have been operating that little more can be said than that shifts of motivation did occur. It is probable that concern for physical safety displaced some of the love and esteem frustrations and hence prevented what otherwise would have been neuroses. But equally important in preventing neuroses in some cases was the arousal of new positive motives as, for example, the motive to work and receive public and self approval for contributing to the national effort, thus taking attention from self through the physical activity of work and gratifying an esteem need at the same time.

An additional important and relevant fact may be generalized from Gillespie's book. It is that some individuals became neurotic during the Blitz because of love and esteem deprivations dating back to childhood, and change in their life situations in wartime did not prevent the neurosis. The early influences had produced unstable personalities and the personalities remained unstable and maladaptive regardless of shift in need or environment. This means that if the hierarchical theory of needs is later proved, it is not to be expected that a forced shift to more basic needs will cause disappearance in all cases of a neurosis which has been caused by frustration of less basic needs (love, for example). In other words, how different individuals react to shift to a more basic frustration will depend on the personality make-up—one will entirely "forget" his neurosis and begin to work with efficiency to satisfy physical and safety needs; another, whose past has been particularly unfavorable, will "fold up" and, at best, inefficiently go about meeting his physical needs.

10. The Trend in Motivational Theory

Gordon W. Allport

MOTIVATIONAL theory today seems to be turning a corner in the road of scientific progress. In attempting to characterize this change in direction I wish to pay special attention to the problem of psychodiagnostic methods. For the successes and failures of these methods can teach us much about psychodynamic theory.

Let us start by asking why projective methods are so popular in both diagnostic practice and research. The answer, I think, is to be found in the history of motivational theory during the past century. All of the major influences have pressed in a single direction. Schopenhauer, with his doctrine of the primacy of the blind will, had little respect for the rationalization invented by the individual's intellect to account for his conduct. Motives, he was sure, could not be taken at their face value. Darwin followed with his similar anti-intellectual emphasis on primordial struggle. McDougall refined the Darwinian stress on instinct, retaining in his horme the flavor of Schopenhauer's will, Darwin's struggle for survival, Bergson's *elan,* and Freud's libido. All these writers were irrationalists—confident that underlying genotypes in motivation should be sought rather than the surface phenotypes. All of them were reacting against the naive intellectualism of their predecessors and against the rationalizations offered by self-justifying mortals when called on to account for their conduct. Among these irrationalists who have dominated western psychology for the past century Freud, of course, has been the leading figure. He, like the others, correctly perceived

Abridged from *The American Journal of Orthopsychiatry,* 1953, 23, 107-119. Reprinted by permission of the author and the American Orthopsychiatric Association.

that the main-springs of conduct may be hidden from the searchlight of consciousness.

In addition to irrationalism modern dynamic psychology has developed another earmark: geneticism. The original instincts laid down in our nature are regarded as decisive, or if not, then the experiences of early childhood are held to be crucial. At this point, the leading nondynamic school of thought, stimulus-response psychology, joins forces with geneticism. Stimulus-response theorists agree with instinct psychologists and psychoanalysts in viewing adult motives as conditioned, reinforced, sublimated, or otherwise elaborated editions of instincts, drives, or an id whose structure, Freud said, "never changes."

Not one of these dominating theories of motivation allows for an essential transformation of motives in the course of life. McDougall explicitly denied the possibility; for our motivational structure is laid down once and for all in our equipment of instincts. New objects may become attached to an instinct through learning, but the motive power is always the same. Freud's position was essentially identical. The concept of "sublimation" and of shifting object "cathexis" chiefly accounted for whatever apparent alterations occur. Stimulus-response psychology is likewise geared to the assumption of remote control operating out of the past. We respond only to objects that have been associated with primary drives in the past, and we do so only in proportion to the degree that our responses have been rewarded or gratified in the past. From the stimulus-response point of view the individual can hardly be said to be *trying* to do anything at all. He is simply *responding* with a complex array of habits that somehow were rewarded year before last. The prevailing dictum that motivation is always a matter of "tension reduction" or of "seeking equilibrium" is consistent with this point of view, but scarcely consistent, I think, with all the known facts.

This prevailing atmosphere of theory has engendered a kind of contempt for the "psychic surface" of life. The individual's conscious report is rejected as untrustworthy, and the contemporary thrust of his motives is disregarded in favor of a backward tracing of his conduct to earlier formative stages. The individual loses his right to be believed. And while he is busy leading his life in the present with a forward thrust into the future, most psychologists have become busy tracing it backward into the past.

It is now easy to understand why the special methods invented by Jung (forty years ago), Rorschach (thirty years ago) and Murray (twenty years ago) were seized upon with enthusiasm by psychodiagnosticians. At no point do these methods ask the subject what his interests are, what he wants to do, or what he is trying to do. Nor do the methods ask directly concerning the subject's relation to his parents or to authority figures. They infer this relationship entirely by assumed identifications. So popular is this indirect, undercover approach to motivation that many clinicians and many university centers spend far more time on this type of diagnostic method than on any other.

Occasionally, however, a client may cause the projective tester consternation by intruding his unwanted conscious report. The story is told of a patient who remarked that a Rorschach card made him think of sexual relations. The clinician, thinking to tap a buried complex, asked him why. "Oh, because," said the patient, "I think of sexual relations all the time anyway." The clinician scarcely needed a Rorschach card to find out this motivational fact.

Still it is probably true that most psychologists prefer to assess a person's needs and conflicts by going the long way around. The argument, of course, is that everyone, even a neurotic, will accommodate himself fairly well to the demands placed upon him by reality. Only in an unstructured projective situation will he reveal his anxieties and unmasked needs. "Projective tests," writes Stagner, "are more useful than reality situations for diagnostic purposes." To my mind this uncompromising statement seems to mark the culmination of a century-long era of irrationalism, and therefore of distrust. Has the subject no right to be believed?

Fortunately, the extensive use of projective methods at the present time is yielding results that enable us to place this technique in proper perspective, and to correct the one-sided theory of motivation upon which their popularity rests.

Let us consider first the wartime research conducted with 36 conscientious objectors who lived for six months on a semistarvation diet. Their diet was so rigorously meager that on the average they lost one quarter of their initial body weight in the course of the six months. The food need was agonizingly great; their incessant hunger most poignant. Unless occupied with laboratory or other tasks they found themselves thinking of food almost constantly. Typical daydreaming is reported by one subject as follows: "Today we'll have Menu No. 1. Gee, that's the smallest menu, it seems. How shall I fix the potatoes? If I use my spoon to eat them I'll be able to add more water . . . . If I eat a little faster the food would stay warm longer—and I like it warm. But then it's gone so quickly." Now the curious thing is that while these men were clearly obsessed by their food drive, and all their energy seemed directed toward its fulfillment, yet on projective tests the need failed to appear. The investigators report that among the tests used (free word association, first letters test, analysis of dreams, Rorschach, and Rosenzweig's P-F Study) only one gave a limited evidence of the preoccupation with food, viz., the free association test.

Here is a finding of grave significance. *The most urgent, the most absorbing motive in life failed completely to reveal itself by indirect methods.* It was, however, entirely accessible to conscious report. Part of the explanation may be that the subjects turned in relief to laboratory tasks to forget for a while their obsessive motive. They responded to the projective tests with heaven knows what available, habitual associational material. The failure of night dreams to reveal a significant amount of wish fulfillment is somewhat more perplexing. It can scarcely be ascribed to a defensive mental set. But both types of result suggest a possible law: Unless a motive is repressed it is unlikely to affect distinctively the perception of, and responses to, a projective test. It is too early to tell whether this is a valid generalization, but it is a hypothesis well worth testing.

Other studies on hunger seem to yield supporting evidence. Their trend suggests that on projective tests the number of explicit food associations actually declines in longer periods of fasting, apparently because the motive itself gradually becomes completely conscious and is not repressed. It is true that instrumental associations (ways of obtaining food) continue to appear in the subject's word-responses as the state of hunger grows. This finding, however, is quite consistent with the hypothesis, since while hunger is fully conscious, the subject in the experimental situation is prevented from seeking satisfaction, and thus is still repressing his instrumental action-tendencies.

Another revealing line of evidence comes from the research of J. W. Getzels. This investigator utilized two forms of a sentence completion test—one couched in the first person and one in the third. His pairs are of the following type:

When they asked Frank to be in charge he . . . . .
When they asked me to be in charge I . . . . .

When Joe meets a person for the first time he usually . . . . .
When I meet a person for the first time I usually . . . . .

In this experiment, of course, the items were randomized. In all there were 20 diagnostic items of each type. The subjects were 65 veterans, 25 diagnosed as well adjusted; 40 were psychoneurotic cases discharged from service with disability involving personality disorder.

It turned out that to a highly significant degree the well-adjusted men gave *identical* responses to the first and to the third person completions. If we assume that the third-person sentence is "projective method" then the results obtained by this method for well-adjusted subjects squared almost perfectly with the results obtained from the direct, first-person questioning. The psychoneurotics, on the other hand, to a highly significant degree varied their responses. They said one thing when queried directly (e.g., "When they asked me to be in charge I agreed") and another on the projective item (e.g., "When they asked John to be in charge he was afraid.") The first-person completion is so direct that in the psychoneurotic it invokes the mask of defense and elicits a merely conventionally correct response.

Thus the direct responses of the psychoneurotic cannot be taken at their face value. The defenses are high, the true motives are hidden and are betrayed only by a projective technique. The normal subjects, on the other hand, tell you by the direct method precisely what they tell you by the projective method. They are all of a piece. You may therefore take their motivational statements at their face value, for even if you probe you will not find anything substantially different.

This research adds weight to the tentative judgment we formed in the case of the starving subjects. It is not the well-integrated subject, aware of his motivations, who reveals himself in projective testing. It is rather the neurotic personality, whose facade belies the repressed fears and hostilities within. Such a subject is caught off guard by projective devices; but the well-adjusted subject gives no significantly different response.

There is, however, one difference between the two researches. The starving subjects actually *avoided* any betrayal of their dominant motive in the projective tests. The well-adjusted veterans, on the other hand, gave essentially the *same* type of response in both direct and in projective testing. It may be that the dissimilar nature of the tests used in the two situations accounts for this difference in results. But this detailed difference need not detain us here. What seems to be important is the implication of these researches that a *psychodiagnostician should never employ projective methods in the study of motivation without at the same time employing direct methods.* If he does not do so he will never be able to distinguish a well-integrated personality from one that is not. Nor will he be able to tell whether there are strong conscious streams of motivation that are entirely evading the projective situation (as in the case of the starving subjects).

The trend of evidence that I have presented seems to indicate that a normal, well-adjusted individual with strong goal-directedness may on projective tests do one of two things: 1) either give material identical with that of conscious report—in which case the projective method is not needed; or 2) give no evidence whatever of his dominant motives. It is only when emotionally laden material comes forth in projective responses that is contradictory to conscious report, or to other results of direct assessment, that we find special value in projective testing. And we shall never know whether or not a neurotic situation prevails unless we use both diagnostic approaches and compare the yield.

Consider for a moment the diagnosis of anxiety. Using various responses on the Rorschach and TAT cards the clinician might infer a high level of anxiety. Now this finding taken by itself tells us little. The subject may be the sort of person who is enormously effective in life because he harnesses his anxiety to performance. He may know perfectly well that he is a harried, worried, bedeviled overachiever. Anxiety is an asset in his life, and he has enough insight to know the fact. In this case the yield by projective technique was not really needed, but it does no harm to use it. Or, as in our starvation cases, we might find that projective protocols reveal no anxiety while in actuality we are dealing with a person who is as harried, worried and bedeviled as our first subject, but who effectively controls his jitters. In this case we assume that his large measure of control enables him to tackle the projective tests with some mental set unrelated to his anxious nature. But we may also find—and here is where projective methods have their uses—that an apparently bland and calm individual, denying all anxiety, reveals profound disturbance and fear in projective performances. It is this type of dissociated nature that projective tests help to diagnose. Yet they cannot do so unless direct methods also are employed.

In speaking so frequently of "direct" methods I have referred chiefly to "conscious report." To ask a man his motives, however, is not the only type of "direct" method that we may employ. It is, however, a good one—especially to start with.

When we set out to study a person's motives we are seeking to find out what that person is trying to do in this life, including of course what he is trying to avoid, and what he is trying to be. I see no reason why we should not start our investigation by asking him to tell us the answers as he sees them. If the questions in this form seem too abstract they can be recast. Particularly revealing are people's answers to the question, "What do you want to be doing five years from now?" Similar direct questions can be framed to elicit anxieties, loyalties and hostilities. Most people, I suspect, can tell what they are trying to do in this life with a high degree of validity, certainly not less on the average than the prevailing validity of projective instruments. Yet some clinicians disdain to ask direct questions.

But by "direct methods" I mean also to include standard pencil-and-paper measures, such as the Strong Interest Inventory and the recently revised Allport-Vernon-Lindzey Study of Values. Now it often happens that the yield on such instruments is not what would come from the subject's conscious report. The subject may not have known, for example, that compared with most people his pattern of values is, say, markedly theoretical and aesthetic, or far below average in economic and religious interest. Yet the final score on the Study of Values is itself merely a summation of a series of separate conscious choices that he has made in 45 hypothetical situations. While his verbal report on the pattern as a whole may be faulty, yet this pattern not only squares with all his separate choices, but is known on the average to have good external validity. People with certain patterns of interests as measured by the test do in fact make characteristic vocational choices and do in their daily behavior act in ways that are demonstrably consistent with the test results.

To sum up: direct methods include the kind of report that is elicited in careful interviewing, whether it be of the simple psychiatric variety, the sort employed in vocational or personal counseling, or in non-directive interviewing. Autobiographic methods when employed at their face value are likewise direct. So too are the results of any kind of testing where the final scores represent a sum or pattern of a series of conscious choices on the part of the subject.[1]

The currently fashionable term *psychodynamics* is often equated explicitly with psychoanalytic theory. Projective techniques are considered psychodynamic because they are thought to tap deepest layers of structure and functioning. We have already indicated reasons for doubting the sufficiency of this assumption. Many of the most dynamic of motives are more accurately tapped by direct methods. At the very least the discoveries by projective techniques cannot be properly interpreted unless they are compared with discoveries yielded by direct methods.

Devotees of psychodynamics often say that no discoveries are of value unless the unconscious is explored. This dictum we find in the valuable book by Kardiner and Ovesey, *The Mark of Oppression,* dealing with the seriously disordered and conflictful motivational systems of Negroes in a northern city. Unless I am greatly mistaken, however, the authors discover little or nothing about their cases through psychoanalytic probes that is not evident in the manifest situation. The conscious handicaps of a Negro in our society, the economic misery, the deteriorated family situations, the bitterness and despair, constitute a painful psychodynamic situation in individual lives that in most instances receives no further illumination when depth analysis is employed.

Most of the psychodynamic evidence given by Kardiner and Ovesey concerning their cases is, in fact, drawn from straightforward autobiographical report. Their use of this method is acceptable and their findings highly instructive. But their theory seems to me out of line with both the method actually used and the findings obtained. Psychodynamics is not necessarily a hidden dynamics.

This point is well made by the psychiatrist J. C. Whitehorn, who correctly

---

[1]For the purposes of the present argument this simplified discussion of "direct" and "indirect" techniques is adequate. Psychodiagnosis requires, however, a much more discriminating classification of the methods currently employed, and of the "levels" of organization that each normally taps. An excellent beginning is Rosensweig's proposal that three classes of methods be distinguished, each adapted in principle to tapping three levels of behavior. What he calls *subjective* methods require the subject to take himself as a direct object of observation (questionnaires, autobiographies). *Objective* methods require the observer to report on *overt* conduct. *Projective* methods require both subject and observer to "look the other way" and to base the diagnosis on the subject's reaction to apparently "ego-neutral'" material. Broadly speaking, Rosenzweig's subjective and objective procedures correspond to what I here call "direct" methods, and projective procedures to "indirect" methods.

Especially noteworthy is the author's statement that the significance of projective methods (e.g., his own P-F Study) cannot be determined unless the subject's projective responses are examined in the light of his subjective and objective responses.

holds that psychodynamics is a general science of motivation. Into its broad principles one may fit the specific contributions and insights of psychoanalysis. But psychoanalysis itself is by no means the sum and substance of psychodynamics. Whitehorn insists that the proper approach to psychotic patients, especially to those suffering from schizophrenic or depressive disorder, is through such channels of their normal interest systems as remain open. It is not the region of their disorder that requires primary attention, but those psychodynamic systems that still represent sturdy and healthy adaptations to reality. In Whitehorn's words, the therapist should seek "to activate and utilize the resources of the patient and to help him thereby to work out a more satisfying way of life with a less circumscribed emphasis upon these special issues."

Sometimes we hear it said that psychoanalytic theory does not do justice to psychoanalytic practice. What is meant is that in the course of therapy an analyst will devote much of his time to a direct discussion with his patient of his manifest interests and values. The analyst will listen respectfully, accept, counsel and advise concerning these important, and *not* buried, psychodynamic systems. In many instances, as in the cases presented by Kardiner and Ovesey, the motives and conflicts are taken at their face value. Thus the method of psychoanalysis as employed is not fully sustained by the theory that is affirmed.

Nothing that I have said denies the existence of infantile systems, troublesome repressions, or neurotic formations. Nor does it deny the possibility of self-deception, rationalization and ego defense. My point is merely that methods and theories dealing with these aberrant conditions should be set in a broad conception of psychodynamics. The patient should be assumed insightful until he is proved otherwise. If you ask a hundred people who go to the icebox for a snack why they do so, probably all would answer, "Because I was hungry." In ninety-nine of these cases we may—no matter how deeply we explore—discover that this simple, conscious report is the whole truth. It can be taken at its face value. In the hundredth case, however, our probing shows that we are dealing with a compulsive overeater, with an obese seeker after infantile security who, unlike the majority of cases, does not know what he is trying to do. It is peace and comfort he is seeking—perhaps his mother's bosom—and not the leftover roast. In this case—and in a minority of all cases—I grant we cannot take the evidence of his overt behavior, nor his account of it, at their face value.

Freud was a specialist in precisely those motives that cannot be taken at their face value. To him motivation resided in the id. The conscious, accessible region of personality that carries on direct transactions with the world, namely the ego, he regarded as devoid of dynamic power.

It is a misfortune that Freud died before he had remedied this one-sidedness in his theory. Even his most faithful followers tell us now that he left his ego psychology incomplete. In recent years many of them have labored to redress the balance. Without doubt the principal current in psychoanalytic theory today is moving in the direction of a more dynamic ego. This trend in theory is apparent in the work of Anna Freud, Hartmann, French, Horney, Fromm, Kris, and many others. In a communication to the American Psychoanalytic Association, Kris points out that the attempt to restrict interpretations of motivation to the id aspect only "represents the older procedure." Modern concern with the ego does not confine itself to an analysis of defense mechanism alone. Rather it gives more respect to what he calls the "psychic surface." Present psychoanalytic techniques, he tells us, tend to link "surface" with "depth." In a similar vein Rapaport has argued that a measure of true autonomy must now be ascribed to the ego.

To illustrate the point at issue, we might take any psychogenic interest of maturity, for example, the religious sentiment. Freud's handling of the matter is well known. To him religion is essentially a neurosis in the individual, a formula for personal escape. The father image lies at the root of the matter. One cannot therefore take the religious sentiment, when it exists in a personality, at its face value. A more balanced view of the matter would seem to be this: *sometimes* one cannot take this sentiment at its face value, and *sometimes* one can. Only a careful study of the individual will tell. In a person in whom the religious factor serves an obvious egocentric purpose—talismanic, bigoted, self-justificatory—we can infer that it is a neurotic, or at least immature, formation in the personality. Its infantile and escapist character is not recognized by the subject. On the other hand, in a person who has gradually evolved a guiding philosophy of life where the religious sentiment exerts a generally normative force upon behavior and confers intelligibility to life as a whole, we infer that this particular ego formation is not only a dominant motive, but that it must be accepted at its face value. It is a master motive and an ego ideal whose shape and substance are essentially what appear in consciousness.

Let us consider a final example. It is well known that most boys around the age of four to seven identify with their fathers. They imitate them in many ways. Among other things they may express vocational aspirations for daddy's job. Many boys when grown do in fact follow their fathers' footsteps.

Take politics. Father and son have been politicians in many families: the Tafts, Lodges, Kennedys, LaFollettes, Roosevelts, to mention only a few. When the son is at a mature age, say 50 or 60, what is his motivation? Is he working through his early father identification or is he not? Taken at its face value the interest of the son in politics now seems to be absorbing, self-contained, a prominent factor in his own ego structure. In short, it seems to be a mature and normal motive. But the strict geneticist would say: "No, he is now a politician because of a father fixation." Does the geneticist mean that an early father identification started him in a political direction of interest? If so, the answer is yes, of course. All motives have their origin somewhere. Or does he mean, "This early fixation now, today, sustains the son's political conduct?" If so, the answer is normally, no. The political interest is now a prominent part of the ego structure, and the ego is the healthy man's source of energy. To be sure, there may be cases where a person mature in years is still trying to curry father's favor, to step into his shoes, to displace him with the mother. A clinical study of a second-generation politician may conceivably show that his behavior is compulsively father-identified. In such a case his daily conduct is in all probability so compulsive, so ungeared to realistic situational needs, so excessive, that the diagnosis can be suspected by any skilled clinical observer. But such instances are relatively rare.

To sum up: we need in our motivational theory to make a sharper distinction between infantilisms and motivation that is strictly contemporary and at age.

I am fully aware of my heterodoxy in suggesting that there is in a restricted sense a discontinuity between normal and abnormal motivation, and that we need a theory that will recognize this fact. Discontinuities are distinctly unpopular in psychological science. One theory of abnormality tells us that we are merely pleased to regard the extremes on our linear continuum as abnormal. Further, some culture theorists insist that abnormality is a relative concept, shifting from culture to culture, and from one historical period to another. Likewise, there are many borderline cases which even the most experienced clinician could not with confidence classify as normal or as abnormal. Finally, and most important, is the fact that in many normal people one can by scratching deeply enough find *some* infantilism in their motivation.

Granted all these familiar arguments, there is still a world of difference—if not between normal and abnormal people—then between the healthy and unhealthy mechanisms involved in the development of motivation. What we call integrative action of the nervous system is basically a wholesome mechanism that keeps motivation up to date. It tends to bring about both an internal consistency and a reality testing among the elements entering into motivational patterning. Effective suppression is another healthy mechanism, not only harmless to the individual, but making possible the arrangement of motives in an orderly hierarchy. With the aid of effective suppression the individual ceases to act out infantile dramas. Insight, a clear self-image, and the little understood factor of homeostasis may be mentioned among the balancing mechanisms.

As Getzel's experiment shows, direct and projective performances in healthy people are all of a piece. A further test of normality—unfortunately one psychologists have not yet developed—may lie in the harmony of expressive behavior (facial expression, gestures, handwriting) with the individual's fundamental motivational structure. There is evidence that discoordination between conscious motives and expressive movement is an ominous sign.

This lead for research should be followed through.

In unhealthy motivation, unbalancing mechanisms have the upper hand. There is always some species of dissociation at work. The individual represses ineffectively; repressed motives erupt in autistic gestures, in tantrums, in nightmares, in compulsions, perhaps in paranoid thinking. Above all, self-knowledge is lacking in large regions of the life.

My point is that normally the balancing mechanisms have the upper hand. Sometimes, in certain badly disordered lives, the unbalancing mechanisms take over. Occasionally too, we find them operating in a segmental way in lives that are otherwise healthy. When the clash in mechanisms is marked, diagnosis is then aided by the use of projective techniques. But when there is essential harmony within the personality system projective methods will teach us little or nothing about the course of motivation.

From what has been said it is clear that a satisfactory conception of psychodynamics will have the following characteristics. 1) It will never employ projective methods nor depth analysis without allowing for a full diagnosis of motives by direct methods as well. 2) It will assume that in a healthy personality the great bulk of motivation can be taken at its face value. 3) It will assume that normal motivation of this order has a present and future significance for the individual that is by no means adequately represented by a study of his past life. In other words, it will allow that the present psychodynamics of a life may in large part be functionally autonomous, even though continuous with early motivational formations. 4) It will at the same time retain the epochal insights of Freud and others to the effect that infantile fixations frequently occur, and that we do well to check on conscious report and to supplement direct methods by indirect.

Before such an adequate conceptualization can be achieved there is one current dogma in motivational theory that demands re-examination. I refer to the oft-encountered statement that all motives aim at "the reduction of tensions." This doctrine—found in instinctivism, psychoanalysis, and in stimulus-response psychology—operates to keep us on a primitive level of theorizing.

We cannot, of course, deny that basic drives seem to seek "reduction of tension." Oxygen need, hunger, thirst, elimination are examples. But these drives are not a trustworthy model for all normal adult motivation. Goldstein remarks that patients who seek only tension reduction are clearly pathological. They are preoccupied with segmental irritations from which they seek relief. There is nothing creative about their interests. They cannot take suffering, or delay, or frustration as a mere incident in their pursuit of values. Normal people, by contrast, are dominated by their "preferred patterns" of self-actualization. Their psychogenic interests are modes of sustaining and directing tension rather than escaping it.

We should, I think agree with Goldstein that tension reduction is not an adequate statement of the functioning of mature psychogenic motives. At the time of his inauguration as president of Harvard, James Bryant Conant remarked that he was undertaking his duties "with a heavy heart but gladly." He knew he would reduce no tensions by committing himself to the new job. Tensions would mount and mount, and at many times become almost unbearable. While he would in the course of his daily work dispatch many tasks and feel relief, still the over-all commitment—his total investment of energy— would never result in any equilibrium. Psychogenic interests are of this order: they lead us to complicate and strain our lives indefinitely. "Striving for equilibrium," "tension reduction," "death wish" seem trivial and erroneous representations of normal adult motivation.

Recent years, as I have said, have brought a wholesome turn in theorizing. Few authorities on war neuroses, for example, wrote in terms of tension reduction. They spoke rather of "firm ego structure" or "weak ego structure." Grinker and Spiegel say, "As the ego becomes stronger the therapist demands increasing independence and activity from the patient."

After successful therapy these and other writers sometimes remark, "The ego now seems in full control." In such expressions as these—and one encounters them with increasing frequency—we meet post-Freudian ego psychology again. True, the flavor of these theoretical statements varies. Sometimes they still seem close to the conception of the ego as rationalizer, rider and steersman. But often, as in the statements just quoted, they go far beyond. They imply that the ego is not only normally able to avoid malignant repression, chronicity and rigidity, but that it is also a differentiated dynamism—a fusion of healthy psychogenic motives that can be taken at their face value.

There is no need to take fright at the conception of an "active ego." As I see the matter, the term "ego" does not refer to a homunculus, but is merely a shorthand expression for what Goldstein calls "preferred patterns." The term means that normally healthy personalities have various systems of psychogenic motives. They are not limitness in number. Indeed in a well-integrated adult they may be adequately indicated on the fingers of two hands, perhaps one. What a person is trying to do persistently, recurrently, as a function of his own internal nature, is often surprisingly well focused and well patterned. Whether these leading motives are called desires, interests, values, traits or sentiments does not greatly matter. What is important is that motivational theory—in guiding diagnosis, therapy and research—should take these structures fully into account.

11. Measuring Motivation In Phantasy: The Achievement Motive

David C. McClelland

CONTEMPORARY psychological theory stresses the importance of motivation, but provides no satisfactory method for measuring it, at least at the human level. The present research was begun with the idea of remedying this defect. Psychology needs a measure of human motivation and we set out to find one. This report represents a brief description of some of the main findings obtained by our entire research group which has included the following people: David Angell, John W. Atkinson, Robert C. Birney, Russell A. Clark, Gerald A. Friedman, Jules Holzberg, Alvin M. Liberman, Edgar L. Lowell, John Perkins, Thornton B. Roby, Benjamin Simon, Joseph Veroff, and Josef Zatzkis.

In retrospect, at least, our search appears to have been guided by three hypotheses. First, the method of measurement for maximum theoretical usefulness should be at least partially independent of the methods of measurement used to define the other two main variables in contemporary psychological theory, namely, perception and learning. The field of sensation and perception received a great boost when the psychophysical methods were invented or systematized and put into wide use over a century ago. Theoretical development in this field continues to draw heavily for its vitality on the application of these methods. Similarly, learning theory received a great boost around the beginning of the twentieth century when methods for studying problem-solving behavior (*e.g.*, conditioning, serial rote learning, maze learning, and the like) were developed. It seemed logical that motivation in turn would get its greatest lift as a theoretical variable if some

From H. Guetzkow, (Ed.) *Groups, Leadership and Men,* Carnegie Press, Pittsburgh, Penn., 1951. Reprinted by permission of Dr. McClelland, Dr. Guetzkow and the Carnegie Press.

methods for measuring it could be developed that were not identical with those that were already in use to measure perception and learning.

The second hypothesis which guided our search was that motives might be best measured in phantasy. There were two bases for this assumption. In the first place, phantasy fulfills our first requirement: it differs quite radically from problem-solving behavior on the one hand the veridical perception on the other. In the second place, clinical psychologists from Freud to Murray have found phantasy of immense practical value in developing the dynamic or motivational theory of personality. In fact, one could argue that the whole psychoanalytic school of thinking is built, operationally speaking, on an analysis of imaginative behavior, whether it be the free association of adults on a psychoanalytic couch or the imaginative play of children.

Our third hypothesis was that motives could be experimentally aroused by manipulating external conditions. Here we were guided by the immensely successful assumption of animal psychologists that motives are states of the organism which can be aroused normally by deprivation. While we felt that the animal model has so far not proven particularly useful in its direct application to measuring motivation at the human level, nevertheless it has proven so theoretically fruitful in the construction of elementary behavior theory that it should not be wholly ignored.

Quite simply then, our problem became one of attempting to arouse human motives experimentally and to measure the effects on phantasy. As a preliminary check we decided to test one of our basic hypotheses, namely, that phantasy would be sensitive to changes in conditions which everyone would agree were motivating. So Atkinson and McClelland conducted and reported (2) an experiment in which they demonstrated that human subjects deprived of food for one, four, and sixteen hours wrote brief imaginative stories which changed in a number of important ways as hunger increased. From the shifts in the content of the stories they were able to develop a composite score which gave a rough idea of how long the subjects had been without food. This preliminary evidence together with earlier work done by Sanford (9) seemed to clear the track for work on what became the main objective of the study, namely, the measurement of the strength of the achievement motive in phantasy.

PROCEDURE

How could the achievement motive be experimentally aroused in human subjects? This was our first problem. Fortunately, there are several standard laboratory procedures for producing achievement orientation which are usually lumped together under the heading of "ego-involvement." They have in common the attempt to orient the subjects around success in some task which is or should be of great importance to them. In our case, we decided to define certain tasks as achievement-related for the subjects and to control their experiences of success or failure on these tasks. In this way we hoped to be able to control the intensity of the achievement motive aroused in various groups of subjects and to measure the effects of the different intensities on subsequent imaginative behavior. Specifically, we worked finally with six different "arousal conditions": (1) a *relaxed* condition in which the tasks the subjects performed were introduced casually as part of the blind exploration of some graduate students into a new problem, (2) a *neutral* condition in which the tasks were seriously introduced as ones on which the department of psychology wanted some norms, (3) an *ego-involved* condition in which the tasks were described as measures of intelligence and leadership capacity, (4) a *success* condition in which the subjects were allowed to succeed on the ego-involved tasks, (5) a *failure* condition in which the subjects were caused to fail on the ego-involved tasks, and (6) a *success-failure* condition in which the subjects first succeeded and then failed on the ego-involved tasks. In this way we attempted to explore the effect of the entire range of achievement-related experiences on imaginative behavior, although in the end our primary attention focused on the difference between the relaxed and ego-involved orientations rather than on the specific effects of success and failure.

How were we to measure the effects of these various arousal conditions on phantasy? Since our design calls for the scoring of a large number of records from sizable groups of subjects, we necessarily had to eliminate the type of elaborate phantasy production normally used by clinical psychologists. Instead we decided in favor of getting small, relatively standardized samples of imaginative behavior from each subject. In time our routine procedure involved asking a group of subjects to write brief five-minute stories in response to each of four pictures exposed for twenty seconds on a screen in front of the group. The stories were written around the following four questions spaced on an answer sheet:

What is happening?
What has led to this situation?
What is being thought?
What will happen?

The instructions given were the standard ones for the Thematic Apperception Test. Their general tone is to urge the subject to be as creative as possible and not to think in terms of right and wrong answers. There were four slides in all, two of which came from the Murray Thematic Apperception Test and two of which were made up especially for this test. They suggested respectively a work situation (two men working at a machine), a study situation (a boy seated at a desk with a book in front of him), a father-son situation (TAT 7BM), and a young boy possibly dreaming of the future (TAT 8BM). Considerable work has been done by Atkinson (1) with slides suggestive of other situations, but most of the work reported is based on these four which represent an attempt to sample the range of achievement-related activities.

The stories obtained by this method average about ninety words in length. How are they to be scored? Again we had to eliminate complex scoring systems and in the end hit upon the scheme of analyzing the stories in terms of the action sequence suggested by the questions on the answer sheet. That is, a plot or story usually has a beginning (or instigation), a middle (containing instrumental acts and obstacles), and an end (containing goal responses). Thus the categories we finally chose to score were aspects of the instigation action or problem-solving sequence commonly used as a model in contemporary learning theory. They included the following (arranged in accordance with the time order in which they normally appear in a story): statements of need or wish, instrumental activities, blocks or obstacles either internal or external in nature, anticipations of the outcome, positive or negative affect accompanying success or failure in reaching a goal, and the like. Details about scoring definitions and other aspects of the procedure can be found either in the published preliminary report by McClelland, Clark, Roby, and Atkinson (6) or in the monograph now in preparation by McClelland, Atkinson, Clark, and Lowell (5). This scoring system is general enough to fit an action sequence centered around any motive and was also used in scoring for hunger in the Atkinson and McClelland study (2) previously mentioned. The critical problem is that of finding a scoring definition for deciding whether statements are related to the motive in question—in the present instance, the achievement motive. What constitutes achievement imagery? This presented many serious and complicated problems but in the end we were able to formulate a definition which stated that any imagery (*e.g.*, statement in the story) which suggests *competition with a standard* is achievement related. In its simplest terms this means that someone in the story is *trying to do better* in relation to some achievement goal such as doing a better job or getting ahead in the world.

RESULTS

Methodological

Scoring the stories for various achievement-related categories as finally defined is highly reliable. After training, two judges working together agreed on 91 per cent of the categories on two successive scorings of the same records. The agreement on individual n Achievement (need for Achievement) scores derived from summation of these categories is even higher. The correlation is .95 between n Achievement scores obtained on two different judges working together. One judge, after experience with the system for three days, has obtained a correlation of .92 between his scores and those obtained by another judge more experienced with the system. Furthermore, after practice the system can be applied rapidly; it takes from three to five minutes on the average to score the four stories obtained for a given individual.

Many significant differences in the scoring categories were produced by the various methods of arousing the achievement motive. In general, there were large and significant increases in the number of subjects and number of stories showing achievement-related imagery as the experiences the subjects had just had became more achievement-oriented. For the sake of simplicity, we will disregard specific differences in the effects of success and failure and turn our attention only to the derivation of an over-all index of the strength of an individual's achievement motive, an index which we refer to as his n Achievement score, following Murray's convention (8). First, we noted all those characteristics such as stated need for achievement, anticipation of success and failure, *etc.*, which increased significantly from a lower to a higher state of achievement arousal; then we argued that the number of those characteristics in the stories written by a subject under normal or non-ego-involved conditions would indicate the normal strength of his concern for achievement. That is, we could look for the characteristics in a person's stories which we had found to be sensitive to experimental changes in achievement orientation, sum them up, and derive an over-all n Achievement score for that individual.

One of our first concerns was to see whether or not a measure derived in this way was applicable to groups of persons other than the male college students who had been the subjects in the various arousal conditions. To test the generality of the n Achievement measure, Veroff (10) compared the stories written by high school students, both boys and girls, after neutral and ego-involving experiences. He found that the high school boys, representing a much larger segment of the population than our college men, also showed a significant over-all increase in mean n Achievement score from the neutral to the ego-involving condition. This strongly suggests that the characteristics scored are not peculiar to the highly selected portion of the population represented in college. In the second place, Veroff found no significant change in n Achievement score for girls following ego-involvement. There are many interesting explanations for this finding, but the conclusion it leads to here is that the method cannot be applied to women without some additional assumptions.

Finally, we went outside our culture altogether and compared the stories written by Navaho high-school-age males under neutral and ego-involving conditions, and found once again that even in this different culture, our scoring system was applicable and showed a significant increase in mean n Achievement score from a condition of low achievement arousal to one of higher achievement arousal.

Our next concern was with the reliability of a person's n Achievement score. In other words, what are the chances that he will get the same or a similar score on two different occasions? Our reliabilities are on the whole low. A test-retest correlation for two three-picture measures taken a week apart was only .22 (not significant with $N = 40$). However, the two measures agreed significantly (72.5 percent) in placing subjects above or below the mean on the two occasions, and the split-half reliability for a six- or eight-picture test runs over .70 (corrected for halving the test). On the whole, in the present state of development, the n Achievement measure appears adequate for classifying individuals into high and low achievement groups, or at the most into high, middle, and low achievement groups, but not for finer discriminations or for individual testing purposes. It is always possible, of course, that with a projective instrument of this sort high test-retest reliabilities cannot be obtained because the subject is "spoiled" by having taken such a test once previously. This may mean that the measure is more valid in the sense of being related to other types of behavior than it is reliable in the sense of being related to itself as obtained on a second occasion.

RELATION OF N ACHIEVEMENT SCORE TO OTHER KINDS OF BEHAVIOR

While our method of deriving the n Achievement score from differences in achievement arousal conditions gives the measure a kind of validity, the skeptical observer would still want to know more. In particular, is our presumed measure of motive strength related to other kinds of behavior in ways that on a theoretical or common-sense basis we would expect motivation to be related? For this reason, much of our energy has gone into exploring the relation of the n Achievement score to other variables. Chief among these are performance and learning. On theoretical, experimental, and common-sense grounds one would expect that more highly motivated subjects would, at least under certain circumstances, perform more quickly, and, under certain others, learn more efficiently than poorly motivated subjects. Thus, if our n Achievement score is an index of the strength of the achievement motive in individuals, we should be able to demonstrate that people with high n Achievement scores show evidence of better learning and performance. Of the several studies designed to test this hypothesis, the one by Lowell (4) is perhaps the most definitive. He first administered a three-picture form of the TAT n Achievement Test to a group of male college students and then asked them to work on a twenty-minute Scrambled Words test which required them to rearrange a nonsense series of letters (for example, WTSE) until they had constructed a meaningful word (*e.g.*, WEST). The test was arranged in such a way that the subjects worked for two minutes on each of ten different pages of Scrambled Words, which were randomized from subject to subject to equate for difficulties. One week later Lowell administered to the same group of subjects another set of three TAT pictures and asked them to work on solving some simple addition problems for ten minutes. The n Achievement score for an individual was obtained in the usual manner by summing the significant characteristics in the stories obtained from all six pictures on the two different occasions. Figure 1 summarizes how groups of subjects with high and low n Achievement scores performed in different periods of the scrambled words task.

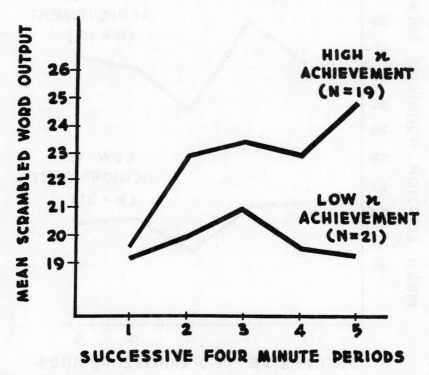

Figure 1. Mean output of scrambled words for subjects above and below the mean in n Achievement score in successive four-minute periods.

The rather regular increases in performance from the first to the fifth four-minute period for the high n Achievement subjects strongly suggest a learning curve, while variations in output for the low n Achievement subjects display no consistent trend. The high need group shows a mean gain in output from the first to the last period of 5.32 words, whereas the low need group shows a gain of only .43 words, a difference in gain of 4.89 words which is well beyond the 1 per cent level (t = 3.76). In short, our expectations are confirmed: there is definite and statistically significant evidence for superior learning in the high as compared with the low n Achievement group.

Figure 2 shows the results for the addition task. Here it is clear that the high n Achievement subjects solved more problems at every point in the test so that their over-all output is significantly greater than for the low n Achievement subjects (t = 2.40, P < .05).

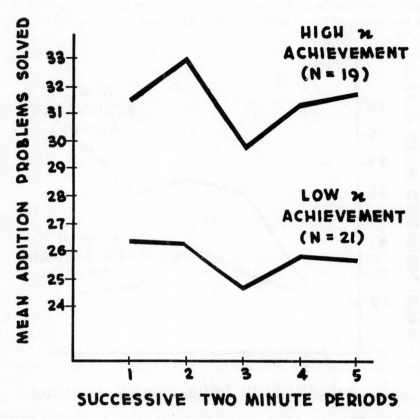

Figure 2. Mean output of addition problems solved by subjects above and below the mean n Achievement score in successive two-minute periods.

The difference in the findings reported in Figures 1 and 2 is important. Presumably the reason why the more highly motivated subjects showed learning in connection with the Scrambled Word task is because this task is sufficiently complex for the subjects to find new and better ways of performing at it as they practice it. The Additions task, on the other hand, is so simple that presumably subjects are about at their maximum level of efficiency when they begin; no new methods of adding are likely to be discovered in the course of a ten-minute task. Thus we can argue that where learning is possible in a complex task, the highly motivated subjects will show it; where it is not possible or at least not likely in a very simple task, high n Achievement produces faster performance but not learning. Both of these findings support the hypothesis that the n Achievement score is measuring motivational strength.

Another psychological variable to which n Achievement should be related is level of aspiration. Atkinson conducted a study (1) in which he obtained a four-picture measure of n Achievement on the day of a final examination in a course. He also asked the subjects to report the grade they *expected* to make on the examination on the back of the story form. The raw correlation between n Achievement score and *expected* examination grade was .24, which falls short of significance with a sample of thirty-eight subjects. Since asking the question in terms of expectancy calls for a reality estimate, he sought to eliminate some of the reality determinants of the level of aspiration by selecting from the thirty-eight subjects those twenty-three who, on the basis of past experience, might have been uncertain as to what to expect. The twenty-three consisted of those men who stood in one third of the distribution of general averages and a different third of the distribution of grades in this particular course. For these subjects the correlation between n Achievement score and level of aspiration was .45, which is significant at less than the .05 level. In other words, when the reality determinants of an aspiration judgment are ambiguous or in conflict, then motivation enters more largely into the determination of aspiration. This, too, confirms the hypothesis that the n Achievement score is a measure of motivational strength.

Motivation should also have some demonstrable connection with perception and memory. Out of several experiments done in this field, two are particularly striking and confirm each other. The first is the one reported by McClelland and Liberman (7) on the effect of n Achievement on the recognition of need-related words. Having previously obtained n Achievement scores on their subjects, they measured how quickly a subject could recognize achievement-related, security-related, and neutral words when they were exposed repeatedly at increasing illuminations for only .01 second. They found that subjects with high n Achievement scores were able to recognize positive achievement words like *success* and *strive* faster than subjects with low n Achievement scores. When they obtained a somewhat more stable measure of n Achievement by combining the score obtained from imagination with one based on a performance task to produce an over-all index of n Achievement rank, they were able to make a finer analysis of the data. That is, they found that subjects in the lowest third of the distribution of n Achievement ranks showed no particular trend with respect to recognizing either positive achievement words or negative achievement words like *unable* and *failure*. The subjects in the middle third of the distribution, however, showed a *slower* recognition time for the negative achievement words than did either the low or high thirds, and the high n Achievement third showed a much *faster* recognition of the positive achievement words than did either the middle or low thirds. In short, it looked as if, as n Achievement increased in intensity, it tended to orient subjects first around avoiding failure (decreased sensitivity to failure words) and then around attaining success (increased sensitivity to success words). Some further evidence that the middle n Achievement subjects were security-minded lay in the fact that they were also quicker at recognizing security-related words like *friend* or *comfort*. McClelland and Liberman concluded that "the group of subjects with moderate n Achievement are security-minded and chiefly concerned with avoiding failure, or with achieving a minimal level of aspiration, whereas the group of subjects with high n Achievement are concerned more directly with achieving success or attaining a maximum level of aspiration." (7, p. 251).

These findings were confirmed in a study reported by Atkinson (1) on the memory for completed and incompleted tasks. In addition to having subjects who could be classified low, moderate, or high with respect to n Achievement on the basis of their stories, he had three types of test situations: (a) a relaxed orientation in which the experimenter was introduced quite informally as a "graduate student who wants to try out some tasks"; (b) a task orientation in which the experimenter simply directed the students' attention to how the tasks were to be performed without any effort to create an experimental atmosphere; and (c) an ego orientation in which the experimenter described the tasks as being measures of intellectual ability, leadership, *etc.*, and urged the students to do their best. Atkinson found in line with work previously reported that the number of *completed* tasks recalled, irrespective of motivation, increased from relaxed to task to ego orientation. But when a breakdown was made according to n Achievement score, he found strikingly opposite trends for the subjects in the high and middle thirds of the n Achievement distribution with respect to the incompleted tasks. For the subjects with high n Achievement there was a regular *increase* in the number of incompleted tasks recalled, whereas for the subjects with moderate n Achievement there was a regular *decrease* in the number of incompleted tasks recalled. For the subjects with lowest n Achievement there was no trend in the number of incompleted tasks recalled. In short, the data look very much like those obtained with perception. The subjects with moderate n Achievement are defensive; they appear to regard their inability to complete a task as a failure as they become more ego-oriented, and consequently attempt to avoid remembering it. Subjects with high n Achievement, however, apparently tend to regard their incompleted tasks as challenges which they remember better as the situation becomes more ego-oriented, presumably in order to complete them. Both of these studies strongly suggest that there are at least two kinds of achievement motivation, one of which appears to be oriented around avoiding failure and the other around the more positive goal of attaining success. It cannot be stated, of course, which type of motivation is more efficient, since either an excessive concern with success or with avoiding failure may be madadaptive, depending on the requirements of the situation.

Having demonstrated the relation of our measure to important behavior variables, we come to the more traditional validity checks. Is the n Achievement score related in any significant way to how much achievement "drive" a person is judged to have either by himself or by a clinician after careful study? Apparently not. There is no significant relationship between imaginative n Achievement score and either a psychiatrist's judgment of n Achievement or a person's own judgment of his n Achievement intensity. This is not as disturbing as it might at first seem to be. If ratings of motivational strength were adequate measures of motivation (e.g., were significantly related to performance, level of aspiration, etc.), there would be no need to develop any such elaborate system as this for measuring motivation. The fact of the matter is that such judgments must necessarily be complexly determined. When a psychiatrist, for example, attempts to estimate the strength of an individual's achievement motive, he must take into account a great many factors—the person's actual performance, his goals in life at least as they are consciously realized, his relation to his father, etc. The final rating, whether it be the psychiatrist's or the person's own, represents a synthesis or integration of these many factors and is not therefore, at least in the theoretical sense, "pure." That is, it does not represent any one aspect of personality but is a judgment involving many. It was just to avoid such complexly determined measures of motivation that the present research was undertaken.

The n Achievement score has been related to many other variables besides those so far reported, but the relationships obtained are either so complex or so tentative that they cannot be reported in any detail here. For example, we have obtained a highly significant correlation between n Achievement scores and college grades on two occasions and an insignificant correlation on another occasion. The problem obviously needs further exploration. Similarly we have explored the relation of n Achievement score to other projective tests, namely, the Sentence Completion Test and the Rorschach, in both cases with some interesting but not completely comprehensible results. We have found that n Achievement score is significantly related to the kinds of linguistic categories that a person uses in attempting to express himself, at least in an achievement-related situation, and so forth. Rather than dwell on any of these findings, let us turn to our attempts to explore the origins of n Achievement, assuming for the moment that our measure of it is valid.

The first study in this area was a cross-cultural one performed by Friedman (3). Quite surprisingly, he found that he could apply the n Achievement scoring system developed on male American college students to folk tales collected from eight different American Indian cultures. By selecting twelve such tales from each of the cultures and using the standard scoring system, he found he could obtain an over-all achievement index for each of the cultures which represented the amount of achievement-related imagery in the stories in his sample. He then correlated this index with ratings which had been made independently of data in the Yale cross-cultural files for a study by Whiting and Child on various child-rearing practices in the eight cultures. On theoretical grounds we predicted that n Achievement scores would be highly related to the amount of stress in the culture which was placed on independence training. Friedman found a relationship that was significant well beyond the 1 per cent level even with only eight cases, indicating that severity of independence training in childhood is highly correlated with the amount of achievement imagery in the folk tales current in a culture. This supports the hypothesis that achievement motivation develops out of parents' concern that children "stand on their own feet" rather early in life and learn to do things for themselves.

A more direct confirmation of this hypothesis was obtained by correlating n Achievement scores of male American college students with their own ratings of their parents' behavior toward them on several different dimensions, namely, Democratic-autocratic, Acceptance-rejection, Indulgence, and Casualness. The correlation for the Acceptance-rejection dimension was significant, being .49 for the father, .33 for the mother, and .48 for both parents combined. In other words, the higher the n Achievement score the more the student tended to rate both parents, but particularly the father, rejectant. Again this suggests that the son was either forced to stand on his own feet by his parents or *thought* he was forced to stand on his own feet (and therefore "rejected"). The sons were also asked to rate their parents on several different personality characteristics including the following: friendly, helpful, domineering, selfish, successful, clever, self-confident. Table 1 shows the results when the personality characteristics were grouped according to similarity.

TABLE 1

Correlations between n Achievement score and
personality traits attributed to parents (N = 30)

	FATHER	MOTHER	COMBINED
1. Friendly-Helpful	—.56	—.39	—.57
2. Domineering-Selfish	.10	.14	.14
3. Successful-Clever-Self-confident	—.37	—.41	—.44

Correlations of .36 and .46 are significant at the 5% and 1% levels respectively.

Apparently, again, the sons who rated their parents as unfriendly, unhelpful, and unsuccessful tended to have higher n Achievement scores. In reverse, the sons who found their parents (especially their fathers) to be helpful, nurturent, friendly, and successful tended to have low n Achievement scores. Again this makes theoretical sense. Apparently n Achievement develops out of an insistence on independence, or doing things for oneself which is interpreted by sons later on during college as rejection and unfriendliness.

Contrariwise, boys who are greatly helped by clever fathers and mothers never get a chance to want to achieve by themselves. There are other bits of evidence in our data on this general point, but they all support the same conclusion: n Achievement score is significantly related to severity of independence training in childhood.

CONCLUSIONS

The general outcome of our research to date may be summarized briefly as follows:

(1) It has demonstrated the great potentiality of an n Achievement score based on phantasy as a measure of the achievement motivation of individuals irrespective of their cultural background.

(2) By providing an independent measure of motivation, it has opened up great new areas for further research, such as the relation between achievement motivation and school grades.

(3) It has demonstrated that the method of deriving a measure of motivational strength from experimentally produced changes in phantasy is a practical one which could theoretically be applied to the measurement of any motive.

(4) It has led us to question seriously prevailing theories of motivation and to attempt a revision of those theories, which is to be elaborated along with many more detailed research findings in a monograph now in preparation (5).

BIBLIOGRAPHY

1. Atkinson, J. W. The projective measurement of achievement motivation. Unpublished Ph.D. Thesis, Univ. Mich., 1950.

2. Atkinson, J. W. and McClelland, D. C. The projective expression of needs. II. The effect of different intensities of the hunger drive on thematic apperception. *J. exp. Psychol.*, 1948, *38*, 643-658.

3. Friedman, G. A. A cross-cultural study of the relationship between independence training and n Achievement as revealed by mythology. Unpublished A. B. Thesis, Harvard Univ., 1950.

4. Lowell, E. L. A methodological study of projectively measured achievement motivation. Unpublished M. A. Thesis, Wesleyan Univ., 1950.

5. McClelland, D. C., Atkinson, J. W., Clark, R. A. and Lowell, E. L. The achievement motivation. Unpublished Manuscript.

6. McClelland, D. C., Clark, R. A., Roby, T. B., and Atkinson, J. W. The projective expression of needs. IV. The effect of the need for achievement on thematic apperception. *J. exp. Psychol.*, 1949, *39*, 242-255.

7. McClelland, D. C. and Liberman, A. M. The effect of need for achievement on recognition of need-related words. *J. Personality*, 1949, *18*, 236-251.

8. Murray, H. A. *Explorations in Personality.* New York: Oxford Univ. Press, 1938.

9. Sanford, R. N. The effects of abstinence from food upon imaginal processes: a further experiment. *J. Psychol.*, 1937, *3*, 145-159.

10. Veroff, J. A projective measure of the achievement motivation of adolescent males and females. Unpublished. A. B. Thesis, Wesleyan Univ., 1950.

REFERENCES—SECTION ONE

Allport, G. W. Motivation in personality. *Psychol. Rev.*, 1940, *47*, 533-554.
———. *The Nature of Personality: Selected Papers.* Cambridge, Mass.: Addison-Wesley, 1950.
———. *Becoming: Basic Considerations for a Psychology of Personality.* New Haven: Yale Univ. Press, 1955.
———. *The Nature of Prejudice.* Garden City, New York: Doubleday Anchor Books, 1958.
———. *Personality and Social Encounter.* Boston: Beacon Press, 1960.
———. The open system in personality theory. *J. abnorm. soc. Psychol.*, 1960, *60*, No. 5.
Angyal, A. *Foundations for a Science of Personality.* New York: Commonwealth Fund, 1941.
Arnold, M. B. Motivation and the desire to know. *Education*, 1956, *77*, 220-226.
Atkinson, J. W. The achievement motive and recall of interrupted and completed tasks. *J. exp. Psychol.*, 1953, *46*, 381-390.
———. Motivational determinants of risk-taking behavior. *Psychol. Rev.*, 1957, *64*, 359-372.
———, (Ed.). *Motives, Action and Society: A Method of Assessment and Study.* Princeton, N. J.: D. VanNostrand, 1958.
———, and Raphelson, A. V. Individual differences in motivation and behavior in particular situations. *J. Pers.*, 1956, *24*, 349-363.
———, and Walker, E. L. The affiliation motive and perceptual sensitivity to faces. *J .abnorm. soc. Psychol.*, 1956, *53*, 38-41.
Ausubel, D. P. Introduction to a threshold concept of primary drives. *J. gen. Psychol.*, 1956, *54*, 209-229.
Binderman, A. D., and Zimmer, H. (Eds.), *The Manipulation of Human Behavior.* New York: Wiley, 1961.
Bindra, D. *Motivation: A Systematic Reinterpretation.* New York: Ronald Press Co., 1959.
Borton, W. M. Correlates of occupational attitudes and consistency with motivational theories. *Soc. Sci.*, 1957, *32*, 159-165.
Boss, B. M. Effects of motivation on consistency of performance in groups. *Educ. Psychol. Measmt.*, 1959, *19*, 247-252.
Brown, J. S. *The Motivation of Behavior.* New York: McGraw-Hill, 1961.
———, and Jacobs, A. The role of fear in the motivation and acquisition of responses. *J. exp. Psychol.*, 1949, *39*, 747-759.
Bühler, C. Motivation and personality. *Dialectica*, 1951, *5*, 312-361.

Cantril, H. *The "Why" of Man's Experience*. New York: Macmillan Co., 1950.

Cattell, R. B. *Personality and Motivation and Measurement*. New York: World Book Co., 1957.

Champion, R. A. The 'directing' properties of motivation. *Aust. J. Psychol.*, 1957, *9*, 31-40.

Cofer, C. N. Motivation. *Annu. Rev. Psychol.*, 1959, *10*, 173-202.

Coleman, J. V. *Personality Dynamics and Effective Behavior*. Chicago: Scott, Foresman and Co., 1960.

————. Motivation of the volunteer in the health and welfare fields. *Mental Hyg.*, 1957, *41*, 217-221.

Coopersmith, S. A method for determining types of self-esteem. *J. abnorm. soc. Psychol.*, 1959, *59*, 87-94.

Davis, C. M. Self selection of diet by newly weaned infants. *Amer. J. Dis. Child.*, 1928, *36*, 651-679.

Davis, R. C. The domain of homeostasis. *Psychol. Rev.*, 1958, *65*, 8-13.

De Martino, M. F. *Sexual Behavior and Personality Characteristics*. New York: Citadel Press, 1963.

Dollard, J., and Auld, F. *Scoring Human Motives: A Manual*. New Haven: Yale Univ. Press, 1959.

Duffy, E. The psychological significance of the concept of 'arousal' or 'activation.' *Psychol. Rev.*, 1957, *64*, 265-275.

Dyal, J. A. Secondary motivation based on appetites and aversions. *Psychol. Rept.*, 1958, *4*, 698.

Farber, I. E. The role of motivation in verbal learning and performance. *Psychol. Bull.*, 1955, *64*, 265-275.

Fleck, S. Recognition and utilization of the motivation of volunteers. *Mental Hyg.*, 1957, *41*, 222-227.

Frank, L. K. The fundamental needs of the child. *Ment. Hyg.*, 1938, 22, 353-379.

Frenkel-Brunswik, E. Motivation and Behavior. *Genet. Psychol. Monogr.*, 1942, *26*, 121-265.

Goldstein, K. *The Organism*. New York: American Book Co., 1939.

Hall, J. F. *Psychology Of Motivation*. Chicago: J. B. Lippincott Co., 1961.

Hall, C. S., and Lindzey, G. *Theories of Personality*. New York: Wiley, 1957.

Harlow, H. F. Mice, monkeys, men and motives. *Psychol. Rev.*, 1953, *60*, 23-32.

————. The nature of love. *Amer. Psychologist*, 1958, *13*, 673-685.

Henle, M. On field forces. *J. Psychol.*, 1957, *43*, 239-249.

Henry, H. *Motivation Research: Its Practice and Uses for Advertising. Marketing, and Other Business Purposes*. New York: Frederick Ungar, 1958.

Herzberg, F., Mausner, B., and Snyderman, B. *The Motivation to Work*. New York: Wiley, 1959.

Hilgard, E. R. *Theories of learning*. 2nd Ed. New York: Appleton-Century-Crofts, 1956.

Irwin, F. W. An analysis of the concepts of discrimination and preference. *Amer. J. Psychol.*, 1958, *71*, 152-163.

Jahoda, M. *Current Concepts of Positive Mental Health*. New York: Basic Books, 1958.

James, W. *Principles of psychology*. 2 vols. New York: Holt, 1890.

Jones, M. R., (Ed.). *Nebraska Symposium on Motivation*. Lincoln: Univ. of Nebraska Press, Vol. I, 1953; Vol. II, 1954; Vol. III, 1955; Vol. IV, 1956; Vol. V, 1957; Vol. VI, 1958; Vol. VII, 1959; Vol. VIII, 1960; Vol. IX, 1961.

Jourard, S. M. *Personal Adjustment*. New York: Macmillan, 1958.

Katz, D. Some fundamental laws of the psychology of needs: Hunger. *Character and Pers.*, 1935, *3*, 312-326.

Koch, S. The current status of motivational psychology. *Psychol. Rev.*, 1951, *58*, 147-154.

Kluckholm, C., Murray, H. A., and Schneider, D., (Eds.), *Personality in Nature, Society and Culture*. 2nd. Ed. New York: Knopf, 1953.

Lazarus, R. S., and Baker, R. W. Motivation and personality in psychological stress. *Psychol. Newsltr., N.Y.U.*, 1957, *8*, 159-193.

Lecky, P. *Self Consistency*. New York: Island Press, 1945.

Lee, D. Are basic needs ultimate? *J. abnorm. soc. Psychol.*, 1948, 43, 391-395.

Leeper, R. The role of motivation in learning: A study of the phenomenon of differential motivational control of the utilization of habits. *J. genet. Psychol.*, 1935, *46*, 3-40.

————. What contributions might cognitive learning theory make to our understanding of personality?, *J. Pers.*, 1953, *22*, 32-41.

————, and Madison, P. *Toward Understanding Human Personalities*. New York: Appleton-Century-Crofts, 1959.

Levy, D. M. Capacity and motivation. *Amer. J. Orthopsychiat.*, 1957, *27*, 1-8.

Lichtenberg, P., Kohrman, R., and MacGregor, H. *Motivation For Child Psychiatry Treatment*. New York: Russell and Russell, 1960.

Lillis, J. C. Motivation: what makes Sammy run? *Advanc. Mgmt.*, 1958, *23*, 5-8.

Lindzey, G., (Ed.). *Assessment of Human Motives*. New York: Grove Press, 1960.

Lundin, R. W. *Personality: An Experimental Approach*. New York: Macmillan, 1961.

Mace, C. A. Homeostasis, needs and values. *Brit. J. Psychol.*, 1953, *44*, 200-210.

Madsen, K. B. *Theories Of Motivation: A Comparative Study of Modern Theories of Motivation*. Cleveland, Ohio: Howard Allen, 1961.

Martineau, P. *Motivation in Advertising: Motives That Make People Buy*. New York: McGraw-Hill, 1957.

Maslow, A. H. Human motivation in relation to social theory. In Shore, M. (Ed.) *Twentieth-Century Mental Hygiene*. Social Science Publishers, 1951.

————. *Motivation and Personality*. New York: Harper, 1953.

————. The instinctoid nature of basic needs. *J. Pers.*, 1954, *22*, 326-348.

————. Cognition of being in the peak-experience. *J. Genetic Psychol.*, 1959, *94*, 43-66.

————. Critique of self-actualization: I. Some dangers of being—cognition. *J. Indiv. Psychol.*, 1959, *15*, 24-32.

————, (Ed.). *New Knowledge In Human Values*. New York: Harper, 1960.

————. Health as transcendence of environment. *J. Humanistic Psychol.*, 1961, *1*, 1-7.

————. *Toward a Psychology of Being*. Princeton, N. J.: D. Van Nostrand, 1962.

Maze, J. R. One some corruptions of the doctrine of homeostasis. *Psychol. Rev.*, 1953, *60*, 405-412.

McClelland, D. C., (Ed.). *Studies in Motivation*. New York: Appleton-Century-Crofts, 1955.

————. Atkinson, J. W., Clark, R. A., and Lowell, E. L. *The Achievement Motive*. New York: Appleton-Century-Crofts, 1953.

McDougall, W. *An Introduction to Social Psychology*. Boston: Luce, 1908.

Miller, N. E. Effects of drugs on motivation: the value of using a variety of techniques. *Ann. N. Y. Acad. Sci.*, 1956, *65*, 318-333.

————. Experiments on motivation: studies combining psychological, physiological and pharmacological techniques. *Science*, 1957, *126*, 1271-1278.

————. Central stimulation and other new approaches to motivation and reward. *Am. Psychologist*, 1958, *13*, 100-108.

Moeller, G., and Applezweig, M. H. A motivational factor in conformity. *J. abnorm. soc. Psychol.*, 1957, *55*, 114-120.

Mowrer, O. H. Motivation. *Ann. Rev. Psychol.*, 3, 1952, 419-438.

Murphy, G. *Personality: A Biosocial Approach to Origins and Structure*. New York: Harper, 1947.

————. Social motivation. In G. Lindzey (Ed.) *Handbook of Social Psychology*. Cambridge, Mass.: Addison-Wesley, 1954.

————. *Human Potentialities*. New York: Basic Books, 1958.

Murray, H. A. Basic concepts for a psychology of personality. *J. gen. Psychol.*, 1936, *15*, 241-268.

————. Some basic psychological assumptions and conceptions. *Dialectica*, 1951, *5*, 266-292.

Olds, J. *The Growth and Structure of Motives*. Glencoe, Illinois: The Free Press, 1956.

Oppenheimer, O. Toward a new instinct theory. *J. soc. Psychol.*, 1958, *47*, 21-31.

Osgood, C. E., and Walker, E. G. Motivation and language behavior: a content analysis of suicide notes. *J. abnorm. soc. Psychol.*, 1959, *59*, 58-67.

Peters, R. S. *The Concept of Motivation*. New York: Humanities Press, 1958.

Piotrowski, Z. A. Basic human motives according to Kurt Goldstein. *Amer. J. Psychother.*, 1959, *13*, 553-560.

Rogers, C. R. Some observations on the organization of personality. *Amer. Psychologist*, 1947, *2*, 358-368.

————, and Dymond, F., (Eds.). *Psychotherapy and Personality Change: Co-ordinated Studies in the Client-Centered Approach*. Chicago: Univ. of Chicago Press, 1954.

————. *On Becoming A Person*. Boston: Houghton Mifflin, 1961.

Ryan, T. A. Drives, tasks, and the initiation of behavior. *Amer. J. Psychol.*, 1958, *71*, 74-93.

Sappenfield, B. R. *Personality Dynamics*. New York: Knopf, 1954.

Schreier, F. T. *Human Motivation*. Glencoe, Illinois: The Free Press, 1957.

Seward, G. *Psychotherapy and Culture Conflict*. New York: Ronald Press, 1956.

Seward, J. P. How are motives learned? *Psychol. Rev.*, 1953, *60*, 99-110.

Shaw, M. E. Some motivational factors in cooperation and competition. *J. Pers.*, 1958, *26*, 155-169.

Stagner, R. Industrial morale (a symposium): II. Motivational aspects of industrial morale. *Personnel Psychol.*, 1958, *11*, 64-70.

Stellar, E. The physiology of motivation. *Psychol. Rev.*, 1954, *61*, 5-22.

Strunk, O., Jr. Theological students: A study in perceived motive. *Personnel guid. J.*, 1958, *36*, 320-322.

Suojanen, W. W., and Hoyt, G. C. Differences in motivation among whitecollar workers. *Personnel*, 1957, *34*, 26-31.

Symonds, P. M. *Dynamics of Psychotherapy*. New York: Grune and Stratton, 1957.

Taylor, J. A. Drive theory and manifest anxiety. *Psychol. Bull.*, 1956, *53*, 303-320.

Telford, C. W. The problem of motives. In P. F. Valentine, (Ed.) *Twentieth Century Education*. New York: Philosophical Library, 1946.

Terrell, G. Manipulatory motivation in children. *J. comp. physiol. Psychol.*, 1959, *52*, 705-709.

Thompson, W. R. Motivational factors in development. *Aust. J. Psychol.*, 1958, *10*, 127-143.

Tolman, E. C. The nature of fundamental drives. *J. abnorm. soc. Psychol.*, 1925-26, *20*, 349-358.

————. The nature and functioning of wants. *Psychol. Rev.*, 1949, *56*, 357-369.

————, Hall, C. S., and Bretnall, E. P. A disproof of the law of effect and a substitution of the laws of emphasis, motivation and disruption. *J. exp. Psychol.*, 1932, *15*, 601-614.

Toman, W. A general formula for the quantitative treatment of human motivation. *J. abnorm. soc. Psychol.*, 1959, *58*, 91-99.

Troland, L. T. *The Fundamentals of Human Motivation*. New York: VanNostrand, 1928.

Turek, E. V., and Howell, R. J. The effect of variable success and failure situations on the intensity of need for achievement. *J. soc. Psychol.*, 1959, *49*, 267-273.

Veroff, J. Development and validation of a projective measure of power motivation. *J. abnorm. soc. Psychol.*, 1957, *54*, 1-8.

Vogel, W., Baker, R. W., and Lazarus, R. S. The roles of motivation in psychological states. *J. abnorm. soc. Psychol.*, 1958, *56*, 105-112.

————, Raymond, S., and Lazarus, R. S. Intrinsic motivation and psychological stress. *J. abnorm. soc. Psychol.*, 1959, *58*, 225-233.

Weber, C. O. Homeostasis and servo-mechanisms for what?, *Psychol. Rev.*, 1949 *56*, 234-239.

Weiss, F. A. Kurt Goldstein and his concept of human nature. *Amer. J. Psychoanal.*, 1959, *19*, 143-148.

Woodworth, R. S. *Dynamics of Behavior*. New York: Holt, 1958.

Young, P. T. *Motivation of Behavior*. New York: Wiley, 1936.

———. The role of affective processes in learning and motivation. *Psychol. Rev.*, 1959, *66*, 104-125.

———. *Motivation and Emotion*. New York: Wiley, 1961.

Zalezink, A., Christensen, C. R., and Roethlisberger, F. J., with the assistance of Homans, G. C. *The Motivation, Productivity, and Satisfaction of Workers: A Prediction Study*. Boston: Division of Research, Graduate School of Business administration, Harvard University, 1958.

Ziegler, H. P. Electrical stimulation of the brain and the psychophysiology of learning and motivation. *Psychol. Bull.*, 1957, *54*, 363-382.

Zimmerman, J. F. What motivates students? *J. higher Educ.*, 1956, *27*, 449-453.

2

FUNCTIONAL AUTONOMY
OF MOTIVES

As was noted in the previous section, there are two broad categories of motives, namely, the physiological and the social or learned. One of the most challenging problems in the field of human motivation is that of explaining the origin of learned or social motives. Thus far the available research has not revealed any organic basis for the social motives. Although everyone would agree that the physiological drives are of extreme importance, social motives may be in many instances more powerful or influential as determiners of behavior.

Because of the significance of these social motives a number of theoretical attempts have been made to explain their origin. One such attempt is contained in Allport's theory of the *functional autonomy of motives*. Allport, it should be noted, protests strongly against the Freudian explanation of motivation. He does not believe that adult motivation is simply a continuation of infantile motivation. According to Allport's theory of functional autonomy, habits which once have been well learned become initiators of behavior and assume the nature of powerful driving forces. That is, they now function as independent (autonomous) motives, unrelated to any underlying organic needs. Thus, habits become motives in their own right and activate behavior. Moreover, Allport "regards adult motives as infinitely varied, and as self-sustaining, *contemporary* systems, growing out of antecedent systems, but functionally independent of them." He says, "Each motive has a definite point of origin which may possibly be in instincts, or, more likely, in the organic tensions of infancy. Chronologically speaking, all adult purposes can be traced back to these seed–forms in infancy, but as the individual matures the tie is broken. Whatever bond remains, is historical not functional." (Paper No. 12)

Stimulating and interesting as the theory of functional autonomy may be, it has met with severe criticisms. (Papers No. 13 and No. 15). Some of the main criticisms leveled at this theory are that: a) it does not provide an adequate explanation of how or why this process of functional autonomy occurs, b) there is no statement as to the exact point at which the transformation of motives occurs, and c) it is too general in that not enough attention has been paid to its relation to other psychological processes such as learning, perception and individual differences.

Rethlingshafer (Paper No. 16) evaluates the experimental evidence introduced by Allport and related studies with the aim of determining whether or not the theory of functional autonomy can be supported. Her conclusion is that, "The present experimental evidence for functional autonomy of motives cannot be considered adequate." As with many theories, the ultimate acceptance, rejection, or modification of Allport's theory of functional autonomy must await more definitive experimental and clinical research.

12. The Functional Autonomy of Motives

Gordon W. Allport

FOR fifty years this Journal has served both as a rich repository for research and as a remarkably sensitive record of the psychological temper of the times. These two services are of great historical value. Since there is no reason to doubt that *The American Journal* will continue to hold its position of leadership in the future, one wonders what new currents of psychological interest its pages will reflect in the coming half century. With what problems will psychologists be chiefly concerned? What discoveries will they make? What types of scientific formulation will they prefer?

To predict at least one of these trends accurately requires no clairvoyance. On all sides we see the rising tide of interest in problems of personality. Up to a few years ago the somewhat segregated field of clinical psychology alone was concerned; but now theoretical and experimental psychology are likewise deeply affected. As never before the traditional portrait of the "generalized human mind" is being tested against the living models from which it is derived. As compared with particular minds it is found to lack locus, selfconsciousness, organic character, and reciprocal interpenetration of parts, all of which are essential to personality. Unless I am greatly mistaken the coming half-century will see many attempts to replace the abstract datum (mind-in-general) with the concrete datum (mind-in-particular), even at the peril of a revolutionary upset in the conception of psychology as *science*.

Some of the best known definitions of psychology formulated in the past fifty years have given explicit recognition to the individuality of mind-that is, to its dependence upon the person. But these definitions have not as yet noticeably affected the abstractive tendency of psychological research-not even that of their authors. Wundt, James, and Titchener serve as examples. The first wrote: "It (psychology) *investigates the total content of experience in its relations to the subject.*" The second: *"Psychology is the science of finite*

Abridged from *The American Journal of Psychology*, 1937, 50, 141-156. Reprinted by permission of the author and The American Journal of Psychology.

individual minds;" and the third: *"Psychology is the study of experience considered as dependent on some person."* None of these authors developed his account of mental life to accord with his definition. It is as though some vague sense of propriety guided them in framing their definitions; they *knew* that mind (as a psychological datum) exists only in finite and in personal forms. Yet their historical positions-the spirit of the times in which they worked-prevented them from following their own definitions to the end. Had any one of them done so, the psychology of personality would have had early and illustrious sponsorship.

In line with what I regard as a certain development in the psychology of the future I venture to submit a paper dealing, I think, with the one issue that above all others divides the study of mind-in-general from the study of mind-in-particular. Motivation is the special theme, but the principle involved reaches into every nook and cranny of the evolving science of personality.

TWO KINDS OF DYNAMIC PSYCHOLOGY

Any type of psychology that treats *motives,* thereby endeavoring to answer the question as to *why* men behave as they do, is called a *dynamic psychology.* By its very nature it cannot be merely a descriptive psychology, content to depict the *what* and the *how* of human behavior. The boldness of dynamic psychology in striking for causes stands in marked contrast to the timid, "more scientific," view that seeks nothing else than the establishment of a mathematical function for the relation between some artificially simple stimulus and some equally artificial and simple response. If the psychology of personality is to be more than a matter of coefficients of correlation it too must be a dynamic psychology, and seek first and foremost a sound and adequate theory of the nature of human dispositions.

The type of dynamic psychology almost universally held, though sufficient from the point of view of the *abstract* motives of the generalized mind, fails to provide a foundation solid enough to bear the weight of any *single* full-bodied personality. The reason is that prevailing dynamic doctrines refer every mature motive of personality to underlying original instincts, wishes, or needs, shared *by all men.* Thus, the concert artist's devotion to his music is sometimes 'explained' as an extension of his self-assertive instinct, of the need for sentience, or as a symptom of some Repressed striving of the libido. In McDougall's hormic psychology, for example, it is explicitly stated that only the instincts or propensities can be prime movers. Though capable of extension (on both the receptive and executive sides), they are always few in number, common in all men, and established at birth. The enthusiastic collector of bric-a-brac derives his enthusiasm from the parental instinct; so too does the kindly old philanthropist, as well as the mother of a brood. It does not matter how different these three interests seem to be, they derive their energy from the same source. The principle is that a very few basic motives suffice for explaining the endless varieties of human interests. The psychoanalyst holds the same over-simplified theory. The number of human interests that he regards as so many canalizations of the one basic sexual instinct is past computation.

The authors of this type of dynamic psychology are concerning themselves only with mind-in-general. They seek a classification of the common and basic motives by which to explain both normal or neurotic behavior of *any* individual case. (This is true even though they may regard their own list as heuristic or even as fictional.) The plan really does not work. The very fact that the lists are so different in their composition suggests—what to a naive observer is plain enough—that motives are almost infinitely varied among men, not only in form but in substance. Not four wishes, nor eighteen propensities, nor any and all combinations of these, even with their extensions and variations, seem adequate to account for the endless variety of goals sought by an endless variety of mortals. Paradoxically enough, in many personalities the few simplified needs or instincts alleged to be the *common* ground for all motivation, turn out to be completely lacking.

The second type of dynamic psychology, the one here defended, regards adult motives as infinitely varied, and as self-sustaining, *contemporary* systems, growing out of antecedent systems, but functionally independent of them. Just as a child gradually repudiates his dependence on his parents, develops a will of his own, becomes self-active and self-determining, and outlives his parents, so it is with motives. Each motive has a definite point of origin which may possibly lie in instincts, or, more likely, in the organic tensions of infancy. Chronologically speaking, all adult purposes can be traced back to these seed-forms in infancy, but as the individual matures the tie is broken. Whatever bond remains, is historical, not functional.

Such a theory is obviously opposed to psychoanalysis and to all other genetic accounts that assume inflexibility in the root purposes and drives of life. (Freud says that the structure of the Id *never* changes!) The theory declines to admit that the energies of adult personality are infantile or archiac in nature. Motivation is *always* contemporary. The life of modern Athens is *continuous* with the life of the ancient city, but in no sense *depends* upon its present "go." The life of a tree is continuous with that of its seed, but the seed no longer sustains and nourishes the full grown tree. Earlier purposes lead into later purposes, and are abandoned in their favor.

William James taught a curious doctrine that has been a matter for incredulous amusement ever since, the doctrine of the *transitoriness of instincts*. According to this theory—not so quaint as sometimes thought—an instinct appears but once in a lifetime, whereupon it promptly disappears through its transformation into habits. If there *are* instincts this is no doubt of their fate, for no instinct can retain its motivational force unimpaired after it has been absorbed and recast, under the transforming influence of learning. Such is the reasoning of James, and such is the logic of functional autonomy. The psychology of personality must be a psychology of *post-instinctive* behavior.

Woodworth has spoken of the transformation of "mechanisms" into "drives." A mechanism Woodworth defines as any course of behavior that brings about an adjustment. A *drive* is any neural process that releases mechanisms especially concerned with consummatory reactions. In the course of learning, many preparatory mechanisms must be developed in order to lead to the consummation of an original purpose. These mechanisms are the effective cause of activity in each succeeding mechanism, furnishing the drive for each stage following in the series. Originally all these mechanisms were merely instrumental, only links in the long chain of processes involved in the achievement of an *instinctive* purpose; with time and development, with integration and elaboration, many of these mechanisms become activated directly, setting up a state of desire and tension for activities and objects no longer connected with the original impulse. Activities and objects that earlier in the game were *means* to an end, now become *ends* in themselves.

Although Woodworth's choice of quasi-neurological terminology is not the best, his doctrine, or one like it is indispensable in accounting for the infinite number of effective motives possible in human life, and for their severance from the rudimentary desires of infancy. Further discussion of the operation of the principle and a critique of Woodworth's position will be more to the point after a review of the evidence in favor of principle.

EVIDENCE FOR FUNCTIONAL AUTONOMY

We begin in a common sense way. An ex-sailor has a craving for the sea, a musician longs to return to his instrument after an enforced absence, a city-dweller yearns for his native hills, and a miser continues to amass his useless hords. Now, the sailor may have first acquired his love for the sea as an incident in his struggle to earn a living. The sea was merely a conditioned stimulus associated with satisfaction of his 'nutritional craving.' But now the ex-sailor is perhaps a wealthy banker; the original motive is destroyed; and yet the hunger for the sea persists unabated, even increases in intensity as it becomes more remote from the 'nutritional segment.' The musician may first have been stung by a rebuke or by a slur on his inferior performances into mastering his instrument, but now he is safely beyond the power of these taunts; there is no need to compensate further; now he loves his instrument more than anything else in the world. Once indeed the city dweller may have associated the hills around his mountain home with nutritional and erotogenic satisfactions, but these satisfactions he now finds in his city home, *not* in the mountains; whence then comes all his hill-hunger? The miser perhaps learned his habits of thrift in dire necessity, or perhaps his thrift was a symptom of sexual perversion (as Freud would claim), and yet the miserliness persists, and even becomes stronger with the years, even after the necessity or the roots of the neurosis have been relieved.

Workmanship is a good example of functional autonomy. A good workman feels compelled to do clean-cut jobs even though his security or the praise of others, no longer depends upon high standards. In fact, in a day of jerry-building his workmanlike standards may be to his economic disadvantage. Even so he cannot do a slipshod job. Workmanship is not an instinct, but so firm is the hold it may acquire on a man that it is little wonder Veblen mistook it for one. A business man, long since secure economically, works himself into ill-health, and sometimes even back into poverty, for the sake of carrying on his plans. What was once an instrumental technique becomes a master-motive.

Neither necessity nor reason can make one contented permanently on a lonely island or on an isolated farm after one is adapted to active, energetic city life. The acquired habits seem sufficient to urge one to a frenzied existence, even though reason and health demand the simpler life.

The pursuit of literature, the development of good taste in clothes, the use of cosmetics, the acquiring of an automobile, strolls in the public park, or a winter in Miami-all may first serve, let us say, the interests of sex. But every one of these instrumental activities may become an interest in itself, held for a life time, long after the erotic motive has been laid away in lavender. People often find that they have lost allegiance to their original aims because of their deliberate preference for the many ways of achieving them.

The maternal sentiment offers a final illustration. Many young mothers bear their children unwillingly, dismayed at the thought of the drudgery of the future. At first they may be indifferent to, or even hate their offspring; the 'parental instinct' seems wholly lacking. The only motives that hold such a mother to child-tending may be fear of what her critical neighbors will say, fear of the law, a habit of doing any job well, or perhaps a dim hope that the child will provide security for her in her old age. However gross these motives, they are sufficient to hold her to her work, until through the practice of devotion her burden becomes a joy. As her love for the child develops, her earlier practical motives are forgotten. In later years not one of these original motives may operate. The child may be incompetent, criminal, a disgrace to her, and far from serving as a staff for her declining years, he may continue to drain her resources and vitality. The neighbors may criticize her for indulging the child, the law may exonerate her from allegiance; she certainly feels no pride in such a child; yet she sticks to him. The tenacity of the maternal sentiment under such adversity is proverbial.

Such examples from everyday experience could be multiplied *ad infinitum*. The evidence, however, appears in sharper outline when it is taken from experimental and clinical studies. In each of the following instances some new function emerges as an independently structured unit from preceding functions. The activity of these new units does not depend upon the continued activity of the unit from which they developed.

1. *The circular reflex*. Everyone has observed the almost endless repetition of acts by a child. The good-natured parent who picks up a spoon repeatedly thrown down by a baby wearies of this occupation long before the infant does. Such repetitive behavior, found likewise in early vocalization (babbling), and in other early forms of play, is commonly ascribed to the mechanism of the circular reflex. It is an elementary instance of functional autonomy; for any situation where the consummation of an act provides adequate stimulation for the repetition of the *same* act does not require any backward tracing of motives. The act is self-perpetuating until it is inhibited by new activities or fatigue.

2. *Conative perseveration*. Many experiments show that incompleted tasks set up tensions that tend to keep the individual at work until they are resolved. No Hypothesis of self-assertion, rivalry, or any other basic need, is required. The completion of the task itself has become a quasi-need with dynamic force of its own. It has been shown, for example, that interrupted tasks are better remembered than completed tasks, that an individual interrupted in a task will, even in the face of considerable opposition return to that task, that even trivial tasks undertaken in a casual way become almost haunting in character until they are completed.

Conative perseveration of this order is stronger if an empty interval of time follows the period of work, showing that *left to itself,* without the inhibiting effect of other duties or activities, the motive grows stronger and stronger. The experiment of Kendiz proves this point, as well as that of C. E. Smith. The latter investigator demonstrated that there is more success in removing a conditioned fear if the de-conditioning process is commenced immediately. After a twenty-four hour delay the fear has become set, and is more difficult to eradicate. Hence the sound advice to drivers of automobiles or airplanes who have been involved in an accident, that they drive again immediately to conquer the shock of the accident, lest the fear become set into a permanent phobia. The rule seems to be that unless specifically inhibited all emotional shocks, given time to set, tend to take on a compulsive autonomous character.

3. *Conditioned reflexes not requiring reënforcement*. The pure conditioned reflex readily dies out unless the secondary stimulus is occasionally reënforced by the primary stimulus. The dog does not continue to salivate whenever it hears a bell unless sometimes at least an edible offering accompanies the bell. But there are innumerable instances in human life where a single association, *never* reenforced, results in the establishment of a life-long dynamic system. An experience associated only once with a bereavement, an accident, or a battle, may become the center of a permanent phobia or complex, not in the least dependent on a recurrence of the original shock.

4.   *Counterparts in animal behavior.* Though the validity of a principle in human psychology never depends upon its having a counterpart in animal psychology, still it is of interest to find functional autonomy in the lower organisms. For example, rats, who will first learn a certain habit only under the incentive of some specific tension, as hunger, will, after learning, often perform the habit even when fed to repletion.

Another experiment shows that rats trained to follow a long and difficult path, will for a time persist in using this path, even though a short easy path to the goal is offered and even after the easier path has been learned. Among rats as among human beings, old and useless habits have considerable power in their own right.

Olson studied the persistence of artificially induced scratching habits in rats. Collodion applied to the ears of the animal set up removing and cleaning movements. Four days later the application was repeated. From that time on the animals showed significantly greater number of cleaning movements than control animals. A month after the beginning of the experiment when the ears of the rats as studied by the microscope showed no further trace of irritation, the number of movements was still very great. Whether the induced habit spasm was permanently retained the experiment does not say.

5.   *Rhythm.* A rat whose activity bears a definite relation to his habits of feeding (being greatest just preceding a period of feeding and midway between two such periods) will, even when starved, display the same periodicity and activity. The acquired rhythm persists without dependence on the original periodic stimulation of feeding.

Even a mollusc whose habits of burrowing in the sand and reappearing depend upon the movements of the tide, will, when removed from the beach to the laboratory, continue for several days in the same rhythm without the tide. Likewise certain animals, with nocturnal rhythms advantageous in avoiding enemies, obtaining food, or preventing excessive evaporation from the body, may exhibit such rhythms even when kept in a laboratory with constant conditions of illumination, humidity, and temperature.

There are likewise instances whose acquired rhythms in human life have taken on a dynamic character. Compulsive neurotics enter upon fugues or debauches, apparently not because of specific stimulation, but because "the time has come." A dipsomaniac, in confinement and deprived for months of his alchohol, describes the fierceness of the recurrent appetite (obviously acquired) as follows.

Those craving paroxysms occur at regular intervals, three weeks apart, lasting for several days. They are not weak, nambypamby things for scoffers to laugh at. If not assuaged with liquor they become spells of physical and mental illness. My mouth drools saliva, my stomach and intestines seem cramped, and I become bilious, nauseated, and in a shaky nervous funk.

In such states of drug addiction, as likewise in states of hunger, lust, fatigue, there is to be sure a physical craving, but the rhythms of the craving are partially acquired, and are always accentuated by the mental habits associated with it. For instance, eating in our civilized way of life takes place not because physical hunger naturally occurs three times a day, but because of habitual rhythms of expectancy. The habit of smoking is much more than a matter of craving for the specific narcotic effects of tobacco; it is a craving for the motor ritual and periodic distraction as well.

6. *Neuroses.* Why are acquired tics, stammering, sexual perversions, phobias, and anxiety so stubborn and so often incurable? Even psychoanalysis, with its deepest of depth-probing, seldom succeeds in effecting *complete* cures in such cases, even though the patient may feel relieved or at least reconciled to his difficulties after treatment. The reason seems to be that what are usually called 'symptoms' are in reality something more. They have set themselves up in their own right as independent systems of motivation. Merely disclosing their roots does not change their independent activity.[1]

7. *The relation between ability and interest.* Psychometric studies have shown that the relation between ability and interest is always positive, often markedly so. A person likes to do what he can do well. Over and over again it has been demonstrated that the skill learned for some external reason, turns into an interest, and is self-propelling, even though the original reason for pursuing it has been lost. A student who at first undertakes a field of study in college because it is prescribed, because it pleases his parents, or because it comes at a convenient hour, often finds himself absorbed, perhaps for life, in the subject itself. He is not happy without it. The original motives are entirely lost. What was a means to an end has become an end in itself.

Furthermore, there is the case of genius. A skill takes possession of the man. No primitive motivation is needed to account for his persistent, absorbed activity. It *is* just the alpha and omega of life to him. It is impossible to think of Pasteur's concern for health, food, sleep, or family, as the root of his devotion to his work. For long periods of time he was oblivious of them all, losing himself in the white heat of research for which he had been trained and in which he had *acquired* a compelling and absorbing interest.

A much more modest instance is the finding of industrial research that when special incentives are offered and work speeded up as a consequence,

---

[1]The case of W. E. Leonard, *The Locomotive God*, 1927, is instructive in this regard. An intense phobia was not relieved by tracing its history backward to the start of life. Even though he could explain why he was once frightened for a very good reason (by a locomotive), the author is quite unable to explain why now he is frightened *for no particular reason.* Such neuroses, and psychotic delusional systems as well, often acquire a "strangle hold," and the task of dislodging them is usually more than therapeutic skill is equal to.

and then these special incentives removed, the *work continues at the speeded rate.* The habit of working at a faster tempo persists without external support.

8. *Sentiments vs. instincts.* Every time an alleged instinct can by rigid analysis be demonstated not to be innate but acquired, there is in this demonstration evidence for functional autonomy. It is true enough that material conduct, gregariousness, curiosity, workmanship and the like, have the tenacity and compelling power that instincts are supposed to have. If they are not instincts, then they must be autonomous sentiments with as much dynamic character as has been attributed to instincts. It is not necessary here to review all the arguments in favor of regarding such alleged instincts as acquired sentiments.

9. *The dynamic character of personal values.* When an interest-system has once been formed it not only creates a tensional condition that may be readily aroused, leading to overt conduct in some way satisfying to the interest, but it also acts as a silent agent for selecting and directing any behavior related to it. Take the case of people with strongly marked esthetic interests. Experiments with the word-association test have shown that such people respond more quickly to stimulus-words connected with this interest than to words relating to interests they lack. Likewise, in scanning a newspaper they will observe and remember more items pertaining to art; they also take a greater interest in clothes than do non-esthetic people; and when they are asked to rate the virtues of others, they place esthetic qualities high. In short the existence of a well-established acquired interest exerts a directive and determining effect on conduct just as is to be expected of any dynamic system. The evidence can be duplicated for many interests other than esthetic.

CRITIQUE OF FUNCTIONAL AUTONOMY

Objections to the principle of autonomy may be expected from two sides. Behaviorists will continue to prefer their conception of organic drive with its capacity for manifold conditioning by ever receding stimuli. Whereas purposivists will be unwilling to accept a plurastic principle that seems to leave motives so largely at the mercy of learning.

The behaviorist is well satisfied with motivation in terms of organic drive and conditioning because he feels that he somehow has secure anchorage in physiological structure (The closer he approaches physiological structure the happier the behaviorist is). But the truth of the matter is that the neural physiology of organic drive and conditioning is no better established, and no easier to imagine, than is the neural physiology of the type of complex autonomous units of motivation here described.

Two behavioristic principles will be said to account adequately for the instances of functional autonomy previously cited, viz., the circular reflex and cross-conditioning. The former concept, acceptable enough when applied to infant behavior, merely says that the more activity a muscle engages in, the more activity of the same sort does it engender through a self-sustaining circuit. This is, to be sure, a clear instance of autonomy, albeit on a primitive level, oversimplified so far as adult conduct is concerned. The doctrine of cross-conditioning refers to subtle recession of the stimuli, and to the intricate possibility of cross-connections in conditioning. For instance, such ubiquitous external stimuli as humidity, daylight, gravitation, may feed collaterally into open channels of activity, arousing mysteriously and unexpectedly a form of conduct to which they have unconsciously been conditioned. For example, the angler whose fishing expeditions have been accompanied by sun, wind, or a balmy June day, may feel a desire to go fishing whenever the barometer, the thermometer, or the calendar in his city home tells him that these conditions prevail. Innumerable such crossed stimuli are said to account for the arousal of earlier patterns of activity.

Such a theory inherits, first of all, the well-known difficulties resident in the principle of conditioning whenever it is made the sole explanation of human behavior. Further, though the reflex circle and cross-conditioning may in fact exist, they are really rather trivial principles. They leave the formation of interest and its occasional arousal almost entirely to chance factors of stimulation. They give no picture at all of the spontaneous and variable aspects of traits, interest, or sentiments. These dispositions are regarded as purely *reactive* in nature; the stimulus is all-important. The truth is that dispositions *sort out* stimuli congenial to them, and this activity does not in the least resemble the rigidity of reflex response.[2]

A variant on the doctrine of cross-conditioning is the principles of red-integration. This concept admits the existence of highly integrated dispositions of neuropsychic order. These dispositions can be aroused *as a whole* by any stimulus previously associated with their functioning. In this theory likewise, the disposition is regarded as a rather passive affair, waiting for reactivation by some portion of the original stimulus. Here again the variability of the disposition and its urge-like quality are not accounted for. The stimulus is thought merely to reinstate a complex determining tendency. Nothing is said about how the stimuli themselves are selected, why a motive once aroused becomes insistent, surmounting obstacles, skillfully subordinating conflicting impulses, and inhibiting irrelevant trains of thought.

---

[2]The basic facts that complex "higher" centers have the power of inhibiting, selecting, and initiating the activity of simpler segmental responses is a fact too well established to need elaboration here. It constitutes the very foundation of the psychophysiological theories advanced by Sherrington, Herrick, Dodge, Kohler, Troland, and many others.

In certain respects the principle of autonomy stands midway between the behavioristic view and the thorough going purposive psychology of the hormic order. It agrees with the former in emphasizing the acquisition of motives, in avoiding an a priori and unchanging set of original urges, and in recognizing (as limited principles) the operation of the circular response and cross-conditioning. It agrees with the hormic psychologist, however, in finding that striving-from-within is a far more essential characteristic of motive than stimulation-from-without. It agrees likewise in distrusting the emphasis upon stomach contractions and other "excess and deficit stimuli" as "causes" of mature behavior. Such segmental sources of energy even when conditioned cannot possibly account for the "go" of conduct. But functional autonomy does not rely as does hormic theory upon modified instinct, which after all is as archaic a principle as the conditioning of autonomic segmental tensions, but upon the capacity of human beings to replenish their energy through a plurality of constantly changing systems of a dynamic order.

The hormic psychologist, however, will not accept the autonomy of new motivational systems. If mechanisms can turn into drives, he asks, why is it that habits and skills as they become exercised to the point of perfection do not acquire an ever increasing driving force? The mechanisms of walking, speaking, or dressing, cannot be said to furnish their own motive-power. One walks, speaks, or dresses in order to satisfy a motive entirely external to these learned skills.[3]

The criticism is sufficiently cogent to call into question Woodworth's form of stating the principle, viz., "mechanisms may become drives." It is not an adequate statement of the case.

Looking at the issue more closely it seems to be neither the perfected talent nor the automatic habit that has driving power, but the imperfect talent and the habit-in-the-making. The child who is *just learning* to speak, to walk, or to dress is, in fact, likely to engage in these activities for their own sake, precisely as does the adult who has an *unfinished* task in hand. He remembers it, returns to it, and suffers a feeling of frustration if he is prevented from engaging in it. Motives are always a kind of striving for some form of completion; they are unresolved tension, and demand a "closure" to activity under way. (Latent motives are dispositions that are easily thrown by a stimulus or by a train of associations into this state of active tension.) The active motive subsides when its goal is reached, or in the case of a motor skill, when it has become at last automatic. The novice in automobile driving has an unquestionable impulse to master the skill. Once acquired the ability sinks to the level of an *instrumental* disposition and

[3]Though this objection is usually valid, it is not always so, for there are cases where the liking for walks, for talking for the sake of talking, or for dressing, playing games, etc., seems to be a self-sustaining motivational system.

is aroused only in the service of some other *driving* (unfulfilled) motive.

Now, in the case of the permanent interests of personality, the situation is the same. A man whose motive is to acquire learning, or to perfect his craft, can never be satisfied that he has reached the end of his quest, for his problems are never completely solved, his skill is never perfect. Lasting interests are recurrent sources of discontent, and from their incompleteness they derive their forward impetus. Art, science, religion, love, are never perfected. Motor skills, however, are often perfected and beyond that stage they seldom provide their own motive power. It is, then, only mechanisms-on-the-make (in process of perfecting) that serves as drives. With this emendation, Woodworth's view is corrected, and McDougall's objection is met.[4]

IMPLICATIONS OF FUNCTIONAL AUTONOMY

The principle of functional autonomy accounts, as no other principle of dynamic psychology is able to do, for the concrete impulses that lie at the root of personal behavior. It is thus the first step in establishing a basis for the more realistic study of unique and individual forms for personality. "But how—" the traditionalists may cry, "how are we ever to have a *science* of unique events? Science must generalize." So it must, but it is a manifest error to assume that a general principle of motivation must involve the postulation of abstract or general motives. What the objectors forget is that *a general law may be a law that tells how uniqueness comes about.*

The principle of functional autonomy is general enough to meet the needs of science, but particularized enough in its operation to account for the uniqueness of personal conduct. Its specific advantages stand out in the following summary.

(1)   It clears the way for a completely dynamic psychology of *traits, attitudes, interests, and sentiments,* which can now be regarded as the ultimate and true dispositions of the mature personality.

(2)   It avoids the absurdity of regarding the energy of life now, in the *present,* as somehow consisting of early archaic forms (instincts, prepotent reflexes, or the never-changing Id). Learning brings new systems of interests into existence just as it does new abilities and skills. At each stage of development these interests are always contemporary, whatever drives, drives *now.*

(3)   It dethrones the stimulus. A motive is no longer regarded as a mechanical reflex or as a matter of redintegration, depending entirely upon the capricious operation of a conditioned stimulus. In a very real sense dispositions *select* the stimuli to which they respond, even though *some* stimulus is required for their arousal.

----

[4]This theory embraces very easily the work of K. Lewin and his associates upon the nature of "quasi-needs." The urgency of these needs is greatest just before a goal is reached, after which time the motive subsides completely.

(4) It readily admits the validity of all other established principles of growth. Functional autonomy recognizes the products of differentiation, integration, maturation, exercise, imitation, suggestion, conditioning, trauma, and all other processes of development; and allows, as they do not, considered by themselves, for the preservation of these products in significant motivational patterns.

(5) It places in proper perspective the problems of the origin of conduct by removing the fetish of the genetic method. Not that the historical view of behavior is unimportant for a complete understanding of personality, but so far as *motives* are concerned the cross-sectional dynamic analysis is more significant. Motives being always contemporary should be studied in their present structure. Failure to do so is probably the chief reason why psychoanalysis meets so many defeats, as do all other therapeutic schemes relying too exclusively upon uncovering the motives of early childhood.

(6) It accounts for the force of delusions, shell-shock, phobias, and all manner of compulsive and maladaptive behavior. One would expect such unrealistic modes of adjustment to be given up as they are shown to be poor ways of confronting the environment. Insight and the law of effect should both remove them—but too often they have acquired a strangle hold in their own right.

(7) At last we can account adequately for socialized and civilized behavior. The principle supplies the correction necessary to the faulty logic of *bellum omnium contra omnes.* Starting life, as a completely selfish being, the child would indeed remain entirely wolfish and piggish throughout his days unless genuine transformations of motives took place. Motives being completely alterable, the dogma of Egoism turns out to be a callow and superficial philosophy of behavior, or else a useless redundancy.

(8) It explains likewise why a person often *becomes* what at first he merely *pretends* to be—the smiling professional hostess who grows fond of her once irksome role and is unhappy when deprived of it; the man who for so long has counterfeited the appearance of self-confidence and optimism that he is always driven to assume it; the prisoner who comes to love his shackles. Such *personae,* as Jung observes, are often transformed into the real self. The mask becomes the *anima.*

(9) The drive behind genius is explained. Gifted people demand the exercise of their talents, even when no other reward lies ahead. In lesser degree the various hobbies, the artistic, or the intellectual interests of any person show the same significant autonomy.

(10) In brief, the principle of functional autonomy is a declaration of independence for the psychology of personality. Though in itself a general law, at the same time it helps to account, not for the abstract motivation of an impersonal and therefore non-existent mind-in-general, but for the concrete, viable motives of each and every mind-in-particular.

13. A Critique of Gordon W. Allport's Theory of Motivation

Peter A. Bertocci

IN *Personality: A Psychological Interpretation,* Professor Gordon W. Allport presents a theory of human motivation and personality development which is designed to account for the uniqueness, variety, and continuity of personal growth. With his mind trained on these undeniable phases of personality, Allport evaluates various attempts to account for them but finds each theory, including instincts, incapable of providing an adequate theoretical basis for individuality. His own solution is in terms of functional autonomy and traits.

In this first part I propose a defense of an essentially McDougallian theory of motivation against Allport's objections. In the second part I shall try to indicate the difficulties which Allport's theory of traits encounters and the necessity of a more adequate motivational base for traits.

Hormic theory should profit much from the avalanche of criticism which Allport lets loose on the instinct hypothesis. In his discussion many criticisms repeatedly directed in current textbooks against a McDougallian view are strengthened and focussed on the problem of personality. Nor can one accuse him, as he might others, of throwing word-javelins like 'not scientific' at the distorted dummy of instinct! Hence, it is all the more desirable that Allport's criticisms should be carefully reviewed as we study his view of original human nature.

I

INSTINCTS VERSUS UNIQUE MOTIVES

1. The "Givens" of Human Personality

That there is "some Original Cause or Source of Animation is assumed explicitly or implicitly by all biological and psychological sciences."[1] Con-

Abridged from the *Psychological Review,* 1940, 47, 501-532. Reprinted by permission of the author and the American Psychological Association, Inc.

[1]All quotations and references involving Allport are from *Personality: A Psychological Interpretation,* New York: Henry Holt and Co., 1937.

troversy arises only when the exact nature of the dynamic force reflected in the stream of living activity is probed. As Allport suggests, the postulates of a vitalistic Horme, Will, or Élan Vital, and of a "more scientific-sounding principle of 'Protoplasmic Irritability,' " are both equally mysterious. Hence he passes over the controversy and begins with the "observable stream of activity." On his view, this stream of activity is differentiated at birth into gross patterns of random movement or into specific reflexes. These activities in turn are "set into motion and sustained" through the sensitivity of the organism's receptors and *either* by segmental drives or tensions such as hunger and thirst *or* by goal-seeking processes (instincts, needs, or entelechies). Allport makes clear, however, that many psychologists including himself regard goal-seeking processes as "a superfluous assumption." We may note to begin with, therefore, that for Allport to favor segmental drives or tensions rather than goal-seeking processes would seem to head him toward the mechanistic postulate of protoplasmic irritability. In his choice between mysteries he favors, in infancy at least, non-hormic, mechanistic postulates.

In pursuing our analysis we need not dwell on the remaining "givens" of personality which are employed in the differentiated stream of activity: intelligence, temperament, physique, and adapative mechanisms, like maturation, conditioning, and integration. Let us turn directly to Allport's objections to goal-seeking processes.

2. *The Essence of McDougall's Theory*

The problem is well put in the question Allport raises: "Does the primordial stream of activity contain within itself directions which determine its own course of development?" Is there any propensity in the individual which, according to McDougall's definition, "determines the individual to perceive (pay attention to) any given object of a certain class and to experience in its presence . . . an impulse to action which finds expression in a specific mode of behavior in relation to that object"? I have left out of this description the words "a certain emotional excitement" which McDougall thinks is always present in propensitive activity, for I am interested in defending the essential aspects of innate motivation rather than the specific variations different psychologists may introduce.[2] The

---

[2]It is important to note that McDougall himself emphasizes the goal-seeking phase of propensitive behavior. In *Energies of Men,* he especially states: "In higher mammals each innate propensity is recognizable only through the *general nature* of the goal (italics mine) towards which it sets, toward which it impels, and from the attainment

essence of a defensible theory seems to me to be the contention that the human psycho-physiological organism does, independent of training or learning, orient itself, as it responds to the environment, in directions intrinsic to that organism (but not necessarily operating under *any* conditions). That is to say, on the human level we should insist that goal-directed activities do not operate automatically and in machine-like fashion as to the *means* of achieving the goals toward which they strive.[3] The actual means chosen for the expression or achievement of the general directions intrinsic to organismic functioning depend on the abilities possessed by the organism and by the environmental situation. We are now ready to consider specific objections to such a theory, which, to summarize, holds that human psycho-physiological organisms share common goal-seeking processes which predetermine *in a general way only* the directions of active response.

3.   *The Argument Against Maturation*

First, as Allport says, instinctivists, confronted by the lack of "such elaborately purposive dispositions" in newborn infants, have found it necessary to claim that goal-seeing processes take time to mature at different levels.

But surely there is no logical or psychological absurdity involved here? Whether he believes in instincts or not, any psychologist must appeal to maturation to explain unlearned development. Why should the instinctivist be denied this same appeal? Can his opponent quote the stanza and verse of empirical evidence against, say, the maturational development of self-assertive and sympathetic behavior? The empirical study of Lois G. Murphy, *Social Behavior and Child Personality,* which outlines the development of sympathy, reveals what can be done to support the instinctivist at this point. To be sure, the instinctivist must continue to support his view of temporal maturation not only by logical argument but by gathering data indicating the advent of a new drive.

4.   *The Argument from Parsimony*

The second difficulty Allport suggests against the instinctivists' 'some-

---

of which satisfaction results." The emphasis here is on the general nature of the end, not the specific manner or means of expression. On the same page, McDougall classified himself with those who, "fixing their attention upon general propensities towards goals common to the species (rather than upon innate abilities)," regard these goals "as of the essence of instinct," and maintain that "the life of man is just as truly rooted in instincts as that of animals."

[3]With McDougall we would use the word instinct strictly speaking for the exclusive or restrictive gearing of abilities to particular goals, and reserve the term propensities for the relatively loose gearing of abilities to various innate goals.

what extravagant portrayal of human purposes' is: "It seems to many psychologists to violate unnecessarily the requirement of parsimony in a scientific theory." This objection, the unnecessary violation of the law of parsimony, constitutes the basic logical objection Allport aims at the instinct theory. It is obvious that there are many individuals in whom particular instincts, like the acquisitive, or gregarious, or parental, do not appear. Hence, the instinctivist is forced to the extravagant logical alternative (for Allport) of explaining away exceptions to the universality of given instincts, a procedure which is "not simpler" than accounting for the various types of interests, "if and when they are present."

Dealing with this objection on the purely logical level, we must grant that the instinctivists may have violated the law of parsimony. But an objection from parsimony is *logically conceivable* against any theory of personality development. It must be remembered, however, that reality is not the servant of the law of parsimony. Unless the actual empirical evidence is adduced in favor of a second simpler theory which still does justice to the total data, any appeal to parsimony against the instinct-theory is gratuitous. Logic aside, in matter of fact Allport does *not* provide specific evidence against the instinctivist's view that the lack of universal drives in particular individuals is due to special conditions explaining the exceptions. Indeed, here the instinctivist is supported by the usual procedure of science. When psychologists, for example, attribute general or universal characteristics to man they thereby demarcate (in part) the definition of normal man. The normal man is normal, we are told, because in common with other persons who are men he enjoys certain characteristics. If he is normal, he may be expected to enjoy, for example, a certain number of senses, glands, vertebrae, etc. . . . The fact that a man turns up without one of these general characteristics does not destroy the class, but it does qualify his normality! We do not give up the classification because some creatures do not live up to it in part.

In other words, any thinker who generalizes is forced to explain the exception to the rule which seems to him to embrace the data most adequately. Complex and unstructured data can be organized and clarified much more conveniently if they lend themselves to generalizations which then help to call attention to the exceptions. It is much simpler logically and methodologically to organize data thus than to proceed as if there were no common characteristics (if one could proceed at all under such conditions!). Exceptions can be explained by appealing to other general principles (such as maturation, or environment, or ability) as they apply to the specific case.

Having indicated the scientific procedure underlying his plea, the instinctivist can also defend himself on independent grounds against the charge of theoretical extravagance. For instinctivists of the type here defended do not claim that human goals are expressed regardless of individual ability

and environmental stimulation. Particular individuals may have been subjected to training or conditions that would inhibit in their lives the active
expression of goals which the majority of mankind pursue. The woman
whose behavior shows no indication of a felt parental urge, who in fact hates
babies, turns out, as in one instance, to be the girl whose mother and father
had been very brutal, had resented her birth, and wanted to "dump me in
the ash-can." This woman wanted nothing to do with children or, more,
with marriage, because she was determined not to be in a predicament that
would even lead to the temptation of mistreating her child. Indeed, one
might say, not that she lacked the parental urge, but that she was obsessed
by the fear of a possible denial of its fulfillment in a desired way. The explanation of such exceptions is by no means a psychological monstrosity.
Are her actions, in fact, not explicable by her desire to be tender to helpless
offspring?

5. *The Argument from Individuality of Purpose*

The heart of Allport's critique of instinct-theory, however, is found in
his refusal to "view personality as a matter of individual modification of
universal instincts or common needs." So many are the permutations of
personality that no verifiable list of instincts would be adequate to explain
them. "But are not the purposes of different people far too diverse and too
numerous to be traced to a few primal motives shared by all the species?"
Once more Allport is appealing to *psychological conceivability,* for, asking
this question, he treats it as one which involves a negative answer. Here
we are nearing the crux of the problem, the explanation of uniqueness.

The plea for uniqueness considered. The inspection of individuals certainly reveals a multiplicity and variety of purposes. Uniqueness lies about
and within us. This fact is basic to future discussion on either view.

Still, to accept uniqueness as alone ultimate is to destroy the possibility
of rational knowledge of any sort. Uniqueness can be felt, lived through,
but not expressed or understood in relation to other common factors. If
it is ultimate, as it seems, there could be no justifiable public knowledge of
it. Now it might well have seemed psychologically inconceivable that this
intricate universe, from the peculiarities of this paper and ink to the peculiarities of the Milky Way, exhibited common elements. Nevertheless,
common characteristics indicative of ninety-two classes of physical elements
have been found to be present in the multiform diversities expressed in the
known physical universe.

So also, similarity, common goals of striving, may be found common to
the apparent variations of human purposes. One thing is certain, that in
similarity or recurrence there is dependability and understanding. If a view
can be suggested which allows both for universality and for individuality of
purposive striving, then psychology may contribute much to the explana-

tion of human behavior in its individual, social, and political manifestations. Hence, apart from specific evidence showing that certain common directions of striving do not exist, psychology would do well to search for whatever universality may be found in human motivation. Without dependable common factors (even within the individual's life temporally studied) there is no theoretical basis for statistical prediction, let alone a more adequate understanding of human *natures*.

Specifically, it makes all the difference in the world for me to be able to anticipate certain kinds of actions from my fellowmen. With certain hypotheses in mind as to the goals his activities can be depended upon to express, I can orient myself until I discover which of the drives are being satisfied by certain activities in this particular individual. Of course I shall never be able to understand him completely as a particular concretion of unique desire, abilities, and temperament. My understanding can assimilate unique individuality only by noting the extent to which it is similar to and different from other individuals known to me. Again, I am quite likely to make mistakes in determining whether a given human act is an expression in a particular situation of one motive (sympathy) or another (fear). But if I must confront an individual with *no* hypothesis about his basic wants, I have nothing at all to guide me in interpreting the behavior of this biped before me. There must be some common bridge between us, or we strain forever to join hands of understanding. There can be no understanding without common characteristics: The individual is never completely understood because, in his individual nature the class-concept cannot find him except negatively. We cannot give up the search for the common pattern underlying various purposes simply because our predecessors and contemporaries disagree about the number and kinds of irreducible unlearned motives!

Nor should we pass on without noting that, despite the so-called disagreement among instinctivists, an inspection of recent psychological literature reveals considerable unanimity with regard to the innateness of hunger, sex, fear, and anger, while learned derivations like mastery, recognition, curiosity, sympathy, adventure, submissiveness are repeated so often as to seem inevitable components of human motivation. The very fact that they are chosen indicates that they are recognized as unusually dominant, common, though learned, motives.

Explanation of common purposes in terms of culture. Allport realizes that people do seek goals in common. His explanation of the fact is the critical point in question. "When people do seek the same goals, may the fact not be explained by the more parsimonious assumption that similarly constructed individuals living in similar environment, influenced by similar culture, would develop similar goals and employ similar modes of obtaining them?" The individuals referred to here are similarly constructed in that they possess "that degree of homogeneity which the human species shows including a few biological drives more uniform in infancy than in later life."[4] Such individuals, interacting in a similar environment, will learn the similar goals which the instinctivist mistakenly considers to be innate.

We shall treat the transformation of infantile uniform drives in Part II. Here we must ask a more fundamental question: Does the actual psychological predicament of individuals allow us to take a similar environment for granted? Can there be a similar environment for individuals unless these persons already possess, along with similar abilities, similar innate goal-seeking tendencies?

It would seem to me that no two *similarly* endowed individuals live in the abstract, similar environment, mentioned here. The psychological situation to which Allport is committed envisions an individual, plastic within limits, confronted with an environment which is psychologically unstructured. The *geographical* environment of things and people makes possible for him and his neighbors an indefinite number of *behaviorial* environments. His actual choice among stimuli is determined by his abilities and the guidance of his culture, to be sure. But one cannot explain the similarity of goals by appealing to the similarity or identity of cultural pressure. For the culture itself needs to be explained, since culture exists, after all, in individuals who construct this common thing called culture. To explain the similarity of individuals by culture is to overlook the basic cause of culture and its similarity in the first place.

If individuals did not have common motives to begin with, would they ever build a shareable culture even though they were blessed with equal abilities? This same point may be developed with regard to the similar non-social environment.

So far as we know, the similarity of 'physical' environment consists not in mere structural similarities, but in their *functional equivalence*. But functional equivalence depends largely upon what the individuals require or want from the forces beyond themselves. Our private worlds become public, common environments because our abilities for action and discernment are similar. But our abilities do not find their sphere of operation all alone. They operate in a world to which they have already been directed by needs, lacks, or urges. If the abilities of two individuals were the same and their purposes different, it is quite probable that they would partition incoming stimuli into compartments suiting their different interests. If they had no common strivings to begin with, even given similar abilities they would not develop common behaviorial environments. Our known environments are always by-products of our total natures and the nature of the independent world. Accordingly, to have a common environment we must have, to begin with, not only common abilities but commonness of goal-

---

[4]Quoted from personal correspondence.

seeking which directs us in the same directions as we exploit incoming stimuli. Hence, the attempt to derive similar goals from a non-purposive individual by resorting to a similar environment involves putting the cart before the horse. For the environment became functionally similar because men with common goals harnessed abilities to the satisfaction of those goals in a given situation. Unless you begin with individuals who have common purposes (circumscribed in expression by abilities) how can you have a common human world enjoyed by men on this planet (as opposed to that of animals)?

If this reasoning is valid, the appeal to a similar environment to explain common goals fails. Indeed, the existence of a common environment is additional evidence in favor of innate goal-seeking tendencies, even though a particular list be inadequate. We seem forced to conclude that the psychological organism is constituted both by abilities and by fundamental purposes, and that the two work together from the beginning of individual existence to modify each other and be modified by external stimuli. Because individuals do have relatively common abilities and common purposes, they find themselves seeking and satisfying the same objectives in an independent geographical environment. On no other ground does the similarity of human culture (as opposed to animal modes of living) seem to be explicable. Meanwhile, the differences between individuals and culture can be largely explained not by giving up instincts, but by differences present in the offerings of Nature and the abilities of the individual.

6. Can Purposive Action be Derived from Non-Purposive Activity?

Our basic contention that innate goal-seeking tendencies participate in, rather than result from, the construction of the cultural and behavioral world (which in turn modifies them) must now face the attack from another source. For Allport asks: "Are the directions of striving after all innately determined? Is it not necessary to allow for the learning of *new* motives and for the acquisition of *novel* interests as personality matures?" If Allport's criticism of instinct were valid, instinct would "turn out to be nothing more than constellations of emotions, habit, foresight, better called *sentiments* or *interests,* and regarded as acquired rather than innate. Learning would then serve not merely as a way of extending and modifying purposes, but also *creating* them." Our attention must now be focused, therefore, on the problem: Can urges be acquired or created?

The meaning of 'newly-created interests.' Let us first be clear as to the meaning of *created,* and the sense in which the instinctivist would have to use the term. The creation of an entity involves the creation *outright* of an entirely new or novel quality or thing, the abrogation of its continuity with what preceded it so far as human knowledge is concerned. To maintain that new interests or purposes are created involves, therefore, the premise that new interests or needs occur in the organism (by other means than maturation of the givens) without any continuity in essential *quality* and *direction* with the givens.

Instinctivists of the McDougallian type would deny that there can be creation of purposes in this sense. Learning is not the process of creating interests which add outright to the purposive tendencies involved in the givens of the organism. On McDougall's view, to be a human being is to be limited (though plastic) to certain basic motives or generic directive urges.

But no psychologist talks about the outright creation of a new ability within the life-time of a given individual. A 'new' ability would be a particular, environmentally provoked, development of a given ability. What fact alters the use of this same logic when we come to motivation? Surely then we cannot speak of the outright creation of an interest, but rather of the manifestation or modification of a basic tendency in accordance with available abilities and possibilities.

The instinctivist, therefore, uses the term *create* in its secondary sense, of proximiate (rather than ultimate) creation. McDougall might well talk of the creation of a proximate motive, the sentiment—which, as we recall, is the product of learning as ultimate needs seek satisfaction in particular situations. The main directions of striving are not created. For example, curiosity is not a creation but is a given motive. But in a particular environmental situation the individual finds, with his abilities, a certain means of satisfying that curiosity which becomes the focus for a sentiment of curiosity.

The claim that basic motives can be created is weakened when we realize what would be involved by outright creation as opposed to modification. But our difficulty increases when we confront the fact that in Allport's view purposive activity is not only acquired but derived from givens that are mechanistic in learning, namely, protoplasmic irritability! The concept of purpose may be inscrutable, but it is not more inscrutable to say the least, than emergent evolutions of purpose especially in a theory with mechanistic postulates. We are now touching on the problem of transformation of motives which is left for extended treatment in the next part. But here we must pause to urge further caution. To say that through learning we create interests is to load the dice gratuitously against the probability that learning presupposes original motivation.

To be sure, any psychology of motivation must allow for the learning of new motives. The novelties in human motivation are the empirical facts which break the back of any mechanical theory of instinct as the mere unfolding of a pattern of life pre-ordained in detail. For such an "unfolding" theory makes learning nonsensical and cannot explain novelties of development. But to substitute for such a view of instinct an organism devoid of lines of purpose (and yet capable of acquiring them!) is also to fly in the face of reasonable and empirical probability, unless one thinks it is an empirical probability that we have "similar" environments, and being non-purposive, can become purposive!

The bareness of the Will-to-Live: The careful student of Allport might interpose an embarrasing question at this point. "You have been imputing mechanistic meanings to Professor Allport without taking into consideration passages which clearly favor the purposive 'Will-to-Live'!" Does he not say, "goals and purposes are not inherited unless one grants the vague primordial need-to-live?" Again, "All motives—diverse as they are—*may* be regarded as so many channels of the original Will-to-Live." Such a monistic underpinning to a theory of motivation is preferable to a list of arbitrarily distinguished propensities or instincts. "But, as was previously pointed out, the Will-to-Live, however acceptable it may be in the under-lying metaphysics of personality, does not in itself aid in the task of psychological analysis." On page 170 he speaks of the "vague, though unquestionable primordial 'will to live.' "

These passages speak for themselves. The Will-to-Live seems to be accepted as a metaphysical possibility which has no particular psychological explanatory value. At one point it is considered to be synonymous with the self-esteem which is "basically co-extensive with life itself," and "enters into all sentiments and traits, which are after all merely channels of the primordial (non-psychological) life-principle." It would be indeed a 'psychological redundancy' and question-begging as an explanatory principle. "It must be broken up and studied in its manifold operations."

All in all one cannot claim that Allport takes the Will-to-Live seriously at the psychological level. At one point he prefers it to a pluralistic theory of instincts, and at another he thinks it must be broken up to be at all useful. Since he does not consider it any more than a psychologically 'harmless' hypothesis, he seriously impairs, as we have seen and shall see, the internal consistency and continuity of his system. It is a curious "metaphysical abstraction" indeed which holds that the ultimate reality of human nature has little effect on the apparent, phenomenal reality!

It would, in fact, be surprising if such a bare and empty concept could have meaning in any realm, metaphysical, or psychological, or demonological! What can the concept mean? The emphasis is on 'live,' but the very point at issue is the concrete meaning of living for human beings. The instinctivists have been trying to overcome the vacuity, the vagueness, and the harmlessness (!) of the doctrine by indicating that *to live equals to want certain goals achieved*. The Will-to-Live is something-I-know-not-what until it is defined by the acutal empirical goals. To reduce instinctivists' goals to a vague Will-to-Live and then to consign the Will-to-Live to vaguer metaphysical regions is, unfortunately, a double-edged method which destroys both sides alike.

7. The Existential Referent of 'General Goal'

Nevertheless, one cannot blame the psychologist of personality for fighting shy of any formulation of human motives which "misrepresent them" by saying that they are "only changes rung upon universal themes."

As a matter of fact, it may well be that the observation of the more mechanical operation of pre-arranged structure and function in animals has prejudiced the interpretation of innate motivation in humans. At any rate, the very phrase 'modification of generic purposes' is a very unfortunate one, foisted upon us by economy of expression but leading almost inevitably to inferences totally incongruous with the data. Since I have used the phrase myself, the last section of this part must be devoted to clarification of phrases like the 'particularization or modification of general goals.'

A moment's careful reflection reveals that there cannot be in concrete human beings 'general abilities' or 'general goals.' There is no such reality as Life in general. As Allport says in a statement to which the remainder of his book is a commentary, "Life exists in individual forms." The term Life refers to a common pattern of function penetrating the individuals to whom it is attributed. Life does not exist before living beings or apart from them.

So also there are no pre-existing general goals. All actual, existential goal-seeking, as opposed to the conceptual description of it, is specific and individual. One never seeks food in general or recognition in general, but his actual seeking is always undergoing particular psycho-physiological processes in relation to particular foods, people, and so on.

The concept of the generality of goals, on the other hand, results from our recognition or realization that not only in the particular striving of the individual, but also in that of large numbers of individuals, there is a recurrence of the same function or pattern, the assimilation of the environment for equivalent satisfactions. The common pattern which is abstracted, for descriptive purposes, from the individual strivings is never exhaustive of the uniqueness and detail of the particular acts of striving which in turn exemplify to some extent, in some novel way, the common functioning. The statement: "Men hunger for food," is a highly abstract description of the concrete unique hunger-pangs and the concrete, unique foodseeking which are actually involved.

The instinctivist, then, is really led to his claim, that there are universal goal-seeking tendencies in men which develop in a variety of ways, dependent upon ability and environment, by an empirical generalization based upon his observation of the similarity pervading or persisting through the specific strivings of men. Hence, his particular empirical generalizations may fail to be valid because his classification of concrete interests may be a distortion or forcing of the data, but mistakes in empirical generalizations are to be held against the observer and interpreter rather than against the broad outlines of his theory.

To be sure, if this similarity of objectives could be accounted for by the similarity of environment, the instinctivist would be confronted by a serious alternative, but we have dealt with this objection. The instinctivist, though he may fail to subsume the manifold interests of man accurately, may still insist on his basic tenet, that striving, in directions to be revealed as the individual develops according to his abilities in his world, is an unlearned dynamic aspect of human nature which creates the problem of goal-fulfillment in particular environments.

II

PROPENSITIES, FUNCTIONAL AUTONOMY, AND TRAITS

1.   The Limitations of Infantile Motives

As we have noted, Allport renounces the instinct-hypothesis in favor of drives originating in persistent intraorganic stimuli. But this drive-hypothesis does justice only to infantile motivation and is to be considered merely as a 'starting point' for a theory of adult motivation. "After the level of infancy is passed primitive segmental drive rapidly recedes *in importance* [italics mine], being supplanted [note the word] by the more sophisticated type of motives characteristic of mature personality, and commonly represented by such terms as instinct, sentiment, value, trait. . . attitude."

According to the drive-hypothesis, especially as developed by E. J. Kempf, the organic cravings (of nutrition, sex and fear) account, by way of conditioning, for the rest of man's desires. The filial sentiment, for example, develops from the child's first connecting his mother with the satisfaction of bodily needs and then keeping that new attachment even when the specific organic craving is lacking.

But Allport, though accepting this biological theory, in its "broader outline," as a starting point, nevertheless condemns it for "its superficial conception of learning."

> It is all to easy to say that the primitive organic tensions become conditioned and by a bit of verbal magic to think that one has accounted for all the motives of the adult person whose desires include not only nutritional and sexual satisfaction but likewise fine music, rare books and the answer to puzzling problems in science, politics, and theology. What really happens is that an elaborate process of learning and growth intervenes between the

organic wants of infancy and the cultural wants of adulthood involving all manner of linguistic, imaginal, and rational factors
that ultimately *transform* [italics mine] the segmental cravings of
infancy into desires having no longer any functional connection
with them, but holding in their own right an autonomous place in
personal life.

Thus Allport consistently rejects any list of instincts or drives which
would presume to be 'all-sufficient' for the whole life of an individual. For
any person, as he develops, transforms such simple drives in the process of
finding modes of expression which themselves come to function as drives
independently of their sources. Consequently, Allport introduces his theory
of functionally autonomous traits which become theoretical substitutes for
instincts in individuals past the stages of infancy. Impressed as he justly is
with the uniqueness of personality as it develops, Allport is as much, if not
more, concerned to point out the *consistency within uniqueness* of personality development, bounded as that is by temperament and environmental
forces. Significant reference is made to the manner in which "distinctive
qualities noticed early in life tend to persist."

In other words, because Allport is concerned to emphasize the uniqueness of personality against an instinct-theory, his own theory must adequately deal with the basic problem of the psychology of personality,
namely, the unity and continuity as well as uniqueness and differentiation
of personality; in fact, one should say the distinctive continuity and the
distinctive differentiation of normal personal experience. But will the principle of functional autonomy do justice to the datum, namely, the observable continuity of personal development?

It is obvious, furthermore, that the principle of functional autonomy assumes especial importance in Allport's psychology of personality. For it
must avoid the fixity of instinct-views, the cloudiness and limitations of
physiological explanations, and yet keep intact the continuity, unity, and
differentiation of personality. Since all accounts of such integrative growth in
physiological terms are "still in the limbo of scientific mystery," Allport
finds additional grounds for his statement: "The characteristics of integration
are known far better through psychological investigations."

So clear and emphatic is Allport's decision to "escape from the deceptive
snare of pseudo-physiology," so firm is he in his agreement with J. S. Mill
that the psychological level of description is preferable to the physiological,
that one cannot refrain from asking: But why begin with the psychological
(purposive) level of description at the age of two or three? What is so clear
about 'organic tensions' in infancy which warrants a change in the nature
and level of description for that period? In the last analysis, the inadequacy
of explanations in organic terms lies in their inability to account for the
functional or *purposive* data of human experience. For this very reason the

hormist starts with the psychic level of purposive striving and maintains it throughout.

Allport would accept a "push" in infancy and a "pull" in later life as a tenable theory of motivation.[5] "Push" and "pull" might both be consistent with the premise of an *élan vital* which Allport would now favor to a non-purposive protoplasmic irritability. We previously pointed out the difficulty with a so completely vague abstraction as the *élan vital*. Here we need simply comment that if the non-purposive "push" of infancy gives way to the purposive "pull" of increasing maturity, we are left with another mystery. Whence the purposes which later appear in human behavior? By what magic are these new purposes born? Are they sprung full-born from the head of Zeus? Granted that Allport has committed himself, tacitly at least, to an ontogenetic emergent evolution (and emergent evolution, after all, articulates but does not solve the dilemma) there are still difficulties untouched.

These difficulties will be seen more clearly if, before proceeding to a direct analysis of functional autonomy, we study an account of functional autonomy which Allport himself would consider incomplete.

> At first the infant's cravings are only for bodily comfort. The mother becomes associated with this comfort; later her presence is sufficient to bring pleasure and her absence provokes a longing for the comfort of her companionship. Such extensions and conditioning may continue until objects, tastes, ideas, associated with the mother become satisfying when they are present and set up desire and longing when they are absent. Due to such conditioning, maternal ideas are accepted with emotional conviction and violation of parental teaching even in later life brings restlessness, pangs of conscience, and feelings of guilt.

Now we are not bothered by the multitude of children and grandchildren this one nutritive drive accumulates. But the anomaly occurs in the kind of children it has! The realm of needs and purposes seems to be pervaded by no laws of inheritance! More concretely, can a need of given limitations be the father of a need which is totally different? In the present example, we can understand why the infant would feel bodily comfort owing to the presence of his mother. She indeed does become functionally related to his need of bodily comfort and becomes the promise of more physiological comfort. But the magic begins when we are told that her absence provokes a longing for the 'comfort of her companionship' especially if 'companionship' means more than simple bodily comfort. For whence this desire for social, aesthetic, or mental companionship in an organism which by definition wants only

[5]This opinion of Professor Allport's was obtained through personal correspondence. It would seem that he wavers between 'protoplasmic irritability' and *'élan vital'* or 'Will-to-live,' but the common factor in all three would seem to be, in infancy, the mechanical 'push' as opposed to the purposive 'pull.'

physical comfort and the pleasure attendant thereupon? A white rabbit and a black cat have suddenly appeared in the tall white hat which a moment ago contained only one innocent white rabbit! But examples of this peculiar magic can be found galore in almost any text which prides itself on the 'scientific' rejection of the instinct-theory-only to resort to a deeper, more mysterious magic.

Can the kind of pleasure which is attendant upon the satisfaction of a bodily need (eating-pleasure) give birth to aesthetic, social, or intellectual pleasure without the entrance of any other need or desire? After all, there is no such thing as *pleasure in general,* but only pleasures which in turn are defined by the very drive-fulfillment precedent to or involved in them. Is physical-pleasure somehow the source of a totally different type (social-pleasure) as empirically known?

As the situation now stands, we can appeal to the mysterious concept of ontogenic emergent evolution to account for the appearance of new needs and consequent pleasures. Or we can appeal to an instinct-theory which attempts to delineate what these basic drives (and consequent pleasures) are in the first place and then shows how they are modified by ability and environment to constitute the uniqueness and the continuity of the individual personality.

To be sure, this passage on the development of the filial sentiment is used by Allport to show how biological psychologists like Kempf would account for such seemingly basic motives. He too doubts that such a theory can do justice *to the complexity* of adult motivation and he provides the alternative of functional autonomy. But this latter is pervaded with the same magic. Allport's unwillingness to attempt an empirically specific account of the *élan vital* keeps him from providing a psychological, purposive base for functional autonomy, and forces him to switch horses mid-stream from "push" to "pull." But he also fails to account, as we shall now see, for the transition from one specific type of motive to another type. We can best develop and clarify our point, however, by a closer description and analysis of functional autonomy.

2. *Two Views of Functional Autonomy*

Functional autonomy is 'a substantive designation' for a psychological process underlying the observable facts (a) that "the manifold potentialities and dispositions of childhood coalesce into sharper, more distinctive motivational systems" and (b) that these systems, as they emerge, "take upon themselves effective driving power, operating as mature, autonomous motives quite different in aim and in character from the motivational systems of juvenile years, and very different indeed from the crude organic tensions of infancy." Briefly, the mechanisms or means used to satisfy certain needs themselves become drives which are not mere 'changes rung on universal themes.'

First let us note that in these words we have not only a description of empirical fact, that mechanisms can become drives (which I certainly do not doubt), but also a *theoretical explanation* of this datum, namely that these mechanisms, once the servants of drives, sever their connections with their masters and become themselves autonomous and unique goals subjecting other activities to themselves.

It is this form of functional autonomy which an instinctivist calls in question. For can he not hold, as an alternative, that servants of one drive do indeed become independent of their master, without, however, gaining independence from *all* master tendencies or drives? Indeed, our very difficulty with Allport's theory is that if mechanisms do cut loose not only from the original but also from all innate purposive drives, the unity and longitudinal consistency of any acquired personality is no longer guaranteed. On the other hand, the significant fact which functional autonomy correctly emphasizes may be preserved without weakening or threatening the unity of the personality, by the realization that mechanisms which served one master well may in time serve another master even better (or worse). Thus, though these acquired motivational systems may indeed become different in aim and character from the motivational systems of juvenile or infantile years, they are supported and derive their 'effective driving power' not from themselves, but from the new goals for which they are means. Mechanisms seem to become drives because they are driven by some other prior or co-existent drive of the psycho-physiological organism. To use a crude figure, mechanisms are like the horse-riders that do indeed affect the nature of the horses which support them in any given instance but which can switch from the saddle of one horse (propensity) to the back of another (changing their activity somewhat to suit the new horse). But they do not drive themselves!

In McDougall's terminology—the sentiment which was once a focus for the expression of given instincts may become quite different 'in aim and in character' as it becomes the new means of expression for other propensities. The love-sentiment which the child develops for his mother may become a means for expressing his love for his wife, or mother-in-law, or God. At least this alternative is a definite possibility which must be proven false before the explanation of functional autonomy can be accepted with full confidence.

As we might expect, Allport, with his eyes trained on the uniqueness of personality, replies: "Not four wishes, nor eighteen propensities, nor any and all combinations of these, even with their extensions and variations seem adequate to account for the endless variety of goals sought by an endless variety of mortals." And the controversy seems to be at a stalemate! For the instinctivist simply will insist that though it may seem *psychologically in-*

conceivable that either extension, variation, or condensation, of propensities could account for the 'endless variety of mortals,' there is no logical inconceivability here, and the *empirical* evidence is not arbitrarily forced.

3.   *Can Autonomous Traits Explain Continuity Best?*

Thus, the question must once more be carried further with renewed consideration of the difficulties involved in turn by the trait-without-supporting-propensity theory. In Part I of this paper we questioned the possibility of accounting for our understanding of human beings without reference to common, underlying motives. No common propensities, then no mutual understanding, we asserted. Here we insist: no underlying drives common to various stages of the same life, then no adequate understanding of the unity and continuity of personality. Both of these difficulties are dissolved by a theory of flexible generic propensities common to men and common (only) in basic aim through the various stages of a given life. These more nearly ultimate motives, however, expressed in accordance with the temperament, physique, and intelligence of a given individual, eventuate, in a given environment, in proximate motives, namely, sentiments, attitudes, *and traits*. These proximate motives in turn explain the uniqueness of the individual personality, itself a mode of adjustment as the self takes advantage of the indefinitely varied ways of expressing its propensities.

This in general would be our contrasting hypothesis in so far as the problem of motivation affects the longitudinal unity of personality. We are not unaware of the fact that, as Allport carefully points out, memory and imagination have much to do with the possibility of unity. But given the strength of memory, cognitive capacity, imagination, and temperament in any particular individual, his concrete unity for the moment and for successive periods will be very much affected by the nature of the drives or urges which play such a large part in determining the way in which these different abilities will function to give unity. Motives are so intimately related with the functioning of the aspects of the self which contribute to unity, that an inadequate theory of motives might make empirical unity insufficiently explicable by these factors alone. Our view is that the theory of traits and their interrelation is not as adequate or intelligible as a support for the unity and continuity of personality as it might be with the aid of propensities. This thesis must now be explicitly justified.

Allport concedes that the "definite point of origin" for his own "self-sustaining, *contemporary* systems" of motives "may lie in the hypothetical instincts," but he thinks that they are "more likely" to depend on the organic tension and diffuse irritability we distrusted earlier in this paper. In either case the tie with these 'seed forms' in infancy is broken as the individual matures, and though there is historical continuity with the past, the contemporary motives 'in no sense' depend upon it for their present 'go'.

But this objection to such dependence seems to be founded upon an unnecessary or distorted view of the opposing theory. It would indeed be valid if, according to instinct-theory, the present motive had somehow to reach back into the non-existent past for its 'go.' It would also be true that the offspring could derive no further support from the seed-forms of infancy, or at any other point of maturation, if such forms were fixed in structure and purposive detail. Or if we supposed that propensities were constant streams of energy, piped in fixed ways through the individual, then again the objection would hold.

Such, however, is not the situation. Rather the total psycho-physiological organism, modified in particular ways, even as body-cells are, still functions in certain directions though focusing at this moment or stage on one available means of satisfaction, and at another, on whatever its ability and its environment make possible. The present, proximate or instrumental motives (sentiments and traits) are the means which the ultimate motives have found in their struggle for satisfaction. Sever all connections with any or all ultimate motives in their present state of existence and the individual has no basis for wanting what he now wants! The motivational stream cannot be cut up into temporal bits, externally continuous historically, and independent functionally. The continuity can be biographical or descriptive only, but not existential. For any one propensity or the whole group are not longitudinal streams along which the observer may find different motives (sentiments and traits) bobbing up and down. The whole organism of purposive action is functioning in the present as modified by the (now non-existent) past. The only 'go' any motive, ultimate or proximate has, is in the present. The fact that the present means of expression *cannot be explained or understood* without reference to a more enduring and general striving must not lead us to think that the more ultimate drive is a substantive reality independent of this and other particular ways of expression.

Hence, all motives are specific existentially. But the very psychological continuity of organismic action depends on the continuity of the purposive energizing which avails itself of suitable or (seemingly suitable) methods or objects of expression at its disposal. Laboring as he seems to under a different, more substantive conception of propensitive action, Allport is forced to deny its existence. In order to avoid such misconceptions we must plead for the same caution with regard to instinctive energizing as he calls for with regard to trait activity, when he says: "Unless full recognition is given to this continuous, variable and convergent character of behavior the theory of traits [propensities] will become a purely fanciful doctrine of 'little men within the breast' possessing, by hypothesis, exclusive control over each and every separate activity . . . . Though traits [propensities] are never directly observed, they are *of necessity* inferred. For without some inference of a flexible underlying structure in personality it would be impossible to account for the recurrent quality of the separate observable acts."

Again, the full meaning of an instinctive drive is not exhausted by any one moment of its history, any more than is a propensity to be divorced from all its manifestations as if it could exist apart from them! Instinctive drive is a distinguishable (not existentially separate) mode and direction of striving. It provides the understandable transition between successive modes of striving which, different in detail, yet can be subsumed under a more generic basic direction or goal. Hence we can agree with Allport that "earlier purposes lead into later purposes, but are abandoned in their favor" only if we can understand what the dynamic basis for the transition is, or, how earlier purposes lead later to self-sufficient power-sources. In order to arrive at such an understanding, however, it is necessary to modify Allport's contention by submitting that the later purposes are the earlier purposes being satisfied in a better or worse way.

Indeed, this is the only legitimate basis for talking about the *transformation* of motives! Otherwise we would have to consider original motives not transformed but *supplanted*. If it is true that "whatever the original drives or 'irritabilities' of the infant are, they become completely transformed in the course of growth into comtemporaneous systems of motives," how do we know that the originals are not *supplanted*? (Allport himself uses this very word on p. 113.) If they are not supplanted but transformed, what is the base for the continuity involved in transformation. Without such a base or common factor, must we not suppose that the individual motivational system is supplanted in different stages by another system which emerges (!) I know not whence? In either case, without the conception of purposive striving which outlasts particular manifestations, it seems impossible to account for the observable continuity between motives in personality.[6]

We might as well ask further: How account for the very fact of *change from* one motivational system *to* another? Let us answer by further analysis of every-day experience which Allport adduces as evidence of functional autonomy.

[6]In correspondence Professor Allport says: "Your discussion concerning the terms 'transformation' versus 'supplanting' makes me realize that I did not stress sufficiently my belief that not all motives are to be viewed as functionally autonomous. Some motives are, no doubt, rigidly persistent from childhood onward. Some are partially transformed, through a changing cathexis (which I think is the theory you favor); whereas some, I am convinced, are so utterly transformed that the term 'supplanted' is the best one to use. I admit that degrees exist in the phenomena under discussion." Two brief comments must be made. First, what are the 'rigidly persistent' motives? Are they the same in most children? If not, how do we tell which they are, why their rigidity, what end they subverse? Second, differences in degree of transformation involve an underlying similarity in function, goal, or purpose here advocated in the form of propensities. (*Cf.* next footnote.)

The sailor who had developed a craving for the sea as a means of satisfying nutritional needs still craves for the sea even now that he is a banker. Instance also the city-dweller with a yearning for the hills. "Once indeed the city dweller may have associated the hills around his mountain home with nutritional and erotogenic satisfactions, but these satisfactions he finds in his city home, *not* in the mountains: whence then came all his hill-hunger?" Again, a good workman may feel compelled to work with unusual accuracy even though his security and prestige no longer depend on the high standard of work. In each instance an 'instrumental technique' becomes a self-sufficient motive.

These instances are very effective against a theory of three basic drives like Kempf's, but they might also be used as evidence that there must be other basic drives as well! If the sea, by hypothesis, could satisfy only the nutritional drive, then it would indeed be difficult to explain the sea-hunger under altered circumstances. But if the sea satisfied not only the nutritional, but submissive, self-assertive, curiosity, as well as gregarious drives, then it would not be difficult to account for such perseveration when only one drive was lacking. Even for the banker nothing else could replace the object of drive-expression (or sentiment) of earlier days. The sea which was once a means for the satisfaction of several drives still continues to operate with perhaps some alteration as a means of drive-satisfaction. There is functional autonomy from one need, *but not from all needs!*

Going still deeper, however, it is difficult to explain why the ex-sailor still loves the sea unless we can discover the desire it *now* satisfies, whether originally present or not. Does sea-going create a new desire apart from the nutritional which it no longer satisfies? Or is it a mechanism of satisfaction which the individual happens to possess and can be remodelled as it now comes to *satisfy* another drive earlier undreamed of in that connection,— like the old wedding dress or coat which we never dreamed would fit our offspring! The same reasoning applies to other instances of functional autonomy, to the city-dweller and the workman. The fact that they *keep* the old instrumental attachments suggests that these means were attached to more than one goal, or that they could become means for satisfying originally neutral or indifferent drives, or both.

If these contentions are rejected, we must ask Allport to explain *why all old mechanisms* do not become self-sufficient drives! Why does the ex-sailor have a present hankering for the sea but not for his captain, his boat, and a multitude of other objects of early instrumental value? There seems to be *a basis for the selection of the means* which we rejuvenate. That basis is, we suggest, the onward going and striving individual, using old achievements according as they serve the present status of his drive development. Otherwise, whence the motives which mechanisms now satisfy? To say that "some new function emerges as an independently structured unit from preceding functions" is merely to state the problem without accounting for the continuity. Again, does curiosity 'emerge' from nutrition, pride from lust, sympathy from fear? The word 'emerge' still covers a multitude of mysteries.[7]

We may ask still another question. Why does the seafaring man ever become a banker? The answer is obvious, except on a theory of strict functional autonomy. For if every motive is to be understood as self-sufficient and not as dependent on any other more basic drive, what is it that produces the change which leads to dissatisfaction with present satisfactions of the need? What produced the dissatisfaction with the sea which led to other pursuits and finally to banking? The instinctivist would argue that seafarer's and banker's ways (sentiments) are functionally equivalent for the individual whose various wants were constant in goal but developing or being frustrated in various ways. The serial development and improvement of habits in functionally continuous fashion is not explicable by a theory of functional autonomy where habit-means become self-sufficient, independent drives. If "the activity of these new units does not depend upon the continual activity of the units from which they developed," then how understand the functioning of the present units without references to another need which they are now satisfying? And whence that need?

Allport does answer by saying that "functional autonomy does not rely . . . upon modified instinct . . . but upon the capacity of human beings to *replenish their energy* [italics mine] through a plurality of constantly changing systems of dynamic dispositions." The instinctivist is trying to give some sort of a psychological (as opposed to biological or physical) account of the meaning of the italicized words. For if there is to be 'functional equivalence' of systems of dispositions, that equivalence cannot be understood without presupposing an underlying identical goal-seeking. Hence the 'energy' must be conceived in terms of goal-seeking tendencies which outlive as a whole any particular mode of satisfaction.

Before leaving this aspect of our discussion, we must study a more specific account Allport gives of the continuity of personality. Recalling the fact that unfinished tasks are completed to avoid motive-frustration, he notes that the incomplete motives subside when their goal is reached, or when satisfaction at a given level becomes automatic. Hence, an ability like driving a car, aroused first by a motive, sinks when once acquired, "to the level of an instrumental disposition and is aroused only in the service of some other driving

---

[7]In personal correspondence Professor Allport has remarked "that to my mind the most incomplete aspect of my theory consists in my failure to give criteria whereby one might distinguish functionally autonomous from unchanged motives." This is the point I have been suggesting, but Professor Allport adds: "I can simply say that I believe the problem to be soluble . . ." Obviously, our appeal to propensities is an attempt to solve this very problem, as well as others.

[unfulfilled] motive."[8] Hence Allport actually modifies the conception of mechanisms becoming drives. The truth is that "only skills in the process of perfecting (mechanisms-on-the-make) serve as drives." In the end, therefore, Allport meets the objection of the hormic psychologist by saying that since the 'permanent interests' of the personality are never satisfied, instrumental mechanisms are never perfect, and may be displaced for better ones, or used in the service of some other motives.

But if Allport must resort to 'permanent interests' to explain the drive of mechanisms, is he not in fact denying that instruments are capable of becoming ends in themselves? For if mechanisms are perfected, they are aroused only in the service of other drives. If they are not perfected, they are still dependent instruments, and not functionally self-sufficient. Each instrument is maintained until it is superseded by better means for the completion of the underlying drive. And that is exactly what we have been suggesting.

In any case, we are driven back once more to our basic issue! Whence the more enduring permanent interests of personality? If they are not innate, or if they are not changes rung on innate tendencies, then they are mechanisms-on-the-make. But on the make for what? Since instrumentalities must have reference sooner or later to something outlasting and underlying them, how can we avoid the conclusion: They are mehanisms-on-the-make for the satisfaction of innate drives which are not themselves functionally autonomous? These propensities *transcend the discontinuity* of particular instruments of satisfaction *while preserving the function* for which the instruments are successively equivalent.

If our argument thus far is valid, it would seem that trait-psychology cannot dispense with propensities and at the same time account for the continuity of personality development which manifests itself in the various stages of successive development or degeneration of traits. The constancy of a trait is determined not by its own self-sufficient energy, as Allport would hold, but by its capacity to satisfy the total needs of the psycho-physiological organism. Traits do not simply change, but they change in directions which increase satisfaction of basic needs, as the individual conceives completion. We may paraphrase a sentence from Allport and say: For without some inference of a flexible, underlying (purposive) structure in personality it would be impossible to account for the recurrent quality (growth, and discard) of the separate observable traits which in turn account for the recurrent quality of the separate observable acts (p. 313). Without a hormic base, traits may indeed "come to stand for an assembly of separate and self-active faculties, though to govern behavior all by themselves, without interference." Interrelated and cooperating traits do indeed help to explain the stability and consistency of personality in successive stages. But so long

---

[8]This is a thesis which in its own way parallels our suggestion.

as that consistency is a functional or purposive consistency, we are forced to go beyond the traits themselves to the underlying goal-seeking tendencies which traits are trying to express or satisfy at a given time and place. In the last analysis the stability and consistency of traits is not explicable without reference to underlying propensities as well as to memory and imagination.

4.   *Is a Synthesis of Propensities, Sentiments, and Traits Possible?*

The problem, after all, is not to choose *between* traits *and* instincts! The hormic psychologist who is concerned to given an adequate account especially of the contemporary and unique phase of personality development must indeed find a place not only for sentiments but also for traits. The existence of traits is undeniable though their origin be in question.

There is no reason why traits cannot be one of the levels at which the hormic energy organizes itself in the life of a given individual. For example, on the McDougallian view, sentiments (proximate motives, instruments) do not account for the fact that individuals come in time to act in certain ways without being stimulated by any object. *Sentiments are not adequate* to explain the persistent and continuously functioning characteristics of given individuals which are uniquely expressive of their form of adjustment rather than of the environment. Why cannot a trait be defined as the product of propensities conditioned or developed to the point where the objects of the sentiments are no longer essential to the operation of the propensities involved? The trait would represent a stage of development beyond the sentiment, though influenced by sentimental organization. The trait would be a residue of the manner in which many past expressions of propensities have transformed the individual, and traits in turn would help or hinder the further expression of the direction implicit in innate striving. A human personality is always in a state of transition in the pursuit of general ends implicit in its very being. But its definition at any moment is impossible without due regard to the interacting effects of its various contemporary commitments or sentiments (themselves in process) and the characteristic modes of expressions which have resulted from these previous conative expenditures.

Such a view of personality as essentially involving in its development,

[9]In another article, 'Sentiments and Attitudes' (*Journal of Social Psychology*, May, 1940), the writer has attempted to delineate two levels of proximate emotional expressions, the sentimental accounting for the intense and more highly valued emotional attachments, and the attitudinal for the less intense, less valued affective attachments. Traits might also be pitched at different levels, depending on whether they develop from earlier sentimental attachments or from attitudinal attachments. Those on the sentimental, intense, level would be classed as 'driving,' while those on the less intense attitudinal level would be 'directive.' Such a conception of 'driving' and 'directive traits' seems to provide as intelligible an account of the differentiation of these two types of traits as that which Allport gives.

propensities, sentiments, attitudes,[9] and traits would seem to preserve (a) the basis for understanding the common ends underlying the differences between personalities, (b) the uniqueness of individual striving owing to differences in temperament, abilities and environment, and (c) the stability and persistent continuity resident in the manner of purposive striving as the individual is transformed during successive stages of his development.

14. Motivation in Personality: Reply to Peter A. Bertocci

Gordon W. Allport

Mr. Bertocci has written an accurate and challenging critique of my views regarding the nature of motivation in human personality. Because he has read my work sympathetically and checked his understanding of my position with care his criticisms are helpful and relevant. Where on rare occasions misunderstanding still remains, it is I and not my critic who must take the blame.

1. Introduction

It will be noted that Mr. Bertocci shapes his attack essentially from the McDougallian point of view. When McDougall died shortly after the publication of my book I gave up hope of ever benefiting from his fierce but friendly criticisms. Mr. Bertocci has now rescued me from disappointment and has laid upon me with the same hefty cudgels that McDougall would have used, and for good measure has employed a few additional cudgels of his own.

His attack, as I see it, must be met on seven fronts, viz., (1) the argument for hormic purposivism, (2) the sufficiency of instinct, (3) the neces-

Abridged from the *Psychological Review*, 1940, 47, 533-554. Reprinted by permission of the author and the American Psychological Association Inc.

sity in science for employing universal dimensions, (4) the 'mystery' of ontogenetic emergence, (5) the nature of functional autonomy, (6) adequate accounting for continuity in personality, and (7) the place of sentiments in the structure of personality. Each of these lines of attack calls for extensive defense and counter-offense, but since space is limited and since some of the disputed issues are by their very nature insoluble, I shall try to content myself with the briefest possible rebuttal.

2.   *Purpose versus Mechanism*

Mr. Bertocci accuses me of wobbling between the principle of purpose and the principle of mechanism. Specifically he does not like the emergent step implied in my contrast between the apparently mechanistic 'push' in infancy and the apparently teleological 'pull' in maturity. In later pages I shall attempt to meet his objections to emergence, but for the moment confine myself to one or two general comments on the nature of purpose and of mechanism.

In modern times it seems to me that the former sharp antagonism between these two principles of explanation has been somewhat overcome. Mechanistic reflexology has certainly been vanquished; and in recent times its adherents seem to have been re-aligning themselves either with the operational creed which is frankly sceptical of the principle of causation, or else with the organismic position that redefines both purpose and mechanism, reconciling them within the new concepts of *structure* and *system*. From this latter point of view—to which I subscribe—it seems unnecessary to ask whether reflex irritability defines and limits goal-seeking responses, or whether goal-seeking is an initial property to which reflex irritability merely holds various 'keys.' The modern tendency is to deal with systemic properties in nature, conceived as neither mechanistic nor purposive but as *organismic*. Just as modern physics has redefined the meaning of 'contact' in such a way that 'push' and 'pull' give place to the concept of interacting molecular systems, so too psychology largely under the influence of Gestalt theory is dealing these days with patterned events, contexts that constrain, structural wholes.

When I remarked to Mr. Bertocci in personal correspondence which he quotes that I saw no difficulty in embracing a principle of 'push' in infancy and of 'pull' in maturity, I did not intend to commit myself to so extreme a paradox as he has made of it. Whether the system that we call gravitation 'pushes' or 'pulls' at my feet it is, as Eddington has shown, impossible to say. Similarly the pattern of hunger behavior in an infant is marked by a sequence of events that may be viewed as either mechanistic or purposive, but preferably as systemic and self-regulating. Yet—and this is the important point— as compared with the corresponding events in adulthood this infantile hunger-system lacks foresight, respect for taboo, epicurean embellishments, idiosyncrasy of taste and all other ideational features. I think, therefore, that we may truly say that the infant is, *relative to the adult,* 'pushed' by immediate, simple, vegetative and proximate features in his hunger system. The adult is to a greater degree 'pulled" by the delayed, ideational, non-proximate features in his system of hunger-behavior. Push and pull are therefore relative terms, signifying respectively the presence of less or more of the personalized and planful components in a system of events and the presence of a slight and limited environmental stimulus field, or the presence of a richly extended and diversified stimulus field.

Were I *forced* to choose between mechanism and purposivism as an ultimate principle of motivation, I should unhesitatingly choose—as I think my book amply indicates—purposivism. Yet I think it entirely proper to see in infancy *less e*vidence of purposive behavior than in adulthood. Infant behavior, I submit, conforms more closely to the alleged characteristics of drive-impelled conduct. Adult behavior with its widened consciousness of goals, and with its lavish use of symbols and all higher mental operations, on the other hand, shows the working of a type of motivation that can only be expressed in terms of *interest, attitude, value, desire, will*—terms quite inappropriate to infancy.

Bertocci, I believe, agrees with me concerning the barrenness for psychology of the postulate of an initial *Hormé.* Neither of us is disposed to deny it metaphysical status, but we both want it broken up into particular manifestations—he into McDougallian propensities; I into individualized motivational systems. His complaint is that in accepting an *élan* and in denying instincts I am guilty of metaphysical abstractions with a vengeance. My reply is that to me individualized motivational systems seem just as saturated with *élan,* ego-involvement, urge, or *Hormé* as do the alleged instincts; but as expressions of *élan,* they are variable, personal, and empirically discovered rather than universal, external, and *a priori.*

3. *The Sufficiency of Instincts*

And so we come to the instinct controversy. Let it be remembered that only instincts in McDougall's sense are here the issue, for Bertocci does not rest his case on such innate sensory-motor co-ordinations as have been empirically established. The principal difficulty with McDougall's set channels of purpose is precisely this: They never can be discovered empirically. Two assumptions make them fatally elusive: (a) the contention that "propensities are but loosely geared to goals,"—this contention making it possible always to interpret any case as fitting the formula; and (b) the reliance on maturation of purposes, another proposition unverifiable. It is recognized that some course of learning invariably precedes alleged maturation. It would be impossible, I think, ever to demonstrate that sympathy matures as a 'non-specific innate tendency' because two or three years of individualizing personal experience precede its overt manifestations. Since purposes never ripen in an experiential vacuum I think it is wiser to order the phenomenon of the growth of motives to the psychology of progressive mental organization—in other words, to the psychology of learning. My critic, on the other hand, prefers to believe that learning can best be subordinated to the doctrine of fixed motives which throughout life predetermine 'in a general way' the direction of active response. Later I shall give other reasons for thinking that learning rather than inheritance is the leading category in the psychology of motivation.

To another of my objections—that the assumption of universal instincts is not a parsimonious procedure—Mr. Bertocci rightly, but not altogether relevantly, retorts that it is the scientist and not nature that shows a partiality for parsimony. (Certainly in my ascribing 'an infinite variety of motives to an infinite variety of mortals' I myself am in no danger of saddling nature with the canon of parsimony.) But the point is that instincts explain *too much*. Even McDougall admits that people can be found who seem to lack one or more of the 18 primary propensities. If this is so, then to regard the 18 (or any other number) as 'normal' and the exceptions as 'abnormal' is clearly an extravagant convention. In nature, we must assume, there are no exceptions; every case is completely and adequately determined by law. If then, certain purposes seem to be absent in some people, why should we suppose they were ever meant to be there? Only if purposes can empirically be shown to be present are we obliged to account for them. In the psychology of personality we need a law of motivation that will have no exceptions. Even a formula of considerable subsumptive power is not enough, for unlike other branches of science, the psychology of personality is bound to account for *individuality*. Instincts being universal in their reference lack individualizing power.

Before expanding this last remark I should like to call attention to one promising feature of Mr. Bertocci's position. He admits that in the course of development a person's abilities and individual temperament, as well as the exigencies of his peculiar environment, have an individualizing effect on his purposes so that his goals are not exact duplicates of other people's goals. He admits likewise that "all actual, existential goal-seeking, as opposed to the conceptual description of it, is specific and individual. One never seeks food in general or recognition in general, but his actual seeking is always undergoing particular psycho-physiological processes in relation to particular food, people, and so on." These admissions seem to show that Mr. Bertocci is impressed by precisely what impresses me—by the concrete and individual character of 'actual, existential goal-seeking.' Am I wrong in believing that in the passage just quoted he admits a contradiction between the impressively concrete, unique, and personal character of goal-seeking, and the 'conceptual description' of it that he is defending?

4. Necessity for Universal Dimensions

While admitting—in the passage just quoted and in others—that uniqueness is the mark of personality, that "life exists in individual forms," Bertocci, like other of my critics, insists that "to accept uniqueness as alone ultimate is to destroy the possibility of rational knowledge of any sort. Uniqueness can be felt, lived through, but not expressed or understood in relation to other common factors." He writes also: "My understanding can assimilate unique individuality only by noting the extent to which it is similar to and different from other individuals known to me." In these passages Bertocci is stating the traditional view of psychological science that the data of human nature must be treated nomothetically (in terms of general dimensions) and that scientific understanding of these data proceeds through inference (associative comparison).

Readers of my book will perhaps recall that I endorse the use of nomethetic procedures and admit the importance of inference in the process of understanding people. Certainly I would subscribe to Mr. Bertocci's statement that "psychology would do well to search for whatever universality may be found in human motivation." But unlike Bertocci and my other critics I am unwilling to stop here. I believe there is—in addition to these nomothetic and inferential procedures common to all science—something quite special about the pyschology of personality that marks it off from all other branches of science, namely, its obligation to deal with integrated individuality. In order to fulfill this special obligation I submit that the psychology of personality needs not only the customary procedures and habits of thought employed by nomothetic and inferential science, but needs to develop likewise new idiographic methods and intuitive skills. "A complete study of the individual," I have written, "will embrace both approaches."

Freud, Adler, Spearman, McDougall, Murray, Kretschmer, Thurstone, Guilford, and others have produced nomothetic dimensions to which personalities are to be ordered. But consider the differences, and even the contradictions, between these d'mensional schemes! Think too of the lists of 'primary motives' in textbooks of psychology. I doubt that there is justification for Bertocci's statement that we know some of the 'inevitable components of human motivation.' Even where agreement seems to be reached—Bertocci suggests hunger, sex, fear, anger—the biological capacities mentioned have nothing much to do with the personal level of conduct, and they illuminate little if at all the concrete needs and specifiable desires of actual individuals.

The question is this: Can we not, even while we make use of many maps prepared my many nomothetists, get still closer to the structure of personality by fixing our attention upon individual lives? So to fix our attention requires, of course, a certain re-centering of our theories; (I suggest, for example, the theory of traits and the principle of functional autonomy). Required also are new and different methods of study (greater use, among other techniques, of *intra-individual* statistics, case studies, matching, interviews, expressive and stylistic procedures, and the like). McDougall's map of the propensities is suggestive—so too are all other maps. They serve to call attention to *probable* emotional foci in certain lives. I say 'probable,' not because Providence has endowed all men with eighteen channels of purpose; but because "similarly constructed individuals living in similar environments influenced by similar culture, *would* develop similar goals and employ similar modes of obtaining them."

This last quotation (from page 113 of my book) offends my critic deeply. He accuses me of placing too much weight on culture, of overlooking instincts, which alone can be 'the basic cause of culture and its similarity in the first place.' My reply is that the universal features in cultural practices all over the earth appear to be too few in number to argue from them to common instinctive causation. Of course, universal features in the bodily structure of *Homo Sapiens* lie at the root of certain bodily needs; but there is not one of these needs which is not strangely revised and transformed at the psychological level before it becomes an actual, integrated motivational system. (I have just been reading a well-attested account of orthodox Jews who in Nazi concentration camps suffered inanition and not infrequently death by refusing to violate the food restrictions of their religion.) It is for this reason that I think of biological needs or tissue change as offering a wholly inadequate, sub-personal, picture of psychological motivation.

As I pointed out in the preceding section this personalizing of motives, different in each life, seems to be admitted by my critic. He writes "The statement: 'men hunger for food,' is a highly abstract description of the concrete unique hunger-pangs and the concrete, unique food seeking which are actually involved." Such admissions, it seems to me, prepare the way for a more concrete theory of motivation which will account for the fact that systems of desires are well integrated, and that the object of desire is by no means arbitrary and detachable—as the cathexis theory holds—but is rather a firm part of the system itself.

To summarize: As a first approximation I have no objection to the use of a conceptional schedule of two drives, four wishes, eighteen propensities, or twenty-five needs in approaching the motives of men. Such maps are useful in calling attention to the sort of things that people (physically similar in structure) exposed to roughly similar environments and cultures commonly desire. But this type of nomothetic procedure runs its course on a plane of abstraction that is not within reach of actual personalities. A full-bodied psychology of personality (as opposed to a general psychology of motives) must do a better job. A law of motivation that accounts for the individual organizations of desires is in order. Although I am aware of the argument made by Bertocci and others that "we cannot give up the search for the common pattern underlying various purposes simply because our predecessors and contemporaries disagree about the number and kinds of irreducible unlearned motives," yet I am a bit pessimistic. Within 2000 years of self-conscious psychologizing no stencil to fit human desires has yet been found, because, I suspect, there is none to find. May it not be that the 'irreducible unlearned motives' of men are—excepting in early infancy—a scientific will of the wisp?

To the instinctivist it seems that 'the extension, variation, condensation of propensities' can account for all variety that is needed. To this view I reply that Procrustes had a similar ambition for his bed. Of course cases can be sheared to fit. But unless academic psychologists concern themselves with the problem of the integral individuality of the motivational pattern (as some clinical psychologists do) I fear they will forever be wrangling about the relative merits of their respective Procrustean couches. All stencils fit concrete cases only with the loosest approximation. They seldom help the clinician or the average man in understanding the structure of the individual life.

5. The Principle of Ontogenetic Emergence

Mr. Bertocci asks, "Can a need of given limitations be the father of a need which is totally different?" He thinks it cannot; I think it can. He believes that it would abrogate continuity in personality to have 'outright novelties' emerge; he holds that learning is not a process of adding in number to the purposive tendencies resident in the original nature of man, and he regards it as all very mysterious how any new purposes can ever evolve. He concludes: "As the situation now stands, we can appeal to the mysterious concept of ontogenetic emergent evolution to account for the appearance of new needs and consequent pleasures. Or we can appeal to an instinct-theory which attempts to delineate what these basic drives (and consequent pleasures) are in the first place, and then show how they are modified by ability and environment to constitute the uniqueness and the continuity of the individual personality." To me it seems that personal interests undergo marked and essential change in the course of life: that when we become men we put away for the most part the desires of childhood. It is not merely the 'object cathexis' that is altered; it is the basic structure of motivation.

Mr. Bertocci himself thinks of human personality as 'always in a state of transition,' but he regards the transition as applying to skills and abilities rather than to the 'general ends implicit in its very being.' Just why *transition* should characterize the *Rüstungsdispositionen* and not the *Richtungsdispositionen* is not evident to me. So far as the directional dispositions are concerned I incline toward Wundt's view expressed in his almost forgotten principle of the 'heterogeny of ends.' Primitive man—to cite his somewhat florid example—entered a cave to take refuge from a storm, and finding there a wild dog likewise taking shelter, he emerged from the cave with a desire and plan for domesticating the dog. New purposes have their seeds in old purposes, but the satisfactions they yield are so unexpected, so unpredictable, that only some such principle as the 'heterogeny of ends,' or 'functional autonomy' seems to cover the obvious facts.

My critic argues—and I am glad to agree with him—that the logic of learning must apply to both skills and motives equally. The dispute then comes to a head in the question whether learning creates *novel* skills and purposes or mere variations on the *old*. Since Mr. Bertocci does not favor the emergence of new purposes (although he has written, "novelties in human motivation are the empirical facts that break the back of any mechanical theory of instinct"), he is forced to deny the creation of novel abilities (although he has admitted that human personality is 'always in a state of transition'). "No psychologist," he says, "talks about the outright creation of a new ability within the lifetime of a given individual. A 'new' ability would be a particular, environmentally provoked, development of a given ability. What fact alters the use of this same logic when we come to motivation?" I agree that the same logic must prevail, but I doubt that every psychologist would look upon new skills as mere variations on the old. Is the dextrous piano playing of Horowitz 'a particular, environmentally provoked, development' of his infantile grasp reflex (or some other 'given' ability)? Is the oratory of a Demosthenes essentially a modification of his infant babble? And what functional continuity with some 'given' ability can be demonstrated in the case of skills employed in surgery, aviation, or writing verse? If skills can change until they are wholly unrecognizable and no longer dependent functionally on their seed-forms, so too can motives. I am glad Mr. Bertocci admits that the same logic must apply to both. (In making this admission I think he is on sounder ground than some critics who seem to hold that while learning may transform skills it somehow passes motivation by, leaving it preserved in the water-glass of infancy. Just why learning should reintegrate patterns of skill and not of motives no one has yet explained.)

The emergent step regarded by my critic as most outrageous is my apparent shift (in discussing the ontogenetic course of development) from a mechanistic to a purposive view of motives. "Why begin with the psychological (purposive) level of description at the age of two or three?" he asks, and adds, "the hormist starts with the psychic level of purposive striving and maintains it throughout." I think I have met this objection in my denial that I would regard 'push' and 'pull' as essentially opposed principles. They are merely convenient terms for expressing the fact that the infant seems to be a more vegetative creature than the adult. Bertocci regards it as inconceivable that sophisticated purposes should emerge from vegetative urges. It is black magic, he thinks, to hold that out of the young infant's demand for only the physical comfort its mother can give, should eventually grow a craving for the 'social, aesthetic, and mental' comfort of her companionship. This proposition does not seem magical to me, but on the contrary about as simple and straightforward a statement of empirical fact as we are likely to find in the realm of motivation.

We do need, I admit, a psychology of learning that will explain how transformations come about from the pre-social or vegetative drives to social, aesthetic, and spiritual desires. This particular problem has not, I believe, been adequately considered. Although I cannot discuss it here, I would call attention to two helpful principles in learning, both of them strangely neglected not only by motivationists but by psychologists in general. (1) Sheer familiarity seems to engender positive valuing (demand) on the part of an organism. Ask a child if he thinks American children are nicer than the children of any other nationality. He will reply yes. If you ask why, the child with naive insight will probably say, "Because I *know* American children and don't know the other." Even an infant, through sheer habituation, without human companionship, develops free locomotion and play in a strange room after 8-10 trials: another sign of the affective value of familiar situations. Let psychologists explore the dynamic effects of an accustomed situation, if they would discover one reason why motivation becomes transformed, why habits become 'drives' (2) The psychology of learning has not, I think, given adequate recognition to the dynamic character of the task-attitude. Let a task be accepted for any reason at all, and the attitude engendered seems to furnish its own drive until accomplishment is reached. If it is objected that this perseverative principle depends upon ego-involvement, I shall agree; but the important point is that while the ego is set upon completing an enterprise it has temporarily adopted, this enterprise itself helps to reconstitute the demands and desires of the ego. For example, a young man in college studies his psychology hard in order to reward his immature ego with a pat on the back from his professor. The subject gradually gets under his skin, and high grades come to mean less to him than the solution of intellectual puzzles. Finally, through years of study he equips himself to become a researcher, a teacher, or, perhaps a clinician. All along the line the ego is served, but in the process it is also redefined and reconstructed. The study of psychology serves the *élan,* but the tasks imposed in the course of study create ever new demands and satisfactions on the part of this *élan*. To generalize the illustration, the progressive acceptance of adaptive tasks throughout one's lifetime results inevitably in continuous change in the motivational demands at successive stages in the individual's development. The following section amplifies this proposition which, I submit, represents a second neglected principle of motive-learning.

6.   *The Nature of Functional Autonomy*

The principle of functional autonomy holds (1) that all motives are contemporary, that whatever drives must drive now; that the 'go' of a motive is not bound functionally to its historical origins or to early goals; but to present goals only; (2) that the character of motives alters so radically from infancy to maturity that we may speak of adult motives as *supplanting* the motives of infancy; (3) that the maturity of personality is measured by the degree of functional autonomy its motives have achieved; even though in every personality there are archaisms (infantilisms, regressions, reflex responses), still the cultivated and socialized individual shows maturity to the extent he has overcome early forms of motivation; (4) that the differentiating course of learning (reflecting ever more diversified environmental influence), acting upon divergent temperaments and abilities, creates individualized motives. The dynamic structure of every personality is unique, although similarities due to species, culture, stages of development, climate, may produce certain resemblances that justify—so long as they are admitted to be approximations—the use of universal dimensions for the purposes of comparing individuals in reference to a norm, or for the purpose of constructing convenient 'types' according to the special interests of the investigator. While not denying the possible existence of instincts in infancy—or even the persistence of some instinctive (or reflex) forms of activity throughout life—still the principle of functional autonomy regards the *developed* personality as essentially a post-instinctive phenomenon.

Bertocci believes that the instinct doctrine is sufficiently flexible to account for the known modifiability of motives. He thinks that my arguments would be valid if "according to instinct-theory the present motive had somehow to reach back into the non-existent past for its 'go' " or if "we supposed that propensities were constant streams of energy, piped in fixed ways through the individual." But he concludes that I labor under too substantive a conception of propensitive action, and that McDougallian propensities are so 'generic' and so loosely 'geared,' that they escape my criticisms.

I can only reply that McDougall's account of propensities seems to me highly substantive. To quote one illustrative passage.

Thus a man's efforts to attain success in the practice of his profession may be sustained by tendencies springing from *several propen-*

*sities; at one moment one of these, at another some tendency of a
very different source, playing the predominant part . . . .* And he is
fortunate and happy in so far as these *several powerful motives,*
tendencies springing from *several distinct and very different propensities,* cooperate harmoniously and successfully . . . . (Italics mine.)

From this passage and many like it it seems to me that McDougall does regard purpose as fixed and constant streams of energy.

Bertocci believes that what I call functionally autonomous motives are only
proximate—"the means which the ultimate motives have found in their
struggle for satisfaction." What I see as the growing independence of a motive
from its source he views as a mere tranfer of instrumentality from one ultimate motive to another: "Mechanisms which served one master well may in
time serve another master even better (or worse)." Or, "in McDougall's
terminology, the sentiment which was once a focus for the expression of given
instincts may become quite different in aim and in character as it becomes the
new means of expression for other propensities." Now, if interests and sentiments can be passed around from propensity to propensity (instead of constituting, as I maintain, ultimate facts of motivational structure) it is fair for me
to ask what psychological cement holds a sentiment together? I had supposed
that according to McDougall's theory a sentiment is anchored to one or more
instincts. If this is so, how can it be detached and passed around—unless indeed it has some organization of its own? If the sentiment is detachable from
the propensity must it not have some degree of functional autonomy? If so,
Bertocci has admitted my point, even though he may choose to hold to instincts as an *additional* factor in motivation.

The next issue raised by my critic betrays a defect in my previous exposition: "Why don't all old mechanisms become self-sufficient drives? Why does
the ex-sailor have a present hankering for the sea but not for his captain, his
boat, and a multiude of other objects of early instrumental value." I reply,
the functional autonomy which a motive may demonstrate was never intended
to indicate autonomy of the Self, or ego. Mechanisms do not become drives
unless in so doing they produce some satisfaction for the *person* (though not
necessarily) for an innate purpose planted by Original Nature within that person). I can readily endorse Bertocci's statement that functionally autonomous
motives do not form themselves in a person unless they "serve the present
status of his 'drive development'." I regret ever implying (to some readers)
that motives fly off at a tangent and have no bedrock anchorage in the satisfaction of the ego. In spite of my stress upon the importance of self-esteem,
my assumption of a 'will-to-live,' and, more specifically, my discussion of the
'extension of the self' my exposition seems to have been faulty. Motives, I
contend, may be autonomous in respect to their origins but never in respect
to the ego.

When are we to tell whether a motive is to be regarded as functionally autonomous of its origins? Bertocci as well as other critics has raised this question. The reply, I think, is that the plasticity of the organism under conditions of learning is such that in any given case of a mature individual *unless proof to the contrary is forthcoming all motivational systems that can be empirically identified should be regarded as autonomous of their origins.* It is obvious that on occasion infantile structures persist and serve a somewhat neurotic function in the adult personality. It is obvious too that sneezing, sleep, elimination, and like bodily functions persist throughout life with relatively little personalizing. Furthermore, if one *wishes* to take the biological functions of feeding, anger, sex, fear, stripped of all their individual variability and regard them as abstract categories of motivation—they too may be regarded as unchanging potentialities. But most *concrete* motivational systems, I submit, are individually integrated with unique emotional patterning and peculiar object attachments. As such they differ from person to person and from one period of an individual's life to the other.

Bertocci criticizes me for using the phrase 'permanent interest of personality.' In my sphere of discourse this phrase is intended merely to convey the undisputed fact that in the course of life, sometimes earlier, sometimes later, an interest (sentiment, value, trait) may become essentially fixed in its organization, remaining in that form because it produces adequate satisfaction for the person who in adulthood finds himself in a fairly stable environment and in possession of the basic psychological systems that are to serve as his *modi vivendi.* The standardization of a personality at thirty, and in some respects earlier, seems to be a fact, and I think, therefore, that no paradox is involved between the principle of functional autonomy and the assumptoin of 'permanent interests.'

A final word about habits. Like James, Dewey, Woodworth and the behaviorists, I place relatively more stress upon the driving power of habits than do Bertocci and McDougall. But it is not that I believe each one to be a self-sufficient dynamo. Habits may remain instrumental or they may turn into interests. While 'on the make' most habits seem to *be* interests. After a time they either slip into a state of mere instrumentality, or else, as Dewey points out, become integrated into new motivational systems that are forming. It is not, I think, particularly pertinent for Bertocci to ask what habits are 'on the make' *for* as I have indicated previously conative perseveration as represented in task attitudes,—e.g., learning to drive a car—is a dynamic condition simply because it is accepted by the individual as 'something to be done.' Tasks once accepted are always ego-involved, but for many reasons and in many ways. It is not necessarily their 'instinctive' appeal that makes them accepted. They may be accepted because of suggestion, previous habits of obedience, simple association with the routine of living, or any other mode of involvement in the developing ego.

Bertocci tears to pieces some of my illustrations of functional autonomy. But I am not dismayed. He asks how we are to know that the ex-sailor did not find other satisfactions than the nutritional at sea; so that today, although the need for making a living is no longer present, he is still in love with the sea for the satisfaction it brings to his instincts of submissiveness, self-assertion, curiosity or gregariousness. We are not to know that this is *not* the case, neither are we to know that it *is*. In this particular illustration I am, of course, assuming that the sentiment is a motive in its own right. I cannot prove it. When Masefield wrote, "I must go down to the sea in ships," he too felt that he was expressing an ultimate, not merely a proximate motive. It seems to me, as I have previously indicated, that it is more reasonable to take a motive at its face value, to assume that it is pretty much what it seems to be, *unless* proof is adduced that instincts are actually at the basis of the motive, or that it is sustained by some infantile fixation. These demonstrations, I submit, are rarely forthcoming.

7. *Continuity Within Personality*

Bertocci's remaining objection to functional autonomy is that it fails to account for unity and continuity within personality. My critic fears that without a hormic base the doctrine of functional autonomy may come to stand for an assembly of separate and self-active faculties, thought to govern behavior all by themselves without interference. I hope I have met this objection by admitting that all motives imply some form of ego-satisfaction. I agree with Bertocci's statement that "the constancy of a trait is determined not by its own self-sufficient energy, but by its capacity to satisfy the total needs of the psychophysiological organism." Let me add, however, that to my way of thinking, these 'needs' are not instincts, nor any other de-personalized desires, but rather whatever integral demands the individual organism happens to have. To be sure no motive ultimately runs itself; it serves the organism. But the organism is, after all, but a living system of interdependent motives. Hence it comes about that evolving motives reconstitute the ego even while dependent upon it for their viability.

The view presented by the hormist differs. The ego is not reconstituted. It remains forever the same. The picture is one of an eternal *élan,* running its course in pre-established channels, thereby guaranteeing the essential fixity of the individual life. One consequence of this view is the necessary belief that instincts, which are common to the species, serve as identical cores in all personalities, so that all personalities are at bottom the same. My preference is for a more individual view of personality. Its identity is its own, guaranteed not by unchanging purposes, but by *sui generis* motivational systems, some more or less permanent (especially in adulthood, when the subjective sense of unity is at its maximum). Its identity is guaranteed likewise by individual threads of memory, habits of expectation, recurrent plans, hopes, and ideas of future goals. These and other psychological processes discussed in . . . my book seem to me to provide adequately for all the unity any life possesses. It is, . . . easy to over-state the degree of integration in personality. I fear that the hormist by putting his stress on permanent instincts does in fact overstate the case. In so far, however, as he puts his stress on the 'sentiment of self-regard' (as McDougall sometimes does), he seems to be moving in the direction of functional autonomy, for this sentiment can most reasonably be viewed as constantly in the process of restructuration.

8. *Sentiments versus Traits*

The final section of Bertocci's critique should be considered along with another of his recent papers. He states his willingness to accord a prominent place to both *traits* and *attitudes* in social psychology, and proceeds to work out a plan for co-ordinating these concepts with *sentiment* and *instinct* as defined by McDougall. His plan briefly is this: Let instincts be acknowledged as *ultimate* prime movers, the mainspring of energy behind all behavior; but let it be admitted that unique organizations of instinctive energy take place in the course of each life-history so that we may for many purposes of analysis be content with a *proximate* picture of motivation, in terms of sentiments, attitudes, and traits.

Among the proximate motives the most dynamic are the *sentiments* which are compelling organizations of love and hate. It is characteristic of the sentiments that they beget lively emotions (not merely an attitudinal feeling of favor or disfavor), and that their symbol-attachments are personalized or personified (wife, mother, country, God, Hitler, sin, etc.).

Attitudes are less dynamic, representing mere postures of feeling—for or against. They are secondary in importance. Though like the sentiments in being *proximate* motives, they stand farther down a dynamic continuum, being less driving and more *directive* in character (less energizing and more instrumental); they are not laden with emotion but only with feeling. "In sum, then, sentiments are aroused (we are driven) when the objects of the environment are seen as imminent, effective (or enduring) friends or foes, through personalization or ego-involvement, while attitudes are aroused (we are favorably or unfavorably disposed toward) by the multiplicity of objects and ideas which are neither of great promise or portent (less personalized, less ego-involvement)."

Finally, in his system Bertocci introduces traits, representing 'a stage of development beyond the sentiment, though influenced by sentimental organization.' A trait would be 'the manner in which many past expressions of propensities have transformed the individual' and be 'uniquely expressive of their form of adjustment rather than of the environment.' In short, traits are needed because sentiments do not adequately represent the persistent and continuously functioning characteristics of the individual's adaptive and expressive history. Dominant, greedy, courteous, ruthless, grave, pessimistic *manners* of conducting oneself are 'residues' of past expressions of propensiites and must be admitted as a development beyond sentiments, having no specific objects of attachment, but representing still 'one of the levels at which the hormic energy organizes itself in the life of a given individual.'

In reply to this ingenious scheme for structuring the personality I may say that with one of its principal features I fully agree, and that is with the view that attitude, trait, and sentiment are all indispensable concepts. I agree likewise in giving sentiment an especially prominent place in the psychology of personality for it is with hierarchical and lasting organizations that we have here to deal. But whether the *term* sentiment is always to be used is not so clear. In one passage in my book, I wrote, "After the level of infancy is passed primitive segmental drive rapidly recedes in importance, being supplanted by the more sophisticated type of motives characteristic of the mature personality, and commonly represented by such terms as *interest, sentiment, value, trait, ambition, attitude, taste,* and *inclination.* Obviously none of these motives are found full-fledged in the newborn child." Thus it seems there are many terms available for expressing the dynamic unit we have in mind. Because no other generic term was available I have designated this *class* of structural units as *traits.* Perhaps my choice was not the wisest, but from my point of view a sentiment is one form of trait. All the units listed in the above quotation have essentially the properties of traits as set forth in Chapters XI and XII of *Personality.* Although the principal properties are the same, yet there are slight differences so that in some contexts *value* fits best, in some contexts *interest,* in some *sentiment,* in others one has no alternative but to use the simple term *trait.* This last term, then, is used by me generically as referring to several kinds of motivational units differing only slightly from one another; or else it is used to designate a motivational integer for which no other special term is available (*e.g.,* 'stylistic traits').

Bertocci's suggestion that sentiments have more 'driving' power than attitudes is partly acceptable to me. General usage would seem to favor this suggestion. Difficulty arises, however, in cases where the motivational complex is well integrated and contains both sentimental and attitudinal features. In such a case I believe it does violence to the organized character of the motive to insist upon the distinction he proposes. For example, a young man is heart and soul bent upon becoming a doctor. As I see it this goal may represent a simple, integral fact of motivation in his personality.

It would falsify this organization to dissolve it into a component sentiment (*e.g.*, love for suffering humanity), an attitude (*e.g.*, liking for materia medica), and a trait (*e.g.*, a friendly manner). It is much better in this case to scrap all these three terms and speak only of an *ambition*. (In the generic sense, of course, the *ambition* is itself a *trait*.)

We need diversity and flexibility in our terminology respecting motives. Sometimes we may speak more appropriately of *sentiment,* sometimes of *attitude,* or of *trait.* (There are borderlines where all three seem equally appropriate, as when we speak with propriety of a sentiment, attitude, *or* trait of *patriotism.*) Or we may, if the case requires, employ such terms as *value, frame of reference, ambition, taste, inclination, interest.* For careful thinking in the sphere of motivation these terms should all be distinguished from one another. Elsewhere I have attempted to contribute something toward this clarification of terminology, but do not need to repeat my thoughts on the subject here.

Although these distinctions are not unimportant, what matters most to me is that *all of these units of motivational structure be regarded as dynamic, unique, personal and ultimate.* Hence I cannot accept Mr. Bertocci's proposal to regard them as merely 'proximate' factors in motivation. He has given his arguments for wishing to stand by McDougall's propensities as 'ultimate' causes. I have given my reasons for not wishing to do so. Respecting the immediate structural components we agree quite well. If only he would not insist upon viewing these components (which are all that can be established empirically) as proximate! To my way of thinking they offer as *ultimate* a representation of human motivation as psychological knowledge today warrants.

15. The Functional Autonomy of Motives

Oscar Oppenheimer

THE theory of the functional autonomy of motives forms a vital part of G. W. Allport's theory of personality, and, by itself, it is a very interesting contribution to the field of motivation. Allport states:

Somehow in the process of maturing the manifold potentialities and dispositions of childhood coalesce into sharper, more distinctive motivational systems. *Pari passu* with their emergence these systems take upon themselves effective driving power, operating as mature, autonomous motives quite different in aim and in character from the motivational systems of juvenile years, and very different indeed from the crude organic tensions of infancy.

Elaborating on it, he states further:

The dynamic psychology proposed here regards adult motives as infinitely varied, and as self-sustaining, contemporary systems, growing out of antecedent systems, but functionally independent of them . . . . Each motive has a definite point of origin which may lie in the hypothetical instincts, or, more likely, in the organic tensions and diffuse irritability described in Chapter IV. Theoretically all adult purposes can be traced back to these seed-forms in infancy. But as the individual matures the bond is broken. The tie is historical, not functional.

How does the functional autonomy come about? Is it a result of mere growth, as these quotations would suggest? No, for the illustrations which the author offers in order to make his point clear present a second explanation: elements which first have been accidental in a certain situation gain a superior importance, and become autonomous motives. In fact, in examining his evidences we will find that most of them serve this latter idea, and only very few illustrate his basic description of the origin of the new motives. Allport gives much space to his presentation of evidences, so we will do well to inspect a large majority of them. His first illustration deals with an ex-sailor.

Abridged from the *Journal of Social Psychology,* 1947, 25, 171-179. Reprinted by permission of the author and The Journal Press.

He "has a craving for the sea . . . . He may have first acquired his love for the sea as an incident in his struggle to earn a living. The sea was merely a conditioned stimulus associated with satisfaction of his 'nutritional craving'. But now the ex-sailor is perhaps a wealthy banker; the original motive is destroyed; and yet the hunger for the sea persists unabated, even increases in intensity as it becomes more remote from the 'nutritional segment'." Does the author give a satisfactory explanation for the ex-sailor's present craving for the sea? Did the ex-sailor acquire his love for the sea, on which his present craving is based, only as an incident in his struggle for making a living, as Allport wants us to believe? It may be true that he discovered his love for the sea because he went to the sea. But seeing the sea was nothing but a precipitating cause. The deeper-lying predisposing causes were some instincts in him. As far as the precipitating cause is concerned, the sailor may have hit on it by sheer accident: he was looking for work and he saw a poster of the Merchant Marine, pay and living conditions looked good to him, so he took it. But then, when he was at sea, he realized that his new life satisfied some instincts in him which had been unsatisfied for a long time, perhaps a romantic desire for adventure or for a more irregular life than he had had before, or the motive of scientific curiosity or a longing for natural beauty, or a combination of some or of all of them. If he would have passed a poster of the Pennsylvania Railroad instead of one of the Merchant Marine, the love for his new life and the craving for it afterward would never have developed because the section work on the railroad could not satisfy either his desire for adventure or his scientific curiosity, or his longing for natural beauty. Or, to look at the same thing from another angle, if he would have been another type of fellow who would not care for adventure or for any of the other aspects of the life at sea, the sea as a precipitating cause would never have led to the love for it. To present my last point, his going to sea may have been not accidental at all as far as his love for the sea is concerned. He may have gone to sea because all his life he had been dreaming of it, and now he went in order to satisfy his instincts. All that I have said so far shows how tiny the role is which the accidental element plays in our situation, and that, therefore, it would be very superficial to say that the new motive of longing for the sea grew out of this accidental element. It also disproves Allport's second account of the origin of new motives. The longing for the sea did not grow out of old motives, and then become autonomous while the old motives vanished. On the contrary, the longing will remain strong, if the underlying romantic or esthetic motive will remain strong. If it should happen one day that he does not care any longer for their satisfaction, his longing will die with them.

Before I draw more conclusions from this analysis, let us examine more of Allport's evidences. "A musician longs to return to his instrument after an enforced absence . . . . He may first have been stung by a rebuke or by a slur on his inferior performances into mastering his instrument, but now he is safely beyond power of these taunts; there is no need to continue, yet he loves his instrument more than anything else in the world." How would we answer the question: why does the musician love his instrument? He loves it because playing it gives him thorough satisfaction of instincts like creative expression or social prestige or self-esteem, or of combinations of them. Again, as in the sailor's case, there may or may not have been a mere accidental precipitating cause for learning to play the instrument, and this cause may have vanished, but the motive for playing the instrument does not become autonomous after the initial cause has gone. There will be underlying motives from which it draws its strength and on which it depends. There are two points which become clearer by this illustration than by the ex-sailor evidence. First: the basis on which a certain motive rests may change. What was social prestige first, hurt by his friends' taunts shifted to creative expression or self-esteem or social prestige coming from the praise of the friends. While Allport noticed the disappearance of the first underlying motive, he overlooked the existence of other motives coming into play after the disappearance of the first. Secondly: It is true the new motives originate in adulthood. But they are secondary motives based on primary motives which existed before and which in the years before may have been the basis of other secondary motives. We know that a primary motive forms the basis for a variety of secondary motives.

"A miser continues to amass his useless horde . . . . He perhaps learned his habits of thrift in dire necessity, or perhaps his thrift was a symptom of sexual perversion (as Freud would claim), and yet the miserliness persists, and even becomes stronger with the years, even after the necessity or the roots of the neurosis have been relieved." Here again, the miserliness does not rest mainly on the dire necessity or on sexual perversion, although one or both may have been present at the beginning. Therefore, when they disappeared miserliness did not disappear. What was also present at the beginning, or what appeared after these first motives had gone, was an abnormally strong instinct for security. This instinct is so strong in a miser that it makes him irrational, that means, no horde amassed can satisfy it, even the one which would appear over-sufficient to the rational mind. Therefore, a millionaire can remain a miser.

"Workmanship is a good example of functional autonomy. A good workman feels compelled to do clean-cut jobs even though his security, or the praise of others, no longer depend on high standards. In fact, in a day of jerry-building, his workman-like standards may be to his economic disadvantage. Even so he cannot do a slipshod job. Workmanship is not an instinct, but so firm is the hold it may acquire on a man that it is little wonder Veblen mistook it for one." Contrary to our author's opinion, I hold workmanship as poor an example of functional autonomy as all the others. What we find here again is a shift from one underlying primary motive to another. The motive prompting the workman to do a decent job after the motives of self-preservation or social prestige have gone, may be self-esteem. He thinks now he owes it to himself to do as good a job as possible. A new angle offered by this example (but not one which strengthens Allport's interpretation) is in the fact that the motives of self preservation and of social prestige, which formed the basis of workmanship first have become motives hostile to work-manship, and that the new primary motive of self-esteem must be stronger than they so that we may have sufficient motives for workmanship. Allport's assertion to the extent that "what once was an instrumental technique be-comes a master-motive" is not true in the case of good workmanship. It is not a master-motive, but a secondary motive, based on primary motives, as we realize when we analyze it. Besides, how can an instrumental tech-nique become a motive? An instrumental technique, as the term says, is a technique instrumental for realizing a motive, but not identical with a motive. It belongs in another logical category. I must have a motive first, and then I may look for an instrumental technique to realize it.

Let us take the maternal sentiment as the last illustration of this group of Allport's examples. He says:

The maternal sentiment offers an excellent final illustration. Many young mothers bear their children unwillingly, dismayed at the thought of the drudgery of the future. At first they may be in-different to, or even hate, their offspring; the "parental instinct" seems wholly lacking. The only motives that hold such a mother to child-tending may be fear of what her critical neighbors will say, fear of the law, a habit of doing any job well, or perhaps a dim hope that the child will provide security for her in her old age. However gross these motives, they are sufficient to hold her to her work, until through the practice of devotion her burden becomes a joy. As her love for the child develops, her earlier practical motives are forgotten. In later years not one of these original motives may operate. The child may be incompetent, criminal, a disgrace to her, and far from serving as a staff for her declining years, he may continue to drain her resources and vitality. The neighbors may criticize her for indulging the child, the law may exonerate her from allegiance; she certainly feels no pride in such a child; yet she sticks to him. The tenacity of the maternal senti-ment under such adversity is proverbial.

Allport's description of the initial relations between mother and baby holds true in many single cases. He is also right in further stating that all motives which operated originally as a basis for maternal behavior may dis-appear. But does he really think that the maternal motive for a child that is incompetent, criminal, or a disgrace to the mother, that continues to drain her resources and vitality, could be as strong as it often is if the only explanation for it was the practice of devotion, an instrumental technique?

Is not, on the contrary, the burden which child rearing meant to the mother a factor which would destroy her maternal instinct, rather than strengthen it, if, by its behavior, the growing child shows very little appreciation for all the mother went through in the interest of the child? The real motives which account for sustained maternal behavior are instincts like self-esteem and altruistic motive and sociability. The mother discovers that by her work a young living being grows up, and under her care reveals new gifts every day. She sees its dependence on her and experiences the joy of helping this help-less creature. In thus living very closely and intimately together she over-comes her own lonesomeness. All these motives, to be sure, may not have operated in the beginning, as in the case of the ex-sailor. At the start she did not know that the life with the child would satisfy them. But then she dis-covered that she could satisfy them, and again, the maternal motive is merely a new secondary motive, not an autonomous primary motive, but based on "old" primary motives.

As weak as all the examples from everyday experience which we examined are, as weak are his examples taken from experimental studies, even he himself contends that here "the evidence appears in sharper outline." There is first the circular reflex, the case of the baby who taxes the parent's patience by throwing down the spoon many times, the case of the small child who babbles the same syllables for a long time, or the case of the boy who rides on his bicycle up and down the same sidewalk for time on end. Are such acts satisfactorily explained by "the consummation of an act providing adequate stimulation for the repetition of the same act," as Allport thinks? Does it really "not require any backward tracing of motives?" If this were true, why do we not have much more of this circular reflex in our lives? Is it not more plausible to think that a strong motive became satisfied, and that we anticipate new satisfaction of this motive by repetition of the action? The baby likes to tyrannize the father or enjoys his new gift of babbling or of riding the bicycle, or gets rid of more and more surplus energy by riding it. The act is not self-perpetuating, but the new performances are founded on the same basic motive. If this motive would fall away, the mere fact of repetitive behavior would not produce a new act.

His second example in this category of experimental evidence deals with conative perseveration. He says: "Many experiments show that incompleted tasks set up tensions that tend to keep the individual at work until they are resolved. No hypothesis of self-assertion, rivalry, or any other basic need, is required. The completion of the task itself has become a quasi-need with dynamic force of its own." Motives of self-assertion and rivalry are no *hypothesis,* the "quasi-need with dynamic force of its own" is hypothetical (why does he call the need "quasi"?). And there is no need for turning to a hypothesis when out of numerous experiences we know that motives like self-assertion and rivalry make us desire to finish an uncompleted task. The reason we remember the unfinished task better than the finished one is that we find satisfaction of the afore-mentioned motives in the finished task and that we are still looking for it in the unfinished task.

His third example is a strange one. He presents conditioned reflexes in order to tell us that they are no evidences. But then he goes on to say: "But there are innumerable instances in human life where a single association, *never* reinforced, results in the establishment of a life-long dynamic system. An experience associated only once with a bereavement, an accident, or a battle, may become the center of a permanent phobia or complex, not in the least dependent on a recurrence of the original shock." Let us first disregard the fact that these single associations have nothing to do with conditioned reflexes with which he started out. When the veteran who had a mental collapse on the battle field, years later still winces every time he hears a whistle blow because it reminds him of the screaming of the shells which was in his ears when he collapsed, the explanation is that part of the fear which he suffered once when the realization of the motive of self-preservation was terribly endangered is still in him. Therefore, in order to cure him we go to the underlying motive, to make him feel so secure that the fear of not being able to realize the motive of self-preservation disappears.

How good a point for Allport's theory is the relation between ability and interest? He says:

> A person likes to do what he can do well. Over and over again it has been demonstrated that the skill learned for some external reason, turns into an interest, and is self-propelling, even though the original reason for pursuing it has been lost. A student who at first undertakes a field of study in college because it is prescribed, because it pleases his parents, or because it comes at a convenient hour often ends by finding himself absorbed, perhaps for life, in the subject itself. He is not happy without it. The original motives are entirely lost. What was a means to an end has become an end in itself.

What we find here again by digging a little deeper, is a shift from a first group of underlying motives to another one. The student becomes absorbed in his studies because he discovers in the course of time that doing them well brings satisfaction of various motives of social prestige or of scientific curiosity or of self-esteem. The means to an end, namely studying, has not become an end in itself, it remains a means, but for the realization of new motives. I must say it is fantastic if Allport thinks that he can explain Pasteur's life-long and life-filling devotion to his work by the skill which he acquired in it. It was the scientific thirst crying for satisfaction of the motive of scientific curiosity which was the driving power of Pasteur.

In summarizing my criticism of Allport's theory, I would say his evidences do not prove the existence of new autonomous motives in adulthood, neither in the way that old motives out of which the new ones are supposed to grow, disappear and leave the new ones as autonomous new motives, nor by way of accidental elements in a situation, e.g., instrumental techniques, becoming autonomous new motives. All that we find are new secondary motives, i.e., new motives which are not autonomous, but based on primary motives which existed before. These primary motives may or may not be realized for the first time by the realization of the new secondary motives.

There is one comparatively small field in which we find true evidences for Allport's theory—namely, the field of habits. Strangely enough, Allport puts only small emphasis on this point. "The acquired habits seem sufficient to urge one to a frenzied existence, even though reason and health demand the simpler life." And yet here we find that something originally established on the basis of primary motives, acquires motivating force of its own and becomes independent from its basis. How strong this force can become, we see from the cases in which we do things out of habit which other strong motives would prevent us from doing: e.g., being forced into work that first we dislike thoroughly and yet learn to like in the course of time by dint of habit. While this is the only phenomenon that would back up Allport's theory, even here we have to be cautious, so that we will not overlook the fact that it does not hold true for all habits, and not completely for each single habit. Many habits are not autonomous, but are secondary motives based on the primary motive of self-preservation. For many times habits may give us the illusion of security, the idea that life could go on this way infinitely, and in that case it is the motive of self preservation that we think we satisfy in doing things by habit. Other times a certain habit may be a motivating power partly in an autonomous, partly in a secondary way.

The last question which I would like to raise is: How is it possible for Allport to conceive a theory which holds true only in a small section of motivation, and is wrong for all the rest of the field? The theory has not sprung from an observation of facts. This theory is the child of other Allport theories, and is wrong because those theories are wrong. They are his theory of the uniqueness of personality, and his other theory which holds that the variety of adult motives cannot be traced back to a few childhood motives. Of the first theory, Allport says: "The stress in this volume is constantly on the ultimate and irreducible uniqueness of personality." (I am giving one quotation for many.) A quotation like this shows clearly how Allport strains the meaning of a basically sound theory. All students of personality, starting with Boethius, consider variety of personalities and, resulting from it, uniqueness "main characteristics of personality." Uniqueness, however, does not imply that each personality is completely different from another. The tremendous number of different elements of which each personality consists makes it possible to have a large number of such elements in common with others and yet differ as to many other elements. Therefore, the work of psychology of personality does not need to consist of finding only a general law governing the ways in which uniqueness operates, but also of finding types of personality which have many features in common. Two individuals may differ as to intelligence and strength and kind of emotions, and have in common a strong will and a lack of moral sense. Their personalities will be unique even if they are partly alike. If this were not true, psychology would have to despair because of the lack of material. To quote Allport in regard to his second theory: "The theory declines to believe that the energies of adult personality are infantile or archaic in nature." "It avoids the absurdity of regarding the energy of life now, in the *present,* as somehow consisting of early archaic forms (instincts, prepotent reflexes, or the never-changing *Id*)." As we may gather from the last quotation, Allport, in developing this theory, criticizes McDougall, Freud, and related theories. His excellent criticism of them, however, does not pave the way to a sound theory of his own. He says: "Not four wishes, nor eighteen propensities, nor any and all combinations of these, even with their extensions and variations, seem adequate to account for the endless variety of goals sought by an endless variety of mortals." Very true, but do we therefore have to accept the theory of the functional autonomy of motives? Most modern psychologists do not agree with the instinct psychologists who say that instincts must be present at birth, common among all men and few in number. Many instincts appear later in life, many of them are possessed only by a certain number of people, and there are many instincts. Nothing in the concept of instinct prevents us from assuming this, and there are many facts which substantiate it. Because there are many instincts, there is no need for a theory which tries to create new autonomous motives on the basis of the old ones, or by a transformation of accidental elements in a situation into motives. All that is new, are secondary motives. They are not autonomous, but their large number helps to account for the great variety of motives and for the relative uniqueness of personality. While Freud overrates, I think that Allport underrates the importance of instincts appearing in early childhood. There are a number of instincts, and among them those which play a very important role in the lives of most individuals, as self-preservation and social prestige, which appear early and accompany us through life. They do not change: what changes are the secondary motives on the realization of which their own realization depends.

In concluding, it may be said that Allport's theory belongs to the class of theories which, while wrong, are more thought-provoking than many a stale truth is.

16. Experimental Evidence
for Functional Autonomy
of Motives

Dorothy Rethlingshafer

THE emergent principle of functional autonomy of motives has been stressed by Allport. When activities exhibit this functional autonomy, "some new function emerges as an independently structured unit from preceding functions. The activity of these new units does not depend upon the continued activity of the units from which they developed." The strength, the long duration, the apparent independence from the original motives that may characterize the activities with this functional autonomy is indicated by his illustrations: "An ex-sailor has a craving for the sea," "a workman feels compelled to do clean-cut jobs even though his security . . . no longer depends upon high standards," "the miser continues to amass his usless horde," etc.

It is the purpose of this paper to evaluate the experimental evidence given by Allport, and certain related studies, in order to determine if the principle can be supported or if the systematic behavior of his illustrations might not be better interpreted by other factors.

Allport first suggests the circular reflex as an elementary instance of functional autonomy and later quarrels with it as support for adult behavior. Hence we will accept his own criticism.

Next he cites the experiments which show that "incompleted tasks set up tensions that tend to keep the individual at work until they are resolved." Freeman found task tension increased after interruptions as shown in tendon deformation, palmar skin resistance, and muscular action potentials, but Freeman's measurements of physiological changes were at the moment of interruption, or very near, with no substitute activities intervening. His investigations, therefore, lend only inferential support to the existence of a tension sufficiently long to explain the resumptions of activities when an extended period

Abridged from the *Psychological Review,* 1943, 50, 397-407. Reprinted by permission of the author and the American Psychological Associatiion, Inc.

has intervened between the interruption and the opportunity to return to the original activity. Freeman's explanation, it should be emphasized, is in terms of immediately competing patterns of neural excitation rather than in terms of psychic energy systems.

Abel found that individuals with low Schneider index—indicating instability in neuro-circulatory activity—recall more completed tasks, while interrupted tasks are recalled more by those with high index. This result would suggest that the behavior at an interruption is determined in part by a somewhat consistent physiological condition, rather than by a condition created by the interruption.

Experimental evidence of *behavior* following interruption is given by the work of Zeigarnik, and substantiated by Pachauri, Marrow, etc. But the Zeigarnik ratio rests upon the superior recall of only the names of interrupted tasks. Moreover these tasks are simple and brief. They frequently require only 3 to 5 minutes for completion, and are usually concerned with familiar material. The recall must also be within a short time after the interruption, or completion; otherwise the U-C ratio declines. This decline results from the fading of the interrupted activities, while the completed activities with no unresolved tension do not disintegrate. If tension from the interruption is to be considered as significant in understanding activities possessing autonomy, then the interrupted acts should stand up under the pressure of time. The Zeigarnik ratio is certainly not support for any long-continuing 'striving-from-within' operating in complex and difficult activities.

Ovsiankina's findings that there is a greater resumption of interrupted activities than of non-interrupted acts has been confirmed by various studies, etc., although this resumption is significantly lowered when substitutes are introduced. However, the experimental records are obtained after brief interruption periods, usually on the same day, or more frequently within the same hour. Moreover, if the subjects do not resume their original activity within the first minutes, they are very unlikely to return to them. Ovsiankina noted that resumption would generally follow immediately or within 20 seconds. The writer found in 638 records of behavior following interruption with 58 subjects, that there were only 5 delayed resumptions after four minutes of delay. Eighty-four per cent of the delayed resumptions were within the first two minutes following the opportunity to resume.

It should also be remembered that resumption is lowered or destroyed whenever barriers are introduced between the original interrupted activities and the subjects. The writer found that resumption was cut approximately one-half by the use of quite simple objective barriers. It would appear that 'stimulation-from-without' is as essential as 'striving-from-within,' though the reverse of this was assumed by Allport in discussing functional autonomy of motives.

No doubt the techniques of Ovsiankina and Zeigarnik illustrate the immediate effect of an interruption. But even if resumption (or greater recall) of interrupted acts can be attributed to mounting task tension during the interruption, there is still no evidence that such tension can be considered responsible for the continuance of long-lasting activities un-reinforced by any motives. To do this such tension would have to continue through such interruptions as sleep, varying interrupting activities, periods of time measured in days, or weeks, or years, rather than minutes or hours.

The writer has recently emphasized the wide individual differences in the scores of tendency-to-continue as measured by the interruption technique. These scores were, in part at least, explained by a factor which was identified as the "general habit of keeping on at any task once started." To the extent that a person was strong in this habit, he would tend to keep returning to *any* activity and thus the appearance would be given of an act carrying itself. No experimental evidence has been obtained as to the length of time such a general habit might operate, but it seems conceivable that some people might tend to carry on their activities over long periods of time when apparently the original motives were dead, being restimulated at intervals by such verbalised attitudes as "I always finish what I start."[1]

Evidence other than the interruption experiments is also given by Allport in the field of conative perseveration, and many studies could be reviewed in the related topics of retroactive inhibition, reminiscence, reproduction of forms, etc. Some experimenters have interpreted their results as illustrating the dynamic nature of the process of forgetting; others are more in line with Woodworth's conclusion that the evidence is "against the assumption of any positive formative process in retention itself." Certainly the specific experiments cited could not be considered crucial. Kendig found a five-minute interval most favorable for recurrence effects as compared to no interval or 30 minutes. Smith found that the deconditioning process for a fear is more successful if begun immediately than if a delay of 24 hours intervenes though a 15-minute interval was not significantly inferior to 24 hours (C.R. of .83).

Next under the heading of Animal Behavior, Dodson's work is cited by Allport as illustrating how rats will often perform a habit, learned under hunger, when they are fed to repletion. This study, along with other satiation experiments, is subject to the criticism that unsatisfactory criteria of satiation were used.[2] Particularly in the field of animal behavior there are

[1]This behavior might be considered evidence for functional autonomy of motives, but such an interpretation does not consider the emergent properties that are present when the principle is operating. Allport accepts a "habit of doing any job well" as one of the *early* motives that might be present in the development of the maternal sentiment as a functionally autonomous motive.

[2]Moreover the 'habit' began to disintegrate in 10 test trials, approaching chance behavior.

studies which emphasize the dependence of performance upon some original drive. When the animals were not rewarded, *i.e.,* being deprived of food on the maze, or satiated with food after learning, they would not perform correctly in the learning situation, although earlier and later tests indicated superior performance. When both the drive and the incentive were absent, rats did not persist longer than a few days in a learned sand-digging habit. When the drive remained constant, and incentives were changed in various ways, we again find the maze performance altered. Mann tested for the effect of a changed incentive when the rats were 'approaching mastery' of the problem. The results when the inappropriate reward was introduced before mastery were not significantly different from the results when introduced after mastery.

Allport writes of the 'dynamic character' of acquired rhythms of activity. In this regard Richter found that rats will, even when starved, display the same periodic activity whicn their former feeding habits had forced on them. But the mere removal of the specific stimulus of feeding need not bring about an immediate cessation of activity, since it has been shown that such a physiological reaction as conditioned salivation to morphine may be evoked by the total situation. We also find that if the light-dark stimulation is reversed, the rhythm will follow the stimulation, but there is a lag in the reversal indicating an internal as well as an external control. Hemmingsen and Krarup's results would likewise indicate that these rhythms are not free from their internal control. They were unable to establish in rats a rhythm to fit a 16-hour day, 8 hours dark, 8 hours light. This result suggests that the 24-hour rhythm is inherent in the bodily processes themselves, and not imposed from without, nor learned. Such evidence would indicate that there may be a continuance of the internal control of rhythms even when the external stimulating situation is altered.

Since the above citations would indicate that experimental evidence for the emergent principle of functional autonomy of motives is at least limited, if not non-existent, the question remains as to what may the long-lasting systematic behavior of human adults be attributed? The factors which may be instrumental in giving the appearance of functional autonomy for such behavior will now be considered.

(1) *Motive supplied by conditioned expectancy.*—It is known that the expectancy of previously received reward or punishment may operate in the absence of the objective incentive. Miller has shown that two new methods of escape from a recently charged grid could be *learned* under this 'anxiety' state. This acquired drive though persistent was finally extinguished unless trials with shock were given. Adults may operate on the expectancy of a distant reward, or on the anxiety of a possible punishment,[3] and the rein-

---

[3]Since the above was written, McClelland has developed the same suggestion in greater detail.

forcement could be infrequent, yet sufficient to continue activities over so long a period of time that they might appear functionally autonomous.

(2) *Substitute motives in higher order conditioning.*—There may be present some general energizing agent in the building and maintenance of higher order conditioned responses, as is illustrated by the work of Finch and Culler, Brogden. It is possible that some of the activities of adults which appear free from the original drive were built up by the use of substitute motives in higher order conditioning.

(3) *Sub-goal reinforcement.*—Some long sequences of responses of humans may be given to conditioned sub-goals (tokens, symbols) whose occasional but necessary reinforcement by primary drives may not be so apparent as in the animal studies.

(4) *Rewarded practice of an activity.*—Activities that have been well practiced under a rewarded drive may continue, at least temporarily,[4] when the drive is removed. To explain this continuation, Anderson has advanced the theory of externalization of drive, *i.e.*, late in learning the drive mechanism is externalized; the drive can be aroused even in the absence of the internal components by the external stimulus situation (the food reward, the food box, etc.). This theory has been identified as a special case of an autonomous motive. However, the experimental results which show such a continuance of performance are capable of other interpretations, as Anderson himself suggests. Also even with the primary drive removed, some slight motive may continue to operate so that generalized habits of attacking new problems, learned in the previous successful experience, could lead to quick error elimination.

(5) *Continued learning under drive when incentive is removed.*—After training 40 rats to press a bar in a Skinner box, Fitts removed the food reward but *maintained the hunger drive.* He continued to obtain records of bar-pressing behavior over a seven months period that were superior to a control group not conditioned. Fitts writes: "habituation may serve as a quasi-motive and . . . 'operates as a determining factor of such weight as almost to seem a force in itself.'" However, there is evidence within this experiment that the hungrier the animals were, the more they pressed the bar.[5] It is possible that in the narrow environment of the animals, there was

[4]Brogden refers to externalization of drive as an interpretation of the significant difference he found between the experimental extinction of satiated rewarded dogs and satiated non-rewarded dogs. Unfortunately the experiment was discontinued when the satiated rewarded animals were starting, apparently, to decline in their C.R.'s.

Wherry in an unpublished factor analysis of maze errors under the varying motivating conditions used by Anderson, emphasizes the decrease in efficiency of performance with even the externalized rewarded animals as the final phase of maze learning is reached, *i.e.*, when the actual learning factor is probably at work.

[5]Under two periods of food deprivation, not only did the animals exhibit different rates of responding upon the removal of the reward, but they continued to remain apart.

a continuation of learning under their hunger drive, a possibility which is strengthened by the work of Elliot and Treat.[6]

(6) *Generalized incentives and drives.*—Elliott found that rats continued to exhibit a maze habit with only slight disturbance, even though they started their learning on one drive (with its appropriate incentive) and then were switched to another drive (with its appropriate incentive). Bruce used varying, instead of specific, incentives and drives and finally found no decrement in performance under the generalized motive. These experiments suggest methods of developing an activity free from the original need on which it started but not from all needs. The adult activities of humans which seem so far removed from their original drives that they give the appearance of possessing functional autonomy may have developed under varying drives but have never been entirely free from some drive. There may be "functional autonomy from one need, but not from all needs."

(7) *'Useless' habits may be the expression of some need.*—Allport cites Gilhousen's experiment as illustrating that "Among rats as among humans, old and useless habits have considerable power in their own right." However, behavior which may appear 'useless' may be 'psychologically useful.' Lewin has emphasized the difference between 'psychological' and 'geometrical' space. Snygg has set up a situation in which some short paths were ignored in favor of a long path because of rat's preference for centrifugal swing. Yoshioka found that a pattern difference *may* be a determining factor in a choice between paths. O'Kelly has suggested that in regressive behavior we have an attempt to relieve the tension caused by some preceding frustration.

In studies where some behavior may appear to have no value for the rat, we find the experimenter usually giving a reason for the animal indulging himself: strength of drive, over-learning, electric shock, strong problem solving situation, emotional disturbance, etc. Fixation behavior is usually aroused in strongly motivated situations, and the supposed 'useless' habits may be attempts to relieve the tension present in such situations. Any survival of a supposed useless act after the opportunity for subsidence of the tension might also be traced to spontaneous recovery, lack of differential reinforcement between the efficient and the less efficient act, or to remnants of the original situation. The last point is illustrated by Elliott who found that rats fixated on one path under an intense hunger drive did not return to variable behavior at the 5-way point when the hunger drive was lessened, but, it should be noted, not entirely removed.

The present experimental evidence for functional autonomy of motives cannot be considered adequate. Certain factors have been considered which

---

[6]McClelland has excellently summarized various factors which will delay extinction when the reward is removed. The continuation of a learned act after removal of reward may also be attributed to these factors.

may in part be responsible for the long-lasting adult activities that *appear* to be functionally autonomous. These factors, however, have by no means been completely developed. No studies in which they appear have been carried over any long period of time, and certainly they alone cannot be considered sufficient to account for the multiple systematic enduring activities of humans. However, they may be considered as possible substitutes for the principle of functional autonomy.

REFERENCES—SECTION TWO

Allport, G. W. *Personality: A Psychological Interpretation.* New York: Holt, 1937, Chapter 7.
Anderson, E. E. The externalization of drive. I. Theoretical considerations, *Psychol. Rev.*, 1941, *48*, 204-224.
———. The externalization of drive. II. The effect of satiation and removal of reward at different stages in the learning of the rat. *J. Genet. Psychol.*, 1941, *59*, 359-376, 397-426.
Kaul, J. N. How autonomous is functional autonomy? *J. Educ. Psychol., Baroda,* 1959, *16*, 481-491.
Mc Clelland, D. C. Functional autonomy of motives as an extinction phenomenon. *Psychol. Rev.*, 1942, *49*, 272-283.
Miller, N. An experimental investigation of derived drives. *Psychol. Bull.*, 1941, *38*, 534-535.
Seward, J. P. Note on the externalization of drive. *Psychol. Rev.*, 1942, *49*, 197-199.
Woodworth, R. S. *Dynamic Psychology.* New York: Columbia Univ. Press, 1918.

3

THE EGO IN MOTIVATION

Today the concept of "ego" or "self" is recognized as extremely important in the study of motivation and personality. This has not always been true. For many years these concepts were ignored by psychologists. As Allport (Paper No. 17) points out, "One of the oddest events in the history of modern psychology is the manner in which the ego (or self) became side tracked and lost to view. I say odd, because the existence of one's own self is the one fact of which every mortal person—every psychologist included—is perfectly convinced." Historically, one of the first psychologists to concern himself seriously with the concept of ego or self was William James. In his book, *The Principles of Psychology*, (1890), his entire chapter, "The Consciousness of Self," is devoted to the problem of self (ego). Other social scientists who paid much attention to the concept of ego or self were Baldwin, Dewey, Calkins, Prince, Cooley and Mead. It is important to remember that Freud too always placed much emphasis on the importance of the ego in his theories on personality development.

From about 1910 to the late 1930's the concept of self or ego assumed an essentially non–existent role in the thinking of American psychologists. This was due principally to the rise of and emphasis on objective experimental psychology. During this period most psychologists were of the opinion that the concept of self or ego was too vague, indefinite, intangible and subjective to warrant any serious consideration. In the late 1930's, however, a resurgence of the ego concept in the field of psychology was brought about, in large measure, by an attempt to explain more fully the experimental findings resulting from the research on level of aspiration (See Section 4) and related areas in behavior. In this regard Allport remarks that "historically the aspiration level may well be regarded as the door by which the ego re–entered the cloisters of academic psychology" (Paper No. 17). Some of the individuals most responsible for this resurgence in interest in the concept of the ego were Sherif, Cantril and Allport (Paper No. 17).

Allport's provocative and stimulating paper is undoubtedly one of the most outstanding. He discusses in detail the reasons for the fall and rise of the concept ego or self, some of the most important conceptions of the ego found in psychological literature, the significance of the results derived from experimental studies dealing with ego–involved behavior and the nature of the ego. Allport's attitude concerning the importance of the ego concept is exemplified by his concluding statements that "we may safely predict that ego psychology in the twentieth century will flourish increasingly. For only with its aid can psychologists reconcile the human nature that they study and the human nature that they serve." The ideas developed by Allport in this paper served to stimulate the following articles by Rice, Bertocci, and Chein.

The paper by Rice (No. 18) is devoted primarily to a criticism of Allport's arguments concerning the inadequacy of the Law of Effect to deal with ego–involved behavior. In this paper Rice presents a three-fold thesis: "1) that Allport's criticisms are such to force a reformation or at least a clarification of the Law of Effect, but 2) that his evidence is such as to support rather than to refute the Law when it is so reinterpreted, and 3) that the Law when thus clarified may supply us with precisely the principle that we need in order to account for some central characteristics of the ego's development." Bertocci (Paper No. 19) attempts to solve and clarify some of the problems involved in Allport's discussion of the ego. He suggests the hypothesis that "*I* refers to a complex, unitary activity of sensing, remembering, imagining, perceiving, wanting, feeling and thinking. These *activities are the dynamic unity* referred to by the word *self*." Chein (Paper No. 20) endeavors to meet the challenge of describing what the ego is, as well as to present an inclusive theory of the ego, both of which, he points out, were left undone by Allport. Basic to Chein's theory are his beliefs that except for infants, some philosophers and some psychopaths, everyone is aware of one's self and the self is not identical with the ego. Chein concludes by stating that "the ego is a motivational–cognitive structure built up around the self." Hilgard (Paper No. 21) defends the thesis that all of the defense mechanisms (rationalization, repression, etc.) or mechanisms of adjustment, imply a self-reference and that the mechanisms can not be understood unless the concept of the self is accepted. He believes that in order to understand the dynamics of a person's defense mechanisms it is essential that we know something about his self-image or self-concept. Klein and Schoenfeld (Paper No. 22) set for themselves the problem of answering this question: Would the confidence ratings of a group of subjects acquired in a variety of neutral tasks (non ego-involved) change significantly in another situation where ego factors (prestige, self–esteem, academic standing) are involved in the tasks? In terms of their experimental findings the authors conclude that confidence appears to be a personality trait when the ego is involved but that it is specific to each situation when the situation is neutral (not ego–involved).

While present day psychologists are fairly well agreed that the concept of ego or self is basic and integral to any theory of personality or motivation, there is not complete unanimity as to its nature, development and function. This is not to imply, however, that there is little or no agreement on the fundamental aspects of the ego. Actually, there is much agreement. The main source of difference appears to be in terms of emphasis. It seems very likely that theorists in the field of human behavior will devote more and more attention to a systematic and organized approach to the concept of ego (self) as a dynamic component of personality.

1. INTRODUCTION

17. The Ego in Contemporary Psychology

Gordon W. Allport

ONE of the oddest events in the history of modern psychology is the manner in which the ego (or self) became sidetracked and lost to view. I say it is odd, because the existence of one's own self is the one fact of which every mortal person— every psychologist included— is perfectly convinced. An onlooker might say, "Psychologists are funny fellows. They have before them, at the heart of their science, a fact of perfect certainty, the one warrant for the being of all other things, and yet they pay no attention to it. Why don't they begin with their own egos, or with our egos—with something we all know about? If they did so we might understand them better. And, what is more, they might understand us better."

Back in the 1880's, of course, it was good form for James, Royce, Dewey and their contemporaries to speak freely of the ego, the self, or even the soul. The soul, to be sure, was giving way under Wundt's onslaughts, and everyone was finding it exhilarating to shake off the alleged 'theological domination,' and to emerge unfettered and positivistic into the era of the New Psychology. They forgot that their predecessors had not endorsed the soul because of their theological leanings, but rather, because associationism did not recognize or explain to their satisfaction the *coherence, unity and purposiveness* which they thought prevailed in mental life. Granted that the 'soul' also failed to explain these properties, it at least called attention to their existence.

After the expulsion of the soul, these unifying properties of mental life were occassionally referred to under the designation of 'self.' For a time, thanks to James, Calkins, Prince, and the French psychopatholigists, 'self' was a reasonably popular concept. But gradually it too fell into disuse.

Abridged from the *Psychological Review*, 1943, *50*, 451-476. Reprinted by permission of the author and the American Psychological Association, Inc.

The total eclipse of soul and the partial eclipse of self were due in part, as I have just said, to the rise of positivism in psychology. Positivism, we all know, is a scientific program for moral re-armament, whose imperatives include absolute monism, absolute objectivity, and absolute reductionism—in short, absolute chastity. From this ascetic point of view, subjective certainties are suspect, selves seem a bit indecent, and any hint of metaphysics (that is, of non-positivistic metaphysics) savors of laxness. As Gardner Murphy pointed out to this Association one year ago there was no prestige to be gained from a psychology of the self.

But for all its sumptuary control, positivism had one undisputed merit: it engendered a wholesome dislike for question-begging explanations. Much of the older psychology, it showed, suffered from a tendency to labor over words as if words were the essence of things. Thanks to positivism faculty psychology, resting as it did on verbal realism, became discredited, and dialectics fell into disrepute. Much of self-psychology we must now admit, dwelt on the unenlightening plane of dialectics. Its statements were often redundant or circular. In the manner of Gertrude Stein it sometimes asserted that a self is a self is a self. Not being, by nature, especially lyrical, psychologists failed to see any deeper significance in this exalted formula. Quite understandably they refused to admit such a stammering self to the gray citadel of their laboratories.

But when a concept becomes taboo it is probable that the taboo will irradiate to cover a whole range of problems associated with the concept. Something of this sort seems to have happened. It is not only the soul and the self that suffered ostracism, but along with them a vast array of problems having to do with the coherence and unity of mental life, with pride, ambition, and status, with values, ideals, and outlook on the future. The eclipse, of course, has not been total, but it has been considerable.

As if to compensate for the neglect of these interests within the field of psychology proper, psychoanalysis rose upon the horizon emitting a spectacular, if sporadic, light. Small wonder that the world at large turned to psychoanalysis for guidance in dynamic psychology. There was precious little other guidance to be had. I am inclined to believe history will declare that psychoanalysis marked an inter-regnum in psychology between the time when it lost its soul, shortly after the Franco-Prussian War, and the time when it found it again, shortly after World War II.

Until psychoanalysis becomes finally fused into a broader and more adequate psychology, it may take pride in having preserved and advanced the study of certain functions of the self that positivistic psychology had consigned to oblivion. It may take credit too for preserving one term, more or less cognate with 'self,' from the dark taboo of which I have spoken. 'Ego' has featured prominently in psychoanalytic literature from its beginning.

This term I am now appropriating to signify the recentering that is taking place in psychological theory.

But it is not from psychoanalysis alone that we draw our threads. The position of the ego in contemporary psychology is determined by certain other historical trends as well.

II.   MAIN CONCEPTIONS OF THE EGO

Among the different conceptions of the ego found in psychological literature the following are certainly the most important.

1.   *The ego as knower.*—The nominative form of the word ego implies that some subject is busily engaged as Brentano would say in 'intending' his relations to the universe. The problem of the knower or 'Pure Ego' has been of little interest to psychologists since James gave it his lengthy *coup de grace* in the *Principles.* It is enough, says James in effect, to admit that knowing goes on. A separate knowing-ego is not a necessary assumption. For phenomenologists and personalists of course, the problem of the subject-object relationship remains uppermost. But for the most part, since the time of Brentano and James, psychologists have passed the problem by.[1] For our purposes, we need only record the first usage, and note its relative rarity.

2.   *The ego as object of knowledge*—Some investigators have set themselves the problem of the nature of our experience of the self. This approach, limited as it is to the deliverances of introspection, has not been particularly rewarding. It yields relatively unenlightening localizations for the ego which is felt to lie 'between the eyes,' or to consist of 'motions in the head,' or to be situated 'between right and left,' 'between up and down,' 'between behind and before.' Following this line of investigation Horowitz came upon such a diversity of results (reports locating the ego in the head, heart, chest, face, brain, genitals) that he concludes "the localization of the self as it is reported in the literature quoted, in the responses on our questionnaire, in informal discussion, in the investigation of children, is not the basic phenomenon one might hope for to ease an anlysis of the structure of the self and personality."

There seem to be only two facts upon which there is general agreement. (1) Infants, all writers concur, do not recognize themselves as individuals; they behave in what Piaget calls an 'undifferentiated absolute' composed of self and environment. Only gradually and with difficulty does a segregated ego evolve. (2) The ego of which we are aware is variable in its dimensions.

[1]Private correspondence with Koffka concerning his own usage of the term brought out the interesting fact that in writing his chapters on the ego he had never thought of the ego in the role of the knower. "To be quite frank, I never put this question to myself." He adds, "That my solution will be similar to Brentano's I doubt. At the moment it seems to me that it will be found in the theory of Ego subsystems, more particularly in the relation of the Self-system to other Ego-systems."

Sometimes it includes less than the body and sometimes more. In a semi-doze we lose all sense of our egos though we may be conscious enough of impersonal items. Our feet perhaps are suddenly perceived as strange objects not belonging to us. In pathological conditions, we know, remarkable experiences of depersonalization take place. Conversely, we sometimes think of a tool we are using as parts of our extended ego-system, and at times we regard our children, our lodge, or our ancestors as an intimate part of our extended selves. It is agreed that in this manner the ego-systems of which we are aware contract and expand in a most variable fashion.

3. *The ego as primitive selfishness.*—A century ago Max Stirner wrote *Der Einzige und Sein Eigenthum,* a volume in which he developed the thesis that man is by nature unalterably eogistic. In 1918 the French biologist Felix Le Dantec handled the same theme more brilliantly in his *L'egoïsme: seule base de toute société.* Unquenchable eogism is the foundation of the social edifice, says LeDantec, and hypocrisy is its keystone. Psychologists are partial to such hardheaded realism, and have themselves gone far in unveiling the hypocrisy in man's nature. Projections, rationalizations, defense mechanisms have been exposed for what they are—the whitewashing of ego-centric motivation. During this century psychologists have joined with historians, biographers, novelists in the fashionable sport of debunking human motives.

4. *The ego as dominance-drive.*—Related to this view of primitive egoism, we find many investigations that deal with dominance feelings, with ascendance, with pecking orders, with euphoria. From this point of approach the ego is that portion of the personality that demands status and recognition. The negative states of anxiety, insecurity, defensiveness, resistance are just as truly indicators that whenever the ego is debased there arise impulses for its defense and restoration to status.

5. *Ego as a passive organization of mental processes.*—Psychoanalysis, we all know, has contributed much to the interpretation of human nature in terms of egoism. Its whole theory of motivation is based upon the assumption of hedonistic self-interest. But in psychoanalysis egoism, oddly enough, is not ascribed to the ego, but to the urges arising from the id. For Freud the ego proper is a passive percipient, devoid of dynamic power, 'a coherent organization of mental processes' that is aware of the warring forces of the id, superego, and external environment. The ego, having no dynamic power, tries as well as it can to conciliate and to steer the warring forces, but when it fails, as it often does, it breaks out in anxiety. The ego is born of restraint of the instinctual impulses, and it continually needs strengthening. But even when through the analytic process it is strengthened, it is still essentially nothing more than a passive victim-spectator of the drama of conflict.

Dissatisfied with Freud's denial of dynamic power to the ego, we know that later psychoanalytic writers, French and Hendrick among them, have ascribed more *momentum* to the ego. It is the agent that plans, that strives to master as well as to conciliate the conflicts. One analyst, Heinz Hartmann, departing considerably from Freud, holds that "adaptation to reality—which includes mastery of it—proceeds to a large extent from the ego and in particular from that part of the ego which is free from conflict; and it is directed by the organized structure of ego-functions (such as intelligence, perception, etc.) which exist in their own right and have an independent effect upon the solution of conflicts." To such writers the ego-ideal is no longer, as it was with Freud, a passive reflection of the superego, which in turn is conceived as a mere legacy of the parent. The ego through its ideals reaches into the future, becomes an executive, a planner, a fighter.

6. *Ego as a 'fighter for ends.'*—We are brought then, by some of the more modern psychoanalysts to a position not unlike that of McDougall, or of James in his more teleological moments. For McDougall self-regard was the master and controlling sentiment in whose interest all other sentiments function. The phrase 'fighter for ends' I borrow from James, who at times was intensely dynamic and personalistic in his conception of the self.

The purposive view of the ego may be linked to Koffka's postulate that there is ever active "a force which propels the ego upwards." The position is represented too in those dynamic psychologies that recognize the subservience of the biological drives to one central drive of ego-satisfaction. One of the most forceful expressions of this point of view is to be found in Goldstein's *Human nature in the light of psychopathology.*[2]

7. *The ego as a behavioral system.*—In spite of his postulation of "a force which propels the ego upwards," Koffka's position is characteristically somewhat less dynamic than that just described. The ego, he says, is only one segregated system within an homogeneous field. Much behavior occurs with no reference to the ego. Not all perception, not all action, not all emotion, not all consciousness, are related to an ego-system. The ego varies widely in its boundaries from time to time, and under certain circumstances acts as a system which determines the course of events as does any other dynamic system according to the theory of Gestalt. But much of the time behavior is free from the influence of an ego-system.

More influential because of its experimental fruitfulness is Lewin's treatment of the subject. Although he seldom uses the term ego he too allows for a central subsystem within the person. Not all behavior is ego-linked, but many kinds of experimentally obtained results cannot be accounted for with-

[2]"On the basis of our discussions I believe we are in no way forced to assume the existence of special drives . . . . They are special situations, and represent the various forms by which the organism as a whole expresses itself . . . . The traditional view assumes various drives which come into the foreground under certain conditions. We assume only one drive, the drive of self-actualization, but are compelled to concede that under certain conditions the tendency to actualize one potentiality is so strong that the organism is governed by it."

out referring to the special types of tension that exist whenever the ego is 'engaged.' The shifting aspiration level is, most obviously, a phenomenon of ego-tensions. Satiation, substitution, encapsulation, resistance, irreality, power-field are among the Lewinian concepts whose characteristics represent various properties of ego-tensions.[3]

It is clear that Lewin, no less than Koffka, wishes to avoid thinking of the ego as a single entity, and prefers to regard it as the variable set of forces that are aroused whenever the person enters into some novel and perhaps dangerous relation to his environment.

8. *Ego as the subjective organization of culture.*—In recent years, as everyone knows, there has been a drawing together of psychology, psycho-analysis and social anthropology. The resulting commensalism has produced a new conception of the ego. The picture of the selfish and unsocialized ego bequeathed us by Stirner and Le Dantec has been broadened. Sherif, for example, points out that although the ego is a 'genetic psychological forma-tion,' yet it is acquired by the child under the ceaseless impact of influence by parents, teachers, and associates, with the result that we must say that the ego "is chiefly made up of social values." Since the process of segregating the ego in childhood is achieved largely by giving the child a name, a status, a code of behavior, a social sense of guilt, and social standards for making his judgements—Sherif concludes that the ego is nothing but the social part of man. This author's position is extreme, for if the ego is nothing but 'the social in man,' one wonders what to call all the anti-social impulses and the solitary strivings that are normally called *egoistic?* Cantril's view is similar to, but less extreme than, Sherif's. Cantril admits that "a person's ego and, con-sequently, the way in which he regards himself, are by no means always entirely bound by the surrounding culture." But yet what an individual regards as himself is undeniably, in large part, socially determined. When his nation's flag is torn down *he* is insulted; when disparaging remarks are made of his parents, *he* is involved; when his political candidate loses a contest, *he* has been defeated.

By stressing the cultural content of the ego, these authors in effect eradi-cate the artificial Freudian distinction between ego and superego. They also rescue the ego from the anti-social solipsism of Stirner and Le Dantec and make it a socialized agent ready to enter as an integrated unit into the complex relations of social life.

From this historical glance I have omitted many writers who have made their contribution to the literature of the ego. But, nevertheless, I believe, I

---

[3]A particularly suggestive contribution of Lewin pertains to the difference between nationalities in terms of the relative ease with which the ego becomes 'engaged'. Thus the American is less defensive, less touchy, less reticent than the German, due to the fact that the barriers of the German's ego lie near the 'surface'. He protects himself against familiarity and intrusion; whereas the American leads a much more 'public' life and protects only the 'core' of his personal life from public gaze.

have mentioned the chief ways in which, up to now, the ego has been conceived, viz., (1) as knower, (2) as object of knowledge, (3) as primordial selfishness, (4) as dominator, (5) as a passive organizer and rationalizer, (6) as a fighter for ends, (7) as one segregated behavioral system among others, (8) as a subjective patterning of cultural values.

The question immediately arises as to whether these eight uses of the term ego have anything in common, or whether as is often the case, a single term is allowed to obscure entirely different problems. Is the ego as knower the same ego that seeks status? Is the me that is known also a fighter for ends? Has the ego system proposed by Koffka any kinship with Freud's ego who attempts through insight to reclaim the id?

These are questions that cannot yet be answered. We cannot say whether these eight conceptions reflect irreconcilable theories, whether they shade imperceptibly into one another, or whether they are all ultimately to be subordinated under one inclusive theory of the ego.

In favor of the last possibility I should like to point to recent experimental studies which, if I mistake not, lend support to several of these conceptions simultaneously. The experiments result in one common finding, namely, that ego-involvement, or its absence, makes a critical difference in human behavior. When a person reacts in a neutral, impersonal, routine atmosphere, his behavior is one thing. But when he is behaving personally, perhaps excitedly, seriously committed to a task, he behaves quite differently. In the first condition his ego is not engaged; in the second condition it is. And it is my belief that in most of the experiments I shall report one finds that the ego is acting in several, if not all, of the eight capacities I have listed. In other words, *ego-involvement* is, as the phrase implies, a condition of total participation of the self—as knower, as organizer, as observer, as status seeker, and as socialized being. But now for the experimental evidence.

III. EXPERIMENTAL EVIDENCE

1. *Generality and specificity.*—A few years ago I found myself involved in a controversy in the field of personality. Certain experimenters claimed that their findings demonstrated a situational specificity in human conduct. For example, a child, honest in one situation, would not be found honest in another; a person confident of one judgment would not be confident of another. Whole books were written in defense of specificity. Other investigators, by other methods, found a person honest in one situation to be honest in another; a person confident in one judgment to be confident in another; and whole books were written in defense of generality. It was a pleasant battle while it lasted. An arbitrator arose, a peacemaker by temperament—Gardner Murphy was his name—and he proposed a compromise. "Honesty," he sug-

gested, "is either a general characteristic or a set of specific habits, depending on your interest and your emphasis." Murphy was right, but it was not until recently that the deciding interest and critical emphasis became clear at least to me. For my own belated insight I am indebted to an experiment by Klein and Schoenfeld.

These investigators gave to a group of subjects a series of mental tests under two experimental conditions. In the first, the atmosphere was neutral, dull, *non ego-involved*. The workers were merely laboratory subjects going through routine motions. After each of the six tests they were required to rate the degree of confidence they felt in the accuracy of their performances. Between the six tests there was little consistency in these certainty ratings. After an interval of time, a second equivalent set of tests was administered and the atmosphere was markedly changed. The subjects were placed under greater strain, were told to try hard since the results of these 'intelligence' tests would be entered on their college records. The shift in atmosphere was effective. The confidence ratings became markedly consistent. A student who felt assured in one test felt assured in the other five; whereas a student who lacked confidence in one of his performances generally lacked confidence in the other performances. The authors conclude that confidence is a personality trait when the ego is involved, but that it is specific to each situation when the subject has no deep interest at stake.

This experiment supplies the hypothesis needed to settle a long-standing controversy. When there is ego-involvement there are general traits; when there is no ego-involvement there are no general traits.

From an entirely different source comes evidence of the same type. In connection with its polling investigations the Office of Public Opinion Research has found that *intensity* of feeling goes with *consistency* of opinion. For example, in the pre-Pearl Harbor era it was found that those who felt most intensely in favor of aid to Britain were, by and large, those who endorsed all sorts and varieties of interventionist propositions. On the other hand, those who were lukewarm in their support of aid to Britain were far more inconsistent and specific in their answers. Sometimes they gave interventionist, and sometimes isolationist, replies. The measure obtained between the intensity scale and the generality of the attitude was a coefficient of correlation of +.63.

2. *Judgment.*—Eli Marks worked on judgments of skin-color among Negroes. He found it, in part, to be a function of the objective scale but, in part also, a function of an ego-centric scale. A Negro of medium coloration is likely to be judged dark by a Negro of lighter complexion, and as light by a Negro of darker complexion. For decades psychophysicists have dealt with judgments of hue as a function of wave length, but Marks makes clear that judgments of hue may be also a function of one's sense of social status.

Wave length is perceived by the sensitized retina, but it is perceived no less by the sensitized ego.

In the field of simple predictive judgment, it was found in the public opinion polls of 1940 that of the people who were strong Willkie supporters, 71 per cent predicted that he would win the election; of those who were weak Willkie supporters, only 47 per cent made this prediction. Assuming as we must that intensity of an attitude indicates ego-involvement, we find here a clear quanitative demonstration that a 24 per cent difference in the number of predictions exists when the ego-regions of the personality are engaged. Admittedly, the ego's wish is only one factor in predictive judgments, but if conditions are right it can become the crucial factor as it did in these 24 per cent.

Polling research has uncovered yet another important fact concerning judgment. If you ask respondents to tell you to your face what they think about our allies, the British, or about some minority group in this country, or even about their own educational level, you obtain one set of results; but if you ask them to write their answers to the same questions privately and deposit them in a padlocked ballot box, on the average your results will be significantly different. Now this difference between open and secret expressions of opinion seems to exist only when the answers might jeopardize the respondent's sense of status or affect his prestige in the interviewer's eyes. The discrepancy is great enough to warrant the use of secret balloting whenever questions are of a type that might expose the person to humiliation.

Judgments concerning one's self are remarkably interesting things to study. We know, for example, how inaccurate people are in rating their own economic status. Nearly all prefer to overlook the objective evidence and to identify themselves with the great middle class. We know something about the distortions that result when people report their own traits. Frenkel-Brunswik found the self-protective devices so powerful that her subjects would omit, justify, or completely reverse the facts, in their accounts of their own deficiencies. Although it is trite to point out what all psychologists know so well, that lack of objectivity is the rule when our egos are involved yet it is not trite to remark that very little work has been done on the extent and nature of the distortion, nor upon the curious and momentous question why it is that some personalities attain objectivity even in the face of extreme ego-involvement. Insight, it would seem, grows more and more difficult to achieve as the inner regions of the personality are approached. And yet some individuals accomplish remarkable feats of self-objectification. Why do they succeed and others fail?

3. *Memory.*—Thanks to Bartlett we know how cultural schemata alter our memory traces. Here, of course, is an example of the silent influence of an ethnocentric frame. But within any given culture striking memory-efforts can be traced to egocentric frames as well.

Edwards has demonstrated that if memory material fails to fit comfortably into an ego-involved frame, it contorts itself until it does so. Using three groups of students, each with a different attitude toward the New Deal (favorable, neutral, or opposed) he first read them a 10-minute passage concerning the relations of the New Deal to communism. The subjects knew they were to be tested for the accuracy of their retention.

Immediately after the reading, a multiple choice recognition test consisting of 46 items was given to the subjects. Half or 23 of the items on the test were answered in the passage in a manner favorable to the New Deal, the other 23 were answered in a manner unfavorable. The items on the test offered opportunities for rationalization of one's answer, if the correct answer was opposed to one's attitude. The subjects were re-tested after an interval of 21 days.

Analysis of variance of the data showed that rationalization was directly associated with the degree of conflict between the correct answer and the attitudinal frames of reference of our subjects. In general the results show—as do many other studies—that it is almost impossible to expect objectivity and accuracy in perception, learning, remembering, thinking, etc., when ego-involved frames of reference are stimulated.

Here one might cite also the memory experiments of Zillig which show how members of the male sex recall fewer aphorisms favorable to women than to men. Or, the Watson and Hartmann study concerning the distortions that occur in memory for theological arguments depending upon the subject's previous commitment to atheism or to theism. Or, Wallen's ingenious demonstration that after an interval of time subjects recall ratings of their own personalities in a manner that makes them compatible with their own preconceived opinions of themselves.

In a recent investigation Levine and Murphy demonstrated that pro-Communist sympathizers memorize pro-Communist textual material more easily than they do anti-Communist textual material. What is more, they forget the antipathetic text more rapidly and more completely than the sympathetic text. In anti-Communists the effects are exactly reversed. It was a brilliant stroke for these authors to demonstrate in one experiment that both learning and forgetting are functions of the political identifications of the ego.

4. *Frame of reference.*—Some of the studies I have mentioned have been conducted in relation to what their authors have called a 'frame of reference.' Now, a frame of reference seems to signify any *spatial-temporal or cultural orientation, that relates many of an individual's attitudes, habits and judgments to one another, and influences the formation of new judgments, attitudes, and habits.* A general orientation favorable to the New Deal will, according to Edwards, determine our specific remembrance of items from

speeches concerning the New Deal. A general orientation regarding various other subjects, Sells has shown, will affect our logical reasoning in all matters pertaining to them.

Now it is important to note that not all frames are ego-involved. If I locate 9th Avenue or East 12th Street readily it is because I have a geographic frame in mind for New York City. In my case this spatial orientation is not at all ego-involved. The point I am making is that research on the problem of frames of reference is not necessarily research on the problem of ego-involvement. Many cultural frames having to do with language, etiquette, or dress, determine our perceptions, our memory, our conduct, but their influence is not felt as personally relevant. Margaret Mead has expressed her anthropological astonishment at the odd custom Americans have of appearing at her lectures with clothes on; but to most of us this quaint folkway causes no ego-concern, at least as long as it is operative.

But an interesting discovery has come to light in these days of war and violence. Certain cultural frames which were previously indifferent have suddenly become acutely personal. Probably no one in Alsace felt concerned about the bilingual frame of reference until the Nazis decreed that only German should be spoken, and that only Germanized names and inscriptions should appear on the tombstones. Bilinguality had always been taken for granted, but when this familiar, habitual frame was suppressed and placed under attack, then it became of central importance, and people reacted as to a personal insult. Many of us have recently discovered that hitherto indifferent frames of reference, such as the Constitutional guarantees we enjoy, previously taken for granted, have suddenly become ego-involved, and now in jeopardy are defended as if they were parts of our physical bodies. Suppose we in this room were forbidden to speak the English language. How enraged we would become. What had always been a mere ethnocentric frame would immediately become ego-involved.

Ethnocentric and egocentric frames both affect our conduct, and, as I have just pointed out, under certain conditions the ethnocentric frame is experienced also as an egocentric frame. But I think it is a mistake to confuse the concept of the ego with that of the socius (or cultural portion of our personalities) as Sherif has done. Under normal social conditions only a relatively small portion of our culture is ego-involved.

5. *Learning*.—The longest and most difficult chapter in psychology, no one will deny, is the chapter on learning. The latest Yearbook of the National Society for the Study of Education is devoted entirely to this subject. One searches its 463 pages in vain for any mention of the ego, and almost in vain for any recognition of the importance of *interest*. True, one finds occasional remarks to the effect that "the teacher who neglects the simple but powerful word of praise does so at her pedagogical peril," but the potential significance of such remarks for learning theory seems lost to view.

Clinical, educational, and industrial psychologists know that the first rule of all applied psychology is that every child and every adult needs some experience of success and social approval. John E. Anderson advises the teacher to go far out of her way if necessary to find an area in which these feelings can be engendered, and he adds

> Success in one area may more than compensate for failure in
> many areas; some accomplishment furnishes an integrating center
> about which the personality may be integrated.

Note especially Anderson's statement that "success in one area may more than compensate for failure in many areas." Only in terms of ego-psychology can we account for such fluid compensation. Mental health and happiness, it seems, does not depend upon the satisfactoin of *this* drive or *that* drive, it depends rather upon the *person* finding *some* area of success *somewhere*. The *ego* must be satisfied, not the hunger drive, nor the sex drive, nor the maternal drive, however temporarily insistent these segmental tensions may be.

Now most theories of learning lean heavily upon the assumptions of multiple drives. A segmental tension exists, the organism behaves, the tension is relieved, and the response set. In this sequence it is often assumed that all drives are equally potent for learning. The satisfaction of any drive, through the principle of reward or confirming reaction, is held to bring about an equal degree of learning. If this is so, how can we account for the fact that praise is found almost uniformly to be the leading incentive in school, in factory, and in ordinary life? If we are to hold to the theory of multiple drives at all, we must at least admit that the ego-drive (or pride, or desire for approval—call it what we will) takes precedence over all other drives.

Not only does human learning proceed best when the incentive of praise and recognition is used, but the individual's *capacity* for learning actually seems to expand under this condition. Every psychometrist knows that in order to obtain a valid I.Q. the subject must be encouraged. Terman's instructions on this point are well known.

> Nothing contributes more to a satisfactory *rapport* than praise of
> the child's efforts. . . . In general, the poorer the response, the
> better satisfied one should appear to be with it. . . . Exclamations
> like fine! splendid! etc., should be used lavishly.

In other words, to maximize the child's intelligence we must maximize his ego. For psychological theory this is really a momentous fact. Intelligence is the ego's tool for solving its own problems. It is manifestly unfair to estimate intelligence on the basis of performance in which the individual himself has no interest. For this reason, through the device of praise, the subject must be encouraged to make the test-items into ego-involved problems which he can attack with maximally motivated effort. Intelligence is the individual's capacity to solve problems of importance to himself.

There is one unfavorable condition for learning that must be admitted lest we oversimplify the issue. Too intense an ego-involvement may be disruptive. Its normal integrative value may be actually undetermined when eagerness or self-consciousness reach a degree of intensity that lead to embarrassment or over-anxiousness. No one learns or performs well if his autonomic nervous system is in a turmoil. We need a rule that will help us determine the optimum degree of ego-involvement required for enhancing efficiency of learning and performance.[4]

One word about the law of effect. Its principal shortcoming, I think, stems from the assumption that rewarded *responses* tend to recur. Many experiments, in fact, show that rewarded responses do not blindly recur whenever an appropriate stimulus returns. Hoppe points out that people normally do not strive again for a goal successfully achieved. What they do is to raise their aspirations to a point where they clearly risk failure. A student who makes an A record in a course in college, shows no tendency to repeat that course. He prefers to take new risks in the same general area. And an experiment by Rosenzweig indicates that it is definitely infantile to choose to repeat successful acts. For example, a puzzle once solved, even if accompanied by a burst of elation, no longer attracts the mature individual. He wants new worlds to conquer. Reward may bring merely satiation and boredom.

The fallacy, I repeat, lies in our speaking of rewarding a *response*. The law of effect would be truer if it held simply that a *person,* being rewarded, employs his past successes in whatever way he thinks is likely to bring him satisfaction in the *future.* Israeli has shown that, excepting for certain psychopaths, people are much more interested in their futures than in their pasts. Since this is so, an individual's past performances often mean little nor nothing to him. Only if the ego would be served thereby, does he engage in a repetition of the successful act. More often he chooses to vary and refine his behavior so that he may feel that he himself is growing toward new successes in the future.

The relation between success and repetition, I suspect, is much closer in the case of non ego-involved behavior than in the case of ego-involved behavior. Over and over again I use the same motor combinations in typewriting, in driving my car, in dealing with tradesmen. They are reasonably successful acts; why should I change them? But I do not repeat successful research work, do not repeat a gratifying conversation with a friend, nor do I restate the same goal in an aspiration-level experiment. Ego-involved tasks often demand changing goals and new responses. Rewarded behavior, it

---

[4]One formulation of the needed rule is suggested by French: "So long as the tension does not exceed the available energy of the integrative mechanisms, so long will the integrative capacity of the goal-directed striving increase with increasing tension. But as soon as the tension of the need begins to exceed the available energy of the integrating mechanism, the effect of increasing tension will be the opposite."

would seem, becomes stereotyped only in lower animals, or in such human activities of a routine nature that fail to engage the ego.

To summarize this brief discussion, it would seem that in order to employ the law of effect with human learning we must view it as secondary to the principle of ego-involvement. The law of effect, like cue reduction, conditioning, bond-formation, and most other popular principles of learning, have been worked out for the most part on animal subjects or on human beings deprived for the duration of the experiment, of their egos. The principles may be good ones, but I submit that when the ego is engaged they operate in a contingent fashion. Learning theory of the future, let us hope, will not remain so peripheral to the ego.

6. *Motivation.*—You may be thinking, "But, we've always known that one must be motivated in order to secure a response. Are you talking about anything more than the importance of motivation?" Yes, I am saying that there are two forms of motivation, one ego-involved and one not, and I am attempting by repeated citations from experiments to show the differences that exist between them.

Take, for example, the work of Huntley and Wolff on judgments based upon records of expressive behavior. These investigators working independently instructed their subjects to make judgments concerning the personalities of many people from their handwritings, from their recorded voices, from photographs of hands, and from their style of story telling. The subjects were motivated in a routine manner as is any laboratory subject. But, suddenly, in the midst of the series they were confronted with samples of their own expressive behavior which had been recorded without their knowledge. In the large majority of cases the subjects did not consciously recognize their own records and continued innocently with their characterizations. But something had happened. The characterizations began to take a different form. Even though a judge was wholly unaware that a certain expression was his own, he gave it a much more favorable rating than he gave similar expressive records taken from other subjects. Occasionally he gave it a vehemently unfavorable rating, but practically never did he give it an indifferent rating. Other people's records might arouse no affect, but not his. Whenever a subject became half-conscious, as it were, that a record might possibly be his, his judgments were still more intensely partisan; but when he fully recognized his own record then his social sense of modesty prevailed, and his judgments returned to the noncommital level.

In these experiments we have a particularly neat demonstration of the fact that ego-involved systems may operate in a wholly silent manner, affecting judgments in a most extreme way without the subject knowing the reason. The experiments also prove that the limen of ego-involvement is lower than the limen for self-recognition, an interesting finding which warns us once more that conscious report and introspection will never be a sufficient method for exploring the operations of the ego-system. But the important point for our present purposes, is to note that routine motivation to perform a task is one thing, and that ego-charged motivation is quite another. Routine motives yield one set of results, ego-motives a different set.

When is motivation ego-involved and when is it not? A partial answer seems to lie in the degree of frustration involved. As we have already noted many customary frames of reference are not felt to be personally relevant, and do not behave like egocentric frames, until their continuance is threatened (as in wartime). Many drives, too, run their course without engaging the ego unless they are interfered with. But serious frustration may instigate the clamor, the jealousy, the possessiveness, often characteristic of ego-involvement. And yet frustration by no means always produces this effect, especially if one has compensated for drive-frustration by success in other realms. And then, to complicate the situation further, we cannot say that ego-involvement is absent when there is no frustration. Many smooth-running instances of goal-seeking behavior are obviously ego-involved. A mother feels just as closely identified with her child when it is in good health as when her maternal care meets with frustration. A business man is as much absorbed in his enterprise in times of prosperity as he is in times of adversity. Let us say, then, that frustration of goal-seeking behavior or any kind of threat to the individual, is very likely to engage the ego-system; but that normally this ego-system is made up of the ordinary values which spell out the significance of life to the individual.

7.   *The level of aspiration.*—The history of ten years' research on this Lewinian problem is too intricate to trace here, but unless I am mistaken every investigation has directly or indirectly confirmed Hoppe's initial claim that the subject behaves in such a manner as to maintain his self-esteem at the highest possible level. Of course, many investigators have not used the conception of the ego at all. Yet whatever results are found they all seem to point to the essential inescapability of Hoppe's original hypothesis. Frank for example, found that subjects in whom 'self competition, and consciousness of social pressure' were present, had D-scores three to seven times as large as did subjects who had no such sense of personal involvement in the situation.[5] Frank also found that subjects who are ego-involved do not change their estimates with every little variation in their performance. They try and try again before trimming their aspirations to fit their capacities; subjects not ego-involved on the other hand, quickly yield to the immediate realities of the situation, and lower their aspiration level. We know too that competitiveness, surely a symptom of ego-involvement, usually produces a rise and

---

[5] D-Scores, of course, indicate the discrepancy between performance and the goal that the individual wishes or expects to achieve.

greater consistency in the aspiration level. But we cannot say that competitiveness always has this effect because subjects who dread competition will lower their level of aspiration consistently in order to avoid the risk of humiliation. In short, it seems always to be the ego-demand of the individual subject that determines the behavior of the aspiration level. Some subjects are adventurous, some cautious; their egos demand different types of satisfaction, and it is this fact that is repeatedly reflected in the results of the experiments. It is worth pointing out that historically the aspiration level may well be regarded as the door by which the ego re-entered the cloisters of academic psychology.

8. *Industrial psychology.*—Most of us, I suppose, have been impressed in recent years by the demonstrations of Roethlisberger and Dickson, of Watson, and others, that employees in industry are not 'economic men' so much as they are 'ego men.' What they want, above all else, is credit for work done, interesting tasks, appreciation, approval, congenial relations with their employers and fellow workers. These satisfactions they want even more than high wages or job security. Now, the employer's estimate of the worker's wants correlates just about zero with the worker's own report of his wants. The employer thinks that wages and security are the dominant desires, whereas in reality the ego-satisfactions are primary. What a different outlook there would be on our economic life if we took firm hold on the issues of status and self-respect in industry, and re-planned our industrial society in a manner that would rescue the worker's ego from oblivion.

IV. THE NATURE OF THE EGO

In the experiments I have cited, and in many others of analogous nature, it turns out that one group of subjects (those who are personally aroused and committed to a task) behave in ways quite unlike other subjects (who are not so committed). In some instances there are measurable quantitative differences as great as 50 to 60 per cent, sometimes much more. In other instances there are qualitative changes that elude measurement. In short, we are here confronted with some parameter that makes a vast difference in our experimental results.

We have seen that under conditions of ego-involvement the whole personality manifests greater consistency in behavior, reveals not specificity in conduct but generality and congruence. In the field of judgment, we have seen how ego-involvement results in significant distortions of the ordinary psychophysical scales. In memory, we find that retention is characteristically superior (though at times repressions also may be more likely to occur, and rationalizations may creep into ego-involved memory). In intelligence, we note that ego-involvement is indispensable if we would obtain optimum performance.

In learning theory, reforms seem indicated to make room for the demonstrable influence of the ego upon the acquisition of skill and knowledge. In motivation, the craving for recognition, status, and personal appreciation turns out to be supreme, so much so that our conceptions of procedure and policy in industrial relations, in education, and in psychotherapy, are profoundly affected. And these are only a few of the operational criteria by which we may demonstrate the existence of the ego.

Its admittance to good standing in contemporary psychology has been advocated by several psychologists besides myself. Koffka, Lewin, and the psychoanalysts have done so; as has Murray who makes a distinction between 'peripheralist' psychology and 'centralist' psychology. The thesis set forth in Rogers' recent book *Counseling and psychotherapy* seems to me especially clear evidence that the ego is coming into its own. Rogers, in effect, asks counselors to sit back and with little more than an occasionally well-placed *m-hm,* to encourage the patient himself to restructure and re-plan his life. The patient's ego takes command. It's about time it should.

Although we have given an adequate operational demonstration of the ego, we have not yet faced the difficult problem of definition. Earlier we saw that eight conceptions seem to prevail. But whenever we encounter ego-involvement the ego in several of its historical senses seems to be active. Furthermore, these historical conceptions seem to have much in common.

For one thing, it seems clear that all of the conceptions are less embracing than 'personality.' All writers seem agreed that the ego is only one portion, one region, or as the Freudians say, one 'institution,' of the personality. Many skills, habits, memories or components of personality but seldom, if ever, become ego-involved. Writers seem also agreed that the ego is non-existent in early childhood, evolving gradually as the child comes to mark himself off from his environment and from other human beings. They seem also to agree in viewing the ego as the portion of the personality that is in proximate relation to the external world. It senses the threats, the opportunities, and the survival of significance of both outer and inner events. It is that portion of the personality, so to speak, that meets the world head-on. It is the contact-region of the personality. For that reason it is also the conflict-region. Yet it is co-extensive with neither consciousness nor with unconsciousness, for much that we are conscious of is indifferent to our egos, and many unconscious stimuli silently but effectively engage them.

There is also agreement that the subjective sense of the ego varies greatly from time to time, now contracting to include less than the body, now expanding to include more. Its content keeps changing, for at certain moments the ego seems preoccupied with one activity and soon thereafter with a wholly different activity. This shifting scene however does not mean that there is no stable and recurring structure. On the contrary, if you know a person well enough, you find that you are able to predict with marked success what items will and what items will not be linked to his ego. By many writers the ego is represented as a layered structure. Certainly there are *degrees* of ego-involvement. A person may be intensely partisan or moderately partisan.

There seems to be one other property of the ego, less often discussed, namely its customary preoccupation with the future. Israeli, it will be remembered, reports that among his subjects over ninety per cent expressed themselves more interested in their futures than in their pasts. This finding is worth stressing, for as a rule, psychologists are more interested in a person's past than in his future. In other words, the psychologist and his subject customarily face in different directions, and that is unfortunate.

V.   PSYCHOLOGY DURING THE WAR AND AFTER

You and I are ego-involved in the course of the war and in the outcome of the future peace. Likewise, for different reasons, we are involved in the development and progress of psychology as a science and as a profession. Now it is typical of the generalizing tendency in the ego that matters having a high degree of personal relevance do not ordinarily remain apart. They tend to become fused into an integrated plan of action. Thus, in order to help win the war approximately a thousand psychologists have transferred their professional activity to camps, factories, or government offices. And most of those who have remained in colleges have rearranged their lives in such a way as to blend their war interests with their professional activity.

Although it is too early to evaluate the work we all are doing, I wonder if you have the same impression I have concerning the utility of our previous training in psychology. It is my guess that insofar as our war work deals with sensory, perceptual, and psychometric problems, the transfer value of our previous psychological training is very high. But in so far as our war work deals with problems of morale, public opinion, national character, scapegoating, ideology, guidance, rehabilitation—any of the areas where the major hates, fears, and hopes of men are concerned—the transfer value of our previous training is much less. In other words, the psychology that treats the non-ego involved functions of the human organism has developed to a point of immediate utility, whereas the psychology of the 'central' regions of personality has not. I make this statement with full appreciation of the admirable work of our colleagues in OSS, in OWI, FBIS, and in other similar bureaus. But most of them, I think, would agree that the psychology available for application to their problems has shown itself to be both meagre and inept.

It might be argued that, being a young science, psychology has moved, as it were, from the surface inward. Given time we shall have as much to contribute to an understanding of the central layers as of the surface. But is it merely a matter of time? Is it not rather that the sumptuary regulations of our science have been unhealthy for the ego?

Everywhere we encounter the paradox: As a group, psychologists are liberal, internationally minded, and devoted to the welfare of the common man. They believe in providing a soil where the infinite varieties of the human ego may freely grow. At the same time their assumptions, their methods, their theories have not been well suited to the attainment of their objectives.

For the past ten years we have become increasingly aware of this paradox. As evidence, there is the mounting tide of experiments of the type I have reviewed. As further evidence, there is the widespread recasting of our activities in wartime and the notable turning of psychologists' interests to the formulation of conditions for a lasting peace. In all this work there is a somewhat novel co-operative spirit. The coming Inter-Society Constitutional Convention is one instance of what I have in mind. As never before we seem to desire to have our productions fit together. Ego-satisfactions, we are discovering, are not necessarily competitive. One is reminded here of the experiments of Helen Lewis (unpublished) which have demonstrated that *your* tensions may be resolved by *my* work and *my* tensions may be resolved by *your* work, provided only that we regard ourselves as co-operating members in a common undertaking.

The admittance of the ego to good standing in psychology does not mean a re-importation of the *deus ex machina* of pre-Wundtian psychology. It does mean, however, a recognition of the fact that our predecessors who regarded psychology as the science of the soul, were not wrong in setting the problems of unity and personal relevance before us. What they called the soul, we may now, with good conscience, call the ego. In so doing, no clocks need to be set backward. Dialectics has already given way to experiment and to the clinic, and to still newer methods for studying the common man in his normal social setting.

But disregarding the problems of method, which are beyond the scope of my paper, we may safely predict that ego-psychology in the twentieth century will flourish increasingly. For only with its aid can psychologists reconcile the human nature that they study and the human nature that they serve.

I

18. The Ego and
the Law of Effect

Philip Blair Rice

IN a provocative paper, G. W. Allport has argued that psychology made a mistake in throwing overboard the 'ego' or 'self' along with the 'soul,' and that the time may have come when it is both possible and necessary to rehabilitate the first two of these concepts on a scientific rather than a theological basis. The eclipse of the self, he points out, became almost total when reflexology and the more mechanical versions of behaviorism chose to concentrate, for experimental purposes, on a segmental approach to behavior and thereby lost sight of the larger patterns and unifying features of the organism's activity. Allport cites a number of indications that not only psychoanalysis but several other schools of psychological inquiry are making an effort to rediscover the self, and he offers valuable suggestions as to the directions which this enterprise may take. In his treatment of the problem, however, he sometimes gives the impression that the 'ego' refers to something ultimate, unanalyzable and lawless. Though elsewhere he makes it clear that he rejects such notions as a substantial self and an ego 'instinct,' and that he holds the self to develop gradually under the nurture of experience and not by maturation alone, we are not given any clear principles to account for its genesis and transformations.

More particularly—and this is the section of his paper with which I am here concerned—Allport argues that the Law of Effect, at any rate in the form in which it is usually understood, is inadequate to deal with what he calls 'ego-involved' behavior. This is a charge that must be taken seriously. The last fifteen years have witnessed a widespread tendency to revive the Law of Effect, which had suffered from general disfavor during the 1920's, and to erect it into the principal, and even for some writers the sole, law of learning and acquired motivation. The thesis which I should like to present is three-fold: (1) that Allport's criticisms are such as to force a reformulation

Abridged from the *Psychological Review,* 1946, 53, 307-320. Reprinted by permission of Mrs. Philip Blair Rice and the American Psychological Association, Inc.

or at least a clarification of the Law of Effect, but (2) that his evidence is such as to support rather than to refute the Law when it is so reinterpreted, and (3) that the Law when thus clarified may supply us with precisely the principle that we need in order to account for some central characteristics of the ego's development.

Before taking up Allport's criticisms, I shall first indicate the present state of opinion with regard to the Law of Effect. In earlier formulations by Thorndike, the Law of Effect stated that a connection between a stimulus-situation and a response tends to be strengthened by success or satisfaction or reward, and to be weakened by frustration or annoyance or punishment; the strengthening or weakening is proportional to the degree of the satisfaction or annoyance, and to the promptitude with which this follows upon the response. Later, as a result of many experiments both by himself and by others, Thorndike abandoned the negative clause, and held that (a) punishment may strengthen a connection, but when it does so the reinforcement is much less than in the case of reward, so that if an alternative rewarded response occurs it tends to replace the punished response and (b) escape from punishment is itself rewarding, and tends to strengthen responses avoidant of punishment. In both cases the net tendency of punishment to weaken a connection follows from the positive clause, so that the negative is superfluous as well as inexact.

In its revised form the Law of Effect has been shown by an impressive mass of experimental evidence to work well for many types of animal behavior and for simple human reactions where certain complicated interests, such as self-assertiveness, are not present. Many psychologists who once opposed the Law of Effect, including a number of leading behaviorists, are now coming around to respect it, believing it to be a more adequate principle of learning than the Law of Exercise or the Pavlovian and Watsonian principle of learning by simple conjunction and repetition. The Law of Effect has been restated in an elaborate set of postulates by Hull in his doctrine of reinforcement by need-reduction. Freud at first offered the Pleasure Principle, roughly equivalent to the Law of Effect, as the sole law of motivation; he later added the Death Instinct, or repetition compulsion, which is in opposition to it. Many psychoanalysts, however, have refused to accept the Death Instinct as an original principle, and have tried to derive the death wish and the repetition compulsion from the Pleasure Principle. Recently Mowrer and Ullman have supported the Law of Effect as the sole principle of learning, and have suggested ways in which the repetition compulsion may be derived from it. In his latest treatment of the subject, however, Thorndike himself accepts both the principle of repetition (Law of Exercise) and the principle of reward (Law of Effect) as independent laws, but he holds the latter to be much more important than the former.

The chief theoretical difficulty that remains on this score would seem to center about the status of punishment after the elimination of the negative clause. Thorndike's latest position implies that the occasions on which punishment directly strengthens a connection are taken account of by the Law of Exercise, so that it is repetition and not the accompanying punishment as such that reinforces a connection in cases where reward is absent.

Mowrer and Ullman do not recognize the existence of such cases, but hold that all cases of apparent reinforcement by exercise are due to the indirect operation of reward. Miller and Dollard have upheld a similar position. Further evidence would seem to be required, however, on so difficult a question; by accepted neurological principles, it is hard to see how mere exercise or repetition, without satisfaction or need-reduction, could fail to have some effect on the associative neural tracts, even though this effect may be slighter than the 'retroflex' action of reward.[1] So it is perhaps safer to conclude that the repetition compulsion has not yet been absorbed entirely by the Law of Effect. One may hope that it will be possible to abolish the repetition compulsion as an original principle, so that we may adopt a more optimistic view of human nature, but the prudent course at present would be to suspend judgment.

In this discussion I am not concerned to try to resolve such difficulties, but I prefer to leave it an open question whether the Law of Effect can be taken as the sole principle of learning, or whether a Law of Exercise is also needed, perhaps together with still other principles. And I shall defer until later in the paper consideration of the weighty criticisms of the Law of Effect that have been advanced by the Gestalt school, since I believe that the Gestalist charge that the Law has been tested chiefly by experiments on trial-and-error learning and rote learning, to the neglect of genuinely productive ("insight") thinking, may have been dismissed too cavalierly.

My primary purpose at this point is to consider some other objections to the Law of Effect that have been advanced by Allport in the paper which has been cited. To summarize these criticisms very briefly: Allport adduces some experiments by Hoppe and Rosenzweig and some observations of his own where successful executions of a response do not strengthen but

[1]In support of their contrary view, Miller and Dollard point to Adrian's evidence that "the sudden onset of a new stimulus produces at first a strong burst of impulses from the sense organ which rapidly diminishes in strength till a plateau of stimulation is reached," and infer that it is the satisfaction produced by the diminution of stimulation, and not the annoying stimulation itself, that gives the reinforcement. This explanation would seem to overlook: (a) the possibility in certain cases that the stimulation may not fall to a plateau where it is rewarding rather than punishing, and (b) those cases where the stimulation in question is replaced centrally by another stimulus before the level of excitation has had time to drop below the satisfaction-annoyance threshold— Adrian's experiments deal with an isolated source of stimulation to a sensory nerve and therefore do not take such a situation into account.

weaken the tendency to repeat it. Children who successfully perform assigned tasks do not usually go back to do these tasks over, but prefer to
tackle something else. A student who gets an A in a course does not repeat
that course, but may take another in the same field. Repetition of successful
acts is ordinarily a mark of infantile, deficient or pathological behavior
rather than of intelligent adult activity. Allport concludes: "The relation
between success and repetition, I suspect, is much closer in the case of non
ego-involved behavior . . . . Ego-involved tasks often involved changing goals
and new responses . . . . In order to employ the Law of Effect with human
learning we must view it as secondary to the principle of ego-involvement."

These objections are valid against a segmental or mechanical application
of the Law of Effect which ignores the complexity of motives involved in
most human activity, and the variability of our responses to similar situations
and in pursuit of similar goals. The Law cannot be upheld if it means that
success or satisfaction necessarily enhances the tendency for either or both
(a) the specific response sequence to be repeated, and/or (b) the particular,
or even the specific, goal object to be chosen again. Repetition of *both* these
elements occurs chiefly in very young children, in mental defectives and in
compulsion neurotics. With normal adults, both are repeated mainly in the
case of routine habits and recurrent appetitive drives: like many of my com-
patriots, I nearly always have orange juice, bacon, scrambled eggs and coffee
for breakfast, when I can get them, and I consume them with a fairly stereotyped sequence of acts. Even here repetition occurs only in the absence
of a problem-solving interest (the desire to negotiate a new kind of dish in
a strange country), or ego-involvement (the wish to impress one's distinguished hosts by showing a capacity to master fried kippers), or the quasi-
aesthetic demand for variety (my aesthetic tendencies are usually not awake
by breakfast time).

When normal adults repeat one of these two elements — the response as
a whole or the choice of the particular goal object—after success, it is usually
with a variation in the other. If one puts the same puzzle together twice
(*i.e.,* repeats the choice of a goal object), it is usually to do so in a different
way (*i.e.,* to master a new response sequence). If a college boy repeats the
same 'line' (response sequence) it is with a different goal object (to impress
a new girl). Successful use of a response sequence in attainment of one goal
may nevertheless encourage its repetition in pursuit of a similar but not identical goal; and successful pursuit of a goal may lead to adoption of a similar
but not identical goal in the future, and to use of a similar response sequence.
Or, we may vary both the response and the goal, so far as the details go,
while repeating with variations the same general *kind* of response and selecting the same *kind* of goal that brought us success in the past.

When we change both the specific response sequence and the particular goal, it may still be true that *something* about the activity is repeated, and that satisfaction from this aspect of the activity is the ground of the repetition. We may have several different levels of specificity and generality here. Varied, but partially similar, response sequences and goals are involved in solving different problems in algebra; success with one algebraic problem may encourage us to tackle another algebraic problem. Or, success in algebra may encourage us to take up trigonometry: both have the common property of setting mathematical problems.

These examples suggest that it is not the response sequence as a whole, or even any stereotyped segment of it, that necessarily tends to be repeated, but only certain general features of it, such as the 'interest' that is involved. The only possibility of saving the Law of Effect, then, would seem to consist in finding *what* is reinforced by success or satisfaction, and therefore *what* it is that tends to be repeated. This implies that we should either replace 'response' by some other concept, such as 'interest,' in the statement of the Law, or else try to find some *aspect* or *feature* of the response, rather than the response as a whole, which is reinforced by satisfaction; in the latter case, the feature selected must include for human activity, and possibly for some animal behavior, the core of what is intended by the vague term 'interest.'

II

The examples cited by Allport against the Law of Effect always have one or more aspects in common, and these aspects are more general than either the response mechanism or the class of goal object. The individual cases share at least one of these characteristics: they are examples of *problem-solving,* or they involve- *satisfaction of the ego,* or they embody the *interest in novelty*. If the Law of Effect can be upheld, it must take into account the shifting levels of generality and prepotency that may be involved in motivation. It follows that the satisfactions and dissatisfactions in question must include those attaching to the interests in problem-solving or self-assertion or variety.

Can we then establish a correlation between satisfaction and a tendency to repeat types of acts containing these characteristics?

1. *Problem-solving.* By definition, this excludes repetition of both the same goal and the same response sequence. When both of these are repeated, there is no 'problem'—except in the special case where we 'want to see if we can do it again,' and here whether we can do it again is itself the problem to be solved, and a different stimulus-situation from the original one. All the cases Allport and Hoppe have stressed are cases where the primary *interest* is in problem-solving, or in ego-gratification dependent upon problem-solving. Where there is no such interest, and where the interest in

novelty is not involved—as in the case of my breakfast—then a fairly simple application of the Law of Effect is possible. The Law applies only to the total nexus of interests, and its use must take into account their relative strengths and their subordination.

I cannot get satisfaction from problem-solving unless there is a problem. So it is unfair to cite against the Law of Effect cases, like working puzzles a second time, in which the primary motivation would be problem-solving if such motivation existed, but in which by hypothesis it cannot exist. A puzzle no longer puzzles me when I have learned how to solve it. The stimulus-situation has changed.

The question would seem to be, then: Does satisfaction of the interest in problem-solving tend to reinforce that interest, in the absence of conflicting interests, and does frustration of it tend to replace the interests by some other? Here again we must discuss the question on at least two levels of generality.

(a)   Does success in solving a given *kind* of problem, other things being equal, reinforce the interest in that kind of problem? None of the evidence cited refutes the hypothesis that this is the case: The apparent exceptions involve the intervention of some stronger interest. In general, with the people who devote themselves to mathematical problems, or chess problems, or psychological problems, or amatory problems (I am thinking here of the Don Juans and Casanovas, who have a connoisseur's interest in these problems for their own sake), success in the long run tends to reinforce the interest, and failure to lead them to devote themselves to some other interest in which they have achieved a greater measure of satisfaction. Either the individual goal or the specific response always varies, but the interest when stimulated tends to be repeated with success. When we persist in such activities despite repeated failure, another type of interest to which the one in question is auxiliary can usually be found. The persistent desire to be an engineer may keep a student at mathematics despite repeated failures; but unless he has some partial success in solving some of his engineering tasks, or unless some more embracing ego-motive is involved, he will tend eventually to seek some other vocation, if there is another skill in which he attains proficiency. And his persistence despite failure may be explained in part by the fact that 'satisfaction' and 'success' are only roughly equivalent concepts: the individual may get some satisfaction out of trying, even though he fails. It is a truism that some people are so constituted by their training that to fail at a difficult task gives more satisfaction to the ego than to succeed at an easy one.

We do not find people who are always passing on from one *kind* of problem to another, even though they are sucessful with all kinds. But here also the interest in the specific kind of problem seems subordinate to some ego-motive, or to some more general and powerful interest in novelty, both of which require special treatment.

(b)   Is the most general of interests in problem-solving—problem-solving as such, irrespective of the *kind* of problem—itself subject to the Law of Effect? I believe that everyday experience bears this out, still making allowance for more embracing motives. Except for some mental defectives, there is perhaps no one who has no interest in problem-solving, either for its own sake or as a means to the satisfaction of some specific interest. But there are considerable variations in the intensity of the interest, and in whether problem-solving is undertaken as a means or as an end. We all know people who are not eager to face problems, much less to seek them out, and who put off their solution as long as possible. When such people do solve problems, it is rarely the intellectual or dramatic interest in problem-solving as such that gives them satisfaction, but the ulterior interests which generated the particular problem. But repeated success in solving problems that are forced upon him may make such a person adventurous and may lead him to seek out problems. The best educational practice seems to assume such a hope. The person who is incompetent at reaching solutions, on the other hand, will 'take things as they come' and rely upon more passive or receptive interests. So it would seem that the general interest in problem-solving is, like other interests, enhanced by satisfaction and stiffled by frustration, except where organic needs or ego-involvement complicate the picture.

2.   Allport makes an exception to the Law of Effect in the case of *ego-involvement*. He writes: "The relation between success and repetition, I suspect, is much closer in the case of non ego-involved behavior than in the case of ego-involved behavior." Even here, however, he might accept the Law of Effect in a revised formulation. What I am suggesting is that ego-involved behavior is on a different level of generality of interest, and that the Law of Effect may apply here too unless we try to restrict it to a lower level.

We must avoid two extremes—conceiving the self as a bundle of separate and unrelated reflexes or even unrelated interests, and conceiving it as a mystical unity not subject to analysis and genetic explanation.

The ego is a system of interests; 'system' implies unity, and 'interests,' being plural, implies multiplicity. The unity is presumably supplied by such factors as the hierarchy of dominant and subordinate interests, the level of aspiration, and the 'style of life,' with attendant attitudes such as self-respect, shame and the like, evoked by satisfaction or frustration of the interest-cluster in question. Very likely the unity of the self is to be conceived, like any Gestalt, as an emergent factor, and therefore one that is capable of becoming functionally autonomous. But this does not mean that we cannot go behind it to study its genesis, to find principles governing its changes, and to analyze the various conditions that regularly give rise to its configuration. If not the Law of Effect, then some other law or set of laws specifying the conditions of reinforcement must hold of the ego's development—this would be the assumption of a scientific psychology.

The Law of Effect has not been shown to be inapplicable to the development of the ego as so conceived. The most sustained attention to the problem of defining the ego and tracing its genesis has been found in the work of the psychoanalysts, Freudians and post-Freudians, who have sought the origin of 'basic personality structure' in the relationships involving affection and authority between parent and child. Though the depth psychologists have given little explicit mention to the Law of Effect in dealing with such matters, their stress on the importance of satisfactions and frustrations, rewards and punishments, in character formation suggests that the development of the ego itself may be subject to Thorndike's Law. Level of aspiration and ego-level are surely affected in any given society or any given life by rewards and punishments. And these influence not only the level but also the specific content of the ego-cluster. A 'high' level of aspiration to monetary success is fostered in this country by advertising, the movies and public opinion; it seems to be discouraged among the Marquesans and Zuñis. A high level of meditative absorption is rewarded among the Brahmans. A high level of literary aspiration is fostered by the *cenacles*. A high level of honesty, financial or intellectual, may be encouraged by one's family training. In large part, at least, the level of aspiration here, and its specific direction, do not seem to be ontogenetically emergent from simpler interests of the individual, but to be implanted directly as a unit trait by the social pattern, through society's ability to award and withhold satisfactions and dissatisfactions.

What can cause an individual to persist in a 'style of life,' or the pursuit of it? Observation suggests that he does so because he has found satisfaction, actual or imaginative, from that style of life, or because it promises to integrate the scattered elements of past satisfactions and lessen past dissatisfactions, or because social rewards and punishments promote its adoption. But all these are operations of the Law of Effect.

Since the self is a system of interests, self-assertiveness in general is extinguished only when these interests are extinguished, and when no other system of interests has supervened to take their place. Self-assertiveness is not downed easily, and takes subtle revenges when thwarted, as the psychoanalysts, and before them the novelists, have shown. We should expect this from the Law of Effect itself, because the interests which go to make up the ego-cluster are those which supply continuity to the individual's life pattern, those which have constituted the area of his conflicts, those to which he has given most thought, and therefore those which have been reinforced most often in anticipation and retrospect, even if not by the actual achievement. But self-assertiveness can be deadened, and even to a large extent stamped out. We occasionally find people in whom it has been largely extinguished, and who go through life responding mechanically to external demands and executing their minimum organic drives. In such people the interests which constitute the ego-cluster, and their successive substitutes, have been frustrated so completely that they have been very nearly stamped out: their persistence is to be accounted for by the inability to find any rewarded responses to take their place. Such persons are usually found among slaves—legal or economic—the extreme victims of war, and browbeaten husbands and wives.

3.   Another interest on something like the same level of generality as problem-solving and ego-involvement is the interest in *novelty* or *variety*. This interest may arise through dissatisfaction with routine, or be implanted by a frivolous society or an aspiration for intense asthetic rewards from life. But when it once appears, it seems to be subject to the Law of Effect. The individual to whom novelty brings satisfaction will, other things being equal, seek more of it; the individual whom it bewilders will return to use-and-wont.

The upshot of all this is that the validity of the Law depends on *what* is conceived to be satisfied or thwarted, and therefore reinforced or extinguished. Only because many proponents of the Law, influenced by the cruder forms of reflexology, have focused on response mechanisms and goals rather than interests, and have ignored interests of high generality, has their proof of the Law been so inadequate.

Let us apply this to the case, cited by Allport against the Law, of a student who does not repeat a course even though he has obtained great satisfaction from receiving an A in it. He does not repeat the response involved in registering for the course and attending class, because this would interfere with interests motivating the original act, such as those in obtaining credits (the registrar has a say here), in problem-solving, in novelty and in proving to himself that he can master a new subject. But it may be precisely the past satisfaction of these interests that will determine him to choose a *new* course rather than to repeat the old, and he may choose the new course for its probable capacity to gratify those interests further. So that the example seems to substantiate the Law of Effect rather than to refute it, when completely analyzed.

The Law of Effect, so applied, is also compatible with what Allport has said about the 'functional autonomy of motives'; indeed it, or some principle with a similar scope, is needed to explain how some motives become autonomous and some do not. His discussion of the subject leaves this point in the air. Let us take Allport's case of the person whose interest in literature was first subservient to an interest in sex but persists despite the satiation or extinction of that interest, or independently of it.

Here we have simply a case of mixed motives or complexity of interests.

If the individual has received satisfaction from the non-erotic elements of poetry, whatever his original motives in reading it, he will tend to repeat the activity in cases where sexual interest is not aroused. But would he retain the literary interest independently of the sexual interest if the former had given him no satisfaction, or if it has not become yoked to some new interest? It is precisely when the originally subordinate interest gives intrinsic satisfaction that it becomes autonomous.

This separation of interests originally entwined may take place at either a reflective or a sub-reflective level. Generally it is more effective, *i.e.*, satisfaction is maximized, when we learn to analyze and disentangle our interests, than when we leave it to the fortuitous play of external stimulation alone. But our tendency to be reflective seems itself to be subject to the Law of Effect; the tendency is reinforced only in those people in whom it is successful, *i.e.*, those who have learned to think straight. Those who think crookedly usually get themselves into trouble, and would do better to rely on intuition, or custom, or the guidance of a spiritual adviser—this is, in fact, what in the long run they will do.

These remarks fit in with Thorndikes' own later statements about the Law of Effect, though he has not given a precise reformulation of it. There he has tended to treat reinforcement in terms of 'wants,' 'interests' and 'attitudes,' as well as in terms of stimulus-response connections; and where he does refer to responses he says that reinforcement can attach to any 'part or feature' of them, that the response may consist of an idea, a mood, a liking, a craving, as well as a motor act, and that the reinforcement operates upon the 'relevant' or 'belonging' aspects of the response. And for human motivation, Thorndike has stressed the 'confirming reaction' or 'O.K. reaction' as the kind of reward that is most potent. The confirming reaction is strongest when it is a gratification of the ego by way of self-esteem or a gratification of the super-ego by way of 'conscience.'

In such cases, the confirming reaction is something 'internal' to the individual, and not always, or primarily, an externally administered reward. The external reward operates, anyhow, only when it evokes an affective response, which may or may not issue immediately in overt behavior. We may have here the foundation for a restatement, in scientific terms, of the age-old ethical insight that it is what goes on inside a man that is decisive; and we may be able to see more clearly why a person in whom such tendencies to self-approbation have been established may persist, in his heroism or folly, with course of action that will bring him physical hardship, social punishment and even death. But such considerations require us to take into account complexities of human motivation that have been hitherto ignored by most of the experimental work on the Law of Effect.

III

So far we have seen that there is good reason to hold that *something* about the organism's reaction tendencies is reinforced by satisfaction. For certain types of human activity, we have found it useful to treat this something in terms of 'interests.' It is now time to analyze this vague concept more carefully, and to try to overcome the disjunction between human and animal learning, or between ego-involved and non ego-involved motivation, that the foregoing discussion has seemed to assume, so that the Law of Effect may be conceived in such a way as to comprehend both the simpler and the more complicated types of behavior. We need particularly to understand why satisfaction on one occasion reinforces a stereotyped response sequence, and on other occasions reinforces a general interest which may require changing goals and varied responses.

I have suggested that it may be possible to interpret reinforcement in terms of 'responses,' if the reinforcement is held to attach selectively to some 'parts or features' of the response, including those features of it which constitute the core of an 'interest.' Whether it is helpful, as Thorndike has continued to do, to retain the notion of a *connection* between a stimulus-situation and a response as the basic notion in the statement of the Law is another question. The initiating stimuli in the case of such a reaction tendency as an interest may vary considerably, and these stimuli as a whole may be novel or unique or 'accidental.' Efforts have been made to deal with this difficulty in terms of 'stimulus generalization' and 'response generalization.' But the question is so complicated that it would be wise to restrict the present inquiry to finding some features of the reaction that is reinforced by satisfaction, whatever may be the stimulus which evokes it, and even though it may be held to supply, in some cases, its own recurrent stimulation.

In accordance with a recent paper by Mowrer and Ullman, I should like to suggest that the Law of Effect should take into account the human being's capacity for symbolization. The confirming reaction for humans, and to some small extent for the higher animals, can attach directly to symbols, rather than to those features of the act that are symbolized, or to those features that are not sufficiently 'relevant' to be taken account of by symbolizing them.

That core of the act which constitutes the 'interest' is the feature of it which is most likely to be symbolized and repeatedly confirmed through approval of its symbol. It is therefore impossible to define the interest adequately for all cases in terms of any one feature of the act, such as the goal-object, or the terminal consummatory reaction, or the preliminary response sequences. In some activities, *e.g.*, the economic, we are primarily interested in the goal-object, money or the things that money can buy. In amatory activity, we may be interested in the preparatory features of the act as well as the consummation. When we are playing a game for the sport and not primarily to win, our chief interest is in the performance of certain skills rather than in the attainment of the ultimate goal. In listening to music, we are especially interested in the pattern of sounds, that is to say the perceptual elements of the situation, together with our immediate affective responses to them. In these cases the interest is defined by various features of the act, but always by those to which satisfaction chiefly attaches, and it is consequently these several phases of the act that are reinforced.

Rational or reflective activity requires singling out, by responding to their symbols, such general characteristics of the act in advance of its performance; and we speak of the crucial features as constituting the 'purpose.' Rational behavior is distinguished from non-rational by analysis and symbolization of the purpose, and by the implementation of this through symbolization of the means of achieving it. What is most reinforced by success is the purpose rather than the intention or the specific response sequence as a whole or even any particular temporal slice of the latter. The purpose is that aspect of the act for the sake of which it is done, that to which satisfaction has attached in the past or to which it attaches by way of anticipation; the intention includes the projected means as well as the end. There is no necessary tendency to repeat the instrumental or auxiliary responses after success unless they have also acquired consummatory or end value, that is, have given satisfaction autonomously and are recognized to have done so, or unless their symbols have been so conjoined with the symbol of the purpose that the satisfaction 'spreads' to them too. We show great flexibility in adapting our means to our ends, and we may change our goal-objects freely provided that the pursuit of them is expected to provide, somewhere in the process, those qualities or structures of the act to which satisfaction has adhered.

How then, in accordance with the Law of Effect, does reinforcement occur in the cases of reflective and non-reflective activity respectively? Two concepts may help us here: (a) Thorndike's notion of the 'snow ball' effect of the confirming reaction, and (b) that sub-principle of the Law of Effect known as the 'gradient of reinforcement.'

In animals capable of symbolization, an act that receives approval does not give us just a single satisfaction upon the completion of it. It gives us satisfaction by anticipation and in retrospect. Our symbol of the purpose *intervenes* between the stimulus and the overt response, and we O. K. it before we respond. There may be many such anticipatory reinforcements while we are planning the details of the act, or waiting for an opportunity to perform it. As we are carrying out the successive phases of the act, we keep the symbolized purpose in mind, mull it over, and confirm it repeatedly; unswerving concentration on the purpose, as it begets auxiliary goals, is necessary to keep us going. Successful execution of the act gives the purpose further reinforcement; then after the act we may reflect upon it and obtain repeated satisfaction in retrospect. So the reinforcement 'snow balls,' or multiplies itself.

A dynamic connection must, of course, be established between the symbol of the purpose and the responses necessary to execute it, or else the reinforcement remains at the level of fantasy and wish fulfillment. But this dynamic connection seems to spring from acquired habits of implementing a given kind of symbols by action, and not to require the previous execution of a specific response to the particular configuration of symbols involved in any given act. Otherwise, novel situations would never be met intelligently.

The gradient of reinforcement—according to which reinforcement is an inverse function of the time elapsed between a given feature of the act and the confirming reaction—is obviously operative along with the snow ball effect. In all the above phases of the reflective act, the confirming reaction is simultaneous with, or follows immediately upon, the symbol of the purpose, and so attaches more directly to it than to the other features of the act, which in anticipation and retrospect may not be constantly present at all. So it is the purpose, or interest, that is reinforced more strongly than the details of the response, and the crucial instrumental acts are reinforced next most strongly. It is this attachment of the confirming reaction to the symbolized purpose, and to the crucial means, which constitutes the 'relevance' or 'belongingness' in the rational act which Thorndike recognized but was unable to explain adequately, and which may help us to dispel some of the haze surrounding these concepts in the writings of the Gestaltists.

In the case of ego-involved behavior the purpose may be to exceed our previous performances, or to prove our versatility by mastering a new kind of response. Such interests preclude the exact repetition of a previously successful response, but this does not imply that the general purpose itself is not reinforced by satisfaction.

In non-rational or non-symbolic activity, where effective learning occurs, reinforcement attaches—also according to the principle of the gradient—most strongly to the immediately preceding phase of the response to the 'last open path,' i.e., to the consummatory reaction and the penultimate preparatory response. This accounts for the fact that in animal learning, as well as in human, it is only certain selected features of the response that are reinforced, and that there is consequently a great deal of variability in the means employed to reach a given type of goal. In the case of irrational or non-integrative learning, the confirming reaction attaches to some 'accidental' (non-causal) feature of the situation, or to faultily devised symbols. But in both sub-rational and irrational behavior, as in effective symbolic learning, the feature of the act which immediately precedes the repeated satisfaction is most strengthened. It follows that, when allowance is made for the differences in the situation created by the presence or absence of symbols, and by the correctness or incorrectness of the symbols, all these types of learning alike may be brought under the Law of Effect.

IV

In the above, I have not attempted anything like a 'proof' of the Law of Effect, nor even a precise and detailed reformulation of it. These would require much more experimental and observational evidence than has been advanced, and attention to different kinds of evidence from those that are usually cited for or against the Law. What I have tried to further is analysis of the problem, and in particular a way of applying the Law of Effect to ego-involved and rational behavior in such a manner as to meet Allport's objections. In conclusion, I should like to suggest some further considerations that must be taken into account before a proper application of the Law to learning and motivation becomes possible.

Allport and others have urged as an objection to the Law that the driving power in an immediately operating motive comes from a dissatisfaction rather than from a satisfaction. Only the dissatisfied person, the person who is deprived of his goal at least temporarily, strives to achieve it.

Most proponents of the Law, I believe, would agree with this point, but would hold that it is an objection to the Law only if we look to the Law of Effect to do what it is neither suited nor intended to do. It is not a principle to describe the dynamism of immediate motivation. Its scope is the acquisition and long-run reinforcement of motives, or the influence of the past on the present. It constitutes, as Troland called it, a 'hedonism of the past.' For an understanding of the immediate motivational situation, we must examine the play of forces operating in the present, as well as the influences controlling these from past experience.

A complete analysis of the complex state of affairs with regard to motivation would need to include the following facts. A given interest, unless interfered with by other interests, tends to be fixated by satisfaction. When the goal object has been attained, the interest seeks to hold on to it, to sustain the satisfaction as long as that persists (in the absence of inhibiting stimulation). Before the goal object has been achieved, in order that the interest may operate at all, there must be a gap between its arousal and its satisfaction. The dynamic character of an act in progress, in the latter case, derives from an immediate dissatisfaction, from an interest which in the particular case has not achieved its goal. But the interest as an enduring disposition, a general tendency of the organism which outlasts its particular activations, will be reinforced by repeated satisfaction.

The Law of Effect, then, is a law of retention of interests or dispositions;

it does not deal with the mechanism of the particular striving, except in so far as that is determined by past fixation of interest as one of its conditions. The tendency of particular striving to persist despite repeated frustrations is limited by the relative strength of the interest, which in turn is dependent upon its reinforcement by past satisfactions where it is autonomous, and upon the strength of other interests where it is subservient.

It may be along these lines that we should look for a reconciliation between the proponents of the Law of Effect and the Gestaltists, who have generally been its opponents. The Gestalt school have concerned themselves scarcely at all with the effect of the past upon present motivation, but almost entirely with catching the flying vectors of immediate motivation upon the wing. And they have devoted themselves especially in learning theory, to the psychology of discovery, to the complex and creative types of learning where a problem is solved for the first time and where intelligent manipulation of symbols replaces blind trial-and-error and mere repetitive drill. In particular, they have tried to describe the way in which the elements in a situation character- ized by dissatisfaction regroup themselves in order to provide satisfaction or closure.

I see no reason why the Law of Effect should be expected to provide the complete answer to such problems, nor, on the other hand, why it should be *prima facie* irrelevant to them or incompatible with the solutions offered by the Gestaltists themselves. Where we have a novel problem to be solved, no repetition of a past act, or stereotyped combination of features of it, will be adequate to give us the type of learning called for. But it still remains possible that the habits or tendencies that contribute to 'insight' are them- selves fostered by past experience, and are reinforced by success or satisfac- tion. A growing, if somewhat grudging, recognition of this may be found in some of the writings of the Gestaltists themselves, and particularly in the recent book of the late Max Wertheimer:

> "In short, the role of past experience is of high importance, but what matters is *what* one has gained from experience—blind, un-understood connections, or insight into structural inner re- latedness. What matters is how and what one recalls, how one applies what is recalled, whether blindly, in a piecemeal way, or in accordance with the structural requirements of the situation."

> *"Learning on the basis of success* may mean that an action is singled out because of the success that follows the action only factually, but is not understood; or it may mean that, in learning, a subject grasps why just this kind of action leads to just this effect for intrinsic structural reasons. It is the latter form of 'learn- ing by success' that enables the subject to vary his action in a structurally sensible way when the situation is no longer the same."

In Section III above, the attempt has been made to suggest, through a discussion of the part that symbols play in the process, how reinforcement may attach to the 'relevant' or 'required' features of the act, so that some of the mystery that has accompanied the concept of relevence in the writings of the Gestalitists may be dispelled by the Law of Effect. The implication is that both the Gestaltist description of immediate motivation and the treatment of long-term reinforcement by a revised Law of Effect are needed to supplement and buttress each other.

19. The Psychological Self, the Ego, and Personality

Peter A. Bertocci

IN a recent article in this Journal, Professor Gordon W. Allport, called attention to the pervasive, unifying, and motivating function which the ego plays in the organization of human activity. He called attention also to the growing status accorded to the ego by contemporary psychologists. Readers of that exploratory paper will recall his recognition of, and concern with, the confusion among contemporary conceptions of the ego. In this paper we shall attempt to reduce the confusion and at the same time solve problems implicit in the discussion of the ego. Let us re-state the problem.

I.   THE EGO-PROBLEM AND THE FUNCTION OF THE SELF

As the concept was presented by Allport, there seemed to be a perpetual squinting on the part of the ego. By our author it is used at one moment in the *substantive* sense as a subject producing changes in behavior. For example: "The patient's ego takes command." "It senses the threats, . . . meets the world head-on." ". . . one other property of the ego . . . [is] its customary preoccupation with the future." But while the ego in these instances is itself the agent producing effects, it is also the object (and objec-

Abridged from the *Psychological Review*, 1945, 52, 91-99. Reprinted by permission of the author and the American Psychological Association, Inc.

tive) of an implied subject. The ego has its own possessions and is itself *possessed*. This sense may be called the *objective* sense. It is now the object of knowledge, of striving, on the part of a knower, striver, feeler, and purposer. It is the development by something and 'in' something.

The ego, then, functions in both substantive and objective senses. The article leaves no doubt that the ego itself is a development, that it is not always involved in behavior, that it changes. When it is involved, it is an integrating and purposive magnet, but it is itself not a continuous function. The question, therefore, arises inevitably: What develops it, involves it, participates in it, and explains whatever continuity it does have? This question, 'What or who involves the ego?,' may remind one of the futile infinite regress, but before declaring this verdict let us see if an answer can be given which accounts for what we do know about the ego and personality.

What seems to be called for is a psychological agent whose activities endure throughout changes in egos, personalities, and, for that matter, all other experiences which are identified as 'my' or 'his' experiences. My ego and personality may change, but it is clear to me that they are *my* readjustments, and that *I* am never completely exhausted or absorbed in any one adjustment. What, then, is the referent for the *I* or *he, my* or *his* to whom egos, personalities, or experiences are attributed?

The hypothesis here suggested is that *I* refers to a complex, unitary activity of sensing, remembering, imagining, perceiving, wanting, feeling, and thinking. These *activities are the dynamic unity* referred to by the word *self*. This hypothesis presupposes that there is no acceptable reason for postulating an inactive or unchanging substantive self or soul beyond or underlying these activities in the manner of many scholastic and modern philosophers. The activities are distinguishable aspects, not distinct parts, of the total unitary activity of what I am calling the psychological self.[1]

From birth onward these functions of the self mature and change through

[1] I am using the term *psychological self,* first, because this conception is here being advanced to clarify certain psychological problems, and second, because the philosophical conceptions of the self have invariably considered it to be non-physiological. My discussion here skirts the mind-body problem and defines the self in terms of certain psychological activities, leaving the problem of whether they are 'mental' or 'physiological,' both, or neither, to further analysis.

Perhaps I should add, however, that for psychological and philosophical reasons I am more sympathetic with interactionistic views like that of James, Calkins, Brightman, Pratt, and McDougall which restrict the term 'self' to the purely mental, rather than with the psychophysically neutral views like that of Stern, the isomorphic contentions of the Gestaltists, the 'organismic *neutralism'* with attendant parallelism of J. B. Brown, or double-aspect views like H. Murray's or Moore's.

However, let our individual theoretical solutions of the mind-body problem differ as they may, the empirical data for the psychologist and philosopher seem to be interrelated knowing-wanting for which mind-body theories must account. These interrelated activities, whatever the final conclusion be as to the 'mental' or 'physiological' components, I am calling the psychological self.

learning as the self interacts with the social and physical environment. While much influenced by the kind of environment it has, this psychological self discriminates and selects, within hereditary limits and environmental opportunities, its living adjustments to other selves and things. As a vital part of this adjustment-process, it develops a personality and an ego. The exact meaning of these terms will be discussed in a moment. What needs emphasis here is that the self's thinking, remembering, feeling, wanting, etc., are not identical with the ego and personality (or any developed 'sub-systems'), for these change as the self evaluates its adjustments in a different way.

The activities which constitute this self, such as sensing, remembering, perceiving, imagining, thinking, feeling, and emoting, constitute the 'acts' of man discussed in chapter after chapter of texts in general psychology. There may be debate as to the exact relation between these activities, as to whether these are all the irreducible aspects, as to whether they are completely dependent on bodily activities. There have been fascinating arguments as to what man's essential wants are, and what the sources of his knowledge are, but there has been no denying of knowing and wanting (we telescope the other activities into these two). What we are suggesting is that these processes are phases of one ongoing process which is itself not an abstraction from them but which *is they*. They are, in Stern's term, a *unitas multiplex* and constitute, in Bergson's sense, *durée réelle!*

The psychological self, then, is a knower and a fighter for ends. And here we find the clue for the unification of the eight different conceptions of egos listed by Allport. As he says, "the ego has been conceived, viz., (1) as *knower,* (2) as *object* of knowledge, (3) as primordial selfishness, (4) as dominator, (5) as a passive organizer and rationalizer, (6) as a *fighter* for ends, (7) as one segregated behavioral system among others, (8) as a subjective patterning of cultural values." But if we unify the functions of knower and fighter for ends as activities of the psychological self, then the other egos may be seen as possible modes of adjustment by this conative and cognitive self in interaction with the world. They become not egos but properties of the ego which, as we shall see, is the variable region of the personality which the self evaluates. It is a knowing and striving self, (I, individual, organism, or person) which knows and preserves itself, be it through selfishness, domination, rationalization, as a particular behavioral system, or as a pattern of cultural values. All of these egos *presuppose* some form of knowing and wanting in their development, alteration, and preservation.[2]

One word should be added perhaps about the self *and* ego as 'object of

---

[2]As Paul Schilder has said: "The individual has to compare again and again, and must not only know that he perceives but must also be aware of his effort in the construction of perception." For the ambiguous word 'individual' I would substitute psychological self, and agree that it brings experiences 'into an ego context.'

knowledge' (2 above). Among the things which the *self* can know as existing is itself,[3] and *in this sense* the self is an object of knowledge. The self knows, in reflective self-consciousness especially, *that* it is knowing, feeling, as well as *what* it is knowing. If the self is an object of knowledge, it may be asked, how does it differ from the ego? Haven't we got the squinting substantive and objective ego back again, and if we have, why not leave the matter there instead of multiplying entities needlessly?

The answer is two-fold. First, the self in knowing itself is itself the knower. The ego in the sense being discussed here is known but is *never a knower*. It is an object of the knowing-fighting self, but itself is not a knower or fighter. Such expressions as "My ego is hurt" or "My ego won't stand that," suggest that the ego is a knower and a fighter but they really mean: "I (the self) don't like, and disagree with, the evaluation you are putting on my activities and what is more I'll fight to prevent your doing that again." In other words, the self can know itself and its relation to the world, and the ego *symbolizes* for the self *a particular evaluation* of that self's predicament. The self knows its ego, as a phase in its adjustment, and fights to maintain it. The adolescent, who knows that his 'place' in the gang's esteem depends in large part upon his ability to 'swat' the ball, or to 'strike 'em out,' will carefully protect that arm and seek to develop that system of abilities on which his 'ego' depends. If conditions change substantially, he may strive to change his ego to the extent desired, as for example, when the problem becomes that of getting into college with most of 'the crowd.'

Thus the second difference between the self and the ego becomes explicit. The ego is the self's evaluation of its activities in the life-situation. The self knows and fights, and can know that it knows and fights, as the ego cannot. But the ego represents the evaluation of the self's activities, influenced of course by the evaluations placed on the self's activities by others. What has been said about the ego will be developed and made clearer after we discuss the relation between the psychological self and the personality, but an analysis of Wallen's experiment, cited by Allport, may here clarify further the need for and function of the self.

Wallen in his experiment, 'Ego-Involvement and Selective Forgetting,' discovered that subjects, in recalling ratings of their personality traits after a period of time, tend to alter them "in such a way as to make them more compatible with subjects' opinion of themselves." The explanation offered for the alteration of these ratings or 'trace-systems' is 'inter-action between the ego-field and the trace-system of our material.' In sum, "the similarity

---

[3]Professor Helge Lundholm gives a description of the conditions under which the self expands and contracts. The self as he describes it is an *object* of knowledge. This expansion and contraction of the self's boundaries is, I should say, a function of the cognitive-conative activities of self which finds itself thus contracting and expanding.

between a particular structure in the ego-field and the trace-system of the material [or ratings] must have partially accounted for the substitution of function."

Now, the desirable traits, similar to the ego-system, certainly did not realize their own similarity or 'ego-relatedness' and relate themselves to the ego-system. Nor can the ego-system to which they are assimilated relate them, or see the similarity, for the ego is the subjective standard to which they are related. What, then, *noting* the similarity, relates them? The hypothesis offered to explain such communication is the cognitive-conative psychological self which has certain evaluations of itself (ego), relates other ratings to them, and alters the ratings ego-ward to avoid conflict. Similar considerations would apply to other investigations of this sort.

Should we, perhaps, substitute the term self-involvement for ego-involvement in such experiments? The answer is negative, for the purpose of such experiments is to discover what factors influence the self—in the instance cited remembering is influenced by the factor of ego-formations *et cetera*. The self, as Brightman has said, is involved as the pre-supposition of every experiment, and there is no point in referring to self-involvement especially when the psychologist is trying to study the particular course self-activities take. As James said about the faculty of memory, so we can say about the self: it "does not exist absolutely but works under conditions and *the quest of the conditions* becomes the psychologist's most interesting task." Note he did not say the *only* task! Intellectual clarity and avoidance of confusion is also a scientific objective. When we overlook the unobtrusive but inescapable self, we tend not only to bring back 'the squint,' but also create the artificial problem of how 'communication' and 'interaction' between aspects of experience can take place. When we forget the self, we tend to reify its 'systems' or aspects, and misplace concreteness by attributing activities to them which belong only to the self.

II.   THE SELF AND ITS PERSONALITY

"Personality is the dynamic organization within the individual of those psychophysical systems that determine his unique adjustments to his environment." In this definition the personality is clearly a function of the undefined 'individual.' Let 'the individual' mean the complex unity of cognitive-conative activiites. This is our definition of the self. The definition would therefore read: "A self's personality is its dynamic organization of its own unique psychophysical wants and abilities which renders adjustments to its environment unique." The personality is indeed a *self's* mode of survival, unique because no two selves have the same basic inherited constitution. These adjustments or maladjustments are what they are, in large part, because the acting self is reacting to the world as it perceives, imagines, or conceives that world and as it compares or evaluates the power of its activities and wants in a given socio-geographical situation. The personality a self develops is probably the most important by-product of the self's encounters with the world, for the personality is the particular adjustment the self has *learned* to make to the conceived world.

We need not stress here the importance of self-consciousness in the development of personality. But, as Allport says, "the advent of self-consciousness is gradual." There is consciousness before there is self-consciousness. Whatever the exact nature of the experiences whereby the infant becomes aware of himself as a being distinct from the natural and social environment, consciousness of self presupposes a knowing-wanting self to begin with which as yet was not aware of itself. Nor can there be 'successive moments of consciousness with their imbrication of temporal reference and content,' unless there is an enduring knowing-wanting self. For a succession of experiences to be known *as a* succession, as consistent or inconsistent, similar or dissimilar, involves an embracing unity persistent through change. If the organization of personality, in particular, 'must be regarded as constantly evolving and changing, as motivational and self-regulating,' then, unless we are going to have separate and disparate globs of organization following each other, we must have a knowing-wanting self, an associative functioning, to whose destiny these organizations are related, for whom they exist, and by whom they are altered.

The personality, we have seen, represents the accessible organization of the self's functioning in a given world, which endures as long as that self and its environment allow it. But we must not even suggest that the personality is a mere mask which the self can put on or take off at will. For the self in 'determining' one mode of adjustment, in 'selecting' within limits, as it were, its battering ram and its defense, is restricting its activities to certain channels, and may indeed find itself 'stuck' with its own evolved personality. Personality is anchored in a self, but a self's further actions are modified by or anchored to the personality developed.

This conception of a self-personality throws light on the nature of multiple personalities. Dr. Jekyll can switch to Mr. Hyde only because Dr. Jekyll represents one functional system of the knowing-wanting self which cannot at the moment control all of the self's activities including the system represented by Mr. Hyde. But the self's activity is the mediating activity which may curb the development of Dr. Jekyll or Mr. Hyde, or relinquish itself completely to the one adjustment-system.

III.   THE SELF, THE PERSONALITY, AND THE EGO

In his article, Professor Allport suggested that the ego and the personality are not coextensive or identical. The ego "is only one portion, one region

. . . of the personality." Again, "Many skills, habits, memories are components of personality but seldom, if ever, become ego-involved." The ego, furthermore, 'varies greatly from time to time' and "its content keeps changing, for at certain moments the ego seems preoccupied with one activity and soon thereafter with a wholly different activity." (This last clause illustrates the ego's squint, for it is now reified into a knowing agent.)

It is clear from the above that the ego, like the personality, is acquired, and that it is *not an entity* separate from the personality, but a distinguishable *functional unity* within the system of personality. However, there seems to be no answer to the question: Why changes in the ego? Perhaps the functioning of the psychological self can clarify this situation also.

We have seen that the knowing-wanting self, in its interaction with the socio-geographical environment, is forced to extend its functioning in concrete ways (develop abilities, habits, sentiments, attitudes, traits, secondary personalities), which eventually become the self's more or less organized mode of adjustment, or personality. The personality does not have *independent* thinking-wanting functions, but represents the unique adjustment-system in which a given self has used and is using its inherent energies. The complexity and degree of unity within a given personality, or, in general, the kind of personality developed, indicates the degree of 'success' a given self has had in meeting the demands of the sociogeographical environment with its own intrinsic potentialities. For example, a self may so develop its inherent needs and activities through the years that a genial, trustworthy, industrious, social and theoretical personality results. However, careful analysis often reveals a growing religious interest also. In other words, the self's investments in life have taken a fairly definite form, but not a final form. At the moment, let us say, this person is an appealing public speaker, but he takes special pride in his capacity for theoretical analysis which experts have praised. If he were asked what he prized most in his personality from the point of view of the public speaking, whereby he earned a good living, he would stand by his geniality and golden voice, but if asked what he prized most in his achievements, he would immediately refer to his analytical ability which experts have admired. It is the analytical ability which constitutes the ego at one point, while the geniality and golden voice, other aspects of his personality, comprise his ego at others. Challenge either, and there will be a persistent attempt to show you how incorrect your evaluation is. In each instance he (the *self*) has identified his long struggle for achievement with the traits (parts of the personality) now questioned. His ego, the self's ego, is involved. Strike at the ego and you indeed strike at the self.

The ego, accordingly is that portion of the personality with which the self has identified its greatest value or adjustment-segment at the time. The rest of the personality the self may be aware of and evaluate in different ways at different times, depending on where the stress or threatening conflict happens to fall in the total life-situation. For the ego represents a roughly determinable portion of his mode of survival which he evaluates as 'central' and essential to his welfare at the time. Generally speaking, then, the ego will be the core or cluster of values (perhaps actually embodied in traits) with which the self identifies its 'security' or success at the time. When its ego is involved, the self's value-citadel is in question, its investment in life is at stake. That is why what is relevant to the ego produces tensions in the self, for the conflict with or threat to the ego is really conflict with or threat to the self's prized achievement (ego). To say, as Allport says, that there are "two forms of motivation, one ego-involved and one not," is to say that in some instances the greatest values conceived by the self are involved, and in other instances less critical needs, segmentally conceived, are involved. "Ego-involved tasks often demand changing goals and new responses." When this is true, it is because the self has put a premium on growth. Again, "many cultural frames having to do with language, etiquette, or dress, determine our perceptions, our memory, our conduct, but their influence is not felt as personally relevant." The reason is not that the self does not value them at all but because at the moment they can be taken for granted. But if the situation changes and the connection between them and the security of the self's acknowledged values is clarified, they change their psychological status and become 'personally relevant.'

It will be seen, then, that the ego, though it may be a fairly stable focus of activity and of further organization in any personality, is not a separable organization in personality. The ego could not be understood unless the personality pattern were understood, though an understanding of the personality pattern at a given time would not be complete without understanding the ego, or the critical-value-complex.

IV. THE SELF AS UNIFIER OF SUB-SYSTEMS

Lack of complete understanding, and not of respect, has made me hesitant to relate the psychological self with the concept of the ego as developed by Koffka and Lewin. But what I do comprehend leads me to suspect an underlying squint and lurking disunity in their ego-concept. Professor Koffka stresses the importance of the ego as a unifying, enduring system which maintains "its identity in the stream of varying conditions" and develops "in accordance with the disturbances to which it is exposed and the kind of Ego it is." This passage would describe the psychological self admirably if that were all there were to it. But the subjective-objective squint appears as soon as it becomes clear that the ego is itself one type of experience among others: "discomfort may be experienced without an ego." At one moment we are told that the ego *is* segregated and in the next we read: "No Ego could exist, as a special system, unless it *segregated itself* (italics mine) from other systems." Can it be that something like the psychological self might fill in the gap which Koffka admits when he says that "we have, at the moment, no real knowledge of the forces which keep the Ego unified and segregated from the rest?" Koffka simply rested at this point with the assumption that the ego is 'a particular field part in constant interaction with the rest of the field.'

Another resemblance to the psychological self appears when Koffka finds that the ego is a complex of subsystems with a 'permanent sub-system' which he calls 'the Self.' This 'Self' is the core of enveloping sub-systems interacting with each other and with it, comparable to different layers in surface-depth organization. But is this inner self simply the deepest and permanent layer? Are the other systems ultimately unified by its activities, or do they have their own? Are the tensions which originate in the Self related to the tensions in the sub-systems?

Lewin, as if to reply, not only tells us that "a dominant system 'uses' a subordinate system as its tool," but that a tension from the 'inner-personal region' may spread throughout the personality. The exact inter-relation is not clarified, and we are not told that these sub-systems are nourished by the inner-personal (as I should contend). It may be that the topographical methodology gets in the way of clarity at this point. Yet, when the inner-personal system is itself said to be differentiated into 'central and peripheral inner-personal systems,' we begin to wonder what the differentiating agent is. To speak of 'a central need' setting up "a peripheral 'quasi-need' as a tool for its fulfillment," is meaningless unless it is a linguistic short-cut for something like: "The concrete cognitive-conative self, in order to fulfill one of its most intense or highly valued needs, is forced in a given situation to find a different or devious route for its satisfaction." Better, with Stern, to say *"Keine Gestalt ohne Gestalter,"* and to emphasize that the self, as Stern said of the Person, *"is a living whole, individual, unique, striving toward goals self-contained and yet open to the world around"* it. We shall then more readily realize that the self, its personality, and the ego are not like layers of an onion, but one interpenetrating psychological organization.

In closing, one other theoretical consequence emerges which we would here reemphasize. Most recent discussion of the formation of personality has labored the enormous part played by the cultural situation in which the individual finds himself. Now, it certainly is impossible to account for the self's development without preponderant attention, perhaps, to the cultural environment. If the self, for example, identifies its well-being with social norms and social objectives, like democracy, then in action this social norm becomes the self's highest ego-value, by which the self judges and controls the future course of its activities. But should these major considerations for the course of development not be more closely connected with the *co-generator* and *co-director* of specific human changes in a personality, namely, the functioning self? After all, it is the activities of this self which create demands *for* the environment and society to challenge, fulfill, or frustrate. The self challenges the culture in which it is born even as it responds to its moulding norms. Thus, the ego and the personality are never merely the 'subjective side of culture.' They are always, in varying degree, the means a self has taken in developing itself among the possibilities suggested to it by the surrounding world. The great abstraction or artifact, psychologically speaking, is the word 'environment' or 'society' in the singular. Every self senses, feels, needs, perceives, and thinks about the stimuli which impinge upon it; it relates them in various ways, but always with some uniqueness, to its own developing conception of itself. For the self stands as the unique active unity, ready to be influenced and sometimes forced by demands outside itself, but always eking out its own style and mode of adjustment. Indeed, 'society' represents what selves have more or less agreed upon as valuable aims for self-development.

V. SUMMARY

The concept of the *psychological self,* as an enduring, unique, complex unity of knowing-wanting activities, not only serves to unify diverse descriptions of the ego, but to clarify the function of the ego in personality-organization. The adoption of this self, as the agent ever organizing its activities in relatively stable personality patterns and evaluating its adjustments in the light of environmental demands, helps us (1) to understand the close functional relationship between ego, personality, and self, and (2) to explain the possibility of continuity, succession, and interaction within the personality-ego systems.

The self does not, of course, explain the existence of any one system, or any specific development within personality; it has no specific experimental value. But if we experiment in order to improve our understanding and interpretation of human experience, then this interpretative concept may be found useful, even as it may have to be modified or expanded as empirical data pile up.

20. The Awareness of Self and the Structure of the Ego

Isidor Chein

I. INTRODUCTION

Professor Allport's presidential address to the Eastern Psychological Association on THE EGO IN CONTEMPORARY PSYCHOLOGY with its brief, but exceptionally able review of the main conceptions of the ego and its summary of cogent experimental studies, will undoubtedly serve as a landmark in the history of psychology and as a rallying and focussing point for further studies in ego psychology.

Allport considers eight main conceptions of the ego: "(1) as knower (2) as object of knowledge, (3) as primordial selfishness, (4) as dominator, (5) as a passive organizer and rationalizer, (6) as a fighter for ends, (7) as one segregated behavioral system among others, (8) as a subjective patterning of cultural values." He writes that "We cannot (yet) say whether these eight conceptions reflect irreconcilable theories, whether they shade imperceptibly into one another, or whether they are all ultimately to be subordinated under one inclusive theory of the ego." Professor Allport adds his belief that recent experimental studies favor the last possibility and comments that "it is my belief that in most of the experiments I shall report one finds that the ego is acting in several, if not all, of the eight capacities I have listed."

Professor Allport's paper is, in many ways, challenging as well as provocative. For, while everything seems to point to one unitary ego rather than to a number of different referents, each sometimes called 'ego,' Allport does not indicate what the "one inclusive theory of the ego" might be. In the section of his paper dealing with 'The Nature of the Ego,' he points out that the various conceptions under consideration and the views of various writers on the subject have much in common. Specifically, he lists the fol-

Abridged from the *Psychological Review*, 1944, 51, 304-314.   Reprinted by permission of the author and the American Psychological Association, Inc.

lowing points of agreement: (1) The ego is less embracing than personality. (2) It is in proximate relation to the external world. (3) The subjective sense of the ego (self) varies greatly from time to time. He adds a fourth point which he regards as of great importance, that the ego is customarily preoccupied with the future. But he does not tell us, even hypothetically, what the ego *is*.

Allport's paper is thus a challenge to psychological theorists to provide "one inclusive theory of the ego," and the present writer, for one, believes that this challenge can, at present, be met.

What, however, can be expected of such a theory? Certainly not that each of the main conceptions should find an equally important place in the theory, nor even that these conceptions be accepted without modification. These conceptions have, after all, been advanced by individuals of varied interests and competences. What can be expected is that the theory make clear what each of these conceptions is after, and that the significance of each of the conceptions should emerge from the theory and have some 'organic' relation to it. It may further be expected that the theory perform a similar task with regard to the four points developed by Allport in his consideration of the nature of the ego and that, perhaps above all, it make clear the meaning of 'ego involvement.'

II. AWARENESS OF SELF

We take, as a starting point in the search for a theory of the Ego, two rather obvious, but nonetheless important, facts:

First, the fact that everyone, with the possible exceptions of infants, some philosophers, and some psychopaths, is aware of one's self. The possibility of exceptions is freely admitted, because exceptions would not be critical for the argument. Actually, however, it is doubtful whether many of the seeming exceptions are genuine. There are many disorders of self-awareness, but such disorders do not constitute an absence of awareness of self. Similarly, with regard to the philosophers, it is quite evident that Hume, for example, despite his denial of its reality, did have an awareness of self. His argument did not simply lead to his discovery that he, of all people had no self. Rather, he importuned his readers to examine their own awareness and see whether they did not observe what he himself observed when he examined his awarenesses. A color-blind person does not, on discovering his deficiency, confidently invite others to investigate themselves and see that they, too, are lacking in awareness of color; his discovery is likely to come with a shocked realization that he is missing something which other people are experiencing. In other words, Hume knew perfectly well what other people were talking about when they spoke of their selves and he also knew that he was talking about a corresponding referent in his own awareness. Hume did not try to prove that there was no awareness of self, but rather that this awareness was illusory or delusory, that there was no self to be aware of. We shall return to Hume's difficulty with regard to the reality of the self, but at the moment, we are only concerned with the point that awareness of self is a common experience of mankind.

Second, the fact that the self is not identical with the ego. If it were, then the knowledge of the ego would be as immediate as the knowledge of the self. It is true, of course, that the word 'ego' has been used as a synonym of 'self.' Psychologists, however, generally have something else in mind when they speak of the ego. For, while each individual recognizes himself, he has no immediate knowledge of ego processes such as repression or self-actualization. To be sure, he may know that he, John Doe, is selfish, or domineering, or submissive. But, if you said to him that it was not he, John Doe, who was selfish and so on, but his self that was selfish or domineering, he would regard you with, to say the least, suspicion. It is not selfishness or submissiveness of which the individual is aware when he is aware of his self; it is something quite different.

What that *something* is, everybody knows from a *knowledge of acquaintance.* The trouble began when philosophers, such as Hume, and numerous psychologists tried to transform that *knowledge of acquaintance* into *knowledge about,* particularly when they attempted to localize that something.

Now, in order to localize something, it is necessary to do so with reference to something else. Hume, and James, and Titchener, and many others fell into the pitfall of attempting to localize the self with reference to the body. Why this is a pitfall, will be explained shortly. Suffice it to say for the moment that the foregoing found no self, but only various bodily sensations which, to add to our troubles, were not always the same. In this extremity, Hume flatly declared that there was no *one* thing, nor even a group of intrinsically related things, that could be called the self. This, despite the almost universal experience of mankind to the contrary. Nor was there any ready explanation forthcoming as to why people (including Hume who was talking, as we have seen above, about his self) related these intrinsically unrelated sensations.

It was Köhler who, according to Koffka, was inspired to localize the self, not with reference to the body, but with reference to the environment. This, as a matter of fact, is the way people will spontaneously localize themselves[1] and Köhler's formula is so obvious that it sounds silly even to say it. Yet, because of the seemingly great philosophical problems involved, it is necessary to elaborate upon the obvious.

Koffka presents Köhler's arguments as follows:

It starts with the behavioural environment: . . . space is not only

---

[1]Ask someone where he is and he will answer in terms of environmental coordinates. He will never say, "I am here, in the form of certain sensations around 'my' eyes and throat." To press him further, creates an artificial situation.

in front and at the sides, space is also, though less articulated, less clearly defined, behind . . . . Now then, Köhler's argument continues, what is there between the last thing just in front and the behind? Is space absolutely empty there? The answer is: Certainly not; here, between the 'in front' and the 'behind,' is that part of the behavioural world which I call my Ego. It has a very definite place in that world, and well-defined, if variable, boundaries. From this argument we can take the following answer to our question: 'in front,' 'to the left and right,' 'behind,' and 'above and below' are characteristics of space which it possesses with regard to an object which serves as the origin of the system of spatial coordinates. This object, then, is functionally different from all others, inasmuch as it determines fundamental space aspects.

Koffka's presentation is unnecessarily complicated and, particularly as it is couched in terms of a conceptual framework which is still foreign to a large body of American psychologists, it seems worthwhile to translate it into more familiar terms.

Elsewhere, the present writer, following a respectable psychological tradition (particularly among American psychologists), has briefly presented the point of view that *awareness* refers to the discriminatory activity of the organism. Applying this view to the present problem, we may say that the organism (in this case, we can only speak definitely about *man*) is aware of (i.e., it discriminates) space-in-front, space-behind, space-to-the-right-and left, space-above, and space-below. In between these spaces, it is aware of (it discriminates) something else. That awareness of something in between is *the awareness of self*.

This seems so obvious and clear that it is astonishing that anyone should have gotten into trouble on this score. Yet, there are three reasons for the trouble which can more readily be comprehended in our terms than in Koffka's.

First, there is the problem of two things being in the same place at the same time. In between the 'in front' and the 'behind,' is the body. Yet, experientially, the awareness of self is not the awareness of the body. In terms of the logical principle that two things cannot occupy the same space at the same time, this seems impossible. *Where* in-between is the self? It is not the body and it is not *in* the body, for the internal bodily space is well accounted for in terms of various organs and so on. Where, then, is it?

The impossible paradox is readily resolved if we remember that the awareness of self and the body are not the same order phenomena. The turning of a wheel has a spatial locale, but it has no spatial dimensions. The turning of a wheel occurs in space, but it is not the wheel, nor is it in the wheel; it is a relation between the wheel and the various objects. Similarly, awareness, any awareness, is a relation between the organism and various objects which it is discriminating.[2] The awareness of self is no exception. Being, like all awareness, an action, it has a *locale,* but no physical-spatial dimensions.

Second, there is the common failure to distinguish between the object of awareness and the content. The *content* refers to *what the organism discriminates* and the *object* refers to *what is there to be discriminated.* The content is the discrimination, the object is, to use Tolman's terminology, the *discriminanda* (the properties of objects or situations whereby they can be discriminated). It is important to distinguish the two because they do not always correspond perfectly. Thus, with regard to eye movements, the object of discrimination is the jerky eye movements, the content of discrimination is the smoothly moving eyes. Or, with regard to the Muller-Lyer illusion, the object of awareness is the pair of equal lines, the content is a pair of unequal lines.

This is important with regard to the awareness of self. For the object of awareness is indisputably the body. That is what is in-between. Yet, the content of awareness is not the body; nor does it correspond perfectly to the body. Such a lack of correspondence between object and content is not unusual and it is one of the tasks of psychology to explain such discrepancies wherever they do arise. In this particular instance, it is not especially hard to explain the discrepancies, but that will not be attempted here.[3]

Earlier it was stated that the *awareness* of self and the body were phenomena of different orders. It may now be added that the *self* and the body are also phenomena of different orders: the self being a content of awareness and the body being a *physical* reality.

Third, there is the frequent failure to realize that different contents may be functionally equivalent, just as different things may be functionally equivalent. Earlier, we mentioned that there was no ready explanation forthcoming as to why the different experiences which are arrived at in the attempt to localize the self within the body are normally experienced as *my self* and not simply at one time, as a tension in the eyes and, at another time as aching feet. No explanation *can* come forth so long as we regard these experiences as disparate phenomena, without any coordinating principle. An explanation is, however, readily found when we realize that the awareness of something between the 'in front' and the 'behind.' What these 'different'

[2]It will be recalled that Koffka does attribute spatial dimensions to the self, but this is space in the behavioral environment, which is a different order space than that of the geographic environment (ordinary physical space). Similarly, when Boring in his *The Physical Dimensions of Consciousness,* speaks of *extensity* as one of the attributes of awareness, he cannot mean that the extensity of awareness has reality in *physical* space. This point will become clearer when we contrast the content of awareness with the object of awareness (see below).

[3]The approach to the problem of discrepancies is in terms of the answer to the question: Under what conditions must a given discrimination be made?

experiences have in common is that they all carry the burden of being that something in-between. In this respect all of these experiences are the same, even though in other respects they are different. This is what accounts for the apparent fluctuations in the 'spatial' boundaries of the self. My hand can very readily be experienced as being outside of myself if it is discriminated as belonging to the 'in front.'

These, then (the failure to realize that body and self are phenomena of different orders, the failure to distinguish between the content of awareness and its object, and the failure to realize that different mental contents may be functionally equivalent), are the main reasons for the intellectual muddle that has arisen with regard to the self. There seems, however, also to be some difficulty with Köhler's conception.

The difficulty arises from the possibility of identifying oneself with some other person or of identifying some other person with oneself.[4] In both cases, the awareness of self seems to cross a spatial gap separating the person from the object of identification. It seems as if "here I am, there I am not, and there I am again." What happens, in these cases, to the discrimination of something between the 'before and behind'?

This difficulty disappears with a closer inspection of these phenomena. The writer frequently is unable to identify himself with the characters of a motion picture because of the intrusion into his awareness of what is actually going on to the right, left, and behind. The extent of this awareness is not appropriate to the 'in-front.' The more successful the identification, the less of a 'clash' there is between the 'in-front' and the other directions. In other words, in successfully identifying oneself with the characters in a motion picture, one does not experience oneself as being in one's seat, but as being there, in the picture-world; and, to do this successfully, all directions must be appropriately experienced. Similarly, if one identifies some love object with oneself and some danger threatens that object, then one experiences the danger as occurring 'here,' where one oneself is. With lesser degrees of such identification, one may experience the danger as being both 'here' and 'there'; but the more the danger is experienced as being 'there,' the less of such identification there is.

Köhler's solution of the problem of the awareness of self and of the phenomenal nature of the self holds. It should be clearer than ever, however, that the awareness of self is not an awareness of the ego, that the ego is not simply 'something' between the 'before and behind.' What, then, of the ego?

---

[4]These are phenomenally and dynamically different. The first may be exemplified by an identification of oneself with some character in a motion picture, the second by the phenomenon of 'falling in love.' Both forms of identification are dependent on ego processes. We are, however, only concerned here with the relation of these phenomena to the awareness of self.

III. THE STRUCTURE OF THE EGO

Elsewhere[5] the writer has developed a set of concepts which are very relevant here: the perpetuation, derivation, and imbrication of motives.

In terms of the concept of the perpetuation of motives, any frequently recurrent motive (organically determined or derived) which meets with some frustration results in the development of expectations of its recurrence and the development of a need on the part of the organism to prepare for its recurrence. In other words, the motive becomes broader in its implications and, in this broader sense, continues to function even though the *critical* conditions for its existence are no longer operative. Such a *perpetuated* motive can never, in a very genuine sense, be satisfied; for it is always pointing toward the future and is not concerned with present circumstances; its goals are not attainable. It is only in terms of such motivational perpetuations that we get something that endures and is not transient like ordinary behaviors and awareness.

In terms of the concept of motivational derivation, any environmental situation which requires that the organism have commerce with a given means in order to attain a given end, or that the organism satisfy certain conditions in order to attain that end, results in the development of a need on the part of the organism to have commerce with that means or to satisfy the necessary conditions, provided that it already has a need to attain that end. Such motives, like organically determined motives, may also become perpetuated and enduring, provided that the conditions for such perpetuation are satisfied.

More complex motivational derivations are also possible, as where a derived motive is an indirect result of the derivational process previously described. Here belongs the problem of the psychoanalytic superego, but that is too complex a problem to discuss at this point. A simpler case is to be found in the indirect derivation of elimination motives. So long as excretion takes place spontaneously and without interference, as the 'need' arises, there can be no elimination motives. With the development, however, of a need for control, there occurs an interference with spontaneous elimination and a consequent building up of bodily tensions leading, in this case, to a genuine appetitive drive.

By the imbrication of motives is meant the fact that perpetuated motives do not remain isolated from one another, but rather that they influence each other in the most complex ways. The same perpetuated-derived motive may

---

[5]The writer makes no claim to originality in connection with these concepts. With the possible exception of the concept of perpetuated motives, they have been clearly anticipated by other psychologists in various terminologies and contexts. He is not aware, however, of their having been explicitly put together in this way for the purpose of elucidating problems of personality and ego structure. For the concept of derived motives see, e.g., Tolman. For the imbrication of motives, see Horney. With regard to perpetuated motives, see Hunt.

derive support from a number of parent motives. Thus the need for approval may be related to a host of other motives. Moreover, the derivation of motives involves not merely transitive or simple hierarchal relationships, but circular relationships as well. Thus, while the need to earn money may be in part derived from the need of the approbation of others, the need for approval is, in turn, in part derived from the need to earn money.

The result of the process of motivational imbrication is the development of a structured motivational system, a genuine Gestalt, in which anything which affects any part of the system affects the system as a whole. The fact that the motives involved are perpetuated motives implies that the system is relatively enduring, although not necessarily unchangeable. In the paper to which reference has already been made, the writer suggested that such a system satisfies the essential logical requisites of what may properly be called personality. Here, we shall consider the relation of the above described development to the ego.

The essential key is provided in a reconsideration of the foregoing remarks concerning the structurization of motives. It has to be observed that motives are polarized processes. Consider, for example, the dependence (need to be cared for) motive. Such a motive is bipolar.[6] At one pole are the persons or institutions from whom something is demanded or expected. With reference to these persons or institutions, appropriate actions have to take place such as will elicit the demanded or expected solicitude and care. At the other pole, however, there is something else. It is not the body, except insofar as the 'body image' is incorporated into the awareness of self. At the other pole of the dependence motive there is, precisely, the self of which one is aware. The awareness of self is, in fact, part and parcel of the dependence motive.

The polar situation is even clearer with regard to the so-called self-preservative motive. Here the motive is, basically, unipolar, although motives derived from self-preservative motives may also have outer poles. Again the essential pole is not the body, although here a great deal of confusion reigns, particularly among laymen, but too often among psychologists. Even Freud, who so clearly recognized the derivation of the self-preservative motive (*via* the cathexis of the self), could sometimes, for example confuse hunger as a self-preservative motive. With the development of the theory of the life and death instincts, Freud made a similar error in assuming that reproduction was intrinsically a psychological affirmation of life. The fundamental error is the confusion of the *consequences* of an act with its *aim*.[7] The writer remembers a philosophy instructor who argued that "dogs have a philosophy of life, for why should they copulate if they did not value offspring?" This instructor could not, rationally, conceive of copulation apart from reproduc-

6Bateson is, of course, not talking of motives, but of *social motifs,* i.e., of the environmental setting in which various motives develop.

tion. The error would have been just as great if he had said, "Why should they eat, if they do not value life?" The homeostasis of physiological processes is not a motive although it may sometimes give rise to appetitive drives. It is true, of course, that people sometimes eat in order to preserve the bodily health, but such a motive is itself *derived from* a self-preservative motive; it is not, in itself, a motive of self-preservation; and, often enough, eating has no relation to either self- or body-preservation.[8]

Bearing in mind, then, the many confusions which arise in connection with self-preservation, we may again say that the essential pole of the self-preservative motive is the self of which the individual is aware, not the body. It thus often happens that, to the individual, self-preservation may be perfectly compatible with the destruction of the body.

As with the dependency motive and the self-preservative motive, so with the prestige motive and numerous others; these motives are built up around the awareness of self and do not have any meaning without reference to the self.

We have, then, if the above argument is correct, a structured set of inter-related motives centering about the awareness of self. It is now suggested that *this structure is the ego.*

It must be remembered that not all perpetuated motives, certainly not all motives, necessarily have direct relevance to this structured set of motives. Or, to express the matter differently, the frustration or alteration of any one motive need not be as critical for the total structure as would be the frustration or alteration of another motive. The less direct relevance a given need has for the total structure of self-centered needs or the less critical a role it plays with reference to the total structure, the more peripheral it is to the ego.

It may still be a problem for investigation whether, and to what extent, the ego-involvement of needs is correlated with their intensity, particularly in the case of peripheral or non-ego-involved needs. The need to solve a problem or to earn a high score on a test may not be of much moment, for example, from the point of view of critical ego needs, but can it, under these circumstances constitute a strong motive for the organism? Can appetitive hunger or thirst become so intense that the ego structure becomes temporarily irrelevant in the psychological economy of the organism? If this does happen, in the case of appetitive drives, can it also happen with various derived motives?

---

[7]In defense of Freud, it may be urged that he often had reason to believe that the seemingly *accidental* consequences of acts were actually the *intended* consequences. Each case, however, as Freud well knew, has to be judged on its own merits. The frequent coincidence of seemingly accidental consequences with intended consequences justifies, as a working hypothesis for the further exploration, the assumption that *any* consequence may have been *intended.* A careful distinction must, however, be drawn between a working hypothesis for further exploration and a conclusion that the hypothesis is correct.

[8]Freud realized the difference between hunger and eating for pleasure.

It must also be remembered that the ego structure may be more or less stable. If it is composed of mutually complementary and compatible needs, it is stable and resistant to any change which would destroy the motivational equilibrium. If it is composed of mutually incompatible and dystrophic needs, it is easily disrupted. Any disruption of the ego, however, must follow the lines of cleavage that are natural to the particular structure. In any case, it cannot be stressed too much that a unitary structure does not necessarily imply unity within that structure. The different motives involved may be mutually supporting but they may also be mutually antagonistic. One of Horney's great contributions is her analysis of areas of conflict within the ego structure.

Finally, it should be noted that, by virtue of the central role it plays in the ego structure, the significance of the self becomes enormously enhanced. From the center of the person's awareness, it becomes the center of his existence. From an item, in a universe of observable items, it becomes a supreme value and the core of an evaluative system.

IV.   MAIN CONCEPTIONS OF THE EGO

We may now return to Allport's list of eight main conceptions of the ego and to his four points concerning the nature of the ego, to see how they fare in terms of the theory.

1. *The ego as knower.*—It is the organism that knows, the organism that discriminates, the organism that is aware. As Allport himself writes, "it is enough, says James in effect, to admit that knowing goes on. A separate knowing-ego is not a necessary assumption."

At the same time, we may note that there are numerous cognitions and cognitive functions bound up in the ego structure. The perpetuation of motives is dependent upon the development of expectations and anticipations of the recurrence of episodic motives. The derivation of motives is dependent on the apprehension of means-end relations. The functioning of all motives is dependent on the awareness of the environment, save, perhaps, for the effect of random restlessness. The ego system, therefore, is not merely a motivational system, but, by that very fact, a cognitive system as well. If the theory is correct, then this much is valid concerning the ego as knower.

2. *The ego as object of knowledge.*—As Allport deals with the conception, it is concerned with the self, not with the ego. We have already dealt with this problem at greater length above. The ego is not, spontaneously, known; it becomes the object of knowledge in the same way that any phenomenon becomes known in the course of scientific investigation.

3. *The ego as primitive selfishness.*—We have already noted that the self, by virtue of its central position in the ego structure becomes a supreme

value and the core of an evaluative system. By implication, the ego is selfish. Yet, a great deal would be missed if we let the matter go at that. There is possible, if we may so express ourselves, a selfish selfishness and an altruistic selfishness, a short-sighted selfishness dominated by the pleasure principle and a long-sighted selfishness dominated by the reality principle. In addition, because the self of which the individual is aware is not identical with his body, various transformations of the self are possible, through identification, etc., which destroy the popular meaning of selfishness. In general, we may add, the more fully developed the ego, the less selfish (in the popular sense) the ego is. This is so because there are so many motives involved which must not interfere with one another. Through the interaction of motives, greater scope, and consequently, less essential selfishness is demanded.

4. *The ego as dominance drive.*—Without denying the reality of dominance drives, we may say that this conception mistakes a part for the whole, an ego motive for the ego. How important a role dominance drives play in the ego structure will depend on many factors: the specific pattern of ego development, the importance of dominance in the psychological economy of the individual from the point of view of the requirements for coping with the environmental situations that the individual has met, and the other perpetuated motives developed by the individual. That is to say, the dominance drives are not necessarily basic in the ego structure.

"The negative states," Allport writes, "of anxiety, insecurity, defensiveness, resistance are just as truly indicators that whenever the ego is debased there arise impulses for its defense and restoration to status." With this statement, our theory demands whole-hearted agreement. For, such negative states carry with them threats of frustration and deprivation with regard to the whole motivational structure that comprises the ego.

5. *Ego as a passive organization of mental processes.*—This conception is erroneously ascribed, by Allport, to Freud. Allport misinterprets Freud's discussions of the relative 'smallness' of the ego when faced with a world not built according to its specifications. He writes: "The ego, having no dynamic power, tries as well as it can to conciliate and to steer the warring forces (id, superego, and environment), but when it fails, as it often does, it breaks out in anxiety." As a conciliator, it is not passive and, according to Freud, it is the ego that represses and rationalizes and so on. Freud is talking about the ego when he writes, "A reaction which combines features of both these is the one we call normal or 'healthy'; it denies reality as little as neurosis, but then, like a psychosis, is concerned with effecting a change in it. This expedient normal attitude leads naturally to some active achievement in the outer world and is not content, like a psychosis, with establishing the alteration within itself; it is no longer *auto-plastic* but *allo-plastic.*" This is not a passive victim of external forces. Similarly, when Freud writes,

"One might compare the relation of the ego to the id with that between a rider and his horse," he is talking about the *mastery* of the id by the ego. If he adds that "all too often . . . the rider is obliged to guide his horse in the direction in which it itself wants to go," *all too often* does not mean always, and the obligation does not imply a cessation of struggle for mastery. The therapeutic objective "to strengthen the ego, to make it more independent of the super-ego, to widen its field of vision, and so to extend its organization that it can take over new portions of the id," likewise, does not deal with the ego as a passive organization of mental processes.

Allport quite properly rejects the passivity theory, to whomever it may be attributed, in favor of an activity theory. In terms of the theory we are expounding, all of the above mentioned processes can be comprehended in terms of the interplay of ego motives and factors external to the ego structure. To discuss them in detail would take up too much space.

6. *Ego as a 'fighter for ends.'*—This is implicit in the theory we have advanced of the ego as a dynamic system of motives.

7. *The ego as a behavioral system.*—Allport is here concerned with behavior that is ego-involved. Concerning this we have already commented above. We may here add, however, that in a very genuine sense the ego, as we have developed the theory, is a behavioral system. For motives are incomplete behaviors. It is in the nature of *perpetuated* motives that they are never completed.

8. *Ego as the subjective organization of culture.*—It is intrinsic to the concept of perpetuated derived motives that these motives and the cognitions that are implicit in these motives refer to the environment as the individual finds it. How he finds it is, to a large extent, determined by the culture in which he resides. It is not true, however, as Allport states that "By stressing the cultural content of the ego, these authors in effect eradicate the artificial Freudian distinction between ego and superego." The distinction between ego and superego is not in the fact that one has cultural content and the other has not, but in the mode of derivation and of functioning of the motives involved and in the relations to the environment of the two systems.

Turning to Allport's four points concerning the nature of the ego: The ego *is* less embracing than personality, for the latter includes motives with respect to which the self is not a critical pole. As most psychologists use the word 'personality,' it also includes a good deal more. The ego *is* in proximate relation to the external world, for it is not merely a motivational structure, but, by that very fact, a cognitive structure as well. The subjective sense of self *does vary* from time to time, but in terms of specific content, not in terms of functional significance. Finally, the ego is customarily preoccupied with the future, because that is the nature of motives, in general, and of perpetuated motives, in particular which Allport cites point very strongly to the existence of *something* which may be called 'the ego.' These experiments, to a slight degree, and psychoanalytic and related clinical investigations, to a very large degree, have thrown a good deal of light on the workings of this something. Yet, *what* is this mysterious something which works in these diverse ways? Until this question is answered, all the rest seems vague and empty. In this extremity the theorist is called upon to answer the question, "Well, what *can* be there?" To this question, it is clear, the answer is not, 'the self.' For the self is a content of awareness; it has no reality apart from awareness and it does not correspond closely to the real *object* of awareness. Such a *content* cannot be selfish, or strive for dominance, or look to the future. If there is something which does these things, it must have reality apart from awareness. What we have done here, is to suggest *what* that something *can* be and, until someone suggests something else that it *can* be that fits the facts better, we must assume that our description of the ego is correct: the ego is a motivational-cognitive structure built up around the self.

21. Human Motives and the Concept of the Self

Ernest R. Hilgard

NO problems are more fascinating than those of human motivation, and none are more in need of wise solution. To understand the struggles which go on within economic enterprise, to interpret the quarrels of international diplomacy, or to deal with the tensions in the daily interplay between individuals, we must know what it is that people want, how these wants arise and change, and how people will act in the effort to satisfy them.

American psychologists typically believe that adult motivational patterns develop through the socialization of organic drives. Our preference for such an interpretation is undestandable because our science is rooted in biology. Man is assuredly a mammal as well as a member of society, and we begin to understand him by studying what he has in common with other

Abridged from *The American Psychologist*, 1949, 4, 374-382. Reprinted by permission of the author and the American Psychological Association, Inc.

animals. When we accept as the biological basis for motivation the drives present at birth or developing by maturation, it is natural to think of the learned social motives as grafted upon these or in some way derived from them. Despite the variations in the detailed lists of primary drives which different ones of us offer, and some alternative conceptions as to the ways in which socialization takes place, we find it easy to agree that adult motives are to be understood through an interaction between biology and culture.

Without reviewing any further the genetic development of motives, I wish to turn to some of the problems arising as we attempt to understand how these motives affect conduct. In our textbooks there is usually some important material left over after we have finished the chapters on physiological drives and social motives. I refer to the problems raised by the so-called defense mechanisms of adjustment.

THE MECHANISMS OF ADJUSTMENT IN MOTIVATIONAL THEORY

The mechanisms of adjustment were the features of Freudian theory that we earliest domesticated within American academic psychology. They now have a respectable place in our textbook writers.

The mechanisms did not burst all at once upon the psychological scene. Freud had begun to write about them in the '90's, and by the time of his *Interpretation of dreams* (1900) he had named repression, projection, displacement, identification, and condensation. In his *Three contributions to the theory of sex* (1905) he added fixation, regression, and reaction formation. It remained for Ernest Jones to give the name rationalization to that best-known of the mechanisms. He assigned this name in an article in the *Journal of Abnormal Psychology* in 1908. Among the books which brought the mechanisms together and called them to the attention of psychologists none was more popular than Bernard Hart's *Psychology of insanity,* which appeared in 1912 and went through several editions and many reprintings. Hart treated especially the manifestations of identification, projection and rationalization, and introduced that by now familiar friend, logic-tight compartments.

It remained for Gates to collect the mechanisms into a list in a textbook intended for the general student. The evolution of his chapter on mechanisms is itself instructive by showing how styles change in psychology. In his *Psychology for students of education* (1923), Gates called the chapter "The dynamic role of instincts in habit formation." In the first edition of his *Elementary psychology* (1925) he changed the title to "The dynamic role of the dominant human urges in habit formation." Then in the next edition (1928) he used the contemporary sounding title: "Motivation and adjustment." The content of the chapter underwent only minor revisions with these changes in title. These widely used books did much to place the mechanisms on the tips of the tongues of psychology students and professors twenty years ago, for by that time the mechanisms were already part of the general equipment of psychology, and not reserved for abnormal psychology or the clinic.

Some of the tendencies found in Gates' early treatment have persisted in more recent discussions of the mechanisms. For one thing, we took over the mechanisms when as a profession we were hostile to other aspects of psychoanalytic teaching. As a consequence, we often gave only halting recognition to their psychoanalytic origins. Nearly all the mechanisms do in fact derive from Freud, Jung, Adler, and their followers. Among the mechanisms in Gates' 1928 list, psychoanalytic writers originated introversion, identification, rationalization, projection, defence mechanisms, and compensation. Yet Gates' only mention of psychoanalysis was in some disparaging remarks about the "alleged adjustment by repression to the unconscious," an explanation of adjustment which he rejected as neither true nor useful.

In subsequent discussions of the mechanisms, textbook writers have seldom felt called upon to take responsibility for serious systematic treatment. In order to avoid a mere listing of mechanisms, many writers have attempted some sort of classificatory simplification, but there has been little agreement on which mechanisms belong together. Gates, for example, had included four mechanisms under rationalization: projection, sour grapes, sweet lemon, and logic-tight compartments. He gave defense and escape mechanisms separate places, although psychoanalytic practice has been to consider all the mechanisms as forms of defense. Shaffer separated adjustments by defense from adjustments by withdrawing, but he took back much of the distinction by treating withdrawing as a defense. In his recent books concerned with the mechanisms, Symonds provides a rich collection of descriptive material, frankly psychoanalytic in orientation, but he succeeds little better than those who preceded him in giving a unified treatment of the mechanisms in relation to motivation.

The lack of systematic treatment of the mechanisms has had consequences for their development as part of psychological science. When there is no effort to be systematic, problems are not sharply defined. When problems are not sharply defined, anecdotal evidence is used loosely, and sometimes irresponsibly. A consequence is that very little evidence of experimental sort is introduced into the chapters on the mechanisms. This does not mean that evidence does not exist. It means only that problems have to be more carefully formulated before the relevance of existing evidence is seen, and before gaps in knowledge are discovered which evidence can fill.

THE MECHANISMS AND THE SELF

It would take us too far afield to review the individual mechanisms at this time, and to consider evidence in relation to them. Instead, we may examine some of their most general characterization, as they relate to motivational theory. These characteristics lend support to a thesis which I propose to defend: the thesis that all the mechanisms imply a self-reference, and that the mechanisms are not understandable unless we adopt a concept of the self.

The thesis that the mechanisms imply a self-reference need come as no surprise. Psychoanalysts have thought of the mechanisms as protecting the ego. Anna Freud's book on the subject bears the title: *The ego and the mechanisms of defense*. Non-psychoanalysts have occasionally endorsed a similar thesis. In their recent text, for example, Guthrie and Edwards have given a very straightforward account of the defense mechanisms. Although their text remains within the broad framework of behaviorism, they do not hesitate to relate the mechanisms to the ego. In fact they define defense mechanisms as "the reaction patterns which reestablish the ego."

Let us examine two of the characteristics of the mechanisms to see how the thesis of self-reference is applied. We may choose to view the mechanisms as defenses against anxiety, or we may see them as self-deceptive.

1. *The mechanisms as defenses against anxiety.* The natural history of anxiety in relation to learning has been much illuminated by the series of experiments with animal subjects performed by Mowrer, Miller, and their collaborators.

A white rat is confined in a rectangular box of one or more compartments. The animal can escape electric shock either by some action within the shock compartments (such as depressing a lever to shut off the current), or by escaping from the dangerous place (as by leaping a barrier). Both Mowrer and Miller find that in situations like this a new drive is acquired, sometimes called anxiety, sometimes called fear. This new drive can motivate learning very much like any other drive. They accept the general position that drive-reduction is reinforcing. Anything which reduces the fear or anxiety will reinforce the behavior leading to this reduction. Thus any sort of activity or ritual which would reduce fear of anxiety might be strengthened. Such activities or rituals might have the characteristics of defense mechanisms.

The natural history of anxiety, according to this view, is somewhat as follows. First, the organism has experiences of pain and punishment—experiences to be avoided. These are followed in turn by *threats* of pain and punishment, which lead to *fear* of the situations in which such threats arise. Other situations are assimilated to these fear-provoking ones, so the added circumstances may lead to apprehension. Fears with these somewhat vaguer object-relations become known as anxiety states. Sometimes as the apprehensive state becomes more and more detached from particular frightening situations, clinicians refer to it as a state of free-floating anxiety. All of these acquired states of fear, apprehension or anxiety are tension-states. Any one of them may serve as an acquired drive and motivate learning.

Activities which lessen fear and anxiety are reinforced because tension is reduced. Thus behavior mechanisms become reinforced and learned as ways of reducing anxiety.

The Mowrer-Miller theory of the origin of fear, and of its role as an acquired drive, is acceptable as far as it goes. But it needs to be carried one step further if it is to deal with the kinds of anxiety which are found in the clinic. This step is needed because in man anxiety becomes intermingled with *guilt-feelings*. The Mowrer and Miller experiments with animals carry the natural history of anxiety through the stages of fear and apprehension, but not to the stage of guilt-feelings.

In many cases which come to the clinic, the apprehension includes the fear lest some past offense will be brought to light or lest some act will be committed which deserves pain and punishment. It is such apprehensions which go by the name of guilt-feelings, because they imply the responsibility of the individual for his past or future misbehavior. To feel guilty is to conceive of the self as an agent capable of good or bad choices. It thus appears that at the point that anxiety becomes infused with guilt-feelings self-reference enters. If we are to understand a person's defenses against guilt-feelings, we must know something about his image of himself. This is the kind of argument which supports the thesis that if we are to understand the mechanisms we shall have to come to grips with a concept of the self.

2.   *The mechanisms as self-deceptive.* Another way of looking at the mechanisms is to see them as bolstering self-esteem through self-deception. There is a deceptive element in each of the mechanisms. Rationalization is using false or distorted reasons to oneself as well as to the world outside; using reasons known to be false in order to deceive someone else is not rationalization but lying. It is entirely appropriate to consider self-deception as one of the defining characteristics of a mechanism. As another example of what I mean, let us consider when aggression should be thought of as a mechanism. Aggressive behavior which is a form of fighting directly for what you want or as a protest against injustice is not a mechanism at all, even if it is violent and destructive. It is then simply a direct attempt at problem-solving. But displaced aggression has the characteristics of a mechanism, because false accusations are made, and the object of aggression may be related only remotely to the source of the need to express aggression. Displaced aggression thus contains the elements of self-deception, and fits the pattern of the mechanisms.

There are two chief ways in which we deceive ourselves. One is by *denial* of impulses, or of traits, or of memories. The second is through *disguise,* whereby the impulses, traits, or memories are distorted, displaced, or converted, so that we do not recognize them for what they are. Let us see what evidence there is for denial and for disguise.

The clearest evidence for denial comes through amnesia, in which memories are temporarily lost. If such memories can later be recovered without relearning, support is given to an interpretation of forgetting as a consequence of repression. Often in amnesia the memories lost are the personal ones, while impersonal memories remain intact.

The man studied by Beck, for example, had no trouble in carrying on a conversation, in buying railroad tickets, or in many other ways conducting himself like a mature adult with the habits appropriate to one raised in our culture. It is a mistake to say that he lost his memory, for without memory he would have been unable to talk and make change and do the other things which are based upon past experience with arbitrary symbols and meanings. But he did lose *some* of his memories. He could not recall his name, and he could not recall the incidents of his personal biography. The highly selective nature of the memory loss is an important feature of many amnesias. Under treatment, the man referred to recovered most of his memories, except for one important gap. This gap was for a period in his career in which he conducted himself in a manner of which he was thoroughly ashamed.

Disguise, as the second form of self-deception, shows in many ways. The most pertinent evidence from the laboratory comes in the studies of projection defined as the attribution of traits. Undesirable traits of his own of which the person prefers to remain unaware are assigned in exaggerated measure to other people. In some cases, the deception goes so far as to become what Frenkel-Brunswik calls "conversion to the opposite." In one of her studies it was found that a person who said, "Above all else I am kind," was one likely to be rated unkind by his acquaintances. In the studies of anti-Semitism which she later carried on collaboratively with the California group she presents evidence that anti-Semitism is sometimes a disguise for deep-seated attitudes of hostility and insecurity having to do with home and childhood, and nothing to do directly with experience with Jews.

If self-deception either by denial or by disguise is accepted as characteristic of a mechanism, the problem still remains as to the source of or reasons for the self-deception. The obvious interpretation is that the need for self-deception arises because of a more fundamental need to maintain or to restore self-esteem. Anything belittling to the self is to be avoided. That is why the memories lost in amnesia are usually those with a self-reference, concealing episodes which are anxiety or guilt-producing. What is feared is loss of status, loss of security of the self. That is why aspects of the self which are disapproved are disguised.

In this discussion of the mechanisms I have tried to point out that they may be integrated with other aspects of motivation and learning provided their self-reference is accepted. Then it can be understood how they provide defenses against anxiety, and why they are self-deceptive through denial and disguise.

THE SELF PRESENT IN AWARENESS

The mechanisms are comprehensible only if we accept a conception of the self. This poses us the problem of the nature of the self-concept that we may find acceptable. Two main approaches lie before us. One approach is to look for the self in awareness, to see if we can find by direct observation the self that is anxious, that feels guilty, that tries various dodges in order to maintain self-respect. The second approach is to infer a self from the data open to an external observer, to construct a self which will give a coherent account of motivated behavior. Let us examine these two possibilities in turn.

We enter upon the task of discovering the self in awareness with the warnings from the past failures. Any naive person who started out to develop a psychology of the self would expect to find the task relatively easy because self-awareness seems to be commonplace. Everybody knows that people are proud or vain or bashful because they are self-conscious. But the psychologist knows that this self-evident character of self-awareness is in fact most illusive. You presently find yourself as between the two mirrors of a barbershop, with each image viewing each other one, so that as the self takes a look at itself taking a look at itself, it soon gets all confused as to the self that is doing the looking and the self which is being looked at. As we review the efforts of Miss Calkins and her students to demonstrate that there was a self discoverable in every act of introspection, and find how little convinced Titchener and his students were, we are well advised not to enter that quarrel with the same old weapons. Introspection was taken seriously in those days and psychologists worked hard at it. There is little likelihood that we can succeed where they failed.

Their difficulty was not due to the insistence upon trained observers. Self-observation of a much freer type by naive subjects is little more satisfactory. Horowitz' study of the localization of the self as reported by children was not very encouraging in this respect. Children located their selves in the head or the stomach or the lower jaw or elsewhere, each individual child being reasonably consistent, but the whole picture not being very persuasive as to the fruitfulness of an approach through naive self-observation.

But the reason for rejecting a purely introspective approach to the search for the self is not limited to the historical one that earlier attempts have proved fruitless. It is based also on the recognition that defense mechanisms and self-deception so contaminate self-observation that unaided introspection is bound to yield a distorted view of the self.

Having said all this by way of warning, we may still allow some place for self-awareness in arriving at our concept of the self. Two aspects of the self as seen by the experiencing person appear to be necessary features in understanding self-organization.

The first of these is the continuity of memories as binding the self, as maintaining self-identity. To the external observer, the continuity of the bodily organism is enough to maintain identity, but the person himself needs to have continuous memories, dated in his personal past, if he is to have a sense of personal identity. One of the most terrifying experiences in the clinical literature is the state known as depersonalization, in which experiences are no longer recognized as belonging to the self. Break the continuity of memories and we have dissociation, split personalities, fugue states, and other distortions of the self.

The second feature of self-awareness which cannot be ignored in forming our concept of the self is that of self-evaluation and self-criticism. I earlier pointed out that we need to understand the feelings of guilt which go beyond mere anxiety. Guilt-feelings imply that the self is an active agent, responsible for what it does, and therefore subject to self-reproof. The other side of self-evaluation is that the self must be supported and must be protected from criticism. One component of the self is provided by those vigilant attitudes which are assumed in order to reduce anxiety and guilt. It is this vigilant self-criticism in its harshest form which is implied in Freud's concept of the superego. Evaluative attitudes toward the self, including both positive and negative self-feelings, come prominently to the fore in the interviews recorded by Rogers and his students.

Another way of putting this is to state that the self of awareness is an object of value. McDougall referred to the sentiment of self-regard, as in some sense the master sentiment. Murphy, Murphy, and Newcomb put it tersely: "The self is something we like and from which we expect much." Perhaps I might amend the statement to read: "To some people the self is something they dislike and from which they expect little." In any case it is an object about which attitudes of appreciation and depreciation are organized. Snygg and Combs state as the basic human need the preservation and enhancement of the phenomenal self. It would be easy to multiply testimony that one of the fundamental characteristics of self-awareness is an evaluative or judging attitude toward the self, in which the self is regarded as an object of importance, and preferably of worth.

Despite the difficulties in introspective approaches to the self, we find that our self-concept needs to include some information based on private experience. The continuity of memories maintains personal identity, and the awareness of the self as an object of value organizes many of our attitudes.

More is needed, however, to enrich the concept of the self and to make it square with all that we know about human motivation.

THE INFERRED SELF

This points up the need for a more inclusive self-concept, one which will make use of all the data. Such a self-concept I shall call the inferred self. Like any other scientific construct, it will prove to be valid to the extent that it is systematically related to data, and it will be useful to the extent that it simplifies the understanding of events.

I wish to suggest three hypotheses needed in arriving at an inferred self. Each of these, although plausible, is not self-evident, and therefore requires demonstration. In order to be scientifically useful, it is important that the inferred self should go beyond the obvious. The inferred self will prove acceptable only if these hypotheses, or closely related ones are supported.

The first hypothesis is that of *the continuity of motivational patterns*. This means that the organization of motives and attitudes that are central to the self is one which persists and remains recognizable as the person grows older. Reactions to present situations will be coherent with reactions to past situations. For those who prefer the habit concept, the inferred self may be thought of as a pattern of persisting habits and attitudes. The organization or structure which is implied is a learned one, and like any habit structure it carries the marks of the past in the present. When new goals are substituted for old ones, there is continuity with the past in the ways in which the goals are selected and in the ways in which gratification is obtained. This is all plausible, but it is by no means self-evident, and it is greatly in need of empirical study. It is a matter for study and demonstration whether or not a continuity can be traced between nursing arrangements, thumb-sucking, nail-biting, cigarette-smoking, and overt sexual behavior. The first hypothesis implies that there is such a continuity, whatever motivational strands are being followed, so that one form of gratification shades imperceptibly into the next. If we but knew enough, we could trace the continuity throughout the life span. The second hypothesis supporting the inferred self is that of *the genotypical patterning of motives*. This hypothesis suggests that motives unlike in their overt or phenotypical expression may represent an underlying similarity. It will do no good to try to appraise personality by a study confined to its superficial expression. What we know about the mechanisms of denial and disguise tells us that the genotypical pattern will have to be inferred. Unless we move at the level of inference and interpretation, much behavior will be baffling or paradoxical.

The inferred self goes beyond the self of awareness by including for purposes of inference much that is excluded from self-awareness. Awareness includes the not-self as well as the self. In dreams and hallucinations we have products of the self, present in awareness, but products for which the self takes neither credit nor responsibility. It is hard to see the self as giving the stage-directions for the dream, or as selecting the epithets hurled by the hallucinated voices. Yet, in making a reconstruction of genotypical motives, these products of the self enter as evidence. Some items, then, remain in awareness, but are not part of self-awareness. Other items are excluded from awareness by inattention or amnesia. Facts such as these necessitate indirection in the inference to motivational organization. A description of overt conduct is not enough to permit an accurate appraisal of motivational patterning.

These assertions may be made with some confidence, but again confidence of assertion does not constitute proof. We need to show by rigorous proof that predictions based on the concept of genotypical patterning of motives will account for behavior either more economically or more accurately than predictions based on phenotypical manifestations of motivated action.

3.   The third hypothesis is that *the important human motives are inter-personal both in origin and in expression.* Despite the fertility of Freud's mind and the penetration of his observations, this is one hypothesis about the self which he never fully grasped. By good fortune he laid his emphasis upon the one organic need—sex—which is inevitably interpersonal in its fullest expression. Even so, he remained within the instinct tradition. Once we reject the self as the unfolding of an inevitable pattern, but see it instead as an individual acquisition, we are impressed by the part which other people play in the shaping of an individual self. Because the parents and others who transmit the culture are themselves a part of the culture, there are some uniformities in socialization, producing pressure in the direction of a modal personality. In addition, there are diverse roles which are ready-made for the individual, to which he conforms with greater or less success. There are the roles of man and of woman, of eldest and youngest child, of mother and father and in-law, of employer and employee, of craftsman and white-collar worker. Finally there are the individualizing influences of heredity, of birth accidents, of childhood experiences. There are many details to be filled in, but there is little doubt about the general course of socialization, leading in the end to internalizing much of the culture in the form of personal ideals and standards of conduct.

The self is thus a product of interpersonal influences, but the question remains whether the end-product is also interpersonal in its expression. Does the self have meaning only as it is reflected in behavior involving other people, either actually or symbolically? Is it true that you can describe a self only according to the ways in which other selves react to it? I am inclined to believe that the self, as a social product, has full meaning only when expressed in social interaction. But I do not believe that this is obvious, because I can conceive that it might not be true or might be true in a limited sense only.

These uncertainties about the truth of the hypothesis regarding the inferred self need not be regarded as signs of weakness in the concept. On the contrary, the concept has greater potential richness of meaning precisely because it goes beyond the self-evident and requires empirical study and justification. If it turns out that in some meaningful sense motivational patterns are continuous, that we can unravel their genotypical organization, and that we can know in what precise way they are interpersonal, then we will have a concept of an inferred self that will be genuinely useful.

What does the inferred self imply as to the unity of personality? It does not necessarily imply unity. Conflict as well as harmony may be perpetuated through genotypical organization. The healthy self, however, will achieve an integrative organization. Note that I say integrative and not integrated. It is the integrative personality which can handle the complexity of relationships with other persons in a culture like ours, a culture which makes plural demands. An integrated personality soon leads to its own isolation or destruction if it is not also integrative. Lest this seem to be an idle play on words, let me point out that the paranoid psychotic with highly systematized delusions is among the best integrated of personalities. He is integrated but not integrative. The genotypical patterns of motivation which comprise the inferred self may or may not be integrative.

A LABORATORY FOR THE STUDY OF PSYCHODYNAMICS

I have argued that we need a self-concept if we are to understand the richness of human motivation, and I have proposed that we adopt an inferred self as the unifying concept. Now what shall we do about it?

Perhaps this all sounds very much like clinical psychology, so that the answer might come: "Leave it to the clinicians." I believe this to be the wrong answer, not because I have any lack of confidence in clinicians, but because I believe it represents a faulty conception of the appropriate division of labor within psychology. The problems of human motivation and personality belongs to all psychologists. The problems of the self-concept are general problems of psychological science.

Instead of assigning these problems to any one group of psychologists, I propose that we proceed to establish laboratories for the study of psychodynamics fully commensurate with laboratories for the study of perception or learning or other problems of general psychology.

A laboratory for the study of psychodynamics differs from the clinic in its intent, though there will be overlap in staff, in procedures, and in problems. I am assuming that people are referred to a clinic or come there voluntarily in order to be helped with their personal problems. By contrast, subjects are invited to come to a laboratory because they fit into an experimental design. The laboratory permits delimitation of problems and control of variables in a manner usually less possible in a situation geared to service.

In order to make the picture of the psychodynamics laboratory concrete, we may sketch a few specimen problems likely to be worked upon. Many of these problems will have had their origin in clinical experience, and many fruitful hypotheses will have come from the clinic. But the task of achieving precision in the testing of scientific generalizations belongs to the laboratory.

Of first moment are the problems involved in the natural history of the self. This will mean concentrated study of young children, under arrangements which permit the testing of hypotheses. For many years we have given assent to the importance of language as an instrument of socialization, but we have a paucity of data. Piaget asked many of the right questions, but his conjectures have to be refined and put to the test in a manner more convincing to American psychologists. I should assign the study of the child's language as a task of high priority in the psychodynamics laboratory. This is but one aspect of discovering in what ways the self is a social product.

Other problems include the details of influence by important people in the child's environment. Some studies now under way at Stanford suggest that patterns of sibling rivalry among young children are often traceable to unresolved rivalries going back to the parents' childhoods. A parent may act as a director of the drama, assigning the roles to the children, and calling the turns on a new performance that largely reenacts one of a previous generation. While there is satisfactory evidence from case histories that this sort of parental influence goes on, just how it comes about, and just how the parent is protected from becoming aware of what is being done, need to be studied under laboratory-type controls.

Another developmental problem worthy of careful exploration has to do with the magical ideas of childhood, sometimes referred to as the feeling of omnipotence. While the stubborn realities of the environment soon trim down the sense of power to more finite proportions, magical conceptions continue even into adult life, influencing the interpretations of causal sequences. I do not refer simply to superficial manifestations, as in the prevalence of superstition. When the investigator begins to look, he finds that there are many ways in which individuals believe themselves to have magical powers, to be among the specially gifted, to be so precious as to be specially vulnerable, to be able to shape events through willing them to be. In a scientific age like ours, these magical ideas are taboo, and consequently may influence behavior while being largely out of awareness. If we understand this desire to gain satisfaction through the expression of magical power, we would better understand some of the most puzzling aspects not only of an individual's behavior, but of the dynamics of economic and political life.

I have chosen these few illustrations (language, sibling rivalry, and the magic of power) to illustrate the sorts of problems which can be studied in arriving at a natural history of the self.

Let me turn now to a set of problems in the answer to which experiments with animal subjects are particularly promising. These are defining experiments on the concepts of anxiety, shame, and guilt. I have already referred to the excellent start made by experiments on fear and anxiety in rats. It may take a more sociable animal, such as the dog, to exhibit the behavior we call shame. There is no doubt that the dog can act as if ashamed. I do not know whether or not a dog can act as if guilty. Shame may be thought of as a response to being caught by someone else in socially disapproved behavior; guilt may be thought of as a response to catching yourself in behavior discordant with your own conscience. Can both shame and guilt go on outside of awareness, or is guilt alone subject to unconscious expression? Is the concept of guilt applicable only to man? We need better definitions, but we also need to know what is the case. I should like to see the psychodynamics laboratory work on the problem of clarifying what is meant by anxiety, shame, and guilt, and instructing us about the principles according to which these processes occur.

The psychodynamics laboratory is the place in which to make a direct study of the self-organization which permits conflicts within the self as dramatized in the Freudian notions of id, ego, and superego. This particular partitioning of the self is probably too rigid to be acceptable, but they are genuine problems which the partitioning is designed to explain, and these problems are still in need of explanation. Anna Freud suggests that under hypnosis the hypnotist sets aside the subject's ego. Others have suggested that the superego is soluble in alcohol. If appropriate hypotheses are clearly stated, it ought to be possible to design experiments to test them by biasing the outcome of the wars within the self. That is, through appropriate techniques, perhaps using hypnosis or alcohol, one or the other of the fighters in the battle could be strengthened or weakened. Thus it should be possible to determine with greater precision the nature of the participants in self-conflict.

Another problem is that of rapport which arises because we need to know the circumstances under which a person can freely report private experience with a minimum of distortion. Consider the following three situations. First is the administration of projective tests, say the Rorschach or the TAT. It is assumed, rightly or wrongly, that rapport with the test-administrator can be established fairly promptly. It is also assumed, rightly or wrongly, that once rapport is established, responses are primarily to the stimulus cards rather than to the test administrator. All this needs study, but we may accept this situation as involving a relatively low order of rapport. Next in our scale is the ordinary interviewing situation, in which the subject, alone with the psychologist, reports private experiences. Here it is plausible to assume that rapport is more important than in the test situation, so that what the person reveals becomes more closely related to the inter-personal situation the interviewer is able to create. The third situation, with rapport at a maximum, is that of hypnosis, in which rapport is exaggerated beyond that ordinarily found in the interviewing situation. These graded situations provide an excellent series in which to study what rapport does to the possibility of reporting personal experiences with varying degrees of distortion.

Another problem is that of insight as a factor in personality reorganization. Here we have a problem directly pertinent to clinical practices, and to psychotherapy, but there is pertinence to general psychology also. How is the insight of which the psychotherapist speaks related to that of which the animal psychologist speaks? There is a similarity in that both have to do with sensible problem-solving, based on the ways in which situations are perceived.

In studying the achievement of insight we have an opportunity to compare the self present in awareness with the inferred self. What we mean by insight in this context is essentially that the self of which the person is aware comes to correspond to the inferred self,—in other words, that the person comes to see himself as an informed other person sees him. This is what is meant by an objective attitude toward the self. The self may be granted the privilege of privacy, but even the view of the self held in private is such as could be communicated to a trusted outsider. This explains the enigmatic statement of the late Harry Stack Sullivan that one achieves mental health to the extent that one becomes aware of one's inter-personal relations. When the relations to other people become communicable to oneself and potentially to another, then these relations are no longer confused by the distortions of neurotic mechanisms.

It is sometimes said that the mechanisms are blind and inflexible, little subject to the ordinary principles of learning. But they can be unlearned; this is, in fact, one of the chief tasks of psychotherapy. There are perhaps two main ways in which, through insight, the mechanisms can be defeated.

The first of these methods is to become aware of the mechanisms, so that the person can catch himself using them. He may learn to interpret his own headaches and his own outbursts of temper. Because he knows what he is doing, he is able to control his conduct. Insight here is into symptoms and the chain of events of which these symptoms are a part. Following insight the chain of events may be broken, so that the sequences do not flow to their usual conclusions. Guthrie has made use of a notion very like this (despite his discomfort with insight as a concept) in urging that the way to gain control over a habit sequence is to identify the cues. By alienating these cues, the objectional habit sequence is interrupted.

The second method overlooks the detailed action of the mechanisms entirely, while seeking insight into whatever has made the mechanisms necessary. There is a reevaluation of the self and its motives, a willingness to accept features of the self which were previously unacceptable. If more security can be achieved by abandoning the mechanisms than was achieved by them, they do not have to be fought. The mechanisms simply dissolve because they are no longer needed.

It is important to know whether or not this is a two-stage process, or an interaction between two methods of solving the same problem. This is not something to be debated, but something to be studied and understood.

We are ready today, as we might not have been a few years ago, to establish psychodynamic laboratories to attack and answer many of the questions which I have raised. Such laboratories will provide opportunities for cooperation between experimental and clinical psychologists on problems of mutual concern. The staff to be invited to work in these laboratories will include psychologists with a variety of backgrounds, united in their acknowledgment that the search for the self is a significant scientific endeavor.

PROBLEM

22. The Influence of Ego-Involvement on Confidence

George S. Klein and Nathan Schoenfeld

OUR experiment relates to the range of validity of the finding that there is a general factor of confidence underlying the degree of confidence shown in individual judgments.

One of the bases upon which the claim of generality rests is the discovery that the confidence of an individual is relatively unvarying for a variety of tasks. Our hypothesis proposes that while an unvarying general level of confidence may be maintained by a subject over a series of different tasks, it is the experimental context in which the tests are applied that contributes both to the level of confidence and to the degree of its generality. It is possible that the confidence level might persist through a group of unlike tasks in a neutral or objective situation, yet might undergo some change under a different experimental atmosphere in which the subject's drives, preferences, and goals—i.e., his "Ego"—are bound up in the tasks. Moreover, even if such uniformity of confidence were found in the latter situation, it might well be on a distinctly different level from that in the neutral situation. The variable of situation-set would in either instance be thereby shown to be important.

The problem we set for ourselves, then, is: Would the confidence ratings of a group of subjects in a variety of tasks change significantly in another situation where important Ego factors, e.g. social prestige, self-esteem, fear of academic standing, are closely bound up in the tasks, and where, because of this, performance is of more vital consequence to the subjects?

Abridged from *The Journal of Abnormal and Social Psychology*, 1941, 36, 249-258. Reprinted by permission of the authors and the American Psychological Association, Inc.

HISTORICAL BACKGROUND

The generality of the confidence in judgments which an individual reports has not been given much study. Trow raised the question whether there is enough consistency in the reports of any individual to warrant the conclusion that confidence might be considered as a personality trait. A rank-order comparison of the confidences of a group of subjects on several tests led him to believe that confidence was not a character trait. He did not compute inter-correlations of the rank orders on the tests. His findings were rendered more ambiguous by the fact that he did obtain some degree of generality between the confidence on subjective-judgment tests and the confidence on objective-judgment tests.

Jersild has done some work using true-false tests on reading assignments and lectures. He has found that the mean confidences of the subjects on the two tests are nicely correlated. The material on the two tests, however, was practically the same; hence the conclusion as to generality is dubious.

It is from Johnson's study that the present paper takes off. Johnson, recognizing the shortcomings of the previous work, attacked the problems anew. He devised tests which were dissimilar in content, in an effort to avoid the complication of generality of confidence by generality of ability, as had occurred in Jersild's experiment. They were constructed, furthermore, so that a reliable measure of mean confidence could be obtained. In that way the extent of generality of confidence could be interpreted through the size of the intercorrelations of the separate tests, a step which Trow had not taken.

Johnson finally selected four tests permitting of two-category judgments: (a) judgments of the comparative lengths of lines; (b) judgments of the truth or falsity of statements involving the meanings of words; (c) judgments as to hand position; (d) judgments of recognition of figures. These tests he found could be standardized over a wide range of difficulty; they could be objectively scored for correctness; they were independent; *i.e.,* they varied in content.

From his results, Johnson concluded that there existed in his subjects a rather high degree of generality of confidence for all the four tests. He found, furthermore, that generality did not depend on generality of ability in those tests, since the sizeable intercorrelations of confidence scores were accompanied by low intercorrelations of error scores on the four tests. He held, therefore, that the "confidence an individual expresses in his judgments depends, not only upon the stimulus material, but also, to a considerable and measurable degree, upon the individual's characteristic level of confidence." He drew the implication: "The results at hand support the conclusion that, for the limited area sampled by the tests of the present study, confidence in a judgment is a personality trait, conforming to any reasonable definition of the term."

In a second experiment, Johnson attempted to change his subjects' attitudes toward the tasks by instructions emphasizing speed at one time and accuracy at the next. Such variations in "attitude" he found led to large variations in speed of judgment but had no significant effect on confidence.

Our own study seeks to extend this work beyond the "limited area sampled" by Johnson's investigation. It should be noted that although Johnson obtained indices of confidence under two instructional situations, these involved little, if any, change in the subject's personal rapport with the tasks. Johnson recognized himself that his tasks "involved impersonal, or intellectual, judgments. It may be that in judgments of more vital consequence, or judgments made under emotional stress, less generality, or more, would be found." He thought to take account of this possibility by working his subjects under different instructions, apparently in the belief that he was thereby changing the degree of emotional stress. He found this change had no significant effect on the confidence reports.

It is our opinion that Johnson's change of instruction did not introduce a situation of "more vital consequence" or of more "emotional stress." Our experiment was set up to test the generality of confidence under a situation of actual Ego-involvement. If such generality does exist as a personality trait, it should show up even more clearly under these changes in the situation-set, namely changes introducing Ego factors.

METHOD

1. *Subjects.* The preliminary subjects were 14 male undergraduates of a class in elementary psychology at the College of the City of New York. They served to help select and perfect the tests and the mechanics of the actual experiment, and their data are not included in this report. A second group of 36 subjects, similarly chosen, provided the experimental data. Of this second group, 5 were female. All 50 subjects were relatively homogeneous with regard to age, intelligence, and educational background.

2. *The tests.* We used four crucial tests: (a) Opposites; (b) Mental Additions; (c) Definitions; (d) Dot Apprehension. Since our experiment was divided into two sessions, and the experimental variable was situation-set rather than test content or difficulty, we devised two comparable forms of each of the tests.

The Opposites Tests were constructed with words taken from the material which Gould used in her study. She had prepared a list of words and had had a large number of subjects give opposites, being able in this way to determine the difficulty value of each word in terms of the percentage of correct responses. In arranging our own two lists of words, we paired words of equal difficulty. Each list contained 10 words chosen to give a wide range of difficulty.

The Mental Additions Test we constructed ourselves. Each addition involved two numbers of equal length, but the number of digits varied from one problem to the next. Each test contained 10 problems: two 2-place, two 3-place, two 4-place, two 5-place, and two 6-place additions, thus assuming a wide range of difficulty. Two criteria of construction were followed in order to have approximately equated additions on the two lists; (a) there was no "carrying" involved in the summation of any problem; (b) no digit appeared more than twice in a given problem.

The Definitions Tests also consisted of 10 words each. The words on each list were matched for difficulty on the basis of the frequency reported in Thorndike's *Word book,* and were chosen to give a wide range of difficulty.

The Dot Apprehension Test consisted of seven groups of dots numbering from 8-14. The dot groups were thrown as dots of light upon a dark screen by a slide projector. Timed exposures were obtained by means of a rotation disk adapted to slow speeds. The same stimuli were used in both experimental sessions.

In addition to the fact that each test supplied a wide range of difficulty, it is clear that these tests varied in content. Generality of confidence was thus to be tested over a number of different tasks without necessary complication by generality of ability. Our tests also had the merit of being more or less easily scored for correctness.

On the second experimental session, two dummy tests were included to further the subjects' belief than an intelligence-test battery was being administered. They were (a) Figure Reproduction Test, and (b) Syllogisms Test. Naturally, the results on these were disregarded in the treatment of our data.

3. *Procedure.* The experiment was broken up into two sessions.

a. The purpose of the first session was to have the subjects perform, in succession, four tests without introducing any undue emotional strain. They were informed in an easy manner that they were to participate, for the space of half an hour, as observers in an experiment. Each was given an answer sheet on which to record responses. These sheets contained instructions as to procedures and the use of the confidence scale. When the class had finished reading, these instructions were amplified by an experimenter.

We adopted the use of the 7-category confidence scale for the experiment, with 1 representing extreme uncertainty and 7 extreme certainty. The subjects were given practice in the experimental mechanics and the use of the scale by means of a sample test of 5 words for which they were to give synonyms. A general instruction was given to the effect that they were not to omit an answer to any item of the tests.

Since the same time relations between the items of each test, as well as the same sequence of the item-pairs within each test, were followed during the two sessions, we shall not detail these minutiae of procedure. It will suffice to mention that the subject always had to record an answer to an item before indicating his confidence in that answer; and that the seven dot-groups of the Dot Apprehension Test were arranged in random order and the series was gone through three times, making 21 presentations in all. The four tests were given in the following order: Opposites, Mental Additions, Definitions, Dot Apprehension.

b. The second session of the experiment came eleven days later without the subjects having been informed on the first occasion that there was to be a second. This time they were told that the tests they were taking comprised an intelligence test, the results of which were to be recorded for them in the Personnel Bureau of the college. They were informed that both sessions were an attempt, under different motivation conditions, to standardize some of the tests of a battery. This time they were to try hard to do their very best, since these results were to be recorded for them on their college records. In the discussion which followed the second session, it was apparent that this rationalization had deceived the great majority of the group. Everyone, not excepting the few who had doubted the genuineness of the situation, reported greater strain and effort on the second occasion than on the first, a statement which accorded well with the observations made by the experimenters during the period. In reality, of course, these tests were the alternate forms of those employed in the first session, together with the dummy Figure Reproductions and Syllogisms Tests previously mentioned.

The order in which the tests were given was: Opposites, Mental Additions, Figure Reproductions, Definitions, Dot Apprehension, Syllogisms.

Each subject occupied the same seat for both experimental sessions.

RESULTS AND DISCUSSION

Before presenting our findings it is necessary to point out how we treated our data. The "score" of a subject on any test was the number of items he got right. Thus, on the Opposites, Mental Additions, and Definitions Tests the maximum score was 10; while on the Dot Apprehension Test the maximum was 21. The "confidence" of a subject on any test was the mean of the separate item-confidences. All omissions of response were given a confidence of 1 automatically. The validity of averaging confidence ratings in this way is in the opinion of the writers a very questionable practice. In view of the fact that the widths of the categories of any confidence scale

such as ours are unknown, some degree of error is certainly introduced
when the categories are treated arithmetically. This procedure was followed
in the present study, however, because it seems to be generally accepted
by workers in the field, and the present writers could not concern themselves with the special problem of scaling.

The Opposites Tests were scored generously. An answer was taken as
correct if it obtained the agreement of the experimenters, and if it could
be found in *Allan's synonyms and antonyms.* The Definitions Tests were
also scored generously. Here, the agreement of the experimenters was a
requisite; and adequate synonyms were acceptable in lieu of a formal definition. Responses to items of the Mental Additions and Dot Apprehension
Tests had to be absolutely correct to be accepted.

In the computations of the *r*'s and their PE's, we followed Garrett (*Statistics in psychology and education,* 1937, formulae 52 and 57). Skewness
and the significance of skewness were also computed according to Garrett.
Inasmuch as it was found that no score or confidence distributions was significantly skewed, it was assumed, therefore, that the product-moment coefficient of correlation could be used, and the following considerations are
based on that assumption.

Table I gives the intercorrelations of the scores and of the confidences on
each test with every other test, for the two sessions. Let us first examine

TABLE I

Intercorrelations of the Scores and Confidences on Each Test with Every
Other Test, for the Two Experimental Sessions Separately

	Opposites-Additions	Opposites-Definitions	Opposites-Dot Appr.	Additions-Definitions	Additions-Dot Appr.	Definitions-Dot Appr.
Session I:						
Score	$-.27\pm.10$	$.24\pm.11$	$-.41\pm.09$	$.09\pm.11$	$.22\pm.11$	$.18\pm.11$
Confidence	$.16\pm.10$	$.58\pm.07$	$.38\pm.09$	$-.05\pm.10$	$.28\pm.10$	$-.03\pm.11$
Session II:						
Score	$-.06\pm.11$	$.27\pm.10$	$.38\pm.10$	$.15\pm.11$	$.23\pm.11$	$-.11\pm.11$
Confidence	$.23\pm.11$	$.69\pm.06$	$.48\pm.09$	$.20\pm.11$	$.66\pm.06$	$.43\pm.09$

the results for the first session. It is clear that the score intercorrelations
are low, showing that no generality of ability operated in the tests. Only
one of the six score intercorrelations is reliable, namely the Opposites-Dot
Apprehension correlation of $-.41\pm.09$, since the coefficient is more than
four times its PE. The intercorrelations of confidence are all low also; and
only two of the coefficients are reliable. Underlying the separate judgments

there was apparently little, if any, generality of confidence such as Johnson had found.

Turning to the results for the second session, we see that the score intercorrelations are again low enough to warrant the conclusion that generality of ability did not operate. Only one coefficient approaches significance. The confidence intercorrelations are this time higher than for the first session. All are positive, and now four coefficients are reliable. These results would seem to indicate that our second experimental condition induced a notably higher degree of generality.

It will be recalled that in our statement of the problem, we assumed Johnson's finding as to the generality of confidence to be correct for the tests he used; and we set out to see whether this generality breaks down with other tests and under experimental conditions of greater Ego-involvement. We felt that even if generality persists during such changed experimental conditions, at least the confidence distribution of a group of subjects would be on a different *level*, although the individuals in the group might still retain their relative positions. While we obtained little evidence for generality under our first experimental condition, we seem to have obtained a measure of generality of confidence in our second experimental situation.

Our data, moreover, provided an opportunity to consider a related prob-

TABLE II

Correlations of the Scores and Confidences on Each Test Obtained in the First Session with the Scores and Confidences Obtained on the Comparable Form of the Same Test in the Second Session

	OPPOSITES	ADDITIONS	DEFINITIONS	DOT APPREHENSION
Scores	$.60 \pm .07$	$.68 \pm .06$	$.78 \pm .04$	$.47 \pm .09$
Confidence	$.83 \pm .03$	$.75 \pm .05$	$.80 \pm .07$	$.76 \pm .05$

lem, namely, the relation of confidence to the nature of the task. Table II gives the intercorrelations of the scores and the confidences on the comparable forms of each test as these forms were employed in the two sessions. The score intercorrelations are rather high, as would be expected since the two forms of each test were of the same nature and of approximately equal difficulty. The correlation of the scores on the two forms of the Dot Apprehension is rather low, probably because of the difficulty of presentation in the classroom; the subjects were somewhat inconvenienced in taking the test in a darkened room, and therefore the reliability of performance was not high.

Interestingly enough, however, the correlations of the confidences on the two forms of each test are higher than those of the scores. Thus the confidence reliability of two comparable forms of the same test is greater than the performance reliability. Subjects tend to approach similar tasks with similar degrees of confidence; or at least the relative confidence positions of the subjects in the group tended to remain constant for similar tasks. We may conclude, therefore, that confidence is definitely related to the nature of the task, since it remains relatively the same for the *same* tasks even though the actual performance may vary on those same tasks.

It may be possible to tie up our findings with those of Johnson by means of an interesting speculation. It will be remembered that we found a measure of generality of confidence in the second session. This was less, however, than the degree of generality Johnson reported, and we were cautious in the handling of our finding. Perhaps the increase in generality of confidence in the second session over that found in the first was due to the operation of the increased tension of the second occasion. It is possible that generality does not exist in considerable degree, but that it is evoked only under special conditions. It should not be forgotten that we worked with grouped subjects, whereas Johnson used his subjects singly. In our first period, the atmosphere was "neutral," that is, the subjects worked without strain, and with very little competitive spirit. Probably they relied much more upon their actual ability for their feelings of confidence, and less upon what they would have liked, or wished, to achieve. When on the second occasion the Ego-involvement created an active desire to do well on the tests, their confidence ratings may have reflected this desire as well as, or in addition to, the objective ability to perform. There was no doubt from the reports of the subjects that there was much greater effort expended, and anxiety experienced, during the second session. *This fact would mean that "confidence" would appear as a personality trait when the Ego is involved, but that it would be a function of the nature and difficulty of the tasks when the situation is "neutral."* We are inclined to believe that the investigation of the generality of any personality trait may be expected to yield dubious results unless the experimental situation is so constructed as to introduce Ego-feelings as factors. Johnson worked his subjects individually, and there can be little doubt that being under the personal surveillance of the experimenter contributes, by and large, to a subject's tension and desire to do well. Johnson himself did not think of this circumstance as an important factor in his experimental situation, for he spoke of the desirability of testing his finding under conditions of "more emotional stress." Yet it is possible that it was the very stress inherent in his individualized experimentation which gave him the degree of generality he reported.

This line of reasoning would lead to the conclusion that "confidence" ratings may at one time be really ratings of accuracy or ability, and thus related to the nature of the task, and at another time a measure of aspiration and thus related to the personality of the subject. There is no inconsistency in this view, and it would be of great interest to check upon it.

CONCLUSIONS

1. Under the "neutral" experimental situation-set of the first session, both score intercorrelations and confidence intercorrelations were low. Thus neither generality of ability nor generality of confidence was found.

2. Under the "stress" or "Ego-involvement" situation-set of the second session, score intercorrelations were low; but confidence intercorrelations were all positive and four were significant. Thus some degree of generality was found under these changed experimental conditions.

3. It is possible to conclude from our own and Johnson's experiments that generality of confidence may be evoked under certain conditions of situation-set, especially those which bring into play Ego or personality factors like the "level of aspiration."

4. Testing the inter-session correlations for the scores on each test's comparable forms, we found that the coefficients were fairly high. Their size may have been kept down by the increased tension of the second session and consequent disturbances in performance.

5. Testing the inter-session correlations for the confidences on each test's comparable forms, we found that the coefficients were higher than for the scores. Such a finding was taken to mean that subjects tend to approach similar tasks with similar degrees of confidence, hence that confidence is related to the nature of the task as well as to the personalities of the subjects.

REFERENCES—SECTION THREE

Allport, G. W. Geneticism *versus* ego-structure in theories of personality. *Brit. J. educ. Psychol.*, 1946, *16*, 57-68.

Alper, T. G. Predicting the direction of selective recall: Its relation to ego strength and n-achievement. *J. abnorm. soc. Psychol.*, 1957, *55*, 149-165.

Amen, E. W. Experimental study of the self in psychology. *Psychol. Monogr.*, 1926, *35*, No. 165.

Ausubel, D. P. Ego development among segregated Negro children. *Ment. Hyg.*, 1958, *42*, 362-369.

Beck, S. J. Implications for ego in Tillich's ontology of anxiety. *Phil. phenomenol. Res.*, 1958, *18*, 451-470.

Berkowitz, L., and Levy, B. I. Pride in group performance and group-task motivation. *J. abnorm. soc. Psychol.*, 1956, *53*, 300-306.

Brownfain, J. J. Stability of the self-concept as a dimension of personality. *J. abnorm. soc. Psychol.*, 1952, *47*, 597-606.

Calkins, M. W. The self in scientific psychology. *Amer. J. Psychol.*, 1915, *26*, 495-524.

Combs, A. W., and Soper, D. W. The self, its derivative terms, and research. *J. indiv. Psychol.*, 1957, *13*, 134-145.

———, and Snygg, D. *Individual Behavior.* Rev. ed. New York: Harper, 1959.

Cowen, E. L. The "negative self concept" as a personality measure. *J. consult. Psychol.*, 1954, *18*, 138-142.

Diller, L. Conscious and unconscious self-attitudes after success and failure. *J. Pers.,* 1954, *23,* 1-12.

Elkin, H. On the origin of self. *Psychoanal. Rev.,* 1958-1959, *45,* 57-76.

Engel, M. The stability of the self-concept in adolescence. *J. abnorm. soc. Psychol.,* 1959, *58,* 211-215.

Frenkel-Brunswik, E. Mechanisms of self-deception. *J. soc. Psychol.,* 1939, *10,* 409-420.

Freud, A. *The Ego and the Mechanisms of Defense.* New York: International Universities Press, 1946.

Grauer, D. How autonomous is the ego? *J. Amer. Psychoanal. Assn.,* 1958, *6,* 502-518.

Gutheil, E. A. Dreams as an aid in evaluating ego strength. *Amer. J. Psychother.,* 1958, *12,* 338-357.

Hartmann, H. Technical implications of ego psychology. *Psychoanal. Quart.,* 1951, *20,* 31-43.

———. *Ego Psychology and the Problem of Adaptation,* New York: International Universities Press, 1958.

Harvey, O. J., Kelley, H. H., and Shapiro, M. M. Reactions to unfavorable evaluations of the self made by other persons. *J. Pers.,* 1957, *25,* 393-411.

Helper, M. M. Parental evaluations of children and children's self-evaluations. *J. abnorm. soc. Psychol.,* 1958, *56,* 190-193.

Hendrick, I. Instinct and the ego during infancy. *Psychoanal. Quart.,* 1942, *11,* 33-58.

Hill, T. J. Attitudes toward self: an experimental study. *J. educ. Sociol.,* 1957, *30,* 395-397.

Horowitz, E. L. Spatial localization of the self. *J. soc. Psychol.,* 1935, *6,* 379-387.

Huntley, C. W. Judgements of self based upon records of expressive behavior. *J. abnorm. soc. Psychol.,* 1940, *35,* 398-427.

Iverson, M. A., and Reuder, M. E. Ego involvement an experimental variable. *Psychol. Repts.,* 1956, *2,* 147-181.

Jung, C. G. *The Undiscovered Self.* New York: New American Library of World Literature, 1959.

———. *Researches Into The Phenomenology of the Self.* New York: Pantheon Books, 1959.

Katz, D., McClintock, C., and Sarnoff, I. The measurement of ego defense as related to attitude change. *J. Pers.,* 1957, *25,* 465-474.

Kuenzli, A. E., (Ed.). *The Phenomenological Problem.* New York: Harper and Bros., 1959.

Livson, N., and Mussen, P. H. The relation of ego control to overt aggression and dependency. *J. abnorm. soc. Psychol.,* 1957, *55,* 66-71.

Lunholm, H. Reflections upon the nature of the psychological self. *Psychol. Rev.,* 1940, *47,* 110-126.

Marmor, J. Some comments on ego psychology. *J. Hillside Hosp.,* 1958, *7,* 26-31.

Martin, J. G. Relationships between the self concept and differences in the strength and generality of achievement motivation. *J. Pers.,* 1956, *24,* 364-375.

Milton, T. Authoritarianism, intolerance of ambiguity, and rigidity under ego- and task-involved conditions. *J. abnorm. soc. Psychol.,* 1957, *55,* 29-33.

Moore, J. S. The problem of the self. *Phil. Rev.,* 1933, *42,* 487-499.

Moustakos, C. E., (Ed.). *The Self: Explorations in Personal Growth.* New York: Harper, 1956.

———. The sense of self. *J. Humanistic Psychol.,* 1961, *1,* 20-34.

Mowrer, O. H. The law of effect and ego psychology. *Psychol. Rev.,* 1946, *53,* 321-334.

Murphy, G. Self-realization and mental health. *Bull. Menninger Clin.,* 1959, *23,* 81-84.

Mussen, P. H., and Jones, M. C. Self-conceptions, motivations, and interpersonal attitudes of late- and early-maturing boys. *Child Develpm.,* 1957, *28,* 243-256.

———, and Porter, L. W. Personal motivations and self-conceptions associated with effectiveness and ineffectiveness in emergent groups. *J. abnorm. soc. Psychol.,* 1959, *59,* 23-37.

Nagelberg, L., and Spotnitz, H. Strengthening the ego through the release of frustration-aggression. *Amer. J. Orthopsychiat.,* 1958, *28,* 794-801.

Nahinsky, I. D. The relationships between the self-concept and the ideal-self concept as a measure of adjustment. *J. Clin. Psychol.*, 1958, *14*, 360-364.

Novey, S. A re-evaluation of certain aspects of the theory of instinctual drives in the light of modern ego psychology. *Int. J. Psycho-anal.*, 1957, *58*, 137-145.

Phillips, E. L. Attitudes toward self and others: A brief questionnaire report. *J. consult. Psychol.*, 1951, *15*, 79-81.

Rapaport, D. The autonomy of the ego. *Bull. Menninger Clin.*, 1951, *15*, 113-123.

———. The theory of ego autonomy: A generalization. *Bull. Menninger Clin.*, 1958, *22*, 13-35.

Romanow, C. V. Anxiety level and ego involvement as factors in concept formation. *J. exp. Psychol.*, 1958, *56*, 166-173.

Rosenzweig, S. Preferences in the repetition of successful and unsuccessful activities as a function of age and personality. *J. genet. Psychol.*, 1933, *42*, 423-441.

Rubin, S. A study of the daydream illustrating some aspects of ego functioning. *J. Hillside Hosp.* 1959, *8*, 115-130.

Sarbin, T. R. A preface to a psychological analysis of the self. *Psychol. Rev.*, 1952, *59*, 11-22.

Sherif, M. and Cantril, H. *The Psychology of Ego-Involvements*, New York: Wiley, 1947.

Shippee-Blum, E. M. The young rebel: Self-regard and ego-ideal. *J. consult Psychol.*, 1959, *23*, 44-50.

Smith, G. M. Six measures of self-concept discrepancy and instability: their interrelations, reliability, and relations to other personality measures. *J. consult. Psychol.*, 1958, *22*, 101-112.

Strong, D. J., and Feder, D. D. Measurement of the self-concept: A critique of the literature. *J. counsel. Psychol.*, 1961, *8*, 170-178.

Symonds, P. M. *The Ego and the Self.* New York: Appleton-Century-Crofts, 1951.

Trehub, A. Ego disjunction and psychopathology, *J. Abnorm. soc. Psychol.*, 1959, *58*, 191-194.

Van Krevelen, A. Judgements of personality traits in the self and others. *J. Clin. Psychol.*, 1958, *14*, 178-179.

Vroom, V. H. Projection, negation, and self-concept. *Human Relations*, 1959, *12*, 335-344.

Wallen, R. Ego-involvement as a determinant of selective forgetting. *J. abnorm. soc. Psychol.*, 1942, *37*, 20-39.

Weiss, E. A comparative study of psycho-analytical ego concepts. *Int. J. Psycho-anal.*, 1957, *38*, 209-222.

White, R. W. Adler and the future of ego psychology. *J. indiv. Psychol.*, 1957, *13*, 112-124.

Wyatt, F. Some remarks on the place of cognition in ego psychology. *J. Projective Techniques*, 1953, *17*, 144-151.

Wylie, R. C. Some relationships between defensiveness and self-concept discrepancies. *J. Pers.*, 1957, *25*, 600-616.

———. *The Self Concept.* Lincoln: Univ. of Nebraska Press, 1961.

Zuckerman, M. and Monashkin, I. Self-acceptance and psychopathology. *J. consult. Psychol.*, 1957, *21*, 145-148.

LEVEL OF ASPIRATION

In general terms, the phrase *level of aspiration* refers to the goals which the individual sets for himself and attempts to achieve. In an experimental setting, level of aspiration is defined as the level of future attainment in some specific task which the individual sets for himself. Gardner (Paper No. 24) discusses the history and development of the term from the time that it was first formulated by Dembo and introduced in America by Lewin.

The factors which determine one's level of aspiration are varied —past achievements, interests, abilities, personal needs and group standards, for instance. Consequently, from a psychological viewpoint success and failure are not such simple concepts as is sometimes thought; subjectively they are relative to the individual's level of aspiration. More specifically, success is interpreted by an individual as that level of achievement which is equal to or greater than the goal which he sets up. Likewise, failure is interpreted as that level of achievement which is less than the goal originally aspired to. In short, feelings of success and failure are personal evaluations dependent upon the attainment or the non-attainment of one's level of aspiration rather than on one's objective or actual achievement. For example, a person with a high degree of ability and a relatively low level of aspiration will experience a feeling of success even though his actual achievement may be quite minimal. On the other hand, another person with equally high ability but with an extremely high level of aspiration may experience a sense of failure when his performance doesn't measure up to his aspirations, even though his actual performance is quite good. Another basic point in regard to an understanding of success and failure is one which Lewin makes (Paper No. 23). He states that if a given task is above a certain degree of difficulty ("too difficult" or "objectively impossible") no feeling of failure occurs, and if the task is below a certain degree of difficulty ("too easy") no feeling of success is aroused. In dealing with the problem of the nature of success in relation to level of aspiration, Hilgard (Paper No. 25) points out that success is related to the goals of an individual in at least four ways. He concludes by stating that goals should be kept "realistic and attainable" and that "social pressure toward unattainable goals must be reduced if goals are to be realistic."

As research has indicated, very often an individual's level of aspiration tends to be raised after success and lowered after failure. There is also evidence which suggests a relationship between one's level of aspiration and his underlying personality dynamics. Gruen (Paper No. 26) reveals that emotionally maladjusted adolescents tend to have very high or very low levels of aspiration in relation to their actual performance, and MacKinnon[1] points out that neurotics tend to have extremely high levels of aspiration.

From the standpoint of mental health, it would seem that an individual should set his goals at a realistic level in the sense that they are attainable with a certain degree of effort. Their attainment should be neither too difficult nor too easy.

---

[1]MacKinnon, D. W. *"A Topological Analysis of Anxiety," Character and Personality.* Vol. 12, 1944, 163-76.

23. Psychology of Success and Failure

Kurt Lewin

T HE great importance of success and failure is recognized by practically all psychological schools. Thorndike's law of effect[1], as well as Adler's ideas, has close relation to this problem. Pedagogically, the importance of success is universally stressed.

Indeed, success and failure influence deeply the emotional status of the person, his goals, and his social relations. From the point of view of guidance, one can emphasize the fact that these problems are important throughout the whole age range, and are as basic for the very young child as for the adult.

In spite of the common recognition of these factors, our knowledge about the psychology of success and failure is meager. The law of effect may, for instance, suggest that a person who has succeeded in a special activity will have a tendency to repeat that activity. Indeed, children of two or three years tend to repeat activities again and again. Yet, experiments show, at least for older persons, that a spontaneous repetition of a successful act is not very likely, and that in case it does occur, the activity is generally distinctly changed. As a matter of fact, the tendency to go back spontaneously to a special activity, is, as Ovsiankina has shown, about ninety times as high if the activity is not completed as if it is successfully completed. This shows, at least, that the whole problem is much more complicated than one might expect.

II

The first question one should be able to answer is: Under what conditions will a person experience success or failure? The experiments of Hoppe

Abridged from *Occupations,* 1936, 14, 926-930. Reprinted by permission of the American Personnel and Guidance Association.

[1]Law of effect: One learns quickly those reactions which are accompanied or followed by a satisfying state of affairs; one does not learn quickly those which result in an annoying state of affairs or learns not to make such reactions.

point to some fundamental facts which one could have learned from every-day experience; namely, it is not possible to correlate the objective achievement on the one side, with the feeling of success or failure on the other. The same achievement can result once in the feeling of great success, another time in the feeling of complete failure. This is true not only for different individuals, but even for the same individual. For instance, a person may throw a discus forty yards the first time. The second time he may reach fifty, and feel very successful. After short practice, he may reach sixty-five. If he then throws fifty yards again, he will experience a definite failure in spite of the fact that he got a thrill out of the same achievement but a short time before. This means that the experience of success and failure does not depend upon the achievement as such, but rather upon the relation between the achievement and the person's expectation. One can speak, in this respect, about the person's "level of aspiration," and can say that the experience and the degree of success and failure depend upon whether the achievement is above or below the momentary level of aspiration.

One may ask whether a person always has a definite level of aspiration in respect to a certain task. The answer is no. If one, for instance, does something for the first time, one generally does not set himself a definite goal. It is interesting additional evidence of the relation between success and the level of aspiration that in such situations no strong failure is experienced. If one wishes to avoid or diminish the feeling of failure in the child, one often says to him: "Just try." In this way a definite level of aspiration is eliminated.

Not only is the level of aspiration fundamental for the experience of success and failure, but the level of aspiration itself is changed by success and failure. After success, a person generally sets himself a higher goal. After failure, his level of aspiration generally goes down. There are some exceptions to this general trend which one should notice. In the experiments of Hoppe, success led to a rise of the level of aspiration only in sixty-nine per cent; in seven per cent it remained the same; and in twenty-four per cent the person stopped the activity entirely. After failure, the level of aspiration was never raised, but it was lowered in only fifty per cent of the cases. In twenty-one per cent it remained the same, in two per cent the person consoled himself by the realization of previous successes; and in twenty-seven per cent the person ceased the activity entirely. This varying behavior is due partly to the fact that there are cases which are neither clear successes no clear failures. On the whole, the person is more ready to raise the level of aspiration after success than to lower it after failure.

It is important to note that a person instead of lowering his level of aspiration after failure, may stop entirely. There is a significant difference between individuals in this respect. Some persons are relatively easily influenced to lower their levels of aspiration, whereas others show a stiff backbone. The latter maintain their levels of aspiration in spite of failures, and may prefer to leave the field entirely rather than to lower it. Lack of persistence sometimes has to be attributed to such an unwillingness to yield. On the other hand, there are cases of apparent persistence, in which a person sticks to an activity only at the price of constantly lowering his level of aspiration. This sort of persistency may be found in the hysteric type. In problems of guidance involving unusually high or low persistency, the possible reasons behind such behavior should be carefully examined, because the advisable measures should be different in accordance with the underlying psychological facts.

Surprisingly enough a person may leave the field of activity not only after failure, but after success too. Such abandonment of the field after success occurs generally when this success follows a series of failures. One obviously does not like to quit a task after failure. One continues, eager to find a successful termination, and uses the first occasion to stop, out of fear that further repetitions may bring new failures.

III

One has to consider quite detailed facts in order to understand the forces which govern the level of aspiration.

The first point to mention is that any goal has a position within a set of goals. If a child is asked, "How much is three times four?" the answer, "twelve," determines a definite circumscribed goal he has to reach. The answer will be either right or wrong. But if the child has to write an English composition, or to translate a passage of French, or to build a wooden boat, there is no such absolutely determined goal, but, rather, a variety of possible achievements which may differ greatly in quality. Most tasks are of this nature. It is generally technically possible to order the different possible achievements of a task according to their degree of difficulty. This allows one to compare the achievement and the level of aspiration of different persons, and to determine in a given case, the effect of success and failure. The range of acceptable achievement has often a "natural maximum" and a "natural minimum." In Hoppe's experiment, for instance, the subject had to solve one of a group of puzzles, different in difficulty. A subject who was not able to solve any one of the puzzles, but who was able to return the stones to their proper places in the box would certainly not have reached the natural minimum of the task. On the other hand, it would be above the natural maximum to reach a solution of the most difficult puzzle within one second. Some tasks have no natural maximum. This holds, for instance, for many sport activities—there is always the possibility of jumping higher and running faster. The lack of this natural maximum within the goal structure of many sport activities has led to a biologically unsound race without end.

The individual usually is conscious of the variety of possible goals within the task. He conceives the single action in its significance for a larger field of actions. Besides the goals for the momentary act, he has some general goal in regard to this larger field. For instance, when a person in a competition throws a discus, his goal for a certain trial might be to throw at least fifty yards; his goal for the whole group of actions would be to win! There always exists besides the goal for the next act, or, as we may say, besides the immediate goal, an ideal goal. This ideal goal may be to become the best discus thrower of the college or even to become world champion.

Such a goal can possess any degree of reality or unreality. For the student who does well in the first weeks of his sporting activities, the ideal to become world champion may be only an occasional daydream without any significance. The ideal goal, to become the best player of the university, may have considerably more reality. In a vague way, a student entering college may dream about the possibility of becoming a leading surgeon, and without even confessing this goal to himself. If he progresses in college, and does well in medical school, this ideal goal may become somewhat more real. According to Hoppe, success narrows the gap between the immediate goal and the ideal goal, and brings the ideal goal from the level of unreality gradually down to the level of reality. Failure has the opposite effect: a previously real goal vanishes into the world of dreams. In case the ideal goal should be reached (a case more frequent in experiments than in life) generally a new ideal goal arises.

IV

If it is true that the degree of success and failure depends upon the amount of difference between the immediate goal and the achievement, it should be possible to create a very strong feeling of success by making the task so easy that the achievement will be much better than the task demands. On the other hand, it should be possible to create a very strong feeling of failure by assigning a very difficult task. Experiments show that this is not true. If the task is above a certain degree of difficulty, no feeling of failure arises, and no feeling of success arises if the task is below a certain degree of difficulty. In other words, if one represents the possible degree of difficulty of a task on a scale, this scale is infinite in direction, both to greater ease and to greater difficulty. But an individual reacts with success and failure only to a small region within this scale. In fact, the tasks which an individual considers as "very easy," "easy," "medium," "difficult," and "very difficult," circumscribe only a small region in the scale. Above and below this region lie a great many tasks which the individual calls "too easy" or "too difficult." The "too difficult" tasks are considered as "objectively impossible," entirely out of the range of the individual's ability, and no feeling of failure is attached to such a task. Similarly, in the case of a "too easy" task, the achievement is taken so much for granted, that no feeling of success is aroused. Contrary to the scale of possible difficulties, the scale of possible achievements is not infinite, but has a definite upper limit for a given individual at a given time. Both success and failure occur only if the difficulty of the task lies close to the upper limit of achievement. In other words, the feeling of failure occurs only if there is a chance for success, and a feeling of success occurs only if there is a chance for failure. Behind success and failure, stands therefore always a conflict situation.

This conflict situation makes somewhat understandable the laws which govern the position and the change in the level of aspiration. These laws are probably among the most fundamental for all human behavior. They are quite complicated, and we are only beginning to understand them. If it were true that life is ruled by the tendency to get as much pleasure as possible, one might expect that everybody would keep his level of aspiration as low as possible, because in this case, his performance would be always above his level of aspiration, and he would feel successful. As a matter of fact, there is a marked tendency to keep the level of aspiration down out of fear of failure. On the other hand, there is at the same time, a strong tendency to raise the level of aspiration as high as possible. The experiments of J. D. Frank show that both tendencies are of different strength in different individuals, and that a third tendency may have to be distinguished, namely, the tendency to keep one's expectations about one's future performance as close as possible to reality . A cautious person usually starts with a relatively low level of aspiration, and after succeeding, he raises the level only by short steps. Other persons tend to maintain their levels of aspiration well above their achievements. The rigidity of the level of aspiration, i.e., the tendency to keep the level constant rather than to shift it, shows marked differences among individuals. Frank found that these differences are highly reliable and largely independent of the special nature of the task.

It is important to know whether success and failure change the level of aspiration only in the particular activity in question, or whether success and failure in one task influence the level of aspiration in another task too. This is important for problems of guidance, where the effects of achievement or failure in different fields of activity on each other are of great significance, as for instance, in the realm of school motivation and of delinquency. J. D. Frank found a marked relationship between success and failure in one task and the level of aspiration in another, if the tasks concerned had sufficient psychological relations. Mr. Jucknat's experiments verified this result but showed that this influence is weak or negligible if past experience has rigidly fixed the level of aspiration within a task.

V

These studies point to a relation between the level of aspiration for a specific task and something that one may call the self esteem, which means the feeling of the person about his own status and general standards. All experiments indicate that this relation is very fundamental. There is, for instance, a marked tendency in the case of failure, to blame an inadequate tool or an accident for the lack of achievement. To experience success or failure the person has to attribute the result of an action to himself in a very specific way. In case of inadequate performance, the person often tries to get rid of the feeling of failure by cutting the tie of belongingness between him and the result, and by rejecting his responsibility for the outcome. Also the tendency to raise the level of aspiration as high as possible seems to be closely related to the self esteem, particularly to the feeling of the person about his status in the social group. The level of aspiration is determined on the one side by the upper limit of the person's achievements; in other words, by his ability. A second fundamental factor is the level of achievement prevailing in the social group to which a person belongs; for instance, among his business friends, his comrades, his playmates. The social group can have a strong influence in keeping the level of aspiration either too high or too low for a person's ability. This is especially true for children. The expectation of his parents, or the standards of his group may keep the level of aspiration for the less able child too high, and lead to continuous failure and over-tension. Whereas the level of aspiration for the very able child may be kept too low. (This may be the reason for Wellman's finding that children with a relatively high IQ gain less in IQ in the nursery school than children with a relatively low IQ.)

Fajans has shown that success and failure influence greatly the degree of activeness among active and passive children. Chase found an increase in achievement following success. Fajans has further determined the degree to which praise has an effect similar to real sucess. The effects of being successful, and being socially recognized or being loved, resemble each other closely. This relation is important for adults, and even more so in the case of adolescents and children.

24. The Use of the Term *Level of Aspiration*

John W. Gardner

THE term *Anspruchsniveau* was first introduced into the experimental literature about nine years ago in the work of Lewin and his students, but gained little currency in this country until the appearance in 1935 of Lewin's *Dynamic Theory of Personality*. The term was translated into English as 'level of aspiration,' and in the past several years has gained widespread use. It has appeared in textbooks and other systematic treatises, in discussions of social psychology, motivation and personality. Conversationally, psychologists are increasingly inclined to make use of it as a provocative new term adding spice to old discussions of success and failure, inferiority attitudes, and human motivation. Under the circumstances, a brief discussion of the use of the term 'level of aspiration' seems to be in order.

The concept of 'level of aspiration' was first formulated by Dembo, one of Lewin's students, in the course of an experimental investigation of anger. Her experimental situations employed frustration as a means of evoking anger, the subject being required to perform some task which was either extremely difficult or completely impossible. A by-product of her investigation was the discovery that when a required goal is too difficult the subject will set up an intermediate goal which is easier than, but a step toward, the required goal. This intermediate goal she termed the subject's *momentary level of aspiration*.

It is not the purpose of this paper to review the experimental work on level of aspiration, but it will serve as a useful introduction to the present discussion to describe very briefly a few of the early findings.

Hoppe, who published the first major study of level of aspiration, states that experiences of success and failure in the course of an activity will depend upon whether or not the subject attains these intermediate goals which he himself sets. If the subject attains the intermediate goal (momentary

Abridged from *The Psychological Review*, 1940, 47, 59-68. Reprinted by permission of the author and the American Psychological Association, Inc.

level of aspiration) which he has set himself, he experiences the performance as a success, regardless of whether or not he has achieved a perfect
score or attained the goal set by the experimenter. On the other hand, if
the subject's performance does not come up to his momentary level of aspiration, he experiences the performance as a failure. Hoppe found that the
level of aspiration shifts frequently in the course of an activity. If the individual's performance comes up to his level of aspiration, the latter tends to
shift upward; if he fails to attain his aspiration-level on a given trial, the
aspiration-level is likely to be lowered.

Of most importance to the work of later American investigators was
Hoppe's observation that marked individual differences in aspiration-level
appear, even in the course of simple laboratory tasks, and his suggestions
that these individual differences may be diagnostic of important personality
differences. He found, for example, that an individual may habitually set
intermediate goals (*i.e.,* levels of aspiration) which are far above his level
of performance (thus courting failure-experiences) even though his rate of
improvement offers no grounds whatever for such high expectations. Another
subject may consistently demand so little of himself (*i.e.,* be so careful to
set intermediate goals within easy reach) that he always provides himself
with the presumably satisfying experience of doing "better than he expected."
Hoppe suggests that such individual differences in level of aspiration reveal
differences in ambition, prudence, courage, self-confidence, courage to face
reality, etc.

With this brief introduction, we may proceed to a consideration of the
topic at hand. What do we mean when we speak of an individual's level of
aspiration? How may the term be justifiably used in systematic discussions
of motivation or personality?

Hoppe's delineation of what he understands by the term *level of aspiration*
is contained in the following passage:

> The subject . . . always undertakes the task with certain de-
> mands (Ansprüchen), which can change in the course of the
> activity. The totality of these constantly shifting, now indefinite,
> now precise, expectations, goal-settings or demands in connection
> with one's own future performance, we shall term the level of as-
> piration of the subject.

The meaning of the term level of aspiration bears an intimate relationship
to the methods used in determining level of aspiration. Hoppe's method of
determining level of aspiration is based upon a crude inferential technique.
A subject's aspiration-level may be inferred, he asserts, through the simultaneous use of the three following lines of evidence: (1) the spontaneous
remarks of the subject, (2) the occurrence of success and failure experiences, and (3) the way in which the subject 'goes at' the task. The relev-
ancy of the second line of evidence involves the assumption that success

and failure experiences are dependent upon the attainment (or failure to attain) one's momentary level of aspiration. If this assumption is valid, then the occurrence of an experience of success would permit the inference that the subject's aspiration-level on that trial was at least no higher than he had actually performed; and the occurrence of feelings of failure would permit the inference that the aspiration-level lay somewhere above the subject's actual level of performance on that trial.

Later investigators, while deriving much benefit from Hoppe's important exploratory work, have found it necessary to reject his methods of determining aspiration-level on the grounds of lack of precision and objectivity. Jucknat offers a more precise method. She made use of a series of ten paper-and-pencil mazes, arranged in order of difficulty. The more difficult a maze was the larger it was, so that when the mazes were laid out in orderly arrangement on a table it was easy for the subject to recognize at a glance that he was facing a series arranged in order of difficulty. The subject was told to choose whichever maze he wished and to start working on it. In doing so he automatically revealed his level of aspiration. Thus if his first choice was Maze No. 2 (next to the easiest in the series), his aspiration-level score for the first trial was 2.

The idea of framing the situation so that the subject automatically reveals his level of aspiration without verbal commitments is an appealing one, and represents an unquestionable advance over Hoppe's method from the standpoint of objectivity. It is important to note, however, that in employing this method Jucknat still clings to the hope that she is dealing with the level of aspiration as envisaged by Hoppe. The point is worth considering because it typifies a recurring error in aspiration-level investigation, and because, from a broader viewpoint, it represents a widespread tendency in the study of personality. Students of personality are increasingly eager to employ precise, objective, quantitative methods, but are still notably reluctant to content themselves with the data which such methods yield. The level of aspiration as obtained in Jucknat's situations is not the level of aspiration as conceived by Hoppe. It is clear throughout Hoppe's work that when he uses the term level of aspiration he is referring to the individual's true inner aims and expectations. But as soon as an individual is in a position in which his aspirations are automatically revealed (as in Jucknat's situations), social factors alter the picture. It is a commonplace that an individual's verbal behavior is no valid indicator of his inner attitudes; but the principle will bear re-iteration in its extension to non-verbal behavior. Individuals commonly 'edit' those aspects of their behavior, verbal or non-verbal, which are open to public inspection. When secretly cherished aims are jacked to the surface and forced into behavioral expression, they too become subject to this editing.

These statements are not to be interpreted as a condemnation of Jucknat's method, but only as an argument for explicit recognition of the sort of data which the method yields. In short, if Jucknat wishes to deal with data thus obtained under the term *level of aspiration,* then the latter should be re-defined as, let us say, "that level in a difficulty scale at which the subject is willing to test himself in the presence of the experimenter."

That such a re-definition is necessary under such circumstances was recognized by Frank in his own attempt to provide a more precise method of dealing with levels of aspiration. After each trial in a given task, Frank told the subject his performance score and then asked the subject how well he intended to do next time. He then re-defines level of aspiration as follows:

> The term *level of aspiration . . .* is defined as *the level of future performance in a familiar task which an individual, knowing his level of past performance in that task, explicitly undertakes to reach.*

In his earlier papers Frank makes no comment upon this sharp divergence from the original definition, but in his most recent discussion he states that the reformulation was undertaken "with a clear conscience in the conviction that the concept remains essentially the same as that used by Hoppe." In the light of the present discussion, such a statement cannot be accepted. Hoppe conceives the level of aspiration as the totality of certain highly subjective demands, aims and expectations. With Frank the level of aspiration is the goal which the individual *says* he is undertaking to reach. This amounts to considerably more than a difference in emphasis; the two investigators are talking about two different things. Equating the two involves the assumption that the subjective aims and expectations of which Hoppe speaks are given direct, undistorted verbal expression.

Gould employs Frank's method, but makes clear her conviction that there is "no one-to-one relationship between what we might call 'true aspiration-level' and the quantitative measures of aspiration-level." Following the experimental sessions, Gould conducted lengthy interviews with her subjects, and obtained a wealth of interesting and important material. However, it is interesting to note that while she is keenly aware of the inadequacy of the explicit statements of aspiration-level made in the experimental situation as reflections of inner aspirations, she is rather confident in making generalizations concerning the 'inner level of goal-strivings' (*i.e.,* true aspiration-level) on the basis of the statements made during the interview. For example, after reviewing some of the data of the interview, she states that "explicit estimates yield more rapidly to changes than does the motivating level of goal-strivings . . . ." How the interview statements can provide the basis for such confident knowledge of the motivating level of goal-strivings (*i.e.,* true level of aspiration) is not entirely clear. It is conceivable, to be sure, that considerations of rapport make the interview material less artificial than the experimental material; but in the absence of external evidence to this effect one may question the consistency of permitting the verbal expressions of the interview to achieve the status of valid indicators of inner attitudes, when the verbal expressions of the experimental situation are denied this status.

The issue may now be summarized: Hoppe thought of the level of aspiration as the totality of certain highly subjective aims. Later investigators rejected his methods as inadequate for getting at these aims, and set up more precise and objective methods. These methods were assumed by Jucknat and Frank to be getting at the level of aspiration as originally defined, but actually they were measuring precisely as much as the individual was willing to make public concerning his aims and no more.

The question arises, then, as to the extent to which this constitutes a serious weakness in aspiration-level research. It would seem, at first glance, that we must either give up the research until more piercing methods are developed, or go ahead using the methods at hand with the toughminded but nonetheless wistful assertion that we are dealing with 'manifest' level of aspiration because we simply have no way of getting at the 'true' level of aspiration. Actually, neither alternative states the true case. Such feelings of methodological frustration should be dissipated by consideration of the following question: Is there any 'true' level of aspiration? In the opinion of the present writer the early speculation concerning the nature of the phenomena involved in this line of experimentation produced an *ignis fatuus* which has misled most investigators since. What reason is there to believe, after all, that Hoppe's inner "totality of . . . expectations, goal-settings or demands" is so structured as to warrant the term *level* of aspiration? Might not the subject's striving frequently be characterized by nothing more than an amorphous desire 'to make a good performance' or 'to do better than last time' (which implies a *region* of aspiration, perhaps, or a *direction* of aspiration, but not a level whose height is susceptible to quantitative evaluation to quantitative evaluation)? Might not an individual on a given trial occasionally free himself completely of the scoring scale and concern himself with the improvement of his stance, with the discovery of weaknesses in his technique, with attempts to relax, etc.? Might not an individual in a task such as dart-throwing entertain at one and the same time a wild hope that he will make a perfect hit and a more prudent hope that he will at least hit the target, with perhaps an additional, self-conscious hope that he will not appear too awkward in the eyes of the experimenter? In other words, is there not considerable likelihood that the individual's aims on a given trial are manifold, fluctuant, ephemeral, and differing qualitatively as well as quantitatively, with those aims which involve a specific score often giving way to aims which cannot possibly be described in terms of score values? And may not any or all of these aims, qualitative or quantitative, specific or vague, operate more or less concurrently in a kaleidoscopic pattern, with one aim dominant one moment and another the next? How, then, out of this maelstrom of aims, some quantitatively describable and others not, and all of them contributing to a pattern which is certainly not at present quantitatively conceivable, can we formulate a neat concept of level of aspiration?

There are true aspirations, of course, but what reason have we to suppose that they can justly be described in terms of a *level?* The motivation of such a belief is more obvious than the evidence in its favor. 'Level' implies quantifiability. It means that aspiration can take its place in neat, dynamic formulae such as May and Doob's *Motivation is a function of the discrepancies between level of aspiration and level of achievement.* It is far from our intention to discourage attempts to deal with true, inner strivings; but the way to bring such complicated material within the realm of measurability is not to endow it first with quantifiable characteristics which are utterly spurious.

There is, then, one and only one meaning to the term *level of aspiration:* it can only refer to quantitative indication which an individual makes concerning his future performance in an activity. Such quantitative indications concerning future performance occur sporadically in certain appropriately structured life situations (*e.g.,* on the golf course, in a shooting gallery) but their systematic evocation demands a specially designed experimental situation. This 'specially designed experimental situation' has two important features. In the first place, it demands that the subject make some public indication of what he aims to achieve. Presumably, the subject offers whatever variety of information on this topic it best suits his momentary purpose to give. It may be true or false. It may be true on one trial and false on the next. And after what we have said concerning the subject's true aims, it should be apparent that in many cases the subject's publicly indicated aims may not be appropriately described as either true or false (since there is no underlying truth to adhere to) but only as artificial.

The second important feature of the situation is that the subject is required to put this information concerning his aims in quantitative terms.

Out of these two requirements of the experimental situation—that the subject make some public indication of his aims, and that he make this in quantitative terms—we obtain the concept of level of aspiration. It is manufactured in the laboratory.

Used in this very narrow sense, level of aspiration is a truly quantitative concept. Used in any other sense, it is not only pseudo-quantitative but mythical. It may be objected that in narrowing the concept down to the point where it means something, we have narrowed it down to the point where it means nothing. The only convincing answer to this objection is to be found in the recent experimental literature on the subject, which indicates that even in its strictest meaning the concept represents one of the most interesting personality variables that has been uncovered in recent years.

We have concerned ourselves with what Lewin would term the empirical coordinating definition of the concept of level of aspiration. We would agree with Lewin that knowledge of the 'conceptual properties of the construct' is equally desirable; but the establishment of these conceptual properties remains the task of future experimenters in the field, and will not be hastened by reading more into the concept than is already there.

25. Success in Relation to Level of Aspiration

Ernest R. Hilgard

SUCCESS and failure mean different things to different people, because the measuring rods are so diverse, including money, fame, power, prestige and many less conspicuous forms of personal satisfaction. We can state with assurance that a given person is successful or unsuccessful only if we know what that person is trying to do. As William James put it a long time ago, success can be measured only in terms of pretensions.

Differences in standards of success which pupils and their parents set constitute a familiar and difficult problem in the public schools. At one extreme we find pupils from very poor homes, where the outlook is so depressing that schooling does not seem to matter. A vivid picture is given in some of the cases of Negro children in the South, as reported recently by Davis and Dollard. Truancy is little condemned in such homes, the general value of education is low and school conduct is correspondingly un-

Abridged from *School and Society*, 1942, 55, 423-428. Reprinted by permission of the author and The Society for the Advancement of Education, Inc.

favorable. At the other extreme we have parents overzealous to send their children through college, that they may have opportunities the parents did not have. Such parents often set impossibly high standards for children of ordinary ability.

It is evident that the ways in which individuals set goals for themselves, and their interpretations of success and failure in relation to these goals, constitute interesting psychological problems the answers to which have importance for education. One effort to define these problems was made in 1930 by Hoppe, a student of Kurt Lewin, then of Berlin. He found it somewhat simpler to begin by considering more immediate goals, such as success in a particular task, rather than more remote goals, such as the aims in one's life work. Hoppe used the term *Anspruchsniveau,* which has been translated "level of aspiration," to describe the momentary goal which the individual sets himself. This goal is defined in relation to one's present performance in the task, which may be described correspondingly as the "level of achievement." In line with the usual hope to do better the next time, the most natural relationship between the two levels is for the level of aspiration to be set somewhat above the present level of achievement.

When it is said that success and failure depend on what the individual is trying to do, it is suggested that he must somehow be absorbed in the task if it is to give him the elation of success or the chagrin of failure. This absorption may be called "ego-involvement." Hoppe pointed out that only tasks lying within limited ranges of difficulty can really captivate the person in such a manner as to create the possibility of psychological success or failure. Tasks which are "much too easy" are considered "baby stuff" and there is no satisfaction in getting the right answers. Tasks "much too difficult" are not attempted; they lie, so to speak, beyond the province of success and failure. Only a middle level of difficulty appropriate to the individual has meaning for him. The difficulty level is bounded at the lower end by those tasks which are easy enough to be almost certainly completed satisfactorily, although a slight hazard is present. Perhaps the crossword puzzles in the daily papers represent about this level of difficulty—if by scratching one's head, using the dictionary and calling on other members of the family the puzzle is almost invariably completed. The very difficult task, lying at the other end of the range of potential success or failure, is such that, although the chance of failure is high, there is the bare chance of success. Identifying the authors of books or the composers of music is for many of us a task somewhat of this sort; while the possibility of failure is high, there is so fair a chance of getting some right answers that we are willing to be put to the test, and, because of becoming involved in it, we feel embarrassed at our failures. The matter of ego-involvement is one of the most important problems of good teaching. Tasks appropriate to him—neither too easy nor too hard—are the ideal ones for the learner.

It is possible to design laboratory experiments concerned with ego-involvement, level of aspiration and their relationship to difficulty, to social pressure, to experienced success and failure. A great many experiments of this type have been made in this country, chiefly since 1935. The characteristic experiment consists in having several trials in the performance of a simple laboratory task, such as giving synonyms, sorting cards, substituting symbols for digits. After a first trial the learner is told his score and then asked to state what he is going to "try for" or what he "expects to reach" on the next trial. The actual score is taken as his level of achievement, the estimated future score as an indication of his level of aspiration. Such estimates are always distorted in various ways by the persons participating in the experiment, and few experimenters are so naïve as to believe that the stated level of aspiration necessarily corresponds to the goal at which the person is really aiming. There is, however, much of interest in what the person says he is trying to do, and more subtle methods of getting at the level of aspiration have shown results comparable to those obtained by securing purely verbal statements.

Among the many questions which experimenters have attempted to answer through their studies, several may be mentioned briefly. One question is whether or not goal-setting behavior is characteristic of the individual personality, so that one individual invariably tends to set his goals near to his present achievement, another high above achievement, another perhaps at or below his present level. If this were the case, there should be high intercorrelations among aspiration levels as shown in different situations. Results have been somewhat discordant, most experimenters finding goal-setting to be more highly correlated than the performances on different tasks. A second question has been whether or not goal-setting behavior as shown in the laboratory is related to the typical setting of long-time goals outside the laboratory. Results have for the most part been disappointing, low relationships being the rule. Such low relationships may have been in part a function of the failure to secure ego-involvement in the laboratory corresponding to ego-involvement outside the laboratory. A person does not necessarily attack a parlor game with the same vehemence that he shows while becoming expert in his life's work. Social factors may also distort the correlations found in the laboratory, for other experiments have shown that the group of which one is a part, the prestige of others whose scores are known, all may influence levels of aspiration as individually stated.

One of the experiments, in which care was taken to have ego-involvement in the laboratory similar to that outside the laboratory, yielded results highly significant for educational practices.

Dr. Sears' procedure was to select from the public schools of New Haven three groups of children from the 4th, 5th and 6th grades. The groups differed in their histories with respect to arithmetic and reading. The first group, called the "success" group, had a history of satisfactory results in school in both reading and arithmetic. The second group, matched with the first in respect to age, intelligence, socio-economic status, had a history of unsuccessful work in both arithmetic and reading. This group was designated the "failure" group. The third group, also matched with the others on background items, had a history of success in reading, but of failure in arithmetic. This group was known as the "differential" group. Dr. Sears argued that this known history of success and failure in arithmetic and reading should reflect in the laboratory if the laboratory tasks chosen clearly involved either subject matter. Hence she chose arithmetic and reading tasks, and the children were brought one at a time into the laboratory for testing after the manner of the usual level-of-aspiration experiment.

The most striking finding was that children with a past history of success (whether in both subjects, or in the one being tested at the time) were quite similar in their goal-setting behavior. All tended to "try for" scores close to but slightly better than those which had just been achieved. From the point of view of the teacher this result is potentially of great significance, for it means that children with a history of successful performance behave in a manner which is predictable, and to that extent the learning situation is is under control.

By contrast, the goal-setting behavior of those with a history of failure is quite unpredictable. Only a very few set their goals, like the successful children, close to present achievement. They tended to deviate in one or the other direction. Some, as a consequence of experienced failure, appeared to be so afraid of further failure that they set their goals below present achievement. They appeared to expect to do less well than they had just done. The reaction is something like this: "I'm no good in reading; if it took me only 25 seconds this time, I was just lucky; next time it will probably take me 30 seconds to read something similar." By setting the goal well within reach, the child is protected from the chagrin of further experienced failure. Others of the failure group (and these were the more common) set very high aspiration levels, expecting to improve over present attainment far more than would be predicted on a realistic basis. Their reaction might be described somewhat as follows: "I always seem to have bad luck in my arithmetic, but I'm as good as the next fellow. If anybody can make it in 30 seconds, I can." Or perhaps: "I want to do well in reading. I'll try very hard and see if I can't do *much* better." One can recognize the social approval that this last statement would win in many schools today. We like the child who tries. Actually, of course, this sort of trying is bad from a mental-hygiene point of view, because it is a trying which is uncorrected by the realities of the situation. We should not train children to secure their successes in the realm of phantasy. The results for the children who had a history of repeated failure showed throughout a departure from realistic goal-setting, in the two directions of which neither is wholesome. It is not wholesome for the child to be so beaten down by failure as to cease expecting anything of himself, or to be so inured to failure that what he expects of himself no longer corresponds to reality.

The high specificity of the relationship between the experimental results and the academic achievement was engendered in part by the experimenter's insistence that the laboratory task was continuous with school work in arithmetic and reading. An interesting problem, on which information is incomplete in this study, is the degree to which the consequences of success and failure apply to new situations. This involves some sort of summation of the effects of particular successes and failures, the details of which must prove to be very complicated. Consider, for example, the difficulty in finding the answer to the question, How many good drives does a beginning golfer have to make in order to remain interested in the game in spite of many balls lost in the rough? Or, How many school failures can the child tolerate if he has a margin of successes? Such answers can not be obtained by simple counting, but must be based on an appropriate psychological analysis. So long as the school child has few enough failures and enough successes that he thinks of himself as potentially successful in activities which are to him important, then we may suppose that the failures have not done harm. If, on the other hand, there has been so much failure that the child is afraid to try, or he is so unaccustomed to success that he sets goals which he does not expect to reach, then we may say that he has not succeeded enough.

It was in relation to the problem of the psychological basis of success that the concept of level of aspiration arose, and out of the experiments on level of aspiration have come several suggestions with respect to the meaning of success to the individual. There are at least four ways in which success is related to the goals which the individual sets himself.

1. In the first place, the most obvious basis for success is to reach the goal which one has set. "I made it!" "Eureka!" These are exclamations of genuine private success experiences.

2. To miss the goal is not to fail completely, for to get within the psychological region of the goal is also satisfying. To be nominated to an office is itself a mark of the esteem of one's fellows, even though one may lose the election. There is a tendency in India, when signing a letter, to write the academic degrees earned behind the signature. A curious custom is to include the designation, "B.A., failed," as a mark of prestige. This means that the person concerned has got as far as being admitted to the examination, which is passed by only a small fraction of those admitted. To have arrived so close to the goal is to have had a partial success experience. The

psychological analysis of nearness to a goal is a difficult one, for some goals have very precise boundaries. To get within a few miles of the North Pole, when the North Pole is the objective, is not to get there at all. It is probably a desirable thing educationally to have goals with somewhat fluid boundaries, so that success and failure are not black and white, but to approach a goal is itself to enter the goal region and to have success thereby. Many marking systems have handicapped education through setting too rigid boundaries to the experience of success, and differentiating thereby too sharply between success and failure.

3.   A third source of success in goal-seeking behavior is the partial success which comes through improvement. Even though the goal is still far distant, if we have approached closer that serves psychologically as a successful step. I may not be able to pole vault 12 feet, but I may do better than I have done before. The more forward-looking schools have played up this feature of success, with their emphasis upon what is now loosely called "pupil growth." Change in desirable directions is encouraged as the source of personal satisfaction, somewhat independent of the actual level of performance which has been reached.

4.   Finally, as the fourth source of success, may be mentioned the satisfaction which comes from the setting of desirable goals. It does something for the person's self-esteem to think of himself as the kind of person who is trying to do the right thing. I suppose most of us have at one time or another permitted a salesman to sell us an encyclopedia which we did not use. To have purchased books which remain unread ought, perhaps, to give us a feeling of failure. On the contrary, we gain some satisfaction from our good judgment in selecting books for our library, even though their pages remain uncut.

A similar, perhaps more familiar example, is that of the student in college who carries books home over the Christmas holidays. Does he really intend to study? If a wager were made, the odds would be against it, even before the books were packed. But he takes the books anyhow, even at some inconvenience, for he likes to think of himself as the kind of person who intends to put his vacation to profitable use.

These considerations with respect to the nature of success in relation to aspiration suggest certain responsibilities upon those who have a share in helping children and youth to set their goals.

As a first suggestion, every effort should be made to keep goals realistic and attainable. As goals are permitted to become too remote and unreal, reactions tend to take the form of phantasy, or effort seems futile and discouragement results. It is desirable to have a backlog of success experiences in order to keep the learning situation realistic. The consequence of an unrealistic goal is eventual disillusionment. Consider the plight of the pre-medical student having trouble with his chemistry or physics. He may insist on fighting a losing battle because he is attracted by the prestige of the medical profession, or his work many suffer because he begins to see that his goal is unattainable. How much better it would be if our guidance procedures were more nearly adequate, so that the student would direct his energies along lines in which he would have a high probability of success. The social waste involved in the number of pre-medical students never admitted to medical schools is enormous.

The second suggestion, something of a corollary of the first, is that social pressure toward unattainable goals must be reduced if goals are to be kept realistic. To the extent that all prestige is showered upon the high-school student who wishes to go to college, an unrealistic pressure for a collegiate goal is placed upon those unlikely to go to college. Either this likelihood should be increased through changing the nature of the college and eliminating the economic handicaps that prevent many able students from attending, or the pressure should be changed. Even if we managed to send everyone to college, we should still be up against the stubborn facts of the census; namely, the distribution of available jobs for the products of our schools. So long as a large proportion of workers engage in unskilled labor and in personal services, we must see a corresponding proportion of our youth entering such jobs, unless some unforeseen upheaval greatly changes the complexion of our productive processes. To be realistic is to prepare those who must enter such tasks for finding dignity and self-respect within them. Many of the girls graduating from our high schools will become waitresses, domestic servants, beauty-parlor attendants. And the boys they marry will include chauffeurs, gardeners and window-washers. No decent and useful work must be despised or looked down upon. On the contrary, one of the problems we face is to make every meaningful task one in which an honest and upright citizen may take pride. The unskilled workers must learn how to live on meager salaries, how to find recreation that is inexpensive but satisfying, how to take their share of responsibility as homemakers and citizens. This sets a difficult problem for the school; and if schools fulfill their obligations realistically, they must have to change even more in the future than they have in the past.

Such implications seem rather remote from the limited experimental data now available on level of aspiration. However, educational psychology must not be permitted to develop as a petty little science if it is to be worth its salt. Only by seeing the potential significance of the things done in the experimental laboratory can we direct the more patient collection of data into channels which will ultimately support generalizations of significance for our day and age.

26. Level of Aspiration in Relation to Personality Factors in Adolescents

Emily W. Gruen

INTRODUCTION

T HE aim of this study was to compare the level of aspiration behavior of adolescents differing in selected personality characteristics. Level of aspiration was defined as "the level of future performance in a familiar task, which an individual explicitly undertakes to reach."

Previous studies have indicated that the level of aspiration behavior may be related to underlying personality factors and that it may be used by the subject as an "Ego-protective mechanism," or as a method for maintaining self-esteem and security. The purpose of the present study is to investigate such possible relationships between level of aspiration behavior and certain measures of personality adjustment in adolescents.

The task used in this study consisted of a modified symbol-substitution exercise, using shorthand symbols. It was especially constructed for this study.

Personality adjustment was determined by the Rogers Test of Personality Adjustment. Only those subjects making high total scores, (indicative of mal-adjustment), and those making very low scores (indicative of better than average adjustment), were selected as subjects. Additional criteria, such as teachers' ratings, and classroom observations, were used to supplement the test scores.

SUBJECTS

The Rogers Test of Personality Adjustment was administered to the entire seventh and eighth grades of the University High School. Thirty-two

Abridged from *Child Development*, 1945, 16, 181-188. Reprinted by permission of Child Development Publications.

subjects were selected from the two grades. They included all subjects whose total scores ranged below 34 ("well-adjusted") and above 40 ("maladjusted"). These scores were all corroborated by the teachers' ratings and seemed to reflect feelings of security and insecurity, respectively. The ages of the subjects ranged from 12 to 14 years. The group consisted of eleven girls and twenty-one boys.

THE TASK

The shorthand task consisted of a graded series of cards, containing letters of the alphabet arranged in random order. The subject was required to substitute shorthand symbols for these letters. A reference card, with the letters and symbols arranged alphabetcially, was available to the subject throughout the experiment. Each subject was given a practice period in which to become familiar with the symbols. He was instructed that he was not to memorize, merely to write as many symbols as possible in one-half minute. Ten trials, which were timed, constituted the test series.

The specific instructions for all subjects were as follows:

"Now I think you are ready to start. On these cards I have the letters of the alphabet arranged in different combinations and all lines are equally difficult. The only difference is that on this card there are 5 letters to a line, on the next 6, etc., up to 15. Now I shall time you to see how many symbols you can write in one-half minute. . . . You can choose any card you wish, but I first want you to tell me each time how many letters you *expect* to do on the next trial. . . . I will record the total number of symbols you write on each trial as your score. The idea is to write as many symbols as you can in one-half minute, but also to be as accurate as possible. You will have ten trials."

A record was kept of the subject's estimates and performance. The score was announced as the experimenter wrote it down opposite the estimate previously made. No effort was made to conceal the record from the subject at any time. After each trial, the question was repeated, "Now what do you expect to do next time?"

At the end of the ten trials, the experimenter asked each subject to write as many of the symbols as he could recall without a reference card.[1] He was praised and told that he had done "as well as others in your class," or "better than average," depending on his particular personality needs. The subjects were instructed not to discuss the experiment with anyone, in order to avoid the setting up of a group average, or standard. All subjects seemed

[1]The data were tested as to differences between the two groups in the number of symbols learned, but the difference was not significant.

to enjoy the test, probably because it was presented to them as a test to determine how well they could learn to write shorthand. They seemed highly motivated.

RESULTS

The data thus obtained were analyzed as follows:

(1) *D-scores,* defined as the average discrepancy between the estimate and the preceding performance, were calculated by dividing the algebraic sum of discrepancies on each trial by the total number of discrepancies (i.e., 9). The reliability of these scores for both groups combined was found to be .88, as determined by the split-half method and corrected by the Spearman-Brown formula.

For comparison of the two groups, the mean D-scores were calculated by dividing the algebraic sum of the individual D-scores by the number of subjects in each group (N=16).

The results presented below show a statistically significant difference between the two groups:

	Maladjusted[2] Group (N=16)	Well-adjusted[2] Group (N=16)
Mean D-score	0.08	1.14
Difference	1.06	
"t"	3.155	
Significance	beyond 1%	

These data would seem to indicate that, although both means are on the positive side, the maladjusted subjects tended to average approximately zero as a result of making very large over-estimates and under-estimates, whereas the well-adjusted subjects tended to have low-positive mean D-scores, as a result of more or less consistent positive discrepancies. In other words, the maladjusted subject tended to keep his estimates *below* his performance level, or to make gross compensatory over-estimates. Only in the maladjusted group did negative D-scores occur, whereas none of the well-adjusted subjects showed negative D-scores. This may indicate that for certain maladjusted subjects a possible explanation may be found in their fear of failure and greater need for success. Thus, by manipulating their estimates, they are able to protect themselves against failure and to insure successes, lending support to the hypothesis that the level of aspiration is an "ego-protective mechanism."

The well-adjusted subjected, on the other hand, tended more or less con-

---

[2]The terms "mal-adjusted" and "well-adjusted" shall be used henceforth for convenience in designating those with high and low Rogers scores respectively.

sistently to keep their estimates slightly *above* their performance level. These positive discrepancies appeared to serve the function of incentives, rather than over-estimates, and tended to be realistic, i.e., only one or two points above the previous performance level. Probably one reason that these subjects are able to maintain a positive discrepancy, even despite failures, may be due to their greater feeling of security and self-confidence.

(2) *Average deviations,* defined as the average of the deviations of the individual discrepancies from the D-score, were used as an index of variability. They were calculated by dividing the absolute sum of the deviations from the D-score, disregarding direction of difference, by the number of deviations (i.e., 9). This measure seems important, since two subjects with equal D-scores may have significantly different average deviations.

For comparison of the two groups, the *mean* of the individual average deviations was calculated for each group. The results are presented below, again showing a statistically significant difference between the two groups:

	Maladjusted Group (N=16)	Well-adjusted Group (N=16)
Mean of average deviations	1.24	0.78
Difference	0.46	
"t'	3.833	
Significance	beyond 1%	

These results seem to indicate that the maladjusted subjects tended to show significantly greater variability in their deviations from the D-score than the well-adjusted subjects. In other words, the maladjusted subjects tended either to over-estimate their ability, creating large positive discrepancies, or to under-estimate their ability, yielding large negative discrepancies. The low variability, characteristic of the well-adjusted subjects, probably indicates little more than individual variations and lack of rigidity.

(3) *Reactions to success and failure.* Success was defined as covering all those cases in which performance *surpassed* the previous estimate. Success was differentiated from "achievement," which comprised all those cases in which performance was *equal* to the previous estimate. Failure was defined as covering all those cases in which performance fell *below* the previous estimate. These operationally defined criteria for success and failure were in most cases corroborated by the subjects' verbal reactions, which were recorded verbatim as the score was announced. "Achievement" was usually experienced as success; the distinction was made chiefly to differentiate between the frequency of successes and achievements in each group. Successes seemed to be more characteristic of the maladjusted subjects, while achievements seemed to characterize the well-adjusted group. The differences in the distribution for success, achievement and failure were

found to be statistically significant at the 1 per cent level, as presented below:

Group	Distribution of Successes		Achievements and Failures	
	Total No. possible	Total No. of Successes	Total No. of Achievements	Total No. of Failures
Maladjusted	144	59	20	65
Well-adjusted	144	31	42	71

$X^2 = 16.3$, significant at the 1% level

Reactions to success and failure tended to show significant differences when analyzed in terms of the manner in which the new estimates "E" were shifted in relation to the previous estimate "e." The pertinent data are presented below:

Group	Total No. Successes	Reactions to Success		
		No. of times "E" raised above "e"	No. of times "E" remains equal to "e"	No. of times "E" lowered below "e"
Maladjusted	59	46 (78%)	9 (15%)	4 (7%)
Well-adjusted	31	31 (100%)	0 0	0 0

$X^2 = 5.41$, significant at the 5–10% level

Reactions to success indicate that the well-adjusted subjects tended to *raise* their estimates after success 100 per cent of the time, whereas the maladjusted subjects again appear to have been less consistent and even occasionally (7%) to have lowered their estimates after success.

More significant, and possibly of diagnostic value, are the reactions to failure, as presented below:

Group	Total No. Failures	Reactions to Failure		
		No. of times "E" raised above "e"	No. of times "E" remains equal to "e"	No. of times "E" lowered below "e"
Maladjusted	65	13 (20%)	15 (23%)	37 (57%)
Well-adjusted	71	5 (7%)	46 (65%)	20 (28%)

$X^2 = 21.8$, significant at the 1% level

These data seem to indicate that the maladjusted subjects tended to be much more sensitive to failure, since they lowered their estimates immediately in over 50 per cent of the cases. On the other hand, they tended to compensate for their failures by raising their estimates after failure significantly more often than the well-adjusted subjects. The latter, in contrast, tended characteristically to keep their estimates steady, i.e., they maintained the same estimates and "tried again" despite failure. Only infrequently, and usually after successive failures, did they lower their estimates somewhat. Inspection of the raw data indicates that the maladjusted subjects made much larger and more irregular shifts in their estimates, whereas the well-adjusted subjects tended to make more realistic and smaller adjustments of their estimates in relation to the previous performance.

QUALITATIVE INTERPRETATION OF RESULTS

In order to supplement the above quantitative analyses, certain qualitative analyses were made. The subjects were divided according to their D-scores into (1) high-positive, (2) low-positive, and (3) negative discrepancy groups. The data relative to their personality characteristics were derived from certain pertinent questions on the Rogers test, their verbal reactions to the task, etc. In addition, the subjects' I.Q.'s and grade point averages were available.[3]

(1) *High-positive discrepancy group.* A high-positive D-score was defined as any score above +1.1. Of the total group (N=32) twelve subjects fell into this group, five of whom were classified as maladjusted, and seven as well-adjusted. The maladjusted subjects in this group tended to give verbal evidence of insecurity and to show a need to compensate for failures by raising their estimates after failure.

The well-adjusted subjects in this group, on the other hand, tended to show more "tolerance" for failures. Their verbal reactions showed that they were more determined and they did not tend to compensate for failure by raising their estimates.

(2) *Low-positive discrepancy group.* A low-positive D-score was defined as any score ranging from +0.1 to +1.0. Fourteen of the total group fell into this group, with nine being well-adjusted and five mal-adjusted.

The maladjusted subjects in this group constituted a very mixed group and are difficult to describe. The well-adjusted subjects, however, were all characterized by self-confidence and realistic estimates, evidenced by the preponderance of "achievements" over successes.

An interesting and noteworthy difference between the subjects in this group, was found in the type of answers given to the question as to what they wanted to be when they "grow up." The well-adjusted subjects all gave very *specific* and concrete answers, viz. "research chemist, violinist, ice skater," etc., and in general these tended to be somewhat in accord with

---

[3]It should be noted here that the correlation between I.Q. and Rogers score (total) was $r = .01$, and between grade point average and Rogers score (total) was $r = .38$. Consequently, these measures may be regarded as relatively independent of the Rogers scores.

their abilities. The maladjusted subjects, on the other hand, without exception checked rather vague generalizations and ideals, such as "I want to be a leader in whatever town I live in," or "I want to be a very great person whom people will talk about" (question 4, Rogers test).

Thus it appears that the well-adjusted subjects tended to be more realistic, both in their appraisal of their abilities and in their level of aspiration behavior, while the maladjusted subjects seemed to be somewhat unrealistic and gave evidence of more than average cautiousness.

(3) *Negative discrepancy group.* A negative D-score was defined as any score with a minus sign. *All* the six subjects falling into this group were maladjusted and in every case showed evidence of great insecurity. They were characterized by a tendency toward self-depreciation and a somewhat self-conscious attitude.

The manner in which they manipulated their estimates seemed to indicate a fear of failure and a need to insure success by keeping their estimates *below* their performance level. In view of the fact that none of the well-adjusted subjects fell into this group or showed a negative D-score, the hypothesis may be advanced that a negative D-score might be indicative of personal insecurity and maladjustive tendencies. This, however, would have to be further tested with larger groups of subjects.

SUMMARY

Level of aspiration behavior was studied in relation to personality adjustment in adolescents, as determined by the Rogers Test of Personality Adjustment. The task consisted of a modified symbol substitution task, referred to as the shorthand task.

The results indicate that the differences in D-scores and average deviations are significant at the 1 per cent level between the two groups.

Reaction to failure showed characteristic tendencies toward compensation and/or fear of failure in the maladjusted subjects, in contrast to greater realism for the well-adjusted ones. A negative discrepancy was found to be characteristic of the mal-adjusted subjects only.

Generally, it appears that the level of aspiration behavior seems to reflect underlying personality needs and wants, and that it might be used as another measure of personality adjustment (as defined in this study). Furthermore, these findings suggest that it should be possible to test the hypothesis that, as the personality needs and wants are changed by appropriate training or experiences, a change in the level of aspiration behavior would appear.

REFERENCES—SECTION FOUR

Anderson, H. H., and Brandt, H. F. Study of motivation involving self-announced goals of fifth grade children and the concept of level of aspiration. *J. soc. Psychol.*, 1939, *10*, 209-232.

Ausubel, D. P., and Schiff, H. M. A level of aspiration approach to the measurement of goal tenacity. *J. Gen. Psychol.*, 1955, *52*, 97-110.

Chance, J. E. Personality differences and level of aspiration. *J. consult. Psychol.*, 1960, *24*, 111-115.

Clark, R. A., Teevan, R., and Ricciuti, H. N. Hope of success and fear of failure as aspects of need for achievement. *J. abnorm. soc. Psychol.*, 1956, *53*, 182-186.

Davids, A., and White, A. A. Effects of success, failure, and social facilitation on level of aspiration in emotionally disturbed and normal children. *J. Pers.*, 1958, *26*, 77-93.

Feather, N. T. Level of aspiration and achievement imagery. *Aust. J. Psychol.*, 1958, *10*, 319-328.

Frank, J. D. Individual differences in certain aspects of the level of aspiration. *Amer. J. Psychol.*, 1935, *47*, 119-129.

———. Some psychological determinants of level of aspiration. *Amer. J. Psychol.*, 1935, *47*, 285-293.

Gardner, J. W. Asipration-level in response to a prearranged sequence of scores. *J. exp. Psychol.*, 1939, *25*, 601-621.

———. The relation of certain personality variables to level of aspiration. *Psychol. Bull.*, 1939, *36*, 540.

Gould, R. Factors underlying expressed "level of aspiration." *J. Psychol.*, 1938, *6*, 265-279.

———. An experimental analysis of "level of aspiration." *Genet. Psychol. Monogr.*, 1939, *21*, 3-115.

———, and Lewis, H. B. Experimental investigation of factors governing changes in the meaning of the level of aspiration. *J. exp. Psychol.*, 1940, *27*, 422-439.

Grinder, R. E. Level of aspiration: A clarification. *Psychol. Rep.*, 1958, *4*, 470.

Hausche, J., and Gilchrist, J. C. Three determinants of the level of aspiration. *J. abnorm. soc. Psychol.*, 1956, *53*, 136-137.

Himmelweit, H. T. A comparative study of the level of aspiration of normal and neurotic persons. *Brit. J. Psychol.*, 1947, *37*, 41-59.

Holt, R. B. Level of aspiration: Ambition or defense? *J. exp. Psychol.*, 1946, *36*, 398-416.

Jessor, R., and Hess, H. F. Level of aspiration behavior and general adjustment: An appraisal of some negative findings. *Psychol. Rep.*, 1958, *4*, 335-339.

Kausler, D. H. The effects of a qualitative frame of reference on level of aspiration. *J. soc. Psychol.*, 1958, *48*, 217-221.

———. Aspiration level as a determinant of performance. *J. Pers.*, 1959, *27*, 346-351.

Krugman, A. D. A note on level-of-aspiration behavior and aging. *J. Geront.*, 1959, *14*, 222-225.

Lantz, B. Some dynamic aspects of success and failure. *Psychol. Monogr.*, 1945, *59*, No. 1.

Lewin, K., Dembo, T., Festinger, L., and Sears, P. Level of aspiration. In Hunt, J. McV. (Ed.), *Personality and Behavior Disorders*. New York: Ronald Press, 1944, 333-378.

Maag, C. H. A study of discrepancy between level of aspiration and ability. *USN Sch. Aviat. Med. proj. Rep.*, 1958, Proj. No. NM160111.

Mitchell, L. E. Aspiration levels of Negro delinquent, dependent, and public school boys. *J. Negro Educ.*, 1957, *26*, 80-85.

Neems, R., and Scodel, A. Authoritarianism and level of aspiration scores. *J. soc. Psychol.*, 1956, *43*, 209-215.

Preston, M. G., and Bayton, J. A. Differential effect of a social variable upon three levels of aspiration. *J. exp. Psychol.*, 1941, *29*, 351-369.

Raifman, I. Level of aspiration in a group of peptic ulcer patients. *J. consult. Psychol.*, 1957, *21*, 229-231.

Sears, P. S. Levels of aspiration in academically successful and unsuccessful children. *J. abnorm. soc. Psychol.*, 1940, *35*, 498-536.

————. Level of aspiration in relation to some variables of personality: Clinical studies. *J. soc. Psychol.*, 1941, *14*, 311-336.

————, and Levin, H. Levels of aspiration in preschool children. *Child. Develpm.*, 1957, *28*, 317-326.

Siegel, S. Level of aspiration and decision making. *Psychol. Rev.*, 1957, *64*, 253-262.

Siverstsen, D. Goal setting, the level of aspiration and social norms. *Acta psychol.*, 1957, *13*, 54-60.

Walter, L. M. The relation of sex, age, and school achievement to level of aspiration. *J. Educ. Psycho.*, 1951, *42*, 285-292.

SECTION

5

FRUSTRATION AND AGGRESSION

Usually an individual experiences a sense of frustration when his important motives (desires, wishes) are blocked or thwarted. When he is frustrated, a number of reactions occur. The individual becomes emotionally aroused; this in turn initiates certain forms of behavior. This behavior may be overtly and directly expressed; he may directly attack the frustrating agent. Or it may be expressed indirectly and in substitute fashion through fantasy, rationalization, projection, repression or other well known defense mechanisms. Doob and Sears (Paper No. 30) present four hypotheses (substantiated by objective and quantitative data) bearing on factors which determine substitute behavior and the degree of overt aggression in situations involving aggression. In line with these four hypotheses a number of generalizations are formulated. The effects of frustration, i.e., resultant behavior, depend on many important conditions among which are a) the kind and degree of emotion aroused, b) the importance of the need or motive as perceived by the individual, c) the individual's personality structure, d) his past experience, and e) the way he interprets the present situation. Moreover, the source of frustration may be either situational or external—as objects, other persons or situations; or it may be internal, *ie.*, due to psychological factors such as conflict, fear, low self-esteem, insecurity. Rosenzweig (Paper No. 31) was the first to attempt classifying apperceptive types of conscious reaction to frustration. There has since been a great deal of research on this subject. Rosenzweig describes three types of conscious reaction to frustration: "Extropunitive" (the individual experiences anger and indignation against others, whom he holds responsible), "Intropunitive" (the individual experiences humiliation and guilt, and blames himself), and "Impunitive" (the individual experiences embarrassment and shame, and seeks condonment.)

Fundamental to understanding frustration is a point which has been made by Maslow (Paper No. 29). He emphasizes the need of making a distinction between the concepts of deprivation and frustration, and he contends that not all situations involving deprivation (even of basic needs) necessarily result in frustration. It is only when the deprivation poses a threat to one's main life goals or basic needs (self-esteem or feelings of security) that frustration arises.

While aggression was long thought to be one of the most common reactions to frustration, it was not until publication of the book by Dollard, Doob *et al* entitled *Frustration and Aggression* than an organized hypothesis relating frustration and aggression was highlighted and propounded.[1] In this book the authors presented two basic postulates: a) that the occurence of aggression always presupposes the existence of frustration, b) that the existence of frustration always leads to some form of aggression. Both these postulates—the second in particular—aroused much criticism (Papers 28, 32, 33). Levy (Paper No. 28) illustrates by means of experiments with animals and human infants that there are many frustrating situations which do not evoke aggressive responses in the form of giving vent to hostile impulses "against a social object or its surrogates." Morlan (Paper No. 32) concerns himself primarily with attacking the catharsis aspect of the frustration-aggression hypothesis. He contends that the expression of a certain feeling such as hate or antagonism does not necessarily release and dissipate that feeling; instead the expression of a feeling may serve to strengthen that feeling. Criticisms led the authors to revise their original hypothesis. The authors (Paper No. 27), rephrased their original postulate that "the existence of

[1]Dollard, J., Doob, L. W., Miller, N. E., Mowrer, O. H., Sears, R. R., *Frustration and Aggression,* Yale University Press, New Haven, 1939.

frustration always leads to some form of aggression" to "frustration produces instigations to a number of different types of response, one of which is an instigation to some form of aggression."

One of the more recent and interesting hypotheses concerning frustration and aggression is that presented by Sargent (Paper No. 33), who also criticizes the frustration-aggression hypothesis. Sargent believes that frustration involves a sequence of behavior in which there are four important aspects: a) frustration, b) emotion, c) habit or mechanism, and d) overt behavior. Furthermore, he holds that each of these stages is always influenced by two important factors, the person's past experiences and his interpretation of the present situation.

27. Frustration-Aggression Hypothesis

Neal E. Miller (with the collaboration of Robert R. Sears, O. H. Mowrer, Leonard W. Doob and John Dollard)

THE frustration-aggression hypothesis is an attempt to state a relationship believed to be important in many different fields of research. It is intended to suggest to the student of human nature that when he sees aggression he should turn a suspicious eye on possibilities that the organism or group is confronted with frustration; and that when he views interference with individual or group habits, he should be on the look-out for, among other things, aggression. This hypothesis is induced from commonsense observation, from clinical case histories, from a few experimental investigations, from sociological studies and from the results of anthropological field work. The systematic formulation of this hypothesis enables one to call sharp attention to certain common characteristics in a number of observations from

Abridged from the *Psychological Review*, 1941, 48, 337-342. Reprinted by permission of the authors and the American Psychological Association, Inc.

all of these historically distinct fields of knowledge and thus to take one modest step toward the unification of these fields.

A number of tentative statements about the frustration-aggression hypothesis have recently been made by us in a book. Unfortunately one of these statements, which was conspicuous because it appeared on the first page, was unclear and misleading as has been objectively demonstrated by the behavior of reviewers and other readers. In order to avoid any further confusion it seems advisable to rephrase this statement, changing it to one which conveys a truer impression of the authors' ideas. The objectionable phrase is the last half of the proposition: "that the occurrence of aggression always presupposes the existence of frustration and, contrariwise, that the existence of frustration always leads to some form of aggression."

The first half of this statement, the assertion that the occurrence of aggression always presupposes frustration, is in our opinion defensible and useful as a first approximation, or working hypothesis. The second half of the statement, namely, the assertion "that the existence of frustration always leads to some form of aggression" is unfortunate from two points of view. In the first place it suggests, though it by no means logically demands, that frustration has no consequences other than aggression. This suggestion seems to have been strong enough to override statements appearing later in the text which specifically rule out any such implication. A second objection to the assertion in question is that it fails to distinguish between instigation to aggression and the actual occurrence of aggression. Thus it omits the possibility that other responses may be dominant and inhibit the occurrence of acts of aggression. In this respect it is *inconsistent* with later portions of the exposition which make a distinction between the instigation to a response and the actual presence of that response and state that punishment can inhibit the occurrence of acts of aggression.

Both of these unfortunate aspects of the former statement may be avoided by the following rephrasing: Frustration produces instigations to a number of different types of response, one of which is an instigation to some form of aggression.

This rephrasing of the hypothesis states the assumption that was actually used throughout the main body of the text. Instigation to aggression may occupy any one of a number of positions in the hierarchy of instigations aroused by a specific situation which is frustrating. If the instigation to aggression is the strongest member of this heirarchy, then acts of aggression will be the first response to occur. If the instigations to other responses incompatible with aggression are stronger than the instigation to aggression, then these other responses will occur at first and prevent, at least temporarily, the occurrence of acts of aggression. This opens up two further possibilities. If these other responses lead to a reduction in the instigation to the originally frustrated response, then the strength of the instigation to aggression is also reduced so that acts of aggression may not occur at all in the situation in question. If, on the other hand, the first responses do not lead to a reduction in the original instigation, then the instigations to them will tend to become weakened through extinction so that the next most dominant responses, which may or may not be aggression, will tend to occur. From this analysis it follows that the more successive responses of non-aggression are extinguished by continued frustration, the greater is the probability that the instigation to aggression eventually will become dominant so that some response of aggression actually will occur. Whether or not the successive extinction of responses of non-aggression must inevitably lead to the dominance of the instigation to aggression depends, as was clearly stated in later pages of the book, upon quantitative assumptions beyond the scope of our present knowledge.

Frustration produces instigation to aggression but this is not the only type of instigation that it may produce. Responses incompatible with aggression may, if sufficiently instigated, prevent the actual occurrence of acts of aggression. In our society punishment of acts of aggression is a frequent source of instigation to acts incompatible with aggression.

When the occurrence of acts of aggression is prevented by more strongly instigated incompatible responses, how is the existence of instigation to aggression to be determined? If only the more direct and overt acts of aggression have been inhibited, as is apt to be the case because such acts are the most likely to be punished, then the instigation to aggression may be detected by observing either indirect or less overt acts of aggression. If even such acts of aggression are inhibited, then a different procedure must be employed. Two such procedures are at least theoretically possible. One is to reduce the competing instigations, such as fear of punishment, and observe whether or not acts of aggression then occur. The other is to confront the subject with an additional frustration which previous experiments have demonstrated would by itself be too weak to arouse an instigation strong enough to override the competing responses inhibiting the aggression in question. If the instigation from this additional frustration now results in an act of aggression, then it must have gained its strength to do so by summating with an already present but inhibited instigation to aggression. The presence of the originally inhibited instigation to aggression would be demonstrated by the effects of such summation. Thus the fact that an instigation may be inhibited does not eliminate all possibility of experimentally demonstrating its presence.

At this point two important and related qualifications of the hypothesis may be repeated for emphasis though they have already been stated in the book. It is not certain how early in the infancy of the individual the frustration-aggression hypothesis is applicable, and no assumptions are made as to whether the frustration-aggression relationship is of innate or of learned origin.

Now that an attempt has been made to clarify and to qualify the hypothesis, four of the chief lines of investigation which it suggests may be briefly considered.

1.   An attempt may be made to apply the hypothesis to the integration and elucidation of clinical and social data. Here the fact that certain forms of aggression are spectacularly dangerous to society and to the individual is relevant. This means that acute personality conflicts are apt to arise from the problem of handling aggression and that the problem of aggression is apt to play an important role in shaping certain great social institutions such as the in-group as an organization against the out-group.

2.   An attempt may be made to formulate more exactly the laws determining the different ways in which instigation to aggression will be expressed under specified circumstances. Some of the problems in this field are suggested by the phenomena of displacement of the object of aggression, change in the form of aggression, and catharsis of aggression.

3.   An attempt may be made to secure more information concerning the other consequences which frustration may produce in addition to the instigation to aggression. Such an attempt would lead into studies of rational thought and problem solution as suggested in the classical work of John Dewey, and into studies of experimental extinction, trial-an-error learning, substitute response and regression. Work along this line of investigation may deal either with the clinical and social significance of these other consequences of frustration or with the discovery of the laws governing them.

4.   An attempt may be made to improve or to reformulate the basic frustration-aggression hypothesis itself. The determination of the laws which allow one to predict exactly under which circumstances instigation to aggression may be expected to occupy the dominant, the second, the third, or some other position in the hierarchy of instigations roused by a frustrating situation is a most important problem of this type. Another problem is the reduction of the frustration-aggression hypothesis to more fundamental principles and the more accurate restatement of the hypothesis in terms of these more basic principles. One of the steps in this direction would be to scrutinize any exceptions to the hypothesis as now formulated. Another step would involve a careful study of the early stages of the socialization of the individual in an attempt to analyze the interlocking roles of three factors: first, innate physiological reaction patterns; second, learning mechanisms; and third, the structure of the social maze which poses the learning dilemmas and contains the rewards and punishments. An empirical and theoretical analysis along these lines might lead to a fundamental reformulation giving

a closer approximation of the socially and scientifically useful truths imperfectly expressed in the present frustration-aggression hypothesis.

28. The Hostile Act

David M. Levy

IN *Frustration and Aggression* the situations in which frustration occurs always call for aggression, in terms of an attack on a frustrating agent. If no frustrating agent is present, then some object must be created for the purpose of relieving aggressive tendencies that arise in the frustrating situations. The need varies according to the tolerance to frustration. If the tolerance is poor, then some aggressor must be fabricated. A thwarted individual would then displace the aggression onto a system or onto any group representing a constellation of ideas that evoked hostility, no matter how mild, in the previous experience of the individual. This is all a familiar type of psychodynamics, namely the release of tensions arising from frustration and the use of an available object for its expression. To say, however, that aggression arises as a result of any frustrating experience is a generalization that requires scrutiny.

There are any number of frustrations that do not evoke aggressive response in the sense of discharging hostility against a social object or its surrogates. There are for example, a number of experiments in which animals are frustrated and in which such aggression does not occur. In my own work on the sucking behavior of dogs, an experiment was made in which two puppies were given adequate milk from the bottle, but fed so quickly that their sucking needs were never satisfied. In contrast to the two 'control' puppies who were given adequate satisfactions both of feeding and of sucking, the experimental animals showed no problem in aggression that could be directly traced to the sucking frustration. The result was rather a type of perverted sucking. They sucked each other, their own paws, objects, and later on, after eating, they licked the plate interminably. In terms of general personality description, one of the experimental puppies could

Abridged from the *Psychological Review*, 1941, 48, 356-361. Reprinted by permission of the author and the American Psychological Association, Inc.

be described as more aggressive than the controls, the other less so. But these differences, it could be shown, were modes of reaction that occurred in the beginning of the experiment and were probably reinforced by the particular difficulty of the situation. I do not wish to elaborate this point, except to say that the puppy who was originally aggressive became more so, in certain respects, after the sucking difficulty was established, whereas the other puppy became more submissive.

In chickens in which pecking frustrations were produced, there was also no evidence of increased aggression. In the experiment 100 chicks were fed from troughs in the usual way, but prevented from pecking off the ground by covering it with a raised wire mesh. The control group of 100 in the adjoining half of the same chicken house were fed from troughs, but not prevented from pecking from the ground. The chickens on the wire pecked each other's feathers but, as the experiment revealed, the pecking was not due to increased aggression but to increased pecking needs. This same type of situation has been shown for other animals and for human infants also. The sucking frustrations in infancy cause finger sucking or sucking of other objects, as in the case of the experimental puppies, rather than increased aggression. There is no proof that the so-called weaning traumas of infancy cause more aggression or even more phantasies of hostility and the like than in other children. The same may be said of all those frustrations that have to do with bowel and bladder control.

A distinction may be made between the type of aggression described, especially in regard to sucking habits, and the situations of the type described by Dr. Dollard and his colleagues. The former may be called physiologic, the latter social types of frustration. However, Dr. Dollard has included the type of physiologic frustration I have mentioned as typically provocative of aggression. His generalization could be easily amended. It is a question, however, as to whether numerous situations in which the individual does not deal directly with frustration readily translatable into terms of an aggressor, typically stimulate the aggressive rejoinder, for example, frustrations arising out of one's own inability to solve a mathematical problem and the like. The fact that tension may arise in any such instance, and that this tension is released by some motor action, whether tapping a pencil or pacing the floor, does not mean it is an aggressive act in a social sense. Furthermore, acts that typically call for aggressive behavior in certain individuals may affect others differently. To say that in such cases the aggression should follow but is repressed would require considerable study. Aggression is one of the ways of responding to frustration in a social situation. Presumably it varies in the strength of its impulse and its execution in different individuals. In the phantasies that occur during frustration, or in the choice of behavior to satisfy the particular tensions that arise, various possibilities occur. To state that only one possibility, namely the aggressive act, is the logical response to frustration, all others being forms of extemporizing, needs further proof.

The response of a child to the new baby is a very good example of a frustrating situation commonly evoking aggressive behavior in the form of an assault on the baby or mother, or both. However, though this pattern is seen most frequently, there are instances in which it does not occur. For example, a child may respond to the coming of the baby with, primarily, a desire to possess it, to have it for one's own. This is not an aggressive response in the form of an assault on a social object, yet the reaction may be a very strong one. The new baby may call forth a very strong maternal protective attitude, especially when the prior child is a girl, say eight or ten years older than the new-born. In this situation there is a frustrating experience highly reduced as compared with one in which the age difference is only two or four years. Nevertheless, such situations may reveal frustration and yet show a maternal response as a primary determinant. It may be argued that the maternal response represents jealousy of the mother and hence a concealed aggression against her. That is to say, one may always argue in favor of the theory of aggression as against any other form of behavior in a similar situation. As yet, we have no definite proof that is always the case.

In regard to sibling rivalry, however, the aggressive response to the new baby is so typical that it is safe to say it is a common feature of family life. As seen in 'control situations' the aggressive act in its various forms is depicted so clearly that the dynamic process is worth describing. In the control situation dolls are used representing the baby at the mother's breast and an older child who stands for the patient. If it is a boy the question used to set off the behavior is: "And then the brother sees the new baby at the mother's breast. He never saw him before. What does he do?"

In reviewing the patterns of over 100 S-R experiments of children ranging from two to thirteen years, it is most useful to conceive of the act as an ongoing social process, a dynamic unit of behavior, with various influences brought to bear upon it in every phase. The completed primitive performance is an act in which the child attacks the baby doll and destroys it by biting it, tearing it with his fingers, or crushing it with his feet. If the experiment is repeated, there is, in most of the instances at ages three, four and five, a fulfillment of hostile activity of this type. In others there are varying approaches to this end-point, easily observed and measured. In the beginning of the act when, presumably, the impulse to attack is felt, one observes varying forms of inhibitions to the impulse, so that the act does not come out. These may be in the form of pauses, of saying, "I don't know what to do," of attempting to change the play into some other form, to play with other objects, or even to get out of the playroom. Sometimes the first act is to slap the doll standing for the subject. When a three-year-old girl was asked, "Why did you do that?" she said, "Because she was bad. She wanted to hit the baby." This type of response indicates that the hostile impulse had to be dealt with before the act occurred, that the impulse itself was judged to be bad, that the thought of the act had to be dealt with by punishment as though it were already fulfilled. The inhibition of the impulse may take the form of assumed stupidity like, "I don't know what you mean. I don't know what you want." Such inferences are based on the fact that without any explanation, merely by saying "Go ahead" and repeating the experiment, the hostile act in such cases follows.

Without elaborating the meaning of the various kinds of inhibitions that take place before the act overtly occurs, it may be sufficient to say that we are dealing with repressions and, I believe, the equivalent of superego injunctions; that is to say, the child is in its impulse to act identifying itself with the attitude of a prohibiting parent.

Once the act goes into execution we see a number of efforts to deflect its aim so that the object of hostility will not be reached. At this point a common form of inhibition is a blocking of the act, as, for example, a slapping movement made at the doll which is held back. Another common form is displacement, whereby an object close to the doll is hit and the doll itself avoided. This may be seen also in the form of non-specific aggression, in which the child shoots at the ceiling, or at various objects in a direction entirely different from that of the baby doll.

So far we may say of the modifying influences that occur when the impulse to act is felt, the inhibiting influences tend to block the act when they occur at its initial point (the impulse) and, once the act goes into execution, to reduce it to a gesture or shunt it off.

Even when the object is directly hit, modifications of the attack at the target appear. For example, the hit may change into a touch. Instead of being struck at, the baby is just removed, or dropped. At this point, too, the attack may be disguised. The child takes the baby away and says, "It has to go to the hospital for an operation," and the like. As, presumably, the behavior of the child is released, the attack on the baby becomes free of all modifying forms and the object is destroyed in the manner described.

Even when the baby doll is attacked freely and crushed, the act is not necessarily completed. We are aware at this phase of a number of activities that prove its incompleteness. For example, a child after attacking the baby and crushing it, begins to defend itself for its behavior. The child says, "It was a bad baby." Another child says at this point, "We don't need two babies in one house." Commonly at this stage the doll standing for the brother or sister is attacked, usually with the same method used on the baby. Another common pattern is seen in attempts to restore the baby, to make it come to life again, to fix it up, to deny what happened, and say, "The baby fell apart. Now it's all together again." One child at this stage said it was all a dream, it didn't happen. We see in these various performances that take place in the completion of the hostile attack on the baby, restoring behavior, self-retaliatory behavior, attempts at self-justification, and attempts to wash out the act by attributing to it the aspect of a dream or just play. In several cases children had a kind of war dance after achieving their purpose. In line with other patterns it would be interesting to speculate on this type of war dance as a way of warding off anxiety described in psychoanalytic literature.

Through these control situation experiments we see depicted the type of aggression of which Dr. Dollard and his colleagues have written in clear form, influenced in every stage of their study by the emotional problems of the individual.

29. Deprivation, Threat, and Frustration

A. H. Maslow

It is easy in the discussion of frustration to fall into the error of segmenting the human being. That is to say, there is still a tendency to speak of the mouth or stomach being frustrated, or of a need being frustrated. We must keep in mind constantly the truism that only a whole human being is frustrated, never a part of a human being.

With this in mind, an important distinction becomes apparent, namely the difference between deprivation and threat to the personality. The usual definitions of frustration are in terms simply of not getting what one desires, of interference with a wish, or with a gratification. Such a definition fails to make the distinction between a deprivation which is unimportant to the

Abridged from the *Psychological Review*, 1941, 48, 364-366. Reprinted by permission of the author and the American Psychological Association, Inc.

organism (easily substituted for, with few serious after-effects), and, on the other hand, a deprivation which is at the same time, a threat to the personality, that is, to the life goals of the individual, to his defensive system, to his self-esteem or to his feeling of security. It is our contention that only a threatening deprivation has the multitude of effects (usually undesirable) which are commonly attributed to frustration in general.

A goal object may have two meanings for the individual. First it has its intrinsic meaning, and secondly, it may have also a secondary, symbolic value. Thus a certain child deprived of an ice-cream cone which he wanted may have lost simply an ice-cream cone. A second child, however, deprived of an ice-cream cone, may have lost not only a sensory gratification, but may also feel deprived of the love of his mother because she refused to buy it for him. For the second boy the ice-cream cone not only has an intrinsic value, but may also be the carrier of psychological values. Being deprived merely of ice-cream *qua* ice-cream probably means very little for a healthy individual, and it is questionable whether it should even be called by the same name, *i.e.,* frustration, which characterizes other more threatening deprivations. It is only when a goal object represents love, prestige, respect, or achievement that being deprived of it will have the bad effects ordinarily attributed to frustration in general.

It is possible to demonstrate very clearly this twofold meaning of an object in certain groups of animals and in certain situations. For instance, it has been shown that when two monkeys are in a dominance-subordination relationship a piece of food is (1) an appeaser of hunger and also (2) a symbol of dominance status. Thus if the subordinate animal attempts to pick up food, he will at once be attacked by the dominant animal. If, however, he can deprive the food of its symbolic dominance value, then his dominator allows him to eat it. This he can do very easily by a gesture of obeisance, *i.e.,* presentation as he approaches the food; this is as if to say, "I want this food only to still hunger, I do not want to challenge your dominance. I readily concede your dominance." In the same way we may take a criticism from a friend in two different ways. Ordinarily the average person will respond by feeling attacked and threatened (which is fair enough because so frequently criticism is an attack). He therefore bristles and becomes angry in response. But if he is assured that this criticism is not an attack or a rejection of himself, he will then not only listen to the criticism, but possibly even be grateful for it. Thus, if he has already had thousands of proofs that his friend loves him and respects him, the criticism represents only criticism; it does not also represent an attack or threat.

Neglect of this distinction has created a great deal of unnecessary turmoil in psychoanalytic circles. An ever-recurring question is: Does sexual deprivation inevitably give rise to all or any of the many effects of frustration, e.g., aggression, sublimation, etc. It is now well known that many cases are found in which celibacy has no psychopathological effects. In many other cases, however, it has many bad effects. What factor determines which shall be the result? Clinical work with non-neurotic people gives the clear answer that sexual deprivation becomes pathogenic in a severe sense only when it is felt by the individual to represent rejection by the opposite sex, inferiority, lack of worth, lack of respect, or isolation. Sexual deprivation can be borne with relative ease by individuals for whom it has no such implications. (Of course, there will probably be what Rosenzweig calls need-persistive reactions, but these are not necessarily pathological.)

The unavoidable deprivations in childhood are also ordinarily thought of as frustrating. Weaning, elimination control, learning to walk, in fact every new level of adjustment, is conceived to be achieved by forceable pushing of the child. Here, too, the differentiation between mere deprivation and threat to the personality enjoins caution upon us. Observation of children who are completely assured of the love and respect of their parents have shown that deprivations can sometimes be borne with astonishing ease. There are few frustration effects if these deprivations are not conceived by the child to be threatening to his fundamental personality, to his main life goals, or needs.

From this point of view, it follows that the phenomenon of threatening frustration is closely allied to other threat situations much more than it is to mere deprivation. The classic effects of frustration are also found frequently to be a consequence of other types of threat—traumatization, conflict, rejection, severe illness, actual physical threat, imminence of death, humiliation, isolation, or loss of prestige.

This leads us to our final hypothesis, that perhaps frustration as a single concept is less useful than the two concepts which cross-cut it, (1) deprivation, and (2) threat to the personality. Deprivation implies much less than is ordinarily implied by the concept of frustration; threat implies much more.

30. Factors Determining Substitute Behavior and the Overt Expression of Aggression

Leonard W. Doob and

Robert R. Sears

T HE proposition has been presented elsewhere that aggression is a response to frustration. According to this view a frustration is any interference with a goal-response, whether the interference be caused by some hampering agent or by a conflict of responses within the organism itself. The frustration produces unique changes within the organism which serve as instigation to aggressive behavior. The strength of the frustration-induced instigation, in turn, is reduced by this aggressive behavior and may be called *secondary* to distinguish it more readily from the *primary* instigation to the original (frustrated) goal-response. The situation is similar to that of any response which is dependent on a specifiable drive. When a child, for instance, is hungry, it may be said to be instigated to eat; after carrying out the act of eating, the instigation is presumed to have been reduced in strength, since the eating behavior stops. Aggression differs from many other goal-responses, however, in that the instigation to it is produced by interference with any other pre-established goal-response rather than by recurrent intraorganismic changes such as those involved in hunger, thirst, demands for social approval, etc.

The importance of this distinction between primary and secondary (frustration-induced) instigation lies in the systematic differentiation of substitute responses from aggression. That all frustrating situations do not produce overt aggression is immediately evident. An employee who fails to receive an expected promotion is more likely to double his efforts or

Abridged from the *Journal of Abnormal and Social Psychology*, 1939, 34, 293-313. Reprinted by permission of the authors and The American Psychological Association, Inc.

search for a new job or treat himself to some small luxury than to berate his employer in a face-to-face conversation. While the latter response would be typically aggressive, the more frequently occurring responses to such a frustration seem to contain little or no aggression and may be more appropriately classified as substitute responses. They are substitutes in the sense that they tend to reduce the strength of the primary instigation to the original frustrated goal-response. Redoubled efforts and the search for a new job permit the development of new anticipations of promotion, anticipations which in themselves are rewarding, i.e., constitute goal-responses. The indulgence in a small luxury is a fractional part of the total set of goal-responses which would have occurred had the original frustration of non-promotion not occurred. Such responses may be facilitated by the secondary, frustration-induced instigation but they are, in the main, responses to the original, primary instigation to economic self-betterment.

In so far as any substitute response is "pure", i.e., contains no aggressive component, it will reduce the strength of the primary instigation. Aggression reduces the strength of the secondary, frustration-induced instigation only. But since substitute responses reduce the primary instigation, they likewise reduce the strength of the frustration and hence reduce the probability of occurrence of aggressive behavior.

In many frustrating situations, however, it is difficult to find evidence of either substitute responses or overt aggression in the behavior of the frustrated person. It is necessary, consequently, if the frustration-aggression hypothesis is to be maintained, to postulate some form of unexpressed or *non-overt* aggression. And, in fact, brief questioning of a frustrated individual will often elicit such statements as "I'm angry" or "I'd like to get even with him" or "I'll kill him in my dreams for a week!" While these do not involve any immediate aggressive action against the frustrating agent, they must nevertheless be considered as aggressions from the conceptual standpoint.

It may be said, then, that frustration is followed not only by *aggression which may vary in the degree to which it is expressed overtly,* but also by *substitute responses* as well. The problem attacked in the present study is the isolation of factors which determine the occurrence of these possible alternatives as reactions to frustration and, in the case of aggression, the factors which determine the occurrence of overt or non-overt aggression.

Two hypotheses may be suggested to account for the occurrence of substitute responses rather than aggression: first, that the frequency of substitute responses varies positively with the strength of anticipatory responses to punishment-for-being-aggressive; and second, that the frequency of substitute responses varies inversely with the strength of the frustrated goal-responses.

First hypothesis. It is clear that almost any form of behavior can be suppressed or eliminated by punishment; the law of effect is the most familiar statement of this fact. During the process of learning, an organism develops anticipatory responses to the punishment which on later occasions serve to block or inhibit the proscribed behavior. *It is these anticipatory responses to punishment that are reflected in verbal judgments of anticipating or expecting.* This first hypothesis implies that aggressive behavior is punished more frequently than substitute behavior. While this contention would be difficult to prove categorically even in our own relatively well-documented society, certain logical necessities give the assumption an appearance of validity. Substitute responses are by definition actions that are relatively non-aggressive; when other persons are involved in the situation, therefore, they are not so frustrated as they would be by aggressive actions. Since they are less frustrated, they, in turn, are not so likely to become counter-aggressive. As a consequence, relatively less counter-aggression, or punishment, is anticipated by a frustrated individual when he responds to the frustration with a substitute response than when he responds to the frustration with overt aggression. If then, substitute responses are less often followed by punishment[1] and if the amount of punishment received in the past for a given act determines the extent to which it is eliminated, there should be a greater frequency of substitute responses when subjects express a greater amount of anticipation of punishment for being aggressive.

Second hypothesis. If the above principle is true, it follows that an increase in the strength of instigation to the aggressive responses could overcome the inhibiting strength of the anticipatory responses to punishment. Hovland and Sears have suggested that the strengths of such incompatible or antagonistic responses summate algebraically; and, since in this case the strength of the aggressive responses varies positively with the strength of the frustrated goal-responses, it can be concluded that the amount or frequency of substitute responses will vary inversely with the strength of the drive.[2]

The factors determining the overtness of aggression are somewhat similar to those determining the occurrence of substitute responses and may be expressed in the form of two further hypotheses: third, that overtness varies inversely with the amount of punishment anticipated as a consequence of

[1] All substitute responses are not socially acceptable (e.g., some forms of delinquency, compensations for felt inferiority, etc.), but in general substitute behavior appears to interrupt the activities of others less than does aggressive behavior.

[2] In a previous communication the postulate that *the strength of any frustration-reaction, including aggression, varies positively with the strength of the instigation to the frustrated goal-responses* was presented as necessarily fundamental to any quantitative theory of conflict and frustration.

such behavior; and fourth, that overtness varies positively with the strength of the instigation to the frustrated goal-response.

Third hypothesis. The reasoning which leads to the formulation of the third hypothesis is essentially the same as that described for the first, except for the fact that the assumption concerning the kind of behavior most often punished relates to overt and non-overt aggression rather than to aggression as a whole and substitute responses. Evidence such as the following lends support to the belief that overt aggression is frequently punished in American society. Wickman obtained 511 teachers' ratings on the relative seriousness of a list of 50 school behavior problems. Each problem was rated on a 20-point graphic-rating scale. Of the 50 behavior problems, 12 were clearly overt forms of aggression and were given an average rating of 12.3. The remaining 38 problems (including three which might indicate non-overt aggression: "unhappy or depressed," "easily discouraged," "sensitiveness") were given an average rating of 11.1. Overtly aggressive behavior was placed, therefore, in the upper half of the list in terms of seriousness. That this finding probably reflects the teachers' attitudes toward the reprehensibility of such behavior is indicated by the fact that 30 child psychiatrists judged the same items as having a seriousness rating of only 8.9, while the remaining items were given an average rating of 9.7. If these 511 teachers from New Jersey, New York, Ohio and Minnesota can be considered a fair sample of the disciplining group in the American classroom, it may be said with considerable certainty that overt aggression meets with serious objection from those who are in a position to punish.[3] Direct evidence that people anticipate more punishment for overt than for non-overt aggression has been obtained from the present study and will be presented in the second section of the Results. From this reasoning the hypothesis is derived that the amount or frequency of overt aggression varies inversely with the strength of the anticipatory responses to punishment.

Fourth hypothesis. Here again reference must be made to the assumption that the strengths of incompatible responses summate algebraically. When the strength of the frustrated goal-responses and hence that of the overt aggressive reactions is great, the inhibiting influence of the anticipatory responses to punishment may be overcome, with the result that the overt aggression will occur. The greater the strength of the original goal-responses, the greater is the probability of this outcome.

Although the terms overt and non-overt aggression have been used freely in describing the particular kinds of behavior here studied, it must be remembered that they refer to extremes of a continuum. In actual fact it must be presumed that there are very many discriminable divisions on the

---

[3] Some forms of overt aggression are permissible and encouraged in our culture (e.g., competitive sports, school spirit, chivalric aggression, etc.).

scale of "degree of overtness"; but until some method for equating and ordering these divisions is discovered, only the extremes may be safely used. In the discussion below the following abbreviations are used:

O—Overt aggression
N—Non-overt aggression
S—Substitute responses

The variables presented in the four hypotheses above by no means exhaust the possible list of factors which determine the kind of response to be made in a frustrating situation; they represent simply first approximations. Most seriously lacking is an hypothesis to account for the occurrence of substitute responses rather than non-overt aggression when overt aggression has been punished. Since, however, this differentiation probably is dependent on complex learning experiences during long periods of development, the particular technique of the present investigation has not seemed applicable to a study of the problem.

Additional factors of possible importance in determining overtness of aggression may be suggested.

1. Degree of anticipation of success in overcoming the frustration by being overtly aggressive.

2. Degree of submissiveness ("invitation to aggression") on the part of the frustrating agent.

3. Frequency of the given frustration in the subject's past experience.

4. Degree to which generalization of response exists in the subject; i.e., the degree to which he has a *trait* of being overtly or non-overtly aggressive.

These suggested factors fall within the systematic structure of a reaction psychology and hence are congruent with the four hypotheses tested in the present study.

It has been assumed elsewhere and it is assumed here that overt, direct aggression against the agent which is perceived as the source of frustration is most satisfying to the organism, i.e., is the response to which there is strongest instigation. Whether this tendency to avenge a frustration by attacking the frustrator is original or learned by people in various societies is a question which must be raised but which only future research can answer.

It is known, however, that the most satisfying response is not always the one which is tolerated by society; socialization, in fact, has as one of its functions the inculcation of taboos—the anticipation of punishment for carrying out certain acts. If, even though individuals find a mode of behavior very satisfying, its occurrence is simultaneously inhibited, then it is reasonable to conclude that they have been socialized to the extent that they are able to anticipate punishment from acts which they also anticipate to be satisfying. Evidence concerning the degree of satisfaction and amount of punishment to be anticipated as a consequence of overt and non-overt aggression and substitute responses is given in the second section of the Results.

A psychological systematization of the problem, however, is not necessarily the unique method of formulating it. From a sociological standpoint the question might be phrased: to what degree are various situations frustrating and to what degree do they lead to substitutive behavior or to the overt expression of aggression? In this case, where the *situation* as a measurable social phenomenon is made the key to the problem, an examination can be made either of the behavior of representative members of a society in terms of their conformity to cultural norms or of a situation in the society itself in terms of such behavioral variables as the overtness of aggression. The latter type of analysis permits generalizations concerning culturally described situations; these generalizations not only have behavioral relevance but actually explain social and cultural phenomena by reference to the laws of behavior of the individuals who compose the social body portraying the phenomena. An example of this method of interpretation of social psychological data is given below in the third sub-section of the Results.

METHOD

To test the four hypotheses presented above, data were obtained concerning the previous behavior of subjects in certain frustrating situations which had been fairly common in the lives of all the members of the group. To facilitate uniformity both in the subjects' understanding of the described situations and in their techniques of recall and estimation, a standardized form was prepared on which each subject could record the data from his own recollections.

Construction of the questionnaire. A brief description was prepared of each of 53 situations which either on *a priori* grounds or because of their presence in Cason's list of annoyances seemed to be definitely frustrating and to occur fairly frequently to Yale College students. Three of these descriptions exemplify the list adequately.

1. A policeman reprimands you vigorously and unjustly, perhaps gives you a ticket, for a traffic offense when you are accompanied by a girl whose good opinion you value.

2. You have made extensive and expensive plans for a date. The girl informs you at the last moment that she cannot come and the reason for her breaking the date seems a very inadequate one to you.

3. An instructor announces an unexpected examination for the next meeting of the class.

The list of situations was given to a group of 30 Yale College students enrolled in an elementary course in Personality. The instructions were as follows:

1. Read each item carefully.

2. After reading an item, stop for a moment and recall the last occasion when that or something very similar happened to you.

3. Describe briefly what you did in that situation, what your thoughts were, and what your emotions (if any) were. If you have never found yourself in such a situation, mark a cross in the blank space beneath the item.

From the answers obtained in this fashion, sixteen test items were selected for use in the final form of the questionnaire. Two criteria dictated their selection: first, high frequency of occurrence as indicated by the number who answered each item; and second, the occurrence in each situation of all three kinds of response, O, N, and S. A large number of items had to be discarded because they evidently occurred so infrequently in the students' lives that even in a large group only a few persons would have suffered them. A lesser number were discarded because they elicited, too uniformly, only overt or non-overt aggression or substitute responses.

From these free descriptions at least one characteristic reaction of each of the three types, O, N, and S, was obtained for each of the sixteen situations; for most of the sixteen situations more than three alternatives were secured, but all were classifiable as one of the three types of response (O, N, S). Each reaction was phrased as briefly as possible (see examples below) to insure that the alternatives should be sufficiently extreme in their respective categories. Five psychologists who were familiar with the descriptive concepts employed were asked to rate each alternative under each situation as O, N, or S. Among these judges there was almost complete agreement. Such difference of opinion as there was appeared to derive largely from uncertainty as to the "purity" of a reaction's classification; for example, several of the S reactions were judged to involve a slight degree of N as well. These ambiguities were largely eliminated by rewording the descriptions of the responses.[4]

For each situation a four-point rating scale was prepared on which could be answered quantitatively a question as to the strength of the instigation to the frustrated goal-responses. Each of these questions was examined by the five judges to determine whether it referred accurately to the instigation of the frustrated goal-responses.

[4]Several of the S alternatives appear to represent "substitute gratifications" rather than "substitute responses" to the original instigation. The systematic relationship between these two concepts is not entirely clear at present, and it may be that they operate according to different laws. Since the only effect of combining the two concepts can be to attenuate the differences reported under the first two hypotheses, no attempt will be made to analyze the data differentially in terms of the two concepts.

Final form of the questionnaire. The page of instructions used with the final form of the questionnaire included a sample situation which was not scored in the tabulation of results. The form of presentation of each of the other sixteen situations was the same as that of the first three, which are shown below to indicate more adequately the types of responses presented as alternatives for the subjects to check. After each response is shown in parentheses the category to which the response belongs.

1. You saw an item in the paper which described a case of conspicuous and unnecessary brutality and cruelty on the part of the police.

> I boiled up inside and wanted to do something about it but did not know what I could do. (N)
> I thought what I would like to do to the police. (N)
> I wrote a sharp letter to the newspaper, condemning such actions. (O)
> I quickly began to think of something more pleasant. (S)
> I protested to the chief of police. (O)
> I felt angry. (N)
> I talked to my friends about the brutality of the police. (O)

How strongly did you feel that the police should not use violence?

2. In a semi-formal group you heard a sneering comment about Yale which you felt was unjustified. You discovered that the speaker was a stranger whose appearance you disliked anyway.

> I made a slurring remark in return to put him in his place. (O)
> I unobtrusively left the group. (S)
> I was disgusted or felt resentful, but did not go to the trouble of challenging him. (N)
> I ignored him and diplomatically turned the conversation to another topic. (S)

How warmly did you feel toward Yale at that time?

3. Someone sitting in a seat near you in a theater or concert wiggled and squirmed about in a totally unnecessary way.

> I made some uncomplimentary remarks about him to my companions. (O)
> I moved to another seat. (S)
> He made me sore and disgusted; it almost ruined the performance for me. (N)
> I told him to keep quiet. (O)

How much did you want to enjoy the performance in peace and quiet?

The remaining 13 situations were as follows:

4. You were behaving decorously at a party and an acquaintance who was too drunk spilled some food, his drink, or cigarette ashes all over you.

5. You had to get out of bed after you had gone to sleep in order to

answer the telephone. It proved to be someone who had gotten the wrong number.

6. You tried to have a calm and rational discussion with a good friend about some rather emotional topic (e.g., religion, politics, morals), but he lost his temper and refused to be calm and rational.

7. A guest of yours whom you knew only slightly persisted in telling you how to drive, and in general, pestered you with "back-seat" criticisms.

8. A good friend of yours was driving so recklessly that you were genuinely scared out of your wits.

9. You were in the midst of a task that was taxing your patience (e.g., changing a tire) and a stranger, trying to be helpful, added his cheerful but utterly impractical suggestions.

10. You were bored stiff by a conversation of friends, but the social situation was such that you had to endure it for several minutes at least.

11. In an informal social gathering of people with whom you were not very well acquainted you found you couldn't solve what everyone else considered a very simple parlor trick.

12. A poorly informed foreigner made disparaging remarks about the United States.

13. A very casual acquaintance near you cheated on an examination.

14. You found that although a friend of yours had written a poorer examination than you, he had received a higher grade.

15. When you finally managed to dance with a particularly attractive girl, a good friend of yours cut in.

16. You desired to board a boat or train to see a friend off, or to enter an exhibition or park; the guard forbade you on what seemed to be entirely unnecessary technicalities.

Instructions. The following instructions were memorized and spoken to an elementary class in social psychology composed of 185 Yale undergraduates:

Today I am asking you to fill out a questionnaire. Please be as honest and as truthful as possible. The results, as I have explained to you, are for research purposes. Your name will be kept secret. Please do not look at the rest of the questionnaire until you understand the instructions completely. You will be given an opportunity to ask any questions about points not clear to you.

Let us use the situation on the first page by way of illustration. You must decide whether the situation has actually occurred to you and whether you remember your behavior in the situation sufficiently vividly. If the situation has not occurred to you or if you do not remember the details of your behavior, skip the particular question. There is no social disgrace, of course, in skipping a question, but please make an effort to answer as many questions as possible.

I am asking you to do four things for each question in which the situation has occurred to you:

1. In the first column (three blank columns were ruled in the left margin) check the item or items which best described or describe your behavior at that time. You check those items which describe your behavior and as many or as few as you wish. If you feel that the alternatives described do not cover your behavior, write what you did in the blank space provided for that purpose.

2. In the second column rate the reaction which would have brought you the most satisfaction if you had done it. Perhaps you actually did what brought you most satisfaction. In any case put your rating next to the item which might have brought you, or actually did bring you, the most satisfaction. Put a rating of 1 if this brought you no satisfaction, 2 if it brought slight satisfaction, and so on. These ratings are listed on the first page and are also here on the blackboard.

3. In the third column, rate the reacton which would have brought you the most trouble (or have caused you the most unpleasant consequences) if you had done it. Perhaps you actually did what brought you the most trouble (or caused you the most unpleasant consequences). In any case put your rating next to the item which might have brought you or actually did bring you the most trouble (or caused you the most unpleasant consequences). Put a rating of 1 if it brought no trouble, and so on.

Be sure to recollect what would have or did bring you the most satisfaction and trouble in columns 2 and 3, as these possibilities occurred to you at the time when the incident took place. Do not reconstruct your behavior on what you think about that incident now. In some cases, it may not be possible to rate columns 2 and 3; try to, but, if you can't, then just don't.

4. At the bottom of each incident you are asked an additional question. Give your answer in the form of a rating by checking the alternative which most nearly corresponds to your feeling at the time. There are four possibilities.

The students were told with emphasis that they should answer an item only if that situation had occurred to them. They were given as much time as they wished to answer; all of them finished within 40 minutes. In scoring the items, those responses which subjects added because none of the standardized alternatives described their behavior were judged independently (as O, N or S) by the writers and included in the final tabulation only if the judgments coincided. Otherwise the situation was not tabulated for that particular subject.

This questionnaire was designed to obtain, in a standardized manner, reports of what had actually happened in real-life frustrating situations. The fact that it was standardized implies at once that the answers were limited in certain ways. The nature of the hypotheses under examination determined the kind of limitation. In summary, the data obtained from the 185 subjects comprised the following:

1. What the actual response was to each of the sixteen frustrating situations which had been experienced.
2. What, and to what degree, would have been the most satisfying response to the situation, as the subject recalled his impulses at the time of occurrence.
3. What, and to what degree, would have been the response that would have caused the subject the most trouble or punishment as the subject recalled his judgments and anticipations at the time of occurrence.
4. How strong the instigation was to the goal-responses which were frustrated in the described situations.

RESULTS

I

The standardized recall was made by 185 subjects. The average number of situations for which recalls were made was 12.1; the S.D. was 3.2. In Table 1 are given the percentage of subjects making each type of response to each of the sixteen situations. For each situation the percentages are based on the total number of subjects responding to that situation, as shown in the second column of the table.

First hypothesis. The validity of this hypothesis depends on the demonstration that the proportion of substitute responses (S) was greatest when anticipation of punishment for being aggressive was greatest. With the present data this latter variable can be measured only by a comparison of the size of the ratings given in column 2 (anticipation of satisfaction) and 3 (anticipation of punishment) of the questionnaire. Obviously there would have to be some impulse to do a certain act, and an expectation of pleasure from doing it, before the anticipation of punishment could act as a deterrent. To test this hypothesis, therefore, only those instances were used in which the *same* alternative was checked as providing anticipated satisfaction and punishment; i.e., those instances in which the subject both did and did not want to do a certain thing.[5] Since the hypothesis relates to punishment for being aggressive, furthermore, only those instances from this group were

---

[5]Although it may be presumed that careful introspection at the time of a frustration would reveal one or several impulses both to do and not to do a certain thing, not all of the subjects reported such conflicts. Some of them checked one alternative in column 2 and another in column 3; it is these subjects who have been excluded in the results pertaining to the first and third hypotheses. It was felt that compelling subjects to rate the same alternative in both columns would have increased the artificiality of the questionnaire. Those who rated different columns were probably recalling inaccurately their mental state during the frustration.

TABLE 1

Number of Subjects Who Recalled Each Situation and the Per Cent Who Made Each Type of Response

| Situation | N | Percentage of SS Making Each Type of Response | | | | | | |
		O	N	S	ON*	OS*	NS*	ONS*
1	151	20.5	55.0	4.6	18.6		1.3	
2	136	47.8	33.1	13.2	1.5	1.5	2.9	
3	172	50.6	14.5	16.9	8.7	4.7	2.9	1.7
4	128	13.3	30.4	46.1	.8		8.6	.8
5	125	21.6	36.8	32.8		3.2	5.6	
6	151	32.4	19.9	29.8	2.0	.7	12.5	2.7
7	125	72.0	10.4	6.4	5.6	3.2	.8	1.6
8	165	72.1	15.8	3.0	2.4	4.3		2.4
9	123	16.3	38.2	29.3	3.2	2.4	9.8	.8
10	177	5.6	35.0	48.0	.6	1.7	8.5	.6
11	121	9.1	42.2	23.1	4.1	1.7	19.0	.8
12	85	44.7	29.4	21.2	1.2	1.2	2.3	
13	161	13.0	40.3	22.4	5.6	1.9	14.9	1.9
14	152	16.4	51.3	13.8	4.0	4.6	9.9	
15	152	35.5	17.8	23.7	7.9	5.9	4.6	4.6
16	136	16.9	22.1	31.6	5.9	5.1	8.1	10.3
Average	141							

*The subjects represented in these columns recalled having responded to the situation with more than one of the alternatives; when all the reported responses were the same (O, N or S), the responses were scored as a single response and placed in the appropriate category without differentiation from single responses in that category.

used in which the activity both desired and not desired was either O or N; instances which fitted the first criterion but involved S alternatives were ignored, since they were not relevant to the hypothesis. Within this selected group of cases three degrees of anticipation of punishment can be distinguished: (1) that in which anticipated satisfaction was greater than anticipated punishment, (2) that in which the two were of equal strength, and (3) that in which anticipated satisfaction was less than anticipated punishment.

According to the hypothesis, the proportion of substitute responses should increase from the first to the third degree. In Table 2 are shown, for each of these three degrees, the number of instances in which the above criteria were met and the percentage of these instances in which a substitute response was the only response actually made. These same data are given likewise for all the cases under each of the four strengths of frustration.

The uniform rise in proportion of substitute responses from top to bottom in the table is in accord with expectation on the basis of the first hypothesis, although the critical ratios of the differences (in the right-hand column) are small: between S > P and S = P, 1.2; between S = P and S < P, 0.6; between S > P and S < P, 1.2.

TABLE 2

Data Required for a Test of the First Hypothesis

The rows represent three different amounts of anticipated punishment for being aggressive. The columns represent (N) the number of situations rated as involving each of the four strengths of drive, and (S) the percentage of these situations which evoked substitute responses. The last column is critical for the first hypothesis.

Relative Strengths of Anticipated Sat. and Pun.	Strength of Drive-Instigation									
	Strong						Weak		Total	
	1		2		3		4			
	N	S	N	S	N	S	N	S	N	S
Satisf. > Pun.	241	9.5	203	18.2	79	17.7	22	22.7	545	14.5
Satisf. = Pun.	122	9.8	153	19.0	82	23.2	23	26.1	380	17.4
Satisf. < Pun.	26	15.4	37	13.5	13	30.8	8	50.0	84	20.2
Total	389	10.0	393	18.1	174	21.3	53	28.3	1,009	16.0

Second hypothesis. The number of subjects who answered each item with each of the four degrees of drive strength is too small to permit a test of this hypothesis on each of the sixteen situations. In Table 3, therefore, are given, for all the instances rated under each of the four strengths of drive,[6] the percentage of responses which were O, N, S, and combinations of these. The *N*'s in this table represent all the answers to all sixteen situations by all subjects without reference to the ratings made in column 2 and 3 of the questionnaire. The data of Table 3 are the same as those of Table 1. According to this second hypothesis the proportion of substitute responses should increase with a decrease in strength of instigation. That this condition is fulfilled by the data can be seen from following the row labelled "S" from left to right. The critical ratios of the differences between successive strengths are: between 1 and 2, 3.5; between 2 and 3, 3.3; between 3 and 4, 2.7; between 1 and 4, 7.0.

Third hypothesis. Table 4 presents the data in the way required for determining the validity of the third hypothesis—namely, that the overtness of aggression varies inversely with the degree of anticipation of punishment for being overtly aggressive. As with the test of the first hypothesis above, only those instances were considered in which the same alternative was specified as providing the greatest anticipation of both satisfaction and punishment. In this case, again, a second delimitation of instances was necessary; only those instances were used in which the alternative thus rated was an O alternative. This selection is necessary because the third hypothesis relates to *punishment for being overtly aggressive* and not, as does the

[6]The responses of subjects who gave ratings in the "very strongly" division of the scale below each item are given in the column labelled 1 in Table 3; those in the "cared very little" division are given in column 4; and similarly for columns 2 and 3.

TABLE 3

For the 185 Subjects, the Total Number of Situations Rated as Having Each of the Four Strengths of Drive-Instigation, and the Percentage of This Total Number of Situations Responded to with Each of the Types of Response

Type of Response	Strength of Drive-Instigation				Total N=2260
	Strong 1 N=770	2 N=866	3 N=444	Weak 4 N=180	
01*	35.8	28.2	24.3	17.2	29.2
02*	1.7	1.3		.6	1.1
03*	.3	.1			.1
N	28.3	33.1	31.3	26.7	30.6
S	14.7	21.6	30.4	44.4	22.8
ON	6.5	4.2	3.6	2.2	4.7
OS	3.6	2.4	2.3	1.1	2.7
NS	5.7	8.0	7.2	7.2	7.0
ONS	3.4	1.1	.9	.6	1.8

*Multiple overt responses have been kept separate, in this table, from single overt responses: 01, 02 and 03 indicate the number of overt responses checked.

first hypothesis, to *punishment for any kind of aggression.* The same three degrees of anticipation of punishment were used in the present test (Table 4) as were used for testing the first hypothesis (Table 2).

The hypothesis requires that the proportion of overtly aggressive responses should decrease with increased anticipation of punishment. In Table 4 are given, for the various degrees of anticipation and of strength of instigation, the number of cases which met the criteria mentioned above and percentages of aggressive responses which were overt (number of O responses divided by number of O + N). Even though the number of instances is small in some categories, the predicted trend holds good, both for every degree of drive strength and for the total, which disregards differences in drive strength. For the differences in the right-hand column of Table 4 (Total) the critical ratios are: S > P and S = P, 2.7; S = P and S < P, 2.6; S > P and S < P, 4.3.

Fourth hypothesis. In Table 5 are given the data relevant to the hypothesis that overt aggression varies positively with strength of drive. As in Table 3, these data represent all the responses of all subjects to all situations. For each of the four strengths of drive are shown the percentage of aggressive responses, the percentage of overtly aggressive responses, and the proportion of overtly aggressive responses to all aggressive responses. Not only do total aggressions increase with increase in drive strength (the obverse of the first hypothesis),[7] but the proportion of O in relation to N responses

TABLE 4

Data Required for a Test of the Third Hypothesis

The rows represent three different amounts of anticipated punishment for being *overtly* aggressive. The columns represent (N) the number of situations rated as involving each of the four strengths of drive, and (O) the percentage of these situations which evoked *overt* aggressive responses. The last column is critical for the third hypothesis.

	Strength of Drive-Instigation									
Relative Strengths of Anticipated	Strong 1		2		3		Weak 4		Total	
Sat. and Pun.	N	O	N	O	N	O	N	O	N	O
Satisf. > Pun.	214	65.4	164	56.7	61	59.0	14	42.9	453	60.7
Satisf. = Pun.	105	52.4	119	47.1	60	55.0	17	41.2	301	50.2
Satisf. < Pun.	20	50.0	30	30.0	9	22.2	4	0	63	33.3
Total	339	60.5	313	50.5	130	54.6	35	37.1	817	54.7

increases. The critical ratios of the differences in the bottom line of Table 5 are: between 1 and 2, 5.1; between 2 and 3, 0.8; between 3 and 4, 1.0; between 1 and 4, 4.3.

TABLE 5

In Relation to the Strength of Drive-Instigation, the Number (and Per cent) of All Responses Which Were Aggressive and the Per Cent of Aggressive Responses Which Were Overt

	Strength of Drive-Instigation							
Type of Response	Strong 1		2		3		Weak 4	
	N	Per Cent	N	Per Cent	N	Per Cent	N	Per Cent
Aggressive	657	85.3	679	78.4	309	69.4	100	57.5
Overt-Ag.	395	51.3	323	37.3	138	31.1	39	21.7
Ov.-Ag./Ag.		60.1		47.6		44.7		39.0

II

It is now possible to determine whether these particular subjects have considered overt, direct aggression to be most satisfying. In 2,134 of the

---

[7]This principle has been expressed elsewhere as fundamental to the systemization of the frustration-aggression relationship. It is clear from Table 3 that not only did the percentage of cases in which a single O response occurred increase as drive strength increased, but there were increasing numbers of instances in which two and even three O responses were recorded.

2,260 situations a single alternative was checked as being the most satisfying response. Of these instances, 69.2 per cent were overt aggressions, 7.4 per cent were non-overt, and 23.4 per cent were substitute responses. Among the alternative responses presented with three (Nos. 1, 3, 13) of the sixteen situations, moreover, were responses which represented both direct and indirect overt aggression, i.e., overt aggression toward the frustrating agent or overt aggression not so directed. A far larger proportion of the subjects reacted with direct aggression than with indirect aggression. In No. 1, the third and fifth alternatives represented direct aggression (88 cases) and the seventh alternative represented an indirect (and perhaps partly non-overt) aggression (9 cases). In No. 3, the first alternative was indirect (13 cases) and the fourth was direct (113 cases). In No. 13, a similar pair of alternatives was available: "I griped about it to mutual friends after the examination" (indirect, 12 cases), and "I told him to stop" (direct, 57 cases).

Not only is it clear from the data that the most satisfying response is the overt, direct form of aggression, but it is also evident that overt aggression gives rise to strong anticipations of punishment. In 2,125 of the 2,260 situations recalled, a single alternative was checked as being the response from which most punishment was anticipated. Of these instances, 85.9 per cent were overt aggressions, 6.8 per cent were non-overt, and 7.3 per cent were substitute responses.

III

It is possible, as was suggested in the introductory section, to analyze the data situation by situation. Obviously the findings have certain limitations: only a small sample of social situations has been selected and the individuals studied represent just one segment of the culture, *viz.,* Yale College students. The following discussion, however, may suggest a method of approach to similar problems. For illustrative purposes, three factors have been isolated. They are presented in Table 6. In column 1 is the percentage of subjects who displayed overt aggression in each of the sixteen situations; multiple responses in which 1 or more of the alternatives were O responses are included. In column 2 is given the percentage of subjects who were "strongly" frustrated in the situation; the criterion for "strong" frustration is a rating of "1" for the strength of instigation to the frustrated goal response. In column 3 is given the percentage of subjects who believed they would secure an equal amount of satisfaction and trouble from doing what they wanted to do; again only those are included who rated the same action in both respects. This third factor can be interpreted in terms of conflict. Since the impulse to do something was as strong as the one not to do the same thing (column 2 =

column 3), an internal conflict of Type II variety can be presumed. It cannot be denied that, when the impulse to do something was greater or less than the impulse not to do it, a conflict may also have been present; but here the assumption is made that the conflict was at least *stronger* when the impulses had equal strength.[8] The data are given in percentages also and the situations are ranked with respect to each other for each of the three variables. A high percentage means that the situation evoked, respectively, a great amount of overt aggression, strong frustration, and strong conflict *as these terms have been defined in this connection.*

TABLE 6

For Each Frustrating Situation, the Percentage of Subjects Who Were (A) Overtly Aggressive, (B) Strongly Frustrated, and (C) In Strong Conflict

The total N's to which the percentages for (A) and (B) refer are given in Table 1; those for (C) are given here.

SITUA-TION	OVERT AGGRESSION		STRONG FRUSTRATION		STRONG CONFLICT		
	PER CENT	RANK	PER CENT	RANK	N	PER CENT	RANK
1	39.1	7	27.8	10	50	32.0	12
2	50.7	5	44.9	4	95	32.6	11
3	65.7	3	39.5	6	89	27.0	14
4	14.8	15	27.3	11	61	47.5	2
5	24.8	11	26.4	12	57	24.6	15
6	37.7	9	15.2	14	71	39.4	8
7	82.4	1	46.4	3	67	38.8	9
8	81.2	2	70.9	1	65	30.8	13
9	22.8	12	43.9	5	74	46.0	3
10	8.5	16	16.9	13	105	53.3	1
11	15.7	14	14.9	15	30	40.0	7
12	47.1	6	35.3	9	58	44.8	4
13	22.4	13	11.8	16	42	40.5	6
14	25.0	10	48.7	2	93	34.4	10
15	53.9	4	37.5	7.5	55	21.8	16
16	38.2	8	37.5	7.5	76	43.4	5

In the light of psychological analysis of sixteen diverse situations in the culture of Yale students, these sociological findings emerge:

1. No one situation produced overt aggression, strong frustration, or strong conflict in every individual, but every situation did affect someone in these respects. These particular situations, therefore, even though they bristle with cultural regulations, do not lead to complete uniformity of be-

---

[8]It has been shown by Sears and Hovland that the strength of conflicts, as measured by the difficulty of resolution, varies positively with the approach of the strengths of the two conflicting impulses to equality.

havior, although some of them tend to affect a large percentage of individuals similarly.

2. The range of percentages for overt aggression is from 82.4 per cent to 8.5 per cent; for strong frustration from 70.9 per cent to 11.8 per cent; for strong conflict from 53.3 per cent to 21.8 per cent. This range would indicate that strong conflict varies from situation to situation much less than either of the other two factors.

3. Each situation can be described in two ways: it can be characterized in terms of amount of overt aggression, amount of strong frustration, and amount of strong conflict; and it can be compared in one, two, or all three of these respects with the other fifteen situations. Thus it appears that in situation number 8 ("A good friend of yours was driving so recklessly that you were genuinely scared out of your wits") 81.2 per cent of the individuals were overtly aggressive, 70.9 per cent were strongly frustrated, and 30.8 per cent experienced strong conflicts. In comparison with the other situations, this one ranks second in percentage of those who expressed their aggression overtly and first of those who were strongly frustrated, and thirteenth in percentage of those with strong conflicts. In different words, for Yale students this is a very frustrating situation, more frustrating in fact than any other; it makes a large proportion of them overtly aggressive, more of them in fact than all others except one; and it produces strong conflict in only a little more than one quarter of them, which is a comparatively small number in comparison with most of the other situations.[9] In contrast, situation number 13 ("A very casual acquaintance near you cheated on an examination") is the least frustrating of all, it is low in the amount of overt aggression it arouses, and it stands sixth in respect to the strong conflicts it engenders. In a broad, general way it may be adduced that the students have more strong conflicts in this latter situation than in the former, but fewer of them are affected by the sight of someone cheating and they do not (or cannot) express overtly the aggression they feel.

CONCLUSIONS

Four hypotheses bearing on factors determining substitute behavior and degree of overt aggression have been deduced from the general laws of frustration and of learning, and evidence gathered from a questionnaire designed to permit standardized recall of real-life situations has been presented to substantiate them. The following generalizations may be made:

[9]No comparison of ranks or correlations can be made between the three variables, since the denominators vary systematically in the equations giving the percentage values.

1.   The frequency of substitute responses varies positively with the strength of anticipatory responses to punishment-for-being-aggressive.

2.   The frequency of substitute responses varies inversely with the strength of instigation to the frustrated goal-response.

3.   Overtness of aggression varies inversely with the amount of punishment anticipated as a consequence of such behavior.

4.   Overtness of aggression varies positively with the strength of instigation to the frustrated goal-response.

Three assumptions have also been tested by these data.

5.   Overt aggression is more satisfying than non-overt aggression or substitute responses in the sample frustrating situations used in this study.

6.   Direct overt aggression is more satisfying than indirect or displaced overt aggression.

7.   There is greater anticipation of punishment for overt aggression than for non-overt aggression or substitute responses in the sample frustrating situations used in this study.

31. Types of Reaction to Frustration

AN HEURISTIC CLASSIFICATION

Saul Rosenzweig

THIS paper represents a short excursion in the armchair. We take our place there in the hope of discovering a classification of *apperceptive types of conscious reaction to frustration* that will serve as the basis for further, possibly experimental, research.

If the attempt is made to describe the typical modes of conscious reaction to frustration, one possible result is that summarized in the accompanying table.

Abridged from *The Journal of Abnormal and Social Psychology*, 1935, 29, 298-300. Reprinted by permission of the author and the American Psychological Association, Inc.

Apperceptive Types of Conscious Reaction to Frustration

	Extrapunitive	Intropunitive	Impunitive
Emotions	Anger and Indignation	Humiliation and guilt	Embarrassment and shame
Judgments	Blames others: "You played me dirty. I'll get you for that."	Blames self: "How could I have done a thing like that! I'll never forgive myself."	Condones: "It couldn't be helped. Let bygones be bygones."

In the "extrapunitive" type of conscious reaction to frustration, the individual experiences anger and indignation against others, whom he holds blameworthy. For example, the extrapunitive reaction to being snubbed by a friend would be to regard him as an ill-bred, perhaps ungrateful, person, whatever the objective evidence might be.

In the "intropunitive" type of reaction, the individual experiences humiliation and guilt, for he holds himself blameworthy. For example, the intropunitive reaction to being snubbed by a friend would be to regard oneself as an inferior person, unworthy of the other's attention, whatever the objective evidence might be.

In the "impunitive" type of reaction, the individual experiences embarrassment and shame, and is more interested in condonement than in blame. For example, the impunitive reaction to being snubbed would be to connive at or gloss over the incident as if it were the result of a mere oversight, whatever the objective evidence might be.

The expression "whatever the objective evidence might be" indicates the apperceptive character of our types. We are concerned not with what is objectively present by way of responsibility in the experience of frustration, but rather with what the individual who is frustrated chooses to emphasize or even read into the situation in accordance with his personal traits and needs. In so far as the situation is objectively evaluated, without any degree of apperceptive distortion, our types are inapplicable.

To avoid misunderstanding, at least two further points should be noted.

(1) The present classification applies, in the first instance, not to individuals but to mechanisms. It describes types of reaction, not of reacting persons. While we may assume with relative safety that the majority of normal individuals have a consistently characteristic way of responding to frustration, whether it be extrapunitive, intropunitive or impunitive, we must of course allow that no individual reacts in his characteristic way without exception. Moreover, it is easily possible that a person should consistently respond in some one of the above three ways in one sort of situation and should consistently follow one of the other two in another sort of situation.

(2) The above is a description of the *conscious,* not of the *unconscious,* processes involved in reacting to frustration. The relations of the two—by way of compensation and the like—constitute a fundamental problem that is just beginning to be solved.

In elaboration of the present schema several additional statements may be made.

(1) The above account omits to consider genetic and dynamic factors. We may remedy this to some extent if we avail ourselves of the psychoanalytic classification of needs into aggressive and erotic. We may then speculate that the extrapunitive and intropunitive types are both aggressive in character, the aggression being outwardly directed in the former case, inwardly in the latter. The impunitive type of reaction, on the other hand, may be conceived to draw its energy from erotic sources; it would then not be thought of as intermediate to the other two but as contrasted with them.

(2) It seems likely that each of our types of reaction would have a special relation to memory. One might expect that both the extrapunitive and the intropunitive reactions would entail remembering the occasion of frustration, in the former case, as if in anticipation of revenge, in the latter, as if in preparation for nursing the wounds to one's pride and "eating one's own heart out." It is as if the aggressive impulses were being preserved to be expressed later, in the former case, against outer objects, in the latter, against the subject's own self. The impunitive type of reaction, on the other hand, might be expected to entail a conscious forgetting of the occasion of frustration, as if in order to reconcile one's self—and others— to the disagreeable situation. The impunitive reaction might thus be summed up in the expression "Forgive and forget," whereas the other two types would involve neither forgiving nor forgetting.

It goes without saying that extensive investigation is necessary before the above notions can be correctly evaluated or satisfactorily completed.

32. A Note on the
Frustration-Aggression Theories
of Dollard and his Associates

George K. Morlan

PARALLEL to the confusion in the public debate on civil rights legislation, and perhaps one of the causes of that confusion, are two conflicting psychological theories concerning what happens when an aggressive impulse is expressed. According to some psychologists, the expression of aggression serves as a catharsis; the frustration of an aggressive impulse simply increases the strength of the aggression.

According to another theory, the expression of an aggressive impulse does not result in catharsis, but, on the contrary, sets up a vicious cycle that leads to further aggression.

Thus we have a variant form of the old James-Lange controversy: Do we abuse minorities because we hate, or do we hate minorities because we abuse them? Since psychologists are not clear about this issue, it is no wonder that in public discussion many people are confused and disturbed. Important, practical issues are involved, and a clarification of the underlying psychological theory is urgent, for before supporting or opposing civil rights legislation, we need to know whether laws designed to prevent lynching and the like would make the dominant group more malevolent or whether the net result would likely be pacifying.

These two unreconciled psychological theories have been advanced by John Dollard in different places, but in conjunction with the same general topic of frustration-aggression. Since these two contradictory theories clearly define the issue, Dollard's writings will be used as the basis for the following discussion.

Abridged from the *Psychological Review,* 1949, 56, 1-8. Reprinted by permission of the author and the American Psychological Association, Inc.

CATHARSIS THEORY

In *Frustration and Aggression* under the joint authorship of John Dollard, Leonard W. Doob, Neil E. Miller, O. H. Mowrer, and Robert R. Sears, the authors argue that frustration causes aggression. Childhood, adolescent, and adult experiences are frustrating. Illustrations of each are given, and the resulting aggression is described and explained in terms of frustration. It is asserted that the intensity of frustration varies according to the number of areas that are involved as well as the intensity of the original drive that is thwarted. Other factors that determine intensity or the likelihood of expression need not be reviewed here, but in the conclusion of Chapter Three, two correlative principles, numbered 2 and 4, state in different ways the same fundamental principle of catharsis as follows:

"2.   The inhibition of acts of direct aggression is an additional frustration which instigates aggression against the agent perceived to be responsible for this inhibition and increases the instigation to other forms of aggression. There is, consequently, a strong tendency for inhibited aggression to be displaced to different objects and expressed in modified forms. . . ."

"4.   The expression of any act of aggression is a catharsis that reduces the instigation to all other acts of aggression. From this and the principle of displacement it follows that, with the level of original frustration held constant, there should be an inverse relationship between the expression of various forms of aggression."

Stated more simply in English, these authors conclude that if our urge to hit someone that pushes us at a football game is prevented by law or custom, we resent laws, the police, and Yale, and become more hostile in general. Or if we beat up the alumnus, we are relieved of our hostility and become so tranquil that our aggression (at least temporarily) toward Jews, Catholics, or Senator Taft is reduced. What happens if we are beaten up doesn't seem to come within the preview of this scientific statement.

The practical issue at stake is no trivial matter, for the acceptance of this hypothesis justifies opposition to laws designed to prevent discrimination and lynching. It also follows that people who are oppressed should accept patiently the stings and deprivations they suffer, for in the process of beating up others or similarly relieving their aggression, the persecutors who are filled with the bile of civilization will get rid of their hostile feelings. At peace with themselves, the aggressors will then start loving Negroes and give them equal opportunities in jobs, education and government.

Defined in this operational fashion, this hypothesis appears absurd. Nevertheless, a variety of evidence has been advanced to support it. Since Sargent, in a recent article, has dealt with the aspect of the theory concerning frustration causing aggression, we shall confine ourselves primarily to the catharsis aspect of the hypothesis. Dollard and his associates summarized in their book the evidence available in 1939, but since that time more evidence has accumulated in support of their theory. With one exception, the following reports have appeared since *Frustration and Aggression* was published, but the general point of view is the same.

Appel compared children from two nursery schools, one where there was little supervision and much fighting and the other where there was more adult supervision and fighting was discouraged. Appel found that the following year when the children were in the kindergarten with about equal supervision, the children who had done the most fighting now had fewer altercations. On the other hand, the aggressiveness of the children whose combativeness had been suppressed was now doubled.

H. E. Jones found that babies that cried readily apparently got rid of their emotions and were less tense, as measured by the psychogalvanometer, than those babies that did not cry so readily.

Recent mental hospital practice with the psychodrama and the more common-place use of recreation, arts, crafts, and play therapy support in a general way the view that the expression of feelings even indirectly promotes poise and health, and the treatment of anxiety neurosis in particular is in keeping with the catharsis hypothesis. As might be expected, non-directive counseling has been most successful with anxiety states, but the method of catharsis has been reported as successfully used also in dealing with some aggression in the classroom.

In teaching a course in race relations Gordon W. Allport noticed hostility on the part of the class toward himself. By permitting the students to express their feelings, he observed that they gained insight into their exaggerations and were helped in restructuring their attitudes. Allport concluded that a teacher dealing with race relations becomes more effective if he permits the feelings to be released and thus drained off. Straight lectures on minority rights, he believes, are useless.

> "The listener is often so near to bursting with hostility that nothing new can come into his mind until something old comes out. We have all had the experience of listening to friends who fill us with their woes and who finally say, 'Well, now, that's enough of my troubles. I feel better after spilling them out to you. Let's go to the movies.' Or, instead of going to the movies, it may be that the friend is ready to listen to the opposite point of view. But he could not have done so until his pressure was relieved. If the listener had crossed swords with the complainer at the outset, tenseness and struggle, rather than catharsis, would have been the result."

A similar point of view has been advanced by Dorothy Baruch, and she has criticized a typical group of teachers and supervisors for having

> "no understanding of the emotional genesis . . . of behavior . . . . The fact, for instance, that Negroes or Japanese could be symbols on which to let out aggression to a parent or sibling was unrecognized. The fact that engendering quiet, controlled behavior might hide rather than clear a problem was out of the picture. The emphasis was on repressive, problem-augmenting techniques. It disregarded acceptance of inner emotions and of releasing problem-reducing procedures."

Baruch related how one teacher was able to accept dirty language and abuse a child directed toward her, and how the child was helped to become adjusted by the teacher's accepting this abuse.

In all of these instances, the expression of aggression helped to reduce the tension and promoted healthful adjustment. Following this view through to its logical conclusion, Ellis Freeman has declared that

> "This obliges us to accept some form of expression of hate as an inevitable component of personality. Each one of us must hate something, be it no more than the Devil. The only area of choice lies in the object against which the hate or aggression shall be directed."

But he also went on to assert that if hostility toward Jews were curbed, frustration would be increased, and therefore hostility would break out toward some other group. In other words, as the authors of *Frustration and Aggression* assert on page 1, ". . . frustration always leads to some form of aggression."

This is equivalent to the view that was popular some twenty-five years ago, that if you suppress your sexual urges, a complex will set in; therefore people should let themselves go. Perhaps the frustration-aggression theory is also roughly equivalent in validity to this view on sex.

The catharsis hypothesis has limited value and usefulness, but it does not square with certain obvious facts, and a careful examination of the supporting evidence reveals that some of the material permits more than one reasonable interpretation. In the case of the children who did more fighting in the nursery school and less in kindergarten, one cannot conclude unequivocally that in the process of the fighting the children had gotten rid of their aggressive feelings. Jersild has pointed out that

> "A finding such as this does not mean that a child of three or four has within him a certain amount of fight which he must get out of his system; rather it suggests that children must practice and have experience in order to work out their techniques of dealing with one another."

Neither is play therapy merely a matter of a child's *expressing* his resentment or aggression. In a Veteran's Housing project in one of our Eastern colleges, there is a Polish child who terrorizes the neighborhood. His mother and father were both imprisoned in a Nazi concentration camp when he was a baby. His father died there, and the child suffered terribly at the hands of the Nazis. He and his mother survived, and his mother later married a GI who brought them to this country. The boy still has scars from shrapnel wounds he received during the Nazi blitz, and the scars of his personality are all too evident. He has become so difficult to manage that his mother, who is now pregnant, locks him out of the house during the day. He is a serious behavior problem for his parents and the entire community; yet he is constantly expressing his feelings in an overt way, and some of his play resembles play therapy. He buries any doll he finds, but neither this expression of his feelings nor his attacks on other youngsters serves as a catharsis for his feeling.[1]

In 1944 I also pointed out that more extensive scientific investigation on adult behavior might reveal that expressing our feelings freely can stir us up further.[2]

I related how I had "heard a neurotic janitor swear at a woman tenant, and after she had gone, he continued to rage about her in front of the building until he was sick with fury. An hour later, instead of being sweet and placable, he was consumed with bitterness. Two days afterwards, he was still upset, and I heard him say that he felt so bad he couldn't sleep. He was remorseful, not relieved."

He had been misused and frustrated by the tenant, but his venting his feelings "on the agent perceived to be responsible for this inhibition" did not bring the peace that should have been expected on the basis of the catharsis hypothesis. Indeed, his hurt feelings led to abusive language which stirred him up further, which, in turn, made him still more disturbed.

CIRCULAR INTERACTION THEORY

Strangely enough, reasoning from the same set of principles set forth in *Frustration and Aggression* about frustration causing aggression, in 1938, a year earlier, Dollard concluded that the expression of aggression often

[1]Since the mere expression of feeling may be a pretty futile sort of thing, isn't the term 'non-directive counseling' a psychological misnomer? If the analysis of the Polish child is correct, expression may be less important than direction. There is probably more direction, though more subtle direction, in 'non-directive counseling' than its advocates are willing to admit.

[2]In a foot note on page 50, of *Frustration and Aggression* there is this brief admission. "Also the repetition of a mode of behavior may presumably produce learning of it. Throughout this hypothesis both the role of temporal factors and the influence of learning present problems acutely in need of detailed solution." But nowhere does this admission of inadequacy affect the sweeping formulation of the hypothesis.

leads not to catharsis but to further aggression. His earlier view thus constitutes a refutation of the catharsis theory with which his name is associated.

In the earlier *Social Forces* article, as in the later work he argued that race prejudice develops in a context of frustration that begins with birth in our society. Frustration leads to feelings of aggression, and "It is in part the underestimation of these tendenices which makes 'race prejudice' seem so mysterious." Our social psychology is also inadequate in its "underestimation of the frustrating character of in-group life for its adult participants."

He recognized that some direct aggression results from economic and social competition, but he stressed the fact that childhood and adult frustrations lead to hostile feelings. These feelings, in turn, are channelled by the prejudices that are established in society toward minorities. But instead of the expression of aggression relieving and reducing the tension, as was asserted so categorically in *Frustration and Aggression,* Dollard came to the opposite conclusion that the expression of aggression sets up an interaction that makes one more aggressive.

> Intensive studies of individuals have repeatedly demonstrated the existence of the following mechanism: first, wishes to injure other people or the accomplishment of such injury; second, a fear of retaliation based on what has been done or intended; third, the appearance of new aggression against the wronged object. This vicious circle phenomenon is an example of psychological interaction and can lead to apparently reasonless hostile behavior against those who are guilty only of being the object of hostility.

If this vicious circle, interaction view is true, then it is not true that "The expression of *any* act of aggression is a catharsis that reduces the instigation to *all* other acts of aggression." (Italics are mine.) Indeed, to the extent that the interaction theory is true, the catharsis hypothesis is untrue or limited.

Whether Dollard changed his theory during the interval of a year or whether he did not concur with the extreme statement of catharsis in *Frustration and Aggression* is not clear. In the foreword of the volume, the Director of the Yale Institute of Human Relations pointed out that the cooperative volume was not exactly a 'love feast.' Each author, he said, was probably frustrated by the book's not representing his own convictions at many points. Therefore we cannot assume that Dollard was unaware of the incoherence of these two hypotheses stated in conjunction with the same general topic. However, we are not concerned here with the adequacy of Dollard's distinctive contribution, but with the adequacy of two conflicting points of view, and we have used his name only to help identify the theories.

This second hypothesis also has important, practical implications. If this interaction view is correct, then the expression of antagonisms might wisely be discouraged or even suppressed. Minorities, then, would not only be hurt less, but the oppressors' feelings of hate would be less stirred up. There is also a variety of evidence to support this hypothesis.

The expression of aggression in such acts as stealing (resulting from the frustration of poverty) is not likely to "reduce the instigation" to stealing, but to increase it. One finds habitual thieves; rarely individuals who have broken into houses once. In other words, acting aggressively is one means of strengthening hostile behavior and reducing normal inhibitions.

It is also possbile to find individuals who have never had sexual relations, but rarely does one find an individual who has had intercourse once. The sexually aggressive person does not become less aggressive sexually by seducing every woman he meets, but more confident and habituated to his own behavior.

In the psychodrama there can also be habituation as well as catharsis. Cunningham has related an instance of practice in a role-playing situation that helped a young man reconstruct his behavior patterns.

> He had the insight into his personal problems, but the carry-over into real life was comparatively meager. This set up in itself an unfortunate conflict. He knew what was the matter and what to do about it, but in actual practice he was not able to make the change, with the result that he felt more helpless and angry at himself.

> In searching for ways and means out of the dilemma, he tried a lot of things such as self-hypnotism, prayer, Benjamin Franklin note books, and the driving will of others. Some worked for a while, but none for long. Somehow he couldn't make the grade. Then in a play he experienced some improvement that stuck. He was given the part of an extroverted newspaper man the friend of the great and poor, the woman killer who passed off his conquests and losses with a laugh. He had so much trouble getting into his part, he was continually urged by another to sparkle inside. He found that once that buoyant, light feeling was acquired inside it was comparatively easy to portray the gay and happy reporter.

> He came to enjoy playing the part and found that it was nice to be a friendly guy whom everybody liked even if it was only on the stage. But often the sparkle feeling persisted after rehearsal, and he would carry on in that manner as they went out for a bite to eat.

> Later he discovered that his stage role worked in real life, though he was bothered somewhat, for he knew he was acting. His real self was so terribly depressed. However, in time that out-

going kind of behavior became habitual to the point where the depressed self was losing its grip over many segments of his life. He now finds that he often actually feels friendly toward people and now approaches them with the idea that they will like him and will want to have him around. He no longer considers him-selm habitually as a wet blanket that nobody wants.

Aggression is not directly or primarily involved here, but this case illustrates that expression of a feeling can strengthen that feeling. Evangelists getting people to make public declaration of faith, salesmen getting people to sign on the dotted line, leaders getting people to contribute funds, i.e., act—all of these illustrate the principle that if you want to strengthen an impulse, get people to act or do something in keeping with that impulse.

In Hitler Germany, too, the freedom to release aggression against the Jews did not drain off anti-Semitism or reduce the hostility of Germans toward the rest of the world. There was no "inverse relationship between the expression of aggression" and peacefulness any more than there is today as this paper is being written. Quite the contrary, violence and hate increased (and is increasing) with the expression of violence and hate.

In a race riot or a lynching, the violent expression of aggression does not dissipate the feeling, but increases tension and violence. The catharsis hypothesis is far too simple to be useful for either a comprehensive explanation of social phenomena or a guide for social legislation. The interaction of our own behavior on ourselves, on the other hand, has been too largely ignored.

CONCLUSIONS

Frustration is one among many dynamic factors that influence behavior, and in the flow of life it rarely if ever exists without the blending of other factors. Although the authors of *Frustration and Aggression* have recognized that "a number of antecedent conditions must sometimes *all* be present before any instigation occurs," they have not adequately recognized other complicating factors, and have too largely ignored the correlative complexity of expression of aggression. No aggressive act is the simple atomistic expression of feeling toward another as the catharsis view assumes. Therefore, it is not true that the expression of hate or antagonism necessarily releases and dissipates that feeling as is stated without qualification in conclusion No. 4.

As Dollard pointed out in *Social Forces,* our hurting others may make us fear them, and therefore cause us to be stirred up further. Perhaps people realize that whatsoever they sow, that shall they also reap. Hate still leads to hate. It is probably not true as Gardner Murphy has claimed that "Most people forget that the gun kicks when fired . . ." The fact is that most people do realize that the gun does kick when fired and that is the reason that the expression of hate makes one hate more.

The tension of our feelings may also not be released because we may have a sense of guilt or shame from hurting others. Apparently, in an attempt to be scientifically universal, the aggression hypothesis of the Yale group has been formulated in such an abstract form that it has been stripped of the human variability necessary for it to be psychologically valid. Neither frustration nor aggression is a simple entity to which a specific remedy such as catharsis is applicable in all cases. The theory of catharsis has about as much validity for behavior as castor oil has as a medicine. Because castor oil may be useful for treating certain cases of constipation, we would not be warranted in using it to cure flat feet.

Frustration *often* results in aggression, but frustration does not necessarily cause aggression. Moreover, aggression can occur in the absence of frustration. This conclusion is in agreement with Sargent's view that

> Certain kinds of behavior which are definitely aggressive seem to be the socially sanctioned ways of behaving in some communities (e.g., a tough city slum area or a primitive culture). Such behavior may well be learned and practiced without having its origin, necessarily, in frustration.

The catharsis theory and the interaction theory are both half truths. Since the latter theory has not presumed to be an overall explanation of behavior, it is not subject to the same weaknesses of the former. However, the catharsis hypothesis has limited validity and usefulness, though it needs to be defined more definitely and its scope set more clearly. The likelihood of a healthful catharsis resulting from the expression of aggression is considerably less under some conditions than under others. Some of the conditions and complexities are as follows:

1.   The expression of a feeling may serve as a release for the aggressive feeling or may increase it. To achieve a healthful release, aggression must be expressed in a therapeutic situation. A therapist or one who acts in the role of a therapist must be present and *influencing* the individual or group. A psychiatrist observing a riot would not automatically make that situation a therapeutic one because of his presence. Unless the therapist is interacting in the situation, the expression of antagonism is more likely to strengthen antagonism, and runs the danger of teaching others to share the same feelings.

2.   Those who are expressing their enmity must not be rewarded for doing so. The Woltmans and Peglers have been writing venomous columns in newspapers for years; yet their piled-up aggression has not been dissi-

pated by their freedom of expression. The reason is obvious. They get paid well for hating. So, too, were the hatreds in Germany rewarded. They were whipped up for a purpose, and the people, in turn, got saitsfaction and support from others by their uninhibited hates.

3. If people believe that aggression should not be inhibited, they are more likely to be frustrated and feel more aggressive if they do not vent their worst feelings. If, on the other hand, they accept the interaction hypothesis, the frustration of a mean impulse is not nearly so likely to instigate further aggression. The effect of frustration depends on the attitude of the individuals toward their frustration as well as their attitude and that of society toward the expression of the aggression.

4. If there is doubt about the character of the situation and the possible consequences, we should act on the basis of the interaction hypothesis. Although the expression of some feelings may be dissipated by their expression in a nontherapeutic situation, the expression is just as likely to strengthen the feeling of aggression. Laws enforced against lynching in the long run are more likely to pacify the South than cause serious frustration and increase aggression—as seems to be the result as this is being written. With lynching more effectively frustrated and the poll tax eliminated, Southerners can feel more honest as Christians and citizens in a democracy. Such feelings of personal integrity do not lead to an inverse relationship between hostility and its expression.

5. Finally, whether we should express our feelings or inhibit them should not be determined merely on the basis of the effect on ourselves. We must be guided also by the effect on others. Our own emotions do not exist apart from the attitudes of others. If the expression of aggression harms no one, it is more likely to help dissipate feelings than if others are injured. If the venting of our feelings hurts another, we shall be none the worse off by having the injurious tendencies thwarted. Repression, as D. B. Klein has pointed out, is not only inevitable but essential for individual freedom. It is essential for self-emancipation.

33. Reaction to Frustration:
A Critique
and Hypothesis

S. Stansfeld Sargent

THE problem of frustration has commanded considerable attention during the last decade. Not only psychiatrists and specialists in clinical and abnormal psychology, but also students of personality and social psychology have become interested in frustration. The *Frustration and Aggression* volume by the Yale collaborators, Dollard, Doob, Miller, Mowrer and Sears, has helped focus attention on the subject, as have papers by Maslow, Rosenzweig and others.

While dealing with the concept of frustration in a course in Social Psychology, I became convinced that current treatments of frustration still lack a systematic framework and a clear definition of terms. The major concepts which are used lack integration; for example, frustration, conflict, motives, emotions, defense mechanisms, habit patterns, personality factors of many kinds, and situational influences. Several instances might be cited to illustrate confusion in usage of terms. "Frustration" usually refers to environmental blocking of motives, but sometimes to an unpleasant emotional state resulting from the blocking. At times "hostility" seems to mean actual behavior; again it signifies a strong feeling underlying behavior. "Inferiority," "insecurity," "anxiety," "guilt," and many other concepts are frequently employed in ways which are unclear psychologically. Probably the worst of all is "aggression," which sometimes seems to mean a motive, sometimes an emotional state akin to anger, sometimes a habit or mechanism, and sometimes a type of overt behavior!

I wish to propose a rather simple conceptual scheme for describing behavior resulting from frustration. It is presented as a hypothesis which seems reasonably consistent with clinical and experimental data and also with many of the theoretical formulations which have been advanced.

Briefly the hypothesis is this: frustration evokes a patterned sequence

Abridged from the *Psychological Review*, 1948, 55, 108-114. Reprinted by permission of the author and the American Psychological Association, Inc.

of behavior whose chief stages or aspects are indicated by the terms *frustration, emotion, habit or mechanism,* and *overt behavior.* The nature of each stage of the total process is determined by the interaction of two major factors: the individual's past experience, and the present situation as perceived or defined by the individual. Let us consider each of these in more detail.

It is well agreed that frustration involves the thwarting or blocking of a person's dominant motives, needs, drives, desires or purposes. However, some psychologists place greater stress upon the thwarting than upon the individual's reaction to it. For example, the Yale group defines frustration as "that condition which exists when a goal-response suffers interference". In his recent book Symonds defines it as "the blocking or interference of the satisfaction of an aroused need through some barrier or obstruction." Others emphasize not so much the thwarting, *per se,* as the significance of the thwarting to the individual. Maslow insists that frusrtation involves two concepts—deprivation, and threat to the personality. Sexual deprivation, for example, does not necessarily constitute frustration, but when such deprivation is felt by the individual to represent rejection by the opposite sex, inferiority, or lack of respect, it becomes seriously frustrating. Similarly, Rosenzweig distinguishes between 'need-persistive' and 'ego-defensive' reactions, the latter representing greater frustration. Zander maintains that frustration occurs only when there is interference with "a goal believed important and attainable by a given person." In all probability future studies of frustration will take into account such subjective individual differences as are mentioned by Maslow, Rosenzweig and Zander.

In any event, we turn to the question, What is the immediate psychological consequence of frustration? It is definitely not aggression, as most readers of *Frustration and Aggression* might assume. Nor is it the adoption of some handy defense mechanism, as others might conclude. First in time, and foremost in significance, frustration arouses a *pronounced emotional reaction.*

Most students of frustration refer to concomitant emotional tensions, but they seldom make emotion a central aspect of the whole reaction pattern.[1] According to the present hypothesis, emotion is the core of reaction to frustration. If no emotion is aroused, there is no frustration—at least not in any psychologically meaningful sense.

Furthermore, the emotion aroused may be broad and diffuse, like a generalized anger or fear, or it may be fairly specific, like hostility, jealousy, inferiority or shame. Whether the emotion is general or specific depends largely upon the nature of the whole precipitating situation as interpreted by the individual.

It is clearly established that strong emotional reactions upset the organ-

[1]Maslow and Rosenzweig are exceptions to this statement.

ism and tend to pass over into overt behavior. However, the form of the resultant behavior is not, *ipso facto,* determined by the kind and intensity of the emotion. Behavior is, of course, partly dependent upon the emotion which agitates the organism; anger is more likely to work itself out in aggressive behavior than is anxiety or shame. But the form of the overt reaction is importantly affected by the individual's adjustive habits or mechanisms, and by the way he interprets the situation.

The above analysis agrees rather well with Rosenzweig's interpretation. In studying reactions to frustration, according to Rosenzweig, we must be concerned not with what is objectively present, but instead with what the individual emphasizes or reads into the situation according to his personality needs and traits. He finds three main types of reaction to frustration. The 'extrapunitive' is an aggressive reaction toward others. It arises from anger and indignation and from the individual's judgment which blames others; "I'll get you!" is its thesis. Thus, if snubbed by a friend, the extrapunitive reaction is to regard him as ill-bred and ungrateful. The 'intropunitive' is an aggressive reaction directed toward the self. It comes from feelings of humiliation and guilt, and from judgments of self-blame. The intropunitive reaction to a snub is to regard oneself as inferior and unworthy. The 'impunitive' reaction is unaggressive. It arises from feelings of embarrassment and shame and from the judgment "It can't be helped." A friend's snub would be condoned or glossed over as an oversight.

More than any other interpreter of frustration, Rosenzweig stresses the importance of both emotional and 'apperceptive' or judgmental factors. I feel, however, that he has made the latter too conscious. According to my hypothesis there is a continuously operating, relatively unconscious perceptual process which may be called 'defining the situation.'

This term is taken from the sociologist, W. I. Thomas. It was used by him and by others (*e.g.,* Waller) to designate the process of perceiving and interpreting, and also of exploring the behavior possibilities of a social situation. It has elements in common with Lewin's 'psychological environment' and with Sherif's 'frames of reference.' But 'defining the situation' is more than perceiving; it is a kind of active perceiving, interpreting and sizing up a situation with reference to one's potential behavior in it. We cannot know how a given situation influences an individual unless we know how he defines it for himself.

Strong emotions, then, tend toward overt behavior, but always directed and limited by the individual's adjustive habits and by the way he defines the situation. He may customarily express his emotions freely, or he may repress them. Or he may be adept at utilizing substitute forms—*i.e.,* mechanisms— for expressing his strong emotions which are the essence of frustration. Generally speaking, the more stress or threat he reads into the immediate social situation, the more inhibited and disguised his expressive behavior will be.

Our analysis will be made clearer by the use of an example and a diagram. (See Fig. 1). An individual intent upon an important promotion in his business or profession learns the promotion has been won by another person, which produces real frustration. He becomes emotional—but how? If the event is unexpected and the cause unclear, the emotion is a generalized sort of anger. If he knows, or thinks he knows, whose efforts defeated him, his emotional reaction takes the more specific form of hostility or hatred, quite possibly with components of jealousy. Psychologically this is a different phenomenon from generalized anger (though it may be similar physiologically) since it is directed toward a particular individual.

Let us assume, however, that our individual has no detailed information about the events leading up to the loss of his expected promotion and that, therefore, he is in a state of generalized anger. Then what? If he characteristically expresses emotion in an uninhibited way, he may throw things, kick chairs around and curse vehemently. But he is less likely to do this if persons whose opinions he values are present. If they are, he might rather engage in some substitute type of expression, such as rationalizing or seeking sympathy.

On the other hand, he may be the kind of person who seldom gives free vent to his emotions. He may then displace his anger upon his wife and children if they are present. He might kick the dog or cat, or 'take it out' on a clumsy delivery boy, all depending upon who is present at the time and what his relationship to them happens to be. Or if he were a person of violent prejudices, he might displace his anger upon 'the Jews,' 'the Reds,' 'the Catholics' or some other handy scapegoat. Again, he might regress; if his mother were present he might burst into tears and put his face in her lap as he always did when a child. Or he might engage in one or another kind of comforting fantasy.

Actually he would probably utilize more than one kind of defense mechanism. Seldom does a single outlet relieve all of one's strong emotional tensions. An immediate emotional outburst might well be followed by rationalizing, fantasy, or some kind of compensatory behavior. Clinical data suggest that as children most of us acquire quite a repertory of forms of substitute expression. Hence the particular one or ones we employ depend in large measure upon the social situation as we interpret it.

Another possibility is that, because of past training and/or a very stringent social situation, an individual may inhibit or repress nearly all overt behavior. If so, we would expect some sort of delayed overt expression, possibly in disguised form, as in dreams or physical symptoms of illness.

Does frustration eventuate in aggression? At the beginning of their book the Yale psychologists propose "that the existence of frustration always leads to some form of aggression." This thesis is hard to defend, as two of the authors, Miller and Sears, point out in subsequent articles.[2]

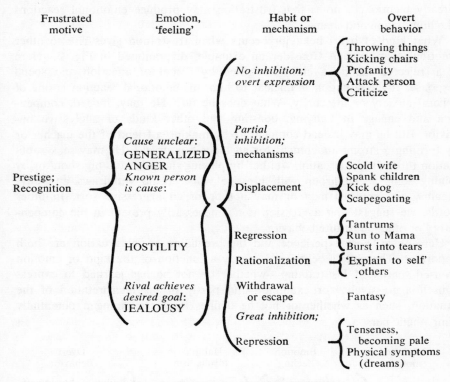

FIG. 1. REACTION TO FRUSTRATION

Much behavior resulting from frustration is, of course, aggressive. Probably the Yale group arrived at their sweeping conclusion partly because the cases they considered were dramatic, short-time, anger-producing kinds of frustration—the young man who was bawled out by the traffic cop while driving with his girl, the boarders and the delayed dinner, and so on. Clinical data, however, suggest that frustration may produce different emotional reactions, such as fear, anxiety, inferiority or shame, sometimes without any

[2]The first part of the same proposition is "that the occurrence of aggressive behavior always presupposes the existence of frustration." We shall not discuss the subject here, except to suggest that it is also difficult to defend as a general statement. Certain kinds of behavior which are definitely aggressive seem to be the socially sanctioned ways of behaving in some communities (e.g., a tough city slum area or a primitive culture). Such behavior may well be learned and practiced without having its origin, necessarily, in frustration.

trace of anger, hostility or jealousy. Symonds considers anxiety a very common reaction to frustration. In fact, he defines anxiety as a "mental distress with respect to some anticipated frustration." Rosenzweig, as already mentioned, notes that frustration may produce emotional reactions like humiliation and shame.

What kind of overt behavior occurs when frustration gives rise to other emotions than anger? Consider an example, diagrammed in Fig. 2. Here is a 'rejected' child—a child frustrated by denial of affection and social response. If the situation is unclear to him, his emotional reaction is one of general anxiety or insecurity. What does he do? He may, indeed, compensate and engage in bullying, boasting and other kinds of aggressive behavior. But he may instead compensate by making a friend of the teacher or by forming a strong attachment for an older boy or girl. He may seek satisfaction through identification—either by playing the role of a 'big shot,' or by joining some social group with prestige value. If he withdraws and daydreams, his fantasies may or may not be of an aggressive sort. In other words, we suggest that aggression is not necessarily present in the compensatory or other substitute behavior.

Here again, past experience and the prevailing social situation are both important. The child's behavior is partly a function of the kind of emotion aroused, partly of his training—whether or not he has learned to express himself aggressively, for example—and partly of his interpretation of the situation, such as whether or not he defines it as containing a potentially sympathetic person.

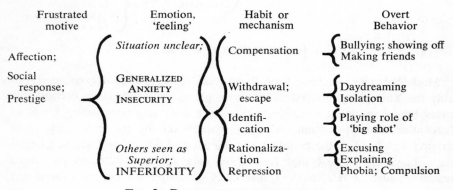

FIG. 2. REACTION TO FRUSTRATION

What about the relation between 'frustration' and 'conflict'? Frustration is usually considered an objective or environmental kind of thwarting; conflict a subjective clash of incompatible motives. The current tendency seems to be to consider conflict a special case of frustration (*e.g.,* Shaffer and

Rosenzweig). Many psychologists, however, treat frustration and conflict separately and do not attempt to relate them. In terms of the present hypothesis the important point is that both frustration and conflict involve dynamic and highly upsetting emotional states which impel the organism toward some sort of overt behavior. Reaction to conflict, as to frustration, follows the same sequence: emotion, habit or mechanism, and overt behavior. For instance, conflict arising from performance of an act considered immoral may arouse a feeling of generalized anxiety, or a more specific feeling of guilt, embarrassment or shame. Habits and mechanisms come into play. Through sublimation the emotional reaction may impel one toward religious or altruistic activity; through projection, toward gossip or scandal-mongering; through repression, toward phobia or compulsion; through a kind of displacement toward masochism or other self-directed aggression. The nature of the frustration largely determines the basic emotional reaction, and the resultant behavior depends upon existing habit-patterns operating in the individually defined social situation.

The above discussion has omitted many important aspects of the problem of frustration. It has not dealt with the efficacy of resultant behavior in reducing emotional tensions evoked by frustration. It has neglected the important matters, so ably treated by the Yale group, of the effects of differing degrees and strengths of instigation, or the effects of anticipated punishment. Nor has it dealt with the concept of 'frustration tolerance' which is taken up by Rosenzweig and others.

The critique and hypothesis presented above is a systematic contribution designed to fill in certain gaps and to fit loose ends together. Some psychologists may object to such an analysis, *per se,* as violating the essential unity or Gestalt-character of behavior. The only answer, I suppose, is that some kinds of behavior are too complex to be treated as a whole; they have to be analyzed, though efforts must be made to put the pieces together again. Other psychologists will undoubtedly object to certain of the statements and interpretations. The whole hypothesis needs, of course, to be verified by clinical or experimental methods.

In addition to setting up the four-stage scheme of frustration-emotion-mechanism-overt behavior, the hypothesis proposes the following things:

It makes emotion the central dynamic factor in reaction to frustration, and distinguishes between generalized emotional states (*e.g.,* anger, anxiety) and more specific and directed states or 'feelings' (*e.g.,* hostility, jealousy, inferiority).

It stresses the interoperation of both past experience and present situations as determining the form and content of resulting overt behavior.

Furthermore, it emphasizes that the crucial present factor is not the situation as it exists in some objective sense, but rather as the individual defines and interprets it.

Most of all, perhaps, this paper represents a protest against what Leeper calls 'peripheralism' in psychology; that is to say, the description of behavior chiefly in terms of stimuli and overt responses, to the neglect of intervening organismic factors. Hence it is, in brief, an attempt to describe all the significant psychological variables which interoperate when a person is frustrated.

REFERENCES—SECTION FIVE

Albino, R. C. Defenses against aggression in the play of young children. *Brit. J. Psychol.*, 1954, *27*, 61-71.

Allison, J., and Hunt, D. E. Social desirability and the expression of aggression under varying conditions of frustration. *J. Consult. Psychol.*, 1959, *23*, 528-532.

Amsel, A., and Hancock, W. Motivational properties of frustration: III. Relation of frustration effect to antedating goal factors. *J. exp. Psychol.*, 1957, *53*, 126-131.

Anastasi, A., Cohen, N., and Spatz, D. A study of fear and anger in college students through the controlled diary method. *J. genet Psychol.*, 1948, *73*, 243-249.

Bandura, A., and Walters, R. H. *Adolescent Aggression.* New York: Ronald Press, 1959.

Barker, R. G. Frustration as an experimental problem. V. The effect of frustration upon cognitive ability. *Charact. and Pers.*, 1938-39, *7*, 145-150.

———, Dembo, T., and Lewin, K. Frustration and regression: An experiment with young children. *Univ. Ia. Stud. Child. Welf.*, 1941, *18*, 1-314.

Bateson, G. The frustration-aggression hypothesis and culture. *Psychol. Rev.*, 1941, *48*, 350-355.

Bennett, C. M., and Jordan, T. E. Security-insecurity and the direction of aggressive responses to frustration. *J. clin. Psychol.*, 1958, *14*, 166-167.

Berkowitz, L. The expression and reduction of hostility. *Psychol. Bull.*, 1958, *55*, 257-283.

———. Anti-semitism and the displacement of aggression. *J. abnorm. soc. Psychol.*, 1959, *59*, 182-187.

Block, J., and Martin, B. C. Predicting the behavior of children under frustration. *J. abnorm. soc. Psychol.*, 1955, *51*, 281-285.

Bornston, F. L., and Coleman, J. C. The relationship between certain parents' attitudes toward child rearing and the direction of aggression of their young adult offspring. *J. clin. Psychol.*, 1956, *12*, 41-44.

Britt, S. H., and Janus, S. Q. Criteria of frustration. *Psychol. Rev.*, 1940, *47*, 451-470.

Brown, J. S., and Farber, I. E. Emotions conceptualized as intervening variables—with suggestions toward a theory of frustration. *Psychol. Bull.*, 1951, *48*, 465-495.

Bull, N., and Strongin, E. The complex of frustration. *J. nerv. ment. Dis.*, 1956, *123*, 531-535.

Child, I. L., and Waterhouse, I. K. Frustration and the quality of performance: I. A critique of the Barker, Dembo and Lewin experiment. *Psychol. Rev.*, 1952, *59*, 351-362.

———, and ———. Frustration and the quality of performance: II. A theoretical statement. *Psychol. Rev.*, 1953, *60*, 127-139.

Cowen, E. L., Landes, J., and Schaet, D. E. The effects of mild frustration on the expression of prejudiced attitudes. *J. abnorm. soc. Psychol.*, 1959, *58*, 33-38.

Davis, J. M. A reinterpretation of the Barker, Dembo, and Lewin study of frustration and regression. *Child Develpm.*, 1958, *29*, 503-506.

Davitz, J. R. The effects of previous training on post-frustration behavior. *J. abnorm. soc. Psychol.*, 1954, *47*, 309-315.

Dollard, J., Doob, L. W., Miller, N. E., Mower, O. H., and Sears, R. F. *Frustration and Aggression.* New Haven: Yale Univ. Press, 1939.

Foulds, G. A. Superiority-inferiority index in relation to frustrating situations. *J. clin. Psychol.*, 1958, *14*, 163-166.

Frederiksen, N. The effects of frustration on negativistic behavior of young children. *J. genet. Psychol.*, 1942, *61*, 203-226.

Gatling, F. P. Frustration reactions of delinquents using Rosenzweig's classification system. *J. abnorm. soc. Psychol.*, 1950, *45*, 749-752.

Goldfarb, W. Psychological privation in infancy and subsequent adjustment. *Amer. J. Orthopsychiat.*, 1945, *15*, 247-255.

Graham, F. K., Charwot, W. A., Honig, A. S., and Weltz, P. C. Aggression as a function of the attack and the attacker. *J. abnorm. soc. Psychol.*, 1951, *46*, 512-520.

Hartmann, G. W. Frustration phenomena in the social and political sphere. *Psychol. Rev.*, 1941, *48*, 362-363.

Himmelweit, H. Frustration and aggression: A review of recent experimental work. In T. H. Pear, (Ed.), *Psychological Factors of Peace and War.* New York: Philosophical Library, 1950.

Jenkins, R. L. Motivation and frustration in delinquency. *Amer. J. Orthopsychiat.*, 1957, *27*, 528-537.

Jensen, A. R. Aggression in fantasy and overt behavior. *Psychol. Monographs*, 1957, *71*, 13 pp.

Jost, H. Some physiological changes during frustration. *Child Develpm.*, 1941, *12*, 9-15.

Kagan, J. The measurement of overt aggression from fantasy. *J. abnorm. soc. Psychol.*, 1956, *52*, 390-393.

Lawson, R., and Marx, M. H. Frustration: Theory and experiment. *Genet. psychol. Monogr.*, 1958, *57*, 393-464.

Lesser, G. S. The relationship between overt and fantasy aggression as a function of maternal response to aggression. *J. abnorm. soc. Psychol.*, 1957, *55*, 218-221.

————. Conflict analysis of fantasy aggression. *J. Pers.*, 1958, *26*, 29-41.

Levin, H., and Turgeon, V. The influence of the mother's presence on children's doll play aggression. *J. abnorm. soc. Psychol.*, 1957, *55*, 304-308.

Lewin, K. Behavior and development as function of the total situation. In L. Carmichael, (Ed.), *Manual of Child Psychology.* New York: Wiley, 1946, 791-844.

————, Lippitt, R. ,and White, R. K. Patterns of aggressive behavior in experimentally created "social climates." *J. soc. Psychol.*, 1939, *10*, 271-300.

Livson, N., and Mussen, P. H. The relation of ego control to overt aggression and dependency. *J. abnorm. soc. Psychol.*, 1957, *55*, 66-71.

Maier, N.R.F. *Frustration.* New York: McGraw-Hill, 1949.

————. Frustration theory: Restatement and extension. *Psychol. Rev.*, 1956, *63*, 370-388.

————, and Ellen, P. The integrative value of concepts in frustration theory. *J. consult. Psychol.*, 1959, *23*, 195-206.

Maslow, A. H. Conflict, frustration and the theory of threat. *J. abnorm. soc. Psychol.*, 1943, *38*, 81-86.

McCary, J. L., and Tracktin, J. Relationship between intelligence and frustration-aggression patterns as shown by two racial groups. *J. clin. Psychol.*, 1957, *13*, 202-204.

McClelland, D. C. Review of Maier's frustration. *J. abnorm. soc. Psychol.*, 1950, *45*, 564-566.

Miller, N. E., and Bugelski, R. Minor studies in aggression: II. The influence of frustrations imposed by the in-group on attitudes expressed toward out-groups. *J. Psychol.*, 1948, *25*, 437-442.

Mobsin, S. M. Effect of frustration on problem-solving behavior. *J. abnorm. soc. Psychol.*, 1954, *16*, 425-428.

Mowrer, O. H. Biological versus moral "frustration" in personality disturbances. *Progressive Educ.*, 1949, *26*, 65-69.

Otis, N. B., and McCandless, B. Responses to repeated frustrations of young children differentiated according to need area. *J. abnorm. soc. Psychol.*, 1955, *50*, 349-353.

Pastore, N. The role of arbitrariness in the frustration-aggression hypothesis. *J. abnorm. soc. Psychol.*, 1952, *47*, 738-741.

Pepitone, A., and Kleiner, R. The effect of threat and frustration on group cohesiveness. *J. abnorm. soc. Psychol.*, 1957, *54*, 192-199.

Roberts, A. H., and Jessor, R. Authoritarianism, punitiveness, and perceived social status. *J. abnorm. soc. Psychol.*, 1958, *56*, 311-314.

Rosen, S. An approach to the study of aggression. *J. soc. Psychol.*, 1957, *46*, 259-267.

Rosenszweig, S. Tests of frustration. *Amer. J. Orthopsychiat.*, 1935, *5*, 395-403.

————. The experimental measurement of types of reaction to frustration. In Murray, H. A., (Ed.), *Explorations In Personality*. New York: Oxford Univ. Press, 1938.

————. An experimental study of "repression" with special reference to need-persistive and ego-defensive reactions to frustration. *J. exp. Psychol.*, 1943, *32*, 64-74.

————. An outline of frustration theory. In J. McV. Hunt, (Ed.), *Personality and the Behavior Disorders*. New York: Ronald Press, 1944, Chapter 11.

————, and Rosenzweig, L. Aggression in problem children and normals as evaluated by the Rosenzweig P. F. study. *J. abnorm. soc. Psychol.*, 1952, *47*, 683-687.

Saksida, S. Motivation mechanisms and frustration stereotypes. *Amer. J. Orthopsychiat.*, 1959, *29*, 599-611.

Scott, J. P. Dominance and the frustration-aggression hypothesis. *Physiol. Zool.*, 1948, *21*, 31-39.

————. *Aggression*. Chicago, Ill.: Univer. Chicago Press, 1958.

Sears, R. R., and Sears, P. S. Minor studies of aggression: V. Strength of frustration-reaction as a function of strength of drive. *J. Psychol.*, 1940, *9*, 297-300.

————, Hovland, C. I., and Miller, N. E. Minor studies of aggression: I Measurement of aggressive behavior. *J. Psychol.*, 1940, *9*, 275-294.

————. Non-aggressive reactions to frustration. Psychol. Rev., 1941, *48*, 343-348.

————, Pintler, M. H., and Sears, P. S. Effect of father separation on pre-school children's doll play aggression. *Child Develpm.*, 1946, *17*, 219-243.

————. Relation of fantasy aggression to interpersonal aggression. *Child Develpm.*, 1950, *21*, 5-6.

————. Effects of frustration and anxiety on fantasy aggression. *Amer. J. Orthopsychiat.*, 1951, *21*, 498-505.

————, Whiting, J.W.M., Nowlis, V., and Sears, P. S. Some child-rearing antecedents of aggression and dependency in young children. *Genet. Psychol. Monogr.*, 1953, *47*, 135-236.

Seashore, H. G., and Bavelas, A. A study of frustration in children. *J. genet. Psychol.*, 1942, *61*, 279-314.

Sherman, M., and Jost, H. Frustration reaction of normal and neurotic persons. *J. Psychol.*, 1942, *13*, 3-19.

Siegel, A. E. Aggressive behavior of young children in the absence of an adult. *Child Development*, 1957, *28*, 371-378.

Singer, R. D., and Fishbach, S. Some relationships between manifest anxiety, authoritarian tendencies, and modes of reaction to frustration. *J. abnorm. soc. Psychol.*, 1959, *59*, 404-408.

Stagner, R., and Congdon, C. S. Another failure to demonstrate displacement of aggression. *J. abnorm. soc. Psychol.*, 1955, *51*, 695-696.

Stanford, J. W., and Hsu, E. H. Experimental frustration in human adults. *J. clin. Psychol.*, 1948, *4*, 269-276.

Swickard, D. L., and Spilka, B. Hostility expression among delinquents of minority and majority groups. *J. consult. Psychol.*, 1961, *25*, 216-220.

White, R. W. *Lives in Progress*. New York: Dryden Press, 1952.

White, W. A. The frustration theory of consciousness: mind as energy. *Psychoanal. Rev.*, 1929, *16*, 143-162.

Worchel, P. Catharsis and the relief of hostility. *J. abnorm. soc. Psychol.*, 1957, *55*, 238-243.

————. Personality factors in the readiness to express aggression, *J. clin. Psychol.*, 1958, *14*, 355-359.

Wright, M. E. The influence of frustration upon social relations of young children. *Character & Pers.*, 1943, *12*, 111-122.

Zander, A. F. A study of experimental frustration. *Psychol. Monogr.*, 1944, *56*, No. 256.

MOTIVATION AND PRECEPTION

Various types of evidence, both experimental and clinical, are responsible for the now generally accepted fact that perception is not solely a cognitive process. Instead, as has been well established, it is a highly selective and active process whose organization is determined not only by external stimuli but also—and more importantly—by the simultaneous operation of an individual's internal states. An individual's internal states may be exemplified by such fundamental needs as sex, hunger, thirst, as well as his attitudes, fears, past experiences, values and purposes. It is important to note that these internal motivating states may be either conscious or unconscious. Hastorf and Knutson (Paper No. 34) elucidate on many of the comments made above.

The remaining articles in this chapter highlight in experimental fashion the influence of motivational determinants on the perceptual process. Bruner and Postman (Paper No. 35) deal "with the problem of threat-produced tension and release from tension in the perceptual behavior of the organism." They concern themselves with solving two related problems: a) whether in the process of perception, the organism tends to accentuate, to minimize, or negatively accentuate threatening objects, and b) what happens to the process of perception when tension is removed? In their second paper (No. 36) Bruner and Postman describe an experiment which shows that the thing considered important, either for positive or negative reasons, "looms larger" (and is accentuated) in an individual's perceptual field than a thing of no importance or value to him. The paper by Smith (No. 37) presents evidence which suggests that one's inner feelings of security and insecurity exert an important influence on the personal (physical) distance spontaneously established between himself and others. The results of this study tend to show that individuals who have feelings of security move toward other persons and those with feelings of insecurity move away from people. Murray (Paper No. 38) illustrates that a person's emotional state may affect his judgment of others. Experimentally, he demonstrates how, in certain circumstances, a feeling of fear will cause some individuals to intensify their judgments of the maliciousness of other people.

Perhaps one of the most significant studies from the standpoint of noting the widespread ramifications of motivation on perception and related psychological processes is that by Franklin, Schiele *et al* (Paper No. 39). This study illustrates the tremendous effect that a minimum diet to the point of semi-starvation has on a group of individuals' basic perceptions, attitudes and interests.

34. Motivation, Perception, and Attitude Change

A. H. Hastorf and A. L. Knutson

PERCEPTION is a central problem in social psychology. In this paper attention is drawn to the manner in which past experience and motivation influence perception in social situations, and, in this way, influence our social attitudes. Any study of

Abridged from the *Psychological Review,* 1949, 56, 88-94. Reprinted by permission of the authors and the American Psychological Association, Inc.

attitudes must take into account the fact that attitudes have a functional value, and that a person perceives social situations in terms of his own past experiences, values and purposes.

PERCEPTION INFLUENCED BY PAST EXPERIENCE AND MOTIVATION

We know that an automobile is perceived as an automobile rather than as the unclassified series of light waves which produces the retinal stimulus. Moreover, different people perceive the same automobile in different ways: the dealer perceives it in terms of its age, make, and sales price; the purchaser sees it in terms of its cost and future use. Purposes and past experience are both known to play a part in this perceptual process.

The view held here is that perception is an active purposive process developed through past experience. Although the role of conscious processes usually referred to as interpretation and judgment is clearly recognized as a factor in some perceptions, it is felt that an even greater emphasis should be given to the essentially unconscious selective aspect of all perception.

It is commonly recognized that in the adaptation of the organism to its environment, perception plays an important role. Those cues which aid the individual in adjusting to his environment are likely to be the ones most quickly learned and longest retained, even though they may not be consciously recognized. In this sense, perception may well be governed by the same general laws applicable to any learning process. The greater pragmatic value for most people of such a distance cue as size as compared with brightness seems to be the most reasonable explanation for the dominance of size over brightness as a distance cue when these two are placed in conflict.

Helmholtz called attention to the experiential and purposive nature of perception in observing that we are not aware of such sensory phenomena as the blind spot, the Purkinje phenomenon and combination tones. His conclusions could well have appeared in a present-day psychological journal:

> We are not in the habit of observing our sensations accurately, except as they are useful in enabling us to recognize external objects. On the contrary, we are wont to disregard all those parts of the sensations that are of no importance so far as external objects are concerned.

There is growing evidence that we learn to perceive, and that perception, like learning, is purposive. Anthropologists have reported many instances which suggest that perceptions serve the values and purposes acquired in a cultural group. Experimental studies by psychologists in recent years give strong support to these observations.[1] Our unique and common needs, values and purposes have been shown to exercise an active functional influence over both what is perceived and how it is perceived.

In the past there has been a tendency to explain these differences in observation only in terms of conscious judgments and interpretations. The word *see* has often appeared in quotes, implying that the stimulus is seen in one way and consciously interpreted in another. The work of the Hanover Institute suggests strongly that perception itself is an unconscious judgmental process—that interpretation occurs at an unconscious, as well as at the conscious, level—and that the *see* may be taken out of quotes.

Past experience and purpose cannot be clearly delineated as controlling factors in the perceptual process. A situation can have meaning to the individual only if he can relate it to his purposes *through* past experience. Purposes are acquired, and in that way represent the conclusions of past experience. The purposive actions of today are evolved from the reward-punishment experiences of yesterday, and to speak of the results of experience in this sense is to speak of acquired purposes. As we learn through experience to perceive, so we learn through experience to evaluate. Thus our present purposes become both functions and representations of our previous successful and unsuccessful activities.

Ames, of the Hanover Institute, has stated his position with respect to this issue as follows:

> It is apparent that there is no 'meaning,' for instance, in the undifferentiated light rays themselves which impinge on the cornea. Nor is there any 'meaning' in the light rays as differentiated by the lens system of our eyes that impinge on the receptors in our retinas; or in the electrical-chemical disturbances that take place between the retinal receptors and the visual center of the brain. 'Meaning' is significance which has been disclosed through prior purposeful action. The significance is related to stimulus patterns existing at the time of the original experience and is reactivated when the organism is later subjected to similar stimulus patterns.
>
> The function of sensations is not to disclose the innate character of a thing as such or its spatial position as such. It is to establish between the evolving organism and the ever-changing environment a relationship on the basis of which the organism may effectively carry out its purpose. This means that sensations are prognostic directives for purposeful action.

---

[1] A very recent study by Riesen provides evidence for the thesis that perception is a learned response. Riesen raised two chimpanzees in complete darkness up to the age of sixteen months. A summary of his observations suggests that these primates appeared to be blind for most practical purposes when first brought into the light.

Ames has developed over sixty demonstrations concerned with the nature of visual perception. Since his conclusions are derived mainly from these demonstrations, it seems pertinent to discuss briefly two of them.

One of the demonstrations is a distorted room so designed that when you look at it from a particular point of view it gives rise to the same uniocular indications that you would get from a rectilinear room. This room is placed behind a screen so that you can see it only with your head in the position from which it appears to you as a rectilinear room.

If you look at the room with one eye from that point of view, your sensations will be of a rectilinear room. You could look at the room forever and, for all that your sensations give you, you would still believe it was a rectilinear room.

Preliminary studies at Princeton[2] of subjects viewing the distorted room reveal considerable individual variation in perception. The distorted room used was not perfect; minor monocular cues still existed and, if perceived, could "tip off" the observer that the room was distorted. These cues included differences in lighting, detail, and minor imperfections in construction. If a subject, viewing the room monocularly, perceived one of these minor cues, it seemed to lead him to discover other evidences of distortion. Some subjects remained unaware of any distortion for relatively long periods of time. Observation of a few subjects, blind in one eye for five years or more, suggests the possibility that they are especially sensitive to monocular cues. This greater discrimination and selectivity on the part of persons with vision in only one eye can be explained in terms of the necessity for the learning and using of these cues for the purpose of adapting to an environment in which accurate judgment of size and distance is so important.

Another demonstration consists of a rectilinear room with one open wall. The inner walls of this room (including the floor and ceiling) are covered with oak leaves. The subject views the room from the open side. With normal vision the room looks perfectly rectilinear, but when the subject views the room through aniseikonic lenses, the room takes on a distorted shape. These lenses alter in specific ways the geometric character of the room, depending on the locus of fixation (e.g., the walls, the floors, etc.). This phenomenon cannot be explained entirely on the basic of optics, because when the same lenses are worn while looking at a room containing such familiar objects as desks, chairs, people, etc., almost no distortions are seen at first unless specifically pointed out by the demonstrator.

In this demonstration, which is somewhat analogous to an early study by Adams, an individual views two situations differing primarily in that one is much more familiar to him than the other. In both instances the visual

[2] The Hanover Institute has provided a complete set of these demonstrations for the Office of Public Opinion Research, Department of Psychology, Princeton University.

sitmulus patterns are distorted, but in the less familiar situations this distortion is observed more quickly and more severely. Thus past experience has an immediate influence upon the perceptual response.

In this section we have attempted to point out briefly that perception is an active process determined by past experience and purpose. The physical stimulus and the physiological state of the organism are also obvious conditions to consider in accounting for individual differences. The evidence suggests that perception takes place in an acquired referential frame, and that situations can have meaning to the individual only in terms of his purposes within such a frame of reference. So viewed, purposes are largely functions of past experience which perform a selective action in the current perceptual situation.

IMPLICATIONS FOR ATTITUDE FORMATION AND CHANGE

If our individual and social purposes are important determinants of what is perceived, as has been suggested above, many of the basic problems of attitude formation, persistence, and change can be seen in a new perspective. It becomes clear that differences in the evaluation of a social situation are not differences in conscious judgment and interpretation alone. Prior to these conscious judgments and interpretations, there very well may be basic differences in the manner in which situations are perceived, depending on differences in past experience and purpose. Fundamental attitude changes are not likely to occur unless there are changes in the individual and social purposes which often play an unconscious selective role in perception. It follows from this thesis that attitudes are functionally related to values and purposes, that a shake-up in the identifications and in the acquired status-strivings or purposes which accompany these identifications is necessary if these attitude changes are to occur.

The attorneys for the N.A.M. and the C.I.O. in debating about the provisions of the Taft-Hartley Bill and the probable effect of its pasasge on the public welfarc really have no parallel topics for debate. They neither perceive the same Taft-Hartley Bill nor the same public welfare. Since the disagreements are more fundamental than differences in conscious judgments or interpretations, no amount of debate is likely to be effecitve. These judgments or interpretations may change, but they will still remain judgments or interpretations of differently preceived situations, unless one or the other of the attorneys first undergoes a complete break-down and reorientation of his identifications and related strivings. In such a case he could no longer effectively represent his group.

If the N.A.M. and the C.I.O. attorneys should honestly attempt to compromise on their points of disagreement, they would not be likely to achieve full success. For the concessions of each would be limited by the framework of the social situation he perceives. Each would unwittingly weigh the other's objectives in terms of his own purposes. What appears to be a minor demand to one may strike at the core of the other's purposes, or may not even come within the framework of the other's perception of the situation. No amount of good will could reconcile the differences in the way they would perceive the same social situation.[3]

The completely different economic and social circumstances attending the development of a middle class child give growth to ego-strivings which do not permit him to perceive a social situation in the same way as a working class child perceives it. The values and purposes acquired in childhood influence both his perception of social situations and his attitudes concerning them. This may in part account for the differences in attitude reported between people in America who identify themselves with the middle class and those who identify themselves with the working class.

In this sense class differences, whether consciously recognized or not, appear to be fundamental differences in acquired purposes, as well as in economics and attitudes. Persons who have acquired their status-strivings in the socio-economic atmosphere of one class are believed incapable by reason of past experience of perceiving the goals of another class. The difference is again thought to be one of perception as well as conscious interpretation and judgment.

This difference makes the crossing of the class lines during a single generation an extremely difficult psychological as well as economic and social problem. At times, however, the attendant uncertainty and insecurity may result in the complete breakdown of the ego and a satisfactory reorientation of group identifications may occur.

It has been suggested that:

> In periods of relative instablity and rapid transition brought about by technological developments, crises in social organization (such as depressions, etc.), personal conflicts are likely to become more widespread and more intense. An individual's loyalties and identifications are, in such a period, torn farther apart. Old loyalties may prove illusory, reference or membership groups that have pro-

[3]President Roosevelt well appreciated this point when he said in his message to Congress (April, 1938): "Government can deal and should deal with blindly selfish men. But that is a comparatively small part—the easier part of our problem. The larger, more important and more difficult part of our problem is to deal with men who are not selfish and who are good citizens, but who cannot see the social and economic consequences of their actions in a modern, economically interdependent community. They fail to grasp the significance of some of our most vital social and economic problems because they see them only in the light of their own personal experience and not in perspective with the experience of other men and other industries. They, therefore, fail to see these problems for the nation as a whole."

vided status may split or disintegrate. In such times, the individual seeks new identifications and loyalties.

This thesis holds, then, that changes in group identifications and status-strivings (acquired purposes) are essential to any relatively lasting attitudinal change. If existing identifications are sufficiently constant and satisfying in terms of ego-strivings for status, lasting changes in attitudes seem improbable. If existing identifications are not satisfying in terms of ego-strivings, however, a person may discard his previous identifications and attendant attitudes, identify himself more or less permanently with some new group or groups, and become personally involved in the purposes of the new group.

In general such re-identifications appear to be facilitated by changing conditions in the individual or his environment which lead to conflicts of identifications. As Sherif and Cantril point out, re-formations of the ego may occur during such critical periods as adolescence, when the existing identifications are rendered particularly unstable.

Changes brought about by sexual maturity, by significant bodily developments with their accompanying serious effects on attitudes of masculinity and femininity, shifts (or preparation for shifts) in economic roles, and actual or more seriously anticipated shifts in social status, all make the period of adolescence a crucial stage of psychological transition involving ego problems.

Breakdowns in the fully developed ego may also occur when some radical change occurs in an individual's environment, such as brought about by war, death, migration, or economic changes. The individual may be forcibly removed from the members and symbols of the group with which he identifies himself. The resulting uncertainties and insecurities may foster the acceptance of new standards, values, and identifications, and in that way, new and lasting attitudes.

At times people of widely different ideologies have been drawn together in support of common purposes. The American First Committee had extremists from both right and left among its membership prior to the German attack on the U.S.S.R. Each group was publicly embarassed by the presence of the other, but, by reason of their temporary purposes, supported one another's arguments. The underlying purposes of the two groups were in conflict even though the situation caused both groups to engage in the same activity. Consequently when the situation changed, the basic conflict in underlying purposes again became apparent.

Such situations may also cause temporary changes in attitude when individuals with conflicting loyalties share purposes and are joined in action to further these temporary purposes. In some situations during the war, white and colored soldiers united for the common purpose of winning; strong group identifications emerged. Racial differences seemed relatively unimportant. When the common purpose was achieved, however, prejudices quickly returned. In other words, the attitude changes observed seemed to be specific to the purposeful action situation, and did not endure beyond this situation.

> Outstanding illustrations of the power of working together on common problems have come from the fighting fronts. In some cases the segregation imposed by the Army and Navy broke down. White soldiers and Negroes, fighting side by side and owing their lives to the bravery of their companions, achieved splendid solidarity. Distinctions between Catholics and Protestants, between Jew and Gentile, mean litle to a bomber crew, a submarine crew, or an advancing patrol. Each man rates on his merits and his service to the group. Common projects required interdependence and fostered appreciation.

In situations involving common purposes and action, such as the war situation, perceptions were changed. For example, the Negro was perceived more as a cooperating fighting soldier than as the member of an ethnic out-group.

Individual strivings for status still occurred in the war situation, but they were overshadowed in importance by major purposes of the identification group. The major purposes of the individual became as one with social purposes of the group, while still being retained as individual purposes by the members of the group. The change in group status was a change in status for every member of the group. Removal of the need for group status-strivings left the members of the group with their old status-strivings; individual conflicts and prejudices returned.

A similar situation may occur under normal peace time conditions. A child may choose a colored playmate in a particular situation because this selection will help him to achieve his purposes in terms of the immediate situation. When the colored playmate no longer helps him to satisfy his purposes after he returns to his old group, the child will no longer select the Negro as a companion. And if the prejudice is the norm of his group, he will not be inconsistent in adopting this norm.

It would seem, therefore, that a greater appreciation of the important relationship of motivation to both perception and attitudes may lead to more productive research on the problems of attitude change. Concentration on the problem of altering an individual's identifications, and thus many of his social purposes, would seem to be getting at both the manner in which a person perceives a situation and his attitude toward that situation.

35. Tension and Tension-Release as Organizing Factors in Perception

Jerome S. Bruner and Leo Postman

PERCEPTION is a form of adaptive behavior. Its operation reflects not only the characteristics of sensorineural processes, but also the dominant needs, attitudes, and values of the organism. For perception involves a *selection* by the organism of a relatively small fraction of the multiplicity of potential stimuli to which it is exposed at any moment in time. In perception, moreover, certain stimuli are *accentuated* and vivified at the expense of others. Finally, what is "habitually seen" in any given perceptual situation is a function of the *fixation* of past perceptual responses in similar situations. Through these three processes—selection, accentuation, and fixation—the adaptive needs of the organism find expression in perception.

In other papers we have been concerned with the role of such factors as need and value in the organization of perception. Here we are concerned with the problem of threat-produced tension and release from tension in the perceptual behavior of the organism. How are threatening objects perceived? More specifically, does the organism vivify them or does one find a process analogous to repression through which such objects are minimized or "negatively accentuated"? What happens to perception in the period of post-tension relief?

Tension has been used by some learning theorists as a synonym for any motivated state of the organism. Without here questioning this usage, *tension* in these pages will be used in a more retsricted sense to denote that state of the organism which arises in the presence of threat, thwarting, deprivation, or any apparently harmful situation. Tension release, then, is the

Abridged from the *Journal of Personality,* 1947, 15, 300-308. Reprinted by permission of the authors and the Duke University Press.

reaction of the organism to the removal of this potentially harmful state of affairs.

In studying the role of tension and tension release in perceptual organization, we have become concerned with yet another problem. Most experimenters who have worked with need and attitude factors in perception have assumed, sometimes quite explicitly, that only in highly equivocal stimulus situations can such "nonsensory" factors operate. In the words of Proshansky and Murphy, for example, "it is necessary to work in a relatively unstructured situation in which the subject's perception is determined in considerable measure by his antecedent training and his present attitude". One is forced to conclude that these authors consider the perception of structured situations to be determined wholly by sensorineural processes, independently of learning and motivation. But all stimulus situations are potentially equivocal and cease to be so only to the extent that selection, accentuation, and fixation have taken place. Perception occurring without the contribuion of such adaptive factors is as unthinkable as perception without the mediation of receptive nerve tissue. In the words of Stern, *kiene Gestalt ohne Gestalter.* Our belief in the ubiquitous operation of adaptive factors in all stimulus situations leads us, therefore, to utilize exclusively in the experiments which follow such stimulus objects as could be perceived easily and clearly.

Briefly, then, the aim of these experiments is to study the perceptual accentuation of "clearly seen" objects when they are imbedded in threatening situations and after threat has been removed.

THE EXPERIMENT

The task assigned to our S's (Harvard undergraduates) was to adjust the size of a variable circular patch of light until it was subjectively equal in size to a bright pink plastic disc 1 inch in diameter and 1/10 of an inch thick. The standard disc was held in S's left palm 6 to 8 inches to the left of the variable light patch. S was seated 18 to 20 inches distant from the variable circle.

S's were divided into a control group and an experimental group of ten each. The procedure for the experimental group was divided into four periods.

Period 1: Preliminary period. No special experimental conditions were introduced during this preliminary period. Each of the ten S's made ten adjustments of the variable circle to the point of subjective equality. Half of these adjustments required the S's to decrease the variable from its maximum diameter (two inches) to the point of subjective equality (*"in"* series). Every other trial the S's increased the size of the patch from its minimum diameter (⅛ inch) to the point of subjective equality (*"out"* series).

Period 2: Mild shock period. In this second period, a grid composed of ⅛ inch copper bars placed ½ inch apart and ½ inch above a plastic platform was put on the table beside the judging apparatus. The floor of the grid measured 3 by 6 inches. This grid was in series with a standard Muenzinger-Walz shocking apparatus. The S was told that he would now engage in a test of motor coordination. A disc, the standard stimulus, was placed under the end bar on the far side of the grid, and S was instructed as follows: "Your task will be to push the disc from under these bars to the open end of the grid nearest you. The best way to do it is to push the disc from one opening between the bars to the next with your finger until you get it out from under the grid." The S practiced this operation until he was able to perform it successfully. Each S was then told that the bars of the grid would be electrically charged, and that he was to decide what magnitude of shock was just perceptible to him. With the apparatus set at 1,000 volts, the range of amperes necessary to elicit this sensation was from .12 to .25 milliamperes, the average being .16 milliamperes. Having removed the disc twice in succession from under the grid, S made two successive adjustments of the variable patch (one "in" adjustment and one "out" adjustment) to the point of subjective equality. Ten adjustments were made in this way. Since the shock sparked easily to the perspiring fingers of the S's, even this mild shock was rather annoying to them.

Period 3: Strong shock period. The procedure in this third period was identical in all respects with that of Period 2, except that S's were now requested to indicate the strongest shock they were willing to tolerate in this experiment. These ranged in strength from .35 to .45 milliamperes, averaging .38. That the shock at this strength was severe was attested by appearance of such somatic signs as sweating and paling as well as by the subjects' reports.

Period 4: Test period. The grid was removed and the shocking apparatus disconnected. The S's were assured that there would be no more shocks. This period was therefore in all respects identical with Period 1.

The procedure for the control group comprised three stages.

Period 1: Preliminary period. This preliminary series of ten judgments was made under conditions which were in all respects identical with those of the corresponding period for the experimental group.

Period 2: Nonshock control period. As in the case of the experimental group, S's were informed that they were to undergo a test of motor coordination. Like the experimental S's, they were required to remove the standard disc from under the bars of the grid. In this case, however, the grid was *not charged* nor was any mention made of electric shocks. The

Muenzinger-Walz apparatus was hidden from view. In all other respects, the experimental procedure was duplicated. On a given trial, S removed the disc twice in succession from under the uncharged grid and then made two perceptual adjustments as before. In all, ten perceptual judgments were made.

Period 3: Control test period. The conditions were in all respects identcal with the test period for the experimental group.

RESULTS

All adjustments of the circular variable patch were scored as per cent deviations from the physical size of the standard disc. The averages obtained under all the experimental conditions are presented in Table 1 and graphically in Figure 1. Before evaluating these results, it is necessary to make sure that the experimental group and the control group were reasonably well matched on their performance in the initial period. The average per cent deviation for the control group was 10.0 and for the experimental group 9.7.[1] This difference yields a *t*-ratio of .13, which obviously lacks statistical significance. The initial equivalence of the two groups may be considered virtually certain.

Let us now examine the difference between the subsequent performances of the two groups.[2] In view of the initial equality of the two groups, any significant differences between them can be reasonably ascribed to the presence of experimentally induced tension in one of the groups.

TABLE 1

Size Estimations of a Standard Disc under Shock and Nonshock Conditions

(Expressed as percentage increase over actual size)

Period	Shock Group	Period	Controls
I (no shock)	9.8	I	10.0
II (mild shock)	8.6	II	8.4
III (strong shock)	7.1		
IV (no shock recovery)	14.3	III	8.6

Mild shock condition: We compare Period 2 for the two groups. The

[1]The initial overestimation of the standard disc is attributable to its vivid light pink color which serves to magnify its subjective size. Comparable gray discs are not overestimated.

[2]There is no statistically significant difference between Periods 1, 2, and 3 of the experimental group or Periods 1, 2, and 3 of the control group.

difference here yields a *t*-ratio of .09, which indicates an absence of a reliable differentiation.

Strong shock condition: The relevant comparison here is between Period 3 of the experimental group and Period 2 of the control subjects. The difference between these two conditions yields a *t*-ratio of .68, which still lacks statistical significance.

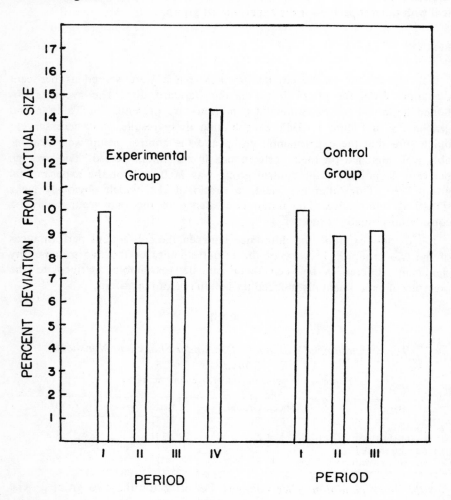

Figure 1. Average percentage deviation of judgments from actual size under various experimental conditions.

Test period: The experimental group has now been released from shock. Inspection of Figure 1 at once indicates that there is now a striking difference between the performance of the two groups. The judgments of the experimental group are characterized by significantly greater magnification. The *t*-ratio is 4.42, which is significant at a level of confidence of less than 1 per cent.

DISCUSSION OF RESULTS

If the experiment had not included a test of the effect of *tension release,* one might have drawn the premature conclusion that the tension induced by the threatening presence of electric shock had not influenced perceptual organization. Not the immediate effect of shock, but its aftermath provides the critical datum. In the presence of shock-induced tension, perceptual objects related to the source of tension seem to remain invariant in subjective size. With release of tension, these same objects become significantly *magnified* in size. What sequence of processes might be responsible?

We should like to propose a conceptualization of these processes in terms of *selective vigilance,* i.e., differential sensitivity to relevant cues. In any given situation, the organism singles out what it considers to be the environment's most relevant aspects—relevant to adaptation in the situation. What is singled out will be accentuated. Presumably, a hungry man will single out cues leading to food. A rat in a maze will, in the process of vicarious trial and error, single out cues which will get him out of the maze and into the food box. In a size-judging experiment such as ours, perception will be selectively vigilant to cues *relevant to accuracy:* the "physical" and "geometric" properties of the environment as we have learned to reconstruct them. Tension or stress introduced into such a situation, rather than rendering cues to accuracy irrelevant, may serve to accentuate them still further. In exacting and threatening situations, the most adaptive perceptual response is frequently the one which coincides most closely to the "physical" characteristics of the stimulus situation. Everyday life provides an illustration. We are never more aware of the geographical environment than walking in the dark over unfamiliar and potentially dangerous terrain. Under such conditions, we grow almost painfully aware of every rut and hummock in our path, ones which we might never have noticed while traversing the same route in the safe daylight.

Emerging from dark, unfamiliar, and dangerous terrain, one may become literally oblivious of the geographical texture of the newly found path. So with our subjects. Made vigilant to accuracy cues both by instructions and by the threatening nature of the situation, the subjects cling to the "physical-geographic" dimensions of the disc. Emphatically freed of its tension signifying quality, the disc becomes the symbol of a relieving, pleasant state of affairs—no more punishing shock. With release from tension, the selective vigilance of the organism is altered; as in previous research the new-found positive value of the stimulus leads to accentuation in the form of size magnification.[3]

One might, at this point, ponder the generality of "post-tension magnification" as a psychological phenomenon. G. W. Allport has remarked, for example, that periods of tension are universally followed by expansion. Expressive and adaptive movements expand following tension release; we are apt to magnify the power and importance of hopeful events after release from the tension of, say, war. "Expansion and megalomania naturally follow release from restriction. The United Nations was our Utopia, for example, in the period immediately following release from war tension."

Such analogies serve to illustrate the generality of the phenomenon with which we are concerned. Like our results, these phenomena indicate the existence of post-tension expansion. What general psychological mechanisms are involved we do not yet know. Our conceptualization has sought to bring to the fore the operation of selective vigilance, which tunes perception to the service of the needs and attitudes of the adapting organism. It is clearly a tentative formulation. We but vaguely understand the nature of vigilance, how it operates in perception, how it relates to other forms of behavior.

The interpretation of our data leads us to a reaffirmation of our insistence upon the role of adaptive factors in perception. *Adaptive factors in perception are not limited to unstable stimulus situations.* Potentially, all stimulus stiuations are equivocal. They do not achieve perceptual organization without selection, accentuation, and fixation by the organism. The need to survive and move about in the world leads us in everyday life to accentuate what we have learned to regard as the "physical properties" of the environment. Vigilance deriving from a strong need to walk, reach, run without mishap keeps the organism bounded to "conventional physical objects" and allows little variability in perception. Such accentuation is highly adaptive behaviorally and, moreover, is rewarded by our culture. Its operation is no more nor less an adaptive and selective response to the environment than is the operation of more bizarre forms of accentuation stemming from strong desires whose satisfaction requires accentuation in a direction away from "physical" size.

---

[3]The reader may well ask for an explanation in terms of learning theory to account for the quick shift from a negative to a positive reaction to the disc. Two points are in order. A stimulus, first, derives its meaning in part at least from the situation in which it is imbedded. A gun on the wall of the study has not the same stimulus value as the same gun in the hands of an assailant. If such a situational explanation were considered insufficient, one is free to draw on any of the theories which have attempted to link the learning of responses to reward and punishment. It may well be that symbolic processes play an important role here just as they seemed to in the experiments of Ellson, in which rapid extinction of a conditioned hallucination was brought about by verbal instruction.

36. Symbolic Value as an Organizing Factor in Perception

Jerome S. Bruner and Leo Postman

THE PROBLEM

IT is by now a truism to say that it is impossible to predict the nature of perceptual organization from a knowledge of the physical properties of the stimulus and/or the characteristics of sensory neural processes alone. But it is not sufficient to pay lip service to the proposition that what is perceived reflects the predispositions, goals, and strivings of the organism at the moment of perceiving. If one is to lend substance to such generalities about the embeddedness of perception in personality, it is necessary to define operationally and to vary systematically such intra-personal factors in perception and to measure their effect on the dimensions of perceptual organization.

One of the parameters of the perceptual situation which cannot, at least for the present, be translated into conventional physical and neural terms is the *symbolic value* of that which is perceived. By symbolic value we simply mean the capacity of a perceived object to evoke reactions relevant not primarily to itself but to some state of affairs which it represents. A perceived object thus may be reacted to as a sign of reward or punishment, threat or security, fulfillment or deprivation. There is already a small body of experimental evidence demonstrating the role of symbolic value as a determinant of perception. Ansbacher, Kardos, and Fazil, for example, have shown the crucial role played by the symbolic value of objects (stamps and coins) in determining judgments of numerical magnitude. Bruner and Goodman have recently demonstrated the complex ways in which monetary

Abridged from *The Journal of Social Psychology*, 1948, 27, 203-208. Reprinted by permission of the authors and The Journal Press.

value affects the judgment of the size of objects. These investigators found that not only is the "culturally" defined value a systematic determinant of size judgments but that such judgments also vary with the individual's *need* for that which is symbolized.

The present investigation was designed to add to our knowledge of the effect of symbolic value on perceptual organization. Thus far, experiments on the role of symbolic value have dealth predominantly with positively valued objects. What of the effect of negatively valued symbols representing a threat, or more generally "an unpleasant state of affairs?" The experiment to be reported was designed to compare and contrast the effects of positive, negative, and "neutral" symbols on perceptual organization.

THE EXPERIMENT

The positive symbol used was a dollar sign, the negative a swastika, the neutral a square with its two diagonals. We are ready to acknowledge at once that these symbols, whether positive or negative, may not have had uniform affective value for all S's. Nonetheless, it is safe to say that in the case of these symbols, the cultural definition was not likely to have been radically different from the definitions applied by the S's we used—undergraduates at Radcliffe College.

The symbols were inscribed in black india ink on bright pink plastic circular discs $1/10$ inches thick, varying in diameter in quarter-inch steps from $3/4$ inches to $1\frac{1}{2}$ inches. Each of the symbols occupied approximately the same proportion of the area of each of the four discs. The symbols were inscribed in a concentric circle whose diameter was one-quarter that of the disc itself.

The task of the S was to adjust the size of the variable circular patch of light until it was subjectively equal to that of a given disc. In short, the method of average error was used. Adjustments were made from an "open" and "closed" position, i.e., starting with a circular opening two inches in diameter or $1/8$ inches in diameter. As for the four different sizes of discs, judgments were made in ascending, descending, as well as random order.

There were two major experimental groups. One of them, comprising 10 S's, made judgments of neutral and *positive* discs, the order of presentation and direction of adjustment (from "open" or "closed" position) being random. The second group of ten S's differed from the first group only in that their judgments were made on neutral and *negative* discs. Each S made 48 judgments, half on neutral discs, and half on either positive or negative ones. In making judgments, S's were seated 18 to 20 inches distant from the variable circle, holding the standard disc in the palm of their left hand, six to eight inches to the left of the variable circle.

RESULTS

The symbolic values of the stimuli proved to be a significant determinant of perceptual organization. Whether a disc was inscribed with a dollar sign, a swastika, or a neutral figure made a reliable difference in its subjective size.

The judgments of all discs were scored as deviations from actual size. These deviations were then plotted against size of discs, with type of symbol as a parameter. The results are presented in Table 1 which lists average deviations from size of disc under all conditions of judgment. The same

TABLE 1

Average Deviations of Judgments From Physical Size of Discs Inscribed With Different Symbols

Size of disc*	Positive symbol (dollar)	Negative symbol (swastika)	Neutral symbol (diagonals)
20	1.9	1.9	1.5
35	5.9	5.1	3.6
50	6.7	6.3	6.0
65	8.2	7.4	6.0

*To facilitate calibration, the diameters of the disc were scaled in arbitrary metric units. Twenty such units equal ¾ inches; 65 units equal 1½ inches.

TABLE 2

Summary of Results of Analysis of Variance

Source of variation	Sum of Squares	d.f.	Mean sum of squares	F	P
Total	27,303.41	959			
Size	3,917.24	3	1,305.75	55.00	.01
Symbols	342.19	2	171.10	7.08	.01
Interaction	117.96	6	19.66	.81	not sign
Error	22,926.02	948	24.18		

results are presented graphically in Figure 1, in which each point is based on 60 judgments in the case of the dollar sign and the swastika discs, and on 120 judgments in the case of the "neutral" discs.

That the differences indicated in Figure 1 are statistically reliable was confirmed by analysis of variance. Two criteria of classification were used, size disc and type of symbol, and as Table 2 shows, both suorces of variation yielded *F*-values significant at the 1 per cent level. It is important to note that the interaction of these two variables was not a significant source of variation.

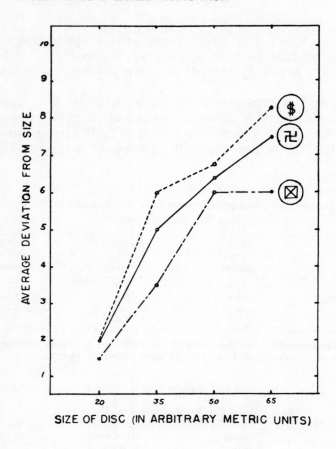

FIGURE 1

AVERAGE DEVIATION OF JUDGMENTS FROM ACTUAL SIZE OF DISCS
(Curves are *average,* not *per cent* deviations . . .)

DISCUSSION

Figure 1 indicates clearly that the dollar discs were judged largest, swastika discs next in size, and neutral discs smallest. This finding suggests an important generalization. *Value,* whether positive or negative, leads to perceptual accentuation. Under the conditions of this experiment, both positive and negative objects were accentuated positively as compared with neutral objects, i.e., subjectively magnified. Apparently, that which is "important" to the subject looms larger in perception.

The positive accentuation of desired objects confirms previous findings. That which is desired or fulfills a need tends to be emphasized in perception through magnification. The organism, as it were, maximizes the reward value of the object. When a negative symbol is of such a nature as to alert the organism to danger or threat, it is reasonable to suppose that positive accentuation may also occur. In terms of the adaptive functions of perception, accentuation of negative symbols may aid under certain conditions in preparing the organism for defense and action. The swastika, the negative symbol used in our experiments, probably had a mildly unpleasant effect, although it very likely did not embody a serious personal threat to the individual, the experiment having been conducted after the end of the war. Hence, it was positively accentuated, although not to any striking extent.

Value, then, whether positive or negative, is a determinant of subjective size. One form which accentuation may take is the kind of shift in subjective size represented by our findings. The *direction* and *magnitude* of accentuation, however, may be a function of the particular values involved. We have demonstrated that negative values can be positively accentuated. It is conceivable, nonetheless, that certain kinds of negative symbols may lead not to positive but to negative accentuation or no accentuation at all. Findings compatible with this hypothesis are presented elsewhere.

An interesting analogue to the positive accentuation of negatively valued objects is to be found in the literature on memory for affectively charged material. Postman and Murphy report, for example, that sheer degree of acceptance or rejection of stimuli was more highly correlated with retention than the values attached by subjects to the stimuli involved. A strongly rejected negative stimulus was retained better than a mildly accepted positive one.

The results of such experiments as these make it clear that one cannot expect a simple one-to-one relationship between the affective symbolic value of objects and perceptual or mnemonic accentuation.

INTRODUCTION

37. Personality Scores and the Personal Distance Effect

George Horsley Smith

IT is a common notion that some individuals are socially oriented so that they relish close personal contacts with their fellows, while others literally keep their distance from the people around them. The former are said to be "sociable," "chummy," "companionable," etc., while the latter are referred to as "distant" and "aloof." In the course of a recent investigation, it was possible to observe this "personal distance effect" in a controlled, non-verbal situation, and at the same time to relate it to scores on two personality inventories. The findings may serve (*a*) to illustrate the way in which needs and dispositions influence overt behavior vis-a-vis other people, and (*b*) to indicate a simple, non-verbal technique for studying certain interpersonal attitudes and social distance frames.

APPARATUS AND PROCEDURE

The apparatus consisted of a table approximately 7 feet 6 inches long and 2 feet wide. A Clason Visual Acuity Meter was mounted at one end of the table, and at the other end a screen was set up on which images could be projected. Images projected by the Clason remain in focus as they vary in size; hence, under proper conditions the observer experiences the image (stimulus object) as undergoing changes in distance with reference to himself. Thus, the faces used in the present experiment could be caused, apparently, to move back and forth in a straight line away from and toward *S*.

S sat at the end of the table closest to the projector. By means of a lever

Abridged from *The Journal of Social Psychology,* 1954, 39, 57-62. Reprinted by permission of the author and the Journal Press.

convenient to his right hand, he was able to control the size (apparent distance) of the image cast on the screen.[1] S viewed this image monocularly (right eye) through an aperture in a partition, just in front of him, which concealed the screen. The room was dark except for a little light that escaped from the projector bulb, and from a small flashlight which E used.

S was instructed as follows:

> You are going to look at several faces of men. They are pictures, of course. If you like, you may think of them as life-size photographs. You may know some of the men, although I doubt whether you do. You are going to be asked to make some very personal judgments about the faces; for example, whether you like them or find them interesting. You will notice that some of the faces are smiling and pleasant, while others are frowning, snarling and unpleasant. These differences will be apparent to you.

S was then shown how to operate the lever and was allowed to observe a neutral stimulus object, a square of light, as it apparently moved away from and toward him in the viewing field. The first face was then exposed, and S was asked to comment on it. He was specifically asked whether he liked the man or not, and whether or not he found him interesting. He was then instructed:

> Put the face where you would like to have it in relation to yourself. This is purely a self-reference setting. There's no right or wrong to it. Just leave the face where it is, put it further away, or bring it closer—whatever makes you feel most comfortable.

When S had finished his setting, the viewing aperture was covered over and E recorded the size of the image. S made one setting each for four different faces.

The faces used were from the Frois-Wittmann series. The details of their selection and preparation have been presented elsewhere. Briefly, two faces describable as friendly and pleasant and two describable as unfriendly and unpleasant were chosen. Slides made from reversed negatives of these were equated for height, width at widest point, brightness, and amount of detail exposed. The projected image of each face could vary in height from 5.5 cm. to 20.3 cm. The height of the image was taken as an index of its size in the present study.[2]

After completing the settings of the faces, each S filled in the Bell Ad-

---

[1]The image was actually directed toward S's end of the table, but was redirected onto the screen by two 45° mirrors.

[2]It should be noted that the Frois-Wittmann faces, while reasonably expressive and life-like, were not made under the best conditions of modern photography; also E may have detracted from their realism by blocking off certain parts of the faces in the interest of uniformity of size. Hence it is possible that the results obtained in this experiment are minimum, and that more pronounced effects might occur with other stimulus faces.

justment Inventory, Student Form, and the Knutson Personal Security Inventory.

Twenty-three male undergraduates served as subjects. Each S participated individually in the experiment.

RESULTS

Analysis proceeded as follows. (*a*) S's were ranked according to the size of their settings of the faces (image sizes). (*b*) Average personality scores were computed for the *11 men who made the larger settings* of the faces and for the *11 who made the smaller settings*.[3] (*c*) Differences between the two sets of mean personality scores were then obtained. Pertinent results are summarized in Table 1.

TABLE 1

Differences In Self-Reference Settings Related to Personality Scores

Subjects[c] ranked by	Bell—Total Score[a]	Bell—Social Score[a]	Knutson—Total Score[b]
Two pleasant faces combined			
Ss who made large settings	26.4	6.5	27.3
Ss who made small settings	44.0	13.6	24.2
Differences	17.6[d]	7.1[d]	3.1
Two unpleasant faces combined			
Ss who made large settings	31.5	8.4	26.1
Ss who made small settings	41.9	11.8	25.1
Differences	10.4	3.4	1.0
"Less ambiguous" unpleasant face:			
Ss who made large settings	28.4	7.3	25.7
Ss who made small settings	44.5	13.0	24.8
Differences	16.1[e]	5.7	.9
All four faces combined:			
Ss who made large settings	30.2	7.3	26.9
Ss who made small settings	43.2	12.9	24.4
Differences	13.0	5.6	2.5

[a]Smaller scores on the Bell Inventory indicate better adjustment.
[b]Larger scores on the Knutson Inventory indicate better adjustment.
[c]All N's = 11.
[d]Difference is significant at .02 level.
[e]Difference is significant at .05 level.

When Ss were ranked by their settings of *the two pleasant faces combined*, the 11 Ss who brought the faces "closer" (made them larger) were apparently better adjusted as estimated by the Bell Inventory than the 11 who sought to push the faces further away (made them smaller). The difference of 17.6 points in the Bell Total Score and of 7.1 points in the Social Sub-

[3]The middle subject in each ranking was excluded from consideration.

scale are both significant at the 2 per cent level. Differences in the three other sub-scales, Home, Emotional, and Health, are in the same direction (not shown on Table 1). On the Knutson Inventory the difference suggests more personal security for the 11 men who brought the faces "closer" to themselves.

Ss were next ranked according to the size of their settings of *the two unpleasant faces combined*. All differences in personality scores point to greater security and adjustment for the men who brought the faces closer to themselves, but these differences are not significant statistically (see table). Ss were then ranked by the size of their settings of each *unpleasant face separately*. For one of the unpleasant faces—apparently the less ambiguous[4]—Ss who brought the projected image "closer" were reliably better adjusted on Total Bell Scores (5 per cent level) than the Ss who "pushed it further away." This trend was confirmed by the differences in all the Bell sub-scales and in the Knutson scores. Rankings by the second unpleasant face confirmed the previously noted trend, but not reliably (not shown in table).

Finally, Ss were ranked by their settings of *all four faces combined*. The 11 men who scored highest on total image settings also averaged 13 points further in the direction of superior adjustment on the Bell Inventory than did the 11 Ss who made the smallest image settings. There are about 90 chances in 100 that this represents a true difference. Differences in the same direction showed up on the Bell Social Scale and on the Knutson Inventory.

In summary, the data suggest a tendency for the men who set the projected faces "closer" to themselves to earn more favorable personality scores than the men who made smaller settings. In several instances the differences in personality scores were too large to be attributed to chance.

DISCUSSION

The findings are in line with common sense, and are about what were expected. What psychological implications do they have? They appear to illustrate *the continuous pressure of inner securities and adjustmental tendencies on the sort of personal distances which one spontaneously establishes between himself and others*. Although the stimuli were pictures Ss seemed to regard them as meaningful and realistic. Typical comments were: "Looks like my brother," "seems friendly," "I could get along with him," "I don't trust him," and "he's somehow beneath me." One gained the impression that Ss were reacting in a free, natural way, giving overt expression to attitudes that were subtle and unverbalized in some cases, sharp and conscious in others. Interpretation of the faces in the light of these ego-involved attitudes

[4]According to average deviations of ratings obtained by Schlosberg.

tudes provided the background out of which emerged the act of setting up a given physical distance between oneself and the "other person."

In everyday life, situations constantly arise in which retiring and insecure persons "push themselves forward," and secure and aggressive ones restrain themselves from being too intimate or assertive. Yet it is a reasonable hypothesis that the sort of person who puts the most distance between himself and the faces in the present experiment would also, in general, sit furthest from other people in a room, walk furthest from companions on the sidewalk, seek a yard well screened from neighbors, etc. Just as Freudian slips, expressive movements, and "occupational postures" tell something about a person, so it is suspected personal distance behavior day in and day out provides a subtle indicator of the structure and purposes of one's personality. The unity of the individual, that is, his attitudes (revealed in the inventories) and his behavior (shown in the size settings), is emphasized.

The personal distance variable is commonly assumed to have practical value in helping one to size up people in daily situations. Whether it could be used in a standardized way for any purpose, such as selecting candidates for certain jobs, might be worth looking into. As a clinical problem, it might be interesting to know more about the sort of people who are able to exercise voluntary control and thus establish personal distances at variance with their felt needs and preferences.

The research technique used in this study, i.e., the projection of images with the Clason, is relatively simple, and could be adapted to a considerable range of clinical and social material. It would seem feasible to devise a set of standardized items, such as faces representing ethnic groups, to which Ss could respond. Attitudes and other information might be revealed that would escape verbal techniques. Some approach such as this, which gets fairly close to full-life social relationships, should at least yield interesting supplementary data in intensive studies of intergroup and interpersonal attitudes.

38. The Effect of Fear upon Estimates of the Maliciousness of Other Personalities

Henry A. Murray

THE present paper describes an attempt to demonstrate in quantitative terms the generally recognized fact that the emotional state of a subject may affect his judgments of other personalities. It is one of several experiments now in progress in this laboratory which have been designed to expose some of the internal—physical and psychical—factors which influence a subject's perceptions, interpretations, and appraisals of the objects and situations in the world about him.

The diagnosis of traits of character from the face depends, it is often said in common language, upon (1) the observation of the features (physical signs) and (2) the interpretation of them on the basis of associations—associations which in the past have been found by the observer to exist between somewhat similar physical signs and particular types of behavior. Psychologically, we speak here of two processes which may for convenience be differentiated, namely, perception and apperception. Such is the nomenclature, at least, which we have provisionally adopted for the purposes of this discussion. The term *perception* is confined to the *conscious* recognition of configurated sense impressions or segregated sensory wholes; whereas *apperception* is used to designate the process—whatever its antecedents—whereby meaning, in other than sensory terms, is assigned to the physical stimulus. This use of the term apperception is at least within the definition given by Stout. For, according to this authority, it is by the process of apperception that " a presentation acquires a certain significance for thought by connecting itself with some mental preformation as this has been organ-

Abridged from *The Journal of Social Psychology*, 1933, 4, 310-329. Reprinted by permission of the author and the Journal Press.

ized in the course of previous experience." The term is used to include understanding, interpreting, classifying, subsuming, and so forth.

The distinction we make between perception and apperception is, of course, somewhat arbitrary. For, under most conditions, the two processes are inseparably fused. For instance, as Köhler has so succinctly remarked: "If in a friendly-looking face we try to separate the mere bodily configuration and the friendliness, we find the task rather difficult, as long as we look at the whole face and do not analyze the face itself as a mosaic of colored spots."

Now, the understanding of other personalities from their features is usually more successful than can be accounted for on the basis of what was consciously perceived. And so, since in such cases the visual apparatus is the only path of communication, there must be some retinal stimulation which is not translated into conscious perception, but which, nevertheless— through some other effects—determines apperception. These other effects are not far to seek when we bear in mind that the external world comes to a subject, not solely in the guise—to use Whitehead's terminology—of *presentational immediacy* (pure sensory experience) but also in the guise of *casual efficacy*. That is to say, physical changes are activated in the body of the subject which are of the sort that may be cognized as feelings, emotions, and kinaesthetic sensations. Such activations are without doubt most fundamental, preceding in ontogenetic development the clear *conscious* perception of the stimulating object. Certain faces, for instance, arouse approach movements and others arouse withdrawal movements in the child long before the capacity for an accurate representation of the perceived object exists. Since experience shows that such movements may be modified by slight changes in the stimulating object, there must be at this time an accurate physical differentiation of sensory impressions. But since no report may be given of them, we must admit that perception—if we wish to use the term—is unconscious. Now, when language is acquired, it is probably that the estimates of other persons which a child expresses verbally are unwittingly made on the basis of how the body responds to their presence. If the child smiles, for instance, the person confronting it is "nice and good," but if it averts the head the person is "bad."

It may also be that unconscious imitation of the expression and gestures of others—a process so common in children—arouses feelings and emotions somewhat comparable to those occurring in the percevied object, and that this too is a factor which aids understanding. In this connection we are reminded of the young lad described by Poe in *The Purloined Letter* who used to mimic the facial expression of his opponent in a gambling game to discover whether it made *himself* feel intelligent. By this means he estimated the mental calibre of the other boy and in accordance with the verdict directed his own moves in the game.

The point is that certain physical features of the object which the subject does not consciously perceive are nevertheless physically affecting his body, and though he may be unable to report upon these internal happenings, they are nevertheless affecting his conscious appraisal of the object.

This is not the place to discuss in detail all the processes which contribute to a knowledge of our fellows. We merely wish to suggest how it may come about that apperceptions of the personality (feelings, motives, and probable behavior) of others are commonly influenced—as experience seems to teach—by the total bodily state of the perceiving subject. Our hypothesis would be, then, that certain meanings, or categories we might call them, such as "friendly" and "unfriendly," become integrated with certain muscular sets and emotions, and when the latter are aroused the former will be mobilized and come to mind. These intermediary physical processes would seem on superficial glance to be entirely irrelevant to the task at hand, but when we consider that they are conspicuously present—at least in an imaginatively representative form—in persons, such as novelists, whose insight into character is generally regarded as most acute, we have cause for reflection.

Now, when such processes can be accounted for by reference to the presented stimulus and its similarity to past stimuli, and hence to *traces* (a fictional concept) in the mind of the subject, we should then consider them—at least for that subject—legitimate, normal, and objectively valid. If they happen to be inappropriate and unadaptive, well, it is a matter of ignorance, insufficient experience, and so forth. When, however, the internal processes which are determining apperception have recently been aroused by some other essentially dissimilar and irrelevant stimulus, or may be shown to be more or less inveterate in the subject, then we must refer to another process—a process which distorts the external world or adds something to it which is not there.

According to the terminology of some psychologists the process whereby psychic elements—needs, feelings, and emotions, or images and contexts of images activated by such affected states—are referred by the experiencing subject to the external world without sufficient objective evidence is called *projection*. When this process is active, what is in truth mental and within the personality comes to appear as if it were outside the personality. We may speak of *perceptive projection* when sensory elements are projected, i.e., when an image takes on the vividness, substantiality, and out-thereness of a real object—as in a dream and in an hallucination—or when an image transforms or makes additions to the actual physical features of an inadequately perceived real object so that the latter is taken for the object of which the image is a representation—as in an illusion. And he may speak of *apperceptive projection* when non-sensory elements are projected. This occurs (1) when imaginal contexts, or the categories under which the activated images are subsumed, are believed, with insufficient objective evidence, to be descriptive of or to pertain to objects in the environment—as in delusions; or (2) when the needs, feelings, and emotions themselves, rather than the images or imaginal meanings activated by them, are believed by the subject to be existent in other personalities—also as in delusions. The former might be termed *complementary apperceptive projection* and the latter *supplementary apperceptive projection*.

An example of perceptive projection would be the case of a girl who mistook a stranger in the crowd for a friend whom she was hoping to meet, or the case of a criminal who believed that he saw a detective with whom he was acquainted following him down the street. An example of complementary apperceptive projection would be the case of a guilt-ridden young man who believed that his elders were secretly condemning him; whereas an example of supplementary apperceptive projection would be the case of an unhappily married woman who believed that most of her married friends were unhappy.

The reader may have noticed that in defining projection we spoke rather nonchalantly of images; we said that hallucinations were projected images, and so forth. How can they be projected images, when for the experiencing subject there are no images; there are only external objects? The answer is that they are projected *unconscious* images—a purely fictional concept. In dreams and in hallucinations we know that they are not external objects which the subject perceives; nor is he conscious of imagery in the usual sense. Common experience, however, bears witness to the inseparable gradations between dreams and phantasies—the latter being admittedly composed of images—as well as to the similarity between memory images and some of the objects which appear in dreams; and consequently some psychologists have been led to speak of projected unconscious images, since *qua* images the subject is unaware of them. It will be remembered, furthermore, that Prince performed experiments upon an hallucinating dissociated subject, and by means of automatic writing demonstrated to his own satisfaction that the hallucinated objects were similar to the imagery of a contemporary unconscious (or co-conscious) mental process.

Despite such considerations and such experiments, the hypothesis of unconscious psychical events is still refuted by other psychologists—principally on logical grounds. This is not the time to debate the point. We ourselves must simply admit that we feel the need of this concept to describe in detail the phenomenon of projection. For, as far as we know, only elements which are not at the moment conscious may be projected. It is supposed that if the subject could adopt the introspective attitude some of these so-called unconscious images would become conscious, but because attention is forcefully and passionately centered upon the external world, or because the subject is in sleep or in some other state hardly to be defined

—abstraction or dissociation—images attain the apparent substantiality of external reality; they appear to be "out there." An illusion exemplifies the same process but to a lesser degree. In this case there is some real object, but what the subject perceives is a composition product of the real object and the unconscious mental image. The greater the ingress of the latter the more does the event resemble an hallucination.

What a subject might say when presented with a vaguely perceived and unrecognizable object is this: "It makes me think of so and so," or: "It arouses images of so and so." That would be conscious imagery and not projection. If the subject "guesses," "supposes," or "imagines" it is "so and so," we speak of a pseudo-projection. For, strictly speaking, the term projection should be used only when the subject is convinced of the true existence outside himself of the object or process in question. A projection is morbid only when it is the result of some obsessive idea or continuously dominant need which frequently operates to transform the real world in a particular way.

Projections, then, by distorting a subject's recognition and interpretation of external reality prevent a detached and disinterested objectivity. They may, nevertheless, serve the cause of truth. For instance, a young man who has suffered undeservedly through the treacherous and malicious behavior of others—he has a fixed feeling of inferiority, let us say—may thenceforth suppose that strangers and acquaintances whom he meets are prompted solely by selfish motives, and at least towards him are critical and scornful. He may, indeed, like Timon of Athens, generalize his particular experiences and become a misanthrope. In so far as such a man overemphasizes the selfishness of human beings to the exclusion of their other more engaging traits he is the victim of a complementary apperceptive projection. We might say that he is mistaken in his proportions, since he attributes so much evil and so little good to others. But we must not lose sight of the fact that in some respects he may be a better observer than the average citizen, since as a result of his particular sensitiveness to malice he may very well discover and precisely analyze subtle and hidden forms of it which others have neglected, and so make a valuable contribution to psychological knowledge.

We have discussed the probable influence of bodily changes upon apperception, and how, when the former are relatively unconnected with the immediate stimulus, misapperceptions or delusions may occur. These we agreed to call apperceptive projections. Finally, we proposed the hypothesis of unconscious images to explain both perceptive projections and complementary apperceptive projections.

Such were the speculations which led us to the present enterprise: an attempt to prove by experiment that a functional relationship between emotional and apperceptive processes exists normally, and, by changing the former, a qualitative or quantitative alteration of the latter will occur. More specifically, we might characterize this experiment as an attempt to produce measurable variations in the apperception of benevolence or malice in other people by the excitation of fear in the apperceiving subject, the variation or exceptionality of the apperception in each case being estimated by comparing it with the subject's habitual apperception of the same object. The particular form of our hypothesis and the technique devised to test it were based upon such a common phenomenon as that of a person who in a fear-invoking situation—for instance while walking through a "tough" neighborhood at night—apperceives some of the strangers whom he encounters as "dangerous characters." It was supposed that, if, for purposes of standardization, photographs of people, rather than living personalities, were used as material to be judged, the subjects—especially children—after a fear-invoking situation would estimate the faces in the photographs to be more malicious than they would estimate them to be when they were free from fear. Such at least was our hypothesis, and when the daughter of the author planned a week-end country house-party of five girls, eleven years of age, it seemed that this might provide an opportunity to test it. It was supposed that during this party there would be many chances for control tests after relatively normal pleasure-invoking circumstances, and, since the children wanted to play the game of *murder* in the evening, it seemed that a fear-invoking situation would occur in the natural course of events.

We judged that the game of *murder* alone would not be sufficiently exciting, so we planned to tell the first half of a ghost story after the end of the game, on the supposition that the combination of the two situations would give rise to a state of anxiety which would perseverate long enough to affect the results on a test given immediately afterwards. At the last minute, however, circumstances interfered with the telling of the ghost story, and so we were forced to depend upon the efficacy of two games of *murder* for the evocation of fear.

TECHNIQUE

Thirty photographs approximately 5.5 x 7.5 cm. in size—most of which were taken from the magazine *Time*—were mounted upon white cards and divided into two roughly comparable series; each of which was composed of eleven photographs of men and four photographs of women, all of them unknown to the subjects of the experiments. The first series of fifteen faces was called Test A, the second series was called Test B.

Tests were given on three occasions as follows:

First Occasion. Test A after pleasure-invoking situation (control). This experiment was performed at 12:30 p.m., Saturday, after the children had returned from motoring about the country.

Second Occasion. Test A and Test B after fear-invoking situation. This experiment was performed at 7:30 p.m., Saturday, after the children had played two games of *murder*. The thirty photographs were arranged in one series so that the even numbers belong to Test A and the odd numbers to Test B.

Third Occasion. Test B after pleasure-invoking situation (control). This experiment was performed at 12:30 p.m., Sunday, after the children had returned from hitching behind a sleigh. In this way each test (A and B) was performed twice—after a fear-invoking situation and after a pleasure-invoking situation (control). We shall speak of the two trials of Test A together as Experiment A, and the two trials of Test B together as Experiment B.

On all three occasions each of the subjects—five girls, eleven years of age (designated as Mary, Jane, Lou, Jill, and Nan)—was seated at the same place, separate from the others, in a well-lighted room. The experiments were conducted as group tests, the photographs being passed around from subject to subject in order.

For the first experiment instructions were as follows:

I shall show you a series of fifteen photographs of persons whom you do not know. Some are nice, some are bad, and some are just average. I want you to guess from the photographs how good or how bad they are.

At this point each S was given a sheet of paper on which were ruled fifteen lines divided into three columns. The instructions were continued as follows:

On the sheet of paper which I have given you there are three columns. In the first column each line is numbered from one to fifteen. These stand for the numbers of the photographs. When you are presented with a photograph—each photograph is numbered from one to fifteen—please look at the face and immediately decide how good or how bad is the character of the person. It has been found that you are more likely to be right if you are guided by your first impression than if you try to reason it out. The mark or rating for goodness or badness which you give the person should be placed in the second column opposite the number of the photograph. The scale for marking runs from one to nine as follows: 1 = extremely good, i.e., generous, kind, loving and tender; 2 = very good; 3 = good; 4 = fairly good; 5 = average; 6 = fairly bad; 7 = bad; 8 = very bad; 9 = extremely bad, i.e., cruel, malicious, and wicked. Remember now: 5 is average, 9 is extremely bad and 1 is extremely good.

In the third column there is space for you to write down what you think the person in the photograph is thinking or saying. You should spend about thirty seconds on each photograph, but I shall allow you more time if necessary.

After these directions were read and explained, two sample photographs not belonging to the series—one of a man smiling and one of a man scowling—were shown to the children and they were asked to announce their ratings so that all could hear. This, so the experimenter could be certain that the directions were understood.

On the second occasion, that is, after the fear-invoking situation, the instructions did not have to be repeated. It was pointed out, however, that there were now thirty instead of fifteen faces to be diagnosed.

For those who are not acquainted with the game of *murder* it may be said that it is played after dark throughout a house with all lights extinguished. The players commence by drawing lots from a hat; one of the players, unknown to the others, drawing the lot of murderer. After the draw, the players, with the exception of the one amongst them who has drawn the lot of detective, sneak about the house in the dark until the murderer "kills"—by touching—any one of the players whom he chooses. The victim, after counting ten, yells aloud, and then all players join the detective, who proceeds by cross-questionings to discover the culprit. Everyone must tell the truth except the murderer, and he may lie as much as he likes.

Among children there are individual differences in sentiment towards this game. Some children love it and play it without disquietude; others wish to play but experience an unpleasant apprehension throughout; still others are afraid to play and avoid it if possible.

RESULTS

At the cross-examination after the "murder" one of the subjects, Mary, said that she was "frightened to death" and again: "I was so scared I hid under the table the whole time." Lou also admitted that she was afraid. No other remarks of a like nature were volunteered, and it was our general impression that the amount of occasioned excitement was less than usual.

That the two games of *murder,* however, were effective in arousing some degree of fear was attested not only by the results of the experiments, but also by an event which occurred in the early morning of the next day— that is, on Sunday. This event bears reporting since it helps to confirm the validity of the tests. It happened in this way. Jane, who had been sleeping in one of the spare rooms with Lou, woke the household at six-thirty in the morning to inform us that for more than an hour two burglars had been prowling about her room. She was in tears and shaking with fright while she explained that it was not a dream but a fact. She had seen the two men clearly with her eyes open; they had taken things from the closet and from the bureaus and had escaped finally by way of the window. She had heard the dogs chase them down the lane, and if we came to the window, she assured us, we would see their tracks in the snow. A careful examination of the premises, however, proved that no one had been about and that nothing had been stolen. Evidently Jane had had a vision, a hypnapomic vision—because, as she explained, it was real and nothing like a dream— due to a perceptive projection. Never before had she had such a vision, so it is probable that the *murder* game was the exciting agent which aroused the imagery. This was more of an effect than we had anticipated. Jane insisted despite the protestations of her companions that the event had really occurred; in fact, it seemed very important to her—as if, let us say, her sanity depended upon it—that she should be believed. None of her friends, however, gave credence to her story during the day. It was not until night- fall that Mary and Lou—but not Jill and Nan—were inclined to believe her. Belief for Mary and Lou seemed to depend upon the uneasiness aroused by darkness. The outcome of the matter was that Jane, Mary, and Lou an- nounced that they would not sleep in the ill-fated room "for anything" and, even when given another room, they insisted that we should look for burg- lars in the closet and under the bed, draw the shades down to the sill, speak in a low voice so that the burglars—supposedly sneaking about the house— should not hear, put a night-light in the room and visit them at intervals throughout the night to make sure that everything was all right. Jill and Nan, however, consented to occupy the spare room where the burglars had been seen and without any ado dropped off to sleep. This difference in attitude between Mary,- Jane, and Lou, on the one hand, and Jill and Nan, on the other, should be borne in mind when the test results are examined.

Now let us turn our attention to the experiments. To discover whether fear affected the subjects' judgments of personality we should compare the results obtained after *murder* in each of the two tests (A and B) with those obtained after normal conditions. In making this comparison we should bear in mind that, according to the adopted method of scoring, an increase in the rating of a photograph signified an increase in the apparent badness (maliciousness) of a face, and a decrease in the rating signified an increase in the apparent goodness (benevolence) of a face.

The results were as follows: In Test A, as compared with the scores obtained after ordinary conditions, the average ratings after the fear-invoking situation remained the same in 1 photograph, were lower (indicating more "goodness") in 2 photographs, and were higher (indicating more "badness") in 12 photographs. In Test B, as compared with the results obtained after ordinary conditions, the average ratings after the fear-invoking event remained the same in 2 photographs, were lower (indicating more "goodness") in 3 photographs, and were higher (indicating more "badness") in 10 photographs. The slightly less significant results in Test B, as compared with Test A, might be explained by supposing that Jane's recital of her burglar vision aroused in her friends (by suggestion) subjective states which were somewhat similar to those which followed *murder,* and so nullified to some extent the significance as a control of the Sunday test trial. If the results of the two experiments (A and B) are taken together, it appears that out of a total of 30 photographs 22 (73%) were scored higher—that is, the character of the faces in these photographs were judged to be more malicious—after the fear-invoking event than after normal pleasure-invoking events; or, to state it otherwise, it appears that out of 27 photographs, the average ratings of which were different under two conditions, 22 (81%) were scored higher after fear.

TABLE 1

S's	EXPERIMENT A			EXPERIMENT B			BOTH EXPERI-MENTS
	Average rating per photograph		Differ-ence in rating	Average rating per photograph		Differ-ence in rating	
	Control	After fear		After fear	Control		Difference in rating
			b—a			d—e	$\dfrac{c+f}{2}$
	a	b	c	d	e	f	g
Mary	4.53	5.73	+1.20	6.47	5.40	+1.07	+1.15
Jane	6.53	7.47	+0.94	7.80	7.00	+0.80	+0.87
Lou	5.67	6.07	+0.40	6.07	5.13	+0.94	+0.67
Jill	5.60	5.93	+0.33	5.33	5.53	−0.20	+0.06
Nan	6.33	6.13	−0.20	6.67	7.27	−0.60	−0.40
Average	5.73	6.26	+0.53	6.47	6.07	+0.40	+0.47

The results might have been more striking if the experimenter had not made the mistake of including several photographs of persons whose faces were so distinctly forbidding that some subjects assigned to them the maximum mark of 9 on the control test, thereby making a further increase of rating after fear impossible. Out of a total of 150 (15 photographs) x 5 (subjects) x 2 (tests) ratings assigned after ordinary conditions, there were 19 ratings of 9 which did not change when conditions changed. Of the 131 remaining ratings, 96 (73%) were different after the fear-invoking situation; and of the 96 ratings which were different, 67 (70%) were higher (indicating more badness).

An examination of the tabulated results reveals the fact that for the five subjects there was an average change per photograph of +0.53 in Experiment A, and of +0.40 in Experiment B; the average of the two tests being +0.465, or approximately one-half a point towards badness per photograph. In other words, after the fear-invoking situation one-half the faces were judged, on an average, to be one point less good (more wicked) than they were judged after ordinary conditions. There are, of course, other methods of scoring the subjects, but, since intercorrelations between the results obtained by a variety of methods indicated that the present system of scoring was the best, the other methods have not been included in this report.

These results seem to show that complementary apperceptive projection did occur in the subjects, or, to state the matter more specifically, that fear tended to increase the apparent maliciousness of other personalities.

Examining Table I from the point of view of individual differences it may be observed that of the five subjects, one (Nan) in Experiment A and two (Nan and Jill) in Experiment B had lower scores after the fear-invoking event; whereas four subjects in Experiment A and three in Experiment B had higher scores after this event. If the two experiments are taken together it appears that one subject (Jill) showed relatively little change in her ratings, whereas the four other subjects did change. Of the four who did change, three, or 75% of them (Mary, Jane and Lou) judged faces as more malicious after *murder* than after ordinary conditions.

As a part of the test the children had been asked to write down what they thought the person in each photograph was saying or thinking. We guessed that fear might make the supposed thoughts more frightening and melodramatic, but there were few differences between the thoughts written under ordinary conditions and those written under exceptional conditions. What changes did occur, however, were for the most part in the positive direction. For instance, in Jane's paper after ordinary conditions a woman said: "What shall I do next?" and after *murder* she said: "So all your children are sick. Well I hope they die"; and after ordinary conditions a man said: "I'll do it if I like," and after *murder* he said: "You brute, you fool, you hypocrite!"; and after ordinary conditions a man said: "Yeah, I understand" and after *murder* he said: "So you *got* them, did you?"

Though the results from this part of the test were inconclusive as far as the verification of our hypothesis was concerned, they did give evidence of both complementary and supplementary projection. They afforded hints, indeed of how the wind was blowing in each subject's mind. Jane, for instance, who hallucinated burglars on Sunday morning, wrote on Saturday the following thoughts for four of her subjects:

"You give me back that money or I'll shoot."

"Gosh. I've gone broke."

"How did you make out? Did you get any money?"

"Have you got the money?"

Since Jane was the only child who made any mention of money or burglars, her written sayings might almost have been taken as prognostically significant. On Sunday, after the hallucination, she wrote the following thoughts for three of her subjects:

"I went in to a room last night in Topsfield" (it was in Topsfield that these events occurred).

"I got the scare of my life last night" (supplementary apperceptive projection).

"Well, well, have any more ghosts come to you?" (this suggests that at this time she was doubting the substantiality of her visionary experience).

THEORETICAL CONSIDERATIONS

To explain the positive results obtained in these experiments it seems that we should take account of at least three processes: (1) the activation of fear by the game of *murder*; (2) the perseveration of this emotion; and (3) the projection of integrated elements into the material to be diagnosed.

All of these processes must have occurred, it seems, in the three subjects who gave consistently positive results (Mary, Jane, and Lou). The two who gave negative results (Jill and Nan) may not have been aroused to anxiety by the game; or, if they were so activated, the emotion may have dissipated itself before the test was given; or, finally, they may have been experiencing some anxiety during the test but the emotion did not affect their judgments of personality.

That the positive results depended to a large extent upon the evocation of fear is suggested by the fact that the only subjects (Mary and Lou) who spoke of being afraid during the *murder* game were both in the positive group. The third member of the positive group (Jane) happened to be the "victim" in the first game of *murder* and the murderer in the second, circumstances which militate against the admission of fear even if the subject is experiencing it.

We must suppose that perseveration and projection were both present to account for Jane's vision of burglars ten hours later. That Mary and Lou were the subjects who gave credence—but only after nightfall—to the substantiality of Jane's vision is a fact which fits in with the other positive responses given by these two children. It demonstrates, moreover, the determining effect of emotion and of projection in the genesis of belief.

It is difficult to give a satisfactory account of the psychological processes revealed by our findings without reference to a theory of motivation. But since the theory which we believe best describes the functional aspect of human nature has not yet found its way into the literature, and hence cannot be referred to by name, and since space does not allow for an outline of it at this time, we shall omit mention of the particular need (instinct) or combination of reflexes aroused in our subjects. In lieu of this, we shall refer all the bodily affections which occurred in our subjects to the emotion of fear, since its existence in children after playing *murder* is easy to establish by means of subjective reports as well as by the observation of its usual objective correlates.

In accordance with our introductory speculations and hypotheses we should attempt to explain the results of this investigation by saying that the bodily processes operative in the subjective experience known as fear were aroused by the game of *murder*; that these in turn mobilized the integrated images and categories (the more general imaginal meanings). We have in mind such categories as "dangerous situations," "criminals and burglars," "malicious characters," and so forth. Then, when the test was presented to the children, the photographs which fulfilled the requirements of sufficient similitude functioned as foci for the projection of these images and categories, a photograph, for instance, being assimilated to the category "very bad" instead of to the category "bad" in which it seemed to fit best when the subject was without emotion.

It was as if the subjects, experiencing an emotion without adequate stimulus, sought something in the external world to justify it—as if the idea had come to mind: "there must be malicious people about." The result of this was that the photographs appeared to change in the direction of adequacy as stimuli. It is clear that we have here a typical complementary apperceptive projection.

Two other processes which usually accompany a state of emotional excitement may have occurred in this experiment—preferential perception and perceptive projection.

By *preferential perception* we refer to the unconscious (unintentional) process by which attention is directed to objects in the environment similar to the traces (or images) integrated with the aroused emotion. The subject simply becomes aware of the external object, the preceding process of selection being unconscious. In the present experiment, it is not unlikely that the children's attention was attracted to special facial parts—parts which indicated "badness"—and that judgments were made on the basis of these.

Perceptive projection has already been defined. It may also have been operating in this test. The children, for instance, may have perceived the faces as physicaly different from what they actually were. In other words, mild illusions may have occurred.

These phenomena can be best explained, though we do not insist upon it, by the hypothesis of activated traces or unconscious images. The traces which are integrated with the bodily processes which make up the emotional state are there, as it were, below consciousness—ready to appear as conscious imagery or to modify events which are conscious, namely, perception and apperception.

That the supposition of active unconscious imagery is not an unwarranted hypothesis is indicated by the frequency with which imagery such as has been described occurs on the fringe of consciousness in the form of a phantasy which can be recalled immediately afterwards. Such imagery is *almost* unconscious in that it may never be in the focus of attention and may be recalled only in part and with difficulty afterwards. The following is an instance of this familiar phenomenon.

One evening a subject was sitting alone in a somewhat isolated farmhouse reading *The Turn of the Screw,* the gruesome story by Henry James (fear-invoking situation). At an exciting point of the narrative the telephone bell rang and a strange man, who said he was a reporter, asked permission to motor over that very evening for the purpose of discussing a matter in which the subject was interested. Though it was already ten o'clock and the reporter was calling from a town twelve miles distant, the subject agreed to see him and returned to his reading. After a few moments he realized that his attention had been divided. Although he could give an account to himself of what he had been reading, he was also aware that an unintentionally initiated phantasy had been developing in the marginal realm of consciousness. In the phantasy an automobile had drawn up to the door and the supposed reporter entered the house. After a few introductory words the latter had drawn a revolver and a skirmish had followed in which the two men had rolled about the floor until by a clever twist of the wrist the revolver had disengaged from the gangster's hand and the subject became master of the situation. This phantasy represented the functional signification assigned to the strange voice on the telephone and the event which was to come. The subject was decidedly of the opinion that this would not have occurred if at the time he had been reading a story of a different kind.

The explanation of this event would be that fear had evoked imagery of "dangerous characters" to which the voice of the stranger had been assimilated; and with these compounded elements the mind swayed by apprehension had constructed a melodramatic reverie in the form of a tentative hypothesis, one might say, of what the future would disclose. This whole phantasy might easily have been unconscious. One might say that it was only by chance that the subject captured it out of the twilight zone of his consciousness (cf. a man capturing, losing, then recapturing the content of a dream as he wakes).

Now, if the subject had been less self-conscious and later had manifested a lowered threshold for the sound of an automobile coming down the drive (preferential perception), and when greeting the reporter had circumscribed his attention to the less kindly aspects of his face (preferential perception) or had unconsciously distorted the features of the stranger so that physically he appeared to be different (perceptive projection) or, though seeing him without distortion, had interpreted his looks and gestures as signifying "bad intention" (apperceptive projection)—if these psychological events had occurred we should have explained them by referring to a mental process (activated in this case by the fear-invoking story) of which the phantasy was a component. If this phantasy had been unconscious—as it might well have been—we should have been forced to resort to the concept of unconscious psychic processes.

If the circumstances of the evening telephone call, however, had been sufficient, as a result of the subject's past experience under similar circumstances, to call forth the fear the resultant phantasy, we should have spoken of the redintegration of danger images and categories without projection—the term projection being confined to the operation of irrelevant affections which in the present instance were aroused by the reading of the book. So much for the projection of unconscious images and meanings.

Now, from the standpoint of an interest in the individual differences of personality, we should like to know whether the two groups distinguished by this test—namely, the susceptible class (Mary, Jane, and Lou) with an average change per photograph of $+.90$ points, and the non-susceptible class (Jill and Nan) with an average change per photograph of $-.17$ points—are characterized by personality differences which are more or less permanent. In other words, would these two groups show approximately the same difference in their responses to other comparable tests or to the same test at a later time or to somewhat similar circumstances in everyday life? We cannot, of course, give a positive answer to this question, but the following facts suggest that the tests did reveal some more or less consistent personality traits:

1. The coefficient of correlation (product-moment methods) between Experiment A and Experiment B was $+.84$.

2. The hostess of the week-end party who knew the children intimately, when the nature of the experiment was explained to her, guessed that Mary and Jane would score the highest. This prophecy was correct.

3. Jane's hypnapomic vision was a manifestation of the same process which was responsible for her high score on the test. Jane had never before experienced such a vision, but in the past few months had had several nightmares in which burglars figured prominently.

4. Mary and Lou came to believe in the truth of Jane's story about the burglars, but Jill and Nan did not.

Thus the behavior of the children during the week-end, the estimations of their temperaments by the hostess, and the results on both tests showed a considerable degree of correlation.

There is no generally accepted concept of type or trait to describe the response of the positive group as differentiated from the negative group. Psychologists have written of emotionality and of subjectivity, but, since these words have been used without precision, it is impossible to say whether our group of projectors should be subsumed under one or both of these headings. By definition there is no projection without affection or emotion, but there is no evidence to show that projection invariably parallels intensity of emotion. Other factors—such as conglomeration and the partial dissociation of the personality itself—seem to be important. *Conglomeration* is a name given to the psychical condition—as found in children—in which little or no differentiation is made between images and objects, between what is internal and psychical and what is external and substantial.

SUMMARY

Five girls, eleven years of age, estimated from photographs the degree of goodness (benevolence) or badness (maliciousness) of other personalities. These estimates were made under two different conditions: (a) after ordinary pleasurable activity in the sunshine, and (b) after two games of *murder* in the dark. A comparison of the ratings assigned under these two conditions revealed the following:

1. Seventy-three per cent of the faces were estimated by a majority of the group as more malicious when judged after the fear-invoking situation than when judged after ordinary conditions.

2. Of the four subjects whose ratings differed under the two conditions, three (75%) estimated the series of faces as more malicious after the fear-invoking situation than after ordinary conditions.

These results may be attributed to complementary apperceptive projection subsequent to the activation of an emotional state. The conclusion which may be drawn from this experiment is that under some conditions the emotion of fear will cause some experiencing subjects to increase their estimates of the maliciousness of other personalities.

INTRODUCTION

39. Observations on Human Behavior in Experimental Semistarvation and Rehabilitation

Joseph C. Franklin,

Burtrum C. Schiele,

Josef Brozek and Ancel Keys

THE primary purpose of the starvation-rehabilitation experiment carried out at the Laboratory of Physiological Hygiene, University of Minnesota, was to investigate under strictly controlled conditions the relative effectiveness of different types of diets in bringing about recovery from prolonged inanition. The starvation which preceded rehabilitation provided a unique opportunity for the assessment of the physiological and psychological concomitants and effects of severe undernutrition. In accordance with the interdisciplinary character of research at the Laboratory, the methods and techniques of physiology, biochemistry, medicine, psychology, and psychiatry were employed in parallel. Preliminary findings were reported for the use of research workers and Allied governmental and military authorities concerned with the problem of nutritional rehabilitation, and the salient aspects were briefly summarized for general use. Numerous journalistic reports, some of relatively high quality, have appeared. A general summary, prepared specifically for relief workers, has been published. The present paper is a detailed descriptive report on behavior in the Minnesota Experiment.

Abridged from the *Journal of Clinical Psychology,* 1948, 4, 28-45. Reprinted by permission of the authors and the Editor of the *Journal of Clinical Psychology,* Frederick C. Thorne.

EXPERIMENTAL DESIGN

Thirty-six "normal" young men between the ages of 20 and 33 (mean age 25.5 years, S.D. 3.5 years) served as volunteer subjects. The body build, physical performance capacity, and personality of these men varied within broad limits.

Excluding the follow-up studies, the experiment lasted for approximately a year. Control data were obtained during three months of standardization (November, 1944 to February, 1945) in which the subjects were maintained on a "good" diet providing a daily average of 3,492 Calories per man. Six months of semistarvation followed (February to July, 1945) when the actual daily average intake was reduced to 1,570 Calories. The diet was planned to simulate in quality and quantity the food available in western and central Europe under the conditions of severe food shortages during the Second World War. The semistarvation period was followed by three months of controlled rehabilitation ending in October, 1945. As we are concerned in this paper primarily with the descriptive, "qualitative" aspects of behavior, there is no need to go into the details of the complex design of the rehabilitation phase of the experiment.

RESULTS: SEMISTARVATION PHASE

Physical Changes and Energy Output. Striking changes occurred in the size and weight of the subjects, the average loss of gross body weight at the end of semistarvation representing twenty-four per cent of the control value. Both the face and the body showed a marked emaciation. Gradual wasting of muscle and subcutaneous adipose tissues made sitting on hard surfaces increasingly uncomfortable and sometimes painful. For the same reason shoes were too large and clothes loose and poorly fitting. By the twelfth week of semistravation, edema became common and was especially noticeable in the knees, ankles, and face. The subjects reported that their nails grew more slowly and that their hair was falling out in large amounts. Shaving became necessary less frequently. The men noted, particularly in shaving, that cuts and wounds bled less than normally and were slower to heal. Physical ability to laugh heartily, sneeze, and blush was reduced or absent during the later stages of semistarvation. Muscle cramps and muscle soreness were reported. Jarring of knee joints, especially when walking on hard pavements, was an annoyance to some. Pigmentation, thinning, and roughening of the skin occurred; however, changes in the sensitivity of the skin, paresthesic and hypesthesic in character, were observed only rarely. There were many complaints that the extremities "went to sleep." Tolerance to heat was greatly increased, *e.g.,* subjects could hold extremely hot plates without discomfort; and they required their food, coffee, and tea served unusually hot. Conversely, cold temperatures were poorly tolerated. Complaints of being cold or of having cold hands and feet were frequent and persistent. In hot summer weather many of the subjects slept under heavy blankets and wore "extra" clothing during the day. Vertigo, giddiness, and momentary blackouts were experienced on rising from lying or sitting positions by almost all during the first months and by some subjects throughout the semistarvation period. Actual fainting, however, occurred on only one occasion. Polyuria and, particularly, nocturia became a common problem.

Objective tests revealed no impairment of visual acuity, but many subjects complained of transient visual disturbances such as inability to focus, eye aches, and "spots" before their eyes. Standard measurements of hearing showed a slight but consistent increase in auditory acuity during the period of semistarvation. It is difficult to determine whether the complaints, that ordinary sounds and noises were disturbing and annoying, had a direct physiological basis in the "improved" auditory sensitivity or were primarily signs of general increase in the irritability of the subjects. Sensations of fullness and ringing were reported by some. Except for hunger pains and some decrease in the frequency of bowel movements, gastro-intestinal symptoms were rare. In several cases periods of transient nausea were experienced.

A marked decrease in pulse rate and in basal metabolism may be regarded as critical indicators of bodily adjustment to reduced food intake, involving a lowering of the speed of the autonomic functions of the body. The overt movements also became noticeably slower, and voluntary energy output was in general markedly reduced. However, overall energy expenditure was maintained on a relatively high level by scheduled physical activity (walking to and from the mess hall, hiking about twenty miles per week, etc.) in order to simulate conditions of natural starvation.

The attitude of the men to physical exertion was ambivalent. It made them tired and as a rule was avoided. On the other hand, occasionally some men exercised deliberately. Thus certain subjects attempted to lose weight by driving themselves through period of excessive expenditure of energy with the object of either obtaining increased bread rations (when weight loss exceeded the prescribed rate) or avoiding reduction in rations (when weight loss lagged). Fatigue, weakness, and hunger were outstanding complaints. The marked reduction in strength and endurance was paralleled by a curtailment of spontaneous activity. The subjects moved slowly and cautiously; they climbed stairs one at a time. Coordination was affected, and the men sometimes tripped over curbstones and bumped into objects which they intended to sidestep.

In general, fewer and fewer things were capable of stimulating overt action. The subjects described their increasing weakness, loss of ambition, narrowing of interests, depression, irritability, and loss of *libido* as a pattern of experience characteristic of "growing old." Even though a defined amount of physical work (principally walking) was required by the experimental regimen, fluctuations in spontaneous activity accounted for large variations in daily energy output. All had periods of well-being when they expended much energy in working, exercise, and occasionally even in sports.

The subjects were not apprehensive about their health. None evidenced anxiety over the possibility of chronic or permanent effects of the stress. They were confident that they would not only receive prompt and adequate care if they became ill but also they would be removed from the experiment if serious consequences were thought likely to develop from their continued participation in it.

Hunger and Appetite. In speaking of "hunger" the subjects referred to sensations vaguely localized in the abdominal region which varied from mild discomfort to intense pain. In total starvation the sensation of hunger rapidly disappears. This is not true in semistarvation. There was no diminution of the desire for food as the starvation progressed. While some subjects suffered relatively little from the distress of hunger, others complained of being hungry all the time. Frequently the men complained of hunger immediately after eating a bulky meal. The most bulky was the most popular menu of the three to which the men were limited.[1] The desire for variety in diet became very strong at times but was always subordinated to the craving for greater quantity.

Eating Habits. Anticipation of eating heightened the craving for food. Consequently, the men dreaded waiting in line while their meals were measured and weighed, each man defensively guarding his place in line. They tended to become irritated when the serving was slow or those who served the food gave any evidence of not taking their business "seriously." The food had to be very hot to be satisfying. This was universally held to be very important. It was as though the starving individual "borrowed" heat from the food ingested as a means of conserving energy.

The subjects exhibited a possessive attitude toward their food. At the table some hovered closely over their trays with their arms placed so as to protect their ration. In eating they were, for the most part, silent, deliberate, and gave total attention to the food and its consumption. Many ingenious devices were used for making food appear to go further and to provide the illusion of variety. As the starvation progressed, the number of men who "toyed" with their food increased. They made what under normal conditions would be weird and distasteful concoctions. There was a marked increase

---

[1]The chief items on the three menus (repeated in rotation) were as follows:

in the use of spices and salt. The subjects were often caught between conflicting desires to gulp food down ravenously or to consume it slowly so that the taste and odor of each morsel would be fully appreciated. Toward the end of starvation some of the men would dawdle for almost two hours over a meal which previously they would have consumed in a matter of minutes.

In order to maximize the pleasure of eating, there was much planning done by the men as to how they would handle their day's allotment of food. Since the subjects went to the dining room only twice a day during the starvation phase of the experiment, many of them saved out part of their meals for later consumption. All food was consumed to the last crumb. The men were cultured and refined, yet they routinely licked their dishes in order to obtain every vestige of food. They quickly became intolerant of food waste and were visibly upset when they noticed others discarding food. There were many bitter comments that any spoilage or wastage of food was prodigal and criminal in a starving world.

Individual food dislikes for such diet items as rutabagas and fish disappeared in the early part of the semistarvation period. Although the subjects were restricted to three rather monotonous menus, the taste appeal of the diet increased rather than diminished throughout the six months of semistarvation.

Food Substitution Habits. Various techniques were developed to approximate or substitute for satisfactions normally derived from eating. Prominent among these were gum chewing and smoking. It was often reported that vivid vicarious pleasure was derived from watching other persons eat or from just smelling food. Large quantities of water were consumed with and between meals, and the subjects increased the bulk of their food by "souping." For example, a man would drink the fluid from his soup, then fill the bowl with hot water, salt it heavily, drink the fluid off again, and repeat this process before eating the solid part of the soup. Satisfaction was also obtained from consumption of coffee and tea (without cream or sugar but with a limited amount of saccharin), both of which were used in large quantities, presumably for their pharmacological as well as their filling and warming effects. It was generally reported that coffee and tea provided a "lift." Because some of the men increased their consumption to fifteen or

Menu No. 1. Morning meal—farina, fried potatoes, jello, bread, jam, milk, sugar. Evening meal—fish chowder, spaghetti, meat ball, potatoes, peas and carrots, cabbage salad.

Menu No. 2. Morning meal—oatmeal, potatoes, gingerbread, bread, jam, milk, sugar. Evening meal—bean and pea soup, macaroni, cheese, rutabagas, potatoes, lettuce salad.

Menu No. 3. Morning meal—pancake, syrup, applesauce, corn bread, bread, jam. Evening meal—potato soup, stew, potatoes.

It should be noted that such items as milk and meat were served only in token amounts.

more cups daily, it became necessary to limit all subjects to a maximum of nine cups per day. A few occasionally violated the spirit of this restriction by brewing nine cups of the strongest possible tea or coffee and then diluting further with hot water. About a half dozen subjects who never drank coffee or tea before the experiment became habitual users of both. For experimental purposes, the subjects were occasionally placed for three-day periods on severely reduced fluid intake; when thus deprived of their beverages, a few complained of headache and greater-than-usual lassitude.

During th early part of the experiment the use of chewing-gum was not limited; however, in time this became excessive. "Heavy gum chewers" would take two or three sticks at a time, chew until the sweet taste was gone, discard them, and then replace with fresh sticks in chain fashion. Finally, some chewed up to forty packages of gum per day. One of the subjects chewed so continuously that he developed a sore mouth. Thereafter, the use of gum was restricted to two packages a day. Several men who had not used tobacco prior to participation in the experiment acquired the habit of smoking during semistarvation because it afforded some degree of relief from hunger.

Preoccupation with Food. Food in all its ramifications became the principal topic of the subjects' conversations, reading, and day dreams. More dreams about food were reported as the stress continued. When subjects read books and attended movies, they were deeply impressed by the frequency with which food and eating were mentioned. Cook books, menus, and information bulletins on food production became intensely interesting reading matter to many of the subjects who previously had little or no interest in dietetics or agriculture. Some men went so far as to re-plan their lives according to their newly-acquired respect for food. For example, one man became impressed by the importance of developing efficient methods of food raising and decided to go into agriculture as a vocation. A few planned to become cooks. In some men there appeared, particularly toward the end of the experiment, a reaction against this "tyranny" of food; they became annoyed by discussions of food and related subjects. One man expressed disgust at this "animal attitude;" another referred to such engrossment as "nutritional masturbation."

Adherence to Diet. The subjects were thoroughly aware of the importance of the experiment, and each man felt that his participation in the experimental program would result in a definite contribution to the body of scientific knowledge in an important area. They were convinced that the findings would aid in the relief and rehabilitation of the starving people of the world. Many of the subjects hoped to be able to go to Europe as members of nutritional relief teams, and they felt that they would be much more able to understand and to minister to famine sufferers by virtue of their first-hand starvation experiences. These factors provided strong incentives to adhere strictly to the diet.

Although some temptation to break the diet was present at times, voluntary commitment to complete the experiment as planned was, with few exceptions, greater than the tantalizing craving for food. This is attested by attainment of the required weight loss (an average of twenty-four per cent). Some men maintained that eating other food than that provided by the diet simply never occurred to them. Direct or indirect evidence of nonadherence to diet was obtained in four out of thirty-six subjects; these men were released from the experiment.

In the beginning of the semistarvation period the subjects were allowed to go about alone but later were required to be accompanied always by a "buddy." If invited out or to a friend's home for a meal, a subject could take a part of his own food (likely a cold macaroni sandwich or a plain slice of bread). Under such conditions the men disclaimed any conscious temptations and even reported annoyance when hosts or others tried to persuade them to take just a little extra food.

The use of subjects on food-handling jobs was discontinued at their request because the temptations under these circumstances became too great; they had found themselves inadvertently licking gravy off their fingers or picking up crumbs.

Emotions and Attitudes. The cumulative effects of the stress were definitely associated with emotional instability. The men experienced transitory and sometimes protracted periods of depression. They became discouraged because of their relative ineffectiveness in daily living. Inability to sustain mental or physical effort contributed much to this feeling of inefficiency. The persistent clamor of hunger distracted the subjects when they attempted to continue their cultural interests, hobby activities, and studies. The discrepancy between what the men wanted to do and what they were able to do resulted in frustration.

During the advanced stages of semistarvation there was a marked lowering of the threshold to depressive reactions. Although clinically, depression reached frankly pathological proportions only on rare occasions and in only a few individuals, the men were always more serious and obviously less happy than during the control period. Unexpected spells of elation, sometimes bordering on ecstasy, occurred. Feeling "high" was sometimes attributed by the men to a "quickening" effect of starvation or to success in adjusting to the semistarvation diet. Feelings of well-being and exhilaration lasted from a few hours to several days but were inevitably followed by ensuing "low" periods. Just as the subjects were unduly depressed by untoward events, their spirits were markedly boosted by such things as fine weather, anticipation of an outing, a profitable "bull session," and other variations in daily routine capable of arousing enough interest or enthusiasm to take them "out" of themselves.

Frequently, both subjects and observers remarked that the group was apathetic. Apathy grew out of repeated failure, with accompanying frustrations, to carry on "normally" during the stress. Things which would arouse their interest tended more and more to fall within the complex of "guinea-pig" life; loss of body weight, hunger, and food. In discussing these, the men would often become animated.

The smooth-temperedness, patience, and tolerance evidenced during the control period gave way under stress to the converse. Irritability increased to the point where it became an individual and group problem. Although the men were aware of their hyper-irritability, they were not altogether able to control their emotionally charged responses. Thus, outbursts of temper and periods of sulking and pique were not uncommon, and a few had strong urges to violence but these were not carried out.

The men exhibiting a large degree of personal and social deterioration easily became objects of aggression for the rest of the group. In particular, one of these subjects, who dramatized himself and his semistarvation role, served as a scapegoat and a ready reference point for favorable self-comparison. The men rated themselves in comparison with their normal condition as lacking in self-discipline and self control, subject to indecisiveness, restless, sensitive to noise, unable to concentrate, and markedly "nervous."

It is likely that the widespread use of coffee, tea, and chewing gum represented attempts to allay nervous tension besides serving as substitutes for food. Similarly, the occurrence of nail-biting (not present during standardization) and the acquisition of or increase in smoking habits were related to increased "nervousness." Personal appearance and care began to deteriorate as the stress progressed. The men often neglected to shave, brush their teeth, and comb their hair. Even those who had been careful or even particular in their grooming now dressed carelessly and presented a slovenly appearance. It should be noted, however, that bathing was not neglected. It was a source of pleasure as it provided means of getting warm as well as a form of hydrotherapy; it was reported to have relieved aches, pains, and fatigue.

Social initiative, and sociability in general, underwent remarkable change. Their earlier interest in having a voice in the making of policies and rules for the conduct of the non-scientific aspects of the experiment dwindled. The men became indecisive, unable to make personal plans, and unwilling to participate in group activities. The subjects spent more and more time alone. It became "too much trouble" or "too tiring" to have to contend with other people. With the decline in the interests which had previously been held in common with others and with the growth of feelings of social inadequacy the men became self-centered. The egocentricity and associated heightened irritability, of which the subjects were well aware, required at times a real effort to maintain socially acceptable behavior. Too often, attempts to keep the interpersonal relationships tolerable, if not gracious, produced an uncomfortable and emotionally charged atmosphere in which politeness was artificial and social interaction stilted. Humor and high morale, which had been an outstanding characteristic of the group during standardization, gradually disappeared. Humor "dried up" and the tone of the group became sober and serious. What humor remained at the end of semistarvation was mainly of the ironic and sarcastic variety.

The men devoted much time and energy to the collection of recipes, studying of cookbooks, and contemplation of menus. The acquisition of coffee pots, hot plates, kitchen utensils, and the like on shopping "sprees" appeared reasonable. Much less so was the buying of old books, unnecessary second-hand clothes, knick-knacks, and other items which came to be known as "junk." Often after making such purchases, which could be afforded only with sacrifice, the men would be puzzled as to why they had bought such more or less useless articles. This acquisitive behavior may be interpreted as a mechanism compensating for the deprivation of food. Several subjects insisted that they had grown unusually anxious to save money for a "rainy day" and attributed this to the insecurity they felt in the experimental situation.

In the later part of semistarvation, housekeeping chores were neglected and non-experimental Laboratory duties were carried out less and less effectively. The educational program, designed to prepare the men for foreign relief work and followed at the start with enthusiasm, in time quietly but decisively collapsed. As the distinction between the men and their non-starved associates became more pronounced, the subjects became strangely and somewhat defensively aware of belonging to a "group." The men exhibited heightened sympathy for an identification with the starving and suffering people throughout the world.

Sex. Sexual feeling and expression declined to the point where at the end of the semistarvation period it was virtually extinguished in all but a few subjects. The decline of sex drive was so dramatic that the subjects were struck by the change and used colorful language to describe it. As one of them put it, "I have no more sexual feeling than a sick oyster." The number of "dates" dropped drastically. Those who continued to "date" found their relationships strained. Some of the men were surprised to find that this was also true in even those cases where their female contacts had appeared to be based on intellectual, social, and group interests. Such situations probably stemmed from decline in sociability as well as loss of sex impulses. Masturbation and nocturnal emissions were reported as absent or greatly reduced. Moreover, sex fantasies and sex dreams were reduced in number and when present were severely attenuated.

Intelligence. Complaints of inability to concentrate for any period of time and of difficulty in developing thoughts became numerous. By the end of the semistarvation period a large proportion of the men felt that their judgment had been impaired. They reported, further, that their alertness and comprehension had declined. Clinically, we had the impression that the intellective capacity was essentially unchanged; this impression was supported by objective test evidence. Memory disturbances and decrease of expressive power were only rarely encountered and did not go beyond the range of normality. Throughout the stress the subjects thought clearly and talked intelligently, and the self-estimates of loss of intellective abilities may be regarded as a function of physical disability and emotional factors. It was the narrowing of their interests, apathy, and lack of initiative in carrying on conversation and study which led the men to conclude that they had suffered actual decline of intellective powers.

RESULTS: REHABILITATION PHASE

The purpose of the rehabilitation phase of the experiment was to measure the relative efficiency of several levels of refeeding in order to secure the most efficient, practical, and economic regimen for dietary rehabilitation. There was little change in the composition of diet, simply more of it. The average caloric intake was 2,448 Calories during the first six weeks, 3,257 Calories from the seventh to the tenth week, and 3,518 Calories during the eleventh and the twelfth week of controlled rehabilitation. Within the context of this report it is not possible to discuss the differential effects of the experimentally varied levels of caloric, protein, and vitamin intake. We shall, therefore, limit ourselves to a qualitative description of behavior during the rehabilitation phase of the experiment.

The process of recovery was slow. It should be emphasized that the psychobiological stress of semistarvation actually continued to a greater or lesser degree (depending upon the level of refeeding) throughout the entire twelve weeks of controlled rehabilitation.

Physical Changes. At the end of twelve weeks of controlled rehabilitation the subjects in the highest caloric group, which received 1200 Calories more than the lowest group, had regained less than sixty per cent of the weight lost. Those in the lowest group gained no weight during the first six weeks and by the end of the twelfth week had regained only twenty per cent of the weight lost in the semistarvation phase. Energy and physical well-being increased roughly in proportion to caloric intake.

Recovery from dizziness, apathy, and lethargy was most rapid. Tiredness, loss of sex drive, and weakness were slow to improve. Although visible edema tended to disappear, in some men there was little change and even an increase in edema. Cramps, vague aches and pains, and paresthesias were unrelieved for some time. Some of the men had new complaints such as flatus, distension, belching, and stomach ache. Those subjects who gained the most weight became concerned about their increasing sluggishness, general flabbiness, and the tendency of fat to accumulate in the abdomen and buttocks.

At the end of three months of rehabilitation even in those subjects who were maintained on the highest caloric intake, the overall physical condition was considerably inferior to the pre-starvation status. Later reports from the subjects indicated that it was not until an additional three months of "normal" living and super-normal eating, beyond the twelve weeks of controlled rehabilitation, that their physical capacity approached pre-experimental levels.

Food. During the twelve weeks of rehabilitation there was relatively little change in the subjects' eating habits and attitudes toward food. The men continued to want more than they received. Even when those on the highest caloric intake were physically full, they wanted more—their appetites were insatiable. The men continued to be concerned with food and their rations above all else. Food substitution habits persisted with only minor alterations. Heavy use of coffee, tea, "souping" of food, and generally high fluid intake continued to be characteristic for most of the rehabilitation period. Keeping foods hot, "formalities" of serving, and creation of mixtures and "concoctions" continued. About half a dozen of the men were more deteriorated in their eating habits and table manners during the first six weeks of the rehabilitation period than during semistarvation. There was little flagging in food interests and culinary matters, although the filing of recipes and the reading of cook books gradually declined.

Emotions and Attitudes. For six months the men had looked forward to the last day of semistarvation as the day which would mark the end of their ordeal. They had anticipated that rehabilitation would bring about early alleviation of their symptoms and distress. This belief was a sustaining motivation during the semistarvation period. The expected "new lease on life" did not materialize. As already stated, weight gains were small or non-existent (a few men even lost weight due to loss of edematous fluid). Weakness, tiredness, pains, and myriad other discomforts continued to contribute to their suffering. Hunger and appetite were not appeased. As one subject expressed himself, "Now I go away from meals hungry three times a day instead of two."

Some men actually became more depressed and irritable than in semistarvation. Many grew argumentative and negativistic. Others professed grave doubts as to the value of the entire project or question the motives and competence of the experimenters. Several subjects confessed that their humanitarian concern for the welfare of mankind had become elusive and difficult to maintain. Impatience, tenseness, and a feeling of a "let down" pervaded the group. After the first few encouraging days of the rehabilitation regimen there was a pronounced and decided slump in morale.

However, the discontent and aggressiveness, as distinguished from the apathy and acquiescence of semistarvation, was an indirect evidence of an increase in energy. It foreran the gradual reappearance of physical, social, and cultural interests which had gone "underground" for the duration of semistarvation. No longer were the men willing to accept without question the formation of policy by those responsible for conducting the experiment. They insisted that the rules and regulations make "good sense" to them. The men became increasingly impatient with the "buddy system" which was maintained until the sixth week of rehabilitation when it was finally removed in the face of imminent wholesale violation. General unrest was reflected in the failure to re-establish efficient non-experimental laboratory and work assignments.

It was difficult for the men to abandon or modify attitudes and habits which they had acquired during semistarvation. In readapting to preexperimental interests and activities, the subjects were often frustrated by lack of supporting strength and endurance. The circumstances of normal living were appealing to the subjects long before they were able to cope with them successfully. This added to the restlessness and complicated the morale problem. In the latter part of rehabilitation the cumulative effects of increased food intake and the nearing prospect of the end of the experiment brought about a noticeable improvement in morale.

Humor, enthusiasm, and sociability progressively reappeared; and irritability and nervousness diminished. The strong sense of group identity was dissipated as the men once again looked forward to developing their own plans for the future and took up interests not immediately related to their participation in the experimental program. The distinction between the "ingroup" and the "out-group" (*i.e.* the starved and well-fed) disappeared.

Sex. The sexual impulses, needs, and interests were very slow in regaining their pre-experimental intensity.

Intelligence. There was a pronounced decline in the number of complaints about the lack of alertness, inability to concentrate, poor comprehension, impaired judgment, and deterioration of memory. However, the inefficiency and poor habits of study persisted. It was apparent that the men by and large did not resume their academic studies and intellectual pursuits with the application and vigor that was characteristic of their efforts during the control period.

RESULTS: POST-EXPERIMENTAL PHASE

On October 20, 1945 (the end of the twelfth week of controlled rehabilitation and the forty-eighth week of the experimental regimen) twenty of
the thirty-two subjects were released altogether from dietary and experimental restrictions. The twelve men selected to remain at the Laboratory
for further study were relieved of all dietary restraints over week-ends. Thus
on the weekend of October 20, the whole group was at long last free to
satisfy their personal food cravings and, most importantly, to eat as much
as they wanted. The men gorged prodigious quantities of food which approximated six to seven thousand calories per day. Many ate more or less continuously throughout the two-day period. Some reported eating as many
as three consecutive lunches. In many cases the men were not content to
eat "normal" menus but persevered in their habits of making "concoctions"
and combinations which could only be described as fantastic. The free
choice of ingredients, moreover, stimulated "creative" and "experimental"
messing with food. Licking of plates and neglect of table manners persisted. Attempts to avoid wasting even a particle continued in the face of
unlimited supplies of immediately available food. An irrational fear that
food would not be available or that the opportunity to eat would somehow
be taken away from them was present in some of the men. This may have
motivated their eating as much as they could hold at any given time.

Generally, the men ate more food than they were prepared to cope with.
This gluttony resulted in a high incidence of headaches, constipation or
diarrhea, intestinal distension, belching, flatus, and unusual sleepiness.
Several men had spells of nausea and vomiting; one became acutely ill and
required hospitalization for a week. Follow-up studies made at thirty-three
and fifty-five weeks after the end of semistarvation showed that the men
had returned, by and large, to their pre-experimental "normal" status
except that a number of men exceeded their pre-starvation weight.

DISCUSSION

Methodological comment. This paper presents clinical observations, impressions, and generalizations derived from formal and informal contacts
with the subjects and from descriptive protocols including diaries and interviews. The subjects were observed under such varied conditions as individual and group testing sessions, personal interviews, clerical and technical
laboratory work, participation in group meetings, at times when the authors
ate with the men, etc. Test results and ratings were mentioned only occasionally and were used as evidence supporting and/or supplementing qualitative
clinical judgment. The parallel use of the clinical approach and standardized

testing techniques facilitates interpretation of the data and has the advantage of providing for cross-validation of the findings.

Magnitude of the semistarvation changes. The fact that it was possible to complete successfully the experiment indicates that neither the physical nor mental health of the group was affected to a pathological degree. At no time was it necessary to omit a test or an interview because of lack of cooperation or incapacity of the subjects which was due to semistarvation alone. Many of the physical and psychological alterations may be considered as adaptive and protective. For example, reduction of basal metabolism conserved energy; likewise, reduction in social participation resulted in decreasing demands upon the energy of the organism. Other changes were frankly deteriorative, such as development of edema, loss of muscle tissue, lack of endurance, reduction in concentration and self-discipline. The character and magnitude of these changes were such as to render the men increasingly inefficient in their daily living. However, persons who came into superficial contact with the subjects did not notice anything strikingly abnormal about their behavior even though it was drastically altered from their pre-starvation norm.

Similarity between experimental and non-experimental semistarvation and rehabilitation. Sorokin critized experimental studies on starvation in man as lacking in realism. In spite of this criticism the picture of semistarvation as seen in the Minnesota Experiment resembled in all essential points the effects of famine as presented by Sorokin in his monograph. For a direct comparison with the changes observed in the Minnesota Experiment, digests of a few representative field reports on war-time semistarvation will be presented.

The severely undernourished persons seen in 1942 in internment camps in southern France universally exhibited weakness, exhaustion, and apathy. Their body temperature was lowered, and they were sensitive to cold; the onset of warmer weather was reflected in an improved sense of well-being. The facial expression was painful ("facies dolorosa"), sometimes mask-like. There was an acute desire for food in large amounts and frequently individuals had to be torn away from refuse cans. Schwarz noted that the increase in the desire to eat (hyperorexia) tended to last long after the patients became well. Even in the treatment of edematous cases the food had to be mixed with large amounts of liquid in order to make up the quantity desired by the patients. The daily bread rations had to be divided into three portions and given out separately, otherwise all the bread would be eaten as soon as it was received. Polyuria and nocturia were universal. Marked neurological changes were observed rarely and then only in the terminal stages of starvation.

Similar findings were obtained in Leningrad in 1941-42. Because of the

German blockade the supply of food to the city decreased rapidly and the progress of starvation approximated the rate of weight loss present in the Minnesota Experiment. The first clinical symptoms of ill-being began to appear in the population about four weeks following drastic reduction in food supply. Emaciation and decrease in strength became noticeable. Numerous cases of generalized weakness and occasional fainting came to the attention of the Leningrad First Aid Service. The effects of the blockade on the health of the population were complex. There were cases of simple semistarvation uncomplicated by symptoms of hypovitaminosis, but frequently there were added the effects of qualitative malnutrition and of intercurrent infectious diseases. In a sample of forty-eight semistarvation patients all but one complained of increased fatigability. All had lost weight, the most frequent loss being between twenty and twenty-five per cent of the prestarvation level with a range of between ten and thirty-three per cent. Polyuria, sensitivity to cold, dryness of the skin and hair, aches and pains in the extremities, and amenorrhea were frequent. No important visual disturbances were reported. Psychologically, various degrees of personality deterioration were observed: apathy, dulling of the emotions, lowering of the moral level, and narrowing down of intellectual interests. Psychotic involvements were rare.

Psychological investigation by means of interviews was carried out on a group of internees who lived through the starvation at the Belsen concentration camp in Germany. The author's main task was to examine patients who needed psychiatric attention and who were referred to him by other physicians. In addition, he examined some sixty cases in the hospital and convalescent areas selected at random to represent a cross-section of the camp population. Unfortunately, in his description the information from these two sources is not clearly differentiated. The nutrition was extremely poor; nine ounces of bread and two pints of turnip soup were given as the daily ration. At the time of liberation, the camp was estimated to contain about 50,000 people with some 10,000 lying dead in the huts and around the camp. In the semistarved inmates of the camp there was a marked reduction in activity, reaching in some cases the form of complete immobility. Many internees did not have enough strength to walk. A common reaction was the loss of appreciation of social ties, each individual living entirely for himself; family had little meaning. Responsiveness to death, cruelty, and humiliation was blunted and the individuals became apathetic to incidents in the camp. Many showed discouragement, seclusion, introversion and depression. Only a minority exhibited aggressive reactions. Impairment of memory appeared common. Carelessness in appearance, particularly in men, tended to persist even after liberation. In women the sense of modesty was dull or lacking. Interests were severely narrowed down to matters of food. The inmates were continually hungry, and it was reported that in the last stages of the camp before liberation cases of cannibalism had occurred. Even after the danger of starvation ceased and anxiety about food was objectively without grounds, the semistarvation reactions such as stealing, hiding, and "saving" food persisted. As nutritional rehabilitation progressed, the pattern of complaints changed. Whereas before the patients complained wearily and hopelessly, later the complaints became fierce, bitter, and resentful. Cases with frank psychopathology were few in view of the harrowing experiences, the physical suffering, and the fear of hunger, torture, and death to which the internees were exposed. There were cases of conversion hysteria, expressed in the inability to hear or see. Delusions were rare. A few patients exhibited maniacal outbursts.

There are many similarities between our experimental findings and the conditions described in the above reports. The loss of weight and the physiological changes were essentially typical of those encountered in non-experimental semistarvation. This was confirmed by Major Marvin Corlette, M.C., who made extensive observations on malnutrition in northwestern Europe at the time of liberation and who visited the Laboratory in July, 1945, at the end of the semistarvation period. He stated:

> . . . . the salient clinical features of the picture we saw at Minneapolis . . . . very closely simulated the picture of semistarvation seen in western Holland as well as in some of the German concentration camps in the early spring of 1945. Except for the absence of filth and secondary skin infections in the experimental subjects, it appears that the fundamental clinical pattern of partial starvation as we observed it in Europe has been duplicated.

The intrinsic psychological effects of semistarvation are also practically identical under both conditions: intense hunger, preoccupation with thoughts of food, marked emotional changes (*e.g.* depression, apathy, irritability), loss of sex drive, and overall suffering. The somewhat inimical social climate in which the men as conscientious objectors had moved prior to participating in the experiment and the unavoidable regimentation of their lives as subjects may be considered to have engendered psychological stresses analogous in some degree to the personal and social insecurity usually experienced by famine victims.

The behavior of the subjects during nutritional rehabilitation in the Minnesota Experiment had its counterpart in patients who suffered from natural semistarvation and were later placed on hospital diets. In this context reference may be made to the released Indian prisoners of war who lost on the average about twenty-five per cent of their body weight during their internment by the Japanese. After admission to the 47th British General Hospital, Singapore, they were served four meals daily. Between the main meals the men were given milk drinks with biscuits, sweets, or choco-lates. The light hospital diet provided an estimated 3,384 Calories; the ordinary hospital diet 4,260. As a rule the men had very large appetites which were not satsified by these diets. Overeating was often followed by flatulence and abdominal distension. Sometimes diarrhea was present. Gas-tro-intestinal discomfort lasted from a few hours to a few days. In severely debilitated persons overeating had serious results including sudden collapse, low blood pressure, a rapid feeble pulse, cold extremities, and stupor. In our group there was only one man who needed hospitalization because of gastrointestinal and cardiac symptoms resulting from overeating although minor distress was experienced by a considerable number of our subjects when they were released from all dietary restrictions.

Factors specific to the Minnesota experiment. In spite of the many simi-larities between the picture of experimental and "natural" semistarvation, we do not wish to minimize the specific factors present in the Minnesota Ex-periment. The subjects were specially selected and constituted a group which was neither a random nor a cross-sectional sample of the population. Certain aspects of the experiment tended to mitigate the severity of the stress as compared with non-experimental semistarvation. The men had clean, healthful living accommodations with adequate sanitary facilities, including soap, hot water, and other comforts. They had sufficient clothing and ade-quate medical supervision and care. All food was skillfully prepared and served. Since the subjects were not permitted to eat off-diet, the danger of ingesting contaminated food or harmful substitutes was eliminated. Neither did they get the opportunity to gorge from time to time. The men had strong intellectual, religious, humanitarian, and ethical values which played an important role in the maintenance of morale and in keeping the men from getting into "trouble." Unquestionably, the subjects possessed a rare capacity for continuous denial of the demands of intensive hunger.

Certain sources of insecurity present in conditions of "natural" famine were absent in this experiment. The subjects knew that the stress would come to an end at a predetermined date and that rehabilitation would follow. They knew when and what food would be served and that it would be available without fail. There was no competition as to who got what to eat, and therefore, no question of fending for it. The men were protected in other ways. When they were too weak or ill, arrangements were made so that their work and "guinea-pig" duties were postponed or re-scheduled. More importantly, they were free from political turmoil and oppression, bombing, threat of sudden death or injury, destruction and loss of property. Furthermore, crime, theft, depravity, exploitation, and other socially dis-ruptive concomitants of non-experimental semistarvation were not present.

On the other hand, some of the provisions and restrictions imposed by the experimental regimen increased its severity as compared with non-experimental situations. The subjects starved in the midst of plenty. The drastic limitations of personal freedom required by the experimental program itself was a hardship. Being volunteers, they could have withdrawn from the experiment; for this reason conflicts and tensions were generated which made the experimental semistarvation more difficult to endure. In the experimental situation the subjects were unable to improve their nutritional condition through ingenuity and individual effort as is often possible in "natural" semistarvation.

It is worthwhile to examine the hypothesis that the necessary controls and grueling regimen of the experiment, aside from diet, heightened significantly the psycho-biological stress and contributed to the behavioral changes. On this point we have only indirect but relevant evidence; twelve subjects serving in another nutritional experiment, who lived in the same quarters as the semistarvation subjects and under similarly controlled experimental conditions but on an adequate diet, gave no evidence of the behavior changes characteristic of semistarvation. It is believed in view of this fact that the rigorous experimental regimen as such did not distort for the group as a whole the personality changes induced by starvation.

Comparison of the Minnesota experiment with other experimental investigations. The psychological effects of semistarvation have been studied in the past primarily during acute and, as a rule, short-term starvation. Since these situations differ radically from prolonged semistarvation, there is no need to review this material.

There is only one experiment, carried out in 1918, which is somewhat similar to the present investigation. The effects of semistarvation on the well-being and personality of our subjects closely paralleled the changes observed by Benedict and his collaborators in their study on prolonged undernutrition. However, in the Minnesota Experiment, the alterations were much more marked. This is understandable because the period of reduced food intake in the present study was one-third longer and the average weight-loss was twenty-four per cent as compared with a decrement of 10.5 per cent in the case of the twelve subjects observed by Benedict. It may be expected that the strain of semistarvation bears an exponential rather than a linear relationship to the loss of body weight.

Use of conscientious objectors as subjects. Because conscientous objectors are members of a small minority group and, as such, known to relatively few people except in a stereotyped and superficial way, some comments on the subjects as persons rather than as "guinea-pigs" may be pertinent. Moreover, descriptive and identifying information may serve to forestall unwarranted criticisms of the experimental findings based on the status of the subjects as conscientious objectors.

Before the men were transferred to Minneapolis to serve as experimental subjects, they had been engaged in a variety of jobs classified as "civilian work of national importance," principally manual labor in work camps but also in special projects where they served as orderlies and attendants in mental hospitals, etc. Over a hundred men responded to the call for volunteers as "human guinea-pigs" in the starvation-rehabilitation experiment. Those candidates whose applications were approved after careful screening were physically examined and interviewed by Laboratory personnel before final selection. The men finally accepted were chosen according to these criteria:

Freedom from history of disabling diseases including mental illness.

Absence of physical disabilities or handicaps.

Ability to cooperate and get along well with others.

Willingness to subordinate personal interests, activities, and welfare
to the requirements of the experimental program.

Active interest in problems of nutritional relief and rehabilitation.

Freedom from marital or familial responsibilities.

The individuals selected were healthy, intelligent, young, white males representing a wide range of body type, physical endurance, personality characteristics, and socio-economic background. According to clinical evaluation as well as the results of objective measures of personality, only their pacifist convictions set these men apart from other men of similar age, health, intelligence, education, and background. The immature and neurotic personality traits evidenced in a few men prior to the experiment were either sub-clinical or mild. The men were highly regarded, both as subjects and as persons, by those with whom they worked and associated. It seems safe to assume that any sample-bias present in the experimental findings errs on the conservative side. The psycho-biological "stamina" of the subjects was unquestionably superior to that likely to be found in any random or more generally representative population sample. It is unlikely that such a sample of subjects could be kept to the grueling regimen for the necessary duration of such an experiment. It should be remembered that the subjects could eat nothing but what the Laboratory prescribed and provided for almost a year. Moreover, for many, at the levels of refeeding used, rehabilitation was, for weeks, little more than a painful continuation of the six months of semistarvation stress.

SUMMARY

Observations are reported on behavioral changes which occurred in 36 volunteer subjects during a semistarvation-rehabilitation experiment.

Six months of semistarvation produced marked deteriorative and adaptive changes in all subjects. The men lost twenty-four per cent of their initial gross body weight. The physiological responses to undernutrition included such changes as decrease in the pulse and basal metabolic rate. A large number of men suffered from edema. The subjects complained of weakness, fatigability, sensitivity to cold, giddiness on arising, polyuria, distressing sensations of hunger, and other aches and pains.

The personality changes were "psychoneurotic" in type and although not grossly pathological, rendered the subjects increasingly ineffective in their daily living. The men exhibited symptoms of depression, irritability, "nervousness," and general emotional instability. Social withdrawal, narrowing of interests, obliteration of sexual drive, and difficulty in concentration were prominent. Food and eating became their dominant concern.

Marked individual differences were present in both the degree of overall deterioration shown in starvation and in the rate of recovery. During the period of rehabilitation, return to "normal" was unexpectedly slow and in general paralleled the levels of caloric intake. Feeling of well being, range of interests, emotional stability, and sociability were regained more rapidly than strength, endurance, normal eating habits, and sexual drive.

REFERENCES—SECTION SIX

Adams, D. K. The organs of perception: sentiments. *J. Pers.*, 1953, *22*, 52-60.
Allport, F. H. *Theories of Perception and the Concept of Structure*. New York: Wiley, 1955.
Altrocchi, J. Dominance as a factor in interpersonal choice and perception. *J. abnorm. soc. Psychol.*, 1959, *59*, 303-308.
Ansbacher, H. Perception of number as affected by the monetary value of the objects. *Arch. of Psychol.*, 1937, *30*, No. 215.
Ardis, J. A., and Fraser, E. Personality and perception: the constancy effect and intraversion. *Brit. J. Psychol.*, 1957, *48*, 47-54.
Aronfreed, J. M., Messick, S. A., and Diggory, J. C. Re-examining emotionality and perceptual defense. *J. Pers.*, 1953, *21*, 516-528.
Beams, H. L. Affectivity as a factor in the apparent size of pictured food objects. *J. exp. Psychol.*, 1954, *47*, 197-200.
Beardslee, D. C., and Wertheimer, M., (Eds.). *Readings in Perception*. Princeton, New Jersey: D. Van Nostrand, 1958.
Beatty, F. S., Dameron, L. E., and Green, J. E. An investigation of the effects of reward and punishment on visual perception. *J. Psychol.*, 1959, *47*, 267-276.
Beier, E. G., and Cowen, E. L. A further investigation of the influence of "threat expectancy" on perception. *J. Pers.*, 1953, *22*, 254-257.
Bender, I. E., Imus, H. A., Rathney, J. W. M., Kemple, C., and England, M. R. *Motivation and Visual Factors*. Hanover, New Hampshire. Dartmouth College publications, 1942.
Bevan, W. Perception: Evolution of a concept. *Psychol. Rev.*, 1958, *65*, 34-55.
Bieri, J., Bradbura, W. M., and Galinsky, M. D. Sex differences in perceptual behavior. *J. Pers.*, 1958, *26*, 1-12.
Bitterman, M. E., and Kniffin, C. W. Manifest anxiety and perceptual defense. *J. abnorm. soc. Psychol.*, 1953, *48*, 248-252.
Blake, R. R. and Ramsey, G. V. (Eds.). *Perception: An Approach to Personality*. New York: Ronald Press, 1951.

Bruner, J. S. Personality dynamics and the process of perceiving. In R. R. Blake, and G. V. Ramsey, (Eds.), *Perception: An Approach to Personality.* New York: Ronald Press, 1951.

————, and Goodman, C. C. Value and need as organizing factors in perception. *J. abnorm. soc. Psychol.*, 1947, *42*, 33-44.

————, and Krich, D. (Eds.). *Perception and Personality: A Symposium.* Durham, North Carolina: Duke Univ. Press, 1949.

————, and Postman, L. Emotional selectivity in perception and reaction. *J. Pers.*, 1947, *16*, 69-77.

Carter, L. F., and Schooler, K. Value, need and other factors in perception. *Psychol. Rev.*, 1949, *56*, 200-207.

Chein, I., Levine, R., Murphy, G., Proshansky, H., and Schafer, R. Need as determinant of perception; a reply to Pastore. *J. Psychol.*, 1951, *31*, 129-136.

Chodorkoff, B. Self-perception, perceptual defense, and adjustment. *J. abnorm. soc. Psychol.*, 1954, *49*, 508-512.

Cohen, B. D., Senf, R., and Huston, P. E. Perceptual accuracy in schizophrenia, depression, and neurosis, and effects of amytal. *J. abnorm. soc. Psychol.*, 1956, *52*, 363-367.

Crockett, W. H., and Meidinger, T. Authoritarianism and interpersonal perception. *J. abnorm. soc. Psychol.*, 1956, *53*, 378-380.

Davis, J. M. Personality, perceptual defense, and stereoscopic perception. *J. abnorm. soc. Psychol.*, 1959, *58*, 398-402.

Dember, W. N. *Psychology of Perception.* New York: Holt, Rinehart and Winston, 1960.

Dixon, N. F. Subception. *New Biol.*, 1958, No. 27, 27-38.

Dunbar, F. *Emotions and Bodily Changes.* New York: Columbia Univ. Press, 1954.

Fishbach, S., and Singer, R. D. The effects of fear arousal and suppression of fear upon social perception. *J. abnorm. soc. Psychol.*, 1957, *55*, 283-288.

Fisher, C. Dreams and perception. The role of preconscious and primary modes of perception in dream formation. *J. Amer. Psychoanaly. Assn.* 1954, *2*, 389-445.

Freeman, J. T. Set or perceptual defense? *J. exp. Psychol.*, 1954, *48*, 283-288.

Frenkel-Brunswik, E. *Personality Theory and Perception.* New York: Ronald Press, 1951.

Gemelli, A., and Cappellini, A. The influence of the subject's attitude in perception. *Acta psychol.*, 1958, *14*, 12-23.

Gilchrist, J. C., and Nesberg, L. S. Need and perceptual change in need-related objects. *J. exp. Psychol.*, 1952, *44*, 369-376.

Goldiamond, I. Indicators of perception: I. Subliminal perception, subception, unconscious perception. An analysis in terms of psychophysical indicator methodology. *Psychol. Bull.*, 1958, *55*, 373-411.

Gordon, I. J., and Combs, A. W. The learner: Self and perception. *Rev. educ. Res.*, 1958, *28*, 433-444.

Gruen, A. A critique and re-evaluation of Witkin's perception and perception-personality work. *J. Gen. Psychol.*, 1957, *56*, 73-93.

Henle, M. Some effects of motivational processes on cognition. *Psychol. Rev.*, 1955, *62*, 423-432.

Hochberg, J. E. Perception: Toward the recovery of a definition. *Psychol. Rev.*, 1956, *63*, 400-405.

Hulin, W. S., and Katz, D. The Frois-Wittman pictures of facial expression. *J. exp. Psychol.*, 1935, *18*, 482-498.

Jenkin, N. Affective processes in perception. *Psychol. Bull.*, 1957, *54*, 100-127.

Kalis, B. L. Some relationships between size perception and ego adequacy. *J. Pers.*, 1957, *25*, 439-450.

Klein, G. S. The personal world through perception. In R. R. Blake, and G. V. Ramsey, (Eds.). *Perception: An Approach to Personality.* New York: Ronald Press, 1951.

————. Perception, motives and personality. In J. L. McCary, (Ed.), *Psychology of Personality.* New York: Logos Press, 1956, 123-199.

————. Consciousness in psychoanalytic theory: Some implications for current research in perception. *J. Amer. Psychoanal. Assoc.*, 1959, *7*, 5-34.

————. On subliminal activation. *J. nerv. ment. Dis.*, 1959, *128*, 293-301.

————, Schlesinger, H. J., and Meister, D. E. The effects of personal values on perception: An experimental critique. *Psychol. Rev.*, 1951, *58*, 96-112.

Lazarus, R. S., Yousem, H., and Arenberg, D. Hunger and perception. *J. Pers.*, 1953, *21*, 312-329.

Leuba, C., and Lucas, C. Effects of attitudes on descriptions of pictures. *J. exp. Psychol.*, 1945, *35*, 517-524.

Levine, R., Chein, I., and Murphy, G. The relation of the intensity of a need to the amount of perceptual distortion: A preliminary report. *J. Psychol.*, 1942, *13*, 283-293.

Levy, L. H. Perceptual defense in tactual perception. *J. Pers.*, 1958, *26*, 467-478.

Lindner, H. Sexual responsiveness to perceptual tests in a group of sexual offenders. *J. Pers.*, 1953, *21*, 364-374.

Luft, J. Monetary value and the perception of persons. *J. soc. Psychol.*, 1957, *46*, 245-251.

Main, T. F. Perception and ego function. *Brit. J. med. Psychol.*, 1958, *31*, 1-8.

McGinnies, E. Emotionality and perceptual defense. *Psychol. Rev.*, 1949, *56*, 244-251.

Miller, J. G. Role of motivation in learning without awareness. *Amer. J. Psychol.*, 1940, *53*, 229-239.

Moffit, J. W., and Stagner, R. Perceptual rigidity and closure as functions of anxiety. *J. abnorm. soc. Psychol.*, 1956, *52*, 354-357.

Murphy, G. Some relations of perception to motivation. In G. S. Seward, and J. P. Seward, (Eds.), *Current Psychological Issues*. New York: Holt, 1958, 23-38.

Murphy, G., and Hochberg, J. Perceptual development: Some tentative hypotheses. *Psychol. Rev.*, 1951, *58*, 332-349.

Niebuhr, H., Jr., and Cohen, D. The effects of psycho-pathology on visual discrimination. *J. abnorm. soc. Psychol.*, 1956, *53*, 173-177.

Pastore, N. Need as a determinant of perception. *J. Psychol.*, 1949, *28*, 457-475.

Postman, L. Perception, motivation, and behavior. *J. Pers.*, 1953, *22*, 17-32.

————, Bronson, W. C., and Cropper, G. L. Is there a mechanism of perceptual defense? *J. abnorm. soc. Psychol.* 1953, *48*, 215-224.

————, and Bruner, J. S. Perception under stress. *Psychol. Rev.*, 1948, *55*, 314-323.

————, Bruner, J. S., and McGinnies, E. Personal values as selective factors in perception. *J. abnorm. soc. Psychol.*, 1948, *43*, 142-154.

Prentice, W. C. H. Perception. *Annu. Rev. Psychol.*, 1958, *9*, 1-18

Proshansky, H., and Murphy, G. The effects of reward and punishment on perception. *J. Psychol.*, 1942, *13*, 295-305.

Rosenbaum, M. E. Social perception and the motivational structure of interpersonal relations. *J. abnorm. soc. Psychol.*, 1959, *59*, 130-133.

Rudin, S. A., and Stagner, R. Figure-ground phenomena in the perception of physical and social stimuli. *J. Psychol.*, 1958, *45*, 213-225.

Salley, C. M., and Murphy, G. *Development Of the Perceptual World*. New York: Basic Books, 1960.

Schlosberg, H. J. A scale for the judgement of facial expression. *J. exp. Psychol.*, 1941, *29*, 497-510.

Schönbach, P. Cognition, motivation, and time perception. *J. abnorm. soc. Psychol.*, 1959, *58*, 195-202.

Smith, G. H. Size-distance judgements of human faces (projected images). *J. gen. Psychol.*, 1953, *49*, 45-64.

Strickland, J. F. The effect of motivational arousal on humor preferences. *J. abnorm. soc. Psychol.*, 1959, *59*, 278-281.

Tajfel, H. Value and perceptual judgement of magnitude. *Psychol. Rev.*, 1957, *64*, 192-204.

Toginni, R., and Petrullo, L., (Eds.), *Person Perception and Interpersonal Behavior*. Stanford, Calif: Stanford University Press, 1958.

Wallach, H. Some considerations concerning the relation between perception and cognition. *J. Pers.*, 1949, *18*, 6-13.

Werner, H., and Wapner, S. Toward a general theory of perception. *Psychol. Rev.*, 1952, *59*, 324-338.

Wiener, M., and Schiller, P. H. Subliminal perception or perception of partial cues. *J. abnorm. soc. Psychol.*, 1960, *61*, 124-137.

Wittreich, W. J. Visual perception and personality. *Scient. Amer.*, 1959, *200*, 56-75.

UNCONSCIOUS MOTIVATION

One of Freud's greatest contributions to the study and understanding of human behavior was his recognition of the importance of unconscious motivation. It was Freud's strong belief that much of an individual's behavior is governed by motives of which he is unaware. Certain motives (wishes, emotions, desires) are repressed, he says, because they are unacceptable to the individual. These motives are primarily sexual and aggressive in nature. However, even though certain wishes, attitudes and desires are unconscious, they express themselves indirectly and in subtle ways, and they exert a significant influence on the individual's everyday behavior. Furthermore, these unconscious motives often express themselves in the form of neurotic symptoms— in dreams and in mistakes of speech, writing, lapses of memory, etc. Freud's book, *The Psychopathology of Everyday Life,* (New American Library, 1951) illustrates dramatically the ways in which unconscious motives intrude themselves in an individual's daily behavior. Robbins (Paper No. 40) presents in a simplified and interesting fashion the different ways in which unconscious motives affect behavior.

It is important to note, however, that while the concept of unconscious motivation, like many other Freudian terms, is generally accepted by social scientists, the Freudian explanation of unconscious motives is not. Some psychologists, for example, prefer to explain unconscious motives in terms of principles of learning, habit formation, etc. McGranahan is one of those who disagree with Freud's theory of repression. In his paper (No. 42) he criticizes the Freudian theory and presents his own: *"Repression will have meaning and significance only when it is the idea, the thought process, that is primarily to be avoided, rather than the external object or situation."* Like Maslow and Mittelmann (Paper No. 41) McGranahan places much importance on the motive of self-esteem in explaining why repression occurs. In addition to pointing up the existence, importance and influence of unconscious psychological processes, Maslow and Mittelmann discuss the reasons why certain needs, emotions and desires are unconscious (repressed). They believe that various psychological processes and reactions are unconscious because they are painful, dangerous, and detrimental to one's feelings of self-esteem and security.

One of the most striking methods by which to exemplify the influence of unconscious motives on everyday behavior is through experimental hypnosis. The paper by Erickson (No. 43) probably illustrates this better than any other available at present. In it he shows the effects on an individual's waking behavior of several post-hypnotic suggestions involving conflict. In Erickson's second paper (No. 44) he explains that a suggestion given to a subject in a deep state of hypnosis will produce not only the expected response specific to a particular modality of behavior, but also that "there may also be elicited, seemingly as coincidental manifestations, marked changes in one or another apparently unrelated modality of behavior." Wolberg (Paper No. 45) demonstrates how unconscious conflicts induced under hypnosis may produce various somatic ailments such as a generalized state of tension, autonomic disturbances, gastrointestinal symptoms, etc. Watkins (Paper No. 46) points out how, under a state of hypnosis, a subject may be forced to perform antisocial compulsive acts.

40. Unconscious Motivation

Lewis L. Robbins

ONE of the most important postulates of modern psychiatric thinking, which came about largely, but not exclusively, through the discoveries and the work of Sigmund Freud, is that most human behavior is determined by forces within the individual of which he is not consciously aware. People often act in ways which they themselves are unable to explain. Some may give explanations for their behavior which they believe are quite correct, which satisfy them, as it were. However, an observer—particularly a psychiatrist—may see that these are not the real motives.

Freud's pronouncements about the dynamic unconscious were about as disturbing to man as the discovery by Copernicus that the earth was not the center of the universe; they were even more devasting than Darwin's theory of evolution. Man liked to think of the earth as the center of everything in the universe. He liked to think of himself as something special and different from lower animals. Above all, he likes to think that he is completely rational. He deeply cherishes the thought that he can always control his behavior and has a great reluctance to relinquish this thought.

Today, most people are somewhat willing to believe man's behavior is unconsciously determined in most instances, but they usually believe this only about the other fellow and not about themselves. They still prefer to think that they are not subject to distant, hidden impulses and motivations.

In psychiatry and psychology, the mind is divided roughly into three areas: the *conscious, pre-conscious, and unconscious.*

The conscious is that segment of the mind which is concerned with immediate awareness. You know you are reading right now. This is conscious.

The pre-conscious is the portion where are stored those things which we can recall more or less at will. You can probably remember the address

Abridged from the *Menninger Quarterly*, 1956, 10, 24-28. Reprinted by permission of the author and The Menninger Foundation.

where you lived when fifteen years old. This awareness is now conscious. A moment before, it was pre-conscious.

The unconscious is that segment containing a great deal of "forgotten" material which cannot be recalled at will. It contains ideas, wishes, and strivings which were once conscious, but now have been buried or, as psychiatrists say, repressed. The unconscious also contains many primitive, instinctual strivings and desires which have never been conscious.

This is a tremendous storehouse of forgotten memories, forgotten experiences. One might say that, like the iceberg, about one-seventh of the human mind is exposed to consciousness or to pre-conscious awareness and about six-sevenths or more is below the surface. But even though the unconscious is not apparent, its effects certainly are.

Is there evidence the unconscious exists? Yes, a great deal.

One of the simplest clinical evidences comes from hypnosis. When a person is hypnotized, it is possible to have him recall many events of his past life which he cannot remember in his normal state of consciousness. Another interesting and easily demonstrated phenomenon is post-hypnotic suggestion. An individual, while hypnotized, is told that after he is awakened he will do something at a given signal. And he does. The impulse on which he acts is determined by suggestion which has become unconscious.

We all make slips of the tongue. Many of them are funny, or embarrassing, because they tell a partial truth and expose a thought or feeling which we may not wish to express consciously. We say what we unconsciously mean or have an impulse to say, but had not consciously intended to say. An example is the mother who carefully warned her children not to stare at or remark about the unusually large, red nose of an expected guest. Then when he came, she introduced him as "Mr. Nose." These slips tell us there is mental activity which is not conscious.

Forgetting is another evidence of the unconscious. We are apt to forget some things about which we have conflict. Some people, for example, often forget important appointments. If they stop and honestly reflect, they will probably find they had been reluctant to keep these appointments in the first place. Of course we may have intense preoccupations and simply forget something which in itself doesn't carry much conflict. If someone in our family is seriously ill, for instance, we're apt to forget little things. But there is much of this other—that is, forgetting because in a sense we do not want to remember. I recall a patient who said, "I always lose my gloves, I don't know why." I knew why. Hers was a very fashionable family in which a lady always wore gloves when in public. She had some conflict about being a fashionable lady all the time. The gloves represented gentility, which was somewhat of a burden to her.

The most comomn example of forgetting is that practically everybody has totally "forgotten" the events of his early childhood. Can you remember when you were weaned, or when you got your first tooth? We may think we recall some early events because we have been told about them over and over again. But most of these memories are really buried in the unconscious and, without knowing it, influencing our behavior today.

In the amnesias, there is gross and pathological forgetting. Some people have particularly horrible traumatic experiences, in war for instance, and not only forget the experience but can't even remember their own names. We can see in such an example some of the function of forgetting. If one remembers who he is, he is likely to recall what he has experienced, and the painful feelings associated with it. So, for psychic self protection, there follows a total blotting out of his own identity.

Dreams also furnish us evidence of unconscious mental activity. We know by the study of dreams that many early childhood events, primitive impulses, and infantile wishes, which somehow have been stimulated by the course of a day's events, reappear in a distorted form in dreams. They are not revealed consciously because when one is conscious he exercises much control. In sleep there is a loss of control which results in mental activity which is reflected in dreams. If we set up proper conditions, it's possible to understand the meanings of dreams. However, only with a certain specific and special relationship to the individual and an understanding of him as an individual, as in the psychotherapeutic situation, could one know what the dreams really mean.

You probably have experienced the interesting phenomenon of solving problems in your sleep. Let us say you were leaving the office yesterday afternoon and could not remember where you put that letter from Bill Smith. You look everywhere, but can't find it. The more you try to think of where that letter is, the further you are from a solution. Finally you quit searching, go home, go to sleep, wake up in the morning, and, while having your breakfast, you know where it is. You solved it in your sleep. Many problems are solved that way. Here again is a curious kind of evidence that an aspect of mental activity is going on without our being conscious of it.

We all have rituals. For instance, each morning nearly everyone puts on the same shoe first, not necessarily the one that comes to hand first. Or some of us feel we *must* straighten every picture that's crooked. These compulsive things we all do may seem illogical or ridiculous, but they all have some meaning. We are forced to do them because of unconscious impulses of which we are not remotely aware. Take the person at the party who goes from one room to the next constantly emptying ash trays. That this has something to do with how he or she was toilet trained as a child may seem very remote, but it does.

Some of us have very marked tics that we, though unaware, do over and over again. We may blink our eyes, or pick at our teeth, or scratch. All these have unconscious meaning which would become apparent to a psychiatrist working with an individual having them. They, too, are evidence of the existence of the unconscious.

There is another broader and most meaningful evidence: "automatic" reactions. For example, you meet people whom you immediately like or dislike for no reason you can explain. These spontaneous reactions are often determined by past events or attitudes within us that come from the past. The reasons we consciously ascribe for such reactions are often very invalid substitutes for the real ones.

Similarly, many of our prejudices and preferences are determined unconsciously, even though we frequently give them conscious reasons. This is true of many political convictions, though certainly not all. Without even thinking about it a great majority of the people in a certain area vote Republican and a similar proportion in another area vote Democrat. They have all kinds of wonderful reasons for political preferences, aside from the one they never thought about: this is the thing to do in this particular culture. Most of us follow the religious precepts we've been taught and are relatively intolerant of those who seem to deviate, who are different from us. We have good reasons, they have good reasons. But most of these reasons are beside the point. The tradition, the culture, the way in which we were brought up—it is these with which we have identified. We have not necessarily learned them. We have acquired them through a rather simple process in which the conscious elements are the least important.

There are other evidences of the unconscious in the change in peoples behavior when they are under the influence of alcohol, drugs, or anesthesia. The facade of conscious control may dissolve in alcohol and the more primitive personality come through. A nice genial fellow may, under the influence of alcohol, pick a fight with somebody. A very sweet, demure, decorous lady may start to flirt. Some people drink to bring about a change in themselves. Rarely does an alcoholic drink because he likes the taste of liquor. He drinks because it does something to him psychologically, because it is a way of bringing a change in himself. We all have heard stories about people who do funny things when they come out of anesthetic—for example, people who had learned a foreign language in childhood and had forgotten it. They talked in that language when they were coming out of an anesthetic. Some drugs have similar effects and occasionally can—as can hypnosis—be useful to the psychiatrist in helping patients express thoughts ordinarily unconscious.

The unconscious is seen in more gross and more bizaare personality perculiarities in severe mental illness. Under this severe stress, some of the methods for maintaining a kind of control, logical behavior, and rationality are weakened; some of the unconscious impulses break through and become part of the conscious behavior. Many of the illusions and hallucinations that people have when severely mentally ill are reflections of this. Severely mentally ill people are just like you and me, only more so, in the sense that lots of the little things that you and I do have the same origins as the more distorted and more persistent behavior seen in certain types of mental disorder.

Basically, what we are is a reflection of this vast area of mental processes which are unconscious. They have a most dynamic effect upon our behavior. Although these unconscious drives, wishes, and conflicts can be made known under certain conditions—psychiatric treatment, hypnosis, drugs, etc.—we usually do not need to know them. Yet an awareness of their existence and their extraordinary functioning can be extremely important to all of us in dealing with other people, for whatever purpose.

41. Unconscious Psychological Processes: Conflict

A. H. Maslow and Béla Mittelmann

UNCONSCIOUS ACTIVITIES

IT has been repeatedly emphasized . . . that the patient cannot adequately account for the complaints and symptoms from which he suffers, but that their meaningful connections can be seen if we assume, on the basis of valid evidence, that he is motivated by needs, goals, and emotions of which he is not aware; in other words, they are unconscious. The existence of unconscious psychological processes can be demonstrated experimentally and clinically by means of hypnosis and in other ways.

Conscious wishes are more controllable than unconscious wishes. The

Abridged from A. H. Maslow and Béla Mittelmann, *Principles of Abnormal Psychology* (Revised Edition), 1951, Chapter 4. Reprinted by permission of Dr. A. H. Maslow and Harper & Brothers, New York.

amazing difference in controllability can be seen most clearly in one of the essential aspects of psychoanalytic therapy. The first task of this therapy is always phrased as "increasing the patient's insight into his own motives, or making the unconscious conscious." . . .

CONDITIONED-RESPONSE EXPERIMENTS AND UNCONSCIOUS ACTIVITIES

. . . These experiments, like certain older ones, prove that we can perceive unconsciously, react unconsciously, and learn unconsciously. They also indicate that unconscious processes seem to proceed in accordance with somewhat different principles than do conscious activities; i.e., they appear to be less controllable and to persist longer. In a word, they seem to be more "powerful" in various ways than when they are conscious. . . .

UNCONSCIOUS AND EMOTIONAL CONDITIONING

Probably the best experimental lead is the work with emotional conditioning. We know that such conditioning can take place in early infancy, even before the age of verbalization. It may persist for a lifetime, the individual remaining unaware of the source of his emotional reaction. These conditioned responses are peculiar in that they may be established in one trial, and they apparently are not easily extinguished. Furthermore— . . . they show a good deal of irradiation; that is, the same emotional response may be evoked by a stimulus which only resembles the original conditioning stimulus. . . .

PSYCHODYNAMICS OF UNCONSCIOUS PROCESSES

In general, we can say that the most important unconscious processes are not unconscious by accident; they do not just happen to be unconscious. They are unconscious for a reason and a purpose. The reason may be complex, but as a rule it includes avoiding pain, danger, and hurt to self-esteem and security. . . .

When all the processes and reactions that are unconscious in a patient are considered, there are strong reasons for their being unconscious and for his shutting them out of awareness. . . . We find that all of them are unconscious because they are all connected with reactions which spring from the anticipation of a catastrophic situation characterized by helplessness, abandonment, worthlessness, fear of humiliation, and injury. To put it another way, various psychological processes must be repressed in their totality by the patient because of his fear of a catastrophic breakdown; he feels that all these processes must remain unconscious, if he had to admit them, if he had to cope with the problems they present, he would be thrown into a catastrophic state of helplessness. . . .

42. Critical and Experimental Study of Repression

Donald V. McGranahan

WE are told that in order to understand the basic concepts of psychoanalysis, a person must be analyzed himself. It was with this thought in mind that I applied for an analysis while living as a student in Vienna during 1935-1936. I was taken on very graciously, though possessed of little financial means, and received about seven and a half months of regular didactic analysis under a Freudian. At the end of that time I felt much better adjusted to the world and duly grateful. But I felt no less mystified as to the nature of certain Freudian concepts than when I went into analysis. This was especially true of the concepts of *rationalization* and *repression,* in which I was much interested. That rationalization and repression take place I was quite convinced; but the underlying dynamics of the process still remained hidden in the mist of theory. It seemed desirable, therefore, to try to understand these concepts from some other approach, and I have accordingly attempted to subject them to experimental analysis. This paper will be concerned only with the concept of repression, which is the more important of the two, and is, in the words of Freud, the very "pillar upon which the edifice of psychoanalysis rests."

In dealing with repression, we must distinguish clearly at the outset between the empirical observations that define repression and the *theory* of repression. There are, on the one hand, certain concrete situations in which the term "repression" is applied; and, on the other hand, there is a vast body of psychoanalytic theory in which repression plays an important

Abridged from the *Journal of Abnormal and Social Psychology,* 1940, 35, 212-225. Reprinted by permission of the author and the American Psychological Association, Inc.

role. Now we may accept as facts the concrete situations that define repression without accepting the theory. But psychoanalysts do not make this distinction, and have an unfortunate tendency to confuse speculation with observation. Consequently, a writer who attempts to apply the term repression on a particular occasion, following empirical criteria, is apt to be told that he is not really dealing with repression at all, because he is not using the psychoanalytic theory. Such an objection is expected by the present writer.

We must first ask, then, what are the concrete situations (or operations, if you will) that define repression. If we make a survey of its usage, we find that the term is commonly employed when certain material consistently remains absent from consciousness, although normal conditions for its appearance are present, and when this material can be made to enter consciousness by changing the individual's attitude or by having him carry out a process of free association in the course of which motivational resistance to the material becomes obvious. Such will be the definition of repression assumed in this paper. Clinical cases in which an individual fails to recall significant incidents of his own past provide the most familiar and typical cases of repression. Post-hypnotic amnesia provides the most clearly demonstrable cases.

CRITIQUE

If we examine the literature dealing with the theory of repression, we find that there are basically two problems to consider. First, what is the nature of the repressed material? And secondly, how is repression carried out; what is the repressing force or agent?

Freud constantly remarks, particularly in his older writings, that repression deals with "unpleasant thoughts" or "painful ideas" or "ideas that might awaken pain." A number of American psychologists have taken this to mean any unpleasant experience whatsoever, and have set out to "test Freud's theory of repression" by seeing whether in experimental situations pleasant experiences are recalled better than unpleasant experiences. Odors, names, life-history incidents, and various other materials have been used. In general, the results have been inconclusive, some showing better memory for pleasant material, some showing no difference, and some showing better memory for unpleasant material. Experiments of one particular type, however, have given consistent evidence of repression—namely, experiments where the material involves shame, guilt, or the lowering of self-esteem. It is the unpleasant examination grade rather than the unpleasant odor that tends to be quickly forgotten. Freud does not himself generally speak of the repressed material as being injurious to self-esteem, although this idea appears when he briefly discusses the relation of the "ego-ideal" to repression.

In his recent technical discussions, where he considers the problem specifically, Freud refers to the repressed material as "instinct-presentations," or ideas that are the conscious "representatives" of libidinal strivings. By this description he appears to mean that the content avoided in repression consists of direct awareness of various primitive, unsocial impulses, including certain feeling-states and thoughts about ends and means. The theory goes further in stating that repression acts as a "defense" against the impulses.[1]

This theory of the repressed material has led to a definite limitation of the concept of repression. For if repression concerns states of consciousness associated with primitive impulses only, then we cannot speak of repression when an individual avoids thinking about his physical or social inferiorities or about his bad examination grades. Awareness of a physical weakness or ineptitude, for example, in no wise represents a libidinal impulse. Nevertheless, it is common, among psychoanalysts as well as other psychologists, to refer to repression when a person fails to admit to himself and others his weaknesses and inferiorities.

In conjunction with the above theory there has also developed a subtle but significant change in the basic meaning of repression. The emphasis has been shifted from restraint upon the conscious or potentially conscious material associated with certain impulses to direct restraint upon the impulses themselves. Freud, and most other analysts as well, now appear to take this meaning of repression. It may be objected that we are splitting hairs and that the two views are essentially the same. Yet in point of fact, two quite different meanings have arisen, one concerning ideas, the other impulses. Even two different definitions of repression are given in Warren's dictionary:

1. (psychoan.) the mental process by which perceptions and ideas which would be painful to consciousness are forced into the unconscious system;

2. (psychoan.) the rejection, by the ego, of impulses emanating from the id (topographic-dynamic conception).

And Lundholm, though not a psychoanalyst, contends that "repression is always repression of an impulse by an impulse. . . . ," even denying that it is proper to speak of the repression of memories.

The view that repression is a matter of direct action upon impulse may seem to the analyst but little different from the view that repression is a constraint upon consciousness; for the analyst tends to conceive of con-

---

[1]It will be impossible in the space allowed to do justice to the many and complicated ideas Freud has expressed about repression. Only the main outlines of his theory can be suggested.

sciousness as a static chamber where various entities come and go. Not being aware of an impulse is thus conceived in the case of repression as a blocking of the impulse from the chamber of consciousness.

But consciousness, far from being such a static affair, where various things can enter or have their entrance blocked, is a dynamic, active process which can be turned in one direction or another. If an item is consistently absent from consciousness, then either the item is removed beyond the possible range of consciousness, or something has been done to the observing system so that it fails to report this particular item. *In repression we must assume that the observing system rather than the observed item is affected.* By definition the item is not physically inaccessible to consciousness, and can be observed by the individual after a change in his psychological state. We can best conceive of repression, therefore, as a matter of direct action and constraint upon the activity of consciousness, a process by which consciousness is turned away and prevented from reporting certain material, rather than a process by which material is turned away from consciousness. The case is similar to what might happen if someone tampered with a galvanometer so that it would never report three amperes, whatever the objective situation, although it reported all other amperage; or to the situation of a hypnotized subject who fails to see a chair because his perceptual system has been so influenced by the hypnotist that he never looks at it but always to one side or another.[2]

If we turn now to the problem of the repressing force or agent, we find that here, too, the literature presents a large number of theories, though none with great confidence and clarity. The "censor," the "ego," the "ego-ideal," the "super-ego," the "ego-instincts," the "death instinct," "fear," "anxiety," the "pleasure-pain principle," "guilt-feelings," "self-estem," the "master sentiment of self-regard," even the "sex-instinct" itself, have all been held responsible for repression in one way or another by some author. McDougall waxes indignant at the large number of theories Freud alone seems to embrace.

In his latest writings, Freud appears to regard anxiety or fear in the ego as the main force determining repression. It is the view that is probably most common among other psychologists as well. At first Freud considered anxiety to be the *result* of repression, but later showed, he claims, that "it is not the repression that creates the anxiety, but the anxiety is there first

---

[2]Repression, so conceived, must be kept distinct from "inhibition," which refers to the blocking of an impulse from expression in overt motor activity. An inhibited impulse may have strong representation in consciousness; and, conversely, an impulse that finds motor outlet may have little or no conscious representation. Repression, as a constraint upon the activity of consciousness, thus may or may not operate in conjunction with motor inhibition. Psychoanalysts, however, seem at the present time to make little distinction between inhibition and repression.

and creates the repression!" Moreover, this anxiety turns out in the last analysis to be fear of external danger (fear of castration in the male, fear of loss of love in the female). The total picture of repression given by Freud is complicated and runs in the following fashion. An instinctual demand arises, and the ego imagines what would happen if it were satisfied. Thereupon anxiety is aroused, for satisfaction would evoke a danger-situation. The anxiety sets into action the automatic pleasure-pain principle, which has direct control over instinctual processes of the id, and restrains the particular impulse in question.

This latest theory of Freud about the manner in which repression is carried out is plainly a theory of direct action upon impulse, rather than upon conscious content. Indeed, it is difficult to see how consciousness comes into the picture at all. An impulse is restrained because its realization in overt action would lead to a danger-situation. But why there should also be no representation of it in consciousness is not clear, especially since, as the analysts themselves admit, impulses can best be controlled by being brought into consciousness.

THEORY

The theory of repression presented in this paper is based on the idea that repression is first and foremost a constraint upon conscious activity; and the questions we must therefore ask are: what kind of conscious material is avoided in repression, and how is the course of conscious activity controlled in repression?

We may approach the first question by inquiring under what conditions it would be useful to the organism to avoid having certain thoughts and ideas. Certainly it would not be of use to repress ideas about objects or situations that are painful and arouse fear. To avoid a frightening object one must think about it and plan a method of escape rather than put it out of mind. If a man walking alone in the woods is confronted with the very real possibility of meeting a bear, it would be biologically foolish to avoid thinking about the situation.

Repression will have meaning and significance only when it is the idea, the thought process, that is primarily to be avoided, rather than the external object or situation. If a thought process can of itself directly lead to pain or frustration, while the object, event, or situation to which it refers is dangerous only derivatively, then it will naturally be of value to the individual to avoid this cognition. Suppose that the man who encountered the bear was actually out hunting for such animals, but when one appeared, he became frightened and ran away. Here would be an occasion for repression. The hunter would have good reason to repress the idea that he ran away because of fear, for to admit the fact to himself or others would be humiliating and frustrating to his self-esteem. If he were asked why he took flight, he might reply that it was because he was in a poor position to shoot, or because at heart he really disliked killing wild animals and went hunting only for exercise. The whole episode might be repressed and become completely inaccessible to memory at a later date.

Now the actual event that took place—running away because of fear— was not in itself physically dangerous or frustrating. Quite the opposite, it dircetly avoided possible physical danger and frustration. But to admit the event, to entertain in consciousness the idea that it took place, would actually be painful and frustrating. In a similar fashion, stealing, cheating, being selfish, having tabooed sexual desires, do not in themselves directly involve pain or frustration, in the way that getting chewed by a bear does. It is the conscious recognition or judgment of their taking place that entails these effects—either judgment by other people or by the self. Thus if a child does not steal but his parents judge that he does, then there are unhappy consequences for him; but if a child steals and no one recognizes it, then no unhappy consequences follow. When he grows older, however, his own judgment that he has stolen may entail unhappy and disturbing experiences, with the result that he will avoid the thought within himself by repression, just as he previously sought to keep his parents in ignorance through the subterfuge of lying.

The close association of self-esteem and shame with repression has already been noted. The relationship is close because the self-esteem motive is essentially a need concerned with conscious content. It is a need to have high judgments and avoid low judgments of the self in certain categories of value (which may vary from individual to individual)—to be judged intelligent rather than stupid, honest rather than dishonest, tactful rather than gauche, possessed of good motives rather than bad motives, and so on. Where there is a strong need to be judged intelligent, for example, we may expect an individual to repress memory of low grades or low intelligence-test scores, and to interpret unstructured situations as implying high intelligence on his part. That it is the subjective judgment rather than the objective phenomenon which is important in matters of self-esteem may be shown simply by the fact that an experimenter can manipulate scores in an aspiration-level test, and the subject will be accordingly gratified or frustrated quite independently of his objective performance.

The judgment that one has anti-social, libidinal motives, we may note, is only one of many types of judgment that must be avoided in order to avoid shame and frustration of the self-esteem motive. Certain humiliating judgments about one's physical, intellectual, social, esthetic, or other qualities must also be avoided, and these correspondingly provide occasions for repression. There is no reason, therefore, to limit repression to material associated with libidinal motives, as does the analytic theory at present.

Furthermore, while the motive of self-esteem is an important source of repression, it is not the only source. Any situation where the presence of certain thoughts would be disturbing and frustrating, and the avoidance of them functionally useful, may provide occasion for repression. There is no reason to deny the possibility of repressing memory of a horrible incident where recall would have only a disturbing effect on the individual, or even the temporary repression of happy thoughts when such thoughts would be distracting and detrimental to the task at hand. If an individual is given an electric shock every time he has a certain thought, as was the case in the experiment to be described shortly, this, too, will provide good occasion for repression.

Let us now turn again to the second problem in the theory of repression: what is the repressing force or agent? We have already seen that the most common view attributes repression to fear or anxiety. There is a plausibility in this view because fear and anxiety are factors in human motivation that determine avoidance. We avoid external objects because of fear, and so, it is easy to believe, we also avoid certain thought processes because of fear. There seems to be a simple formula in the minds of analysts and others who deal with the relation of motivation to thinking: wishes directly cause the appearance of pleasant, gratifying thoughts in dreams and emotional beliefs (wish-fulfillment); fears directly cause the disappearance of unpleasant and frustrating thoughts (repression).

But this formula is based upon a very patent error. It is true, when hungry we think or dream of food objects and ways of getting food; when thirsty, of water; and when sexually aroused, of sexual objects. But it is also true that when possessed by fear, we tend to think of fearful things. Both common sense and literature recognize this fact. Defoe, in his *Journal of the Plague Year,* reports many an incident where the fear that was spread throughout the populace created terrible visions. And Murray has shown experimentally that when a state of fear and anxiety is aroused in children by telling them a murder story, they tend to judge more unknown individuals (presented in photographs) as being malicious and dangerous than otherwise. Yet psychologists, and particularly psychoanalysts, have in general refused to recognize this direct action of fear upon thought. Freud has been much criticized for his failure to deal adequately with the problem. To explain nightmares, punishment fantasies, and the like, the psychoanalyst always conjures up some wish that is being fulfilled, or speaks of these phenomena as "attempts" at wish-fulfillment. Similarly, wish-fulfillment is used to tell the whole story of emotional belief, with the result that many emotional beliefs having unpleasant content and plainly not wish-fulfillment are left without explanation.

The actual situation with respect to the direct effect of motives upon thought seems to be this: when any motivational condition is aroused, there is a direct tendency for an individual to think of objects or situations that are common stimuli for this motivational condition—food, water, frightening objects—depending on what the motivational condition is. *As the stimulus tends to create the motivational condition, so the motivational condition tends to create the stimulus* (as an implicit thought formation). There is thus an integration, a two-way dynamic relation between motivational condition and stimulus.

If this is true, then fear or anxiety cannot be the force directly effecting repression. A condition of fear or anxiety will directly determine the *appearance* of unpleasant, fear-ridden thoughts, rather than the disappearance of them. For integrated with fear and anxiety are unpleasant stimuli and stimulus situations—painful objects and ideas, injuries, punishments, dangers, and the like—which are created as implicit thought formations when these motivational conditions are aroused.

This relation of fear to thought process was brought out in some preliminary association experiments carried out by the author; and these experiments also gave a hint as to what the actual condition is that effects repression. Subjects were told they would receive an electric shock if they thought of "black" or "white." Some subjects appeared to have an unusually large number of "black" and "white" associations under these conditions, others an unusually small number. It appeared also that subjects who were upset and overwhelmed with fear were the ones who gave a large number of such associations, while subjects well organized and confident gave few. The hypothesis was suggested that repression of undesirable ideas depends upon the ability of an individual to carry out organized activity, to subsume his thinking under a set which will determine content of an acceptable kind and avoid content of an unacceptable kind whenever relevant stimuli are present. The following experiment was devised to test this hypothesis.

EXPERIMENT

In this experiment sixteen subjects were given a list of 100 nouns, about one-fifth of which might be expected to suggest color associations (e.g., *grass-green*). The subjects were told they must report the first adjective that occurred to them to describe the object named; but also that if they gave any color response they would receive an electric shock—a shock on the wrist that was as strong as the subject would stand. After the experiment the subjects were asked to report honestly all the cases where they thought of colors but did not give overt associations, and these hold-backs were counted in the totals.

The same association list was given to a group of 15 control subjects who received no shock and had no mention of colors. Whereas the experimental subjects ranged from 4 to 50 color associations, with a sigma of 12, the control subjects ranged only from 13 to 26 color associations, with a sigma of 4.5. Thus the shock situation caused some subjects to have many more color associations than normal, and others fewer than normal.

If the hypothesis suggested above is correct, then those subjects who best repressed (thought of fewest color adjectives) were those who could best carry out organized activity and subsume their thinking under a set or task-motive to think of non-color words; while the subjects who gave the greatest number of color associations were those most disorganized and directly controlled by fear and anxiety. In order to get a separate measure of the capacity of subjects to carry out organized activity under a task-motive and be uninfluenced by such conditions as fear, a pursuit-meter test was employed. On three alternate trials of a minute each, an electric shock was given intermittently on the wrist of the hand performing the task. Its effect on performance was measured by comparing the increments (or decrements) of performance under such conditions with the increments of performance under conditions of no shock (there is a normal learning curve in the pursuit-meter). More specifically, the average increment (or decrement) of the score in seconds of contact for the shock trials was substracted from the average increment for the non-shock trials.

A rank-order correlation of $+.69$ was found between the number of color associations and the amount of disruption of pursuit-meter performance caused by the shock.[3] *Thus a tendency appeared for subjects who were most disorganized and overwhelmed by fear during motor performance to be least able to execute cognitive repression, and those least disturbed to be best able.*

The nature of the data is indicated by Table I. The pursuit-meter performance of Subject A, who gave the largest number of color associations, is omitted because during the performance he broke down and cried; the experiment had to be interrupted and the shock reduced to practically nothing. Subject P, on the other hand, who gave the fewest number of color associations, spontaneously remarked at the end that he always kept cool under tension. These individual reactions of the two extreme subjects lend added support to the general conclusion.

The subjects with but one or two exceptions reported when the experiment was over that they had attempted to avoid color associations by setting themselves to think of adjectives describing size, shape, and the like; and

[3]Various other measures of the effect of the shock on pursuit-meter performance may be used, such as the increment from first to last shock score or the total score achieved in all trials. A positive and significant correlation appears in all such cases.

some even reported that they had quickly and deliberately assembled a supply of non-color adjectives which they held in readiness for familiar nouns suggesting color.

This experiment thus shows that repression can be obtained experimentally by arranging a situation where the presence of certain ideas in consciousness is directly associated with unhappy consequences, making it advantageous for the individual to avoid these ideas; and it indicates that such repression depends directly upon cognitive organization, and only indirectly upon a condition like fear or anxiety. In so far as fear directly affected cognitive structure, fear-associated thoughts appeared.

TABLE I

Summary of Individual Results in Association Experiment and Pursuit-Meter Test

SUBJECT	TOTAL COLOR ASSNS.	NUMBER STATED	HOLD-BACKS	AVERAGE INCREMENT DIFFERENCE
A	50	40	10	. . . .
B	40	24	16	+2.07
C	34	25	9	+3.76
D	29	21	8	+3.43
E	22	15	7	+7.37
F	20	10	10	+1.92
G	19	13	6	+2.52
H	18	17	1	+1.47
I	17	3	14	.00
J	16	6	10	+1.27
K	15	2	13	+9.17
L	15	15	0	+1.58
M	11	9	2	−2.56
N	9	3	6	−7.88
O	6	1	5	−3.75
P	4	1	3	+ .79

SUMMARY AND CONCLUSION

The results of this experiment and the interpretation placed upon them do not agree with the psychoanalytic theory that repression is a mechanism of defense against "libidinal" motives, carried out by anxiety in the ego. Psychoanalysts have based their theory of repression upon spectacular cases of pathological behavior. Patients have been found to possess ugly, unsocial motives, of which they appear quite ignorant, and "repression" is spoken of in such situations. On the basis of these pathological cases, analysts have interpreted repression in *all* cases as a defense against unsocial motives.

We must note that the actual concrete occasion for using the term repression in such pathological cases is an occasion where certain material-aware-ness of unsocial motives—fails to be reported in consciousness although conditions for report are present. This basic situation is similar to the one in the above experiment, and in accordance with the empirical definition of repression used in this study. The theory of repression presented in this study departs from the analytic theory, however, in the following main respects. (1) Repression is conceived as a matter of *direct action and constraint upon the activity of consciousness* rather than upon non-conscious material viewed as trying to enter the "chamber of consciousness." (2) The material avoided in repression may be any material which if reported would be painful and frustrating to certain motivational conditions—typically the motive of self-esteem—which are primarily concerned with the having of one kind of conscious content and the avoiding of another kind. Repression is thus not limited to awareness of unsocial motives, but is considered to extend to any material that would fulfill these conditions. (3) Repression is considered to be a direct function of cognitive organization, rather than of fear or anxiety.

It may be objected that this study deals with a form of "adaptive" repression, whereas the analyst and the clinic are concerned with "maladaptive" repression. The problem of adaptation, however, is a matter of judgment by the observer who takes a long view of things. From the point of view of the subject, every case of repression may be considered to be adaptive in so far as it avoids the pain or frustration that would come with the turning of consciousness to certain thoughts. What is best for the individual in the long run is a problem quite different from the problem of the immediate dynamics of repression, with which we are here concerned.

The objection may also be raised that our theory of repression seems to imply that strongly integrated personalities do the most repressing and neurotic personalities the least, whereas clinical evidence appears to demonstrate just the opposite. But it is claimed here only that a well-integrated personality will do a better job at repression, given the occasion for it, and that his repressing system will be less likely to break down. Such an individual will actually have fewer occasions for repression in daily life than a maladjusted personality. He will also doubtless have greater insight into himself, and a stronger tendency to admit his own weaknesses.

There is an implication from the theory of repression and of the relation of anxiety to thought presented in this study which should be noted. When certain unpleasant and ugly ideas appear in the mind of a disorganized, neurotic individual, these ideas may not be a source of the neurotic condition, as is commonly held, but rather a product of it. For a state of disorganization will favor such ideas by weakening the forces of repression; and a state of anxiety will continually turn consciousness in the direction

of unpleasant thoughts, creating them in imagination, or selectively drawing them forth from the individual's reservoir of past experiences (including childhood experiences, which are full of anxiety situations). Thus what
appears to be a cause may really be only an effect or symptom of maladjustment.

43. Experimental Demonstrations of the Psychopathology of Everyday Life

Milton H. Erickson

INTRODUCTION

THE experiments re-
ported below were
conducted for the
most part in the presence
of a seminar of graduate
students held in New Hav-
en under the leadership of
Dr. Sapir during the spring
of 1933. In addition, a few
experiments which were
performed elsewhere are
included.

The subject who was used for many of these demonstrations had frequently before volunteered for similar purposes. He knew nothing, however, of the plans for these experiments; they represented situations which
were entirely new and problems with which he had never before been
confronted.

In his approach to such demonstrations, this subject customarily reacted
in a way which was fairly characteristic for many others. Ahead of time
he often appeared to be resentful and anxious, or over-eager about the
impression which he and the experimenter would make. Suddenly, however,
with the beginning of the lecture or demonstration, he would seem to shift
the responsibility completely and to lapse into an attitude of complete comfort with loss of all tension and worry.

Abridged from *The Psychoanalytic Quarterly*, 1939, 8, 338-353. Reprinted by permission of the author and The Psychoanalytic Quarterly, Inc.

Following one of the demonstrations described below the subject told the experimenter that his shift in mood had been even more marked than usual. The night before the lecture he had been unable to sleep and had felt more than ordinarily resentful that on so important an occasion no rehearsal or preparatory discussion had taken place. He had even developed some nausea and diarrhea. All of this nervousness had disappeared completely, however, as he entered the lecture room on the morning of these experiments.

I. UNCONSCIOUS DETERMINANTS OF THE CASUAL CONTENT OF CONVERSATION

The subject was brought into a state of profound hypnosis, during which he was instructed that after awakening he would (1) notice Dr. D. searching vainly through his pockets for a package of cigarettes; (2) that he then would proffer his own pack, and (3) that Dr. D. absent-mindedly would forget to return the cigarettes whereupon the subject would feel very eager to recover them because he had no others. He was further told that (4) he would be too courteous to ask for the cigarettes either directly or indirectly but that (5) he would engage in a conversation that would cover any topic except cigarettes although at the time his desire for the return of the cigarettes would be on his mind constantly.

When he was awakened the subject saw that Dr. D. was looking for cigarettes. He thereupon courteously offered his own and at the same time became involved in a conversation during which Dr. D., after lighting the cigarette, absent-mindedly placed the pack in his own pocket. The subject noted this with a quick glance, felt of his own pockets in a somewhat furtive manner as if to see whether or not he had another pack, and showed by his facial expression that he had no others. He then began chatting casually, wandering from one topic to another, always mentioning in some indirect but relevant fashion the word 'smoking.' For example, he talked about a boat on the bay at New Haven, commenting on the fact that the sight of water always made him thirsty, as did smoking. He then told a story about how the dromedary got one hump and the *camel* two. When the question of travel was raised he immediately pictured the pleasure he would derive from crossing the Sahara Desert rocking back and forth comfortably on a *camel*. Next he told a tale of Syrian folklore in which again a camel played a role. When he was asked to tell something interesting about patients he told of taking a patient to see a marathon dance which the latter enjoyed immensely while he himself was reminded by the antics of the dancers of a circus where one would see elephants, hippopotami and *camels*. Asked what he would like to do, he commented on the pleasant weather and said that there was nothing more glorious than paddling in a canoe or floating at ease on the water, smoking.

II. MANIFESTATIONS OF UNCONSCIOUS AMBIVALENT FEELINGS IN CONVERSATION ABOUT A PERSON

During hypnosis, the subject was told that he admired and respected Dr. D. very much but that unconsciously he was jealous of him and that because of this jealousy there would be a cutting edge to complimentary remarks which he would make. He was further told that after awakening a conversation would be started with Dr. D. in which he would take part. The subject was then awakened and the conversation begun.

The topic of traveling and its contribution to personal education was mentioned. The subject immediately brought up the fact that Dr. D. had studied both in the Middle West and in the East and that, having traveled abroad as well, he wight well be called cosmopolitan. He himself, he added, would like to travel and get a cosmopolitan education but in the last analysis that was what was being done by any old tramp who traveled from one part of the country to another by stealing rides on freight cars. There followed a discussion of human behavior as it reflected local environments during which the subject remarked that the man who had traveled showed a broader knowledge and better understanding of people and of cultural things; he added, however, that the same thing might possibly be said of any resident of east-side New York.

III. LAPSUS LINGUAE AND UNCONSCIOUS IRONY

During hypnosis the subject was instructed that after he awakened Dr. D. would begin talking to him about some abstruse subject in which he was not at all interested, and that although he would actually be profoundly bored he would try to appear interested. He was told that he would want very much to close the conversation, that he would wish for some way of shutting off this interminable flow of words, that he would look around him in the hope of finding some distraction, and that he would feel that Dr. D. was terribly tiresome. He was then awakened, whereupon Dr. D. began the conversation. Although the subject appeared to be politely attentive, Dr. D. would occasionally say, 'Perhaps you're not interested?' The subject would reply with excessive emphasis, 'Oh, yes, certainly, I'm very much interested.' Now and then he would interrupt Dr. D., trying to pin him down to some definite point for discussion, but each time this effort was evaded. At length the subject began glancing about the room and noted casually to observe an open door. Finally he interrupted Dr. D. saying, 'Excuse me, I feel an awful draft,' and got up to close the door. As he did so he was asked what he was doing. He replied, 'The air seems to be awful hot ('hot air!'); I thought I would shut off the draft.' When the hypnotist pretended not to understand and asked him what he was doing the subject replied, 'Why I just shut the bore.' His remark was then repeated by the hypnotist for the benefit of those in the audience who had not heard it. When the subject heard his statement given as 'shutting the bore" he started visibly, seemed tremendously embarrassed, and with much urgency turned to Dr. D. saying, 'Did I say that? I didn't mean that. I just meant I closed the door.' He was very apologetic in his whole manner and bearing.

IV. UNCONSCIOUS RESENTMENT EXPRESSING ITSELF IN MASKED FORMS THROUGH A SMOKE-SCREEN OF OVERCOMPENSATORY COURTESY

The subject was told during hypnosis that he felt antagonistic, resentful and jealous of Dr. D., and that this emotional state would persist after he was awakened. He was also told that after awakening he would try to be courteous and acquiescent toward Dr. D. in every way and would appear to be willing to do anything requested of him.

After being awakened the subject seemed to be entirely at ease; he responded courteously to some casual remarks addressed to him by Dr. D. Presently Dr. D. asked him if he would mind changing his seat. The subject replied certainly not, that he would be delighted, but that *he* was quite comfortable where he was; if, however, it would make *Dr. D.* more comfortable, he would be delighted to change his seat. The request was repeated, whereupon the subject arose and asked Dr. D. to designate the precise chair in which he was to seat himself. He walked over toward the designated chair but asked Dr. D. if perhaps a certain other chair might not serve even better since the reason Dr. D. had given for his request was that he was not quite in full view of the audience. When Dr. D. insisted that the designated chair was the better one the subject, with great courtesy, still questioned, seeming nevertheless most willing to do precisely what was desired and to be hesitant only about seating himself before he was absolutely certain of Dr. D.'s wishes. After much insistence by Dr. D. that he seat himself the subject agreed that the chair indicated was precisely the one that he ought to sit in and proceeded to do so; but as he did so he moved the chair about six inches to one side and shifted its position so that it faced in a slightly different direction. Immediately upon seating himself he turned and politely asked, 'Is this the way you would like to have me?' After a few moments of casual conversation Dr. D. found fault with his position and asked him if he would mind taking his original chair. He rose promptly, said that he would be delighted to sit anywhere that Dr. D. wished but that perhaps it would be better if he sat on the table, and offered to move the designated chair to any desired spot, suggesting some clearly unsuitable positions; finally, when urged insistently to sit in the chair he again had to move it.

V. AMBIVALENCE: MANIFESTATIONS OF UNCONSCIOUS CONFLICT ABOUT SMOKING IN THE DISTORTION OF SIMPLE, DAILY SMOKING HABITS

During profound hypnosis the subject was instructed to feel that he wanted to get over the habit but that he felt it was too strong a habit to break, that he would be very reluctant to smoke and would give anything not to smoke, but that he would find himself compelled to smoke; and that after he was awakened he would experience all of these feelings.

After he was awakened the subject was drawn into a casual conversation with the hypnotist who, lighting one himself, offered him a cigarette. The subject waved it aside with the explanation that he had his own and that he preferred Camels, and promptly began to reach for his own pack. Instead of looking in his customary pocket, however, he seemed to forget where he carried his cigarettes and searched fruitlessly through all of his other pockets with a gradually increasing concern. Finally, after having sought them repeatedly in all other pockets, he located his cigarettes in their usual place. He took them out, engaged in a brief conversation as he dallied with the pack, and then began a search for matches which he failed to find. During his search for matches he replaced the cigarettes in his pocket and began using both hands, finally locating the matches too in their usual pocket. Having done this, he now began using both hands to search for his cigarettes. He finally located them but then found that he had once more misplaced his matches. This time however he kept his cigarettes in hand while attempting to relocate the matches. He then placed a cigarette in his mouth and struck a match. As he struck it, however, he began a conversation which so engrossed him that he forgot the match and allowed it to burn his finger tips whereupon, with a grimace of pain, he tossed it in the ash tray. Immediately he took another match, but again introduced a diverting topic by asking the audience in a humorous fashion if they knew the 'Scotch' way of lighting a cigarette. As interest was shown, he carefully split the match through the middle. One half of the match he replaced in his pocket in a time-consuming manner and tried to light his cigarette with the other half. When it gave too feeble a flame he discarded it and had to search for the second half. After striking this another interesting topic of conversation developed and again he burned his fingers before he made use of it. He apologized for his failure to demonstrate the 'Scotch' light successfully and repeated the performance, this time holding the flame in such a way as to ignite only a small corner of the cigarette from which he succeeded in getting only one satisfactory puff. Then he tossed the match away and tipped the cigarette up so that he could see the lighted end. He started to explain that that was how the 'Scotch' light was obtained and noted that only one small corner of the cigarette was lit. He smiled in a semi-apologetic manner and explained that he had really given a 'Jewish' light to the cigarette, whereupon the lighted corner expired. He made a few more humorous comments, and as he talked and gesticulated appropriately he rolled the cigarette between his fingers in such a fashion that he broke it, whereupon he put it aside and took another. This time a member of the audience stepped up and proffered him a light, but as the lighted match drew near to the tip of his cigarette the subject sneezed and blew it out. He apologized again and said he thought he would light his own cigarette. While taking out his matches he commented on the vaudeville trick of rolling cigars from one corner of the mouth to the other and proceeded to demonstrate how he could roll a cigarette in that fashion, which he did fairly successfully. However, in doing so he macerated the tip of the cigarette and had to discard it. He took another, holding it in his mouth while he reached for his matches, started a conversation, and took the cigarette out so that he could talk more freely. It was observed that he took the cigarette out with his hand held in the reverse position to that which he usually used, and after completing his remarks he put the dry end of the cigarette in his mouth, exposing the wet end. He then tried to light this, held the match to the tip in the proper fashion, puffed vigorously, finally got a puff of smoke and then blew out the match. Naturally the wet end of the cigarette did not burn satisfactorily and quickly went out. He looked at it in amazement and in a semi-embarrassed manner mumbled that he had lit the wrong end of the cigarette; he then commented that now both ends of the cigarette were wet, and discarded it for another. After several similar trials he finally successed in lighting the cigarette. It was observed that although he took deep puffs he tended to let his cigarette burn undisturbed, and that instead of smoking it down to a reasonable butt he quickly discarded it.

A little later while smoking the subject attempted to demonstrate the violent gestures of a patient and in so doing knocked off the burning tip. Then while lighting another cigarette he became so interested in talking that he lit the cigarette in the middle rather than at the tip and had to discard it. As usual he showed profound embarrassment at seeming so awkward.

(On other occasions when the subject had demonstrated this phenomenon, he would finally complete the demonstration by selecting a cigarette in a strained and laborious fashion and then, obviously centering all of his attention upon the procedure of lighting it, would hold his hand tensely as he lit the match, applying it with noticeable rigidity to the cigarette and holding it there so long and puffing so repeatedly that all doubt was removed concerning the actual lighting of the cigarette, whereupon his whole manner and attitude would relax and he would appear to be physically comfortable.)

VI. UNCONSCIOUS CONVICTIONS OF ABSURDITIES WITH RATIONALIZATION IN SUPPORT OF THE BELIEF IN THEM

During hypnosis the subject was instructed that he was about to be reminded by the hypnotist of something he had known for a long time, that he had known it both as a result of his own experience and from reading about it in authoritative books. This he was told, was the fact that 'all German men marry women who are two inches taller than they are.' A state of absolute emotional and intellectual belief in this was suggested and he was warned that he might be called upon to defend this statement. He was told that he had read of this in a book written by Dr. Sapir in which the reference occurred on page forty-two. He was informed that he would know this not only in the hypnotic state but also when awake. The subject was then wakened.

During the course of a casual conversation mention was made of the peculiar customs of various nations and peoples. Remarking that he was reminded of a peculiar custom among the Germans, the subject went on to describe the suggested phenomenon in a matter-of-fact way. When his statement was challenged he expressed obvious surprise that anybody should doubt it. He argued that it was entirely reasonable, that customs established originally from some simple purpose could be perpetuated by future generations until, regardless of their absurdity, they were looked upon as rational and commonplace. From this statement he proceeded to draw a social parallel to the attitude of Mussolini regarding compulsory marriage, arguing in a logical, orderly and reasonable fashion. When this failed to convince the doubters he drew upon personal experience, citing examples with a casual, simple, matter-of-fact and convincing manner, and calling upon others in the group to verify his statements. When they failed to do so and cited contrary instances, he smiled agreeably and stated that every rule had its exception and that the failure of the German in the audience to confirm his observation was characteristic of the well-known tendency to overlook the obvious in familiar situations. When he was asked whether any authority in the field was known to hold such a brief he promptly stated that he had read the same observation in a book by Dr. Sapir entitled, Primitive Peoples and Customs. When he was asked where in the book it was described he smiled in a deprecating fashion and remarked that it had been so long since he had read the book that he could not be sure of the page but that, as he recalled it, it seemed to be between pages forty and forty-five—forty-four, perhaps; this despite the fact that the hypnotist had specified page forty-two. He was then asked by a member of the audience what chapter it was in; he stated that as far as he recalled it was chapter two. Asked for the chapter heading, he explained that he had read the book so long ago he realy could not recall it. When a member of the audience then stated that such a belief was contrary to all common sense the subject, in amazement and with some embarrassment, asked rather urgently, 'Surely you would not dispute a man as famous and distinguished as Dr. Sapir?,' nodding his head toward Dr. Sapir. His whole manner was suggestive of intense surprise at such arrogant disbelief.

VII. AUTOMATIC WRITING: UNCONSCIOUS OBLITERATION OF VISUAL IMPRESSIONS IN ORDER TO PRESERVE AN HYPNOTICALLY ORDERED AMNESIA

During hypnosis the subject was instructed that on awakening he would engage in a casual conversation and that as he did so his hand would begin writing, but that he would have no knowledge of what he was doing.

After he had written some incomplete sentences he was asked what he was doing by others in the audience. With some amazement he explained that he had been talking to Dr. D. When he was informed that while talking to Dr. D. he had also been writing, he immediately pointed out that this could not have been since he had been holding a cigarette in his right hand. (He had actually transferred the cigarette from his left to the right hand upon completing the writing.) As the audience continued to insist he pointed out that he had no pencil and nothing to write on, in addition to the fact that *he knew* he had not been writing and that the audience must have been mistaken. His attention was then called to a pencil and some paper on the table; he seemed surprised to see the paper and pencil and insisted that he had not had anything to do with either. He was asked to examine the paper to see if there were not some automatic writing on it, or at least writing. He picked up the paper, glanced at the top sheet, shook his head and began slowly to thumb over each sheet, examining the papers over and over again on both sides, and finally restoring the pile to its original state. He said that he found no writing on any of the sheets. His attention was called to the top sheet which he was asked to examine. He looked it over carefully at the top, turned it over and examined it, seemed to be in doubt as to whether or not he had taken the top sheet and took the second sheet; he examined that, put it away, and glanced at the third sheet; he then seemed to feel that possibly he *had* had the top sheet in his hand, so he reexamined that very thoroughly and carefully and then, still holding it right side up, declared hesitantly, as if he hated to dispute with the audience but felt compelled to disagree, that there was no writing on the paper. One of the audience called his attention to the particular part of the paper on which there was writing. He glanced at it, looked back at his informant in a puzzled way and then reexamined that part of the paper. After turning it over somewhat doubtfully and glancing at it he turned it right side up again. He then began holding it so that the light struck it obliquely and finally declared, still in a puzzled fashion, that there *really* was no writing on the paper. Finally he was given the suggestion by the hypnotist that there *was* writing and that he would see it. He glanced back at the paper in surprise and then an expression of amusement and amazement spread over his face as he saw the writing apparently for the first time. He commented on the juvenility of the handwriting, disowning it. When asked to tell what it said he showed much interest in reading the characters but appeared to have a certain amount of difficulty in deciphering the writing. The last word was incomplete; he read it, spelled it, and stated that it seemed to be only part of a word. When he was asked to guess what the word was he promptly reread the sentence in order to get the context, but was unable to guess. He then wanted to know why the writing had not been finished and was informed by the hypnotist that if he would just watch the pencil on the table it would suddenly lift up in the air and begin writing the rest of the word. He looked doubtfully at the hypnotist and then said, 'Why, it's lifting up,' seeming to have no realization that his own hand was picking up the pencil and holding it poised in position to write. Gradually his hand began forming letters. He was asked what the pencil was writing, to which he replied, 'Wait—wait; let's see'; he appeared to be entirely absorbed in the supposed phenomenon of a pencil writing alone. The hypnotist watched the writing, which was proceeding very slowly, and soon realized that the word in question was 'delicious.' The hypnotist then announced this to the audience while the subject was writing the last four letters and finished by the time the subject had finished writing. The subject looked up upon completing the word and said, 'It's delicious,' and then read the sentence to see if the word was relevant to the meaning. Apparently he had not heard the observer announce the word to the seminar.

VIII. 'CRYSTAL' GAZING: HALLUCINATORY VIVIDNESS OF DREAM IMAGERY
    EMBODYING ANGER DISPLACED FROM HYPNOTIST ON TO DREAM
    PERSON

In a somnambulistic state the subject was instructed that he was to gaze at the wall and that as he did this the wall would become distant, far-away, foggy and blurred, and that gradually a dark point would appear which would become more and more elaborate, that movement would enter the scene and that soon he would see a well-known and emotionally stirring moving picture.

The subject began these observations with faint interest and considerable difficulty at first but gradually a profound change in his manner and attitude occurred as he was seen to watch the moving images with intense interest. He resented any inquiries as to what he was seeing and gave the impression that he did not want to be distracted from the scene. Now and then he would turn slightly to ask, 'Did you see that? Watch.' The moving scene was from Rasputin and the Empress, showing the stumbling and falling of the Czarevitch, to which the subject showed appropriate emotional reactions. He went on to describe the sequence of events in proper chronological order. When the demonstration had gone far enough, he was told that the picture was changing. He disregarded this; when the hypnotist insisted, he declared that he did not want to listen now, that the hypnotist should wait until the picture came to an end. He was obdurate about accepting any suggestions concerning the changing of the picture. The suggestion was then tried of speeding up the movie, making it go faster and faster. When this was done it was possible to shift the scene to a hospital picture which he described as one in which *a nurse shouted loudly at a patient*. Here he manifested great resentment toward the nurse for doing this, apparently hallucinating the nurse's voice. The incorporation into the hallucinatory image of his anger against the experimenter and the child-like and fear-laden exaggeration of his impression of loud and angry voices because of his own inner anger were all very evident.

IX.   IMPLANTATION OF A COMPLEX

During hypnosis the subject was instructed to recall having had dinner at Dr. D.'s home on the previous day. He was then told that the hypnotist would review a certain series of actions which had occurred on the previous day, and that the hypnotist would refresh his memory of certain things that the subject had done which he regretted intensely and which constituted a source of much shame to him. Thereupon he was told to remember how during the course of the afternoon he had stood by the fireplace, leaning against the mantel while talking to Dr. D. about various subjects, when his eye happened to fall upon a package of cigarettes lying behind the clock on the end of the mantelpiece. The tale went on that Dr. D. had noticed his glance and had proceeded to tell the subject that the package of cigarettes was a sentimental keepsake of his marriage, that he and his wife had received this package of cigarettes on their wedding day and had preserved it unused ever since. As Dr. D. added various romantic elaborations the subject had not paid much attention because he was really rather bored by the sentimental story. After fingering the package, Dr. D. had replaced it at the other end of the mantelpiece; but the subject had not paid any attention to this either. Shortly after this Dr. D. and his wife had left the room for a few minutes. During their absence the subject noticed that he was out of cigarettes and glanced about the room to see if his host had some. Noticing a pack of cigarettes at the other end of the mantelpiece, he thought that his host would have no objections to his helping himself. He stepped over and took this pack of cigarettes from the mantelpiece, opened it, extracted a cigarette, lit and smoked it. Not until he had finished smoking did he realize that this was the very pack of cigarettes which Dr. D. had placed at the end of the mantelpiece instead of returning to its original hiding place behind the clock. The subject was then reminded of how distressed he had felt, of his sense of being in a quandary as to what he ought to do, of how he had hastily closed the pack and had replaced it behind the clock and had then decided that he had better put it where Dr. D. had placed it, but how before he could do this his host had returned so that he had been forced to carry on a casual conversation with this burden on his mind. Furthermore he was told that even now and after awakening this burden would still be on his mind.

The subject was roused and after a few brief remarks Dr. D. offered him a cigarette. The subject started, glanced furtively first at Dr. D. and then at the hypnotist and finally in a labored fashion reached out and accepted the cigarette, handling it in a gingerly manner. Dr. D. began an innocuous conversation, but the subject paid little attention to what was said and asked Dr. D. what he thought about sentimentality, uttering the word 'sentimentality' in a tone of disgust. He then stated that he himself was not sentimental and that he tended to dislike people who were sentimental and maudlin. He stated that he hoped that Dr. D. was not sentimental, that he did not impress the subject as being sentimental. Dr. D. made another attempt to change the topic of conversation but the subject persisted with his own line of thought. He raised a hypothetical question about a man who owned an old homestead and who, as a result of the economic depression, had lost much money and was in a quandary about the necessity of selling it. He went on to talk of the burning of the house, of the house going up in smoke, and various allied topics. He then talked of guilt feelings, how everybody stole, how he himself had stolen; he wanted to know how Dr. D. would feel about anybody who had stolen unwittingly. Another attempt by Dr. D. to change the trend of the conversation failed. The subject then told of having once stolen a cigar which belonged to a man who had kept it for sentimental reasons. He said he had taken the cigar and smoked it without realizing that it was a keepsake, and that he had felt very badly about it and wondered about the possibility of replacing it so that the sentimental man would not be angry with him. In a defensive

manner he then expressed a high regard for a person's feelings and contended that nevertheless people should not think too hard of others who had
unwittingly violated some of their sentimental values. After this he stated
that not only had he stolen the cigar but he had even stolen cigarettes (pause)
a pack of cigarettes. As he said this he glanced in a particularly furtive
manner at Dr. D. and also at the hypnotist, and seemed very ill at ease. He
told about having smoked a cigarette and having enjoyed it, but that it had
left a bad taste in his mouth afterwards and that even though he had stolen
the cigarettes long ago he could not get them off his mind, that they still
troubled him though common sense told him it was nothing to be concerned
or worried about.

X.   THE ASSUMPTION OF ANOTHER'S IDENTITY UNDER HYPNOTIC DIRECTION,
      WITH STRIKING UNCONSCIOUS MIMICRY AND THE ASSUMPTION OF
      UNCONSCIOUS EMOTIONAL ATTITUDES

During hypnosis the subject was informed that after awakening *he* would
be Dr. D. and that Dr. D. would be Mr. Blank, and that in the role of Dr.
D. he would talk to the pseudo Mr. Blank. Additional suggestions which
the subject fully accepted were given to complete the trans-identification.
After the subject was awakened a conversation was begun. The pseudo Mr.
Blank questioned him about his work in the seminar, as though he were
Dr. D.; the subject responded by giving an excellent talk about his experiences in the seminar and his reactions to the group, talking in the phraseology
of Dr. D. and expressing the personal attitudes of Dr. D. A chance conversation with Dr. D. on the previous day had supplied him with a great
deal of information which he utilized fully. It was noted also that he adopted
Dr. D.'s mannerisms in smoking and that he introduced ideas with certain
phrases characteristic of Dr. D. When the pseudo Mr. Blank challenged
his identity the subject contradicted 'Mr. Blank' politely and seemed profoundly amazed at 'Mr. Blank's' remarks. Then suddenly, with an expression of dawning understanding, he turned to the hypnotist saying, 'He's in
a trance, isn't he?' and thereafter was only amused at 'Mr. Blank's' remarks. 'Mr. Blank' then questioned the subject about his 'wife', to which
the subject responded in a way that would have been natural for the real
Dr. D. When asked about children he assumed an expression of mild embarrassment and replied, 'not yet, but you never can tell.' 'Mr. Blank' then
began talking to the hypnotist in his ordinary fashion, at which the subject
again seemed tremendously surprised. With a puzzled look on his face he
suddenly leaned over and tested 'Mr. Blank' for catalepsy. When he found
none his face was expressive of some concern; he promptly whispered to

the hypnotist, 'He's coming out of the trance,' but was relieved when the hypnotist assured him that it would be all right if this happened.

Finally, when an attempt was made to rehypnotize him in order to restore his own identity, the subject displayed the emotional attitude of resistance towards the induction of hypnosis which would have been entirely characteristic of the real Dr. D. The subject seemed actually to experience the same emotional responses that Dr. D. would have had at such a time. Finally, because he appeared to be entirely resistive to simple suggestion, it was necessary to induce hypnosis by indirect methods.

This rather astonishing result offers a technique for the experimental investigation of the phenomena of identification, and of the unconscious incorporation of parental emotions by children.

44. Hypnotic Investigation of Psychosomatic Phenomena

Psychosomatic Interrelationships Studied by Experimental Hypnosis

Milton H. Erickson

THE purpose of this paper is to present an account of various psychosomatic interrelationships and interdependencies frequently encountered as coincidental phenomena during the course of hypnotic experimentation on normal subjects. No effort will be made to review the literature for reports on comparable findings made in neurological studies, in research on sensory and physiological psychology or in other allied fields of investigation. Nor is there any intention of offering an extensive discussion of the possible significances of the observations reported, since this is primarily an initial report upon extremely complex and varied observations requiring further controlled studies. Briefly, then, the purpose is to report certain phenomena from the field of hypnotic research, of which the literature on hypnosis makes little or no mention.

These coincidental phenomena are not those usual and expected changes in psychological, physiological and somatic behavior that are essentially

Abridged from *Psychosomatic Medicine,* 1943, 5, 51-58. Reprinted by permission of the author and Paul B. Hoeber, Inc.

common to all hypnotic subjects in profound trances, such as alterations in reaction time, sensory thresholds, muscular tonus, and similar items of behavior. Rather, they are distinct from such psychosomatic manifestations of the hypnotic trance and they are, in all probability, expressive, not of the state of hypnosis itself, but of the interrelationships of hypnotically induced behavior and conditions within the trance state. That is, after a profound trance state has first been secured, specific hypnotic instructions can then be given to the subject to elicit responses of a particular sort and in a chosen modality of behavior. However, in addition to the behavior that is suggested, there may also be elicited, seemingly as coincidental manifestations, marked changes in one or another apparently unrelated modality of behavior. Or, equally significant, hypnotic suggestions bearing upon one sphere of behavior may remain ineffective until, as a preliminary measure, definite alterations are first induced hypnotically in an apparently unrelated and independent modality of behavior. Thus, to cite general examples, effective hypnotic suggestions bearing only upon sensory responses would often elicit additional unexpected and apparently unrelated motor responses; or suggestions directed toward a sensory sphere of behavior would remain ineffective until hypnotic alterations in a seemingly unrelated motor sphere had been first induced.

These various interrelationships and interdependencies, however, were found to vary greatly from subject to subject and, to a lesser degree, for the individual subject, depending in large part upon the nature and the character of the experimental work in progress.

The findings included in this report have been collected over a period of years from a large number of normal subjects. In most cases they were made originaly as an incidental part of the development of other research projects, and hence, could not always be explored adequately. Whenever possible, however, each of the various findings has been confirmed by further experimental work on the same and other subjects.

These findings to be reported are of two general types. The first type consists of specific instances either observed repeatedly in the same subject and confirmed on other subjects or encountered from time to time in a number of subjects. The other type consists of a case report of the psychosomatic interrelationships and interdependencies found to exist between vision, headaches of visual origin and hypnotically induced psychological states in which the subject was regressed to earlier age levels.

Report on the first type of psychosomatic interrelationships and interdependencies is difficult, since they constitute essentially individual manifestations which occur under a wide variety of circumstances and in many different associations. Furthermore, they are not constant in their appearance for all subjects in the same situation nor does the appearance of any one phenomenon necessarily signify the development of other possibly related phenomena in the same subject. However, the findings do tend to remain constant for the specific modality of behavior under investigation in the individual subject, although repeated hypnotic experiences tend to lessen progressively the extent and duration of phenomena likely to cause the subject discomfort.

With this general introduction, we may turn to the experimental situations out of which our findings on psychosomatic interrelationships and interdependencies developed. Many of the findings were made originally in relation to experimental studies on hypnotically induced states or conditions of deafness, blindness, color blindness, amnesia, analgesia, anaesthesia and age regression. (By the latter is meant the hypnotic reorientation of normal subjects to a previous period of life with a revivification of earlier patterns of behavior and response and with an amnesia for all experiences subsequent to the suggested age level.) Some of these studies have been reported in the literature but at best, only brief mention has been made of these special findings which have been further investigated by direct studies. Briefly stated, these findings are that the development of any of these special hypnotically induced conditions or states may lead, in addition to those phenomena properly belonging to it, to any one or more of a great variety of responses and manifestations belonging properly to other modalities of behavior, for example, the development of visual and motor disturbances when only hypnotic deafness is suggested.

For purposes of brevity, these phenomena will be listed under general headings, and this listing will be followed by a citing of specific examples to illustrate the coincidental developments that may be seen in relation to various induced hypnotic states. The listing is as follows:

A. Altered visual behavior.
   1. Decrease in visual acuity with blurring of vision and difficulty in reading.
   2. Contraction of the visual field.
   3. Difficulty in focusing gaze.
   4. Decreased ability in depth and distance perception.
   5. Subjective sense of colored vision, that is, addition of chromatic values to visual stimuli.

B. Altered auditory behavior.
   1. Decrease in acuity.
   2. Inaccuracy in localizing sound.
   3. Distorations in perception of sound qualities.

C. Altered motor behavior.
   1. General muscular incoordination.

    2. Specific motor disturbances:
       (a) Paresis and paralysis
       (b) Apraxias
       (c) Speech disturbances
       (d) Dysmetria
       (e) Ocular fixation, pupillary dilation and nystagmoid movements.
  D. Other types of altered behavior.
    1. Analgesias and anaesthesias.
    2. Subjective reactions of nausea and vertigo.
    3. Anxiety states and phobic reactions with their various physiological concomitants.
    4. Amnesias, usually circumscribed and specific.
    5. Revival of forgotten patterns of behavior.

To explain the above listing, specific examples will be cited as they were observed in various types of experimental work. However, it must be noted that while some subjects showed many of the phenomena listed above, others showed few or none, depending, apparently, upon the specific type of experimentation. Thus, for example, one subject, rendered hypnotically deaf, might show many changes in visual, motor and other forms of behavior but when rendered color blind might show only one or two disturbances in other fields of behavior, while another subject rendered hypnotically color blind might show many disturbances of motor behavior but no changes in the auditory sphere. Some of these alterations in behavior preceded the development of the hypnotic condition being suggested; some accompanied the process of the development of that intended state; but most frequently, they constituted a part of the total picture after the intended hypnotic condition had been established.

In presenting specific examples, not all instances will be cited since this is not intended to be a statistical account. Rather, an effort will be made to select the more typical and informative developments. Also, it is to be noted that there was usually the minimum of interference by the experimenter and, hence, little effort to investigate the unexpected findings. There were two reasons for this, namely, the feeling that more could be learned from simple observation of these spontaneous manifestations which were not readily understood and recognized sufficiently to permit extensive experimental manipulation, and the fact that other experimental work was usually in actual progress.

One of the first instances observed was that of a hypnotically deaf subject polishing and repolishing his glasses and showing peering behavior as if he could not see well. A written inquiry disclosed him unable to read the question although he examined the paper carefully as if trying to find the writing on it, which actually was somewhat faintly written. Finally he handed it back to the experimenter in puzzled silence. He was handed a book and a paragraph was pointed at. The subject started to ask if he were to read but showed a startled reaction immediately upon speaking. This was followed by a puzzled repetition of his question as if speaking to himself, whereupon he asked the experimenter what was wrong. Again the pantomimed instructions to read were given but the subject seemed to experience great difficulty and he explained that the print was blurred, that the lighting of the room was very dim and he made anxious inquiry about his voice since he could not hear it. Examination of his eyes disclosed his pupils widely dilated. To prevent disruption of the experimental situation the subject was reassured by the measure of large script on a blackboard.

Subsequently, the restoration of the subject's ability to hear restored his visual acuity and his pupils contracted to normal size.

Another hypnotically deaf subject showed a marked loss of peripheral vision and seemed to have preserved only central vision. Other subjects showed various degrees of peripheral loss but in no instance was an exact determination made. These subjects also showed ocular fixation and seemed to be unable to move their eyeballs freely.

One hypnotically deaf subject was noted to shift his position, to twist his body and head about and to make strained efforts whenever he attempted to look directly at an object. Inquiry elicited the subjective statement that whenever he tried to look closely at an object it seemed to blur and to move back and forth as if alternately receding and advancing. Examination of his eyes showed a slow irregular alternating contraction and dilation of his pupils.

Another subject, a psychologist, spontaneously discovered that he seemed to have lost his ability for depth and distance perception, a topic he was studying at the time. He was permitted to investigate this to some extent wih available apparatus and the results obtained indicated a definite decrease in his ability to judge distances. Similar results were obtained with one other subject untrained in psychology. Somewhat comparable was the behavior of another subject who became distressed by her tendency to over-reach or to underreach when handed objects and she was most apologetic about her "clumsiness." The only explanation she could offer was that her body did not "feel right," that her arms and legs seemed numb and stiff and there were many evidences of general motor incoordination and muscle paresis but, because of her emotional distress, extensive investigation could not be carried on without disrupting the general experimental situation.

A subject who had been used repeatedly and successfully in conditioned reflex experiments failed to develop a conditioned response based upon a pain-light stimulus complex since he invariably developed a generalized anaesthesia when rendered hypnotically deaf. Another conditioned reflex subject, reported upon briefly in another study, invariably developed a progressive anaesthesia when rendered hypnotically deaf.

Two subjects when hypnotically deaf were found to have a subjective sense of colored vision, explaining respectively that everything seemed to have a reddish or a bluish hue and they suspected the experimenter of secretly employing colored lights to achieve this effect.

Subjective feelings of nausea and vertigo invariably developed in one subject whenever a state of hypnotic deafness became well established for her. She rationalized this by explaining that her voice did not "feel right" in her throat but the measure of keeping silent did not lessen her subjective distress. Additionally, she showed nystagmoid movements and pupillary dilation. Restoration of hearing would immediately correct all of these deviations from the normal and efforts to alleviate her distress tended to remove the hypnotic deafness.

Another subject, who developed hypnotic deafness satisfactorily, seemed to be unable to respond to instructions to recover his hearing. Much effort and investigation finally disclosed that with the onset of hypnotic deafness there occurred an extensive anaesthesia. Until this anaesthesia was corrected he could not recover his hearing except through the experimentally unsatisfactory measure of awakening from the trance state. Several other subjects have shown a comparable inability to recover from induced behavior changes until the coincidental developments were first corrected unless resort was had to the measure of awakening them from the trance state, usually an undesirable method since it disrupts the general experimental situation.

A peculiar circumscribed amnesia for anything pertaining to the radio was shown by one subject, a medical student, whenever he became hypnotically deaf. He readily detected the sound vibrations of the radio when he happened to touch it, showed a lively curiosity about it, but seemed incapable of understanding any information given him about it. He regarded the radio as some form of a "vibrator" such as might be used in physiotherapy and was obviously incredible of the explanations given him by the experimenter. A possibly significant item from his past history related to many reprimands given him by his father for his neglect of his studies in high school because of his excessive interest in the radio. Restoration of hearing always corrected this amnesia. Several other subjects showed somewhat similar circumscribed amnesias in that while in the deaf state they would be unable to call to mind items of memory otherwise readily accessible to them. Thus, one subject could never remember when deaf a certain professor's name and another invariably forgot a certain street address. Comparable findings are reported in a special study on aphasia-like reactions from hypnotically induced amnesias. Yet, in the ordinary trance or waking states none of these subjects showed special amnesic reactions.

More common in hypnotic deafness than the above manifestations were states of anxiety and panic, and phobic reactions with their various physiological concomitants of increased pulse and respiratory rates, tremors and excessive perspiration. Usually these manifestations would be attributed by the subjects to the experience of finding themselves unable to hear and they would especially comment upon the unpleasantness of not being able to hear their own voice. Occasionally, however, a subject would show only increased perspiration, tremors, or other evidence of a state of tension which he would not be able to explain and which were apparently not accompanied by any feelings of subjective distress.

In the development of these types of additional behavior disturbances, the time of their appearance varied greatly. Thus, several subjects given suggestions to develop hypnotic deafness invariably showed a preliminary state of rigidity and immobility with generalized anaesthesia. As the state of deafness became established these preliminary manifestations slowly disappeared completely. Any attempt to prevent these preliminary manifestations seemed to preclude the developemnnt of deafness, but suggestions leading to such immobility and anaesthesia hastened the appearance of deafness. Another subject was found to be resistant to suggestions of deafness until he had first been given suggestions for a generalized amnesia. Following this, deafness could be induced. In large part, however, the additional behavior disturbances seemed to be an essential part of the established state of deafness, and any disruption of them tended to disrupt the state of hypnotic deafness also. These general findings were found to be true for other special hypnotically induced conditions or states.

In brief, the induction of hypnotic deafness in the normal subject may lead to the development of a variety of other behavior disturbances. These aditional manifestations seem to constitute a part of the process of developing the suggested auditory disturbances or of maintaining it, or to be an expresion of the imbalance of the psycho-physiological functioning caused by the induced auditory disturbance.

In studies of hypnotic blindness, color blindness, amnesia, analgesia, anaesthesia, age regression and post hypnotic behavior, the coincidental phenomena, depending upon the exact nature of the experimental work in progress, were found to be essentially similar to those developing in relation to hypnotic deafness. Hence they will not be reported in full detail but instead, emphasis will be placed upon these instances found specifically in various of these special hypnotic states.

In hypnotic blindness, the coincidental phenomena tended to be limited to fear reactions with corresponding physiological concomitants. However, one subject showed a definite decrease in auditory acuity, another developed a marked increase in muscular tonus with a subjective feeling of stiffness and rigidity, while sitll another showed an extensive analgesia and anaesthesia of the legs and arms which persisted throughout the state of visual disturbance. In one study, which is now in course of preparation for publication, it was found that hypnotic blindness could not be induced except as the culminating feature of an induced acute obsessional hysterical state. In general, the feeling of helplessness these subjects experienced and their tendency to become frightened by the situation in which they found themselves made experimental manipulations difficult.

Hypnotic color blindness, like hypnotic deafness, yielded a large variety of unexpected behavior disturbances. Foremost among these were emotional reactions of marked distress accompanied by increased pulse and respiratory rates, tremors and excessive perspiration. These seemed to derive primarily from the feelings of disorientation and confusion caused by the changed appearance of the experimental setting as a result of the visual disturbance. As was briefly mentioned in another study, one subject became seriously distressed by her inability to recognize her dress as her own. Reassurances by the experimenter served to allay in large part these manifestations.

In the sphere of auditory behavior, two subjects with induced color blindness showed an inability to localize sound correctly and both commented spontaneously on their subjective feeling that the experimenter's voice did not seem to emanate from him and that his voice had changed markedly in its tonal qualities. Both were observed to turn their heads and listen in the wrong direction to unexpected sounds and they failed to recognize and identify sounds ordinarily familiar to them. One subject became greatly interested in investigating the altered character of sounds, periodically interrupting her investigation to ask for reassurances to the effect that the experimenter had full control over the situation. A stop watch was described as ticking in an unusually mufflled way, the tapping of a pencil was regarded as having a "thick, dull" sound and the squeaking of certain door hinges familiar to her was found to be extremely unpleasant, having a peculiar shrill quality, although in the ordinary trance or waking state she did not react unfavorably to that particular sound.

One special finding in relation to hypnotic color blindness was the unexpected discovery of two instances of synesthesia, the first of which has been reported upon briefly in the study of hypnotic color blindness. This instance was marked by a loss of conceptual values and meanings for the word *three* and its corresponding numeral upon the development of red color blindness. Restoration of color vision restored conceptual values. The second instance was an association of the color red with the numeral 7. Color blindness resulted in a feeling of unfamiliarity for that number despite its recognition, but there was no actual loss of conceptual values. Nor could the subject explain what way the numeral 7 was changed. Additionally, this subject was found to show synopsia, in that certain sounds always carried a reddish color significance for her. Upon the induction of color blindness these sounds lost their characteristics of warmth and familiarity and in some instances she failed to recognize them, especially in connection with music.

A phonograph record played for her was described as having an "incredible number of mistakes" and she wondered why such a recording should ever have been made. When these two subjects were rendered hypnotically deaf, however, the numerical concepts retained their chromatic associations.

In relation to post hypnotic behavior and amnesia, a not uncommon finding was the development of a headache when the subject was given an unpleasant post-hypnotic task to perform or was asked to develop an amnesia. One example is that of a junior medical student who, because of previous experience as a subject, volunteered for a class demonstration. There were no unexpected manifestations until he was asked to develop an amnesia for all hypnotic experiences including the present one and to awaken with a firm conviction that he never had been hypnotized and that in all probability he could not be. The subject performed this task adequately but soon developed a severe headache which was readily removed by the simple measure of letting him recover his memories. He later explained that he reesnted being asked to develop an amnesia for his past hypnotic experience and that he felt that this resentment had caused his headache.

With other subjects who have failed to develop hypnotic amnesias readily, experience has disclosed that the measure of suggesting that they forget some unpleasant thing, to which suggestion the significant qualification is added "even though it causes you to have a headache" often enables the subject to develop additional amnesias previously impossible and without experiencing an associated headache. Other subjects react to amnesias by the spontaneous development of a headache and still others show peculiar anaesthesias upon the induction of amnesic states even of a limited character. Thus, one subject instructed to become amnesic for certain trance experiences developed a persistent anaesthesia of her hands. This was discovered when she attempted to do some writing. Correction of her amnesia enabled her to write. However, this hand anaesthesia developed only when she was given instructions to forget specific items and it did not accompany spontaneous generalized amnesias.

Two female subjects to whom a phobia for cats had been suggested developed olfactory behavior changes in that one of the subjects became hypersensitive to unpleasant odors and the other inexplicably interested in pleasant odors until the suggested phobia had been removed. However, suggested olfactory sensitivity did not result in phobic reactions.

Another subject to whom a general disorientation for time and place had been suggested developed a very definite speech defect and stammered although he had no history of previous stammering. Several months later in another setting the same subject was instructed to become equally confident that a certain specific event which had occurred only once had happened on two distinctly different days and to defend these beliefs emphatically. He again developed his serious stammering and in addition he became disoriented for time, place, and person with the exception of the experimenter. On still another occasion he was asked to forget that a friend of his had been sitting in a certain chair and to be most confident in his assertion that his friend had occupied an entirely different seat. The subject responded to this task by first developing a stammer but shortly this disappeared and it was replaced by an amnesia for the identity of his friend. He was shortly given a book to read and after he had read aloud from it, he was told he would stammer on the next paragraphs. This stammering resulted in the recovery of the friend's identity.

In relation to regression, two subjects who are reported in another paper, when reoriented to a period of life antedating the development of certain food intolerances were enabled to enjoy the otherwise unacceptable food.

Several adult subjects when regressed to earlier childhood age levels have shown marked changes in their motor behavior. Two other such subjects wrote freely and easily with the backhand slant without error, although special inquiry disclosed that they had changed to a forward slope 15 and 18 years ago respectively. Another subject who habitually wrote with a backhand slope, in the regressed state wrote with a forward slope. An inquiry proved that this change in her handwriting had occurred at the time of puberty. Efforts in the ordinary trance and waking states to secure duplications of their earlier patterns of writing resulted at best in only fair approximation with many errors.

In brief, the hypnotic induction of disturbances in any chosen modality of behavior is likely to be accompanied by disturbances in other modalities. These vary greatly in their nature and variety and in their relationship to the primary induced behavior disturbance.

CASE REPORT

The report of a case history illustrating various psychosomatic interrelationships and interdependencies may be presented by a listing of the pertinent facts. The subject was a medical interne who suffered from a high degree of myopia. Whenever forced to do without his glasses he developed severe headaches. Subsequent to his first hypnotic trance it was learned that he received his first pair of glasses at the age of 10 years upon the recommendation of his school nurse because of his severe headaches from eyestrain. The original prescription for glasses had been changed for one less strong when he was about 14 years old and these he still wore. His mother, fortunately, had kept his first pair of glasses.

For demonstration purposes before a group this subject had been deeply hypnotized and then reoriented to an age of 8 years and awakened in that state of regression.

Promptly upon awakening he removed his glasses, refusing to wear them and seeming to be amazed to be wearing them. When he was persuaded to wear the glasses he complained that they hurt his eyes and shortly he became resentful because, he explained, they made his head hurt and he could not see well. Accordingly, he was allowed to take off his glasses and he was then interested in a series of tasks all involving eyestrain, such as reading books held at the wrong distance, threading fine needles and similar tasks. He cooperated readily for about an hour without subjective complaints. He was then reoriented immediately to his current age and awakened but he was found to be free of subjective discomfort. As a control measure he was subsequently asked to perform similar tasks in the ordinary waking state without his glasses but each time he developed a headache after about one half hour of effort.

A series of trances over a period of weeks then disclosed that the hypnotic regression of this subject to various age levels yielded the following pertinent findings:

I. At 8 and 9 years levels:
    a. Refusal to wear both pairs of glasses and complaints that they hurt his eyes.
    b. No subjective symptoms from deliberate eyestrain.
    c. Denial of headaches at 8 year age level but admission of occasional headaches at 9 year age level.
    d. No subjective symptoms when awakened from these age levels after eyestrain.

II. At 10 to 13 year levels:
    a. Ready wearing of first but not of second pair of glasses.
    b. Prompt development of headaches when induced to dispense with glasses.
    c. Complaint of headache when induced to wear the second pair of glasses.
    d. Persistence of headaches when awakened from the trance state after eyestrain.
    e. Abolishment of headaches when regressed to any previous age level after eyestrain had resulted in headaches.

f. Failure to reestablish headache abolished by reorientation to an earlier age by subsequent reorientation back to the age level at which the headache had been developed unless care was taken to specify the exact date.

III. At 14 and subsequent years:

a. Recognition of first pair of glasses but subjective complaints when induced to wear them more than an hour, and ready wearing of second pair of glasses with no subjective complaints.

b. Development of headaches upon eyestrain.

c. Persistence of these headaches when awakened from the trance after such eyestrain.

d. Abolishment of headaches immediately upon regression to any earlier age level.

e. Failure to reestablish headache abolished by reorientation to an earlier age by subsequent reorientation back to the age level at which the headache had been developed unless care was taken to specify the exact date.

Control tests conducted in the ordinary trance and waking states disclosed the subjects to be unable either to dispense with his current pair of glasses or to wear the first pair without soon developing headaches.

When the subject was informed of the experimental results he was inclined to doubt their validity. He asked that a repetition, while a fellow interne acted as an observer, be made of the various procedures to satisfy him that he could dispense with his glasses without developing a headache when reoriented to an earlier age. The experimental results obtained confirmed the previous results. The subject was much intrigued by the proof offered him that in a certain psychological state he could dispense with his glasses and he made repeated but unsuccessful efforts on his own initiative in the waking state to achieve comparable results.

These findings are comparable to those reported previously in an account of the apparent development of a state of unconsciousness during the reliving of an amnesic traumatic experience and in the repeated findings that acquired food intolerances and phobic reactions are not manifested by subjects regressed to a period of life antedating those developments.

In brief, this case report discloses that, contrary to the actual current physical status of the subject, there were positive and striking correlations between the non-wearing and the wearing of glasses and the development of headaches in accord with past chronological physical states and experiences.

DISCUSSION

Discussion of these findings may be summarized by the statement that they constitute an experimental demonstration of unsuspected and unrealized interrelationships and interdependencies that exist between various modalities of behavior, an understanding of which is most important in any effort to deal effectively with the complex symptomatology of psychopathological conditions. Particularly do these findings demonstrate that psychopathological manifestations need not necessarily be considered as expressive of combined or multiple disturbances of several different modalities of behavior. Rather, they disclose that a disturbance in one single modality may actually be expresed in several other spheres of behavior as apparently unrelated coincidental disturbances. Hence, seemingly different symptoms may be but various aspects of a single manifestation for which the modalities of expression may properly be disregarded. Just as the hypnotically deaf subject manifested, as a part of his state of deafness, additional sensory or motor changes, so it may be that psychopathological manifestations involving several modalities of behavior are actually expressive of but a single disturbance in only one modality of behavior. Furthermore, just as the experimental approach to one modality of behavior was often dependent upon another apparently unrelated sphere of behavior, so it may be that the primary task in the therapy of various psychopathological conditions may be dependent upon an approach seemingly unrelated to the actual problem, even as hypnotic deafness was sometimes best achieved by first inducing an anaesthesia.

In brief, these experimental findings suggest that psychopathological phenomena cannot be understood in terms of the modality of their expression and manifestation alone but rather that an understanding must be looked for in terms of their fundamental interrelationships and interdependencies.

45. Hypnotic Experiments in Psychosomatic Medicine

Lewis R. Wolberg

ONE of the basic tenets of psychomatic medicine is that long continued emotional stress can produce widespread somatic changes. Probably the most insidious form of emotional stress is that which issues from unconscious conflict, since the individual, unaware of the cause of his difficulty, is usually helpless in coping with it.

That unconscious conflict can produce psychomatic illness is confirmed by studies during psychoanalytic therapy. However, few experimental studies have been made reporting on this phenomenon. It is understandable why this is so, since in a field as complex as human behavior it is extremely difficult to provide satisfactory experimental conditions.

Following the important observations of Luria, other workers have demonstrated how hypnosis may be utilized to study the effects of an experimentally induced conflict on the individual. Where posthypnotic amnesia is suggested or where it occurs spontaneously, the subject, while under the influence of the conflict, is not consciously aware of its existence.

This paper deals with experiences under hypnosis which demonstrate in a more or less dramatic fashion how unconscious conflict can produce states of somatic distress. Some of the effects reported are the deliberate product of an artificially induced conflict, while others are accidental by-products of conflicts inadvertently created during hypnoanalytic therapy.

The first case demonstrates how a conflict between an irrepressible impulse and a moral prohibition reflects itself in a generalized state of tension, with muscular tremors and neurocirculatory collapse. The subject was an individual who claimed he had no disturbing neurotic difficulties and had volunteered to act as a subject out of interest. An experimental conflict was induced in a deep trance by giving the subject the following posthypnotic

Abridged from *Psychosomatic Medicine*, 1947, 9, 337-342. Reprinted by permission of the author and Paul B. Hoeber, Inc.

suggestion. "When you awaken you will find next to you a bar of chocolate. You will have a desire to eat the chocolate that will be so intense that it will be impossible to resist the craving. At the same time you will feel that the chocolate does not belong to you and that to eat it would be very wrong and very bad. You will have no memory of these suggestions when you awaken, but you will, nevertheless, react to them."

When the subject was aroused, he looked casually about the room, yet avoided the table near him on which I had placed a bar of chocolate. He complained of a feeling of dizziness and of faintness. He asked for a glass of water and then decided to get it himself. He stood up from the chair, took two or three steps, then fell backward remarking that he felt so faint that he could hardly walk. His face was blanched and when his pulse was taken it was found to be rapid and steady. His forehead was covered with cold perspiration. He complained of feeling chilly. He then began to shiver and shortly after exhibited generalized muscular tremors. Almost compulsively his head moved sideways as he glanced furtively at the table. The moment he caught sight of the bar of chocolate his tremors became much more violent. He breathed deeply and seemed to go into a faint, leaning backward in the chair with his eyes closed. He remarked that he had no idea why he felt so bad and when questioned he had a complete amnesia for suggestions given him. When he was asked whether he would like a piece of candy, he shook his head emphatically and stated that he disliked chocolate bars. When I attempted to hand him the candy he became agitated and complained of such great physical distress that I found it necessary to re-hypnotize him and remove the conflict.

In this subject defensive devices such as avoiding looking at or touching the candy failed to lessen the intensity of his desire for the candy. The threat of yielding to the impulse to eat it was so strong that even the attempted phobic avoidance of the chocolate produced no solution. The resulting conflict caused tension and anxiety with generalized somatic effects.

Why the subject responded in this particular way to the conflict is a most provocative question. A partial analysis of his reaction was attempted later and it was determined that his response was characteristic of his usual reaction to disturbing life situations. Known to his friends as a "good, solid citizen" who rarely transgressed the bounds of social decorum, he suffered from tension and mild anxiety which he managed to control fairly well. From time to time, when under stress, he manifested symptoms of exhaustion and muscular tremors and on several occasions had collapsed physically and had been confined in bed for several weeks with what his family physician had classified as "subfebrile influenza."

Another subject, also without expressed neurotic problems, responded to the same induced conflict with a generalized autonomic disturbance as well as with gastrointestinal symptoms.

Similar suggestions to produce an experimental conflict were given to the subject in the trance state. When he awoke, he appeared to manifest some tension and trembling. There was complete amnesia for the trance events. He talked spontaneously and loquaciously about foods and eating, and then he skillfuly introduced the subject of how in a visit to a mutual friend he had politely refused to eat candy that had been offered to him. However, he insisted, visitors were usually expected to partake of food offered to them. Saying this he reached over, quickly unwrapped the chocolate and ate it with smacking satisfaction. When he had gotten through three-quarters of the bar, he looked up with a puzzled expression on his face and asked if there were something wrong with the chocolate. He remarked that it tasted bitter. He returned the remains of the chocolate to the table, wiped his mouth, and then talked about foods, eating, the virtues of dietary abstemiousness. In the middle of his discourse he began to complain of nausea and stomach pains. He then excused himself and went to the bathroom where he disgorged the candy he had eaten. When he returned to the room he remarked that he felt a great deal better. He kept avoiding commenting about the incident; however, when pressed, he hazarded a guess that the candy was probably spoiled.

The subject probably responded to the conflict situation by satisfying both his impulse and his conscience. He ate the candy, but the symptom of distaste, nausea, and vomiting served a punitive function propitiating the guilt incurred in the process. The conflict was allayed by disgorging the candy.

Another example of how a conflict can produce a generalized psychosomatic reaction is illustrated in an experimental neurosis unwittingly produced in a medical student by myself. During a lecture course in psychiatry, I desired to illustrate the phenomenon of hypnosis as well as the induction process by hypnotizing student volunteers. With one student who volunteered as a subject, I decided that I would demonstrate to the class the phenomenon of posthypnotic suggestion. I instructed the student who had gone into a deep trance that upon awakening he would return to his seat and listen attentively to the remainder of the lecture. As soon as I turned my back to the classroom and wrote the word "psychiatry" on the blackboard, he would have a compulsion to write his name, but as he did, he would misspell it. I then proceeded to arouse him; however, he was so soundly asleep that he seemed to pay no attention to my suggestions that he awaken. After some minutes had passed, I instructed him to stand up and open his eyes, but his only response was violent shaking and tremors.

Believing that I had somehow aroused a conflict in the posthypnotic suggestion I had given him, I acquainted him with this fact and told him that he did not have to comply if he did not want to. He then opened his eyes, but his shaking became more violent. He went back to his seat, but the tremors were so bad that he could hardly sit. I rehypnotized him and attempted to remove the tremors by direct suggestion. They diminished somewhat in intensity but were still present. He was obviously upset, and he complained of nausea, feelings of tenseness, and anxiety. He remarked that he felt "utterly silly," but he could not seem to control himself. He was certain that his reaction had nothing to do with any suggestion I had given him.

I then went to the blackboard and wrote the word "psychiatry." His tremors became much more intense and his right hand suddenly started to move toward a pencil on his desk. He forcibly withdrew his hand, but to his dismay it again began traveling toward the pencil. He tried to restrain his hand with his left hand but his shaking became so violent that he decided to pick up the pencil. He grasped the pencil but his fingers refused to move. When he started writing his hand shook so strongly that he was unable to form letters. He tried to steady his right hand with his left, but the pencil moved so slowly that it took him almost five minutes to write his first name. The letters were large and poorly formed. As he approached the last part of his last name, his hand stopped and he seemed to exhibit an almost superhuman effort to force himself to write. Upon reaching the last two letters his hand refused to go further. Finally after a pause of several minutes he finished his name. To his amazement he had misspelled it. His anxiety and tremors then vanished immediately and he evidenced an extremely cheerful attitude. He reached for the pencil again and wrote his name without any difficulty, this time spelling it correctly.

When asked whether he resented any suggestions given him, he declared that he had no conscious resentment. However, he did admit that people frequently misspelled his name and that this irritated him. He did not know why he was unable to write his name, but he remarked that he had resolved, when he picked up the pencil to write his name and to write it accurately. The misspelling occurred automatically, to his surprise.

A letter written me by the subject is interesting in detailing his subjective reactions:

"When the experiment started, I found it very easy to concentrate. When you told me that I was asleep, I truthfully didn't believe it because I could still hear you talking and was still conscious of the fact that I was being hypnotized. I believe I remember everything you told me to do since I do not feel that I lost consciousness during hypnosis. I simply felt more or less drowsy. The best comparison that I can make is this: I felt that I just ingested some alcoholic beverage (which I very rarely do because I never got into the habit), and was just about to doze off. When you told me that my right arm felt very light, it really did feel that way, and the same holds true when you told me that my left arm felt heavy. And yet throughout all of this, I kept being amazed by it all, because I didn't see how it could be possible. When you gave me the command to write my name incorrectly spelled, I was not conscious of the fact that such a task would be distasteful, no less that it would create an experimental neurosis. When you asked me to dream, I did not dream, but felt very relaxed and saw a soothing red or pink color in front of my eyes. When you tried to waken me, I felt very much as I do when I wake up in the morning; *i.e.,* I hated to waken. I know I trembled while still under hypnosis and even after I came out (I'm not sure that I did come out when you told me to), I could not stop trembling no matter how much self-control I tried to exert.

"When I sat down in the chair, I wanted to write my name on the paper, largely because of curiosity, especially since you began to analyze the situation at the time, referring to experimental neurosis created, etc. When I tried to write, I could hardly hold the pencil since I was shaking so violently. As you well know it turned out to be a child's scrawl. I had difficulty in getting out every single letter. I just 'could not get it out.' All through this performance, I kept murmuring to myself that the whole thing was ridiculous, especially the tremors and trembling which affected my entire body. Finally in exasperation, I murmured, 'what the hell' and ended my name wrong against my will. When I did this, the trembling immediately ceased and I felt kind of relieved. Someone then asked me to misspell my name again and I could do it with no trouble.

"After this I felt tired because of the strain of concentration and trembling. But sure enough, on my way home from school on the train, I felt very gay and lively, in spite of the fact that I was up late the night before and would ordinarily be tired. I was with some friends. I kept joking with them, inviting them to come out with me that night to 'tear the town apart' and felt very contented as one does in the early stages of alcohol intoxication. When I got out of the subway, for some strange reason I ran all the way home and did not feel at all tired when I got there (and I'm hardly in good athletic form at this time). That evening I felt very well, not at all tired as I usually am (from a full day at school), and studied very efficiently. When I turned in I was not tired and I think I could have worked efficiently the entire evening. (We'll have to try this again before finals.)"

In this subject a posthypnotic suggestion to misspell his name created a conflict, since it was opposed to his common sense. He considered the suggestion silly and he resented seeing his name misspelled. Yet he felt obliged to obey the command compulsively. He attempted at first to avoid the conflict by refusing to awaken. My suggeston that he need not write his name inaccurately was sufficient to arouse him, but he felt obliged nevertheless to react to my first command. He attempted unsuccessfully to resist the command by partial paresis of his right arm. The paresis was, of course, produced by forces outside of his awareness as were the shivering and muscle tremors.

Some psychosomatic problems appear to be manifested as a disturbance of a specific organ, rather than as a generalized physiologic reaction such as in the above cases. This was illustrated during the hypnoanalytic treatment of an alcoholic patient, in the course of which a conflict engendered by a transference reaction manifested itself in the form of a gastrointestinal symptom. During the early part of treatment the patient was carrying on a clandestine love affair of which he felt so guilty that he failed to mention it to me. One of the reasons was that the young lady in question was also an alcoholic who helped goad him on to excessive drinking. One evening I received a telephone message from this young woman, who confided to me her relationship with the patient, and declared that the latter had proposed to her the evening before. She also mentioned that she and the patient had engaged in excessive drinking and that on the evening before they had escaped a serious auto accident by a narrow margin.

When the patient came to my office the following day, he took pains to explain to me that he had gone to bed quite early the evening before, a statement that was in contradiction to the actual facts as revealed to me by his fiancee. Because I did not wish to jeopardize the relationship, I decided not to question him about his love affair. Under hypnosis, however, while in a deep trance state, he suddenly mumbled her name. I took this opportunity then to question him about the young woman and asked him whether it were not true that he had been out with her the night before. He admitted this and then confessed carrying on an affair which he desired to conceal from me because he intended to break up the relationship anyway. He stated: "She's a mess, she's been after me for a long time. I try to avoid her as much as possible. Last night she called me up. I was lonely, but I didn't really want to see her. She calls me up all the time." When aroused he showed no particular reaction to the trance events.

The next day he complained of abdominal pains which, he remarked, had started during the night time and had kept him awake most of the night. He was certain that the pains were caused by a Chinese meal he had eaten the night before. However, he confided that following the last session he was for some reason very troubled and preoccupied, although he was unable to understand why. Before going to bed he felt especially jittery. During the night his stomach symptoms appeared and he awoke in the morning feeling depressed. He could not understand why he felt depressed because nothing unusual had happened.

Under hypnosis I gave the patient the suggestion that if there were reasons for his depression, they would become more apparent to him while he was asleep. After a few minutes he remarked: "I had a dream last night that I forgot . . . I dreamt it again. I suddenly remembered it. It's just tied off . . . that's all . . . he tied my stomach off it's the doctor who operated on me . . . he operated on me last night. First, it's about the ether . . . he wanted to give me ether twice and I didn't want that. I believe in spinal anaesthesia . . . I get sick with ether. Then he came in there and said he would give me ether, so I got up and knocked him down. He said I had enough ether, so I knocked him down again. Last night he tied my stomach up so I couldn't digest my food . . . these sutures they use . . . fortunately they don't last too long and I will probably be able to eat again. I figure that if I'm good and sick he won't give me any more ether . . . that's what it is . . . If I'm good and sick my stomach is sick, he won't give me any more ether . . . this was in that hospital."

I then gave the patient the suggestion to dream of his actual feelings toward me. In response to this he stated: "You're the doctor in that dream . . . you could help me, but I'm afraid you don't trust me. We used to walk together, step by step, but you've got other interests. We don't talk about the same things. Maybe you treat someone else in my family. Maybe you treat my girl friend. You talked about her. Maybe I shouldn't expect you to devote your time to me. I guess you've got someone else. We are not together. I fixed that damned woman good. I called her up Friday night. I told her any affection I had for her was all over. I was mad that she called you. She must have called you because you knew of her. I realized something was funny when you mentioned her the other day. I felt you didn't trust me. I felt you didn't believe in me. Maybe my mother called you, and then that woman. I felt you were on their sides and then I got this nervous stomach."

It seemed apparent that the patient's stomach symptoms had followed the dream which was stimulated by the feeling that I did not trust him and must have rejected him for his actions. It appeared interesting that he had repressed the dream completely, possibly because it involved acknowledgment of hostile attitudes toward me, which he could not admit in the waking state at this particular phase of therapy. It seemed to me at the time that his stomach symptoms were a response to feelings of abandonment and, in order to check this, I gave him a suggestion that he would regress in the trance state to a period in his life when he had last had a very bad stomach complaint.

The time to which he regressed was three years prior to his coming to see me, when, in response to difficulties he had gotten into with the law, his family had become infuriated with him. He declared he was certain no one was on his side, that he was all alone, that his mother and father would never again accept him. He complained of severe pains in the abdominal region.

I then gave him a suggestion that he would go back to that time in his life when he first had his stomach illness. He shook his head and declared that he did not want to be a little boy again—that he did not like being a little boy. Nevertheless, after a while he appeared to have followed my suggestion. When he talked to me his language was very childish, but he was unable to tell me how old he was. He declared that he was not yet at school. He said "Daddy's away . . . Mummy's there, but she's not around. Nana . . . I don't like her a bit. She takes me away from Mummy. My stomach hurts. It feels awful. I vomit. It feels awful." Saying this he writhed around on the couch, holding his stomach. He shouted, "Everything is black . . . I want my Mummy!" I then suggested to him that Nana was away, that his mother was holding him on her lap. I asked him how he felt. He smiled and said, "it's soft, it's nice." Then he moved his lips as if he were suckling. I asked him how his stomach felt. He replied, "It feels good. I feel hungry."

From material brought up later in analysis, the patient had felt rejected by his mother and had attributed her securing a nurse for him as abandonment. From time to time he had had gastrointestinal complaints which were related to a fear of abandonment and rejection.

When the patient awoke, he did not remember the incidents that had occurred during hypnosis. He remarked, "You know, my stomach was upset when I came in here. It felt pretty terrible, but right now it feels marvelous. I wonder what you've done to me. It feels as if I never had any difficulty with my stomach. It feels all gone like magic. I wonder if my stomach is nervous, an indicator of this tension. You know, come to think of it, I had a funny dream last night, of a doctor operating on my stomach. Actually, I cannot stand either ether or gas. In the dream I was having an argument about taking the anaesthetic. The doctor was mad at me. He tied my stomach off. It's a funny thing that I did not remember the dream."

This patient demonstrates how emotional situations inspired by relationships with other people, can reflect themselves in disturbances of organ function. In his case a severe trauma had been inflicted upon his security system during his early relationship with his mother. Rejection and fear of abandonment by his mother reflected themselves in feeding disturbances and gastrointestinal symptoms. These repeated themselves later in life under situations symbolically representative of rejection by personages on whom he was dependent. An interview with his parents revealed that he had a severe feeding problem as an infant with intolerance of milk, vomiting and colic. This would indicate that his oral difficulty started long before the age to which he had regressed in hypnosis.

A large group of psychosomatic symptoms appear to serve protective or defensive functions against anxiety. This is illustrated in the case of a patient who was being treated by hypnoanalysis and who had started to become cognizant of the hostility he harbored toward his father. The hostility was, to a large extent, unconscious, being covered up by a façade of submissive character traits. He expressed a profound admiration of authority in general and of his father in particular.

In order to bring his attention to his unconscious attitudes, he was given under hypnosis, at a time when he exhibited a favorable transference reaction, the suggestion that he would dream of his deepest feelings toward his father. The next day he walked into my office limping, complaining that his right leg had become stiff and that the symptoms had increased during the morning. He attributed his difficulty to straining his leg while carrying an item of furniture up the stairs the evening before.

Under hypnosis the patient was instructed that if he had had a dream the evening before, he would dream the identical dream and reveal it to me. After a few minutes he remarked: "I just had a horrible dream. I drove Mother and Father up to this place and I was driving fast. They asked me not to. We had an awful accident; my father was killed. I see my father's face, dead. I am not dead. I should have killed myself instead." The patient was wringing wet with perspiration and, as he talked, I noticed that his right leg was jerking back and forth. I asked him what this signified. He remarked, "Putting on the brake." The stiffness in his leg apparently was an attempt to undo the damage he had done to his father in the dream.

When I explained to the patient how it was possible for him to have had hostile attitudes toward his father which he had misidentified with actual murder attitudes, his right leg suddenly relaxed. After awakening he observed with surprise that the stiffness had disappeared from his leg. Immediately thereafter he repeated the dream to me.

In this case a psychosomatic symptom, spasm of the leg, served to neutralize guilt, symbolically wiping away the damage he had inflicted on his father in his dream. It served also to help repress the dream from consciousness in order to avoid his becoming aware of his hostile attitude.

The defensive significance of certain psychosomatic symptoms is also illustrated by a patient suffering from conversion hysteria in whom I created an experimental conflict similar to that in the first two cases reported; namely, that he would, when he awoke from the trance, have an irresistible desire to eat a bar of chocolate on a table nearby, and, at the same time, feel that his morals would probably prohibit him from so doing.

Upon awakening he showed extreme equanimity and there was not the slightest indication in his free associations that he had reacted to the conflict situation. After a number of minutes, when it seemed apparent that the conflict had had no effect upon him, I asked him whether he would like to have a bar of candy. The patient shook his head and then deliberately changed the subject. He interrupted me several times when I talked on the subject of candy. I finally asked him to hand me the candy on the table near him. He turned his head, looked at the table and remarked, "What candy?" "Why the candy right next to you," I retorted. "There is no candy there," he replied, "Are you kidding?" I walked over to the table, lifted the bar of chocolate in my fingers and said, "Why here it is." He looked at my hand with a puzzled expression on his face. "You do not have anything in your hand," he retorted. When I attempted to hand him the chocolate, he refused to reach out for it. I threw the candy down on the table. He heard the sound of something landing, but was not able to see what had caused the sound. He said, "I suppose you think I'm crazy, but I don't see anything." The negative hallucination for the candy lasted almost twenty minutes, at the end of which time he spontaneously remarked, looking at the table, that there was a bar of chocolate there. Nevertheless, he refused to eat it, rationalizing his refusal on the basis of having shortly before had a full meal.

SUMMARY

A group of cases are presented in whom an unconscious conflict, deliberately or accidentally produced during hypnosis, created psychosomatic symptoms which could be traced directly to the conflict, and which disappeared when the conflict was resolved. Some of the symptoms were random physiological manifestations of tension and anxiety. Others were purposeful reactions which served a symbolic function as an expression of a conflict or as a defense against it.

46. Antisocial Compulsions Induced under Hypnotic Trance

John G. Watkins

A commonly held belief about hypnosis is that under trance a person cannot be made to commit crimes or be forced to do anything which he would not do under normal circumstances or which would violate his ethical sense. The belief is generally held both by laymen and professional psychologists, psychiatrists and physicians.

Rowland conducted a series of experiments at Baylor which indicated that this was not the case and that individuals could be made to perform acts that endangered their lives. Wells, at Syracuse University, has also performed studies in which crime compulsions were induced and subjects made to steal objects under hypnotic trance. While Estabrooks also is quite insistent that criminal behavior can be suggested, Erickson, on the other hand, has carefully performed a group of studies in which he arrives at the conclusion that crime compulsions cannot be induced. The critics of the experiments conducted by Wells, Rowland, and Estabrooks base their arguments on two points: First, that small cues inevitably inform the subject that he will be protected and will not really commit murder, suicide, or robbery; consequently, he goes through the suggested behavior secure in the belief that it is only an act, not the real thing, and that he is not really committing a crime. Secondly, they insist that if the individual actually carried out a crime compulsion it was because he had latent criminal tendencies in his nature; so he was not actually violating his true principles. They also point out the studies of Erickson and others who have not been able to induce crime compulsions. To these, Estabrooks suggests that operator-attitude is extremely important and implies that Erickson indirectly inti-

Abridged from the *Journal of Abnormal and Social Psychology*, 1947, 42, 256-259. Reprinted by permission of the author and the American Psychological Association, Inc.

mated to his subjects that he did not really expect them to carry out the suggested crimes.

In this paper the writer wishes to report a series of experiments which might throw further light on this problem. The controls were certainly not as rigid as one would desire to establish firmly that criminal compulsions are possible, yet the combined weight of evidence from these studies definitely favors that contention.

CASE STUDY A

The subject was an Army Corporal who volunteered for the experiment in off-duty hours. The objective of the study was to determine if information could be extracted from a presumably unwilling subject. The subject was first hypnotized and given the post-hypnotic suggestion that any time the Experimenter handed him a yellow pencil he would have to go back to sleep immediately. The study was then conducted as follows:

E: Do you think that you, as a good soldier (the subject had an excellent record), could be entrusted to keep confidential military information given you?

S: Why, of course.

E: Capt. S. here will give you a bit of information and order you not to divulge it to me under any circumstances. Can you keep it to yourself? Remember, if you tell me you are disobeying a direct military order.

S: Certainly I can keep it. (Subject goes to Capt. S., who whispers the order. He then returns to his chair with a defiant appearance.)

E: (Hands yellow pencil to subject, who immediately goes into a deep trance.) I am Capt. S. I just gave you a piece of information you were not to divulge. I want to see if you remember it, Corporal. What is it?

S: Company B will leave at 2100 tonight. (Capt. S. nods to indicate that this was the message.)

E: (Removes subject from trance.) Did you divulge the message?

S: No, and you can't get it out of me.

E: (Repeats message to the subject who appears amazed, and who then insists that Capt. S. must have revealed it to the experimenter.)

E: What is it I am putting in front of you?

S: Why, that's a ten-dollar bill.

E: I want to try you again. I shall ask Capt. S. to give you another message. That ten-dollar bill is yours if you *do not* tell me the message. Do you understand?

S: It's in the bag. (Goes to Capt. S. and receives another message.)

E: (Places ten-dollar bill on table directly in front of the subject, and, while the subject is looking at the bill, hands him the yellow pencil. S immediately goes into trance, and E secures the second message in the same manner. He then awakens the subject.)

S: The ten-dollar bill is mine, isn't it? (S reaches for it and is greatly disappointed when he is told he has divulged the message. He then becomes angry and indicates he thinks he is being cheated.)

E: Let's try it once more. This time you can earn the ten-dollar bill if you will just stay awake. Do not go to sleep. Fight back and refuse to go into trance.

S: (Rather belligerently) That's easy—just try to put me to sleep.

E: (Hands subject the yellow pencil. Subject blinks a moment or two and then sinks back into a deep trance.)

The above experiment was repeated with similar instructions to seven different subjects. They were all military men and volunteers. Not one of them was able to earn any money. Of course, the seven were picked as readily hypnotizable and did not by any means represent a random sample of humans. However, the desire to earn the money was not strong enough to enable them to overcome the suggestions. In no case could the subject withhold information, nor could he refuse to enter trance when once hypnotized and set for rehypnotization by the post-hypnotic suggestion of the yellow pencil.

CASE STUDY B.

The subject was an enlisted WAC who was working in a military intelligence office. The officer in charge was interested in the possibilities of extracting information under trance conditions and offered his assistants for an experiment to see if information could be secured by the experimenter from individuals ordered to withhold it. He was frankly skeptical of the possibility. Suggestibility tests in the form of arm freeze and postural swaying were administered to some dozen WAC and civilian assistants. One responded positively but only to a small degree. The officer than gave her a message and ordered her not to divulge same. With difficulty she was placed in a light trance through eye-fixation on a bright nickel pencil. The trance was so light that she was fully conscious of all that she was being told to do. If she was requested to perform some "foolish" operation such as picking fruit she would do so slowly and smile about it. The experiment was then conducted as follows:

E: You have a mesage given to you by your Commanding Officer. You are working in a military intelligence office and know the seriousness of not being able to keep confidential information. Furthermore, you **know the consequences of disobeying a military order from a superior** officer. Yet, in spite of this, you are going to tell me that message. It is rising in your throat, and you will not be able to keep it down. It is getting higher, higher, higher. Now it is on the back of your tongue. Now it is in the middle of your tongue. Now it is on the tip of your tongue. Now it is escaping from your teeth. You will endure the most extreme suffering until you release it and speak the message. Speak it! Speak it! (During all this time the subject's anxiety kept constantly increasing. Her face turned a livid red. She writhed all over, wrung her hands, made the most twisted grimaces and facial contortions. Finally the message virtually "exploded" from her.)

S: The WAC detachment will embark tonight at 1930. (She immediately sighed and slumped in her chair. She was then brought out of her trance).

S: My God, you didn't have to choke it out of me!

CASE STUDY C.

The subject this time was a private with a very good record. He was in the same company as the experimenter and was well known to him. He had an excellent military record and was a most conscientious young man, about 20 years of age. He was respected by the other men as sincere and earnest. Several members of the medical staff of the Neuropsychiatric Division of a station hospital were present. The subject was placed in trance.

E: In a minute you will slowly open your eyes. In front of you, you will see a dirty Jap soldier. He has a bayonet, and is going to kill you unless you kill him first. You will have to strangle him with your bare hands. (A Lieutenant Colonel, the head psychiatrist and Director of the Neuropsychiatric Division of the hospital, was placed directly in front of the subject and about ten feet away.)

(The subject opened his eyes. He then slanted them and began to creep cautiously forward. Suddenly in a flying tackle he dove at the Lieutenant Colonel, knocking him against the wall, and with both of his hands (he was a powerful, husky lad) began strangling the man. It will be recalled that for an enlisted man to "attack" a commissioned officer is a serious offense in the Army. It took the instantaneous assistance of three others to break the soldier's grip, pull him off the officer, and hold him until the experimenter could quiet him back into a sleep condition. The Lieutenant Colonel reported that the man's grip was strong and dangerous, and that he might have been killed or injured if assistants had not been available to drag the soldier back.)

It will be noted here that the man did not violate his own conscience. He was attacking what to him was a Jap soldier and not an officer in the Army.

He was acting under an induced hallucination. Yet had he been permitted to continue his act he would have committed murder from the social viewpoint and would have been punished if the prosecution had "proven" to the resulting court martial that "people cannot be made to commit crimes under hypnotic trance."

CASE STUDY D

The subject was a 21-year-old Lieutenant, friendly and non-aggressive in nature. He was a small man, weighing about 120 pounds and short in stature. The same experiment was repeated with him as with the subject in Case Study C. The "Jap soldier" was a friend, a brother officer. In this case the subject acted as did the private in Case C except that he suddenly pulled out and opened a pocket knife. (His possession of this article was not known to any others present.) Only the quick intercession of witnesses and an upward wrist parry by his officer friend (the Jap soldier) prevented a serious stabbing.

CASE STUDY E

The subject was a WAC volunteer for a demonstration of hypnosis before a professional group. She was a visitor at the installation. The subject was questioned prior to trance.

E: If you were captured by the Germans how would you answer questions asked you?

S: With my name and serial number, nothing more.

E: You're certain of that?

S: Certain.

E: Let us pretend I am a German military intelligence officer and you are a prisoner of war. Remember, you will tell me only your name and serial number. (The subject was placed in hypnotic trance.)

E: I am your First Sergeant. I have a few questions to ask you. What's the name of the installation where you are now stationed?

S: The Aberdeen Proving Grounds.

E: What part are you in?

S: The WAC Detachment.

E: About how many are there in the WAC Detachment?

S: Oh, around 1500 girls.

E: What do you do?

S: I'm assisting with a research project.

E: What kind of a research project? (It will be remembered that this interview was taking place in the presence of a group of some 200 people.)

S: We are developing a new secret type of fuel for propelling rockets.

E: Do you know how this fuel is made?

S: Of course. I've watched them make it. (At this moment a high-ranking officer present stepped in and said, "I think we've gone far enough. In the interest of military secrecy we'll have to stop at this point.")

It was apparent to all that this girl would have unconsciously divulged genuine, confidential information, which would have subjected her to a court martial, if she had been permitted to continue.

CASE STUDY F

This subject was a corporal who had been hypnotized once before but had not been connected to any posthypnotic "yellow pencil" suggestion. The purpose of this study was to see if a person could be made to enter trance against his will. The subject was shown a ten-dollar bill which was placed on a table before him. He was seated and told to look at the bill.

E: "Now, George, this ten-dollar bill in front of you is yours under one condition. I want you to look at it carefully. You can have it if you will *just not let me make you go to sleep.* Keep from entering a trance. Remember, you are to try your hardest not to enter a trance . . . But it won't do you a damned bit of good because I am going to count up to twenty-five and by the time I get there you will be sound asleep. 1,2,3, . . . 25." The subject was in a deep trance. His eyes closed at the count of twenty while staring directly at the ten-dollar bill in front of him. Of course, this individual was very highly hypnotizable, but the experimenter has observed several others who were equally so.

CONCLUSIONS

1. Under hypnotic trance some subjects can be made to release, unconsciously, information which they had a prior strong motivation not to divulge. (Cases A and E).

2. Under light hypnoidal trance some subjects who are conscious of what they are doing can be "forced" to divulge information they intend to withhold. (Case B).

3. Under deep trance, hallucinations can be set up in some subjects which will cause them to commit "socially criminal acts," even to the extent of murder. (Cases C and D).

4. If sufficiently suggestible, some subjects can be "forced" into trance against their will. (Case F).

These conclusions are not intended to be drawn for all people. From these studies, however, it seems they apply to some individuals. The subjects were selected from small groups of volunteers and represented about 10 per cent of those volunteering. They were, of course, highly hypnotizable individuals and not random selectees. However, no exhaustive or rigid selection system was employed other than the usual tests of suggestibility. There apparently would be many thousands of individuals like them in the total population.

REFERENCES—SECTION SEVEN

Ambrose, G., and Newbold, G. *A Handbook of Medical Hypnosis.* London: Bailliere, Tindall, 1956.

Bowers, M. K. (Ed.). *Introductory Lectures in Medical Hypnosis.* New York: Institute for Research in Hypnosis, 1957.

Brenman, M., and Gill, M. *Hypnotherapy.* New York: International Universities Press, 1947.

Bull, N. Attitudes: conscious and unconscious. *J. nerv. and ment. Dis.,* 1946, *103,* 337.

DeMartino, M. F. (Ed.). *Dreams and Personality Dynamics.* Springfield, Ill.: Charles C. Thomas, 1959.

Carter, H. D. Effect of emotional factors upon recall. *J. Psychol.,* 1936, *1,* 48-55.

Edwards, A. L. The retention of affective experiences—a criticism and restatement of the problem. *Psychol. Rev.,* 1942, *49,* 43-53.

Ellenberger, H. The unconscious before Freud. *Bull. Menninger Clin.,* 1957, *21,* 3-15.

Erickson, M. Hypnotic psychotherapy. *Med. Clinics North America,* May, 1948, 571-583.

Freud, S. Repression. In *Collected Papers,* Vol. 4, 84-97. London: Hogarth Press, 1925.

———. *New Introductory Lectures on Psycho-Analysis.* New York: Norton, 1933.

———. *Inhibitors, Symptoms, and Anxiety.* London: Hogarth Press, 1936.

———. *The Standard Edition of the Complete Psychological Works.* J. Strachey (Ed.). London: Hogarth Press, 1953.

Gould, R. Repression experimentally analyzed. *Character and Pers.,* 1942, *10,* 259-288.

Heron, W. T. *Clinical Applications of Suggestion and Hypnosis.* (3rd ed.) Springfield, Ill.: Charles C. Thomas, 1957.

Hilgard, E. R. *Unconscious Processes and Man's Rationality.* Urbana, Ill.: Univer. Illinois Press, 1958.

Jones, E. (Ed.). *Collected Papers—Sigmund Freud.* New York: International Univ. Press, Vols. 1-5, 1950-1951.

Kogen, N. Authoritarianism and repression. *J. abnorm. soc. Psychol.,* 1956, *53,* 34-37.

Kline, M. V. *Freud and Hypnosis: The Interaction of Psychodynamics and Hypnosis.* New York: Julian Press, 1958.

MacIntyre, A. C. *The Unconscious: A Conceptual Analysis.* New York: Humanities Press, 1958.

Marcuse, F. L. *Hypnosis: Fact and Fiction.* Baltimore: Penguin Books, 1959.

Margetts, E. L. The concept of the unconscious in the history of medical psychology. *Psychiat. Quart.,* 1953, *27,* 115-138.

McConnell, J. V., Cutler, R. L., and McNeil, E. S. Subliminal stimulation: An overview. *Amer. Psychologist,* 1958, *13,* 229-242.

Meltzer, H. Sex differences in forgetting pleasant and unpleasant experiences. *J. abnorm. soc. Psychol.,* 1931, *25,* 450-464.

Mowrer, O. H. Changing conceptions of the unconscious. *J. nerv. ment. Dis.,* 1959, *129,* 222-234.

Prince, M., *The Unconscious.* Second Edition, New York: Macmillan, 1924.

Rapaport, D. *Emotions and Memory.* Baltimore: Williams and Wilkins, 1942.

Rhine, J. B. On the nature and consequences of the unconsciousness of psi. *J. Parapsychol.,* 1958, *22,* 175-186.

Rosenzweig, S. The experimental study of repression. In H. A. Murray, (Ed.), *Explorations In Personality*. New York: Oxford Univ. Press, 1938.

————. An experimental study of "repression" with special reference to need-persistive and ego-defensive reactions to frustration. *J. exp. Psychol.*, 1943, *32*, 64-74.

————, and Mason, G. An experimental study of memory in relation to the theory of repression. *Brit. J. Psychol.*, 1934, *24*, 247-265.

Shaw, F. J. Two determinants of selective forgetting. *J. abnorm. soc. Psychol.*, 1944, *39*, 434-445.

————. A stimulus-response analysis of repression and insight in psychotherapy. *Psychol. Rev.*, 1946, *53*, 36-42.

Stagner, R. The redintegration of pleasant and unpleasant experiences. *Amer. J. Psychol.*, 1931, *43*, 463-468.

Steckle, L. C. Again—affect and recall. *J. soc. Psychol.*, 1945, *22*, 103-105.

VanPelt, S. J., Ambrose, G., and Newbold, G. *Medical Hypnosis*. London, England: Victor Gollancz, 1953.

Wallen, D. Ego involvement as a determinant of selective forgetting. *J. abnorm. soc. Psychol.*, 1942, *37*, 20-29.

Waters, R. H., and Leeper, R. The relation of affective tone to the retention of experiences in everyday life. *J. exp. Psychol.*, 1936, *19*, 203-215.

Weitzenhoffer, A. M., and Weitzenhoffer, G. Personality and hypnotic susceptibility. *Amer. J. Clin. Hypnosis*, 1958, *1*, 79-82.

Whyte, L. L. *The Unconscious Before Freud*. New York: Basic Books, 1960.

Zeller, A. P. An experimental analogue of repression—I. Historical summary. *Psychol. Bull.*, 1950, *47*, 39-51.

————. An experimental analogue of repression: II. The effect of individual failure and success on memory measured by relearning. *J. exp. Psychol.*, 1950, *40*, 411-422.

————. An experimental analogue of repression: III. The effect of induced failure and success on memory measured by relearning. *J. exp. Psychol.*, 1951, *42*, 32-38.

MOTIVATION AND
DEPTH PSYCHOLOGY

This chapter is concerned with a presentation of some of the theories and concepts underlying motivation from the standpoint of psychoanalytically oriented or depth psychologists. It is generally agreed that Fromm (Paper No. 47) and Horney (Paper No. 48) are outstanding representatives of what has become known as the "neo-Freudian" school of thought. Both these analysts, unlike Freud, have emphasized greatly the significance of cultural and social factors (pressures) on personality development. Fromm and Horney recognize and stress the extreme importance of parent-child relationships and the influence of parents as the representatives of the social structure. Contrary to Freud they hold that the libido is not the one and only source of human motives, but that human motives arise out of a given culture.

Originally, Alfred Adler belonged to the school of thought led by Freud. However, because of certain basic disagreements with Freud's theories, particularly that aspect dealing with the importance of sex, he broke with him and formulated his own theory of personality development and human motivation. His system of ideas came to be known as the school of Individual Psychology. Adler believed that the basic motive underlying all behavior is a *striving for superiority* (Paper No. 50). He maintained that this *striving for superiority* has its origin (from the time of birth) in underlying feelings of inferiority.

Among the major contributions of David M. Levy, one of the foremost contemporary analysts in the field of child psychology, are his studies on maternal overprotection, sibling rivalry and a form of psychotherapy known as "Release Therapy." In his paper (No. 49), he is concerned primarily with what he calls *affect hunger*. To Levy "the term, affect hunger, is used to mean an emotional hunger for maternal love and those other feelings of protection and care implied in the mother-child relationships." Levy feels that primary affect hunger may become as fundamental as any of the other basic needs.

Bibring is the only author in this section who may be classified as belonging to the orthodox Freudian school of thought. In his highly regarded paper (No. 51), he gives an historical overview and explanation of the development of the psycho-analytical theory of the instincts.

47. Selfishness and Self-Love

Erich Fromm

Modern culture is pervaded by a taboo on selfishness. It teaches that to be selfish is sinful and that to love others is virtuous. To be sure, this doctrine is not only in flagrant contradiction to the practices of modern society but it also is in opposition to another set of doctrines which assumes that the most powerful and legitimate drive in man is selfishness and that each individual by following this imperative drive also does the most for the common good. The existence of this latter type of ideology does not affect the weight of

Abridged from *Psychiatry*, 1939, 2, 507-523. Reprinted by permission of the author and The William Alanson White Psychiatric Foundation.

the doctrines which declare that selfishness is the arch evil and love for others the main virtue. Selfishness, as it is commonly used in these ideologies, is more or less synonymous with self-love. The alternatives are either to love others which is a virtue or to love oneself which is a sin.

This principle has found its classic expression in Calvin's theology. Man is essentially bad and powerless. He can do nothing—absolutely nothing— good on the basis of his own strength or merits. "We are not our own," says Calvin, "therefore neither our reason nor our will should predominate in our deliberations and actions. We are not our own; therefore, let us not propose it as our end, to seek what may be expedient for us according to the flesh. We are not our own; therefore, let us, as far as possible, forget ourselves and all things that are ours. On the contrary, we are God's; to him, therefore, let us live and die. For, as it is the most devastating pestilence which ruins people if they obey themselves, it is the only haven of salvation not to know or to want anything by oneself but to be guided by God who walks before us."[1] Man should not only have the conviction of his absolute nothingness. He should do everything to humiliate himself. "For I do not call it humility," says Calvin, "if you suppose that we have anything left ... we cannot think of ourselves as we ought to think without utterly despising everything that may be supposed an excellence in us. This humility is unfeigned submission of a mind overwhelmed with a weighty sense of its own misery and poverty; for such is the uniform description of it in the word of God."

This emphasis on the nothingness and wickedness of the individual implies that there is nothing he should like about himself. This doctrine is rooted in contempt and hatred for oneself. Calvin makes this point very clear; he speaks of "Self-love" as of a "pest."

[1]From "For as it is . . . ." the translation is mine from the Latin original (Johannes Calvini *Institutio Christianae Religionis.* Editionem curavit A. Tholuk. Berolini 1835, par. I, p. 445.) The reason for this shift is that Allen's translation slightly changes the original in the direction of softening the rigidity of Calvin's thought. Allen translates this sentence: "For as compliance with their own inclinations leads men most effectually to ruin, so to place no dependency on our own knowledge or will, but merely to follow the guidance of the Lord, is the only way of safety." However, the Latin *sibi ipsis obtemperant* is not equivalent to "follow one's own inclinations" but "to obey oneself." To forbid following one's inclinations has the mild quality of Kantian ethics that man should suppress his natural inclinations and by doing so follow the orders of his conscience. On the other hand, forbidding to obey oneself is a denial of the autonomy of man. The same subtle change of meaning is reached by translating *ita unicus est salutis portis nihil nec sapere, nec velle per se ipsum* "to place no dependence on our knowledge nor will." While the formulation of the original straight-forwardly contradicts the motto of enlightenment philosophy: *sapere aude*—dare to know, Allen's translations warns only of a dependence on one's own knowledge, a warning which is by far less contradictory to modern thought. I mention these deviations of the translation from the original which I came across accidentally, because they offer a good illustration of the fact that the spirit of an author is "modernized" and colored—certainly without any intention of doing so—just by translating him.

If the individual finds something in himself "on the strength of which he finds pleasure in himself," he betrays this sinful self-love. This fondness for himself will make him sit in judgment over others and despise them. Therefore, to be fond of oneself, to like anything about oneself is one of the greatest imaginable sins. It excludes love for others[2] and is identical with selfishness.[3]

There are fundamental differences between Calvin's theology and Kant's philosophy, yet, the basic attitude toward the problem of love for oneself has remained the same. According to Kant, it is a virtue to want the happiness of others, while to want one's own happiness is ethically "Indifferent," since it is something which the nature of man is striving for and a natural striving cannot have positive ethical sense. Kant admits that one must not give up one's claims for happiness; under certain circumstances it can even be a duty to be concerned with one's happiness; partly because health, wealth, and the like, can be means which are necessary to fulfill one's duty, partly because the lack of happiness—poverty—can seduce a person from fulfilling his duty. But love for oneself, striving for one's own happiness, can never be a virtue. As an ethical principle, the striving for one's own happiness "is the most objectionable one, not merely because it is false, ... but because the springs it provides for morality are such as rather undermine it and destroy its sublimity. . . ." Kant differentiates in egotism, self-love, *philautia*—a benevolence for oneself; and arrogance—the pleasure in oneself. "Rational self-love" must be restricted by ethical principles, the pleasure in oneself must be battered down and the individual must come to feel humiliated in comparing himself with the sanctity of moral laws. The individual should find supreme happiness in the fulfillment of his duty. The realization of the moral principle—and, therefore, of the individual's happiness—is only possible in the general whole, the nation, the state. Yet, "the welfare of the state—*salus rei publicae suprema lex est*—is not identical with the welfare of the citizens and their happiness."

In spite of the fact that Kant shows a greater respect for the integrity of the individual than did Calvin or Luther, he states that even under the most tyrannical government the individual has no right to rebel and must be punished no less than with death if he threatens the sovereign. Kant emphasises the native propensity for evil in the nature of man, for the suppression of which the moral law, the categorical imperative, is necessary unless man should become a beast and human society should end in wild anarchy.

[2]It should be noted, however, that even love for one's neighbor, while it is one of the fundamental doctrines of the New Testament, has not been given a corresponding weight by Calvin. In blatant contradiction to the New Testament Calvin says: "For what the schoolmen advance concerning the priority of charity to faith and hope, is a mere reverie of a distempered imagination. . . . ."

[3]Despite Luther's emphasis on the spiritual freedom of the individual, his theology, different as it is in many ways from Calvin's, is pervaded by the same conviction of man's basic powerless and nothingness.

In discussing Calvin's and Kant's systems, their emphasis on the nothingness of man has been stressed. Yet, as already suggested, they also emphasize the autonomy and dignity of the individual, and this contradiction runs through their writings. In the philosophy of the enlightenment period the individual's claims and happiness have been emphasized much more strongly by others than by Kant, for instance by Helvetius. This trend in modern philosophy has found an extreme expression by Stirner and Nietzsche. In the way that they often phrase the problem—though not necessarily in their real meaning—they share one basic premise of Calvin and Kant: that love for others and love for oneself are alternatives. But in contradiction to those authors, they denounce love for others as weakness and self-sacrifice and postulate egotism, selfishness, and self-love—they too confuse the issue by not clearly differentiating between these phenomena—as virtue. Thus Stirner says: "Here, egoism, selfishness must decide, not the principle of love, not love motives like mercy, gentleness, good-nature, or even justice and equity—for *iustitia* too is a phenomenon of love, a product of love: love knows only sacrifice and demands self-sacrifice."

The kind of love denounced by Stirner is the masochistic dependence which makes the individual a means for achieving the purposes of somebody or something outside himself. With this conception of love could he scarcely avoid a formulation which postulated ruthless egotism as a goal. The formulation is, therefore, highly polemical and overstates the point. The positive principle with which Stirner was concerned[4] was directed against an attitude which had run through Christian theology for many centuries—and which was vivid in the German idealism which was passing in his time; namely, to bend the individual to submit to and find his center in a power and a principle outside of himself. To be sure, Stirner was not a philosopher of the stature of Kant or Hegel, yet he had the courage to make a radical rebellion against that side of idealistic philosophy which negated the concrete individual and thus helped the absolute state to retain its oppressive power over the individual. Although there is no comparison between the depth and scope of the two philosophers, Nietzsche's attitude in many respects is similar to that of Stirner. Nietzsche also denounces love and altruism as the expressions of weakness and self-negation. For Nietzsche, the quest for love is typical of slaves who cannot fight for what they want and, therefore, try to get it through "love."

---

[4]One of his positive formulations, for example, is: "But how does one use life? In using it up like the candle one burns . . . Enjoyment of life is using life up." Engels has clearly seen the onesidedness of Stirner's formulations and has attempted to overcome the false alternative between love for oneself and love for others. In a letter to Marx in which he discusses Stirner's book, Engels writes: "If, however, the concrete and real individual is the true basis for our 'human' man, it is self-evident that egotism —of course not only Stirner's egotism of reason, but also the egotism of the heart—is the basis for our love of man."

Altruism and love for mankind is thus a sign of degeneration. For him, it is the essence of a good and healthy aristocracy that is ready to sacrifice countless people for its interests without having a guilty conscience. Society should be a "foundation and scaffolding by means of which a select class of beings may be able to elevate themselves to their higher duties, and in general to their higher existence." Many quotations could be added to document this spirit of sadism, contempt and brutal egotism. This side of Nietzsche has often been understood as *the* philosophy of Nietzsche. Is this true; is this the "real" Nietzsche?

To answer this question would require a detailed analysis of his work which cannot be attempted here. There are various reasons which made Nietzsche express himself in the sense mentioned above. First of all, as in the case of Stirner, his philosophy is a reaction—a rebellion—against the philosophical tradition of subordinating the empirical individual to a power and a principle outside of himself. His tendency to overstatements shows this reactive quality. Second, there were traits in Nietzsche's personality, a tremendous insecurity and anxiety, which explain that, and why he had sadistic impulses which led him to those formulations. Yet, these trends in Nietzsche do not seem to me to be the "essence" of his personality nor the corresponding views the essence of his philosophy. Finally, Nietzsche shared some of the naturalistic ideas of his time as they were expressed in the materialistic-biologistic philosophy, for which the concepts of the physiological roots of psychic phenomena and the "survival of the fittest" were characteristic. This interpretation does not do away with the fact that Nietzsche shared the view that there is a contradiction between love for others and love for oneself. Yet, it is important to notice that Nietzsche's views contain the nucleus from development of which this wrong dichotomy can be overcome. The "love" which he attacks is one which is rooted not in one's own strength, but in one's own weakness. "Your neighbor love is your bad love for yourselves. You flee into your neighbor from yourselves and would fain make a virtue thereof. But I fathom your 'unselfishness'." He states explicitly, "You cannot stand yourselves and do not love yourselves sufficiently." The individual has for Nietzsche "an enormously great significance." The "strong" individual is the one who has "true kindness, nobility, greatness of soul, which does not give in order to take, which does not want to excell by being kind;—'waste' as type of true kindness, wealth of the person as a premise."

He expresses the same thought also in *Thus Spake Zarathustra*: "The one goeth to his neighbor because he seeketh himself, the other one because would he fain lose himself."

The essence of these views is: love is a phenomenon of abundance, its premise is the strength of the individual who can give. Love is affirmation, "it seeketh to create what is loved!" To love another person is only a virtue if it springs from this inner strength, but it is detestable if it is the expression of the basic inability to be oneself.

However, the fact remains that Nietzsche left the problem of the relationship between self-love and love for others as unsolved antinomy, even if by interpreting him one may surmise in what direction his solution would have been found.

The doctrine that selfishness is the arch-evil that one has to avoid and that to love oneself excludes loving others is by no means restricted to theology and philosophy. It is one of the stock patterns used currently in home, school, church, movies, literature, and all the other instruments of social suggestion. "Don't be selfish" is a sentence which has been impressed upon millions of children, generation after generation. It is hard to define what exactly it means. Consciously, most parents connect with it the meaning not to be egotistical, inconsiderate, without concern for others. Factually, they generally mean more than that. "Not to be selfish" implies not to do what one wishes, to give up one's own wishes for the sake of those in authority; *i.e.,* the parents, and later the authorities of society. "Don't be selfish," in the last analysis, has the same ambiguity that we have seen in Calvinism. Aside from its obvious implication, it means, "Don't love yourself," "don't be yourself," but submit your life to something more important than yourself, be it an outside power or the internalization of that power as "duty." "Don't be selfish" becomes one of the most powerful ideological weapons in suppressing spontaneity and the free development of personality. Under the pressure of this slogan one is asked for every sacrifice and for complete submission: only those aims are "unselfish" which do not serve the individual for his own sake but for the sake of somebody or something outside of him.

This picture, we must repeat, is in a certain sense one-sided. Beside the doctrine that one should not be selfish, the opposite doctrine is propagandized in modern society: have your own advantage in mind, act according to what is best for you—and by doing so, you will also bring about the greatest advantage for all others. As a matter of fact, the idea that the pursuit of individual egotism is the basis for the development of general welfare is the principle on which competitive capitalism has been built. It may seem strange that two such seemingly contradictory principles could be taught side by side in one culture. Of the fact, there can be no doubt. One result of this contradiction of ideological patterns certainly is confusion in the individual. To be torn between the one and the other doctrine is a serious blockage in the process of integration of personality and has often led to neurotic character formation.

One must observe that this contradictory pair of doctrines has had an important social function. The doctrine that everybody should pursue his individual advantage obviously was a necessary stimulus for private initiative on which the modern economic structure is built. The social function of the doctrine "don't be selfish" was an ambiguous one. For the broad masses of those who had to live on the level of mere subsistence, it was an important aid to resignation to having wishes which were unattainable under the given socio-economic system. It was important that this resignation should be one which was not thought of as being brought about by external pressure, since the inevitable result of such a feeling has to be a more or less conscious grudge and a defiance against society. By making this resignation a moral virtue, such a reaction could to a considerable extent be avoided. While this aspect of the social function of the taboo on selfishness is obvious, another, its effect upon the privileged minority, is somewhat more complicated. It only becomes clear if we consider further the meaning of "selfishness." If it means to be concerned with one's economic advantage, certainly the taboo on selfishness would have been a severe handicap to the economic initiative of business men. But what it really meant, especially in the earlier phases of English and American culture was, as has been pointed out before: don't do what you want, don't enjoy yourself, don't spend money or energy for plea-sure, but feel it as your duty to work, to be successful, to be prosperous.

It is the great merit of Max Weber to have shown that this principle of what he calls *innerweltliche Askese* [innerworldly asceticism] was an im-portant condition for creating an attitude in which all energy could be directed toward work and the fulfillment of duty. The tremendous economic achieve-ments of modern society would not have been possible if this kind of asceti-cism had not absorbed all energy to the purpose of thrift and relentless work. It would transcend the scope of this paper to enter into an analysis of the character structure of modern man as he emerged in the 16th century. Suffice it to say here, that the economic and social changes in the 15th and 16th cen-turies destroyed the feeling of security and "belonging" which was typical of the members of medieval society.[5] The socio-economic position of the urban middle class, the peasantry and the nobility were shaken in their foundations; impoverishment, threats to traditional economic positions as well as new chances for economic success arose. Religious and spiritual ties which had established a rounded and secure world for the individual had been broken. The individual found himself completely alone in the world, paradise was lost for good, his success and failure were decided by the laws of the market; the basic relationship to everyone else had become one of merciless competition. The result of all this was a new feeling of freedom attended, however, by an increased anxiety. This anxiety, in its turn, created a readiness for new sub-mission to religious and secular authorities even more strict than the previous

[5]Harry Stack Sullivan has given particular emphasis to the need for security as one of the basic motivating forces in man, while orthodox psychoanalytical literature has not paid sufficient attention to this factor.

ones had been. The new individualism on the one hand, anxiety and submission to authority on the other, found their ideological expression in Protestantism and Calvinism. At the same time, these religious doctrines did much to stimulate and increase these new attitudes. But even more important than the submission to external authorities was the fact that the authorities were internalized, that man became the slave of a master inside himself instead of one outside. This internal master drove the individual to relentless work and striving for success and never allowed him to be himself and enjoy himself. There was a spirit of distrust and hostility directed not only against the outside world, but also toward one's own self.

This modern type of man was selfish in a twofold sense: he had little concern for others and he was anxiously concerned with his own advantage. But was this selfishness really a concern for himself as an individual, with all his intellectual and sensual potentialities? Had "he" not become the appendix of his socio-economic role, a cog in the economic machine, even if sometimes an important cog? Was he not the slave of this machine even if he subjectively felt as if he were following his own orders? Was his selfishness identical with self-love or was it instead rooted in the very lack of it?

We must postpone answering these questions, since we have still to finish a brief survey of the doctrine of selfishness in modern society. The taboo on selfishness has been reinforced in the authoritarian systems. One of the ideological cornerstones of National-Socialism is the principle: "Public good takes precedence over private good." According to the original propaganda technique of National-Socialism, the thought was phrased in a form purposed to permit the workers to believe in the "socialist" part of the Nazi program. However, if we consider its meaning in the context of the whole Nazi philosophy, the implication is this: the individual should not want anything for himself; he should find his satisfaction in the elimination of his individuality and in participating as a small particle in the greater whole of the race, the state or its symbol, the leader. While Protestantism and Calvinism emphasized individual liberty and responsibility even as it emphasized the nothingness of the individual, Nazism is focused essentially on the latter. Only the "born" leaders are an exception, and even they should feel themselves as instruments of someone higher up in the hierarchy—the supreme leader as an instrument of destiny.

The doctrine that love for oneself is identical with "selfishness," and that it is an alternative to love for others has pervaded theology, philosophy and the pattern of daily life; it would be surprising if one would not find the same doctrine also in scientific psychology, but here as an allegedly objective statement of facts. A case in point is Freud's theory on narcissism. He says, in short, that man has a certain quantity of libido. Originally, in the infant, all this libido has as its objective the child's own person, *primary narcissism*.

Later on, the libido is directed from one's own person toward other objects. If a person is blocked in his "object-relationships," the libido is withdrawn from the objects and returned to one's own person, *secondary narcissism*. According to Freud, there is an almost mechanical alternative between ego-love and object love. The more love I turn toward the outside world the less love I have for myself, and vice versa. Freud is thus moved to describe the phenomenon of falling in love as an impoverishment of one's self-love because all love is turned to an object outside of oneself. Freud's theory of narcissism expresses basically the same idea which runs through protestant religion, idealistic philosophy, and the everyday patterns of modern culture. This by itself does not indicate that he is right or wrong. Yet, this translation of the general principle into the categories of empirical psychology gives us a good basis for examining the principle.

These questions arise: Does psychological observation support the thesis that there is a basic contradiction and the state of alternation between love for oneself and love for others? Is love for oneself the same phenomenon as selfishness, is there a difference or are they in fact opposites?

Before we turn to the discussion of the empirical side of the problem, it may be noted that from a philosophical viewpoint, the notion that love for others and love for oneself are contradictory is untenable. If it is a virtue to love my neighbor as a human being, why must not I love myself too? A principle which proclaims love for man but which taboos love for myself, exempts me from all other human beings. The deepest experience of human existence, however, is to have this experience with regard to oneself. There is no solidarity of man in which I myself am not included. A doctrine which proclaims such an exclusion proves its objective insincerity by this very fact.[6]

We have come here to the psychological premises on which the conclusions of this paper are built. Generally, these premises are: not only others, but also we ourselves are the "object" of our feelings and attitudes; the attitude toward others and toward ourselves, far from being contradictory, runs basically parallel. With regard to the problem under discussion this means: Love for others and love for ourselves are not alternatives. Neither are hate for others and hate for ourselves alternatives. On the contrary, an attitude of love for themselves will be found in those who are at least capable of loving others. Hatred against oneself is inseparable from hatred against others, even if on the surface the opposite seems to be the case. In other words, love and hatred, in principle, are indivisible as far as the difference between "objects" and one's own self is concerned.

[6]This thought is expressed in the biblical: "Love thy neighbor as thyself!" The implication is that respect of one's own integrity and uniqueness, love for and understanding of one's own self, cannot be separated from respect, love and understanding with regard to another individual. The discovery of my own self is inseparably connected with the discovery of any other self.

To clarify this thesis, it is necessary to discuss the problem of hatred and love. With regard to hatred one can differentiate between "reactive hatred" and "character-conditioned hatred." By reactive hatred I mean a hatred which is essentially a reaction to an attack on one's life, security, or ideals or on some other person that one loves and identifies oneself with. Its premise is one's positive attitude toward one's life, toward other persons and toward ideals. If there is a strong affirmation of life, a strong hatred necessarily is aroused if life is attacked. If there is love, hatred must be aroused if the loved one is attacked. There is no passionate striving for anything which does not necessitate hatred if the object of this striving is attacked. Such hatred is the counterpoint of life. It is aroused by a specific situation, its aim is the destruction of the attacker and, in principle, it ends when the attacker is defeated.

Character-conditioned hatred is different. To be sure, the hatred rooted in the character structure once arose as a reaction to certain experiences undergone by the individual in his childhood. It then became a character trait of the person; he *is* hostile. His basic hostility is observable even when it is not giving rise to manifest hatred. There is something in the facial expression, gestures, tone of voice, kind of jokes, little unintentional reactions which impress the observer as indications of the fundamental hostility, which also could be described as a continuous *readiness* to hate. It is the basis from which active hatred springs if and when it is aroused by a specific stimulus. This hate reaction can be perfectly rational; as much so, as a matter of fact, as is the case in the situations which were described as arousing reactive hatred. There is, however, a fundamental difference. In the case of reactive hatred it is the situation which *creates* the hatred. In the case of character-conditioned hatred an "idling" hostility is *actualized* by the situation. In the case where the basic hatred is aroused, the person involved appears to have something like a feeling of relief, as though he were happy to have found the rational opportunity to express his lingering hostility. He shows a particular kind of satisfaction and pleasure in his hatred which is missing in the case of an essentially reactive hatred.

In the case of a proportionality between hate reaction and external situation, we speak of a "normal" reaction, even if it is the actualization of character-conditioned hatred. From this normal reaction to an "irrational" reaction found in the neurotic or psychotic person, there are innumerable transitions and no sharp demarcation line can be drawn. In the irrational hate-reaction, the emotion seems disproportionate to the actual situation. Let me illustrate by referring to a reaction which psychoanalysts have ample opportunity to observe; an analysand has to wait ten minutes because the analyst is delayed. The analysand enters the room, wild with rage at the offense done to him by the analyst. Extreme cases can be observed more clearly in psychotic persons; in those the disproportionality is still more striking. Psychotic hatred will be aroused by something which from the standpoint of reality is not at all offensive. Yet, from the standpoint of his own feeling it is offensive, and thus the irrational reaction is irrational only from the standpoint of external objective reality, not from the subjective premises of the person involved.

The lingering hostility can also be purposely aroused and turned into manifest hatred by social suggestion; that is, propaganda. If such propaganda which wants to instill people with hatred toward certain objects is to be effectual, it must build upon the character-conditioned hostility in the personality structure of the members of the groups to which it appeals. A case in point is the appeal of Nazism to the group which formed its nucleus, the lower middle class. Latent hostility was peculiarly the lot of the members of this group long before it was actualized by Nazi propaganda and that is why they were such fertile soil for this propaganda.

Psychoanalysis offers ample opportunity to observe the conditions responsible for the existence of hatred in the character structure.

The decisive factors for arousing character-conditioned hatred may be stated to be all the different ways by which spontaneity, freedom, emotional and physical expansiveness, the development of the "self" of the child are blocked or destroyed.[7] The means of doing this are manifold; they vary from open, intimidating hostility and terror, to a subtle and "sweet" kind of "anonymous authority," which does not overtly forbid anything but says: "I know you will or will not like this or that." Simple frustration of instinctual impulses does not create deep seated hostility; it only creates a reactive hate reaction. Yet, this was Freud's assumption and his concept of the Oedipus Complex is based on it; it implies that the frustration of sexual wishes directed toward the father or mother creates hatred which in its turn leads to anxiety and submission. To be sure, frustration often appears as a symptom of something which does create hostility; not taking the child seriously, blocking his expansiveness, not allowing him to be free. But the real issue is not isolated

---

[7]In recent years, a number of psychologists were interested in the problem of uncovering the hostility, consciously or unconsciously, present in children. Some of them were very successful in demonstrating the presence of strong hostility in very young children. A method which proved to be particularly fruitful was to arrange play situations in which the children expressed their hostility very clearly. According to Bender, Lauretta, and Schilder, Paul, Aggressiveness in Children. *Genetic Psychology Monographs* (1936) 18:410-425, the younger the children were the more directly they expressed hostility, while with the older ones the hate-reaction was already repressed but could be clearly observed in a play situation. Compare also Levy, David M., *Studies in Sibling Rivalry* V; New York, American Orthopsychiatric Association, 1937 (96pp). L. Murphy and G. Lerner have found normal children who seem quite conventionally adjusted to the nursery-school play group, revealing intense aggression in a free play situation, alone with one adult. J. Louise Despert has come to similar conclusions. Hartoch, A., and Schachtel, E. have found expression of strong aggressiveness in Rorschach tests in two to four year old children who did not show proportionate amount of manifest aggressiveness in their behavior.

frustration but the fight of the child against those forces which tend to suppress his freedom and spontaneity. There are many forms in which the fight for freedom is fought and many ways in which the defeat is disguised. The child may be ready to internalize the external authority and be "good," it may overtly rebel and yet remain dependent. It may feel that it "belongs" by completely conforming to the given cultural patterns at the expense of the loss of its individual self—the result is always a lesser or greater degree of inner emptiness, the feeling of nothingness, anxiety and resulting from all that a chronic hatred, the *ressentiment,* which Nietzsche characterized very well as *Lebensneid,* envy of life.

There is a slight difference, however, between hatred and this envy of life. The aim of hatred is in the last analysis the destruction of the object outside of my self. By destroying it I attain strength in relative, although not in absolute terms. In envy of life, the begrudging attitude aims at the destruction of others too; not, however, in order to gain relative strength, but to have the satisfaction that others are being denied the enjoyment of things which—for external or inner reasons—I cannot enjoy myself. It aims at removing the pain, rooted in my own inability for happiness, by having nobody else who by his very existence demonstrates what I am lacking.[8]

In principle, the same factors condition the development of chronic hatred in a group. The difference here as in general between individual psychology and social psychology is only to be found in this: while in individual psychology, we are looking for the individual and accidental conditions which are responsible for those character traits by which one individual varies from other members of his group, in social psychology we are interested in the character structure as far as it is common to and, therefore, typical of the majority of the members of that group. As to the conditions, we are not looking for accidental individual conditions like an overstrict father or the sudden death of a beloved sister, but for those conditions of life which are a common experience for the group as such. This does not mean the one or the other isolated trait in the whole mode of life, but the total structure of basic life experiences as they are essentially conditioned by the socio-economic situation of a particular group.

The child is imbued with the "spirit" of a society long before it makes the direct acquaintance with it in school. The parents represent in their own character structure the spirit prevalent in their society and class and transmit

[8]It should be noted that sadism has to be differentiated from hatred. As I see it, the aim of sadism is not destruction of the subject, but a seeking to have absolute power over it, to make it an instrument of oneself. Sadism can be blended with hatred; in this case it will have the cruelty usually implied in the notion of sadism. It can also be blended with sympathy in which case the impulse is to have the object as an instrument and, at the same time, to further him in any way excepting in one: letting him be free.

this atmosphere to the child from the day of his birth onward. The family thus is the "psychic agency" of society.

The bearing on our problem of the differentiation in hatred will have become clear by now. While in the case of reactive hatred the stimulus which is at the same time the object, constitutes the "cause" for the hatred; in the case of character-conditioned hatred, the basic attitude, the readiness for hatred, exists regardless of an object and before a stimulus makes the chronic hostility turn into manifest hatred. As has been indicated, originally, in childhood, this basic hatred was brought into existence by certain people, but later it has become part of the personality structure and objects play but a secondary role. Therefore, in its case, there is, in principle, no difference between objects outside of myself and my own self. The idling hostility is always there; its outside objects change according to circumstances and it but depends on certain factors whether I myself become one of the objects of my hostility. If one wants to understand why a certain person is hated in one case, why I myself am hated in another case, one has to know the specific factors in the situation which make others or myself the object of manifest hatred. What interests us in this context, however, is the general principle that character-conditioned hatred is something radiating from an individual and like a searchlight focussing sometimes on this and sometimes on that object, among them myself.

The strength of basic hatred is one of the major problems of our culture. In the beginning of this paper, it has been shown how Calvinism and Protestantism pictured man as essentially evil and contemptible. Luther's hatred against the revolting peasants is of extraordinary intensity.

Max Weber has emphasized the distrust for and hostility toward others which runs through the Puritan literature replete with warnings against having any confidence in the help and friendliness of our fellow men. Deep distrust even toward one's closest friend is recommended by Baxter. Th. Adams says: "He—the 'knowing' man—is blind in no man's cause but best sighted in his own. He confines himself to the circle of his own affairs and thrusts not his fingers in needless fires . . . . He sees the falseness of it [the world] and, therefore, learns to trust himself ever, others so far as not to be damaged by their disappointments."

Hobbes assumed that man's nature was that of a predatory animal, filled with hostility, set to kill and rob. Only by the consensus of all, submitting to the authority of the state, could peace and order be created. Kant's opinion of man's nature is not too distant from Hobbes, he too thought that man's nature had a fundamental propensity for evil. Among psychologists, chronic hatred as an inherent part of human nature has been a frequent assumption. William James considered it as being so strong that he took for granted that we all feel a natural repulsion against physical contact with other persons.

Freud, in his theory of the death instinct, assumed that for biological reasons, we all are driven by an irresistible force to destroy either others or ourselves.

Although some of the philosophers of the enlightenment period believed that the nature of man was good and that his hostility was the product of the circumstances under which he lives, the assumption of hostility as an inherent part of man's nature runs through the ideas of representative thinkers of the modern era from Luther up to our days. We need not discuss whether this assumption is tenable. At any rate, the philosophers and psychologists who held this belief were good observers of man within their own culture, even though they made the mistake of believing that modern man in his essence is not a historical product but is as nature made him to be.

While important thinkers clearly saw the strength of hostility in modern man, popular ideologies and the convictions of the average man tend to ignore the phenomenon. Only a relatively small number of people have an awareness of their fundamental dislike for others. Many have only a feeling of just having little interest or feeling for others. The majority are completely unaware of the intensity of the chronic hatred in themselves as well as in others. They have adopted the feelings that they know they are supposed to have: to like people, to find them nice, unless or until they have actually committed an act of aggression. The very indiscriminateness of this "liking people" shows its thinness or rather its compensatory quality as a basic lack of fondness.

While the frequency of underlying distrust and dislike for others is known to many observers of our social scene, the dislike for oneself is a less clearly recognized phenomenon. Yet, this self-hatred may be considered rare only so long as we think of cases in which people quite overtly hate or dislike themselves. Mostly, this self-dislike is concealed in various ways. One of the most frequent indirect expressions of self-dislike are the inferiority feelings so widespread in our culture. Consciously, these persons do not feel that they dislike themselves: what they do feel is only that they are inferior to others, that they are stupid, unattractive or whatever the particular content of the inferiority feelings is.[9]

To be sure, the dynamics of inferiority feelings are complex and there are factors other than the one with which we are dealing. Yet, this factor is never missing and dislike for oneself or at least a lack of fondness for one's own person is always present and is dynamically an important factor.

A still more subtle form of self-dislike is the tendency toward constant self-criticism. These people do not feel inferior but if they make one mistake, discover something in themselves which should not be so, their self-criticism

---

[9]Industry, for instance, capitalizes the unconscious self-dislike by terrorizing people with the threat of "body odor." The unconscious dislike the average person has for himself makes him an easy prey for this suggestion.

is entirely out of proportion to the significance of the mistake or the short-coming. They must either be perfect according to their own standards, or at least perfect enough according to the standards of the people around them so that they get affection and approval. If they feel that what they did was perfect or if they succeed in winning other people's approval, they feel at ease. But whenever this is missing they feel overwhelmed by an otherwise repressed inferiority feeling. Here again, the basic lack of fondness for themselves is one source from which the attitude springs. This becomes more evident if we compare this attitude toward oneself with the corresponding one toward others. If, for example, a man who believes that he loves a woman should feel if she makes any mistake that she is no good, or if his feeling about her is entirely dependent on whether others criticize or praise her, we cannot doubt that there is a fundamental lack of love for her. It is the person who hates who seizes every opportunity to criticize another person and who does not miss any blunder.

The most widespread expression of the lack of fondness for oneself, however, is the way in which people treat themselves. People are their own slave drivers; instead of being the slaves of a master outside of themselves, they have put the master within. This master is harsh and cruel. He does not give them a moment's rest, he forbids them the enjoyment of any pleasure, does not allow them to do what they want. If they do so, they do it furtively and at the expense of a guilty conscience. Even the pursuit of pleasure is as compulsory as is work. It does not lead them away from the continual restlessness which pervades their lives. For the most part, they are not even aware of this. There are some exceptions. Thus, the banker, James Stillman, who, when in the prime of life, had attained wealth, prestige and power reached only by but few people said: I never in my life have done what I wanted and never shall do so.

The role of "conscience" as the internationalization of external authorities and as the bearer of deep seated hostility against oneself has been seen clearly by Freud in the formulation of his concept of the Super-Ego. He assumed that the super-ego contains a great deal of the basic destructiveness inherent in man and turns it against him in terms of duty and moral obligation. In spite of objections to Freud's Super-Ego theory, which cannot be presented here, Freud undoubtedly has sensed keenly the hostility and cruelty contained in the "conscience" as it was conceived in the modern era.

What holds true of hostility and hatred holds also true of love. Yet, love for others and self-love is by far a more difficult problem to discuss; and this for two reasons. One is the fact that while hatred is a phenomenon to be found everywhere in our society and, therefore, an easy object for empirical observation and analysis, love is a comparatively rare phenomenon, which lends itself to empirical observation only under difficulties; any discussion of love, therefore, implies the danger of being unempirical and merely speculative. The other difficulty is perhaps even greater. There is no word in our language which has been so much misused and prostituted as the word "love." It has been preached by those who were ready to condone every cruelty if it served their purpose; it has been used as a disguise under which to force people into sacrificing their own happiness, into submitting their whole self to those who profited from this surrender. It has been used as the moral basis for unjustified demands. It has been made so empty that for many people *love* may mean no more than that two people have lived together for 20 years just without fighting more often than once a week. It is dangerous and somewhat embarrassing to use such a word. Yet a psychologist may not properly succumb to this embarrassment. To preach love is at best bad taste. But to make a cool and critical analysis of the phenomenon of love and to unmask pseudo-love—tasks which cannot be separated from each other—is an obligation that the psychologist has no right to avoid.

It goes without saying that this paper will not attempt to give an analysis of love. Even to describe the psychological phenomena which are conventionally covered by the term "love" would require a good part of a book. One must attempt, however, the presentation necessary to the main trend of thought of this paper.

Two phenomena closely connected with each other are frequently presented as love—the masochistic and sadistic *love*. In the case of masochistic *love,* one gives up one's self, one's initiative and integrity in order to become submerged entirely in another person who is felt to be stronger. Because of deep anxieties which give rise to the feeling that one cannot stand on one's own feet, one wants to be rid of one's own individual self and to become part of another being, thus becoming secure and finding a center which one misses in oneself. This surrender of one's own self has often been praised as the example of "the great love." It is actually a form of idolatry, and also an annihilation of the self. The fact that it has been conceived as love has made it the more seductive and dangerous.

The sadistic *love* on the other hand springs from the desire to swallow its object to make him a will-less instrument in one's own hands. This drive is also rooted in a deep anxiety and an inability to stand alone, but instead of finding increased strength by being swallowed, strength and security are found in having a limited power over the other person. The masochistic as well as the sadistic kind of love are expressions of one basic need which springs from a basic inability to be independent. Using a biological term, this basic need may be called a "need for symbiosis." The sadistic *love* is frequently the kind of love that parents have for their children. Whether the domination is overtly authoritarian or subtly "modern" makes no essential difference. In either case, it tends to undermine the strength of the self of the child and leads in later years to the development in him of the very same symbiotic tendencies. The sadistic love is not infrequent among adults. Often in relationships of long duration, the respective roles are permanent, one partner representing the sadistic, the other one the masochistic pole of the symbiotic relationship. Often the roles change constantly—a continuous struggle for dominance and submission being conceived as *love*.

It appears from what has been said that love cannot be separated from freedom and independence. In contradiction to the symbiotic pseudo-love, the basic premise of love is freedom and equality. Its premise is the strength, independence, integrity of the self, which can stand alone and bear solitude. This premise holds true for the loving as well as for the loved person. Love is a spontaneous act, and spontaneity means—also literally—the ability to act of one's own free volition. If anxiety and weakness of the self makes it impossible for the individual to be rooted in himself, he cannot love.

This fact can be fully understood only if we consider what love is directed toward. It is the opposite of hatred. Hatred is a passionate wish for destruction; love is a passionate affirmation of its "object."[10] That means that love is not an "affect" but an active striving, the aim of which is the happiness, development, and freedom of its "object." This passionate affirmation is not possible if one's own self is crippled, since genuine affirmation is always rooted in strength. The person whose self is thwarted, can only love in an ambivalent way; that is, with the strong part of his self he can love, with the crippled part he must hate.[11]

The term *passionate affirmation* easily leads to misunderstanding; it does not mean intellectual affirmation in the sense of purely rational judgment. It implies a much deeper affirmation, in which one's personality takes part as a whole; one's intellect, emotion and senses. One's eyes, ears and nose are often as good or better organs of affirmation than one's brain. If it is a deep and passionate one, the affirmation is related to the essence of the "object," not merely toward partial qualities. There is no stronger expression of God's love for man in the Old Testament than the saying at the end of each day of creation: "And God saw that it was good."

There is another possible misunderstanding which should particularly be avoided. From what has been said, one might come to the conclusion that every affirmation is love, regardless of the worthiness of the object to be

[10]Object is put into quotation marks because in a love relationship the "object" ceases to be an object; that is, something opposite to and separated from the subject. Not accidentally do "object" and "objection" have the same root.

[11]Sullivan has approached this formulation in his lectures. He states that the era of preadolescence is characterized by the appearance of impulses in interpersonal relations which make for a new type of satisfaction in the pleasure of the other person (the chum). Love, according to him, is a situation in which the satisfaction of the loved one is exactly as significant and desirable as that of the lover.

loved. This would mean that love is a purely subjective feeling of affirmation and that the problem of objective values does not enter into it. The question arises: Can one love the evil? We come here to one of the most difficult problems of psychology and philosophy, a discussion of which can scarcely be attempted here. I must repeat, however, that affirmation in the sense here used is not something entirely subjective. Love is affirmation of life, growth, joy, freedom and by definition, therefore, the evil which is negation, death, compulsion cannot be loved. Certainly, the subjective feeling can be a pleasurable excitement, consciously conceived in the conventional term of love. The person is apt to believe that he loves, but analysis of his mental content reveals a state very different from what I have discussed as love. Much the same question arises with regard to certain other problems in psychology, for instance, the problem as to whether happiness is an entirely subjective phenomenon or whether it includes an objective factor. Is a person who feels "happy" in dependence and self-surrender happy because he feels to be so, or is happiness always dependent on certain values like freedom and integrity? One has always used the argument that the people concerned are "happy" to justify their suppression. This is a poor defense. Happiness cannot be separated from certain values, and is not simply a subjective feeling of satisfaction. A case in point is masochism. A person can be satisfied with submission, with torture, or even with death, but there is no happiness in submission, torture or death. Such considerations seem to leave the ground of psychology and to belong to the field of philosophy or religion. I do not believe that this is so. A sufficiently refined psychological analysis, which is aware of the difference in the qualities of feelings according to the underlying personality structure, can show the difference between *satisfaction* and *happiness.* Yet, psychology can be aware of these problems only if it does not try to separate itself from the problem of values. And, in the end does not shrink from the question of the goal and purpose of human existence.

Love, like character-conditioned hatred, is rooted in a basic attitude which is constantly present; a readiness to love, a *basic sympathy* as one might call it. It is started, but not caused, by a particular *object*. The ability and readiness to love is a character trait just as is the readiness to hate.[12] It is difficult to say what the conditions favoring the development of this *basic sympathy* are. It seems that there are two main conditions, a positive and a negative one. The positive one is simply to have experienced love from others as a child. While conventionally, parents are supposed to *love* their children as a matter of course, this is rather the exception than the rule. This positive condition is, therefore, frequently absent. The negative condition is the absence of all those

---

[12]It would be most unfortunate to assume that these respective readinesses are characteristics of different personalities. Many people present concomitant readinesses of both varieties.

factors, discussed above, which make for the existence of a chronic hatred. The observer of childhood experiences may well doubt that the absence of these conditions is frequent.

From the premise that actual love is rooted in a *basic sympathy* there follows an important conclusion with regard to the *objects* of love. The conclusion is, in principle, the same as was stated with regard to the objects of chronic hatred: the objects of love do not have the quality of exclusiveness. To be sure, it is not accidental that a certain person becomes the *object* of manifest love. The factors conditioning such a specific choice are too numerous and too complex to be discussed here. The important point, however, is that love for a particular *object* is only the actualization and concentration of lingering love with regard to one person; it is not, as the idea of *romantic love* would have it, that there is only *the* one person in the world whom one could love, that it is the great chance of one's life to find that person, and that love for him or her results in a withdrawal from all others. The kind of love which can only be experienced with regard to one person demonstrates by this very fact that it is not love, but a symbiotic attachment. The basic affirmation contained in love is directed toward the beloved person as an incarnation of essentially human qualities. Love for one person implies love for man as such. The kind of "division of labor" as William Jones calls it; namely, to love one's family, but to be without feeling for the "stranger," is a sign of a basic inability to love. Love for man as such is not, as it is frequently supposed to be, an abstraction coming "after" the love for a specific person, or an enlargement of the experience with a specific *object;* it is its premise, although, genetically, it is acquired in the contact with concrete individuals.

From this, it follows that my own self, in principle is as much an object of my love as another person. The affirmation of my own life, happiness, growth, freedom is rooted in the presence of the basic readiness of and ability for such an affirmation. If an individual has this readiness, he has it also toward himself; if he can only *love* others, he cannot love at all. In one word, love is as indivisible as hatred with regard to its *objects.*

The principle which has been pointed out here, that hatred and love are actualizations of a constant readiness, holds true for other psychic phenomena. Sensuality, for instance, is not simply a reaction to a stimulus. The sensual or as one may say, the erotic person, has a basically erotic *attitude* toward the world. This does not mean that he is constantly excited sexually. It means that there is an erotic *atmosphere* which is actualized by a certain object, but which is there underneath before the *stimulus* appears. What is meant here is not the physiologically given ability to be sexually excited, but an atmosphere of erotic readiness, which under a magnifying glass could be observed also when the person is not in a state of actual sexual excitement. On the other hand, there are persons in whom this erotic readiness is lacking. In them, sexual excitement is essentially caused by a stimulus operating on the sexual instinct. Their threshold of stimulation can vary between wide limits, but there is a common quality in this type of sexual excitement; namely, its separateness from the whole personality in its intellectual and emotional qualities. Another illustration of the same principle is in the sense of beauty. There is a type of personality who has a readiness to see beauty. Again, that does not mean that he is constantly looking at beautiful pictures, or people, or scenery; yet, when he sees them a continuously present readiness is actualized, and his sense of beauty is not simply *aroused* by the object. Here too, a very refined observation shows that this type of person has a different way of looking at the world, even when he looks at objects which do not stimulate an acute perception of beauty. We could give many more examples for the same principle, if space permitted. The principle should already be clear: While many psychological schools[13] have thought of human reactions in terms of stimulus-response, the principle presented here is that character is a structure of numerous *readinesses* of the kind mentioned, which are constantly present and are actualized but not caused by an outside stimulus. This view is essential for such a dynamic psychology as psychoanalysis is.

Freud assumed that all these readinesses are rooted in biologically given instincts. It is here assumed that although this holds true for some of them, many others have arisen as a reaction to the individual and social experiences of the individual.

One last question remains to be discussed. Granted that love for oneself and for others in principle runs parallel, how do we explain the kind of *selfishness* which obviously is in contradiction to any genuine concern for others. The *selfish* person is only interested in himself, wants everything for himself, is unable to give with any pleasure but is only anxious to take; the world outside himself is conceived only from the standpoint of what he can get out of it; he lacks interest in the needs of others, or respect for their dignity and integrity. He sees only himself, judges everyone and everything from the standpoint of its usefulness to him, is basically unable to love. This selfishness can be manifest or disguised by all sorts of unselfish gestures; dynamically it is exactly the same. It seems obvious that with this type of personality there is a contradiction between the enormous concern for oneself and the lack of concern for others. Do we not have the proof here that there exists an alternative between concern for others and concern for oneself? This would certainly be the case if selfishness and self-love were identi-

[13]Although the reflexological viewpoint seems to be similar to the one taken here, this similarity is only a superficial one. The reflexological viewpoint means a pre-formed readiness of neurones to react in a certain way to a certain stimulus. Our viewpoint is not concerned with these physical conditions and, what is more important, by *readiness* we mean an actually present but only lingering, or idling attitude, which makes for a basic atmosphere or Grundstimmung.

cal. But this assumption is the very fallacy which had led to so many mistaken conclusions with regard to our problem. Selfishness and self-love far from being identical, actually are opposites.

Selfishness is one kind of greediness.[14] Like all greediness, it contains an insatiability, as a consequence of which there is never any real satisfaction. Greed is a bottomless pit which exhausts the person in an endless effort to satisfy the need without ever reaching satisfaction. This leads to the crucial point: close observation shows that while the selfish person is always anxiously concerned with himself, he is never satisfied, is always restless, always driven by the fear of not getting enough, of missing something, of being deprived of something. He is filled with burning envy of anyone who might have more. If we observe still closer, especially the unconscious dynamics, we find that this type of person is basically not fond of himself but deeply dislikes himself. The puzzle in this seeming contradiction is easy to solve. The selfishness is rooted in this very lack of fondness for oneself. The person who is not fond of himself, who does not approve of himself, is in a constant anxiety concerning his own self. He has not the inner security which can exist only on the basis of genuine fondness and affirmation. He must be concerned about himself, greedy to get everything for himself, since basically his own self lacks security and satisfaction. The same holds true with the so-called narcissistic person, who is not so much overconcerned with getting things for himself as with admiring himself. While on the surface it seems that these persons are very much in love with themselves, they actually are not fond of themselves, and their narcissism—like selfishness—is an overcompensation for the basic lack of self-love. Freud has pointed out that the narcissistic person has withdrawn his love from others and turned it toward his own person. While the first part of this statement is true, the second one is a fallacy. He neither loves others nor himself.[15].

It is easier to understand this mechanism when we compare it with overconcern and overprotectiveness for others. Whether it is an oversolicitous mother or an overconcerned husband, sufficiently deep observation shows always one fact: While these persons consciously believe that they are particularly fond of the child or husband, there actually is a deep repressed hostility toward the very objects of their concern. They are overconcerned because they have to compensate not only for a lack of fondness but for an actual hostlity.

The problem of selfishness has still another aspect. Is not the sacrifice of one's own person the extreme expression of unselfishness, and, on the other

---

[14]The German word *Selbstsucht* (addiction to self) very adequately expresses this quality common to all *Sucht*.

[15]Since Freud thinks only in the framework of his instinctual concepts, and since a phenomenon like love in the same sense used here does not exist in his system, the conclusions to which he comes are all but inevitable.

hand, could a person who loves himself make that supreme sacrifice? The answer depends entirely on the kind of sacrifice that is meant. There is one *sacrifice,* as it has been particularly emphasized in recent years by Fascist philosophy. The individual should give himself up for something outside of himself which is greater and more valuable; the Leader, the race. The individual by himself is nothing and by the very act of self-annihilation for the sake of the higher power finds his destiny. In this concept, sacrificing oneself for something or someone greater than oneself is in itself the greatest attainable virtue. If love for oneself as well as for another person means basic affirmation and respect, this concept is in sharp contrast to self-love. But there is another kind of sacrifice: If it should be necessary to give one's life for the preservation of an idea which has become part of oneself or for a person whom one loves, the sacrifice may be the extreme expression of self-affirmation. Not, of course, an affirmation of one's physical self, but of the self in the sense of the kernel of one's total personality. In this case the sacrifice in itself is not the goal; it is the price to be paid for the realization and affirmation of one's own self. While in this latter case, the sacrifice is rooted in self-affirmation, in the case of what one might call the masochistic sacrifice, it is rooted in the lack of self-love and self-respect; it is essentially nihilistic.

The problem of selfishness has a particular bearing on psychotherapy. The neurotic individual often is *selfish* in the sense that he is blocked in his relationship to others or overanxious about himself. This is to be expected since to be *neurotic* means that the integration of a strong self has not been achieved successfully. To be *normal* certainly does not mean that it has. It means, for the majority of *well-adapted* individuals that they have lost their own self at an early age and replaced it completely by a *social self* offered to them by society. They have no neurotic conflicts because they themselves, and, therefore, the discrepancy between their selves and the outside world has disappeared. Often the neurotic person is particularly *unselfish,* lacking in self-assertion and blocked in following his own aims. The reason for this *unselfishness* is essentially the same as for the *selfishness.* What he is practically always lacking is self-love. This is what he needs to become *well.* If the *neurotic* becomes well, he does not become *normal* in the sense of the conforming *social self.* He succeeds in realizing his self, which never had been completely lost and for the preservation of which he was struggling by his neurotic symptoms. A theory, therefore, as Freud's on narcissism which rationalizes the cultural pattern of denouncing self-love by identifying it with *selfishness,* can have but devastating effects therapeutically. It increases the taboo on self-love. Its effects can only be called *positive* if the aim of psychotherapy is not to help the individual to be himself; that is, free, spontaneous and creative—qualities conventionally reserved for *artists*—

but to give up the fight for his self and conform to the cultural pattern peacefully and without the noise of a neurosis.

In the present era, the tendency to make of the individual a powerless atom is increasing. The authoritarian systems tend to reduce the individual to a will-less and feelingless instrument in the hands of those who hold the reins; they batter him down by terror, cynicism, the power of the state, large demonstrations, fierce orators and all other means of suggestion. When finally he feels too weak to stand alone, they offer him satisfaction by letting him participate in the strength and glory of the greater whole, whose powerless part he is. The authoritarian propaganda uses the argument that the individual of the democratic state is *selfish* and that he should become unselfish and socially minded. This is a lie. Nazism substituted the most brutal selfishness of the leading bureaucracy and of the state for the selfishness of the average man. The appeal for unselfishness is the weapon to make the average individual still more ready to submit or to renounce. The criticism of democratic society should not be that people are too selfish; this is true but it is only a consequence of something else. What democracy has not succeeded in is to make the individual love himself; that is, to have a deep sense of affirmation for his individual self, with all his intellectual, emotional, and sensual potentialities. A puritan-protestant inheritance of self-denial, the necessity of subordinating the individual to the demands of production and profit, have made for conditions from which Facism could spring. The readiness for submission, the pervert *courage* which is attracted by the image of war and self-annihilation, is only possible on the basis of a—largely unconscious—desperation, stifled by martial songs and shouts for the Fuhrer. The individual who has ceased to love himself is ready to die as well as to kill. The problem of our culture, if it is not to become a fascist one, is not that there is too much selfishness but that there is no self-love. The aim must be to create those conditions which make it possible for the individual to realize his freedom, not only in a formal sense, but by asserting his total personality in his intellectual, emotional, sensual qualities. This freedom is not the rule of one part of the personality over another part—conscience over nature, Super-Ego over Id—but the integration of the whole personality and the factual expression of all the potentialities of this integrated personality.

48. Culture and Neurosis

Karen Horney

I N the psychoanalytic concept of neuroses a shift of emphasis has taken place: whereas originally interest was focussed on the dramatic symptomatic picture, it is now being realized more and more that the real source of these psychic disorders lies in character disturbances, that the symptoms are a manifest result of conflicting character traits, and that without uncovering and straightening out the neurotic character structure we cannot cure a neurosis. When analyzing these character traits, in a great many cases one is struck by the observation that, in marked contrast to the divergency of the symptomatic pictures, character difficulties invariably center around these same basic conflicts.

These similarities in the content of conflicts present a problem. They suggest, to minds open to the importance of cultural implications, the question of whether and to what extent neuroses are moulded by cultural processes in essentially the same way as "normal" character formation is determined by these influences; and, if so, how far such a concept would necessitate certain modifications in Freud's views of the relation between culture and neurosis.

In the following remarks I shall try to outline roughly some characteristics typically recurring in all our neuroses. The limitations of time will allow us to present neither data—good case histories—nor method, but only results. I shall try to select from the extremely complex and diversified observational material the essential points.

There is another difficulty in the presentation. I wish to show how these neurotic persons are trapped in a vicious circle. Unable to present in detail the factors leading up to the vicious circle, I must start rather arbitrarily with one of the outstanding features, although this in itself is already a complex product of several interrelated, developed mental factors. I start, therefore, with the problem of competition.

Abridged from the *American Sociological Review*, 1936, 1, 221-235. Reprinted by permission of Marianne Horney Eckardt, M.D., and of the American Sociological Society.

The problem of competition, or rivalry, appears to be a never-failing center of neurotic conflicts. How to deal with competition presents a problem for everyone in our culture; for the neurotic, however, it assumes dimensions which generally surpass actual vicissitudes. It does so in three respects:

(1) There is a constant measuring-up with others, even in situations which do not call for it. While striving to surpass others is essential for all competitive situations, the neurotic measures up even with persons who are in no way potential competitors and have no goal in common with him. The question as to who is the more intelligent, more attractive, more popular, is indiscriminately applied towards everyone.

(2) The content of neurotic ambitions is not only to accomplish something worth while, or to be successful, but to be absolutely best of all. These ambitions, however, exist in fantasy mainly—fantasies which may or may not be conscious. The degree of awareness differs widely in different persons. The ambitions may appear in occasional flashes of fantasy only. There is never a clear realization of the powerful dramatic role these ambitions play in the neurotic's life, or the great part they have in accounting for his behavior and mental reactions. The challenge of these ambitions is not met by adequate efforts which might lead to realization of the aims. They are in queer contrast to existing inhibitions towards work, towards assuming leadership, towards all means which would effectually secure success. There are many ways in which these fantastic ambitions influence the emotional lives of the persons concerned: by hypersensitivity to criticism, by depressions or inhibitions following failures, etc. These failures need not necessarily be real. Everything which falls short of the realization of the grandiose ambitions is felt as failure. The sucess of another person is felt as one's own failure.

This competitive attitude not only exists in reference to the external world, but is also internalized, and appears as a constant measuring-up to an ego-ideal. The fantastic ambitions appear on this score as excessive and rigid demands towards the self, and failure in living up to these demands produces depressions and irritations similar to those produced in competition with others.

(3) The third characteristic is the amount of hostility involved in neurotic ambition. While intense competition implicity contains elements of hostility— the defeat of a competitor meaning victory for oneself—the reactions of neurotic persons are determined by an insatiable and irrational expectation that no one in the universe other than themselves should be intelligent, influential, attractive, or popular. They become infuriated, or feel their own endeavors condemned to futility, if someone else writes a good play or a scientific paper or plays a prominent role in society. If this attitude is strongly accentuated, one may observe in the analytical situation, for ex-

ample, that these patients regard any progress made as a victory on the part of the analyst, completely disregarding the fact that progress is of vital concern to their own interests. In such situations they will disparage the analyst, betraying, by the intense hositality displayed, that they feel endangered in a position of paramount importance to themselves. They are as a rule completely unaware of the existence and intensity of this "no one but me" attitude, but one may safely assume and eventually always uncover this attitude from reactions observable in the analytical situation, as indicated above.

This attitude easily leads to a fear of retaliation. It results in a fear of success and also in a fear of failure: "If I want to crush everyone who is successful, then I will automatically assume identical reactions in others, so that the way to success implies exposing me to the hostility of others. Furthermore: if I make any move towards this goal and fail, then I shall be crushed." Success thus becomes a peril and any possible failure becomes a danger which must at all costs be avoided. From the point of view of all these dangers it appears much safer to stay in the corner, be modest and inconspicuous. In other and more positive terms, this fear leads to a definite recoiling from any aim which implies competition. This safety device is assured by a constant, accurately working process of automatic self-checking.

This self-checking process results in inhibitions, particularly inhibitions towards work, but also towards all steps necessary to the pursuit of one's aims, such as seizing opportunities, or revealing to others that one has certain goals or capacities. This eventually results in an incapacity to stand up for one's own wishes. The peculiar nature of these inhibitions is best demonstrated by the fact that these persons may be quite capable of fighting for the needs of others or for an impersonal cause. They will, for instance, act like this:

When playing an instrument with a poor partner, they will instinctively play worse than he, although otherwise they may be very competent. When discussing a subject with someone less intelligent than themselves, they will compulsively descend below his level. They will prefer to be in the rank and file, not to be identified with the superiors, not even to get an increase in salary, rationalizing this attitude in some way. Even their dreams will be dictated by this need for reassurance. Instead of utilizing the liberty of a dream to imagine themselves in glorious situations, they will actually see themselves, in their dreams, in humble or even humiliating situations.

This self-checking process does not restrict itself to activities in the pursuit of some aim, but going beyond that, tends to undermine the self-confidence, which is a prerequisite for any accomplishment, by means of self-belittling. The function of self-belittling in this context is to eliminate oneself from any competition. In most cases these persons are not aware of actually disparaging themselves, but are aware of the results only as they feel themselves inferior to others and take for granted their own inadequacy.

The presence of these feelings of inferiority is one of the most common psychic disorders of our time and culture. Let me say a few more words about them. The genesis of inferiority feelings is not always in neurotic competition. They present complex phenomena and may be determined by various conditions. But that they do result from, and stand in the service of, a recoiling from competition, is a basic and ever-present implication. They result from a recoiling inasmuch as they are the expression of a discrepancy between high-pitched ideals and real accomplishment. The fact, however, that these painful feelings at the same time fulfill the important function of making secure the recoiling attitude itself, becomes evident through the vigor with which this position is defended when attacked. Not only will no evidence of competence or attractiveness ever convince these persons, but they may actually become scared or angered by any attempt to convince them of their positive qualities.

The surface pictures resulting from this situation may be widely divergent. Some persons appear thoroughly convinced of their unique importance and may be anxious to demonstrate their superiority on every occasion, but betray their insecurity in an excessive sensitivity to every criticism, to every dissenting opinion or every lack of responsive admiration. Others are just as thoroughly convinced of their incompetence or unworthiness, or of being unwanted or unappreciated; yet they betray their actually great demands in that they react with open or concealed hostility to every frustration of their unacknowledged demands. Still others will waver constantly in their self-estimation between feeling themselves all-important and feeling, for instance, honestly amazed that anyone pays any attention to them.

If you have followed me thus far, I can now proceed to outline the particular vicious circle in which these persons are moving. It is important here, as in every complex neurotic picture, to recognize the vicious circle, because, if we overlook it and simplify the complexity of the processes going on by assuming a simple cause-effect relation, we either fail to get an understanding of the emotions involved, or attribute an undue importance to some one cause. As an example of this error, I might mention regarding a highly emotion-charged rivalry attitude as derived directly from rivalry with the father. Roughly, the vicious circle looks like this:

The failures, in conjunction with a feeling of weakness and defeat, lead to a feeling of envy towards all persons who are more successful, or merely more secure or better contented with life. This envy may be manifest or it may be repressed under the pressure of the same anxiety which led to a repression of, and a recoiling from, rivalry. It may be entirely wiped out of consciousness and represented by the substitution of a blind admiration; it may be kept from awareness by a disparaging attitude towards the person concerned. Its effect, however, is apparent in the incapacity to grant to others what one has been forced to deny oneself. At any rate, no matter to what degree the envy is repressed or expressed, it implies an increase in the existing hostility against people and consequently an increase in the anxiety, which now takes the particular form of an irrational fear of the envy of others.

The irrational nature of this fear is shown in two ways: (1) it exists regardless of the presence or absence of envy in the given situation; and (2) its intensity is out of proportion to the dangers menacing from the side of the envious competitors. This irrational side of the fear of envy always remains unconscious, at least in non-psychotic persons, therefore it is never corrected by a reality-testing process, and is all the more effective in the direction of reinforcing the existing tendencies to recoil.

Consequently the feeling of one's own insignificance grows, the hostility against people grows, and the anxiety grows. We thus return to the beginning, because now the fantasies come up, with about this content: "I wish I were more powerful, more attractive, more intelligent than all the others, then I should be safe, and besides, I could defeat them and step on them." Thus we see an ever-increasing deviation of the ambitions towards the stringent, fantastic, and hostile.

This pyramiding process may come to a standstill under various conditions, usually at an inordinate expense in loss of expansiveness and vitality. There is often some sort of resignation as to personal ambitions, in turn permitting the diminution of anxieties as to competition, with the inferiority feelings and inhibitions continuing.

It is now time, however, to make a reservation. It is in no way self-evident that ambition of the "no-one-but-me" type must necessarily evoke anxieties. There are persons quite capable of brushing aside or crushing everyone in the way of their ruthless pursuit of personal power. The question then is: Under what special condition is anxiety invoked in neurotically competitive people?

The answer is that they at the same time want to be loved. While most persons who pursue an asocial ambition in life care little for the affection or the opinion of others, the neurotics, although possessed by the same kind of competitiveness, simultaneously have a boundless craving for affection and appreciation. Therefore, as soon as they make any move towards self-assertion, competition, or success, they begin to dread losing the affection of others, and must automatically check their aggressive impulses. This conflict between ambition and affection is one of the gravest and most typical dilemmas of the neurotics of our time.

Why are these two incompatible strivings so frequently present in the same individual? They are related to each other in more than one way. The briefest formulation of this relationship would perhaps be that they both grow out of the same sources, namely, anxieties, and they both serve as a means of reassurance against the anxieties. Power and affection may both be safeguards. They generate each other, check each other, and reinforce each other. These interrelations can be observed most accurately within the analytic situation, but sometimes are obvious from only a casual knowledge of the life history.

In the life history may be found, for instance, an atmosphere in childhood lacking in warmth and reliability, but rife with frightening elements—battles between the parents, injustice, cruelty, oversolicitiousness—generation of an increased need for affection—disappointments—development of an outspoken competitiveness—inhibition—attempts to get affection on the basis of weakness, helplessness, or suffering. We sometimes hear that a youngster has suddenly turned to ambition after an acute disappointment in his need for affection, and then given up the ambition on falling in love.

Particularly when the expansive and aggressive desires have been severely curbed in early life by a forbidding atmosphere, the excessive need for reassuring affection will play a major role. As a guiding principle for behavior this implies a yielding to the wishes or opinions of others rather than asserting one's own wishes or opinions; an overvaluation of the significance for one's own life of expressions of fondness from others, and a dependence on such expressions. And similarly, it implies an overvaluation of signs of rejection and a reacting to such signs with apprehension and defensive hostility. Here again a vicious circle begins easily and reinforces the single elements: In diagram it looks somewhat like this:

Anxiety plus repressed hostility
    Need for reassuring affection
        Anticipation of, sensitivity to, rejection
            Hostile reactions to feeling rejected

These reactions explain why emotional contact with others that is attained on the basis of anxiety can be at best only a very shaky and easily shattered bridge between individuals, and why it always fails to bring them out of their emotional isolation. It may, however, serve to cope with anxieties and even get one through life rather smoothly, but only at the expense of growth and personality development, and only if circumstances are quite favorable.

Let us ask now, which special features in our culture may be responsible for the frequent occurrence of the neurotic structures just described?

We live in a competitive, individualistic culture. Whether the enormous economic and technical achievements of our culture were and are possible only on the basis of the competitive principle is a question for the economist or sociologist to decide. The psychologist, however, can evaluate the personal price we have paid for it.

It must be kept in mind that competition not only is a driving force in economic activities, but that it also pervades our personal life in every respect. The character of all our human relationships is moulded by a more or less outspoken competition. It is effective in the family between siblings, at school, in social relations (keeping up with the Joneses), and in love life.

In love, it may show itself in two ways: the genuine erotic wish is often overshadowed or replaced by the merely competitive goal of being the most popular, having the most dates, love letters, lovers, being seen with the most desirable man or woman. Again, it may pervade the love relationship itself. Marriage partners, for example, may be living in an endless struggle for supremacy, with or without being aware of the nature or even of the existence of this combat.

The influence on human relations of this competitiveness lies in the fact that it creates easily aroused envy towards the stronger ones, contempt for the weaker, distrust towards everyone. In consequence of all these potentially hostile tensions, the satisfaction and reassurance which one can get out of human relations are limited and the individual becomes more or less emotionally isolated. It seems that here, too, mutually reinforcing interactions take place, so far as insecurity and dissatisfaction in human relations in turn compel people to seek gratification and security in ambitions strivings, and vice versa.

Another cultural factor relevant to the structure of our neurosis lies in our attitude towards failure and success. We are inclined to attribute success to good personal qualities and capacities, such as competence, courage, enterprise. In religious terms this attitude was expressed by saying that success was due to God's grace. While these qualities may be effective—and in certain periods, such as the pioneer days, may have represented the only conditions necessary—this idealogy omits two essential facts: (1) that the possibility for success is strictly limited; even external conditions and personal qualities being equal, only a comparative few can possibly attain success; and (2) that other factors than those mentioned may play the decisive role, such as, for example, unscrupulousness or fortuitous circumstances. Inasmuch as these factors are overlooked in the general evaluation of success, failures, besides putting the person concerned in a factually disadvantageous position, are bound to reflect on his self-esteem.

The confusion involved in this situation is enhanced by a sort of double moral. Although, in fact, success meets with adoration almost without regard to the means employed in securing it, we are at the same time taught to regard modesty and an undemanding, unselfish attitude as social or religious virtues, and are rewarded for them by praise and affection. The particular difficulties which confront the individual in our culture may be summarized as follows: for the competitive struggle he needs a certain amount of available aggressiveness; at the same time, he is required to be modest, unselfish, even self-sacrificing. While the competitive life situation with the hostile tensions involved in it creates an enhanced need of security, the chances of attaining a feeling of safety in human relations—love, friendship, social contacts—are at the same time diminished. The estimation of one's personal value is all too dependent on the degree of success attained, while at the same time the possibilities for success are limited and the success itself is dependent, to a great extent, on fortuitous circumstances or on personal qualities of an asocial character.

Perhaps these sketchy comments have suggested to you the direction in which to explore the actual relationship of our culture to our personality and its neurotic deviations. Let us now consider the relation of this conception to the views of Freud on culture and neurosis.

The essence of Freud's views on this subject can be summarized, briefly, as follows: Culture is the result of a sublimation of biologically given sexual and aggressive drives—"sexual" in the extended connotation Freud has given the term. Sublimation presupposes unwitting suppression of these instinctual drives. The more complete the suppression of these drives, the higher the cultural development. As the capacity for sublimating is limited, and as the intensive suppression of primitive drives without sublimation may lead to neurosis, the growth of civilization must inevitably imply a growth of neurosis. Neuroses are the price humanity has to pay for cultural development.

The implicit theoretical presupposition underlying this train of thought is the belief in the existence of biologically determined human nature, or, more precisely, the belief that oral, anal, genital, and aggressive drives exist in all human beings in approximately equal quantities.[1] Variations in character formation from individual to individual, as from culture to culture, are due, then, to the varying intensity of the suppression required, with the addition that this suppression can affect the different kinds of drives in varying degrees.

This viewpoint of Freud's seems actually to encounter difficulties with two groups of data. (1) Historical and anthropological findings do not support the assumption that the growth of civilization is in a direct ratio to the growth of instinct suppression. (2) Clinical experience of the kind indicated in this paper suggests that neurosis is due not simply to the quantity

[1]I pass over Freud's recognition of individual Constitutional difference.

of suppression of one or the other instinctual drives, but rather to difficulties caused by the conflicting character of the demands which a culture imposes on its individuals. The differences in neuroses typical of different cultures may be understood to be conditioned by the amount and quality of conflicting demands within the particular culture.

In a given culture, those persons are likely to become neurotic who have met these culturally determined difficulties in accentuated form, mostly through the medium of childhood experiences; and who have not been able to solve their difficulties, or have solved them only at great expense to personality.

49. Primary Affect Hunger

David M. Levy

IN a previous study of maternal overprotection an investigation was made of a mother-child relationship featured by an excess of maternal love. This excess was demonstrated overtly in maternal behavior through physical and social contact with the child, infantilization, extra precautions and protective behavior. Definite criteria of a relationship were set up, and cases selected, out of a large number, in which the criteria were satisfied. Case studies were thereby utilized in the form of an experiment, as though to say: If we could make an experimental study of such a relationship, we would have to satisfy certain conditions. Let us see if in a large body of case material such conditions are already satisfied. Naturally, the more definite and numerous the criteria the fewer the number of cases that can be filtered out by this process. The advantage, however, is that the greater the selectivity, the "purer" the relationship to be studied.

During the study of maternal overprotection, it was necessary to select, for the purpose of contrast studies, cases of maternal rejection. In the latter group, however, selective criteria were never adequately worked out. Since the investigation of the overprotective groups was terminated by the

Abridged from the *American Journal of Psychiatry*, 1937, 94, 643-652. Reprinted by permission of the author and The American Psychiatric Association.

closing of the Institute for Child Guidance, a staff was no longer available for study of the numerous details that were part of the undertaking. In the absence of such aids to a companion study of maternal rejection, it is necessary to have recourse to a simpler method. I must, therefore, in this paper, utilize illustrative cases to indicate certain basic dynamic principles, without statistical aids. Furthermore, this study is limited in its orientation to the child who suffers the rejection. It is also limited to the experience of a certain type of rejection, to which I am applying the name "affect hunger."

The term, affect hunger, is used to mean an emotional hunger for maternal love and those other feelings of protection and care implied in the mother-child relationship. The term has been utilized to indicate a state of privation due primarily to a lack of maternal affection, with a resulting need, as of food in a state of starvation. Since the symptoms of affect hunger are clearly manifested in children who receive maternal care and direction to a high degree in a physical and intellectual sense, though without any evidence of affection, the analogy is more accurately related to a vitamin deficiency rather than to a gross starvation. The use of the term affect hunger, rather than affection or love hunger, opens the possibility, also, of a privation of other sources of the emotional life, even possibility of hostility, though this is yet to be investigated. A child who has been overprotected and later, through the birth of another child, thrown into a rejected state, may also suffer affect hunger. In the present paper, however, I am using the term to apply only to individuals who have suffered lack of maternal love in the early years of life. Assuming for the moment the value of maternal love as an essential component in the development of the emotional life, what happens when this element is left out of the primary social relationship? Is it possible that there results a deficiency disease of the emotional life, comparable to a deficiency of vital nutritional elements within the developing organism?

My first example is an eight-year-old girl who was adopted a year and a half before referral. After an illegitimate birth, the child was shifted about from one relative to another, finally brought to a child placing agency, and then placed in a foster home for two months before she came to the referring foster parents. The complaints were lying and stealing. The parents described the child's reaction to the adoption as very casual. When they brought her home and showed her the room she was to have all for herself, and took her on a tour of the house and grounds, she showed apparently no emotional response. Yet she appeared very vivacious and "affectionate on the surface." After a few weeks of experience with her, the mother complained to the husband that the child did not seem able to show any affection. The child, to use the mother's words, "would kiss you but it would mean nothing." The husband told his wife that she was expecting too much, that she should give the child a chance to get adapted to the situation. The mother was somewhat mollified by these remarks, but still insisted that something was wrong. The father said he saw nothing wrong with the child. In a few months, however, he made the same complaint. By this time, also, it was noted that the child was deceitful and evasive. All methods of correction were of no avail. A psychoanalyst was seen. He recommended that the parents stop all correction and give the child a great deal of affection. This method was tried, according to both parents, with no result. The school teacher complained of her general inattention, and her lack of pride in the way her things looked. However, she did well in her school subjects, in keeping with her good intelligence. She also made friends with children, though none of these were close friendships. After a contact of a year and a half with the patient the father said, "You just can't get to her," and the mother remarked, "I have no more idea today what's going on in that child's mind than I knew the day she came. You can't get under her skin. She never tells what she's thinking or what she feels. She chatters but it's all surface."

I have selected this case as my first illustration of a type of difficulty that is familiar to everyone who works with children, because I feel reasonably sure that the parents were distinctly affectionate with children, and also because their own child, aged twelve, was affectionate and well adjusted.

Repeated experience in the treatment of the type of child referred, indicates a poor prognosis. Before considering this phase of the problem, I would like to cite further examples.

An unmarried woman, aged forty, adopted a child aged two years and eight months, through private arrangement. The child was the illegitimate son of a woman of high economic and social status. The family history was negative. The child was turned over to an agency very soon after birth, placed in an orphanage from age 12 to 27 months and then transferred to a boarding home, where he remained until the period of adoption. After a year, the mother gave up the possibility of getting any emotional relationship with the child. She had never been able to get any sign of affection from him. He never accepted her fondling. In the household there was a doting and indulgent grandmother, to whom the child also did not respond. The mother felt she had been taking punishment for a year and could stand it no longer. Besides the lack of emotional response, she complained chiefly of his negativistic behavior. According to tests the child had superior intelligence, and the physical examination was negative.

The third example is that of a boy adopted at the age of three. The previous history was unknown, except that he was illegitimate and had been shifted around from place to place. A Wassermann test and physical examination made at the time were negative. I examined him at the age of eight years. There was a good health history, and the physical examination was negative. According to tests, the intelligence was adequate. He was referred because he had been twice suspended from school for poor work, and the fact that he made a general nuisance of himself. The mother had given up hope of making any relationship with him. He showed no affectionate response. Although she made several trips aways from home, he never asked about her when she was away. Punishment or ordinary methods of correction had no effect. He would "forget" too easily. His behavior in the office was quite infantile, I thought like that of a three year old boy. He showed a complete lack of appreciation of his difficulties at school and at home. There was no question of some distinct emotional deficiency in his response.

The fourth case is another example of an adopted child, a girl aged nine years and ten months at the time of referral to the Institute for Child Guidance. She was referred for general incorrigibility. She was adopted at the age of seven months into a home in which the foster mother could give little affection, but demanded highly conventional behavior. Before the referral, she had been seen by two psychiatrists, one in consultation and the other for a series of about twelve interviews. She had also received thyroid treatment for a period of time, though our findings showed no evidence of physical difficulty. Our examination revealed, besides the problems for which she was referred, fantastic lying, difficulty in making any friendly relationships wth children, and school retardation. The parents noted especially her "failure to profit by experience" and "unresponsiveness to affection." The problem was complicated by the fact that the home was of a superior type in a cultural sense—requirements that were too high for a child with an I. Q. of 80. The entire history led to the conclusion that the patient had some inadequacy in her emotional response and was an unfavorable subject for therapy. The parents were, throughout the long contact that ensued, conscientious in cooperating with every therapeutic effort. The patient was treated by the psychiatrist, utilizing chiefly a psychoanalytic method, for a period of two years. The behavior of the patient during the process of over 200 sessions were markedly negativistic. There were some interesting periods of improvement. Nevertheless, the result of the entire therapy was practically nil. At the end of the treatment, the parents were willing to consider another therapeutic adventure before referring the child to foster care. Through special circumstances, it was possible to send the child to Vienna, where she was treated by a psychiatrist of the Adlerian school, with whom she lived for a period of three years. The results were essentially negative; indeed, the child's problems became more alarming because of her greatly increased aggression. She was thereupon sent to her own mother and very quickly got into difficulty because of her incorrigibility and because, somehow or other, she had managed to collect five revolvers. From there she was sent to an orphanage, from which she ran away on two occasions, and then to a detention home, from which the psychiatrist wrote that he considered the patient an excellent prospect for intensive psychotherapy. At the last notation patient was eighteen. It is interesting that the typical attitude of the psychiatrist was that she would respond to psychotherapy. I have cited this case especially to show the failure of psychotherapy to meet these problems.

These case illustrations are given as examples of emotional pathology caused by primary affect hunger of a severe degree. The symptom-complaints are of various types. They include, frequently, aggressive sexual behavior in early life, stealing, lying, often of the fantastic type, and, essentially, complaints, variously expressed, that indicate some lack of emotional response in the child. It is this lack of emotional response, this shallowness of affect, that explains the difficulty in modifying behavior. The inhibitions to the instinctive impulses, normally strengthened by the response to maternal affection, are no longer in operation. As an instrument in modifying behavior, the power of maternal love may be seen most clearly in life histories where it is absent—a kind of ablation experiment in social life. That the difficulty in these cases is due to a primary affect hunger seems a reasonable assumption, even though not proven by any direct experiment or by statistical checks. Does it follow, necessarily, that any child who suffers complete loss of maternal love, during the infantile period, will develop into a psychopathic personality of the type described? Further, in a number of cases in which a child was given presumably normal maternal love, in the first two years of life, the same difficulties may occur when an attempt at adoption is made at this age. Such cases were sufficiently numerous in my experience to warrant the advice that adoptions be made either in the first year of life, or after the infantile period. It was assumed that when the early emotional attachments were made by the child, as the personality began to grow, a break at this stage caused a situation similar to one in which the child could make no emotional attachment to start with.

There is an interesting bit of evidence on the prognosis in cases of primary affect hunger in a recent issue of the American Journal of Orthopsychiatry. Eighty-one delinquent girls were treated by a combination of social and psychotherapy. Successes and failures were tabulated by follow-up studies varying from one to five years, after discharge from the home. One of the investigators independently analyzed the parent-child relationships and classified them into four groups. The successes and failures were then checked against these classifications. They illustrate a finding already determined in previous studies, to wit that the cooperation of the parent is the most important item in prognosis. One finding, however, is especially striking, namely, that the 17 cases in which there was evidence of complete rejection, showed 100 per cent failure in response to therapy. This is in contrast with the general result of 50 per cent success for the group. The case examples of complete rejection cited are extreme and convincing.

In contrast with the extreme cases of affect hunger we have, at the other end of the scale, a series of children whose difficulties are solved by the restoration of maternal love. In such cases psychotherapy may be either unnecessary or merely a complementary therapy. There are a number of children who do well with affectionate foster parents, or with a psychiatrist who renders the therapeutic relationship primarily supportive. This type of treatment, to which the name supportive therapy has been given, is a recognition of the fact that in certain cases the child's hunger for love must be gratified. It is recognized that in every therapeutic relationship the patient receives some support of this type (transference) but there are cases in which the treatment must be primarily, even exclusively, supportive; a treatment in which the worker acts *in loco parentis*. Favorable results with such children are often utilized to prove the particular merits of this or the other type of psychotherapy, whereas it matters little what technique is used as long as the child feels loved.

A patient was referred to the Institute for Child Guidance at the age of nine years, with a complaint of enuresis and temper tantrums. A visitor to the foster home wrote a letter to the Institute from which the following excerpt is taken: "He is starved for affection. His mother rarely visits him, although she is urged to do so frequently. When she is there, he acts very infantile, climbing up on her lap, always wishing to be with her, and showing off. Then as time elapses after her visit, he becomes more unmanageable and disagreeable." The history of the case is featured by the child's affectionate response to grown-ups, his making up to any stranger, the explosive and dangerous temper tantrums, and marked jealousy of the other children in the foster home. The "hunger" element in the difficulty is seen in the response to grownups and to the mother, with whom he acts in complete disregard of what is usually a strong inhibiting influence—the presence of other boys. When his mother is about he is always sitting in her lap, he holds his face up to be kissed and puts his arms around her neck. According to the foster mother, he acts in these situations quite like an infant. Though affectionate to the foster mother, he makes no such display with her. The severity of the temper tantrums must be mentioned. On one occasion he tried to break up a game which the other boys were playing. The foster mother sent him to his room, whereupon he tore up the bedding and pulled all the pictures off the walls. On another occasion he attempted to hit a boy with an axe. On another, he chased the teacher and the children out of school.

The patient lived with his father and mother in the first year of life. After the death of the father he was placed in an institution for a year, then for two years in a boarding home, from which he was removed by his mother. He was placed again with the previous boarding mother. He was moved again to a foster home in which he had been living for a year and four months at the time of referral. There are certain elements in the history that indicate a certain modicum of affection from the mother and in the homes in which he was placed. In one boarding home there was an affectionate mother. The foster mother also was affectionate with him. Furthermore, his own mother, though very spasmodic and infrequent in her visits, was affectionate while with him.

In this case, treatment consisted in getting placement with a foster mother who could give him a great deal of affection. There were only four interviews with the psychiatrist. They consisted largely of chats about the foster home. Marked improvement in behavior occurred and continued for two years. A follow-up study made when the patient was twelve years six months old, showed complete cessation of the temper tantrums, good school adjustment, growth in responsibility, though no improvement in the enuresis.

The case described illustrates a very frequent problem for social agencies. A number of cases in the Institute for Child Guidance series show a growing adjustment under the care of an affectionate foster mother. Such therapeutic benefit may occur even in the adolescent group. However, the stumbling block is often the mother of the child, who continues sporadic contact. She visits the child once a week, more commonly once in several weeks, and thereby prevents the building up of a stable relationship with the foster parent. Furthermore, the fact that the child is under foster care while his own mother is still in contact with him, stimulates various fantasies of abandonment, confusion about his own place in the world, sometimes even a confusion of self-identity, often an illusion that the mother who has really abandoned him is a loving and protecting mother. Agencies seem to foster this illusion on the part of the child, because otherwise they would feel guilty of encouraging hostile feelings toward the mother. The mother who has given the child to foster care, yet refuses to give up the child for adoption, is motivated by her feelings of guilt over the rejection and thereby acts as a great handicap to the child's stability. Frequently, also, we have instances in which the mother removes the child from one boarding home, has the child live with her for a week, and then through the agency gets another placement. Because of her own guilt, also, she may find all kinds of fault with different foster mothers. It is not unexpected, therefore, that a recent follow-up in the case of this patient, now age 18, shows this type of history: discharged from a foster mother to his own mother, back to another foster mother, truancies to his own mother, then placement in a farm school.

In a similar case, presented by Dr. Blanchard at the last meeting of the American Orthopsychiatric Association, the main psychodynamics are clearly discernible. (1) A group of activities representing responses to the primary need. They are manifested in various manoeuvers to hold closely to a person, to win demonstrations of affection, to plead for love, to utilize pathetic appeals and states of helplessness, in order to stimulate a love response from a mother-person. The kissing-bug reaction represents an avidity for physical affection, as illustrated in the previous case, and belongs in this category of responses. So also a number of the whiners and pleaders and naggers for attention, for closeness and for guarantees that the maternal sustenance will never be withdrawn. Out of this group, also, are derived the mechanisms of constant begging for gifts, also of making overwhelming demands from a friendship later in life, to insure against any possible break in the relationship. (2) A group of activities that represent various hostile acts designed to punish the one who denies love and to prevent the possibility of its withdrawal. The mother who has denied or withheld stimulates a hostile rejoinder in the form of wishes for her death, various sadistic fantasies, even threats to her life, also threats of suicide if she will not respond. The conscious level of these performances varies, but they may be overtly expressed. The temper tantrums, possibly also the enuresis may be manifestations in this group, as may all types of "bad" behavior. (3) A group of symptoms that are based on the child's fear of the hostile impulses. These represent the source of the emotional conflicts and neurotic derivatives of the original state of privation. Fear of death is a manifestation. In fact, for every hostile move there is a retaliatory fear. There are a number of interesting derivatives from this state that have to do with the feeling of being deprived, and its consequences. These have to do with various forms of self-pity, the creation in the individual of helpless states, and even depression, but time does not allow these elaborations.

So far I have cited two types of response to affect hunger, one, the extreme instance in which the emotional development of the child has been adversely affected from the start, with a resulting pathology of affect; the other, an instance in which the renewal of maternal love has a successful restorative function. There now remains a large mid-group of cases in which the problems derivative of the early affect hunger are marked by special and usually persistent relationship difficulties. They follow along the lines in which the denials of maternal love and affection are especially marked.

In the last case cited, a boy who made up to every adult, we have an example of what may become a characteristic of every relationship. Such examples are better seen in those adults, whose social life represents a series of relationships with older people, every one of whom is a substitute mother. They must be single or in combination, the point being simply that the patient must, throughout life, be in contact with a person from whom the same demands are made that were thwarted in the original experience with the mother. The life pattern then becomes dependent on maintaining such relationships. When one of them is broken there is a period of depression, or a feeling that "something is terrifically lacking," until another relationship is made. Another type of reaction is seen in the form chiefly of excessive demands made on the person who is selected to satisfy the privations of early life. Such examples also represent a distinctive cluster of cases seen in social agencies, especially in children who have difficulty in adapting to the foster home. The story is typically that the child makes a good impression, the foster parents are delighted, and then, within a week or two, the demands of the child become so excessive that the foster parents are worn out and insist on release from their charge. The problem is always the same—excessive demands for food, for money, for privileges. Attempts to satisfy them end always in disaster. They represent, it seems to me, the child's need of proof that the adult is a loving parent because he satisfies every requirement that is made, also a hostile motive to destroy by getting things out of them. It is as though the child has to repeat the original frustration. A recent example comes to me of a delinquent boy who, in relation with the social worker, tried to get money from her. It was put on the basis that "if you love me you will do this for me." If the demand was not satisfied, then refrain would be "then this shows that you don't care for me." Every attempt made at giving insight into the relationship failed. The patient showed initiative in getting a job but quit in a short time because he thought he deserved more money, they should give him more time for lunch, etc., etc. Other jobs were terminated for the same reasons. The patient was able to respond only to stern necessity. He was never modified by therapeutic methods.

No doubt there are a number of children who feel a distinct lack that is related to an original privation, who, nevertheless, are in a state of externally good adjustment. Such children naturally are not referred for treatment, since it is rare that a child is not brought to treatment through an adult. There are, certainly, numerous examples of adults, well adjusted according to the criteria of overt behavior, with complaints of various dissatisfactions, chiefly in the form of futility, or depression, that have their origin primarily in affect hunger. How much of the difficulty is related to a true deficiency in the infantile period, and how much is due to neurotic mechanisms is a question that the psychoanalyst is in the best position to solve, but I feel sure that there are numerous instances in which the deficiency is covered by neurosis, and the difficulty mistakenly attributed to the overlying structure. At least, a recognition of this fact will compel a reorientation to the life history.

The responses described seem to pick out special elements of privation in the mother-child relationship. In the social relationship the protective phase of maternal care may be sought; or the giving function in maternal care may be the special point of attack. In others, it may be the mere demonstration of affection, including also genital satisfaction. These elements represent special incompleteness in the early emotional development of the patient and must be demonstrable in numerous phases of the life history, of which this account can only be a rough sketch.

I have tried in this study to indicate certain basic responses to affect hunger, showing a group of cases in which there are pathologic residues due to an extreme deficiency; second, a group in which the restoration of maternal love has marked therapeutic effect; and third, a group which demonstrates specialized difficulties in social relationships that are derivatives of a primary affect hunger.

50. The Feeling of Inferiority and the Striving for Recognition

Alfred Adler

(Translated by Walter Beran Wolfe, M. D.)

I. THE SITUATION IN
EARLY CHILDHOOD

WE recognize the fact that children who have been treated as step-children by Nature have an entirely different attitude toward life and their fellow creatures from that of those to whom the joys of existence were vouchsafed at an early age. It may be stated as a fundamental law that children who come into the world with organic defects become involved at an early age in a struggle with the facts of existence which results only too soon in the suppression of

Abridged from the *Proceedings of The Royal Society of Medicine*, 1927, 20, 1181-1186. Reprinted by permission of The Royal Society of Medicine.

their social feeling. Such children are continually preoccupied with themselves and the impression they make upon others, instead of interesting themselves in an adjustment to their fellows. What holds good for organic defects is equally valid in the case of any social or economic disability which manifests itself as an additional burden capable of producing a hostile attitude toward the environment. The deciding trend becomes determined at an early age, and such children have an intuition, even at the age of two, that they are somehow not as adequately equipped for the struggle as their playmates, and have a sense that they cannot trust themselves in the common games and pastimes. As a result of past privations they have acquired a feeling of being neglected, which expresses itself in their tendency to hold themselves in an attitude of anxious expectation. It is necessary to remember that every child occupies an inferior position in life, and were it not for a certain quantum of social feeling on the part of his environment would be incapable of independent existence. One can realize that, at the commencement of every life, there must be a more or less deep feeling of inferiority. This arises in the weakness and helplessness of children who are at all conscious of their inability to cope single-handed with the problems of existence. This feeling of inferiority is the driving force, the starting point, from which every childish striving originates. It determines how, and whether, this individual child acquires peace and security in life, it determines the very goal of his existence, and prepares the path along which this goal may be reached. The basis of his educability lies in this attitude, this peculiar situation in which every child finds himself, a situation very closely bound up with his organic potentialities. This educability, general as the feeling of inferiority is, may be destroyed by two factors: (1) An exaggerated, intensified, unresolved feeling of inferiority, and (2) a goal demanding not only security, peace and social equilibrium, but power over his environment, i.e., dominance over his fellows. Children who have such a goal are easily recognized and they become "problem" children, (1) because they interpret every experience as a defeat, and (2) because they always consider themselves neglected and discriminated against by both Nature and mankind. One need only consider these factors to see how readily a crooked, inadequate, error-ridden development may occur in the life of a child.

Every child runs the danger of such a development, because he finds himself, at some time or another, in a situation which is precarious.

A child finding himself in an environment of adults is predisposed to consider himself weak, small and incapable of living alone, and in such a situation is quite unable to trust himself to accomplish little tasks, which we would think him capable of performing without making mistakes, and exhibiting clumsiness of action. At this point most of our errors of education commence, and by our demanding more than the child can accomplish, the idea of his own helplessness is thrust upon him. Some children are consciously made to feel their smallness and helplessness. Then, again, there are children who are regarded as merely animated dolls, and those who are considered valuable property that must be carefully watched. Lastly, there are those who are made to feel that they are useless human freight. A combination of these attitudes on the part of parents and adults, generally leads a child to believe that he can accomplish only two things, the giving of pleasure or displeasure to his elders. The type of inferiority feeling which is produced by such an attitude on the part of the parents may be further intensified by other peculiar characteristics of our civilization. The habit of not taking children seriously falls into this category, and a child gets the impression that he is a nobody and without rights, that he is to be seen, not heard, must be courteous and quiet, etc. There are numerous children who grow up in the constant dread of being laughed at. This laughing at children is well-nigh criminal; it retains its effect upon the soul of the child, and upon his reaching adult life is transferred into habits and actions. One often recognizes an adult who was continually laughed at by his parents when a child; such individuals cannot rid themselves of the fear of being made ridiculous even on reaching maturity. Another aspect of this matter of not taking children seriously is the custom of telling children palpable lies, with the result that the child begins to doubt, not only his immediate environment, but also to question the seriousness and reality of life.

Cases have been recorded of children who laughed continually at school, seemingly without reasons, who, when questioned, admitted that they thought school was a joke of their parents, not worth taking seriously!

II. COMPENSATING FOR THE FEELING OF INFERIORITY; THE STRIVING FOR RECOGNITION AND SUPERIORITY

It is the feeling of inferiority, of inadequacy, of insecurity which determines the goal of an individual's existence. The tendency to push into prominence, to attract the attention of parents, makes itself felt in the first days of life. These are the first indications of the awakening striving for recognition which develops itself under the concomitant influence of the feeling of inferiority, and purposes a goal in which the individual is seemingly dominating his surroundings.

The degree and quality of the social feeling also helps to determine the goal of dominance. We cannot judge any individual, whether he be child or adult, without drawing a comparison between his goal of dominance and the quantum of his social feeling. His goal is so determined that its achievement promises the possibility of either a sentiment of superiority, or, at least, an elevation of the personality to such a degree that life seems worth living. It is this goal which gives value to our sensations, which links and coordinates our sentiments, which shapes our imagination, guides our creative powers and determines what we shall remember and what we must forget. We can realize how relative is the value of all our sensations, sentiments, affects, imagination, when we appreciate the fact that not even our sensations are absolute quantities. All are influenced by the striving for a definite goal, so that our very perceptions are prejudiced and always chosen, so to speak, with a secret hint at the final end and toward which the personality is striving.

We orientate ourselves according to a fixed point which we have artificially created, and which does not exist in reality. This assumption, necessary because of the inadequacy of our psychic mode of expression, is very similar to the fictions which are of use in other sciences, such as dividing the earth with meridians; these do not actually exist, but are useful assumptions. In the case of all psychic fictions we have to postulate the following: We assume a fixed point even though close observation forces us to admit that it does not exist. The purpose of this assumption is simply to orientate ourselves in the chaos of existence, so that we can come to some apperception of relative values. The advantage is that we can classify every sensation and every sentiment according to this fixed point, once we have assumed it.

Individual psychology, therefore, creates for itself a heuristic system and method; it regards human behavior, and endeavours to understand it, as though it were possible to produce a final state of affairs out of a set of inherited potentialities which are all tending to strive for a definite goal. Our experience, however, has shown us that the assumption of a striving for a goal is more than simply a convenient fiction. It has proved itself to be largely coincident with the actual facts in its fundamentals, whether these facts are to be found in the conscious or unconscious life. The striving for a goal, the purposiveness of the psychic life, is not only our philosophic attitude, but actually a fundamental fact.

When we question how we can, in a case of the child, best meet and answer the question of the abolition of that striving for power which is a prominent evil of our civilization, we are faced with the difficulty of making ourselves understood. For this striving tendency shows itself in the life of a child long before the time when it is possible to begin making attempts at improvement and clarification. Nevertheless, our living with the child, when such tendencies first occur, does afford us the opportunity of developing his social feeling so that his striving for personal power becomes a negligible factor.

A further difficulty lies in the fact that even children do not express their striving for power openly, but hide it under the guise of gentleness. They conceal their aspirations as if behind a veil, and so modestly expect to escape disclosure in this way. Their uninhibited striving for power, seeking for support, is capable of producing degeneration in their psychic development, with the result that, in their exaggerated striving for security and might, courage becomes changed to impudence, obedience into cowardice, gentleness degenerates into a subtle treachery, and the final result is that every natural feeling or expression carries with it a hypocritical afterthought the final end of which is the subjugation of the environment.

Conscious education works upon the child with the conscious, or unconscious, desire to remove him from his insecurity, to school him in the technique of life, give him a knowledge and educated understanding, and furnish him with a social feeling for his fellows. All these measures, from whatever source they come, are to be understood as attempts to give the growing child new ways of ridding himself of his insecurity and his feeling of inferiority. What happens in the soul of the child during this process we must judge by his character traits which are the mirror of the activity in his soul.

The importance of the feeling of insecurity and inferiority depends largely upon the interpretation given to it by the child; the objective degree of inferiority is important, of course, and makes itself felt.

One must not expect a child to possess the correct estimation of himself in this situation, any more than one expects adults to possess it. Here the difficulties grow apace, as one child will grow up in a situation so complicated that errors concerning the degree of his inferiority are absolutely unavoidable, while another child will be better able to interpret his situation. But taken as a whole the interpretation which the child has of his feeling of inferiority varies from day to day until it finally becomes consolidated and expresses itself as a definite self-estimation. According to this crystallized self-estimation, the compensatory trends which the child creates to guide him out of his inferiority will be directed toward this or the other goal.

The mechanism of the striving for compensation, by means of which the soul seeks to neutralize the torturing feeling of inferiority, has its analogy in the organic world. It is a well-known fact that those organs of our bodies which are essential for life produce an overgrowth and overfunction when, through damage to their normal state, their productivity is lessened. Thus, in difficulties of circulation, the heart enlarges and becomes more powerful, seeming to draw its new strength from the whole body, until it reaches a stage in which it has become more powerful than a normal heart. Similarly so, does the soul under pressure of the feeling of inferiority, of the torturing thought that the individual is small and helpless, attempt with all its might to become master over this "inferiority complex."

Where the feeling of inferiority is highly intensified, to the degree at which the child believes that he will never be able to compensate for his weakness, the danger arises that in his striving for compensation he will be satisfied not with a simple balance of power, but will strive for an extra-compensation and will aim at over-balancing the scales.

This striving for power and dominance may become exaggerated and intensified to a degree that will entitle it to be called pathological. The ordinary relationships of life will never satisfy such children, and varying with their goal, their movements will come to assume a certain grandiose gesture. They seek to secure their position in life with extraordinary efforts, with greater haste and impatience, with more intense impulses, and without consideration for anyone else. Owing to these exaggerated movements toward their exaggerated goal of dominance, such children become more noticeable, and their attacks on the lives of others necessitate defensive measures against their activities. They are against the world, and the world is against them, and this antagonism does not necessarily occur in a bad sense of the word. Such a child may express his striving for power in a manner which does not come into conflict with society for a long time, and his ambition may be considered as no abnormal characteristic. If, however, we carefully investigate their accomplishments and achievements, we shall find that for the most part society at large does not benefit from their triumphs, because their ambition is a social one and will always put them in the path of other human beings as disturbing elements. Gradually other characteristics will appear which will evince a more anti-social colour, if we consider an individual in his full relationship to his fellow-men. In the forefront of these manifestations we find pride, vanity, and the striving to conquer everyone regardless of method, and this striving may manifest itself subtly in the relative exaltation of the individual, through the degradation of all those with whom he comes in contact; the important thing being only the distance which separates him from his fellows. Such an attitude is not only uncomfortable for his neighbours, but it is also very uncomfortable for the individual, because it brings him into continual contact with the dark side of life and prevents him from experiencing any happiness.

By means of the exaggerated straining for power with which these children endeavour to ensure themselves a place over their environment, they soon put themselves in a position of resistance to the ordinary tasks and duties of everyday life. Compare such a "power-hungry" individual with the ideal social being, and one can, after some little experience, specify, so to speak, his social index, that is, the degree to which he has removed himself from his fellow-man.

The student of human nature, in observing one of these individuals, will immediately recognize that some difficulties in the evolution of the psychic

life must have occurred here, even as his eyes are open to any physical
deficiencies and inferiorities. If we keep this fact in mind we shall do no
damage to the individual's social feeling, seeing that we ourselves have
developed an adequate social feeling, and with this attitude only we can
help the individual. Bearing this in mind, we must not blame the bearer of
a psychical defect or a disagreeable characteristic for his attitude of indignation. Indeed, we must admit his right to be indignant to the last limits,
and we must be conscious that we participate in the common blame for his
situation. We share the blame because we, too, have taken part in the inadequate precautions against the social misery which has produced it. If we
abide by this standpoint we may effect improvement, and only thus can we
approach such an individual, not as a degraded, worthless outcast, but as a
fellow human being. Having this attitude toward our patient we must sur-
round him with an atmosphere in which he will find that there are possibilities for feeling himself equal to every other human being in his environment.
We have only to remind ourselves how unpleasant may be to us the sight of
an individual whose organic or bodily inferiorities are externally visible, to
judge the amount of education which we ourselves need in order to arrive
at an absolutely just evaluation of our social feeling, and to judge also how
much our civilization owes to such an individual. It is taken for granted
that those individuals who come into the world with organic defects feel
existence to be a burden from their earliest days—a suffering which most
of us are spared. They thus find themselves in a position of pessimism as
regards the whole structure of existence. Children who have less noticeable
organic defects, but in whom the feeling of inferiority has become intensified,
from whatever cause, right or wrong, find themselves in a very similar
situation. Such a feeling of inferiority may be so artificially intensified, as, for
instance, by over-pressure of education during the critical period, that the
result is exactly the same as though the child came into the world greatly
crippled. They never rid themselves of the thorn which has pierced their
side in the early days of their existence, and the coldness which they have
experienced prevents them from approaching their fellow-beings, with the
result that they believe themselves to be in a world devoid of love and
affection and with which they have no point of contact.

For example: A patient became specially noticeable because he was
continually telling us about his great sense of duty and the importance of
all his actions. He lived with his wife in the worst possible relationship, both
he and she being individuals who measured to a hair-breadth the value of
any event as a means toward the subjugation of the other partner. The result
was seen in continual wrangling, reproaches, and insults, in the course of
which the two had become entirely estranged from one another. This individual certainly retained some small portion of his social feeling for his

fellow-men, but even this was suppressed by his striving for superiority, at least so far as his wife and friends were concerned.

We learned the following facts from the story of his life. Up to his seventeenth year he was practically undeveloped physically. His voice was still the voice of a young boy, he had no hair on his face or body, and he was one of the smallest of the boys with whom he associated. Now at thirty-six years of age his external appearance is normal and is entirely masculine; Nature has seemingly caught up with herself and completed everything which she had hardly begun to fashion when he was seventeen. But for eight years he suffered from this failure of development, and he had no ground for hoping that Nature would ever compensate for the fallow time. During this entire period he was tortured with the thought that he must always remain a "child," and already the beginnings of his present characteristics could be noted. He acted as though he were very important and as if every action had the utmost weight. Every movement served the purpose of bringing him into the centre of attention. In the course of time he acquired those characteristics which we see in him today. During married life he was continually occupied with impressing upon his wife the fact that he was really bigger and more important than she thought, and she was continually busied with showing him that his assertions concerning his value were untrue! Under these circumstances their marriage (both of the partners having already shown signs of disruption during their engagement) could hardly be expected to develop favourably, and the end was a social cataclysm. At this point, however, the patient came to the physician, since the dissolution of his marriage had served only to accentuate the dilapidation of his already battered self-esteem. In order to effect a cure, the first thing to be learnt from the physician was how to know human nature, and to estimate the extent of the error he had made in life. And this error, this wrong evaluation of his inferiority, had coloured his entire life up to the time of his coming for treatment.

51. The Development and Problems of the Theory of the Instincts

Edward Bibring

THE following pages set out to give a short and simplified survey of the development of the psycho-analytical theory of the instincts. It is based essentially upon the works of Freud, since, however, tempting it may be to take into account the whole of the psycho-analytical literature, to do so would complicate our exposition too much. . . . The survey follows a chronological order (except in one place, in connection with the fourth step in the history of the theory) but naturally this does not apply to the detailed discussion of certain points.

Before embarking on my actual theme, let me say a few words about the subdivision of the branch of knowledge of which the theory of the instincts is only a part. The psycho-analytical study of the instincts is made up of two main parts, a general theory of the instincts and a specialized one. The general theory includes, besides the *concept* of instinct, the theory of the instincts in the narrower sense, that is, the question of the number and nature of the instincts, the question of the criteria of their classification, and the question of their causation and function; the general theory further includes the theory of instinctual transformation, i. e., the question of the variability of instincts and the laws which such variations (which are in part the same as what are called instinctual vicissitudes) obey; and it includes, finally, the concepts and problems connected with the energic aspect of the instincts. The specialized theory is concerned with the development of the instincts in the individual, together with the working hypotheses which that development entails and the problems to which it gives rise.

Abridged from The *International Journal of Psycho-Analysis,* 1941, 22, 102-131. Reprinted by permission of the author and The International Journal of Psycho-Analysis.

In the following pages I shall confine myself to the general theory and in particular to that part of it which is devoted to the theory of the instincts in the narrower sense. This field, too, has been the main subject of psycho-analytical discussions upon the instincts, during the last few years.

Let us begin, for the sake of clarity, with a short sketch of the history of instinctual theory. A theory of the instincts can be monistic, dualistic or pluralistic. . . . Freud's theory was a dualistic one from the beginning, and it remained so, in spite of all the changes that it underwent. What was changed was never the *number* but only the nature of the instincts, or rather the groups of instincts, that were to be distinguished.

The theory of the instincts reached its present position in four steps.

(1) The first step was the setting up of two groups of instincts—the sexual and the ego instincts. The sexual instincts were closely studied, whereas the ego instincts remained to begin with a relatively unknown quantity.

(2) The second step was an addition to the theory. The introduction of the concept of narcissism into the libido theory led to the postulation of a libidinal component of the ego instincts. Nevertheless Freud held firmly to the view that besides this libidinal component there must exist a primary, non-libidinal component; this he called 'interest' in a noncommittal way, rather in the sense of non-libidinal egoism.

(3) The third step—a step which has for the most part been overlooked in psycho-analytical writings—was that the aggressive trends were ascribed to the ego instincts as being among their essential constituents. This view was set out by Freud in the last sections of his paper on 'Instincts and their Vicissitudes' and was based upon a discussion of the relation between love and hate, in which he came to the conclusion that hate was to be regarded as a non-libidinal reaction of the ego.

(4) The fourth step was due to a growing knowledge of the structure of the mental apparatus as a whole and its division into a 'vital' stratum (the id) and an organized part (the ego), and, more especially, to a study of the unconscious region of the ego, the super-ego. The gist of this view was that the aggressive trends were no longer regarded as primary attributes of the ego instincts but as independently existent instincts of aggression and destruction existing side by side with the sexual instincts in the vital strata of the mind. The ego instincts ceased to be independent entities and were derived partly from the libidinal and partly from the aggressive instincts.

To this fourth step in the development of instinctual theory there was now added a further theory. It postulated the existence of the primal instincts—what are known as the instincts of life and of death. This postulate served to extend the theoretic basis that underlay the fourth step, to solve certain unexplained problems and to bring together and simplify the various theoretical hypotheses that had been so far set up.

I

Let us now proceed to discuss in detail and in due order these four steps in the development of instinctual theory. The first theory made a distinction between sexual and ego instincts and was set up as a result of clinical observation which showed the central importance of mental conflict in the production of neuroses. In support of it Freud adduced the beliefs of popular psychology and, more emphatically, certain biological lines of thought. In view of what will be said further on, it is important to note the following passage in his 'Instincts and ther Vicissitudes': 'I am altogether doubtful whether work upon psychological material will afford any decisive indication for the distinction and classification of instincts. Rather it would seem necessary to apply to this material certain definite assumptions in order to work upon it, and we could wish that these assumptions might be taken from some other branch of knowledge and transferred to psychology.' Thus, according to him, it is hardly possible to arrive at a classification of the instincts along purely analytical lines.

During the period when this first theory of the instincts held the field, Freud's interest was taken up with developing the sexual theory. His conclusions are mainly to be found in his *Drei Abhandlungen,* where they were given progressive formulation. The sexual theory falls naturally into three parts: (1) the thesis of the component instincts, which is linked to the concept of erotogenic zones; (2) the thesis of an ontogenetic development of the sexual instincts taking place in successive stages and following a fixed order prescribed by biological laws; and (3) the libido theory (which amplifies and underpins the first two theses) and also, perhaps, the theory of the transformations of the sexual instincts in general.

It is necessary to enter into the subject of the sexual theory at this point for two reasons. In the first place, because the concept of instinct which was arrived at in this field of knowledge and which underlay the sexual theory has been used by many writers to challange the later hypotheses put forward by Freud; and in the second place because of the quantitative view of the instincts which was held at this time and which gave way later to a qualitative one.

We will first turn to the question of the concept of instinct. According to the most usual definition, instinct is an energy arising from the vital stratum of the mind and having a direction which is determined inherently. Since many facts seem to indicate that instinct originates in organic phenomena, it can be described, with Freud, as being a borderline concept between the mental and the organic spheres. In this way the concept of instinct comes to be classed under the concept of stimulus: instinct is a stimulus of the mind, distinguishable from other kinds of stimuli in that its operation is constant and comes from the interior of the body and not from outside. Thus one can also regard it as 'a measure of the demand for work imposed upon the mind in consequence of its connection with the body.'

According to this view instinct, whatever may be the form in which it becomes a tension of psychical energy, is always, as being a stimulus, contrasted with the mental apparatus with its postulated methods of functioning. Concerning those methods of functioning themselves some assumptions are necessary, and that necessity, as we know, has led to the laying down of certain principles of mental happening and certain fundamental trends of the mental apparatus. We shall return to this point later; at the moment what we must bear in mind is that the principles or regulative mechanisms regulate the mental apparatus, while the instincts continually impose fresh demands for work upon that apparatus, so regulated. This contrast between instinct and mental activity is perhaps most clearly expressed in a passage in 'Instincts and their Vicissitudes'. There the distinction between sexual and ego instincts is described as an auxiliary construction of a provisional kind, while the thesis that there is a basic trend of the mental apparatus 'to abolish stimuli which reach it, or to reduce excitation to the lowest possible level, or even . . . to maintain itself in an altogether unstimulated condition' is laid down as a necessary postulate.

Since the instincts spring from the organic field, the question of their source becomes an important one in their classification. The three characteristics of an instinct as stressed by Freud—its source, aim and object—can be employed as criteria. Of these, the object is the most variable; the aim is less variable, though still somewhat so; but the source is relatively constant and is therefore the best qualified to serve as a basis for a classification of the instincts.

Thus at this stage, in which the sexual theory was being elaborated, the idea of source was the most important criterion of classification. The source of an instinct, being the site of its inception, is from its very nature thought of as linked to an organic event. Such an organic event is in its turn hypothetically regarded, in accordance with the theory of hormones, as a kind of chemical process—as being, possibly, an accumulation of sexual substances or a concentration of chemico-sexual processes which then undergo a fresh distribution or are perhaps dissolved. The organ from which an instinct arises usually coincides with the place at which it obtains satisfaction; or else the place of satisfaction is an organ from which some other component instinct originates.

The differentiation of the separate component instincts is based upon the various organs from which they originate—what are called the erotogenic zones. The aggregation of the component instincts into the homogeneous group of the sexual instincts is based upon their common characteristics and regular relationships. The concept of erotogenic zones is in the first instance purely descriptive and derived from the oral, anal and genital zones of the body. Their distinctive signs are experimentally verifiable, and are excitation, action and satisfaction; the last of these takes the form of characteristic pleasure-processes, which are different in the case of the oral and anal zones from those in the genital zone.

Instinct, then, is an energy which arises from the vital stratum of the mind, which has a direction that is determined inherently, which presses forward towards a particular aim and is directed somewhat loosely towards things and persons as its object. It is linked to an organ of origin as its source and to a terminal organ as the site of its satisfaction. Its satisfaction consists in the removal of those changes in the zones of excitation which accompany the instinctual tension. Or, to put it more shortly, an instinct is something that 'comes from outside', produces energy and is the cause of particular mental processes.

When the component instincts had been aggregated into the homogeneous group of the sexual instincts and had been assigned to pre-determined biological stages within the framework of sexual development, it became necessary to set up the libido theory to provide a basis and amplication. According to that theory the instincts are to be regarded as purely quantitative amounts of energy which can be variously localized (displaced) and concentrated. The qualities of the component instincts do not belong to the instincts themselves but are derived from their sources. This hypothesis made it possible to describe in a comparatively simple way the inter-relationships between the erotogenic zones, the transformations of one component instinct into another, and so on. As will be seen presently, the distinction which was afterwards made between the instinctual qualities on the basis of their *aim* made it impossible to explain those transformations without making certain other assumptions.

Meanwhile the ego instincts were being somewhat neglected. The concept of ego instincts was only a provisional one, as can be seen from Freud's formulations of it at the time. They were of a purely tentative nature; and so, at bottom, was the whole classification of the instincts. This was due partly to historical and partly to practical factors. On the one hand, it was necessary first of all to solve the problem of the structure and development of the sexual instincts—a problem which was the first to offer itself for investigation. On the other, the manifestations of the ego instincts were much more difficult to recognize. The trends emanating from the ego and their modes of expression were much more complicated and consequently harder to understand. But the main reason was that before anything could be learned about them a certain amount had to be known about the libidinal instincts.[1]

It is important to notice that the ego instincts were not regarded as on the same level as the sexual ones. In 'Instincts and their Vicissitudes' Freud formulated the psychological conflict which can be discovered at the root of every neurosis as a conflict between the demands of sexuality and the demands of the ego. Thus we see that at that time the ego instincts stood for an ego, not as yet accessible to investigation, which was governed by certain tendencies.

The criterion of source which had been used for the classification of the sexual instincts was carried over to the ego instincts, of which the nutritional instincts served as the typical example. They too could be linked with organs of origin and termination, once more with the help of hypothetical chemico-physiological processes.

II

The motive for taking the second step in the development of the theory of instincts came from the field of psychiatry. New facts appeared which could not be explained by any of the existing ideas and which necessitated a new addition to the libido theory, namely the concept of narcissism.

The concept of narcissism made the first breach in the independent existence of the ego instincts. It included three component parts: (1) A stage was introduced at the beginning of the life of the individual in which his instincts have no object. This stage was called primary narcissism. In it the object-libidinal attitude has not yet been differentiated off, just as there is no proper differentiation between the ego and the external world. The libido is either stored up in some way or other, as it is in sleep or in the embryonic state, and is 'quiescent' and perhaps not yet roused to function; or it cannot as yet be distinguished or detached from the energy and functions of the ego—it is only operative, to use Federn's word, in a 'medial' way. (2) The libido, after the separation between the ego and the external world has taken place, can take the subject's own person as its object just as well as any thing belonging to the external world. (3) By means of identification in the ego or the ego ideal, the instinctual energy can be transformed into narcissistic energy. In this case, too, it will act 'medially', that is to say, in a secondary way.

The postulation of a libidinal energy operating in the ego necessitated a revision of ideas about the ego instincts. It implied that the energy of the ego instincts was libidinal in origin and that their aims were derived from the aims of narcissistic libido directed to the subject's own self and acting within and upon it. The ego instincts were nothing more than libidinal instincts directed to the ego and hence somewhat differently organized. Just as the

[1]This applies to the situation as it was then. In the present state of our knowledge it goes without saying that a complete study of the ego pre-supposes an understanding of both the libidinal and the aggressive instincts.

reality principle, for instance, was merely a modification of the pleasure principle and yet could turn against it, so the ego instincts seemed to be libido modified in its aims, which was nevertheless able to turn against the true libidinal instincts. This hypothesis is connected with a particular view of the origin of instinctual aims. According to it the general aim of libido appears to be pleasure, but its particular aims are derived from the particular objects to which it is directed. Mental conflict is no longer a conflict between sexual and ego instincts but between parts of the sexual instinct which are directed to the external world and parts which are directed to the ego—between object-libidinal and ego-libidinal trends. This explanation of conflict as a clash between different interests was a possible one, but not easy to maintain; moreover it was too simplified to take all the facts into account.

It seemed inevitable that this undermining of the independent status of the ego instincts should throw doubts upon the dualistic character of the instinctual theory. For there was now only one group of instincts—the libidinal instincts. Instincts were no longer classified with reference to their source but primarily with reference to their relations to various objects, which in their turn seemed to modify the instincts' aim. In essentials this already implied the view that the sexual and the ego instincts were only differentiated products of a common 'primal libido'.

Nevertheless Freud kept firmly to the idea of the autonomous nature of the ego instincts. This may to a large extent have been because he had classified the instincts in accordance with biological considerations and those considerations were not at first upset by his new discovery of narcissism. The life of the individual seemed to have quite different interests from those concerned with the preservation of the species. Thus it was natural to suppose that different forces were at work. Moreover, the phenomena of sadism in its wider aspects had not as yet been explained. Freud therefore introduced the notion of ego interest in the sense of a non-libidinal egoism; or, to put it more correctly, he asserted that what was known as egoism had two components, a libidinal-narcissistic component and a non-libidinal component. Narcissism, as he wrote, is only 'the libidinal complement to the egoism of the instinct of self-preservation, a measure of which may justifiably be attributed to every living creature.' Originally these two components were undifferentiated.

Thus Freud still upheld the view that the nature of the ego instincts was originally non-libidinal. And this view was supported in the first instance by considerations of a theoretical and heuristic kind.

III

Later on, on the strength of empirical observations and theoretical arguments, the non-libidinal portions of the ego instincts were given some additional attributes which tended to confirm their independence of the libido. This constituted the third step in the development of the theory of the instincts, a step which gave the aggressive trends an independent status *vis-a-vis* the libidinal currents and classed them as belonging to the ego instincts.

Let us see what the observations and arguments were which led to this attempt to classify the instincts in this way. The most important reason was that the theory had not, so far, adequately ordered or explained the known facts.

Where the sexual instincts were concerned, it was primarily the position of their sadistic components which still lacked a sound theoretic basis. At first it had seemed as though sadism was erotogenetically bound. Sadistic impulses were to be found on every level, though in a form which apparently varied with the nature of their source or their erotogenic zone. The oral, anal and phallic levels each had their sadistic constituents. As the field of observation widened it seemed more and more probable that sadism was an independent component instinct which permeated every level, was able to ally itself to any other component instinct, had its own vicissitudes and could be regarded, in accordance with the dominant criterion of that time, as linked to the striated muscular system as its 'source'. Viewed in this way, sadism occupied a more curious position than ever in contrast to the purely libidinal instincts. What was particularly difficult to account for was the contradiction between the *aims* of the two. This contradiction seemed to call for a different genetic history for each. The term 'sadism' undoubtedly included all sorts of phenomena, some of them not of an erotic kind, ranging from sexual perversions to impulses of cruelty and harshness which were devoid of any manifest eroticism; and finally it was also employed for certain ego instincts.

As regards the ego instincts, too, various component instincts could be distinguished. In connection with the criterion of source, hunger and thirst seemed to be the appropriate representatives of the ego instincts. But in the course of time they came to lose that position.

Closer inspection of the ego instincts made it possible to introduce a more fundamental classification of them. Impulses to control could be distinguished from defensive impulses; and instincts of power and of self-assertion could be added to them. The impulses to control seemed to be related to the trends of power and neither differed very much from many sadistic manifestations of instinct. The defensive trends, too, which could be sub-divided into impulses to flight and to attack (destructive impulses) exhibited an unmistakable streak of aggressiveness. Thus most of these ego trends had to be credited with an aggressive character; it became necessary to suppose that, in addition to sexual sadism there was a 'sadism' of the ego instincts, while they in their turn entered into the service of the libido in the form of instincts of dominance. All this made the situation more than a little complicated. It was precisely this concept of the sadism of the ego instincts that showed clearly what an undue extension the notion of sadism had undergone. The terminology used at that time was the result of the absence of any distinction between the relation on the one hand of sadistic phenomena to libidinal phenomena and on the other hand of aggressive phenomena to sadistic ones.

Since the idea of sadism embraced facts of a disparate kind, the question was, how could the relationship be cleared up between the two sets of insintctual components—between those with aggressive and those with libidinal aims? There is only a limited number of ways in which we can imagine this relationship. Either the libidinal and aggressive instinctual phenomena start from something that is primal and common to both and only become differentiated in the course of development; or they each have a different origin and follow separate though at times intersecting lines of development.

The first of these possible views, namely that they have a common origin, is a monistic one and seeks to regard the libidinal and aggressive phenomena of instinctual life as products of differentiation or modes of the manifestation of one and the same instinct—bipolar phenomena which can replace each other.

The alternative view of the relations between the two groups of instinctual impulses is a purely dualistic one. It assumes the existence of two qualitatively different instincts and endeavours to subsume all the relevant phenomena under them. While the first view draws its support from the existence of phenomena which contain both sets of trends in an undifferentiated state and is met by the problem of accounting for their emergence in a differentiated form, in the second view it is precisely the undifferentiated phenomena which constitute a stumbling-block and have to be accounted for with the help of the theory of fusion.

Before committing himself to the dualistic theory, Freud, as has been seen in the passages referred to in his 'Instincts and their Vicissitudes,' put forward the possibility of a bipolarity of instinct as its ordering principle. But, after having compared the aims of the two groups of instinctual trends and established their disparate character, and after having discussed the question of the 'transformation of love into hatred' and denied the possibility of such a thing, he rejected the idea that there was a genetic relationship between the two sets of phenomena.

Thus aggressiveness (including hatred and sadism) and libido differed in regard to aim and origin. But this still left aggressiveness in an uncertain position in the framework of the instinctual theory. Freud's next attempt to solve this point was to ascribe the characteristics of aggressiveness (or 'sadism', to use the then current term for the last time) to the ego instincts and to assume that, side by side with an opposition between the sexual and ego (aggressive) instincts, which expresses itself, among other things, in conflict, certain states of fusion between them also occur.

It is important to notice that in this connection Freud did not as yet talk about instincts of aggression as independent entities but only about the aggressive aspect of the ego instincts. This seemed to offer a provisional answer to the question of the relationship between aggressiveness and the ego instincts—namely, whether there are any phenomena of aggression at all outside the field of the ego-preservative functions. (The problem of erotic sadism is not affected by this question.) The question goes back to the empirical fact that aggressiveness appears only or almost only when the life instincts or the ego instincts are exposed to harm. It is a question which will come up again later on.

This third step, then, furnished provisional solutions to a great many problems. In the first place, sadism was taken out of the category of sexual instincts and put among the ego instincts; and in this way the independent character of the ego instincts was asserted. But this amounted only to a reshuffling of the two big groups of instincts, not to a new classification of them. In the second place, the idea of states of fusion threw a little more light upon the situation. The sadism of the sexual instincts would arise from the aggressiveness of the ego instincts and would emerge 'when the sexual function is governed by the ego instincts': the latter would 'impart to the instinctual aim as well the qualities of hate' (the general name for aggressiveness at that time). Freud attempted to trace the evolution of the influence which the ego instincts have over the sexual instincts, starting from the ambivalence of the oral stage and passing through the sadism of the anal stage to the love belonging to the genital stage, at which love and hate come into direct collision for the first time. Conversely, the ego instincts might themselves receive an admixture from the libidinal side, as in narcissism. In the third place, an alteration in the criterion of the classification of the instincts was thus brought about. The typical example of the ego instincts was no longer hunger but 'hatred', viz., aggression. As we know, the fact of there being different instinctual aims had already led to the problem of the position of sadism. At the same time the question arose whether along with this change of criterion from source to aim there went an alteration in our concept of instinct. As far as the sexual instincts were concerned, this stronger emphasis upon the instinctual aim had entailed no such alteration. It must be remembered, moreover, that the instinctual source still retained its significance as a criterion; and so did the theory of energic tension with its chemical foundation. Even if no chemical hypothesis could be formulated for the ego instincts, the general concept of instinct which had been gained from the sexual instincts could nevertheless be carried over to them. They, too, could be regarded as demands for work imposed upon the mental apparatus, as tensions which set going certain activities which procured satisfaction by the attainment of their aim—hunger, for instance, and its resultant impulse to control—, as stimuli which impinged upon the mental apparatus and produced energy.

Thus this third step in the theory of instinct apparently solved a whole number of problems. It seemed to establish the aggressive ego instincts as independent entities; to render plausible the fact that the aim of 'sadism' was not purely sexual, by means of the theory of instinctual admixture; and to order and clarify the various manifestations of libidinal and non-libidinal aggressiveness.

IV

The Problem of the Instinct of Aggression.—The need to re-model the theory of the instincts and take another step forward was felt as a consequence partly of research into sado-masochistic phenomena in their widest sense, partly of the fuller knowledge of the structure of the mental apparatus which was obtained as a result of the advance from the study of the repressed forces to that of the repressive ones as well.

In describing this fourth step (which must, in my opinion, be separated into two parts) I shall no longer give a purely historical survey, based upon Freud's works in the order of their appearance, but shall discuss it rather from a systematic standpoint.

The necessity for assuming the existence of an unconscious sense of guilt led to a new conception of the structure of the personality. The ego and the id were contradistinguished, and the ego was looked upon as having arisen out of the id and as being an organized portion of it. The id comprised (1) the vital stratum, in which the instincts had their place of origin and which was in free contact with the ego, (2) the repressed portion of the instincts, which was prevented from having free communication with the ego by anti-cathexes, and (3) the unconscious part of the ego, that is, the super-ego.

The fourth step in the development of the instinctual theory consisted in removing aggressiveness from the ego instincts—i.e. no longer viewing it as a component instinct or as a characteristic of the ego instincts—and in putting it, as an independently subsistent instinctual group with aims of its own, in the vital stratum of the mind. In this way the new theory asserted that there are two groups of instincts in the vital layer—the libidinal and the aggressive (or destructive) group. Each instinctual group moves forward towards satisfaction on its own account; and, partly through a free struggle to obtain it, partly through the influence of an ego which is subjected to the pressure of the external world and of the super-ego, each enters into a great variety of relationships with the other, whether of an associative or an antagonistic kind. Both can easily come into opposition with those trends of the system which operate in a self-preservative sense and which are represented in the ego (the ego instincts.) In contradistinction to the instincts of sex and of aggression, which work in the vital layer and are directed to objects, are the ego instincts whose field of operation is the ego.

At this point three questions arise: Why did this fourth step have to be made? What is the advantage of a new instinctual theory which, although dualistic from a genetic point of view, recognizes three sets of instincts? Have the concept of instinct and the criterion for its classification undergone any change?

Since, as we saw from our discussion of the reasons for making the third step in the instinctual theory, it was found necessary to take away the aggressive trends from the sexual instincts and ascribe them to the ego instincts, the whole problem of establishing an instinct of aggression on its own footing is narrowed down to the question of whether aggressive trends of a non-libidinal nature play any role outside the functions of the ego.

There seems to be no doubt that there are in fact aggressive trends which, without betraying any sexual charactristics worth mentioning, do operate outside the field of the self-perservative functions. Moreover, to range aggressiveness completely under the ego instincts is a doubtful proceeding in those cases where its action comes into opposition with those instincts. Manifestations of sexual sadism might possibly be accounted for on the theory of an admixture of the ego instincts; but this is not so easily done with masochistic manifestations. The ego instincts are representatives of the 'instinct which constrains every living thing to cling to life'. That pain, which could only be regarded as a signal acting in the service of this life instinct, should itself become the aim of a masochistic instinct, seemed contrary to the laws of biology, even though the idea of sexualization might offer a possible explanation. But the difficulty became still greater where melancholic depressions exerted a self-destructive power—depressions which Freud described as characterized by 'an over-throw, psychologically very remarkable' of the self-preservative instinct. The same is true of those trends of the super-ego which are turned against the self, as, for instance, in the need for self-punishment, which seems to act like an independent instinct.

These manifestations, against which the ego has to defend itself, just as it has to defend itself against the libidinal impulses, cannot easily be explained as being due to the aggressiveness of the ego instincts. And it is clear that Freud very soon dropped that view. He does not mention it except in the passages from 'Instincts and their Vicissitudes' which have already been quoted. Nevertheless, the problem of whether manifestations of aggressiveness appear outside the defensive functions of the ego does remain in a sense unsolved, and to that problem belongs also the question of the relationship between the intoxication of omnipotence felt by the ego and the degree of intensity attained by the gratified instincts of aggression.

It was only logical that, when the contrast was made between the ego and the id and it was shown that the ego had to defend itself against the instincts of the id, the aggressive trends should have been placed, as autonomous instinctual forces, in the vital layer of the mental apparatus. To do this was, as Freud says in the sixth chapter of his *Civilization and its Discontents,* not to make any fresh change in the theory of instincts but was 'merely a matter of coming to closer quarters with a conclusion to which we long ago committed ourselves and following it out to its logical consequences'.

The postulation of the existence of an independently subsistent instinct of aggression undoubtedly facilitated a description of the facts in question. The ego was now thought of as being obliged to struggle with aggressiveness exactly as it was obliged to struggle with libido; it could give way to it, sublimate it, repress it, alter it by means of reactive formations, mitigate it by adding libidinal elements to it or offer itself as an object and so direct aggression onto itself (perhaps *via* the super-ego). But of course the mere establishment of such an instinct did not solve everything. The problem had come to be not so much one of destructiveness in its outward operation as of destructive trends turned in upon the self, as they could be observed in melancholia, the need for punishment and the *Schicksalsneurose* or neurosis of fatality. Here it seemed to be a matter of a destructive instinct at work inside the subject himself and this was still more difficult to account for on biological lines than was the existence of pleasure obtained from pain in the narrower field of sexual theory. It looked as though our first investigations of the ego had revealed the existence of what was, phylogenetically speaking, the most recent instinct—an instinct which might have arisen along with the civilization of man.

Primary Destructiveness.—It cannot be doubted that the super-ego exists and that it can, in certain circumstances, carry its punitive trends to the length of destroying the subject himself. Nor can it be doubted that to explain the latter fact as a turning of aggression against the self does not furnish an adequate theoretical account of the phenomenon. Such an explanation is merely the starting point for a discussion of the true problem. How is it possible that the aggressive instincts should be turned against the subject's own person to the point of self-destruction?—that is, how can we explain such a state of things from the hitherto accepted biological standpoint? It will be quite in keeping with the methodological principles of psycho-analysis if we assume the existence of some more fundamental thing in virtue of which this turning of aggression against the ego can take place. This thing can be nothing else than an instinctual trend which somehow has a self-destructive effect but whose manner of working is not visible at the first glance.

The problem was already present in some sense in the sexual theory; and Freud stated it when he asked whether sadism or masochism was the primary phenomenon, viz. the older of the two from a biological point of view. Even at that time he adduced the parallel problems from the development of the purely libidinal instincts and established the fact that in sadism, unlike the other component instincts such an exhibitionism, there did not exist, or could not be shown to exist, a stage that was analogous to the narcissistic stage.

The observation of the clinical phenomena mentioned above, as well as the fundamental methodological need to find an original model in analogy with the parallel hypotheses of the libido theory, made it necessary to assume the existence of a 'self-destructive' trend which somehow operated within the self. This trend would be a kind of primary destructiveness and would be analogous to primary narcissism. Aggressiveness directed onto objects would be the counterpart of the object-libidinal trends; and the manifestations of secondary destructiveness would correspond to those of secondary narcissism.

This analogy was supported by the observation that similar fluctuations occur between aggressiveness and self-destructiveness as occur between a narcissistic libidinal position and one which is oriented towards objects. Aggressiveness can become directed inwards in the same way that self-destructiveness, if it reaches a dangerous pitch, can find a safety-valve by being turned outwards in the form of aggression.

Here, then, is the problem. If the hypothesis of a primary stage of the destructive instinct is theoretically unavoidable, how can a trend of this kind be formulated? It was in endeavouring to answer this question that Freud opened up those lines of thought which have led to so much misunderstanding and contradiction. . . .

The Theory of the Primal Instincts.—In order to fill in and gather together the theoretical issues involved in the fourth step and in order to solve the problems raised by it, Freud now introduced the theory of the primal instincts. These, according to him, are the life instincts and the death instincts. The theory was not set up on the grounds of any fresh psychological material or indeed of any question of a psychological nature; it was the result of certain theoretical problems which had been raised by previous hypotheses and which it was designed to solve. It was thus in the nature of a theoretical sub-, or rather, superstructure and was a theory of the second order as compared with the instinctual theory which had so far been directly built up upon clinico-psychological data and problems. It was a biological theory of instinct, since it rested almost entirely upon biological considerations. Instincts of life and death are not psychologically perceptible as such: they are biological instincts whose existence is required by hypothesis alone. This being so, it follows that, strictly speaking, the theory of the primal instincts in a concept which ought only to be adduced in a theoretical context and not in discussions of a clinical or empirical character. In them, the idea of aggressive and destructive instincts will suffice to account for all the facts before us.

By drawing this sharp distinction between the two concepts we are more likely, I think, to avoid certain errors and to ensure the clarity of our clinical descriptions.

Some confusion of thought has been created, especially as to the relation between the death instinct and the repetition compulsion, by the manner in which Freud introduced his theory of the death instinct. Let me therefore at once point out that, although he used repetition compulsion as evidence of the existence of the death instinct, the evidence from that source is not to be regarded as indispensable. His writings show in the main two classes of argument in support of the theory of the death instinct. I should like to contrast these with each other under the name of a *speculative* and a *theoretical* line of argument respectively. The speculative line is fully worked out in *Beyond the Pleasure Principle*; the theoretical one is more lightly indicated and is scattered in various places, but it can be collected to form a whole. We will turn our attention to the speculative line first.

The Speculative Basis of the Theory of the Death Instinct.—It would be beyond the scope of this paper to enter into the reasons which led Freud to the hypothesis of a repetition compulsion and the various problems which are bound up with it. It is enough to say that the result was that he found it necessary to postulate a regulative mechanism which acted independently of the pleasure principle and appeared to be much more primary than it (i.e. earlier from a historical point of view and more elementary), and which must be regarded as a primal principle, a primal characteristic of life, and therefore a characteristic not only of the death instinct but of all instincts.

The concept of repetition compulsion is a complex one and comprises several aspects. (1) Repetition compulsion is an expression of the 'inertia' of living matter, of its 'disinclination to abandon an old position in favor of a new one' and therefore of a conservative trend which always inclines to maintain the existing state of things. (2) In consequence, there is a tendency to keep to certain forms of adaptation and to certain circuitous routes as a reaction to any disturbance of the usual processes. This may be described as the 'impressibility of life'. Adaptations once acquired are retained and reproduced. Under this heading may be placed the basic law of biogenesis and the biological concept of reproduction in general. (3) The conservative nature of life, however, does not express itself only in the maintenance and reproduction of already established processes, but also in a backward-looking trend which aims at surmounting or, as it were, throwing off adaptations which have been imposed upon it and at re-instating more primitive situations, that is to say, historically earlier ones. Here inertia and conservatism have become an active 'yearning for the past', a regressive trend. (This method of formulation was of importance as a ground for the assumption of the death-instinct.) (4) From the energic point of view repetition compulsion is found to be a special case of the trend towards abreaction. The large quantities of energy released by traumatic stimuli are bound by anti-cathexes and then gradually, as the traumatic situation is repeated over and over again, discharged in fractional amounts. Under this heading fall the dreams of persons with a neurosis due to an accident, the play of children, the manifestations of the transference situation in analysis, and so on.

As has been indicated above, the historical formulation of the repetition compulsion—as an endeavour to re-establish the *status quo ante*—was used by Freud as a basis for his assumption of the instinct of death. He started from the fact that the earliest moment at which organic life can be said to exist is the moment when it emerges from inorganic, dead matter. The phenomena of inertia in the world of physics, which is no more than an opposition to any change, becomes, as it were, in the realm of biology, an active trend—from the historical standpoint a retrogressive one, and, from the energic standpoint, a trend towards a relaxing of tension, towards absolute rest. But at this point the difficulties involved in this speculative line of argument become evident. Apart from the many handicaps from which it suffers in the hypothetical field, . . . there is the further objection that it regards the death instinct as the original one and implies that the life instincts came into existence subsequently as a result of the chances of development. The life instincts are thus subordinated to the death instincts, as is seen when Freud says in *Beyond the Pleasure Principle* that fundamentally the life instincts act in the service of the death instincts. According to this, the life instincts would create tensions of every possible kind only to submit them to the death instinct with its inevitable trend towards relaxation of tension. Freud's speculative effort in this field is indeed a pessimistic one; it affirms that the true essence of life is death.

A subordination of this sort of life instincts to the death instincts does not seem, however, to be entirely justifiable theoretically. At any rate, the converse of it is quite as possible and arguable. In his *New Introductory Lectures* Freud emended this view in so far as he treated the two instincts as synchronous and co-ordinate in their operation: life consists of life and death instincts alike.

The Theoretic Grounds for the Theory of the Death Instinct.—Freud's first suggestion, which seemed so pessimsitic, was due to the fact that the need for assuming the existence of instincts of life was not nearly so pressingly felt as the need for assuming the existence of instincts of death. In so far as the existence of the life instincts had to be conceded theoretically, it was done more for biological reasons than for psychological ones. Sexuality as a relationship between germ-cells of different sexes, or rather between the bearers of those cells, does not make its appearance till some way on in the course of phylogenetic evolution. It must, therefore, be either a new acquisition, or, more probably, a modification (made necessary, perhaps, by the need for adaptation) of some older instinct which may have exhibited the most general characteristics of the sexual instincts, such as a trend towards bringing things together or, from the energic aspect, towards creating tensions.

This new conception of the instinctual theory, however, obviously proceeded above all from the necessity for solving the problem of primary destructiveness. We have already seen what considerations led to this problem and need not go into them again; but the question admits of certain further points of discussion.

As we know, psycho-analysis has always had a biological orientation, and the theory of instinct has hitherto rested upon a biological basis. It is therefore quite natural that it should seek to find a pre-existing biological model for the destructiveness at work within the individual. The task before it, then, was to formulate the biological model for the primary destructive trend which operates in the mind and whose existence seems so probable on theoretical grounds. Just as it was found earlier that aggressiveness ran counter to the libido in its aims, so now aggressiveness turned against the self must contradict the self-preservative principle of life—unless there was something in life itself which made possible a turning back of this kind.

The questions which we shall now have to discuss are firstly, how is primary destructiveness to be defined? and secondly, how are we to understand the biological 'compliance' whose existence has been assumed?

The problem of finding the original model of the self-destructive trends (both primary and secondary) leads inevitably to the subject of death; for the question of the nature of death and its place within the scheme of life is in a sense the same as that problem and should help to solve it. Thus the relationship between life and death, if there is indeed a biological model for self-destruction, must be thought of as more intimate than is usually supposed. In other words an essential characteristic of life must be its relation to death. This statement of the problems leads straight to the sphere of biology and narrows down to two alternatives: is death merely the outcome of an injury from without? Or has life a natural end? If the first alternative is true, life is, theoretically, an eternal process which is only terminated by destruction from outside. If the second is true, death is a necessary component of life. Each of these views about the nature of death implies a corresponding view about the nature of life.

It would take us too far afield to bring forward the various relevant biological facts and considerations; we must content ourselves here with answering two questions. The first is the one that has alreay been asked, and it has been answered by Freud in *Beyond the Pleasure Principle* where he expresses the cautious view that there are a number of facts that speak in favour of the occurrence of natural death and none that definitley exclude it.

The second question is: is natural death, which, as we know, overtakes the soma only and not the germ plasm, a phylogenetic acquisition which has been made possible by the emergence of the multi-cellular organism and which has nothing to do with the essential nature of life? Here also, the answer may be that in the course of phylogenetic evolution something has merely become differentiated which was already an integral part of the unicellular organism —that is, that natural death is an original 'character' of life, so that dying, too, is something which instinct strives after.

If this is so, what does it mean in the dynamic sense? If life is regarded as a closed system moving in an orbit, as it were, round a fixed centre of gravity, death must be something that is foreign to that system; it can only be destruction coming from outside. But if life is regarded as proceeding in a linear course, then death is something that is essential to life; it is the goal towards which life is being driven. Living is dying, a process moving towards death, towards zero potential.

But it seems to me that Freud's conception of life is neither of these things, but a third which is a combination of the two. According to him the life system is governed by two trends: it moves towards zero potential but in doing so it creates new tensions. It is, to quote a simile of Aster's, like a self-winding clock. In the individual, life, it would seem, leads inevitably to death; but if life is taken as an integral process including the past and the future and looked at from a larger standpoint than that of individual existence, then Aster's simile holds good. The struggle of the Titans is constantly creating new forms of life and new deaths in an apparently unending and interminable procession.

The Significance of the Theory of the Death Instinct.—What does the concept of the death instinct do towards clarifying the theoretical problems under consideration and towards unifying the various attempted solutions? Not everything, but a good deal. The biological model of primary destructiveness has been seen to be an instinct of death which can be formulated as a tendency moving towards absolute rest, towards zero potential. From that instinct primary destructiveness and aggressiveness, and all forms of them that turn back upon the self, can be derived. This cannot be done, indeed, without the assistance of certain auxiliary constructions which, though doubtless unsatisfactory in many respects, rest upon certain facts of observation.

To begin with aggressiveness. The fact that aggressiveness can be turned back upon the subject's own self and the equally observable fact that this retroverted destructiveness can once more be turned out upon the external world in the form of aggression make it probable that similar processes and connections occur between primary destructiveness and aggression directed outwards—that is to say that in certain circumstances primary destructiveness is 'turned outwards.' The findings of crowd psychology, too, speak for this possibility. In this case the individual who is prepared to be aggressive is bound to an organized group and thus his aggression is diverted to a part of the external world which is outside that group, to a so-called 'enemy', whether that enemy is a hostile idea or a hostile group of persons. This fact, together with the clinical observation just mentioned, provides us with an *ontogenetic* model (to borrow Kris's words) on the strength of which we can proceed to construct a *phylogenetic* model. According to the latter, the emergence of the mulit-cellular organism out of the unicellular one would presumably have the effect of rendering the self-destructiveness of the cells harmless, since they would be bound to one another (perhaps with the help of the libidinal instincts), and of making it in part turn outwards, in some form or other, as an instinct of aggression.

If we now try to tabulate the instinctual classification which we have arrived at in analogy with the parallel concepts of the libido theory, we find the following set of comparisons:—

Life Instincts (Eros).	Death Instincts (Primal Sadism, Primal Masochism).
The Sexual Instincts: Primary Narcissism. Object Libido.	The Destructive Instincts: Primary Destructiveness. Aggressiveness turned against the Object.
Secondary Narcissism.	Aggressiveness turned back against the Self (Secondary Destructiveness).

This symmetrical arrangement is not in any way due to a desire to establish a systematic series, but will be seen to have a role to play when we come to discuss the question of the visible manifestations of the death instincts.

The terms 'life instincts' and 'sexual instincts' on the one hand and 'death instincts' and 'destructive instincts' on the other, are used by Freud synonymously and without any distinction. And indeed it does not seem possible to make any sharp division, especially between the second pair. Nevertheless I should like to attempt to trace certain lines of demarcation for heuristic reasons.

The instincts of life and death are purely biological instincts, which operate in the organic sphere but which are reflected in some form or other in the mental sphere as well. The sexual instincts are only a specialized form of the life instincts. The same is true of the concept of the destructive instincts. The two terms are only generalized names for all libidinal phenomena on the one hand and all destructive, or aggressive phenomena on the other. Thus if we are asked how these instincts manifest themselves we have only to point to all the facts that belong directly or indirectly to the field concerned. The phenomena of the sexual instincts are sufficiently well known; and so are those of aggressiveness, whether turned outwards or back upon the self. All that remains, therefore, is to discover what are the mental representatives of primary destructiveness—these being parallel to the mental representatives of primary narcissism.

Are there any mental phenomena which may be regarded as expressions of this primary destructive trend? The very fact that such a question can be asked at all, and that the existence of a primary destructive trend has had to be deduced in the first instance upon purely theoretical grounds, is tantamount to making the assumption that we are dealing with 'silent' instincts. Primary destructiveness must, therefore, be defined in some such way as that it is the destructive energy in virtue of which we grow old and die mentally, to adapt Weiss's phrase. . . .

We cannot, then, describe primary destructiveness in any way except by definition. But the question remains, whether, though there are no direct products of it, there may not be some indirect ones? Two facts seem relevant to this question: the need for rest and the need to suffer. I do not think that it would be difficult to show that there is probably such a thing as an instinctual desire for rest. The need for rest comes not only as a result of being tired; it is a phase which alternates naturally with phases of activity or which occurs in the middle of the latter as though it was a primary need that had been neglected and was now demanding to be satisfied. The need for rest seems to govern the psychic apparatus quite as much as the need for pleasure. It is precisely the combined appearance of the two trends in the sexual instincts that led to their being equated in the first place. The instinctual need for sleep, too, or instinctual falling asleep, seems to be an expression of this instinctual need for rest.

A much more difficult task is that of demonstrating the relationship between primary destructiveness and the need to suffer. In this connection Freud has introduced the concept of erotogenic masochism, which can be regarded to a certain extent as a normal phenomenon and which is characterized by having for its aim pleasure in pain, or more generally, a need to suffer. It is assumed that not all primary destructiveness is turned outwards but that some portion of it remains operative within, and, libidinally bound or softened, only emerges in the form of what is called erotogenic masochism; and this assumption is an attempt to establish a direct connection between the postulated primary destructive instinct and the phenomena of masochism. . . .

Thus the need for rest would be a more or less direct reflection in the mind of the death instinct, of primary destructiveness; but the need for suffering would be only indirectly derived from that instinct, with the help of the theory of instinctual admixture. Even pleasure in causing suffering to others is not, according to Freud, an immediate expression of primary destructiveness directed outwards but the result of a state of fusion.

To sum up: With the help of the biological theory of the death instinct it became possible to formulate the nature of primary destructiveness, which was a necessary hypothesis from a theoretical point of view; and furthermore (though not without resorting to various auxiliary hypotheses) to obtain a unified view of destructive and aggressive manifestations. The heuristic advantage of these assumptions is, I think, unquestionable. But this is not all that the theory can accomplish in the direction of unifying the facts.

Instincts and Principles.—In discussing the concept of instinct as implied in the sexual theory we have seen that the instincts were contrasted with the functioning of the mental apparatus. On the one hand the characteristics of the instincts were examined, but it was necessary on the other hand to make certain assumptions about the way in which that apparatus worked: It was presumed to be regulated according to certain trends or principles. What, then, was the relationship between those principles and the instincts? The instincts were regarded as tensions of energy which arise from the organic sphere and act in a 'disturbing' way like an external stimulus upon the mental apparatus, and are then dealt with according to the regulative principles governing that apparatus. This is what was meant when instincts were defined as demands for work made upon the mental apparatus. How the disturbing stimuli are to be classified seems a secondary matter compared to the adoption of the view that the mental apparatus has a fundamental method of working in relation to all the stimuli that reach it, whether they come from without or from within.

It must once more be emphasized that in this general view the instincts were not thought of as directing the whole course of mental events, but only as being sources of energy and causes of excitation which set in motion the regulative trends of the mental apparatus.

Freud's basic assumption was that this apparatus is governed by a trend which strives towards a complete relaxation of tension or towards keeping down to the lowest possible level the quantities of incoming stimuli. At first he equated this trend with the pleasure principle, since tension seemed to call out feelings of unpleasure and relaxation of tension feelings of pleasure. Nevertheless there were various facts which could not be made to fit in with this view. The reality principle represented a modification of the pleasure principle according to which pleasure was no longer sought directly and immediately but along devious ways adapted to reality and over an extended passage of time.

But, for reasons which we already know, it proved necessary to detach the pleasure principle from the underlying trend towards relaxing tension and keeping it down to a minimum. Various ideas were put forward about this fundamental trend. It seemed to be a kind of principle of constancy concerned with maintaining tension at a particular level; it was as though, in other words, the individual mental system was regulated at a particular state of equilibrium. Anything which seemed to disturb that balance whether in an upward or a downward direction was brought back by the regulative trend to the normal tension. It was the view which regarded life as something moving in an orbit round a fixed centre of gravity that found expression in the hypothesis of the principle of constancy or stability. It was then possible to define the pleasure principle, which directs mental processes towards an end-state of pleasure, as a modification of the principle of constancy. Everything which led nearer to the constant degree of tension or the state of stability was felt as pleasurable and everything which drew away from them was unpleasurable.

But as soon as the fundamental view of life was changed and it was no longer regarded as moving in an orbit but along a linear course, its basic trend had also to be differently regarded. The principle of constancy was accordingly replaced by the Nirvana principle, the trend of which was to effect a complete levelling down of all difference of potential—to reach zero potential.

Thus, if we leave on one side repetition compulsion,[2] we find that there are three regulative trends directed respectively towards a complete relaxation of tension, towards pleasure and towards adaptation to reality (or the Nirvana principle, the pleasure principle and the reality principle). The reality principle remains, on this view, a modification of the pleasure principle, but the relationship between the Nirvana principle and the pleasure principle becomes a different one from what it was according to the old view, according to which the pleasure principle was regarded as a special form of the principle of constancy. Now each corresponds to a different trend. Desire for pleasure on the one side and desire for rest on the other are the two chief regulative principles of mental life.

It is clear that only a provisional position has been attained by merely contrasting on the one hand the regulative principles of the mental apparatus and, on the other, the instincts which come from the outside and make themselves felt as a demand for work to be done. The heuristic principle, which would lead us to enquire to what extent the entire mental organization and its modes of working are built up upon the instincts, must inevitably raise the question of whether the instincts exert an influence upon the trend of mental processes. But to ask this would be to ask what is the relation between mental principles and instincts.

This question arose all the more easily because the concept of instinct had undergone a change in the course of the development of the instinctual

---

[2]Repetition compulsion should also be reckoned among the regulative trends. It is a general regulative principle and serves to bind energies, i.e. to bring them from a state of 'flow' to one of 'rest'. That a regulative trend of this sort does exist seems beyond doubt. The way in which the ego works, too, presupposes this possibility of binding, and of arresting tensions—of making them static. In the same way the repetition compulsion seems to be a *sine qua non* of all the other regulative trends. The quantities of incoming stimuli (in so far as they have not been confined to certain channels in the course of phylogenetic processes of adaptation, or if they have overflowed the capacity of those channels) must be arrested and bound before the other regulative forces can come into play.

theory. Originally instinct was regarded as an energic tension arising from organic sources and automatically directed towards an inherently determined aim; that aim was attained circuitiously *via* an object and consisted ultimately in a modification of the organ of origin of the instinct—in a return of the organ to the state in which it was before the stimulation occurred. It was in conformity with the view that the idea of instinctual source was chosen as a suitable criterion for the classification of the instincts.

The impossibility of discovering sources of this kind for every instinct and the difficulty of constructing them hypothetically, especially in relation to the ego instincts, brought into the foreground the notion of instinctual *aim* as a criterion. This did not necessitate any radical change in the concept of instinct. The aim consisted externally in the carrying out of the purposive act upon the object and internally in the attainment of a relaxation of tension, as, for instance, in the case of the aggressive instincts.

But the theory of the primal instincts (the life and death instincts) was founded upon an essentially changed concept of instinct. According to it, instinct was not a tension of energy which impinged upon the mental sphere, which arose from an organic source and which aimed at removing a state of excitation in the organ from which it originated. It was a directive or directed 'something' which guided the life processes in a certain direction. The accent was no longer upon the production of energy but only upon the function determining a direction.

But the mental principles, too, were nothing else than a determining 'something' which decided in what direction psychological processes should move. The concepts of 'instinct,' 'principle,' 'regulation,' thus seemed to be very much alike. Just as the instincts regulated the course of biological events, so, naturally, did they regulate the course of mental events. It was no longer possible to maintain a strict contrast between a mental apparatus regulated by principles and instincts pressing in upon it from outside, since the instincts themselves now stood revealed as fundamental principles of life.

This led to the possibility of grouping the principles with the instincts. It would take us too far afield to go into this point in greater detail here. But we know how Freud pictured an arrangement of this sort. He writes: 'The Nirvana principle expresses the trend of the death instincts, the pleasure principle represents the claims of the libido (and thus corresponds to the life instincts), while a modification of the latter, the reality principle, represents the influence of the external world.' The relation between the two main principles was pictured as being that the life instincts effect a modification in the course run by the processes of relaxation of tension, a modification which is associated with the emergence of pleasure. . . .

Let me add a few words upon the question of quantity. So long as the concept of aim was used merely as a criterion for classification, it in no way contradicted the quantitative concept of instinct. But it was otherwise as soon as quality of aim was regarded as a primary characteristic of instincts. To do so involved turning the instincts into mental *qualities* and restricting their *quantitative* aspect to each separate group of them (to the sexual or the aggressive group). There would then be two classes of instinctual energy which would be distinguishable by the quality of their direction, namely, the energy of libido and the energy of aggressiveness—or, as Weiss calls it, 'destrudo'—and no exchange of energy could take place between the two. (The problem of *confluence* of aim is on quite a different plane). Although this view is a consistent one, it brings with it its own difficulties, connected partly with certain clinical facts and partly with the concept of a narcissistic reservoir of libido. The latter, according to Freud, is 'a displaceable energy, which is in itself neutral, but is able to join forces either with an erotic or with a destructive impulse, differing qualitatively as they do, and augment its total cathexis'. Freud finds a solution in the supposition that the aim of the libidinal instincts, which are 'more plastic, more readily diverted and displaced than the destructive ones,' can be reduced to a mere need for 'discharge' or relaxation of tension, in which the object and the paths of discharge are 'relegated to a position of no more than secondary importance'. The neutral reservoir of energy would thus consist of libido sufficiently reduced to be in a position to make contributions to libidinal and aggressive impulses alike. Thus a supply of pure energy—i.e. one in which the quality of its aim is inoperative—would be able to flow only from the libidinal to the aggressive instincts and only by the way of this undifferentiated reservoir of libido.

To sum up the discussion. For the sake of greater clarity we have so far been at pains to make the cleavage between the concepts under consideration as wide as possible. But I should now like to narrow the gap once more and to approach the actual structure of those concepts more closely. On the one hand, the biological life instincts which create tensions, the sexual instincts, the ego instincts, with their aim of maintaining life, and the pleasure principle—all these are somehow related to one another; on the other hand, the death instincts which seek to cancel out tensions, the instincts of destruction at work within, aggressiveness directed outwards, the trend towards a state of rest (the Nirvana principle) and the inclination to suffer—these, also, form a related group.

The 'mysterious' instinctual forces, which lie behind all this, work each in their own direction or against one another or with one another. They become combined in the form of masochistic pleasure in suffering, of sadism, of the need for punishment, of self-hatred, of aggressive ego instincts, and so on.

What we call instinct operates in a directive fashion upon biological events both in the physical and mental field. Under certain influences it becomes differentiated and concentrated into centres of tension which are somehow bound to organic phenomena as sources; it turns outwards upon an object, strives after an aim which consists externally in a particular kind of behaviour towards that object and towards the subject's own body, and internally in the removal of a state of excitation. How it operates to begin with inside the self is not clear. We can see more easily what it is doing when it is directed towards objects upon which it carries out purposive actions. In order to effect this, something has sometimes to happen to the organ of origin, sometimes only to the object. Satisfaction ensues sometimes in the form of a particular process that is run through, sometimes in a more diffused manner. But the instinct can also take the subject's own self as its object in various ways. It can turn into 'motive force' and so increase the energies of the ego. It can enter into a multitude of by-paths and it is so malleable that it can undergo a great variety of changes. We cannot classify it in any single uniform way, but now according to one point of view, now according to another—according to its aim, its object or its source.

All these facts, hypothetical opinions and theories have been formulated in concepts which are often ambiguous and vague. Exact and well-defined notions are not always possible in the region of psychology. But much has been gained if we have been able to advance into a new field and to set up a number of concepts which can shed a mutual light on one another, even if we have done no more than make a first approach to a set of facts which, upon the whole, are still unknown to us.

REFERENCES—SECTION EIGHT

Adler, A. *Study of Organ Inferiority and Its Psychical Compensation.* New York: Nervous and Mental Diseases Publishing Co., 1917.

———. *The Practice and Theory of Individual Psychology.* New York: Harcourt, 1927.

———. *Social Interest.* New York: Putnam, 1939.

———. Suicide. *J. Indiv. Psychol.,* 1958, *14,* 57-61.

———. *The Education of the Individual.* New York: Philosophical Library, 1958.

Adler, G. The concept of compensation and over-compensation in Alfred Adler's and Kurt Goldstein's theories. *J. indiv. Psychol.,* 1959, *15,* 79-82.

Ansbacher, H. L., and Rowena, R., (Eds.). *The Individual-Psychology of Alfred Adler.* New York: Basic Books, 1956.

Colby, K. M. On the disagreement between Freud and Adler. *Amer. Imago,* 1951, *8,* 229-238.

Cohen, M. B., (Ed.). *Advances in Psychiatry: Recent Developments in Inter-personal Relations.* New York: Norton, 1959.

Fenichel, O. *The Psychoanalytic Theory of Neurosis.* New York: Norton, 1945.

Fleming, G. W. T. H., and Walk, A., (Eds.). *Recent Progress in Psychiatry.* Vol. III, New York: Grove Press, 1959.

Fodor, N. Motives in psychological sterility. *Psychoanalysis,* 1958, *6,* 59-73.

Freud, A. *The Ego and The Mechanisms of Defense.* New York: International Universities Press, 1946.

Freud, S. *Basic Writings of Sigmund Freud.* New York: Random House, 1938.

———. *An Outline of Psychoanalysis.* New York: Norton, 1949.

———. *On creativity and the unconscious: Papers on the psychology of art, literature, love, religion.* (Ed. by Benjamin Nelson.) New York: Harper & Bros., 1958.

Fromm, E. *Escape From Freedom.* New York: Farrar and Rinehart, 1941.
————. *Man for Himself.* New York: Rinehart, 1947.
————. *Psychoanalysis and Religion.* Yale Univ. Press, 1950.
————. *The Sane Society.* New York: Rinehart, 1955.
————. *The Art of Loving.* New York: Harper and Bros., 1956.
————. *Sigmund Freud's Mission.* New York: Harper and Bros., 1959.
————, Suzuki, D. T., and DeMartino, R. *Zen Buddhism and Psychoanalysis.* Harper and Bros., 1960.
Gill, M. The present state of psychoanalytic theory. *J. abnorm. soc. Psychol.,* 1959, *58,* 1-8.
Goldberger, E. The id and the ego: a developmental interpretation. *Psychoanal. Rev.,* 1957, *44,* 235-288.
Hall, C. S. *A Primer of Freudian Psychology.* Cleveland: World Publishing Co., 1954.
Hilgard, E. R. Experimental approaches to psychoanalysis. In Pumpian-Medlin, E. (Ed.), *Psychoanalysis as Science.* Stanford, Calif., Stanford Univ. Press, 1952, 3-45.
Hoch, P. H., and Zubin, J., (Eds.). *Current Approaches to Psychoanalysis.* New York: Grune and Stratton, 1960.
Horney, K. *The Neurotic Personality of Our Time.* New York: Norton, 1937.
————. *New Ways in Psychoanalysis.* New York: Norton, 1939.
————. *Our Inner Conflicts.* New York: Norton, 1945.
————. *Neurosis and Human Growth.* New York: Norton, 1950.
James, W. T., Karen Horney and Erich Fromm in Relation to Alfred Adler. *Indiv. Psychol. Bull.,* 1947, *6,* 105-116.
Jocobi, J. *The Psychology of C. G. Jung.* rev ed., New Haven: Yale Univ. Press, 1951.
Johnson, H. Psychoanalysis: Some critical comments. *Am. J. Psychiat.,* 1956, *113,* 36-40.
Jones, E. *The Life and Work of Sigmund Freud.* Vols. I and II. New York: Basic Books, 1955, Vol. III, 1957.
Jung, C. G. *Psychology of the Unconscious.* New York: Dodd, 1925.
————. *Modern Man in Search of a Soul.* Harcourt, Brace, 1933.
————. *The Integration of Personality.* New York: Farrar and Rinehart, 1939.
————, and Pauli, W. *The Interpretation of Nature and the Psyche.* New York: Pantheon Press, 1955.
Kardiner, A., Karush, A., and Ovesey, L. A methodological study of Freudian theory: I. Basic concepts. *J. nerv. ment. Dis.,* 1959, *129,* 11-19.
Levy, D. M. *Studies in Sibling Rivalry.* Monog., No. 2, Amer. Orthopsychiat. Assn. 1937.
————. Release therapy. *Amer. J. Orthopsychiat.,* 1939, *9,* 713-736.
————. Psychosomatic studies of some aspects of maternal behavior. *Psychosom. Med.,* 1942, *4,* 223-227.
————. *Maternal Overprotection.* New York: Columbia Univ. Press, 1943.
————. The deprived and indulged forms of psychopathic personality. *Amer. J. Orthopsychiat.,* 1951, *21,* 250-254.
Mowrer, O. H. Neo-analytic theory. *J. Counseling Psychol.,* 1956, *3,* 108-111.
Munroe, R. *Schools of Psychoanalytic Thought.* New York: Dryden Press, 1955.
Nuttin, J. Human motivation and Freud's theory of energy discharge. *Canad. J. Psychol.,* 1956, *10,* 167-168.
Robbins, I. An analysis of Horney's concept of the real self. *Educ. Theory,* 1958, *8,* 162-168.
Sullivan, H. S. *The Interpersonal Theory of Psychiatry.* New York: Norton, 1953.
Walker, N. How does psychoanalysis work? *Psychoanalysis,* 1957, *5,* 16-27.

MOTIVATION AND EMOTION

Up to this point our book has been concerned mainly with the motivational aspects of human behavior; i.e., the *why* of man's actions. While no direct emphasis has been given to the emotional phases of human behavior it must be realized that every important human reaction of necessity has an emotional concomitant. Motivation and emotion are intertwined and not separated, and some degree of emotion is an accompanying factor in every behavioral response.

Historically, emotion and motivation were viewed as two different aspects of human behavior. This, however, is no longer the case and emotions themselves are being recognized and accepted more and more as significant motivating forces. Perhaps more so than any other individual, Leeper was the one who was most responsible for focussing attention on the motivational aspects of emotion. In 1948, in his highly important and stimulating as well as provocative article (Paper No. 52) Leeper attacks the viewpoint which holds emotion to be a disorganized (or disorganizing) response, and presents his own theory, namely that, "emotional processes are one of the fundamental means of motivation in the higher animals," and that "the discussion of emotion belongs in the discussion of motivation." Leeper believes that since emotions arouse and organize behavior they serve as motives.

Leeper's paper instigated several psychologists to write further on the problem of emotion and motivation. Some of the authors were in agreement with Leeper's general point of view while others opposed it. Duffy, for example (Paper No. 53) sympathizes with Leeper's overall viewpoint, but feels that he "does not go far enough" in that he only attacks one definition of emotion—"that of emotion as disorganized response." She feels that other definitions of emotion are equally unacceptable as is the definition of emotion presented by Leeper. Webb (Paper No. 54) like Duffy is in general agreement with Leeper's view of emotion. In his paper he "attempts to extend the criticisms and theoretical ramifications which were indicated by Leeper." It is Webb's belief that emotion as a motivational concept can be understood best within the framework of the theories of Tolman and Skinner.

Young (Paper No. 55) recognizes the importance of Leeper's contributions with respect to the problem of defining emotion but feels that he has not defined emotion and motivation in either a positive or satisfactory manner. In addition to examining critically Leeper's point of view, Young presents his own theory and definitions of emotion, affective process, and motivation. In Paper No. 56 Waters and Blackwood attempt to examine whether or not emotions should be included in the category of motivation, as propounded by Leeper. After an analysis and discussion of the criteria of motivation, they conclude that emotion may be included within the framework of motivation. The final paper in this section (Paper No. 57) is one which was presented by Leeper at an APA symposium on emotion in 1959. In it Leeper gives a sounder and stronger basis for his motivational theory of emotions which was first published in 1948. In doing so he discusses seven points which he considers important for his theory. As Leeper indicates, his main new idea "is that emotional processes ought to be seen as one type of perceptual process. . . . namely, that emotional processes, basically and fundamentally *are* perceptual processes, just as apparent movement is a perceptual process."

52. A Motivational Theory of Emotion To Replace 'Emotion As Disorganized Response'

Robert W. Leeper

A discussion of current theoretical interpretations of emotion might have two values. Thus, first, it might have some value as a means of studying the theoretical efforts of present-day psychology. Second, it might have value because of the increasing interest of psychologists in many particular fields in which emotional processes play important roles.

Confronted with the problem of the limitations of psychology, psychologists rather oddly have been inclined basically to accept the criticism of outsiders—to wit, that the trouble with psychology is too much theorizing and too little factual evidence. This criticism, however, has not reflected any well-informed study. Actually, psychology now shows a one-sided development of an opposite sort. It has achieved a considerable maturity in its factual material and fact-gathering techniques. But it has failed seriously to make corresponding progress in its task of organizing the descriptive data into general principles or theories.

The problem of the nature of emotion, however, is worth discussing, not merely as a means of studying psychological theorizing, but also as a problem worthy of study in its own right. Psychologists are showing increasing interest in the extension of their work into such fields as psychotherapy, personality, child psychology, and social psychology. In all of such cases, if psychologists are to make a full contribution, they must develop some sound concepts of emotional processes, because emotion clearly plays an important role in personality disturbances, social prejudices, etc.

Abridged from the *Psychological Review*, 1948, *55*, 5-21. Reprinted by permission of the author and the American Psychological Association, Inc.

THE DISORGANIZATION CONCEPT AS DOMINATING CURRENT PSYCHOLOGICAL
THEORIES OF EMOTION

Even though psychologists have taken an increasing interest in such fields
as were just mentioned, the discussions of emotion by psychologists of
experimental background have had little application to such other fields. A
chief reason for this is that such experimental-psychological interpretations
of emotion have been dominated by the concept of emotion as disorganized
(or disorganizing) response. This is so poor a generalization of the known
facts that it has served as a serious obstacle both to good research work on
emotional processes and also to efforts to apply practically the psychological
concepts of emotion.

Admittedly, not all of the textbooks of psychology have presented the
same theoretical interpretations of emotion. It may seem unfair to psychology
as a whole, therefore, to select a limited number of authors as representative
of the trend of interpretation in psychology. I think, however, the evidence
will indicate that the doctrine of emotion as disorganized or disorganizing
response is the favored doctrine in some of the most widely used books.

Let us start with the most recent general text—not merely because it is
the most recent, but also because it apparently is also the most widely used
introductory text. N. L. Munn's *Psychology*, in its chapter on 'Emotion,' says
this:

> Perhaps as satisfactory a definition as can be give at the present
> time describes emotion as 'an acute disturbance of the individual as
> a whole, psychological in origin, involving behavior, conscious ex-
> perience, and visceral functioning' (P. T. Young, *Emotion in Man
> and Animal,* p. 60). However, this definition needs some elabora-
> tion. We say acute because emotion comes over us suddenly and,
> after a time, weakens and disappears. . . . We say disturbance be-
> cause all but the mildest emotions disturb or upset whatever activi-
> ties are in progress at the time of arousal. We say of the individual
> as a whole because when an individual is emotionally disturbed,
> he is disturbed all over.

Another significant example is the introductory text by L. F. Shaffer, B.
Gilmer and M. Schoen. This book has received wide use, and it is noteworthy also because its chapters on emotion reflect the views of L. F. Shaffer,
whose *Psychology of Adjustment* has been the most extensively used text in
courses on personality and mental hygiene. In the glossary of their book these
authors give the definition: "Emotion—A disorganized response, largely
visceral, resulting from the lack of an effective adjustment." Similarly, and yet
also somewhat contradictorily, in the concluding remarks of their 'Chapter
VI. Emotional Behavior,' these authors say:

> As has been stressed throughout this chapter, emotion is a dis-

organized response that hinders an individual from making effective
adjustments.

In their chapter on motivation, these authors do not adhere to this approach,
but offer a number of the same concepts which the present article will advocate. For example: ". . . emotional responses are basic to many important
forms of motivation. . . . Persistence, ambition, rivalry, and cooperation are
motivated to a large extent by emotion. . . . Positive motives are closely
allied to the emotional responses of delight and affection." But in their
abstract discussion of emotion, the authors laid no basis for such interpretations, putting all their stress, instead, on the doctrine of emotion as equivalent
to disorganized and/or disorganizing response.

The same doctrine appears in the two books by Paul T. Young which
represent the two major attempts of psychologists, to date, to organize the
scientific materials on motivation and emotion. Thus, in his *Motivation of
Behavior* in 1936, at the conclusion of his discussion of the definition of
emotions, Young gave this statement with italics:

> *The foregoing discussion leads us to define emotion as a disrup-
> tion or disorganization of behavior.* The purest emotions—such as
> laughing, weeping, extreme general excitement—are those in which
> there is the most complete loss of cerebral control and the least trace
> of conscious purpose. During emotional behavior the subject goes
> wild, his consciousness is a blur, his activity becomes disrupted. . . .
> The one feature common to all emotion processes is their disorgan-
> izing effect upon behavior.

In his book on *Emotion in Man and Animal* in 1943, Young gave the definition quoted above as repeated by Munn. In this later book, too, Young
repeats the suggestion of his earlier book that another characteristic of emotion is the "weakening or loss of cerebral control" as contrasted with the
fact that "During calm, non-emotional behavior the organism usually functions as a unit, the cerebral hemispheres dominating activity of the lower
neural centers."

Among general-psychology textbooks, another example is to be found in
the *Introduction to Psychology* edited by E. G. Boring, H. S. Langfeld, and
H. P. Weld. This case is significant both because this book made a special
effort to present a scholarly report of general psychology and because the
chapter in it on 'Emotional and Affective Responses' was written by Carney
Landis, who has occupied an outstanding place among experimental workers
on emotion. Landis starts his chapter with the statement that, "Emotional
behavior, including the affective experiences of pleasantness and unpleasantness, forms the basis of human motivation." However, instead of pursuing
this lead by defining motives in relation to this asserted motivational influence, Landis proceeds to consider, in his section on 'Nature of Emotion,'

merely such possible criteria as visceral change, affective value, and involvement of the whole organism. He concludes that none of these criteria is a dependable one, and yet he concludes this section with the statement:

> Thus it seems that emotion can best be characterized as a *relationship existing between many diverse elements of experience and reaction.* This relationship is not well specified, but, generally speaking, it is marked by pleasantness or unpleasantness and by disorganization of usually integrated behavior patterns. An emotion is the total of the experience of an individual during any period of time when marked bodily changes of feeling, surprise or upset occur. (italics in the original.)

This is not too clear a statement, of course. It is hard to see how an emotion can be ". . . the total of the experience of an individual during . . ." and yet can also ". . . best be characterized as a *relationship existing between many diverse elements of experience and reaction.*" In general, however, as these statements indicate, Landis's discussion contains to a considerable extent the same suggestion that disorganization is characteristic of emotion.

F. Dockeray's *Psychology*, as will be indicated in some quotations later, is unmistakable in its insistence on disorganization as the characteristic feature of emotion. An even more noteworthy example, however, is R. S. Woodworth's *Psychology*. Even if Munn currently is the best-seller in psychology, Woodworth has certainly held the long-time record. Woodworth's text, moreover, has been respected especially because of its sensible and reasonable treatment of so many problems. But, on this matter, we find Woodworth using basically the same concept as the authors quote above. Thus he says:

> The difference between emotional and unemotional activity . . . depends on the degree to which the individual keeps his head, that is, on the degree to which the brainy life of relation dominates his whole activity.
>
> The degree of emotionality depends on how free the lower centers are at any time from domination by the cerebral cortex. Or, if we do not pin our faith to any particular theory of the brain action, we can say that activity is unemotional in proportion as it consists in observing and managing the situation."
>
> Emotion is . . . a stirred-up state of feeling—that is the way it appears to the individual himself. It is a disturbed muscular and glandular activity—that is the way it appears to an external observer. . .

Clearly there are some differences between Woodworth's portrayal and that, say, by P. T. Young. But there is still the same basic idea of a contrast between adjustive or adaptive behavior and emotional behavior. As, to quote Woodworth again:

> If the brainy life of relation dominates the organism at the moment, the emotional response is minimized. But if the situation gets out of hand, the emotion appropriate to the situation surges up.

From the above survey, I think we can reasonably say that the concept of emotion as disorganized response (or disorganizing response) is held fairly commonly among psychologists. This impression, furthermore, might have been supported still further by mentioning some other features of the books and chapters cited above. For one thing, an author's definitions are given, not merely by abstract statements, but also by the particular examples to which he points. In this respect we find that almost all of the discussion of emotions is in terms of such emotions as fear, anger, excitement, and their variants such as startle, anxiety and rage. In other words, most of the attention is given to those emotional processes that seem to fit, at least half-plausibly, the idea of emotions as disorganized or disorganizing reactions. Some passing mention is usually made of other emotions such as delight, joy, affection, and love; but the space devoted to these is negligible in comparison.

For another thing, in speaking about the relation of learning to emotion, almost all of these chapters talk in terms of the problem of the 'control' of emotion. Woodworth, for instance, says this:

> The practical life of relation dominates more and more over the emotional life, so that the child's behavior becomes less emotional as he grows older. A scale for emotional age, after the analogy of the Binet scale for mental age, would consist in large part of tests for *not* being afraid or angry or grieved or inquisitive over things which regularly arouse these emotions in the younger child.

Emotion, in other words, is something to outgrow! Even Floyd Ruch's *Psychology and Life,* for all practical purposes, expresses the same approach. For, despite the fact that Ruch says that, "The best way to control emotional behavior is, clearly, to acquire useful emotional responses and to lose hampering ones," his chapter on 'Control of Emotions' goes into detail on the problem of how to eliminate such emotions as fear, but contains nothing in the way of suggestions on how to "acquire useful emotional responses."

It would not be correct to say that the above-mentioned authors have dealt exclusively with evidence of emotions as disruptive. Broadly speaking, however, it is only in minor touches that emotions are considered, in these books, in any other sense. The general tenor of the interpretation is the idea that emotions may best be understood as disorganized or disorganizing responses.

CULTURAL ORIGINS OF THE DISORGANIZATION THEORY OF EMOTION

One might wonder whether psychologists have originated this theory from their experimental evidence, or whether they are merely reflecting a concept which has developed from other origins. Rather oddly, several spiritual kin of this disorganization concept are easily found. They are family relations which many psychologists might wish to disavow. But they are there, nonetheless.

We commonly think of the period of Locke and Adam Smith and the French encyclopedists as the age of rationalism. It was the period in which man was held to be primarily and fundamentally a rational creature. Or, at least, it was believed that he *should* be a rational and intelligent creature. Only in the rational or intellectual functions did mankind reach its proper stature. The passions and like weaknesses of human life were unfortunately too often visible, but they were something to be overcome. They were something that made for traditionalism in religious thinking, for respect and deference to authorities, for inertia rather than scientific-mindedness.

We generally pride ourselves that we have come to realize the inadequacies of this rationalistic approach to human nature. We are probably justified in this pride to some extent, because in psychology we have come to realize the rather humble nature of human learning processes in many types of situations. But we should not claim too much difference in our theories, because the view that emotions are basically disruptive, and that a child properly should become "less emotional as he grows older," could almost have been the doctrines of the old rationalists themselves!

Furthermore, when psychologists consider emotion as disruptive, they have another relationship that is even more surprising, especially in view of the resemblance of psychological thought to the doctrine of rationalism just mentioned. For, if any psychoanalytic thinker were asked whether his ideas are comparable to the rationalistic tradition, he would insist proudly that psychoanalytic thought has been the one really effective challenge to that earlier conception of human nature. He would say that psychoanalytic ideas are the opposite of rationalism.

Perhaps they are. But the psychoanalytic theory states that the ego—the ordinary conscious and pre-conscious part of the personality, the main workaday part of the personality—is a reality-recognizing and reality-manipulating part of the personality. The instinctive processes of the personality, with their emotional components, are not a part of the ego functions, but are a part, instead, primarily of the id, and perhaps to some extent of the super ego. Not only that, but these instinctive tendencies, with their emotional aspects or components, are the trouble-makers in the whole personality of the individual. They are not things that are to be enriched and developed, if possible. They are nothing that gives reassurance and stability to the personality, but, at least in one sense, they are the disruptive factors in the life of the person!

A fine expression of this is given in Hanns Sachs' *Freud: Master and Friend* when Sachs speaks of Freud as a courageous thinker. He says:

> To look at the Medusa's head is no parlor game. Freud—and this is the sum of everything that has been said in this chapter— was steady enough to stand firm when he perceived that we are not and never will become the masters of our own soul, even when he made the staggering discovery of what unholy stuff the unknown masters are made. He did not flinch when he had to look down, standing at the brink of the precipice. Most others who followed in his tracks got at first a fit of giddiness and had to hold on to him to steady themselves when the mountains seemed to reel. What could those do who were too proud to be supported by him and yet too weak to stand alone? They covered their eyes with their hands and slunk away.

Now, really, what is Sachs saying by this? What were the facts which were so fearsome to contemplate? In a sense, of course, they were ideas antithetical to the rationalist tradition. They were ideas of intellect as dominated by emotional forces, and they were ideas that these emotional forces were threatening forces of sexual passion, hostility, terror, and the like. But, in this, do we have entirely an abandonment of, or contrast with, the rationalist position? Or do we, on the contrary, have here merely the rationalist disconsolately convinced against himself, still convinced that human life *would* be best if intellectual processes could be the undisputed masters of human life, but forced to admit that this fond hope is unfounded? There is, after all, no confidence here in emotional reactions, no idea of emotional processes as necessary for a full or wholesome human life. There is still another intellectual relative of the disorganization theory of emotion. This third relative has resulted from the whole trend of modern technology. It is the sort of thing which Gustav Ichheiser has emphasized when he has pointed out that some of the views which we are apt to regard as rather original insights of psychology are merely elaborations of ways of viewing life demanded by the social setting of modern psychology.

What I refer to is that our modern world most obviously is a world of skills, factual knowledge, and intellectual processes—or, in short, of nonemotional processes. At least this is the case at the end where goods are produced, as contrasted with the consumers' end of the process. Advertisers of course know that they have to appeal to emotional motives rather typically. But we take the view that, if anything, the folly of people's behavior as consumers (*cf.* the kinds of movies they demand, the kind of radio programs to which they listen, and the kind of newspapers they buy) merely indicates the superiority of the brains involved in production as compared with the inferiority of the emotions involved in consumers' behavior.

Nor is it merely in industry that the broader social scene tends to echo the suggestion that emotion is disruptive. In political life we speak of propaganda (in an unfavorable sense) as appealing to the emotions. We speak of rabble-rousers as depending on appeals to emotion. We know that some very unfortunate political movements, from Ku Klux Klan to fascism and naziism, more or less frankly have built their programs on an emotional basis. In the field of religion we have seen that traditionalism and fundamentalism, often openly allied with emotionalism, have conflicted with other more intellectual tendencies which have sought to revise religious beliefs in the light of historical criticism, scientific knowledge, etc.

Consequently, when we question the doctrine that emotions are disorganizing, it is no straw man that we are considering. It is a view, instead, that has been rooted in our popular thought for several centuries. It appears in psychoanalytic thinking as well as in academic psychology. It is enormously strengthened by the fact that a highly technological society tends to share the view that intellectual processes are *the* worthwhile and appropriate human functions.

It does not condemn a concept in psychology, however, merely to point out that it resembles some concept in psychoanalysis or some concept naturally used in everyday life. We need to turn, therefore, to the question as to whether there really is justification for thinking of emotions as disruptive.

THE DISORGANIZATION DOCTRINE AS RESTING ON UNDEFINED
AND WRONGLY INTERPRETED TERMS

When we consider the pitfalls which beset the path of the scientist who is trying to develop an adequate theory, we are likely to find that there are two main pitfalls: (1) the risk that he will survey too narrow a range of facts when he is trying to formulate or evaluate some abstract proposition, and (2) the risk that he will use vague, undefined terms or poorly defined terms, so that it will be hard for him to see whether he always uses his terms consistently and hard for him to see whether the available factual knowledge supports or contradicts the abstract statement he is considering. It is from these angles, now, that we need to examine the rather common view of emotion cited above. Let us consider first the matter of carefulness of definition, and of consistent use of terms.

First of all, we may note that none of the above-mentioned authors has attempted to give a definition of such terms as 'disorganized' and 'disorganizing.' They are the key terms, or crucial terms, for such a theory. But the authors apparently have assumed that the terms are self-explanatory or self-defining, with their meanings sufficiently indicated by common usage or by the dictionary. But to proceed in this way is dangerous. It is the typical way in which sloppiness and inaccuracy sometimes slip into scientific theory. Where there are no explicit definitions of key terms, it is easy for thinkers to neglect significant factual data and it is easy to fall into inconsistent usages.

As an example of such inconsistent or shifting meanings, we find that these psychologists seem to speak as though the two terms 'disorganized' and 'disorganizing' (or 'disturbance' and 'disturb') are synonymous. Thus, in the quotation from Munn given above, you will remember that, at first, he says that emotion may be defined as "an acute disturbance." Then, to explain this, he says, "We say disturbance because all but the mildest emotions disturb or upset whatever activities are in progress. . ." Now either usage might be clearcut. We might say that the *disturbances* or *disorganization* of behavior is the emotion. Or we might say that the emotion is *what produces this disturbance*. Or, conceivably, we might say that emotion is both the disturbance and that which produces the disturbance of the previous processes. But there can be no claim to scientific thinking when, without explaining our gymnastics, we jump back and forth from one such contradictory usage to another. It is not Munn alone, either, who follows such a shifting usage. It is the typical thing with all of the authors quoted above.

The difficulty is not solely a matter of lack of definitions, however, but is a matter also of sticking consistently to the same definitions, because even when the implied meanings are fairly clearcut, there still exist contradictions in closely-adjacent sentences. Careful thinking takes a lot of time, a lot of turning-over-and-over of the material. The disorganization theory of emotion has not received such careful thought. Let us consider Munn again. He says that " . . . all but the mildest emotions disturb or upset whatever activities. . . ." From this a student might reasonably assume that there are some (mild) emotions that do not "disturb or upset." But, when the student then tries to find out the definition of these emotions, he has to go back to the statement that emotions are "an acute disturbance." This is not acceptable, of course. A definition of a key term in psychology must cover the phenomenon as it appears in all degrees.

Several other examples of such contradictory usages may be found in F. Dockeray's *Psychology*. He says:

WHEN THE BEHAVIOR OF THE ORGANISM BECOMES DISORGANIZED AS THE RESULT OF THE OCCURRENCE OF A SITUATION FOR WHICH IT HAS NO READY RESPONSE, WE MAY CALL THE DISORGANIZATION 'EMOTION.' This is the distinguishing feature of emotional behavior: It can and does occur to all degrees, from the mild disturbances we call feelings to the gross upsets that are called emotions (capitals in the original).

In this statement there is a contradiction in two successive sentences. The first sentence says that *any* disorganization we call 'emotion.' The next sentence, however, says that only *gross* upsets are called 'emotions'—and this even though disorganization in any degree is the "distinguishing feature of emotional behavior"! Still further, on the following page, Dockeray makes this statement when discussing the emotional development of children:

> As the years pass, the child . . . also is acquiring new interests, love of parents, their welfare as well as his own, friends with whom he is willing to share in order to secure more remote goals, and the satisfaction of seeing others happy. From a crude vegetative animal, he is developing into a human being with sympathies, appreciations, adorations, and a host of other *emotionally toned* patterns (italics added).

Now, by any reasonable use of words, an emotionally toned pattern of response is activity which involves at least some mild emotion. But, we were just assured that disorganization is the distinguishing feature of emotions in 'all degrees.' But surely Dockeray does not mean to assert that there is such a disorganization in the examples just quoted. He is simply failing to integrate what he says at one point with what he says at another point.

CONTRADICTIONS BETWEEN THE FACTUAL DATA AND CAREFUL DEFINITIONS OF 'DISORGANIZED' AND 'DISORGANIZING'

The center of the whole discussion, then, obviously lies in the matter of what is meant by such key terms as 'disorganize' and 'disorganization' (or their opposites, 'organize' and 'organization').

First of all, it should be clear that these terms possess no connotation, properly, of 'good' or 'bad'. In fact, they have been used primarily because it was felt that they were terms which avoided any such value-judgments. This is a reasonable view. After all, an organized mob or an organized gang is not necessarily something good. So, 'organized' must not be taken as meaning 'useful' or 'wholesome in its influence.' Instead, a system is 'organized' when one part of it is functioning harmoniously with other parts. Something is 'organized' when the parts fit, or dovetail, or are congruous with one another. And on the other hand, something is 'disorganized' when the subordinate parts operate at cross purposes with each other. Something has an 'organizing' influence in a system when it tends to produce order or cooperation or harmony between different subordinate parts or subordinate activities.

A qualification needs to be added, however, 'Organization 'always is purchased at the price of interfering with what is inconsistent with the main basis of organization. For example, when we say that effective study or effective thinking is an 'organized' process, we need to recognize that the person's activity tends to inhibit or side-track some processes which otherwise would occur, or which were occurring previously. The person does not react to sounds which ordinarily would have diverted him; he fails to respond to a condition of hunger which is developing within him; he is side-tracking a number of competing interests. In the same way, even though we would say that a nation at war is more highly organized than a nation at peace, it also is true that factories often are required to give up their regular work, young men are taken from their schools and home life, many recreational activities are discontinued, and so on. The criterion of organization, consequently, is not a matter of whether there is some interference with preceding activities or with inconsistent subordinate activities. *It is the question whether this interference is relatively chaotic and haphazard, or whether the suppressions and changes of subordinate activities are harmonious with some main function which is being served.* Unless we adopt such a usage, the disorganization theorists must say that problem-solving thinking is an emotion, because clearly it disrupts preceding modes of response and also interferes with incongruous activities at the moment.

Is there any fault with the definitions just suggested? If there is, these various authors have not said so. As we have mentioned, they have simply let their main terms be undefined. It would seem, however, as though they would agree with the above suggestions. Let us see, therefore, whether the factual data are consistent with definitions which seem reasonable.

Rather commonly, the authors mentioned above have said that emotions involve disorganization of three aspects of life: visceral processes, behavior, and conscious experience. Let us examine, first, the asserted disorganization of visceral processes. The asserted facts are that, when a person reacts with strong fear or anger (and in some other emotions, but not all), his digestion is slowed or stopped, his heart beats more rapidly, his breathing becomes more rapid, his blood is driven more extensively into the skeletal muscles rather than into the digestive organs, etc.

Is this to be understood as 'disorganization'? Do these subordinate visceral changes operate at cross purposes with one another, or do they dovetail in high degree? There is interference with digestion, of course. But, from the standpoint of the main function for which the organism is now prepared, is this interference with digestion a mark of disorganization, or is it more truly a mark of organization? In such matters, the disorganization theorists have not attempted to show that the different visceral reactions in fear and anger operate at cross purposes with one another! They have been content to refer to faster breathing, faster heartbeat, etc., as though such changes *ipso facto* are demonstrations of disorganization. But, carefully speaking, the person is organized during fear or anger. He is organized viscerally so that he can most naturally do something consistent with his fear or anger. What he is organized to do may be 'unwise' or 'bad.' But that is irrelevant. Viscerally, the 'individual as a whole' is not disorganized.

Behaviorally, is the person disorganized while afraid or angry? If he is, a football coach typically does some very unwise things, because he puts out considerable effort to get his men emotionally aroused (or even angry!). Of course, in some instances it is easy to demonstrate that such emotions as fear often handicap the behavior which the person (because of some other motive) wants to engage in. The pianist with stage-fright, for instance, cannot play well. But the test of whether fear has an organizing effect on behavior is not the test of whether it tends to help produce some kind of behavior demanded by some other competing or conflicting motives of the person! The fear is tending to make the person avoid the platform appearance. It makes him seek for excuses to get out of such performances; it tends to make him flee even after he gets onto the platform. The stage-fright, in other words, tends to organize behavior along lines consistent with that fear.

In the third place, *from the standpoint of conscious experience*, is there disorganization? Again our general factual knowledge denies any such assertion. When a person is strongly aroused emotionally, as in the psychiatric cases so well described in Landis' chapter, the conscious experience is not disorganized. On the contrary, a persistent, insistent mood prevails. The person finds it impossible to shake off a feeling of personal worthlessness or of discouragement or of danger or whatever. There may be some play of thought, it is true, within the limits of what is consistent with the emotionally-significant situation. But the conscious experience shows strong organization. In fact, a main difficulty with such clinical cases is that of helping the person to get any thoughts or feelings other than he usually has as a consequence of his most prevalent emotional response.

Several answers might be made to these comments, however. In the first place, the disorganization theorists might say, "Yes, that may all be true, but there is a disorganization of the behavior and conscious experience that went before." True enough. But every psychological process has this same effect. When the players in a symphony orchestra see the conductor come out on the platform, this perception causes a cessation of their preceding activity of talking, tuning their instruments, fingering special phrases, and so on. We could say that there is a disorganization of the behavior that was occurring before. But we do not say, because of this, that the musicians have now become emotional. All that we say is that there has been a change of activity and, if anything, a shift from a less organized condition to a more organized condition. When a challenging problem occurs to a scientist he tends to drop what he was working on previously. But we do not say that he is thus becoming emotional. In the same way, then, there is no basis for saying (unless we want to give up all effort at consistency of speech) that emotions are disorganizations because preceding activities are terminated and replaced by other activities.

In the second place, though, the disorganization theorists might say, "Yes, but this shift involves a change from constructive or useful activities to foolish and inappropriate activities." Maybe so. And, correspondingly, if we want to define emotions as 'foolish and inappropriate responses,' this definition might harmonize with the facts to which we would thus be pointing. But, as we said above, the terms 'organize' and 'disorganize' are supposedly neutral with regard to value-judgments. They have appealed to psychologists, rather typically, because they seemed merely descriptive. Well and good, then, we must stick to our meanings. A shift from a wise behavioral organization to an unwise behavioral organization is not a shift from organization to disorganization.

In the third place, however, the disorganization theorists might say, "Now we will play our trump card. Look at what happens when the person becomes *extremely* afraid or *extremely* angry. Then he wants to run, or he wants to call for help, and he cannot do it. He wants to win the football game, but his reaction is so over-intense that he is hampered rather than helped. The boxer becomes so angry that he loses his technical skill and fights ineffectively. What can you say about this—isn't this really disorganization, even in the sense that you defined above?"

In this type of case, indeed, the emotional process does seem to produce disorganization in significant degree. It interferes with reactions that would be consistent or harmonious with what is demanded by the emotion. But are such cases to be the means of deciding the function of emotional responses of all degrees of intensity? If so, there is a queer logic involved. In no other case do we decide on the properties of something by a like procedure. If we did, we would say, for instance, that the function of breathing is to disrupt psychological processes because the person who forces himself to breathe rapidly and deeply will find in a few minutes that he gets dizzy, he begins to tingle all over, and (as is used in electroencephalographic work) if he has a tendency to epilepsy, he will have a mild attack which can be recorded on the electroencephalograph. We do not determine the functions in the body of normal amounts of salt, iodine, fluorine, or any other material by discovering the influence of these same materials when consumed in extreme doses. We are interested, perhaps, in describing such effects also; but we do not use this as the means of determining the normal functions of such products. The same logic, then, should apply to emotional processes.

Let us now consider another slant on this matter. In the above discussion, in considering whether there is really evidence of disorganization in emotional activity, we have been talking only in terms of such emotions as fear and anger. But, although they have spoken somewhat hesitantly, the disorganization theorists have not applied their concept of emotion merely to such emotions. They have included, although to a relatively limited extent, what might be called positive emotions. For example, Dockeray says:

The satisfaction felt in a job well done, the pride of a father in

his son, and the joy of meeting an old friend are relatively mild
emotions as compared with the unpleasant experiences of dissatisfaction, disgust, or hate.

Similarly, in his list of typical feelings and emotions, Woodworth includes
joy, amusement, hope, courage, contentment, and love. Shaffer, Gilmer, and
Schoen, in their chapter on 'Emotional Behavior,' include one section on
'delight, joy, and laughter' and another section on 'affection and love'.

If these are emotions, as the historical usage of the term would suggest, it
would seem that they ought to occupy a rather significant place in these
discussions. For one thing, unless we are to take an extremely pessimistic
view of human life, we might well say that such 'pleasurable emotions' or
'positive emotions' are, in general, just as numerous and important in human
life as are the 'unpleasurable' or 'negative' emotions. It is hard to see, therefore, why they secure merely passing mention and why such emotions as fear
and anger are discussed as though they are the only valid prototypes of
emotion.

However, even beyond this, if these positive emotions are to be spoken
of as emotions, we have a right to ask the disorganization theorists to consider the question whether they also are interpreted as supporting the generalization that emotions disorganize the person viscerally, behaviorally, and
in conscious experience. A scientific writer should be sensitive to empirical
knowledge. As Clark Hull has put the matter very clearly, ". . . wherever
a generalization really conflicts with observation the generalization must always give way." But what we have in this matter is no such sensitiveness to
accepted factual knowledge. Instead, we have the trick of Procrustes: The
facts must lie down on a harsh bed of foreordained proportions, and if the
facts do not fit, it is just too bad for the facts.

It is curious, in fact, to see the contortions through which some of these
authors go in order to make it appear that these emotional reactions do not
rule out the definition of emotion as disorganized or disorganizing. Thus,
let me quote (with comments) from Shaffer, Gilmer, and Schoen:

> Superficially, forms of behavior such as joy, elation, and laughter
> seem very different from the emotions of fear and anger, yet they
> also bear some striking resemblances. The greatest difference, of
> course, is that anger and fear have an unpleasant feeling tone,
> whereas joy and laughter are pleasant. The former are generally
> avoided, but people will deliberately seek the latter. Delight and
> similar functions have much in common with emotion, however."
> [That is, they are *not* emotions, but "have much in common with
> emotion."] "The joyful individual is stirred up and excited. He
> shows some disorganization of ordinary habits. Visceral reactions,
> consisting of changes in heart beat, blood pressure, and respira-

tion, are also present in joy. It is fair to conclude, therefore, that
states of this sort should be called emotional.

Thus, behold! Before our very eyes the miracle is accomplished. Having
warmed to their task, the authors have convinced themselves, at least, that
joy and similar processes do not merely "have much in common with emotion," but that, come to think of it, they *are* emotions! The same miracle
of transformation takes place as these same authors take up the discussion
of affection and love. They start by saying:

> It is doubtful whether affection and love are emotional states
> in the psychological sense, but they have the support of long-
> standing literary usage as 'emotions.' Most conditions of affection
> lack the violent nature of the other emotional habits . . . described
> thus far, and are calming rather than exciting physiologically.

But then, going on, the authors say:

> The phenomenon of love between the sexes, seen in adolescents
> and adults, shows more evidence of being a genuine emotional
> state. The classic lover is distracted and cannot concentrate, his
> heart beats rapidly upon seeing his loved one, his bosom heaves,
> and his blood pressure rises. In short, he shows the signs of a
> first-class case of emotion.

Can we expect that students will take such interpretations seriously? They
are given the statement that emotions are disorganized and/or disorganizing;
they are later told that there are pleasurable emotions such as delight and
joy and romantic love as well as unpleasurable emotions; and then they are
told that, if truth be known, all these pleasurable emotions are probably
disruptive in the same sense, though perhaps not in the same degree, as are
the unpleasurable emotions. If this be true, the student might say, it means
that the person with a life rich in friendships, in aesthetic emotion, in love
for someone of the opposite sex, and in enjoyment of his work probably will
not live to as ripe an old age as will the person not thus marked by these
well-developed emotional interests. We cannot expect that students will believe such artificially manufactured 'facts' as these or that he will keep his
respect for psychology when he sees such twistings of facts and of meanings
of words.

SOME FALLACIES WHICH HAVE OBSTRUCTED THE ACCEPTANCE OF A MOTIVA-
TIONAL THEORY

Our conclusion has been, therefore, that the whole framework of the
discussion of emotion as disorganizing has been absurdly inadequate. It is
not enough to leave the matter in this form, however. It is not sufficient to
criticize such a concept adversely, because the question then would come,
"All right, but how else can we think about emotions?" This is a legitimate

question. Indeed, if there were no alternative concept, we probably would not be inclined to object so strongly to what has been said.

To get some satisfactory alternative, we will need, of course, to get some agreement as to the subject-matter to be covered by such terms as 'emotion,' and we will need to get some abstract statements about this subject-matter which will represent the best of our available factual knowledge.

To begin with, we can use the 'pointing' method of defining emotion. We can say that emotions are such phenomena as fear, anger, feelings of guilt, feelings of grief, affection, pride in the doing of good work, enjoyment of beautiful music, and enjoyment of companionship. Continuing our pointing, we may say that 'emotions' are to be seen, not merely in cases where these processes occur in intense form, but that emotion can exist, as Woodworth says, in all degrees of intensity.

We ask, then, what properties mark all of such a diverse collection of phenomena, at least when they are not carried to rare extremes. We have seen that disorganization is not characteristic. Hardly in any sense do we find any disorganization as a product of such emotions as affection or esthetic emotion. Even in such emotions as fear and anger we saw that disorganization occurs ordinarily merely as the price of achieving some dominating organization, and that consequently it is not truly disorganization.

In fact, we seemed to be moving toward the conclusion that, for all emotions, organization is the typical thing. Organization for what? Organization in what sense? When we come to this point, we have to decide whether to trust factual knowledge or whether to trust a priori conclusions. Our factual knowledge says that if you can arouse anger in a person you can increase the probability that his behavior will be directed and sustained in a certain direction. If you can arouse sympathy and friendliness, you will increase the likelihood that his behavior will be directed and energized in a different direction. The stronger the emotional process aroused (short of extremes that will perhaps run into qualitatively different effects), the more certainly will his behavior be governed in a way consistent with his emotional reaction. This is a principle which permits prediction and control of human behavior and conscious experience. It might be criticized, of course, as being merely a vague, nonquantitative principle. Any principle is likely to have this character at the start. But that is no serious objection. Scientific work must proceed by a process of approximation and correction.

If this line of argument is sound, it means that emotional processes operate primarily as motives. It means that they are processes which arouse, sustain, and direct activity!

Or, at least, this is what it would seem that they are. But the doctrine of emotion as disorganized or disorganizing does not permit such a statement, even though the disorganization theorists have considered it as a possibility. Thus, P. T. Young makes this amazing statement:

. . . there are persistent, purposive activities which arise during emotional upset and which are a part of emotional behavior. Thus, fear is associated with impulses to escape, anger with aggressive attack, sexual emotion with fondling and caressing. Inasmuch as these purposive activities are integrated, they cannot be components of *emotion*—emotion being always disruptive—but they are a part of *emotional behavior*. Thus, emotional behavior includes both integrated components and the signs of disruption.

"The association of certain purposive activities with emotional disturbance is not accidental. The psychological situation which arouses a disturbed state of fear evokes also the precipitate flight from danger. The situation which arouses the emotion of anger also produces aggressive behavior. Thus, organized and disorganized processes normally arise out of the same psychological situation.

Now, where in modern science could one find a better example of the kind of thinking that marked the old scholastics—arbitrary definitions, subtle distinctions unsupported by empirical observations, and then deductive argument from those as unquestionable data! What an amazing thing this would be, if what Young asserts were true! In all of the higher animals there are evidently emotional reactions of fear, anger, affection, playfulness, and what not. And, by some mysterious alchemy, these occur at the same time that the organism struggles with unusual intensity and effectiveness to flee, fight, or whatnot. But these emotional reactions have nothing to do with these unusually-well-motivated actions which they accompany—in fact, though regularly correlated with such, they have exclusively a dragging or hampering influence. As Young insists, "Emotion is always a disruption."

Munn argues in much the same way. He says:

There are several theories of emotion. . . . One, designated the *common-sense theory,* needs little discussion. It assumes that we perceive an emotion-provoking situation, have an emotional experience, and then behave emotionally—as if the emotional experience aroused or stimulated the visceral and skeletal reactions. To the man in the street this is obviously what happens. The psychologist, however, does not accept so naive a view." This is all that he says about this 'commonsense theory.' But why is this commonsense view "too naive for scientific acceptance?

Munn is relying, fairly surely, on the idea that any concept of mind-body interaction is naive and unsound, and that therefore the psychologist cannot say that the conscious experience causes the reaction. Perhaps this is so, but if such is the case, it is equally unsound for him to discuss the James-Lange and thalamic theories as though they might provide some explanation of how certain physiological processes might explain the conscious experience of emotion, because any such theories involve the same assumption of mind-body interaction!

But, after all, in such a matter as this, we do not need to run into such difficulties. If we are willing to talk about conscious experiences, as Munn now is, we can simply state that we conceive of this conscious experience as an aspect of a larger happening or process, partly conscious in character and partly neurological or physiological in character (or partly susceptible to study by neurological or physiological techniques), which occurs under conditions that are presumably discoverable. The James-Lange theory asserts one hypothesis regarding the origins or conditions productive of this complex, partly conscious and partly neurological condition or event. The hypothalamic theory suggests another such hypothesis. But, in the same basic terms, it is quite a possible hypothesis that the perception of the emotion-provoking situation produces the emotional process (which may have a conscious aspect to it, and which may produce also an autonomic discharge, either directly or via some subcortical centers, and which may then be reinforced or supported by widespread bodily changes). And it is quite a possible hypothesis that this emotional process (perhaps as reinforced by interoceptive impulses from visceral reactions or proprioceptive impulses from general tonus changes) then operates to motivate behavior. In fact, from what we know, this seems to be decidedly the least naive of the three theories!

One might well ask, "On what basis, then, did Young and Munn decide that the emotional process is such a parasitic phenomenon, occurring at the same time at which unusually effective organization is needed, but operating solely to produce disorganization?" It may seem odd (and indeed it *is* odd in the work of persons as capable and careful), but the simple fact is that they had no basis other than the doctrinaire premise that emotions are always disruptive. For after all, by the same procedure, we could demonstrate that bodily drives, such as hunger and thirst are always disruptive, basing our argument on the observation that a person's previous activities become disorganized when he becomes hungry or thirsty, his thinking becomes ineffective about other matters, he loses his ability, perhaps, to inhibit certain tendencies, etc. Then, confronted with the evidence that some very effective food-seeking occurs while the person is hungry, we could merely dismiss this with Young's type of argument, as by saying, "The association of such adaptive and integrative activity with hunger is not accidental. The same situation which evokes the hunger also evokes the food-seeking activity. Inasmuch as food-seeking is integrated, it cannot be dependent on hunger—bodily drives being always disruptive!" The logic of such a statement would be exactly parallel to that which Young has used with reference to emotion.

But, obviously, Young and the other workers have not argued in this way about the bodily drives. Why, then, have they reasoned in one way on one matter, and in the other way on the other matter? The answer seems to be that in our thinking about emotion, perhaps because it has been relatively a neglected problem with general psychologists, we have not been doing a reasonable scientific job. We have been dominated by *a priori* conceptions about emotion. Too commonly we have adopted, for all practical purposes, a faulty representation of psychological functions which was started back in the late 1700's—a division of psychological processes into those of cognition, affection, and conation. The view adopted by Young, Munn, and the others is essentially that same view, that matters of feeling or emotion (or, affection) are fundamentally different from matters of striving or motivation (or, conation). But it is time that psychology issued a declaration of independence from this antique tradition, and it is time that this declaration of independence took the form, not merely of change of words, but also of a rejection of the false dichotomy between affection and conation which that eighteenth-century view contained.

THE ESSENTIAL POINT OF A MOTIVATIONAL THEORY OF EMOTION

What would be the view that might be adopted instead of the view that emotions are primarily disorganized or disorganizing? It would be the view that emotional processes are one of the fundamental means of motivation in the higher animals—a kind of motivation which rests on relatively complex neural activities rather than primarily on definite chemical states or definite receptor stimulation, as in the case of bodily drives or physiological motives such as hunger, thirst, toothache, and craving for salt. In lower animals, such as a clam, there probably are no such emotional processes, but merely the physiological motives. But, as evolution proceeded, a need for additional motives appeared. Animals became more complex in their receptor equipment, motor equipment, and capacity for learning. As such complex creatures developed, those that were motivated merely by the long-established physiological motives were not so well equipped for survival. The animal that did not make avoiding responses until it was grabbed by an enemy was less likely to survive than an animal capable of reactions of fear that would be set off by relatively slight stimuli. The animal that had an interest in its offspring—even in the case of the male and in the case of the female even beyond the period of nursing the young—was more likely to reproduce its kind. The primate that had an almost insatiable urge to explore was more likely to get the maximum benefit out of its chief asset—its great potential learning capacity—than the animal lacking such motivation.

In other words, the discussion of emotion belongs in the discussion of motivation. When we omit it from this field we may be doing justice to the motivation of clams, but we are not doing justice to the motivation of human beings, or even to the motivation of chimpanzees or dogs.

If we conceived of emotional processes as motives, however, our conception would have a still further influence. We would no longer be under some pressure to examine, under the heading of emotion, merely those examples, like fear and anger, which half-plausibly have matched the description of emotion as disorganizing. We would no longer be under pressure to say that the emotional development of the child would consist primarily of the child's becoming less emotional as he grows older, as Woodworth has said, but would see this problem in fuller terms.

Indeed, a change of interpretation on this matter could have some highly important applications in our broader psychological thinking as well, and in our modern culture as a whole. We might well learn to see that the task of development and of functioning in human life is not a matter merely of development of skills and of the "brainy life of relation." It is not a matter just of minimizing emotional responses. It is, indeed, a matter of minimizing *some* emotional responses because they are costly physiologically and costly from the standpoint of the happiness of the person. But we would see that the task of development is also a matter of finding means of developing an emotional richness of life. We need to see that emotional functioning is not merely one of the legitimate, but also one of the primary needs of human life. Then we might realize that naziism, for example, was not just an appeal to unhealthy emotional reactions, but that it was probably partly a consequence of the emotional poverty of modern life. We might come to see that education legitimately needs to aim at more than the development of skills and intellectual functions, and that part of the task of education is the development of healthy emotional processes as one of the indispensable assets, after all, of human life.

With this sort of approach, the chapter on emotion could be rescued from its present museum function of collecting little curios on the facial and vocal expression of emotion, the PGR or EDR, some outworn physiological theories of emotion, and so on, and could become really one of the important topics in the field of psychology.

SUMMARY

Psychologists, though resenting the criticism as ill-informed, have too much tended to accept the idea of outsiders that the chief weakness of psychology is an insufficiency of factual knowledge. Actually the chief immaturity of psychology now lies in its theorizing.

Escape from weak theorizing depends on careful definition of terms, on an effort to consider a wide range of relevant factual knowledge, and on taking a lot of time to integrate the thinking on any problem. The common theory of emotion illustrates this analysis. The view expressed by some main textbooks—as by Munn; Shaffer, Gilmer, and Schoen; Young; Boring, Langfield, and Weld; Dockeray; and Woodworth—is that emotion may be understood as a disorganized (or disorganizing) process. This doctrine is not new to psychology. It reflects the supposedly by-gone rationalistic approach to human nature; it is shared in many ways by psychoanalytic thought; and it is encouraged by the emphasis of our technologically highly developed culture.

Such disorganization theorists, however, have not defined their key terms, have not written consistently, and have not related their generalizations to a wide range of factual knowledge. Disorganization properly means that subordinate activities are operating at cross purposes rather than in ways congruous with some main tendency or function. In terms of such a definition, as contrasted with supposedly rejected value-judgments, emotions produce *organization* rather than disorganization—viscerally, behaviorally, and in conscious experience. They disrupt preceding and incongruous activities, but all integrating activities do the same. Disorganization seen in intense emotion does not give the clue to the general influence of emotion because, as in physiology, extremes cannot be taken as evidence of normal effects. Especially awkward have been the attempts to force the positive emotions to fit the characterization of emotions as disorganizing.

Some of these writers have recognized that emotion often accompanies marked integration of behavior, but have insisted that emotion, "being always disruptive," has nothing to do with this organization seen in "emotional behavior." However, if we use the same logic in thinking about emotion as we use in thinking about physical motives, we are led to the conclusion that emotional processes of all sorts (except perhaps in rarely intense forms) are organizing in their influence and should be studied as an aspect of the motivation of the higher animals. Such a change of theory of emotion would have significant implications, not only for many theoretical problems in psychology, but also for much of our practical understanding of human nature.

The whole discussion tends to suggest that the greatest weakness of psychology now lies in its methods of formulating and testing theoretical formulations rather than in its incomplete factual knowledge.

53. Leeper's 'Motivational

Theory of Emotion'

Elizabeth Duffy

IN a recent article in the PSYCHOLOGICAL REVIEW entitled "A Motivational Theory of Emotion to Replace 'Emotion as Disorganized Response,'" Dr. Robert W. Leeper attacks the common textbook definition of emotion as disorganized response and offers in its stead "a motivational theory of emotion." Since I myself have long been interested in theories of emotion, and, following an initial venture in 1932, have written a number of papers on the subject, I find myself impelled to comment on this recent contribution.

I am happy indeed to have so able an ally as Dr. Leeper in the fight against current theories of emotion—even though Dr. Leeper is apparently unaware that he is not waging the battle alone. I have, however, one serious objection to Dr. Leeper's attack: *it does not go far enough.* He directs his guns at only *one* of the current types of definition of emotion—that of emotion as disorganized response. Other varieties of definition, equally vulnerable, are left unscathed. And, finally, Dr. Leeper offers his own definition of emotion which, in the form in which it is stated, is itself untenable.

In 1934, in an article in this journal entitled "Emotion: An Example of the Need for Reorientation in Psychology," I examined the various types of definition of emotion offered by psychologists and concluded that attempts had been made to differentiate emotion from other states or conditions on five bases. These bases, as presented at that time, were as follows:

1. The physiological mechanisms involved in the response, *e.g.*, visceral as opposed to somatic activity; or activity of the thalamus as opposed to activity of the cerebral cortex.

2. Degree of arousal, or intensity of reaction, of the organism.

Abridged from the *Psychological Review*, 1948, *55*, 324-328. Reprinted by permission of the author and the American Psychological Association, Inc.

3. Disorganization, and consequent ineffectiveness, of behavior.

4. Interpretative data of various sorts, *e.g.*, descriptions of the content of consciousness, or of the kind of stimulus-response situation.

5. Various combinations of the above differentiae.

I examined each of these types of definition and pointed out its inadequacies—*including that of emotion as disorganization of behavior.* I concluded that " 'Emotion' does not represent a unique state; it represents merely one end of a continuum. Or rather, it represents various ill-defined points on a number of continua, according to the definition employed." In the summary of the article, I stated, "An examination of these various types of definition of emotion results in the conclusion that in every case the distinction between 'emotion' and other patterns of reaction is one of degree rather than of kind. It further appears that, since the precise degree of a given kind of behavior which is to be called 'emotional' is never stated, the concept is not useful in exact psychological investigation."

Since the article has apparently been *widely unread*, perhaps it would be useful to summarize briefly the arguments presented against each of the proposed types of definition. They were, in part, as follows:

1. The first type of definition is inadequate because visceral changes of some sort occur all the time. "The vegetative mechanisms passes through various cycles of increased and diminished activity as it sustains the organism and provides the bases for the energy used in motor response." Shall we say that we have an emotion whenever there is an increase or a decrease in energy? But, if so, how *much* of an increase or a decrease?

A variant of this first type of definition, description in terms of the part of the nervous system controlling the behavior, is inadequate because, "unless we are agreed upon a statement *of which responses* are emotional responses, it is meaningless to ask whether these responses are always controlled by a certain section of the nervous system. . . . Neurological description is not psychological description."

2. The second type of definition of emotion, that in terms of the *intensity* of the physiological arousal, is inadequate because energy is mobilized in a continuum, ranging from a very low point in sound sleep to a very high point during frantic effort. Not only so-called 'emotional' situations, but also the demands of strenuous physical or mental exertion, result in a high degree of mobilization of energy.

3. The third type of definition of emotion, that in terms of disorganized response, is inadequate because "disorganized responses are clearly found in many situations which would not ordinarily be termed 'emotional,' and well-organized responses are, in the opinion of many psychologists, frequently found in the presence of 'emotional' stimulation." Moreover, "organized behavior shades into disorganized behavior, with no gap between the two."

4. The fourth type of definition of emotion, that which is based upon an interpretation of either certain characteristics of consciousness or the meaning of a given stimulus-response situation, is inadequate because it can never be made exact, and, basically, it is founded upon conventional usage rather than psychological analysis.

5. The fifth type of definition, which represents a combination of two or more of the types described above, shares the inadequacies of the various definitions which it seeks to combine.

This attack upon the concept 'emotion,' which incidentally had been preceded a very short time before by a somewhat similar attack by Max F. Meyer, unseen by me until my own paper was almost ready for publication, had little effect upon textbook discussions of emotion. Hence, in 1941, I attempted in another article to offer an explanation of the experiences commonly called 'emotional' without invoking the concept of a unique condition. The stated purpose of this paper was to show that "these experiences, which appear to be unique, are in fact merely manifestations in extreme degree of phenomena which are of very general occurrence, and which follow the same principles of action throughout the continua of their occurrence, rather than different principles of action during the condition called 'emotion'."

Also, in 1941, I attempted, in an article in this journal entitled "The Conceptual Categories of Psychology: A Suggestion for Revision," to show that the substitution of a smaller number of more basic categories would eliminate the need for such overlapping categories as 'motive,' 'emotion,' and certain others. I proposed, as one of these basic categories, that of *energy mobilization* or the energy level or intensity of a response, pointing out that changes in energy level occur with changes in the amount of effort demanded by the situation *as interpreted by the individual*. Dr. Leeper will find me entirely in agreement with him on the kinship of 'motivation' and 'emotion.' My statement reads in part: "Changes in energy level are assumed to occur, not only as a part of 'emotion', but also as a part of motivation. A motive, like any other activity, originates in a certain stimulus situation which represents a disequilibrium of the organism. The phenomena of motivation are said to be (1) the maintenance of direction in behavior and (2) an increase in energy level. These phenomena are similar to those described under the category emotion, though emotional behavior is said to be characterized at times by a *decrease* rather than an *increase* in energy level, and emotion is said to involve a distinctive (undefined) feeling tone. Certainly motives also, as well as all other states of the organism, involve some feeling, or awareness, of the condition of the organism, and the only difference between the feeling tone of emotion and that of other conditions is that the energy level called emotional represents an extreme departure from the usual energy level and involves, therefore, an unusual heightening or deadening of sensations."

I hope I have made it entirely clear that, from my point of view, Dr.

Leeper's identification of emotion with motivation represents a decided advance over the usual way of regarding the phenomena of emotion. I would cheer him heartily in his attack on the inconsistencies, the ambiguities, and the downright obfuscation of current textbook presentations of the topic of emotion.

But, if I may again take up the fight, I should like to join battle at a point at which Dr. Leeper has laid down his weapons. Not *all* leading textbooks of psychology define emotion as disorganized response. For example, a textbook which is still considered by many psychologists to be the leading textbook in the field, that of Dashiell, defines 'emotion' as follows: "What is the essential nature of those phases of a person's life we call 'emotional'? It may now be formulated. *The changes of diffuse internal conditions in his organism (through external or internal stimuli) act indirectly (neurally) or directly (chemically) upon his organs of overt response. As a result his behavior towards things and people is strengthened and accelerated or is weakened and retarded. He is typically aware of these internal conditions, and may report them verbally as feelings of 'pleasantness,' 'happiness,' 'anger,' 'reproach,' and so on.*" For Dashiell the distinguishing characteristic of emotion is "changes of diffuse internal conditions" by which behavior is "strengthened and accelerated or is weakened and retarded"—in other words, changes in energy mobilization. The implication is, of course, that there are certain internal conditions which strengthen or weaken behavior enough to be called emotional, and others, presumably, which are non-emotional. But where, or by what criteria, shall we draw the line between 'emotion' and 'non-emotion'? And why do we assume a dichotomy rather than a continuum? Does Dr. Leeper hail Dr. Dashiell as an advocate of a motivational theory of emotion, or does he repudiate also *this* textbook definition of emotion, albeit not based upon the theory of emotion as disorganized response?

Turning to Dr. Leeper's proposed substitute for current theories of emotion, that of conceiving of emotional processes as motives, I search in vain for a definition of *emotional* processes which would distinguish them from *other types* of motives. I maintain that no such distinction can be made. But let us see what Dr. Leeper has to say on the subject. I find the following: "To begin with, we can use the 'pointing' method of defining emotion. We can say that emotions are such phenomena as fear, anger, feelings of guilt, feelings of grief, affection, pride in the doing of good work, enjoyment of beautiful music, and enjoyment of companionship. Continuing our pointing, we may say that 'emotions' are to be seen, not merely in cases where these processes occur in intense form, but that emotion can exist as Woodworth says, in all degrees of intensity." Degree of intensity, then, cannot be used to distinguish an emotion from a motive, or, following Leeper, from *other* motives. Dr. Leeper continues: "We ask, then, what properties mark all of such a diverse collection of phenomena, at least when they are not carried to rare extremes. We have seen that disorganization is not characteristic. . . . If this line of argument is sound, it means that emotional processes operate primarily as motives. It means that they are processes which arouse, sustain, and direct activity!"

Is there any difference, for Leeper, between *emotional* processes and other motivational processes? A difference is implied (else why keep two terms for the same thing?), but no difference is explicitly described. The only further discussion of the topic which I can find reads as follows: ". . . it is quite a possible hypothesis that the perception of the emotion-provoking situation produces the emotional process (which may have a conscious aspect to it, and which may produce also an autonomic discharge, either directly or via some subcortical centers, and which may then be reinforced or supported by widespread bodily changes). And it is quite a possible hypothesis that this emotional process (perhaps as reinforced by interoceptive impulses from visceral reactions or proprioceptive impulses from general tonus changes) then operates to motivate behavior." The 'emotional process' is constantly referred to but nowhere defined—unless the previous 'pointing' method of definition be considered adequate. And if it *is* so considered, this means merely that we are in an emotional condition whenever we are in a condition *conventionally classified* as emotional. "It would be the view that emotional processes are one of the fundamental means of motivation in the higher animals—a kind of motivation which rests on relatively complex neural activities rather than primarily on definite chemical states or definite receptor stimulation, as in the case of bodily drives or physiological motives such as hunger, thirst, toothache, and craving for salt. In lower animals, such as a clam, there probably are no such emotional processes but merely the physiological motives." Is an emotional process, then, a 'non-physiological motive'? It is said to rest on "relatively complex neural activities rather than primarily on chemical states or definite receptor stimulation." But what kind of *behavior* or *process is* this process which 'rests upon' these more 'complex neural activities'? Neurological description is not psychological description. If we cannot describe the process, how can we determine by *what* neural or other means it is controlled?

Further on, Dr. Leeper appears to confuse this 'non-physiological' motivation called 'emotion' with the animal's ability to respond to relationships. He says, "As such complex creatures developed, those that were motivated merely by the long-established physiological motives were not so well equipped for survival. The animal that did not make avoiding responses until it was grabbed by an enemy was less likely to survive than an animal capable of reactions of fear that would be set off by relatively slight stimuli." It would appear that the defect of such an animal is not one of drive or energy mobilization, but one of inadequate maintenance of *direction* in behavior, due to the inability to *respond to relationships* among 'relatively slight stimuli.'

As I have attempted to demonstrate more fully elsewhere, it appears that *all* behavior may be described in terms of the two dimensions: *goal-direction* (including responses to relationships) and *intensity* or *energy mobilization*. No other 'cross-sectional' concepts appear to be needed, though we still require such 'longitudinal' concepts as 'learning' in order to describe *sequential* changes in behavior. So-called 'emotional' responses, like all other responses, manifest both *direction* and *intensity*. Much of the confusion in the current discussions of emotion stems from a lack of recognition of this fact. If we should study behavior from the point of view of its *direction* and its *intensity*, we should be able to solve many of the puzzles which have so long resisted attack by means of the atomistic, overlapping, vague and utterly unserviceable categories which constitute our present 'cross-sectional' concepts in psychology.[1]

Dr. Leeper is definitely 'going my way,' but I wish that I might persuade him to continue farther down the path with me.

[1]There has been no attempt in this paper to offer an alternative theory of emotion. The phenomena of 'emotion' appear to be adequately described by the concepts of 'direction' and 'energy mobilization,' presented elsewhere. The experiences commonly referred to as 'emotional' I have elsewhere attempted to explain in terms which do not invoke the concept of a unique condition.

54. "A Motivational Theory of Emotions. . ."[1]

Wilse B. Webb

"THAT whale among fishes—the theory of emotions" has become no less diminutive as a problem with the passage of fifteen years since Meyer so aptly characterized its nature. Leeper is among the most recent to attempt to encapsulate this hulk-

Abridged from the *Psychological Review*, 1948, 55, 329-335. Reprinted by permission of the author and the American Psychological Association, Inc.

[1]Many of the basic ideas presented in this paper were generated in an Action and Emotion class of Dr. Judson S. Brown, State University of Iowa. The author deeply appreciates these ideas as indicated by the present article. Full responsibility, however, is accepted for any criticism which may be leveled at the ideas presented here.

ing concept. In attacking this problem (and incidentally nearly every respectable generaly psychology text), Leeper places the concept in a motivational framework. The present paper, in general agreement, attempts to extend the criticisms and the theoretical ramifications which were indicated by Leeper.

EMOTIONS AS DISRUPTIVE PHENOMENA

Leeper's primary objections seem to stem from a dissatisfaction with viewing emotions as disruptive phenomena. To quote this author, ". . . emotion produces *organization* rather than disorganization. . . . They [emotions] disrupt preceding and incongruous activities, but all integrating activities do the same." Appeal to extreme instances (intense emotions) to maintain the disruptive position or to characterize emotions as accompanying (parasitic) phenomena is logically rejected. Leeper suggests that such a framework of emotions (disruption) stems from a 'bygone rationalistic approach' and is encouraged by our technological culture.

In considering this attack, it should be noted that this battle standard is not a new one nor has it particularly impressed the opposition. Young himself, one of the focal points of Leeper's objections, recognizing the difficulties in forcing emotions into a disruptive paradigm, seems to chafe under his own conclusions. This seems exemplified by the following statements. "The question of whether emotions are disruptive or adaptive is, after all, one of *interpretation* rather than *fact*," and "the writer holds to the multiple-aspect hypothesis which postulates that emotional processes simply exist in nature . . . regardless of the ways in which men of science describe and interpret them." It is true that Young stresses the communality of disruption as characteristic of emotions; however, he persistently stresses that this behavior is a part of the motivational aspect of behavior. "When emotion occurs there is an imbalance of motives . . . the pattern of emotional expression depends upon the kind of motivation which is thwarted and the nature of the inducing stimulus."

More specifically, we find Leeper's attack is historically antedated. Two of the early pioneers in the field of emotions, Darwin and Cannon, propounded theories which were the antithesis of disruption hypotheses. Darwin indicated that emotions should be considered as having been derived from biologically adaptive behavior. Cannon's 'emergency theory' of emotions stated that the bodily components of emotional behavior gave evidence of preparing the organism to more readily cope with the emergency leading to such behavior. All research and thinking grounded in these approaches has logically been in contrast to a 'disruptive hypothesis.' Most importantly it should here be noted that a critique of disruption has led to no clarity of the concept.

Finally, if attack we must, the level of Leeper's attack does not seem the most appropriate possible. It may be desirable to attack *also* the problem at the general psychology textbook level since future psychologists are there first 'contaminated' with concepts. It is felt, however, that to confine one's attack to this level is to hack at symptomatology. Should not the attack be extended to such fountainheads of the disruptive approach as Watson, Laird, Higginson, and others? Here are the systematic, theoretical, and most critically, empirical aspects that must be encompassed by any new theory. Only by formulating a concept which will account for their 'disruptive' data, not just damning these data as extremes or fantasy, will we gain agreement. Any other approach can only lead to a choosing of sides or a compromise of ways.

OTHER ATTACKS ON THE PHENOMENA OF EMOTION

In an overview of Leeper's article, it seems that the problem of emotions has been bifurcated along the lines suggested by Rapaport, *i.e.*, in terms of the emotions as phenomena in contrast to emotions as a dynamic problem. Leeper has obviously chosen to side with the dynamic approach, and in doing so, has stood on the neck of a single phase of the phenomenological approach, emotions as disruptive phenomena. Before considering Leeper's suggestions concerning a dynamic theoretical approach, other criticisms that have been leveled at the area of emotions deserve at least passing mention.

These further critiques of emotions as phenomena seem classifiable under three general categories:

(1) *Inability to develop an adequate criterion*: Much of the research in emotions has been at this level, attempting to find an index of emotion. Many suggestions have been made and countermanded, *e.g.*, body changes, responses, feelings. None has been established as *the* index of *all* emotions. This inability to 'operationally' define emotions has long been a focus of attack.

(2) *Inability to differentiate between emotional and non-emotional*: Partially as a function of the above listed problem, the problem of defining what is meant by 'emotions' in contrast to 'non-emotional' behavior has long been a fulcrum of criticism. Skinner cites the use of weeping as a definition of an emotional response and further indicates its equivocation by noting that this response may readily occur in the non-emotional situation of having a cinder in the eye.

(3) *Inability to differentiate within emotions*: Because of no method differentiating the wide range of emotions, *e.g.*, joy, fear, rage, etc., the entire concept of emotions as an entity has been questioned. Dashiell, and earlier Cannon, wrote papers which seem particularly pertinent on this problem.

Examples of the specific instances of these critical evaluations of emotions are too numerous to attempt to consider here. Innumerable experiments have been performed to promote one or more of these critiques. Many laboratory hours have been spent proving that facial expressions can or cannot be differentiated; that bodily reactions are the same or different for different emotions; that the PGR changes are a concomitant or not a concomitant of emotions. Summaries of these 'pro' and 'con' experiments may be found in nearly any general discussions of emotions.

The ultimate extension of the attack on the phenomenological stronghold may be seen in Duffy's paper (which in itself is a renovation of the earlier Meyer paper). In this paper emotion is described as a relative concept and it is suggested that we consider emotions as a part of a continuum. Specifically, Duffy reviews the so-called differentia of emotions and finds them all an expression of 'degree,' not 'kind,' and further, "since the precise degree . . . is never stated, the concept is not useful. . . ."

An outstanding attempt to patch the phenomenological approach at a descriptive level may be found in the recent article of Hebb. Hebb attempts to trace the 'intuitive' base on which he and others have been able to recognize emotions and concludes that their recognition is an inferred concept, the inference being made on the basis of a behavior deviation from the 'normal' (?) level and in terms of the stimulus, the past history or acquaintance with the organism and the stimulus, the response and associated behavior. As we shall see, this 'intuitive' approach approximates the approach suggested by this paper.

THEORETICAL APPROACHES

In suggesting a motivational approach to emotion, we again find Leeper antedated historically. "By emotions I understand the modifications of the body by which power and action is increased or diminished, aided or restrained." This is not a quotation from Leeper's article but rather a paraphrase of Spinoza's seventeenth century writing as cited by Rapaport. More contemporaneously the approach of McDougall was recognizably motivational. Symonds in his recent book is seen to equate 'preparatory act' with 'emotional tension.'

Other theorists have considered emotion as some sort of energy or drive. Outstanding among these was that of McDougall and Prince's expansion of this thesis. Finally the systematic approaches outlined below which form the base of the present paper all seem to directly or indirectly implicate a motivational approach. We must conclude then that our answer to this problem of emotion cannot be found alone in the label of 'motivational.'

Leeper's original thesis lies in that our failure in the area of emotions has been a failure in theorizing, not in facts. Perhaps, however, a more appropriate analysis seems to be that the failure resulted from a lack of integration between fact and theory. A consideration of a number of theories previous to Leeper's clarion call seems to indicate that motivational theories are not lacking. Further, these theories seem to be similar and only differing in details.

Leeper suggests that 'emotional processes' should be viewed as "one of the fundamental means of motivation in the higher animals—a kind of motivation which rests on relatively complex neural activities rather than primarily on definite chemical states or definite receptor stimulation . . ." This is agreeable but is hardly a theory. Has not this approach been agreed with and in addition been somewhat systematized?

Let us consider two such theoretical approaches. An earlier theory was that proposed by Tolman. Emotion is defined as "a release of relatively generalized sign-Gestalt-expectations" leading to "incipient movements going-off appropriately" and "resulting sets of organic and kinesthetic sensations." Sign-Gestalt-expectations in the Tolman system are defined as 'cognitions' or 'readiness to respond' in a particular manner. These 'cognitions' result in preparatory or consummatory activities compatible with these sign-Gestalt-expectations. Finally, these movements and expectations result in certain sensations which may be 'introspected' as emotional 'feeling.' Each emotion is to be defined "in terms . . . of the process' functional character as an immanent determinant of behavior—i.e., in terms of its character as a demand to and from such and such specific quiescences and disturbances plus also its character as an accompanying mean-ends-relations . . . as distinctive and unique 'directions' of behavior." Most important to an understanding of the nature of this definition is to understand that these terms of 'demand' or 'mean-ends-relation' are not mere descriptive terms but are inferred concepts based upon the experience of the organism, presently operating stimuli and physiological drive conditions and their relation to certain response characteristics which are exhibited.

Skinner has proposed a similar theoretical approach. Skinner first, as with Leeper, rejects the phenomenological approach. "The definition of emotion as a response involving certain effectors . . . is by no means rigorous, since there are probably no effectors involved in emotions which are also not involved in non-emotional behavior." He then describes emotion as ". . . a state of strength comparable in many respects with a drive. If . . . responses are to be called emotional, it is not because of any essential emotional character they possess, but because they are elicited by stimuli which typically induce changes in reflex strength." Further, Skinner states, "The problem is similar in many ways to that of drive. . . . In both cases we must describe the covariation of the strengths of a number of reflexes as a function of a particular operation. . . . The important thing is the recognition of a change in the strength as a primary datum and the determination of the functional relation between the strength and same operation. . . . An emotion is a dynamic process rather than a static relation of stimulus and responses." In summary, emotion is "some more or less temporary state of reduced strength (an increase in strength would fit into the same formulation) that has been related to a disturbing stimulus or some other emotional operation, such as withholding of reinforcement."

A summary paper by Hunt expounds a somewhat similar view by examining and integrating the relevant data up to 1941.

A 'MOTIVATIONAL' THEORY OF EMOTIONS

The theories of Tolman and Skinner and the present paper agree with Leeper in considering emotion as a motivational concept. In addition, the theories of Tolman and Skinner seem to furnish a framework for the dynamic definition of emotions. How have these theories defined emotions and how does the present paper hope to define emotions?

It is proposed that emotion be defined as an inferred concept which results in a change in the organism's behavior, the inference of this concept being posited from an integrated examination of the stimulus aspects and the response aspects of behavior.

More specifically, emotion or emotions would be inferred in a situation in which responses occurred that are not directly definable in terms of the existent conceptual properties of habit or drive. Emotions would be defined when the responses were lawfully related to some measurable property of the stimulus (either antecedent to or existent with the response situation).

It must be admitted that this is no 'differential' definition of emotions; the author, if pressed, would contend that no differential definition does presently exist. It is further admitted that the 'definition' offered is no more (no less) than a description of the now familiar approach utilizing the 'intervening variable' which has profitably been exploited by Tolman, Hull, and Skinner. Such an approach admits no other definition than an experimental one. It is suggested, however, that an experimental definition generated by such an approach may lead to an unequivocal and utilitarian definition of emotion.

CHARACTERISTICS OF A 'MOTIVATIONAL' APPROACH

What would be the nature of the approach generated by the use of such an experimental framework? First, such an approach would demand that experimentation show that we cannot predict the response in a particular situation on the basis of the presently existing concepts, i.e., that emotions are not mere extensions of the presently existing relationships which have been defined among stimulus aspects and motivational aspects and resultant responses. This is to demand of emotion that to be retained as a heuristic concept it justify its existence as a unique variable rather than an instance of some other concept. The drive concept is thus justified from the fact that holding all factors constant and modifying 'drive' operationally (depriving the organism of some goal object) results in variations in behavior.

Secondly, assuming such a demonstration, the 'inferred concept' approach demands that this inferred concept be adequately anchored on both ends (the stimulus and the response ends) and that the relationships be lawfully defined. How would this be done? Does this approach lend itself to the experimental definition demanded?

Fortunately we have examples of the use of such an approach. The feasibility and productive character seem to have been demonstrated in at least three instances. Although 'anxiety' and 'conflict' and 'aggression' are not frequently classified under the typical listing of emotional, it is suggested that general agreement could be reached on the proposition that the reactions exhibited may well fit the present phenomenological paradigm of emotions. Three clear-cut approaches to these specific problems of 'anxiety,' 'conflict,' and 'aggression' may be found in the writings of Mowrer, Miller, and the Yale group, including Dollard, Doob, Miller, Mowrer, Sears, et al. In these instances emotional responses have not been the focal point, but rather an attempt has been made to correlate stimulus conditions (past and present) with the responses of the organism. Although emotional responses of 'fear,' 'anger,' 'rage,' etc., are predominant among the responses occurring, the experimenters have been content to state that certain responses occur as a result of certain antecedent or existent conditions.

More recently Miller has set about to formulate an experimental definition of the acquired nature of fear and in turn its motivational aspects. In these studies we find maximal use of an inferred concept to explain behavior and an exemplification of the program proposed in this paper. These applications of the 'inferred concept' approach, i.e., 'anxiety,' 'conflict,' and 'frustration,' seem characterized by the following design. By observation and/or definition a relevant set of 'stimulus' and/or 'response' variables is selected, e.g., 'aggression,' 'anxiety responses,' 'fear,' 'frustrations,' conflicts.' These variables are operationally defined and capable of objective measurement. The experimenter or theorist then states a hypothesis or series of hypotheses concerning the relationship existing between the 'stimulus' and 'response' variables. His task then is to test these hypothetical relationships in designs which meet the requirements of his definitions. The result of these applied approaches has been the attempt to predict behavior (classically emotional in nature) on the basis of certain antecedent conditions (the past experience with noxious stimulus, the competition of response systems or drives, the blocking of instigated activity).

What do these results of the application of the suggested methodology imply for a 'definition' of the concept of 'emotions'? In general, it is suggested that the definition of emotions should be primarily focused on the integration of the antecedent conditions leading to emotional responses. It must be emphasized that the present paper does not necessarily imply that the term of emotion, or the classical names of emotions, be abandoned.

'Rage' and 'fear' admissibly are responses in three paradigms of 'anxiety,' 'conflict,' and 'frustration.' It is important to note, however, that in each case the conditions leading to (and hence defining) these responses are stated in relation to a prediction of these responses. Certainly such a definition of 'rage' and 'fear' seems more fruitful than the present rather sterile discrete examination of responses or physiology alone.

What are the advantages of this projected approach? A primary advantage, of course, is the fact that the definition is founded in an experimental and empirical test of its character and not a rational definition. More general advantages may be cited. It meets the previously offered critiques head-on. It approaches the problem of 'disruption-non-disruption' by saying it must include all types of responses, rejecting neither but necessarily including both. The continuum approach of Duffy and Meyer is acceptable if the data are shown to be simply an extension of 'non-emotional' behavior. Emotion or emotions as meaningful concepts will result from the empirical demonstration of differences from or similarity with 'non-emotional' behavior. It does not deny but allows full use of what Leeper calls those "little curios of facial or vocal expression, the PGR or EGR," etc., as being well-defined response aspects which should be included (but not deified or reified as emotion per se). Most importantly, it is not only phenomenological but also dynamic in its approach, i.e., it forces a definition of all the relevant variables (learned, physiological, etc.) and an integration of the variables with the resultant responses or phenomena.

On what basis may we reasonably reject this approach? Basically one may object that emotions could not be related to antecedent conditions. Such objections could only be supported by contending that emotions are unlawful, i.e., independent of antecedent conditions or that the task was too difficult or complex. Accepting either alternative would be to deny basic tenets of the science of psychology and could hardly be defended by a serious minded psychologist. A further and more critical objection may be that such an approach would not 'define' emotion. A 'classical' one-sentence or one-paragraph definition of emotions may well not accrue from the present approach. It is suggested, however, that the prediction and definition of all the responses now classified as emotions would result. If by 'definition' we accept this statement 'complete description,' then it is suggested that the present approach would generate an adequate definition. Finally, it may be maintained that our job is to 'classify' the phenomena of emotions rather than 'predict' emotions. It is doubted that even the most ardent phenomenologist would maintain such a statement of purpose.

SUMMARY AND CONCLUSIONS

The present paper agrees with Leeper in its rejection of the phenomenological approach and placing emotions in a motivational framework. It is, however, noted that these arguments *per se* have failed to integrate the problem of emotions. Using the previously suggested theories of Tolman and Skinner as basic frameworks, the present paper points to presently existing experimental programs which seem to be particularly applicable to the definition of emotions.

55. Emotion as Disorganized Response — A Reply to Professor Leeper[1]

Paul Thomas Young

THE view that emotion is a disorganized (or disorganizing) response is held quite commonly among psychologists today. This interpretation of emotion is found in the textbook writings of Munn, Shaffer *et al.*, Young, Landis (in the text of Boring, Langfeld, and Weld), Dockeray, Woodworth, and others. This view, Professor Leeper writes, is such a poor generalization that it has served as a serious obstacle to good research and to application.

The disorganization doctrine, he tells us, rests upon undefined and wrongly interpreted terms. None of the above writers has attempted to give a definition of the terms *disorganized* and *disorganizing*. These key terms must be defined to prevent sloppy thinking and the neglect of significant data. In fact, some of the above writers have used the concept of disorganization in shifting and contradictory meanings.

To help remedy this deplorable condition Professor Leeper gives a definition of the key terms *organize* and *disorganize*. A system is organized, he writes, when one part of it is functioning harmoniously with the other parts. A system is organized when the parts fit, or dovetail, or are congruous with one another. Something is disorganized when the parts do not function harmoniously but work at cross purposes with each other.

Abridged from the *Psychological Review*, 1949, *56*, 184-191. Reprinted by permission of the author and the American Psychological Association, Inc.
[1]In the preparation of this paper the writer has had helpful criticisms from S. S. Dubin, Stanley Roscoe, and R. G. Smith, of the University of Illinois.

Now in anger, to illustrate, the person is definitely organized for attack. His visceral processes are organized for the prolonged and vigorous action required in a biological emergency. His conscious experience is organized along with the basic determination. Instinctive acts of attack or flight or mating are highly organized—viscerally, behaviorally, and in conscious experience.

Again, according to Leeper, a neurotic individual is not completely disorganized. He may be organized around a feeling of worthlessness which is so rigid that he cannot shake it off or around a feeling of discouragement or anger or what not. Organization rather than disorganization is the rule in "emotion."

Professor Leeper admits, however, that disorganization does occur in extreme emotions. A man may be so extremely afraid that he wants to run or to call for help but he may be unable to do so. The boxer may become so angry that he loses his technical skill and fights ineffectively. In these extreme cases "the emotional process does seem to produce disorganization in significant degree. It interferes with reactions that would be consistent or harmonious with what is demanded by the emotion." But, says Professor Leeper, these are extreme cases and we should not use them as a means of deciding the normal function of emotional responses in the various degrees of intensity. A concept should not be defined by the extremes. The concept of emotion must apply to all degrees and intensities of emotion.

Leeper is clear about this point: Emotion exists in all degrees of intensity, but disorganization characterizes only the most extreme or intense emotions. Moderate emotions are *organized* responses. Hardly in any sense, he writes, do we find disorganization in affection, in esthetic emotion, in friendliness, in sympathy. These "emotions," as well as anger and fear, *organize* the individual for action.

"Emotions" operate primarily as motives, Professor Leeper continues, and their analysis belongs within the context of motivation. In contrast with the disorganization theory of emotion, Leeper affirms, emotional processes of all sorts (except perhaps in the rare and intense forms) are organizing in their influence and they should be studied as an aspect of the motivation of the higher animals. In fear or anger, to repeat, the person is organized so that he can most naturally do something consistent with his fear or anger.

Emotional motivation rests upon relatively complex and primitive neural patterns. From the evolutionary point of view animals motivated solely by physiological drives were not well equipped for survival. The animal that did not make avoiding responses until he was grabbed by an enemy was less likely to survive than an animal capable of reactions of fear set off by relatively slight stimuli.

Emotional motivation is indispensable in human life. Emotion is not merely a disturbance or a disorganization.

CRITIQUE OF EMOTIONAL ORGANIZATION AND DISORGANIZATION

Professor Leeper's discussion is interesting and important. He is struggling with a genuine difficulty in the definition of emotion—a difficulty which pervades the whole of affective and dynamic psychology. Terms must be defined, as Leeper has pointed out, so let us press this matter of definition a little further in the light of Leeper's paper. We believe that the difficulty is entirely one of definition.

The first point to notice is that Leeper has not given us a precise definition of the key terms *emotion* and *motivation*, although his paper bears the title "A motivational theory of emotion . . ." and stresses the importance of defining key terms.

Leeper emphasizes the point that an "emotion" is typically an *organized* and *organizing* process, but he admits that in extreme or intense "emotions" there may be disorganization. He states that the definition of a key term in psychology must cover the phenomenon as it appears in all degrees and not merely at the extremes; yet he does not give us a definition of emotion which includes both organized and disorganized "emotions."

Leeper's admission that intense emotions are disorganized psychological processes raises a curious question of logic. Logically the concepts of organization and disorganization are opposed and both concepts are not necessary to interpret the facts. The greatest possible disorganization is at the same time the minimum of organization and *vice versa*. If we hold to the concept of organization exclusively, then these extreme or intense emotions are processes with the minimum of organization. The degree of organization is so low, however, that we find ourself spontaneously using such words as *upset, disturbance, disorganization, disruption,* to describe them adequately.

The attempt to classify emotions into two groups, organized and disorganized, is futile since no sharp lines of distinction can be drawn. The true distinction, rather, is between two aspects of emotional behavior. In his book upon emotion the present writer has described the relationship in these words:

"A true picture of the relation between organized and disorganized behavior is this. At a given time the behavior of an individual is more or less organized, and more or less disorganized. One can view the same bit of behavior from the point of view of its integration or from the obverse standpoint of disintegration. The first point of view reveals an organized, integrated aspect; the second, a disorganized, disintegrated aspect.

We shall use the phrase *emotional behavior* to designate the total process regardless of the standpoint from which it is viewed. The adjective *emotional* implies that the behavior is to some extent disorganized, disintegrated, upset, disturbed. This is the aspect in which we are interested when we are studying *emotion*. But, when examined from another point of view, emotional behavior is found to contain well-organized components—integrated patterns of response, goal-oriented activities. . . ."

Organization and disorganization are thus different ways of viewing and interpreting one and the same event. Even the most completely disorganized emotional process, when viewed from another point of view, is found to contain integrated components of response. There is no real antagonism between the two views of emotional behavior. As stated above, they are simply different ways of interpreting the same facts. Both interpretations are needed and both are legitimate.

Leeper's view that only abnormal or extreme emotions are disorganized and that normal emotions are organized is not an adequate statement of the facts. Starting with the logical opposition of these two words, we are unable to reach the conclusion that psychological processes are of two kinds—organized and disorganized. As a matter of fact only one of these concepts is required logically and any distinction between organized and disorganized is relative and arbitrary.

The confusion lies in the logical opposition of words. Emotional behavior, as an event in nature, simply occurs. It is the psychologist who, with one interest, emphasizes now the aspect of organization and again, with another interest, the aspect of disorganization. But to force the psychologist to choose between these interpretations is ill advised and confusing.

The writer agrees with Leeper in emphasizing the importance of the organized components of emotional behavior. Organized patterns of emotional response include: (a) reflexive patterns such as the rage pattern, the cry, the laugh, the mating patterns, etc., (b) persistent purposive activities such as flight, attack, courtship, etc., (c) culturally determined gestures and postures such as the attitudes of courage (fear-inhibitory), friendliness (inhibitory of hostile attack), the voluntary smile, etc.

Organized patterns assuredly exist as components of emotional behavior. They are important practically and their analysis, as part of the psychology of motivation, must not be neglected. The present writer, certainly, has given adequate emphasis to the organized processes occurring in emotional behavior. Further, in a current paper, based upon experimental findings, he has argued that the enjoyment of food and the relief from distress *organize* determinations to seek specific kinds of food. This frankly hedonic theory of motivation emphasizes the positive role of enjoyment and relief from distress in organizing purposive behavior.

There is no incompatibility between Professor Leeper's emphasis upon organized response in emotional behavior and our own account. Nor is there anything really novel about Leeper's emphasis since other students of emotion, *e.g.*, McDougall, have stressed integrated behavior.

The present writer has argued that the analysis of organized patterns of behavior, and especially goal-oriented behavior, belongs squarely within the psychology of motivation. This is just as true in explaining a race for one's life as in interpreting persistent food-seeking behavior. But the psychologist who would limit his view of emotional behavior to the organized, integrated, aspect alone is thereby closing his eyes to another important aspect: the obverse aspect of disorganization.

Whenever a highly organized activity is blocked, or when success with its release of tension is suddenly achieved, or when some danger threatens, there is an immediate affective upset. Emotional disorganization is a condition which exists in nature as truly as smooth and calm organized activity. There is no gain in ignoring this aspect of the total picture.

EMOTION AND MOTIVATION

In an all too brief positive statement toward the close of his discussion Professor Leeper states that emotions *are* motives and that the analysis of emotional behavior should be made within motivational psychology.

From our point of view an acute affective upset is not itself a motive. An affective upset, however, may result in the formation of a motive which has consequences in future behavior. To illustrate: According to the record, when Abraham Lincoln saw slaves being sold on the New Orleans market he was so disturbed emotionally that he resolved "to hit that thing hard" if ever the opportunity came. This resolution, resulting from an emotional disturbance, was a determining factor in Lincoln's life and in human destiny. The upset, a disorganized event, did not motivate but it led to the formation of a motive.

Now insofar as emotional behavior can be regarded an an *organized* process its analysis, we fully agree, belongs within motivational psychology. In emotional behavior well integrated patterns of response appear. Why not study the motivation of these organized responses exactly as one studies reflex action, behavioral drive, social expression, and other smoothly organized activities? The writer's answer is: Go ahead! Get all the light possible upon these and other integrated activities. Why not?

We should prefer to say, however, that these integrated patterns of response are *motivated* rather than that they are *motives*. Motives are factors which initiate, direct, and sustain action. Disorganized affective states are produced by the frustration of motives, by conflict, by intense and persistent painful stimulation, by the sudden release of tension as in joyful success, by anticipation of harm, and in other ways. These acute affective disturbances reflect the dynamic interplay of motives.

After the story of motivation has been told completely there will remain facts of a different order to be investigated. Acute affective disorganization exists within the individual as a fact of nature. We cannot, therefore, agree with Professor Leeper that the concept of disorganization serves as a serious obstacle to good research and to application. Good research and application must rest first of all upon a true view of the facts.

EMOTION AND OTHER AFFECTIVE PROCESSES

Another point relative to the definition of emotion is the following:

In popular psychology the word *emotion* is used broadly to cover a wide range of affective and motivational processes such as persistent states of anxiety, phobias, attitudes of love and hate, determinations to seek revenge, and the like. This popular usage ignores two important distinctions: (1) the distinction between affective processes in general and a specific form of affective process which is characterized by upset, and (2) the distinction between emotion as an event and an assumed stable state of the subject. These two distinctions will be considered briefly below:

(1) The broad concept of affective process includes at least: (a) simple feelings of pleasantness and unpleasantness, (b) moods of cheerfulness and depression, (c) interests and aversions, (d) organic aches and satisfactions, (e) feelings of hunger, thirst, fatigue, etc., and (f) emotional upsets. The present writer has distinguished six main varieties of affective process, determined by their conditions, and he identified emotion with only one, namely, that form of affective process characterized by upset, or acute affective disturbance. Of course, if emotion is defined as an affective process characterized by acute disturbance, the term must mean exactly that and it must be used consistently in that rather limited and specific sense.

The popular term *emotion*, however, has not been so sharply delimited. It includes moods, sentiments, interests, and other affective processes, in which the factor of upset is definitely less pronounced than with the truly disruptive emotions. The popular term *emotion* clearly covers some effective processes in which organized behavior is very prominent. This broad use of the term *emotion* may be a source of confusion.

To clarify the picture it is fair to ask Professor Leeper these questions: Is *emotion* to be regarded as the equivalent of affective process, in the broad meaning of affectivity? If not, how are emotions to be distinguished from other kinds of affective process?

Our answer would be that emotion is a specific kind of affective process, namely, that kind of affective process which is characterized by acute upset or disturbance involving particularly the smooth muscles and glands. We suggest that the phrase *affective process* be used broadly to include simple feelings, moods, sentiments, interesting and aversive activities, emotions, and similar processes; and that the term *emotion* be restricted to those affective processes characterized by acute upset or disorganization. This suggestion implies that the popular meaning of emotion should be narrowed down to the meaning of acute affective upset or disturbance. Where we now speak of emotional development, emotional maturity, emotional appeal, and the like, we should substitute the more technically correct term *affective* for *emotional*.

(2) There is a further difficulty of definition. As an *observed* event emotion must be distinguished from the *assumed* event within the subject and from his relatively stable affective states. As a psychological datum emotion is revealed in direct conscious experience (conscious emotion), in behavior (emotional behavior), and in internal bodily changes especially in those bodily processes regulated through the autonomic nervous system (physiological emotion). Now an emotion is *assumed* to be an acute affective disturbance within the individual as a whole.

The word *acute* implies that the emotion is brief and intense. In common with other acute events it has a beginning, a relatively brief course, and an ending. The acute affective upset is not to be confused with a chronic state of disorganization within the personality. A neurosis, to illustrate, may be regarded as a chronic disorganization within the subject. The neurosis reveals itself by various symptoms—tics, amnesias, paralyses, sometimes repeated emotional outbreaks, and others. The emotional outbreak is not to be confused with the neurosis. The outbreak is a natural event, a process. The neurosis is an assumed enduring state or condition within the subject.

The distinction between an acute affective disturbance (which is coexistent with the manifest emotion) and a chronic state of disorganization within personalty is not always clearly drawn by psychologists. In psychosomatic medicine, for example, the term *emotion* is used broadly to include any chronic mental disorganization as well as the acute affective disturbance. This confusion is to be regretted. When a student reads F. H. Dunbar's *Emotions and Bodily Changes, a Survey of Literature on Psychosomatic Interrelationships*, he is at a loss to know exactly what constitutes an emotion. When emotion is equated with persistent disorganization within the personality as a whole the concept becomes so broad that it is virtually useless in psychology. It is significant, however, that even in the broad view of psychosomatic medicine emotion is conceived for the most part as a *disorganization* rather than as an organized response.

For the present writer emotion is defined as an acute affective disturbance, an event occuring here and now and revealed to the observer in different ways. An emotion is not a neurosis, nor a persistent state of conflict, nor an attitude, nor a motive, nor a habit structure. All of these are important concepts which are related to the concept of emotion, but they must be distinguished from emotion.

To clarify the picture the writer suggests that the term *emotion* be employed exclusively in the more restricted sense to designate an event or occurrence. The emotion is something that happens here and now, in the present tense. The term *affect* might be used within clinical and dynamic psychology in a broad generic sense to designate all persistent affective states of the individual such as persistent anxiety or depression or euphoria or excitement. An *affect*, then, is a persistent affective state of the individual.

THE DEFINITION OF EMOTION

What is an emotion? Our answer would be as follows: *An emotion is an acute affective disturbance within the individual as a whole, arising from the psychological situation, and manifest in conscious experience, behavior, and especially through bodily changes which are regulated by the autonomic nervous system.*

This definition of emotion rests upon a fundamental distinction between what is given as psychological datum and what is assumed or inferred as hypothesis. The data upon which any definition of emotion must rest are found in three areas of fact: (1) conscious feeling or experience, (2) emotional behavior as observed objectively in animals and men, (3) physiological changes, especially those regulated through the autonomic nervous system and the mid-brain patterns of response, as observed in the laboratory.

The *real* emotion is *assumed* to exist within the psychological individual as a whole. The assumption is based upon facts within all three of the above areas. The experiential, behavioral, and physiological manifestations of emotion are regarded simply as manifestations of an assumed acute event within the subject.

Now when the writer defined an emotion as an *acute affective disturbance within the individual as a whole* he was interpreting the data in terms of an assumed individual. The emotion, so conceived, was distinguished from organized attitudes (of fear, of affection, of hate, of disgust, etc.) and from organized motives (determinations to have revenge, to justify one's self, to woo and win, etc.).

There are two aspects of our definition which have been completely ignored by Leeper. We hope that the reason for this is that he accepts and agrees with them.

First, our definition states that *emotional disturbances originate within the psychological situation*. This part of the definition is important in distinguishing emotion from various illnesses (acute indigestion, headache) which are also disturbed affective states of the organism, and from appetites (hunger, thirst, fatigue) which originate from intra-organic conditions. The psychological situation, whether perceived or imagined, always involves an environmental component. Environmental events such as meeting a bear in the woods, being insulted by a rival, encountering one's love mate (to use William James' now trite illustrations) typically arouse emotions. Also seeing a movie or recalling a past experience may evoke emotional disturbance. Therefore, an environmental factor in the origin of emotion is what distinguishes emotion from various illnesses and from appetitive states.

Second, our definition affirms that *emotional disturbance involves bodily changes regulated through the autonomic nervous system.* The presence of marked changes in the activity of glands and smooth muscles is quite generally recognized as a sign of emotion. In fact, autonomic involvement is what distinguishes emotional from non-emotional disturbances. A distraction of attention can correctly be interpreted as a disturbed state, but unless the disturbance spreads to the involuntary nervous system and involves marked changes in the activity of glands and smooth muscles a simple distraction is not to be described as an emotion.

The above definition of emotion is assuredly imperfect. There is no single criterion which in itself is fully adequate to define emotion. But the three criteria of our definition, when they are met simultaneously, do indicate approximately what processes are and what are not to be regarded as emotions. This is about all one can expect of any arbitrary definition.

CONCLUSION

In conclusion, the problem of defining emotion in a positive and constructive way is still with us despite Professor Leeper's discussion. The following points have been made in the present analysis:

1. It is confusing and illogical to classify emotions into two groups, organized and disorganized. Organization and disorganization are logically opposed concepts and in strict logic only one of these concepts is required. Disorganization is the minimum of organization and *vice versa.*

2. Since emotion is an affective process, it must be defined in relation to other affective processes. The popular term *emotion* covers a wide variety of affective and motivational processes with little specificity.

To clarify the picture it is suggested that the term *affective process* be used broadly to include moods, sentiments, simple feelings of pleasantness and unpleasantness, interesting activities, and the like, and that *emotion* be employed specifically to designate that variety of affective process which is characterized by acute upset.

3. Of great practical importance in the definition of emotion is the distinction between a contemporary event revealed in conscious experience and behavior and bodily change, on the one hand, and an assumed disorganization within the subject, on the other hand. Emotion as an event should be distinguished from neurosis, from attitude, from persistent motive, from persistent conflict, and from habit structure. The present writer's definition of emotion makes it possible to distinguish between emotion as a specific event and relatively stable affective states within the subject.

It is suggested that the term *affect* be employed broadly to refer to a persistent anxiety or depression or euphoria or excitement or other relatively permanent affective state within the individual and that the term *emotion* be reserved to designate a contemporary process or event.

4. To define emotion as an acute affective disorganization, etc., is entirely in agreement with the psychological facts. An acute upset, however, of itself is not a motive (since motives initiate, direct, and sustain action), but rather a condition which results from the dynamic interplay of motivating factors —from frustraton or conflict or persisting pain or the sudden release of tension or the apprehension of some impending injury.

5. In a current paper based upon experimental results, the present writer has stressed the view that food-seeking drives are *organized* to preserve enjoyment and to relieve distress. Thus some affective processes are definitely organizing and the resulting behavior is organized. But despite this, it remains a fact of nature that acute affective disorganization occurs. It is quite proper to designate such disorganization as emotion.

56. The Applicabilty of Motivational Criteria to Emotions

R. H. Waters and D. F. Blackwood

IN a recent paper Leeper suggests that, contrary to outside opinion, present-day psychology needs not more facts and less theory, but theory tailored to conform more closely to the facts which have already been accumulated. As an example of the sort of theoretical revision which is needed to keep psychology abreast of its growing body of factual material, Leeper examines the treatment given the emotions in some of our widely used texts and argues that their treatment of the emotions as disorganized phenomena is obsolescent. He shows that the terms "disorganized" and "disorganizing" are frequently used in a contradictory manner and that a careful survey of the factual material at our disposal shows them to be poor generalizations. According to Leeper the term "disorganized" has been incorrectly applied to data which actually show reorgan-

Abridged from the *Psychological Review*, 1949, *56*, 351-356. Reprinted by permission of Dr. R. H. Waters and the American Psychological Association, Inc.

ization, organization along new lines. Because they arouse and organize behavior along given lines, Leeper holds that the emotions operate as motives and should properly be included within the concept of motivation.

Two other papers have since appeared bearing directly on his proposal. Duffy applauds his stand and discusses some of the theoretical issues involved, such as the difference between emotional and non-emotional behavior and the problem of the nature of emotional processes which would set them off from other motives. Webb also adds other objections to the current treatment of emotion and suggests a possible theoretical orientation for the new view. That neither of these, though contributing significantly to the problem, attack the question along the lines of the present paper will become clear as we proceed.

The suggestion that emotions be included in the category of motivation demands an examination of the concept of motivation to determine whether such an inclusion can be justified. The present paper is an attempt at such an examination. It will be restricted to the applicability of motivational criteria to emotional phenomena.

It should be kept in mind from the outset that a concept is a symbol standing in lieu of a group of specific referents which share some common attribute. The concept "dog," for instance, refers to a group of animals which have some things in common, but all of which are by no means identical. Thus in order to justify the inclusion of the emotions within the category of motivation, it is not necessary to demonstrate that the emotion of fear and the hunger drive are the same thing, but merely to show that fear is similar to hunger in the same way in which hunger is similar to sex need, that is to say, to show that they have comparable dimensions.

Our first move must be to ferret out the criteria of motivation, to determine what common attributes hunger, thirst, sex need and the like have which cause us to think of them as belonging in the same category. These criteria may then be tried on the emotions and tested for goodness of fit. A study of the literature reveals that there have been, in general, two sets of criteria commonly applied to motives. According to Young these may be designated the behavioral and the physiological.

Motivation is a common concept in psychology today and certainly an important one. Why, then, should there be a difference of opinion as to its nature? The answer to this question is that motivation occupies the position of an intervening variable. It is not itself directly observable but is inferred to exist between two units of observable behavior in order to explain a relationship which seems to exist between them. The difference in interpretation depends upon the size of the unit which is observed. For example, according to the behavioral criterion, hunger may be inferred when (a) behavior is aroused, and (b) it is organized in such a way as to lead to the ingestion of food. Many psychologists who insist on a finer analysis of the behavior sequence will not admit the adequacy of this criterion. They will point out that when the rat is observed to enter the food box we are not justified in assuming that he is operating under hunger motivation unless we also know something about his physiological condition. Thus, according to the physiological criterion, it is necessary to demonstrate (a) an atypical tissue condition, followed by (b) gross behavior oriented toward some goal, followed by (c) a change in the tissue condition.

Some writers admit that the physiological criterion is adequate for what are called the biological drives but contend that it is inadequate for the demonstration of higher types of motivation.[1] What, they ask, is the tissue condition characteristic of a desire for social approval? We have, then, a sort of double concept of motivation embracing simple biological drives which have a clear physiological basis and the so-called higher motives in which no such condition is objectively demonstrable.

If a physiological approach is to be used in the area of higher motivation, then the following alternatives present themselves. Some may infer the presence of the physiological condition and make no distinction between drive and motive. They may argue that the physiological basis of higher motives *would* be demonstrated were our techniques sufficiently refined. Others, preferring a broader and safer course, may conceive the higher motives as growing out of biological drives through learning. There is even further division among the latter with some, like Dockeray[2] considering the derivation to be direct and the learning processes involved rather simple. Others, like Allport, hold that the genesis is devious and the learning processes so complex that the resultant motives become functionally autonomous, completely distinct from and independent of their roots in tissue need. The two foregoing examples have been utilized as illustrations of extremes along a continuum of learning imposed upon drive. Not all positions have been so extreme, nor have they been completely consistent.[3] Having determined the criteria of motivation and indicated the alternative positions with regard to the relation of drive to motive, we may now proceed to an examination of the concept of emotion.

Leeper's protest is not the first statement of dissatisfaction with the concept of emotion as an independent category. Meyer, writing in 1933, drew an analogy between the concept of emotion and that of volition, and was so

[1]Those who hold strictly to the behavioral criterion will not admit the adequacy of the physiological criterion even in the area of the biological drives. It is beyond the scope of this paper to examine the validity of the physiological criterion. It is sufficient for the purpose of the present analysis to note that it is a widely held position.

[2]Dockeray's position does not actually represent the theoretical extreme of the continuum, but approximates it about as well as any.

[3]Compare Dashiell's treatment of motivation in his 1928 edition with that in his 1937 edition.

bold as to predict that the term would be cast out of our psychological vocabulary by 1950. (His time is growing short.) Shortly thereafter, in 1934, Duffy suggested that "emotion" simply does not exist as a type of behavior clearly discriminable from other types; and again, in 1941, seven years prior to the publication of Leeper's paper, she argued that in their capacity to release energy in a given direction those phenomena which we call emotions are, indeed, a form of motivation.

In terms of the behavioral criterion it is not difficult to reconcile emotional phenomena with the concept of motivation, nor is it inconsistent with some lines of traditional thought in psychology. Such an approach is generally in harmony with the thinking of the functional psychologists, and lends itself rather well to the evolutionary emphasis for which they have been noted. From time to time a number of writers have considered the motivational aspects of emotion according to the behavioral criterion. Such a concept has been outlined by McDougall who considered that emotional behavior represented innate response patterns calculated to insure the survival of the organism. A similar approach is inherent in Cannon's early "emergency theory," and in the several approaches based upon the biological concept of homeostasis. These last are somewhat closer to the physiological criterion, but lean heavily upon survival in the evolutionary sense.

The behavioral criterion does not depend upon the essential nature of the phenomena, but rather describes the way in which they operate. For example, we observe that an animal directs its activity toward the ingestion of food and infer that it is motivated by hunger. Similarly, we observe the animal retreats from a dangerous situation and infer that it is motivated by fear, that is to say, that the emotion of fear has served to organize behavior in such a way as to remove or alter the exciting stimulus. With his emphasis on the fact that the behavior aroused by the emotions is organized and purposive, Leeper has aptly demonstrated that emotions may legitimately be thought of as motivation in the behavioral sense, which defines motivation as that which serves to arouse, direct, and sustain activity in conjunction with some goal.

Such broad approaches, it may be argued, lay themselves open to criticism because of the teleological leanings. They cannot be acceptable to those who insist upon a strict physiological interpretation of motivation. For these psychologists motivation must be a matter of here-and-now reduction of an immediate tissue need. Can it be shown that emotions meet the physiological criterion of motivation, that is to say, that they may be thought of as growing out of physiological conditions and that these conditions are subsequently altered as a result of behavior?

Although emotions as motivation do not appear to fit so readily the physiological criterion, there have, nonetheless, been some suggestions made in that direction. This sort of inclination is to be noted in the writings of Woodworth, who says:

> Anyone will unhesitatingly classify as emotions: anger, fear, disgust, joy and sorrow; and as states of the organism: hunger, thirst, nausea, fatigue, drowsiness, intoxication. Now that physiology has revealed a peculiar organic state in fear and anger, why do we continue to call them emotions and deny that name to fatigue or drowsiness?

Woodworth has thus indicated that some emotions are comparable, physiologically, to other states commonly called drives. Cannon, writing in 1922, catalogued the tissue changes involved in pain, hunger, fear and rage. The inclusion of hunger among the conditions we call emotions appears particularly significant, for is not hunger one of our more commonly referred to biological drives?

In terms of Dockeray's treatment of motivation derived from drive, an approach fairly common in our texts, the emotions can be fitted within such a framework. Dockeray views a drive as a tissue condition which stimulates the organism to random activity until, through trial and error, it hits upon some response which serves to alter the tissue need. This approach is wholly consistent with the usual genetic description of the development of the hunger motive according to which the organism receives sensory impressions from the stomach, is stimulated to a wide variety of activity which brings it into contact with food, the exciting stimulus (tissue condition) is modified, and the organism, if it be a human one, learns to give the sensory impressions from the stomach the name "hunger."[4] When, through learning conceived as being of a rather simple sort (conditioning), the organism comes to associate the specific tissue need with a specific response which will serve to reduce it, it is called a motive. Motive, then, is equal to biological drive plus relatively simple learning. There is some experimental evidence to indicate that emotions as motives can be similarly interpreted. Miller, working with rats, used an induced fear as a presumably motivating condition in a learning situation and found that it did indeed operate as a motive in that it (a) produced trial and error activity, and (b) served to reinforce the correct response.

Obviously, further research of a similar nature is indicated. While the outlook, on the basis of this one experiment, is promising, it may be well to look to some of the theoretical implications of such an inclusion. Considering emotions as motivation within this framework may afford us some insight into the existential nature of the emotions themselves. Recall that for

---

[4]It will be seen that this represents an oversimplification of the mechanisms involved in the hunger drive whose physiological components are known to include much more than stomach contractions alone. Stomach contractions are here used as an illustration of the sort of tissue condition which Dockeray considers to furnish the drive.

Dockeray the drive which directly produces the motive is a tissue condition. The motive then becomes, in a sense, the organism's interpretation of a specific tissue need. Fitting emotions to such a framework is tantamount to an acceptance of the James-Lange theory of emotion, which holds that an emotion is the perception of certain bodily changes, or, in more behavioristic terminology, an emotion is the name which we learn to give to a particular pattern of sensory impressions. It need hardly be pointed out that this theory is not currently in good repute since it implies that patterns of internal stimulation in the several emotions must be discriminable one from another and since no such discriminable differences have been satisfactorily isolated. If there are no discriminable differences in patterns of stimulation afforded by the physiological components of the various emotions, then we have a situation somewhat analogous to that found in the field of higher motivation. Clearly, if Leeper's idea of emotions as motivation is to be adopted in conjunction with a concept of motives directly derived from tissue need, then further research is needed in the physiology of the emotions, calculated to demonstrate discrete patterns. This is an area which has already received considerable attention and, as has been noted, the results, generally, have been negative.

Fortunately there is another alternative which, while it compromises to some extent the strict physiological viewpoint, effectively circumvents the difficulties inherent in Dockeray's approach. This alternative invokes Allport's idea of functional autonomy. Here motives may also derive from biological drives with a basis in tissue need, but the learning processes involved are so complex that the resultant motivation is completely independent of its physiological roots. The emphasis in functional autonomy is upon the divorcement of the motive from the tissue need involved in its genesis. Thus, when a motive has, through complex learning, become autonomous, it is to all practical intents and purposes psychogenic and one is no longer obliged, when dealing with higher order motives and those areas of emotion which are hazily defined, to demonstrate the present operation of an atypical tissue condition. Hence, as Leeper has held, the theory of emotion which says that emotions are, indeed, psychogenic, and which Munn considers too naive for serious treatment, may in the final analysis be the least naive of all the theories which have been advanced.

It may be argued that in invoking functional autonomy to circumvent the need for the establishment of specific tissue conditions in all cases, we have left the strict physiological criterion and have arrived by indirection at a behavioral approach. The only answer to this must be that any theoretical area in psychology must be broad enough to cover all of the involved phenomena. As Hull has said, when theory and fact conflict, theory must always give way.

From the foregoing review of the status of emotion and motivation, it appears that the concept of emotions as motivation can be conditionally reconciled with a physiological approach to motivation, the conditions being these: In order to insure consistency those who hold to the physiological criterion of motivation will be faced with the alternative of either (a) instituting more intensive research with an eye to the establishment of definite patterns of atypical tissue conditions both in the so-called emotions and in the area of higher motivation, or (b) expanding their theoretical framework to include the concept of functional autonomy. Acceptance of the Leeper hypothesis will serve to combine two vague areas of investigation into one and offer positive suggestions for research in this one area which may lead not only to clarification of the phenomena in question, but also to a narrowing of the gap between those who approach the problem from different directions.

The lines of research indicated by such a concept embrace not only investigation of the physiological components of motives and emotions but also the operational aspects of both. We speak, for instance, of levels of motivation which are presumed to vary directly with goal deprivation. This raises the question of the possible quantification of emotions along similar lines. Again it has often been noted that extreme emotion appears to operate in contradiction to a motivational interpretation. At the same time there has been some suggestion that a similar situation exists in motivation. Too high a level of motivation may inhibit goal-directed activity.

Further consequences of the adopton of Leeper's hypothesis will probably involve such problems as the reconciliation of the genetic development of emotions according to Bridges with some scheme of the genetic development of motives, a treatment of Dashiell's suggestion that emotions may be nothing more than socially determined interpretations of environmental conditions, and investigation in the area of the acquisition of new motives and emotions.

Of course, the final word on the inclusion of emotions within the category of motives must rest with the experimental findings in the above indicated areas. In terms of the narrower topic assumed by this paper, however, it appears that the hypothesis may be tentatively accepted.

57. The Motivational Theory
of Emotion*

Robert W. Leeper

I am glad to have this opportunity to discuss the problem of a motivational theory of emotion. For one thing, as several critics have pointed out, when I published the paper in 1948 on "A Motivational Theory of Emotion to replace 'Emotion as disorganized response' ", I hardly presented anything ample enough to be called a theory. As a matter of fact, I submitted the paper with this longer and more modest title, *"The need for a motivational theory to . . . (so and so)."* Except for the insistence of the editor of the Psychological Review, that would have been the title. But, he ordered, "Chop off the first three words." Being a submissive soul, I did, but at some cost to my conscience. So, even if for no other reason, I have felt some pressure to go back and try to state a motivational theory of emotion in something more than the very sketchy terms that I did then. I think it is also true too, though, that I can discuss these problems in a somewhat more satisfactory way than I was ready to in 1948. . . .

In all, I will discuss seven main points that I see as important for a motivational theory of emotion.

The first of these is the proposal that, when we talk about emotions, we ought not to think of them in the old introspective tradition, but as full psychological processes. That is, we ought to think of them as processes that might conceivably be studied as neurological or physiological processes; and, from another standpoint, as processes that have influences on the rest of psychological functioning. Or, to put the matter in negative terms, we ought not, I think, to conceive of emotions as merely the conscious aspect of some larger events. I am not proposing, on the other hand, that we ought to think of emotional processes merely in behavioristic terms. Sometimes emotional processes are conscious processes, and we may as well use our

Abridged and published by permission of Dr. Robert Leeper.
*Paper presented in a symposium on Emotion at the 1959 APA meeting.

opportunities for subjective observation whenever this is helpful. On this first point, then, I am proposing that we ought to think of emotional processes in the same way that most psychologists regard concept-formation—that is, as a process that may be either conscious or unconscious, but that will have most of its properties the same in either case.

. This is a different view from the Freudian view of affect or emotion. . . . This is surprising, because the Freudians certainly have been insistent, in general, that mental activity cannot be equated with conscious activity. But, with regard to affect or emotion, it seems that the Freudians unfortunately carried over the commonsense tradition that you cannot talk sensibly about a psychological process unless you conceive of it as a conscious process. . . .

In the second place, and central to my whole proposal, is of course the suggestion that emotional processes are motives. In fact, I would submit that, except as we use a motivational criterion, we cannot distinguish between some processes that we call emotions and some other processes that we do not think of as emotions. . . .

But, now, is this actually a reasonable view? Do emotions actually function as motives?

To answer this question, we will need to look first at some processes which psychologists generally would conceive as motives, and ask what means we have for identifying such motives in human beings and animals. For example, take hunger. Can we infer a motive of hunger merely on the basis of some period of food-deprivation? Definitely not. An animal like a shrew has a terrific consumption of food and seems to need to eat almost continuously; a boa constrictor, on the other hand, might go for weeks after a really good meal before it would be inspired to search for any more food. No; basically we have to infer hunger on the basis of influences exerted by hunger on the rest of the life of the individual. One of the most vivid accounts of such influence has been given by Sir Ernest Shackleton, who, with his three companions, tried to reach the South Pole in the old, hard way back in 1909. These men were engaged in very strenuous physical exercise, they were living under conditions of intense cold, and yet they had only the smallest of daily rations.

As Shackleton reports, they thought and talked about food virtually all day long. They dreamed about it at night. They spent an enormous amount of time comparing notes on new recipes that they wished to use when they returned to civilization. They devised special rituals for dividing the food at each meal to insure that no one would get a smaller portion than another person. They gladly hauled their sleds with their food supplies on them, even though they were tired and might have wished for lighter burdens. Even aside from their conscious experience of hunger, these several influences are the means by which we would judge that they were tremendously motivated by a hunger for food. As a matter of fact, their example illustrates the point that the conscious aspect of motivation is not an essential attribute. These men were also strongly motivated to try to reach the South Pole. Each day, at every step and every choice point, instead of turning back to where they could find food, they were moving further and further away from their base camp to the goal that was dictated by whatever motives made them want to reach the South Pole. But it was only in the effects on the rest of activity, and not within conscious experience, that the other motives demonstrated that they were dominant over the motive to seek for food.

Now, if such influences on other psychological functioning are the means of inferring a physiologically-based motive, we need to ask whether these influences also come from emotional processes. That is, do emotional processes tend to dominate the content of thought, do they tend to determine what will be stressed perceptually, and do they make people willing to endure penalties or forego other satisfactions to reach goals resulting from emotional sources? Do emotional motives tend to lead to a learning of new means of acting that would serve such goals?

Suppose we examine a case of emotional reaction. Thus, suppose that you start on a drive with another person and that you quickly observe that he is a rather reckless and clumsy driver. You note, for instance, that he often misjudges when it is safe to pass other cars and that he often wanders across the middle line on the road even when other cars are coming toward him. What are the effects of the fear that gets aroused in you? Does your fear tend to focus your perceptual processes, making it hard to watch the scenery, just as it was true that the magnificent scenery of the Antarctic was wasted on Shackleton's men? Do you tend to engage in problem-solving thinking or trial and error activity trying to find some means to change the behavior of the driver or to extricate yourself from the situation? In all such respects, it would seem, the fear that is aroused in you is functionally equivalent, in its basic effects, to strong hunger. The same would be true of other emotions. Consider, for example, how much sacrifice and efforts at problem-solving a nation will engage in when it thinks it is endangered by some other nation.

So, since emotions have the same fundamental effects that the physiologically-based motives have, we may call them motives. This is the most fundamental fact about emotions. It is our basic means to distinguish between emotions and other psychological processes of a non-motivational sort.

Often we tend to think of emotions as processes that are identified by physiological effects such as visceral reactions or galvanic skin response or the like. But such indices of emotion are not nearly as sensitive or efficient as the behavioral effects of emotions. The case is like that with regard to a qualitative food-hunger after some period with an inadequate diet. The behavioral indications of such qualitative food hungers come long before there are any physiological indications of dietary imbalance.

In the third place, now, if we are to conceive of emotional motives, we need to ask about the relation between emotional motives and motives more generally. What I am assuming is that all motives may be conceived of as two types that are spaced along some continuum. At the one end are the very clearly physiologically-based motives like hunger and thirst. Some of these are dependent on general tissue states. Others, like toothaches or pain from an electric shock or from a blow, are dependent on external stimulation. But, in these cases, the external stimulation is relatively intense and an interruption of the afferent impulses from the point of stimulation, as from the tooth, would bring the physiologically-based motive to an end. Emotional motives, on the other hand, depend on relatively more complex psychological processes. For example, consider the gosling that were studied by Tinbergen. These goslings showed an arousal of fear responses and hiding behavior when the silhouette of a hawk was passed over them, but they were unaffected when the same cardboard model was turned end for end and passed over them in such a way as to mimic the long-necked silhouette of a goose. In this case the perceptual discrimination is apparently innate or instinctive, and yet we would call the process an emotional one.

In most cases, however, learned meanings are involved. Thus, suppose a person consults a physician about a certain symptom and is told that there is some chance that this might indicate cancer and that they should have an exploratory operation in another week. The physician might tell the person not to worry in the meantime and merely go about his usual life. But the effects of all the usual stimuli now are changed because of the person's complex processes of representation on his situation. So, while some emotional motives shade off from almost similar physiologically-based motives, most of them are markedly different, even though they do belong within the large classification of motives.

Some treatments of the topic of emotion, . . . purpose that only the responses to serious frustrations are emotions and that, on the other hand, the processes involved in, or back of, healthy goal-oriented behavior are not emotions. There are differences, of course, between these two sorts of processes, and we need to study these differences. But this difference is not of such a character that we ought to speak of emotions as existing only in the one case. Or, at least, if we use a motivational theory of emotion, we would not speak in that way. For, in both cases there may be processes that depend, as I have just said, on complex representation of the life situation, and that also serve as the basis of goal-directed functioning. Consider a person, like a surgeon, who thoroughly enjoys his work, who believes that it has great value and that it is deeply appreciated by other persons. Such a person shows all the hard work, the willingness to forego other goals, the focussing of perceptions, and so on, that mark emotional processes or emotional motives. But the person who is deeply concerned about the threat of war, which is certainly a frustration effect, also has the same highly organized goal-directedness. It seems to me, therefore, that . . . emotional processes are involved in both kinds of activity and not merely in the frustration case.

As the fourth point, now, I would like to suggest that, in the higher animals, including man, the most important motives are the emotional ones. At least, they are the ones that are particularly developed in the higher animals that use their distinctive biological characteristics, both on the side of excellent distance receptors and on the side of greater perceptual and learning capacity. Take a deer, for example. It can detect a very faint odor or sound that would indicate an enemy. But, what is important biologically is that the deer must do more than merely sense the presence of a cougar. What is important also is that the deer must be powerfully motivated in consequence of this, even though there is, as yet, no condition of tissue injury such as may later occur if the enemy is disregarded.

I do not mean that physiologically based motives are unimportant in our lives. But, particularly when, as Maslow says, we have achieved some fairly adequate means of satisfying cravings for food and water and physical comfort, the main motives of our lives come to be emotional motives. We are strongly motivated creatures in modern society, but the motives that cause this fact are emotional processes. The emotional motives are the ones particularly that can be greatly modified by learning. They operate with reference to distant objectives as well as with reference to immediate ones. They can use very subtle cues. They are the ones, therefore, that particularly fit the requirements of human existence.

As a fifth problem, now, we ought to say something more about the nature of emotional processes. We have been considering the suggestion that emotional processes are motives. But what more about them? What are these processes that are emotional motives?

Particularly what gives rise to this question is the observation that emotional motives are relatively definite, precise processes. We tend to use broad terms that do not suggest this. When an elderly man picks his way carefully along an icy street, we say that he does this because of fear. When a person is reluctant to make a speech, we may say that his hesitancy is because of fear. And so on. But surely the one fear is quite different from another—the one man has a fear of physical injury; the other person has a fear, say, of being criticized or embarrassed. These don't seem like the same process. What is a fear process, then?

What I want to suggest, and I see this as perhaps the main new point of the present paper, though it may seem like a peculiar idea, is that emotional processes ought to be seen as one type of perceptual process. I don't mean that emotional processes *depend on*, or *come from* perceptual processes, though this also is true. I mean a more drastic statement—namely, that emotional processes basically and fundamentally *are* perceptual processes, just as apparent movement is a perceptual process.

Not all perceptual processes, of course, are emotional processes. Most of the processes that have been studied in research on perception have been about as nonemotional or nonmotivational as one could find, as in studies of reversible figures, influence of visual contours, and psychophysical effects. Such nonmotivational perceptions have been focussed on for reasons of expediency. It is much easier to get subjects for experiments on comparisons of lengths of line than it is to get (or at least keep) subjects in a study of discrimination of strengths of electric shock. It is much easier to study simple visual discriminations than to study such complex matters as discriminations of the degree to which one situation is more embarrassing than the other.

Because of such considerations of convenience or expediency, the psychologists doing research on perception have worked with these simple, nonmotivational examples of perception. They also have worked almost entirely with *conscious* perceptual processes, so that they could have the economies of introspective reports, rather than working also with unconscious perceptual processes. And, since they have worked with perceptions that were not motivationally significant, they have worked with processes that are very transitory in character.

But these considerations of expediency of original research ought not to dictate our basic conception of perception. For, with many other examples of perception, the processes shade over into those that are more and more definitely motivational, either in an emotional sense or in a simpler physiologically-based sense. Thus, suppose that an infant who is being given a bath takes a bite from the cake of soap. Is this any less a perceptual effect because it is not a motivationally neutral process? Suppose a person receives an electric shock—is this any less a perceptual process because it is so painful and because the person tends strongly to translate his perception . . . into overt action? Suppose Tinberger's goslings saw the silhouette that had the rough shape of a hawk—was this process any less a perceptual process because of the added fact that it governed their behavior in the way characteristic of a motivational process? In fact, as Dr. Köhler was saying. . . , if a process is to have a motivational effect—that is, a goal-directing influence—it cannot be something as formless as a tissue state or a diffuse affect—it must be something that has a sufficiently precise and definite character that it can operate as a vector—with a direction—rather than merely somehow serve in an energy-releasing fashion.

One objection that this suggestion faces, of course, is that emotional processes often have only a vague conscious character. A person is despondent, say, or suffers from so-called "free-floating anxiety," but cannot say what he is despondent about. And, many psychologists say, perceptual processes are of course an awareness or conscious experience of something or other. But, here again, we are following too narrowly a tradition dominated by considerations of expediency in early research. There is no reason why we should conclude, merely because so much work on perception has concerned merely conscious perception, that all perceptual processes are conscious. When clinicians work with cases of free-floating anxiety, they find that it is not formless and free-floating. It arises in certain situations characteristic for the given person and expresses itself in certain characteristic ways of dealing with those situations. As this indicates, a good portion of the perceptual processes that constitute some emotional processes are unconscious perceptual processes. But they still are fairly definitely structured processes—that is, perceptual processes.

To make this proposal more clear, I might compare perceptual processes to movies. The kinds of perceptions that we ordinarily experiment on are like the black and white movies. Then, from them, let us imagine that other movies might have more and more color added to them. The fact that such color has been added does not mean that such movies have any less precision of detail; that they are any less "movies." Or, as perceptions come to have more and more of a motivational character, or more specifically of an emotional character, this does not mean that they cease being dynamically organized neural processes, involving complex cortical activities—or that, in brief, they cease being perceptual processes.

If we held such a motivational theory of emotion—or, I suppose I should say, such a perceptual-motivational theory of emotion—what are some implications that would flow from it? I would propose two such implications as the sixth and seventh main points of this paper.

In the first place, if emotional processes are perceptual processes, this suggests that, after the earliest period of life, emotional processes will exist in increasingly diverse and highly individualized forms. For, if there is one thing that marks perceptual processes in addition to their dynamic organizational character, it is their great susceptibility to modification by learnng or experience. The small infant, I think it is safe to say, much as Koffka did, or as Hebb has been emphasizing, would have the capacity for only the simplest kind of perceptual organization. To the tiny infant, the face of the mother is probably only a bright patch against a darker background. But, as the child develops, the perceptual mechanisms that were originally so indefinite become sharper and finer. The original neural mechanisms no longer exist. He can no longer perceive things in the undifferentiated way that he did originally. And, different persons learn different perceptual mechanisms. One person develops his perceptual mechanisms for one kind of music, another person for another kind. One person learns to recognize chimpanzee faces, another person picks his friends from his fellow human beings.

This is one of the points where a perceptual-motivational theory of emotion would differ most strongly from the view that Dr. Plutchik has developed.

For, as I understand it, he believes that emotions continue as primary, physio-logically-given emotions even though they may get into new combinations that produce strikingly new effects. It seems to me that one of the main theo-retical and empirical issues regarding emotion would be to determine which of these two hypotheses comes closer to reality.

Finally, another implication of a perceptual-motivational theory of emo-tion would concern questions of how emotional processes and emotional habits are changed. We have a lot of ideas about how emotions are changed, as by permitting "emotional discharge," by "making emotions conscious," by "experimental extinction," and so on. There is some truth in all of these views. But, from the viewpoint that I have been proposing, I think we might say that, wherever any of such means is successful, an influence of a different sort has been responsible and that we would get more command over this problem if we could recognize what this more fundamental process is.

To explain this suggestion, let me use a small example of a non-technical sort, one taken from the little book by Katherine Forbes, *Mama's Bank Ac-count*. In one chapter, the young girl who tells the story is described as sharing, with her aunts, a very unsympathetic and disparaging attitude toward one of her uncles. He had seemed solely preoccupied with himself. He lived in the most miserly fashion, even though it was thought that his work in buy-ing run-down farms, building them up, and selling them, had probably brought him a good income. There was bad feeling because he had sold certain family heirlooms brought over from Norway and apparently pocketed the money. The relatives granted that he had his troubles. They knew he had been somewhat crippled from childhood and had a bad limp, but they re-sented his seemingly entirely self-centered ways.

When he died, the family gathered at the funeral with some interest in the question of his estate. What they found, though, was that there was no money left—only a little notebook with a lot of entries such as these:

"Joseph Spenelli. Four year old. Tubercular left leg. $237. Walks.

"Jamie Kelly. 9 years. $435. Walks.

"Esta Jensen. 11 years. Braces, $121.

"Sam Bernstein. Five years. Club foot. $452.16. Walks."

Now, when this additional material was met, there was a sharp and enduring emotional change as a result. Why? Not because there had been any lack of strength or practice with the preceding emotional reaction to this man. But because, instead, a new and more compelling perceptual organization had been developed which did not deny any of their previous factual knowledge, but which incorporated it into a more powerful and enduring perceptual or-ganization.

To say this does not mean necessarily that any one means of psychother-apy is more effective than another. But it does suggest that, when psycho-therapy is successful, we must look for the development of such new perceptual organizations as the basic happening. Experimental extinction procedures are effective only when they are suited to accomplish this; making an emotion conscious is effective only when it involves conditions that accomplish this; and so on.

As I see it, therefore, our approach to problems of emotion has been greatly hampered by our continuance in certain habits of thought that we carry over from the earlier days of psychology, as with the ideas that we ought to think of psychological processes merely in terms of what is conscious, and as those cases where we have failed to see similarities because we have been so impressed by differences that also exist. I might even suggest that we have been somewhat like the child who is asked, "In what way are an orange and a ball alike?" and who insists, with admittedly some degree of justification, "They aren't alike. You can eat an orange and you can play with a ball." Admittedly there are differences between emotions and other motives; admittedly there are differences between emotions and other motives; admittedly there are differences between emotional processes and other perceptual processes. But, I submit, we would open out some very useful conceptualizations if we would see that there are also major similarities.

REFERENCES—SECTION NINE

Arnold, M. B. *Emotion and Personality, Vol. I. Psychological Aspects. Vol. II. Neurological and Psyiological Aspects.* New York: Columbia University Press, 1960.

Bartley, S. H. Emotion an evaluative feature of all behavior. *Psychol. Rec.*, 1958, *8*, 39-41.

Bridges, K. M. B. A genetic theory of emotions. *J. genet. Psychol.*, 1930, *37*, 514-527

Broadhurst, P. L. Emotionality and the Yerkes-Dodson law. *J. exp. Psychol.*, 1957, *54*, 345-352.

Brown, J. S., and Farber, I. E. Emotions conceptualized as intervening variables—with suggestions toward a theory of frustration. *Psychol. Bull.*, 1951, *48*, 465-495.

Bull, N. Towards a clarification of the concept of emotion. *Psychosom. Med.*, 1945, *7*, 210.

———. *The Attitude Theory of Emotion.* New York: Nervous and Mental Disease Monographs, 1951.

———, and Gidro-Frank, L. Emotions induced and studies in hypnotic subjects. Part II: The findings. *J. nerv. ment. Dis.*, 1950, *112*, 97.

Cannon, W. B. The James-Lange theory of emotions. *Amer. J. Psychol.*, 1927, *39*, 106.

———. *The Wisdom of the Body.* (rev. ed.), New York: Norton, 1951.

Carr, H. Relation between emotion and its expression. *Psychol. Rev.*, 1917, *24*, 369-375.

Darwin, C. *Expressions of Emotions.* London: Murry, 1904.

Duffy, E. Emotion: an example of the need for reorientation in psychology. *Psychol. Rev.*, 1934, *41*, 184-198.

———. An explanation of "emotional" phenomena without the use of the concept "emotion." *J. gen. Psychol.*, 1941, *25*, 283-293.

———. The psychological significance of the concept of "arousal" or "activation." *Psychol. Rev.*, 1957, *64*, 265-275.

Ellis, N. R. The immediate effects of emotionality upon behavior strength. *J. exp. Psychol.*, 1957, *54*, 339-344.

English, H. B. Education of the emotions. *J. Humanistic Psychol.*, 1961, *1*, 101-109.

Gardiner, H. M., Metcalf, R. C., and Beebe-Center, J. G. *Feeling and Emotion.* New York: American Book Co., 1937.

Harlow, H. F., and Stagner, R. Psychology of feelings and emotions: I Theory of feelings, *Psychol. Rev.*, 1932, *39*, 570-589.

————, and ————. Psychology of feelings and emotions: II Theory of emotions. *Psychol. Rev.*, 1933, *40*, 184-195.

Hebb, D. O. Emotion in man and animal: an analysis of the intuitive processes of recognition. *Psychol. Rev.*, 1946, *53*, 88-106.

Hunt, W. A. Recent developments in the field of emotions. *Psychol. Bull.*, 1941, *38*, 249-276.

Lund, F. H. *Emotions.* New York: Ronald Press, 1939.

Marston, W. M. *Emotions of Normal People.* New York: Harcourt Brace, 1928.

Meyer, M. F. That whale among the fishes—the theory of emotions. *Psychol. Rev.*, 1933, *40*, 292-300.

Plutchik, R. Outlines of a new theory of emotion. *Transac. N.Y. Acad. of Sci.*, 1958, Ser. II, *20*, No. 5, 394-403.

————. The multifactor-analytic theory of emotion. *J. Psychol.*, 1960, *50*, 153-171.

Rapaport, D. *Emotions and Memory.* Baltimore: Williams and Wilkins, 1942.

Ruckmick, C. A. *The Psychology of Feeling and Emotion.* New York: McGraw-Hill, 1936.

Sartre, J. P. *The Emotions-Outline of a Theory.* New York: *Philosophical Library,* 1948.

Scholsberg, H. Three dimensions of emotion. *Psychol. Rev.*, 1954, *161*, 81-88.

Simon, A., Herbert, C. C., and Straus, R. *The Physiology of Emotions.* Springfield, Illinois: C. C. Thomas, 1961.

Smith, K. On the inter-relationships among organization, motivation, and emotion. *Canad. J. Psychol.*, 1958, *12*, 69-73.

Spence, K. W. A theory of emotionally based drive (D) and its relation to performance in simple learning situations, *Amer. Psychologist,* 1958, *13*, 131-141.

Thompson, W. R., and Higgins, W. H. Emotion and organized behavior: experimental data bearing on the Leeper-Young controversy. *Canad. J. Psychol.*, 1958, *12*, 61-68.

Tolman, E. C. A behavioristic account of the emotions. *Psychol. Rev.*, 1923, *30*, 217-227.

Triandis, H. C., and Lambert, W. W. A restatement and test of Schlosberg's theory of emotion with two kinds of subjects from Greece. *J. abnor. soc. Psychol.*, 1958, *56*, 321-328.

Watson, J. B. A schematic outline of emotions. *Psychol. Rev.*, 1919, *26*, 165-196.

Wechsler, D. What constitutes an emotion? *Psychol. Rev.*, 1925, *32*, 235-240.

Young, P. T. *Emotion in Man and Animal.* New York: Wiley, 1943.

————. *Motivation and Emotion.* New York: Wiley, 1961.

Zeigler, H. P. Electrical stimulation of the brain and the psycho-physiology of learning and motivation. *Psychol. Bull.*, 1957, *54*, 363-82.